Burnside's Boys

BURNSIDE'S BOYS

The Union's Ninth Corps and the Civil War in the East

DARIN WIPPERMAN

STACKPOLE
BOOKS

Essex, Connecticut
Blue Ridge Summit, Pennsylvania

STACKPOLE BOOKS

An imprint of Globe Pequot, the trade division of
The Rowman & Littlefield Publishing Group, Inc.
4501 Forbes Blvd., Ste. 200
Lanham, MD 20706
www.rowman.com

Distributed by NATIONAL BOOK NETWORK

British Library Cataloguing in Publication Information available

Library of Congress Cataloging-in-Publication Data available

ISBN: 978-0-8117-7264-8 (cloth : alk. paper)
ISBN: 978-0-8117-7265-5 (electronic)

♾™ The paper used in this publication meets the minimum requirements of American National Standard for Information Sciences—Permanence of Paper for Printed Library Materials, ANSI/NISO Z39.48-1992.

*To the archivists, librarians, and other public servants
who have done such a great job preserving Civil War history*

So uncertain is a soldier's life
—HENRY SPOONER, 4TH RHODE ISLAND INFANTRY, 1862

Contents

List of Maps

Acknowledgments

In so many books, spouses are mentioned at the end of acknowl-
edgments. For my second Civil War book, however, Jan gets top billing
again. During the long process to turn an idea into this book, Jan was
there to work hard, provide advice, or to make copious use of a red pen
to suggest textual changes. Her work as a researcher really helped save
time at several locations. She deserves infinite praise for her diligence
and assistance.

My parents proved vital to my interest in history. They bought me
a colorful and map-filled book on the Civil War about forty years ago,
beginning my lifetime of interest. I wish my dad could have read my first
Civil War book. I'm overjoyed that my mom will see my second.

After learning about my work on a Ninth Corps manuscript, John
Gardiner, a fellow resident of northern New Hampshire, reached out
to me. His great-grandfather Charles Read, 58th Massachusetts, wrote
some excellent letters. John's kindness at letting me use his ancestor's
marvelous words enriched this book, as did his mention of a short but
very useful regimental history of the 58th that I had yet to discover. The
preservation of Civil War records by family members remains a leading
way for historians to tell better tales.

Digitization of old books has done a tremendous service, saving time
for historians and making excellent sources available to a wide audience.
Individuals throughout the country have dramatically increased the
number of books that are just a click away. I thank them with an immense
level of gratitude.

Although manuscript research during a pandemic proved difficult,
some individuals assisted greatly with digital materials. One who deserves
special mention is Stephanie Grey, Antietam National Battlefield. I had

an appointment to use the battlefield library before the closure of such facilities became common in the first year of the pandemic. Stephanie kindly did a great deal of work to send me information about some Ninth Corps regiments. I thank her for the help, as well as her service to history and the country.

As before, Hal Jesperson's tremendous knowledge and skill enriched my work with delightful and beautiful maps. Hal has worked well with authors for a long time. I thank him again with much appreciation.

Few Civil War books could ever have been written (certainly not this one) without the incredible letters, diaries, and personal observations of soldiers and veterans. Saving those records to the current extent is a great credit to the dedicated staff across the country at libraries and archives. They deserve special plaudits from this grateful author and their country. I dedicate this book to them.

As before, the great folks at Stackpole worked really well with me. As the years go by, I hope for more chances to laud their professionalism and knowledge in a new book. However much I end up writing, the number one rule an author must respect prevails here: Many help, but I must accept responsibility for any and all imperfections herein.

PREFACE

WHETHER THEY SERVED IN MARYLAND, MISSISSIPPI, OR SEVERAL bloody fields in between during the Civil War, Union soldiers in the Ninth Corps sacrificed greatly for the preservation of one undivided country. One proud Civil War veteran referred to service with the Ninth Corps as "Burnside's Geography Class," while another from New Hampshire labeled the command a "Peripatetic Geography Class." Those pithy phrases hold much truth. Called "a wandering corps," the Ninth covered more ground than nearly any corps in the Union's service. Some regiments that had been attached to coastal expeditions in the Carolinas were the basis of the corps, which officially formed in Virginia on July 22, 1862. Maj. Gen. Ambrose Burnside, who led the Unionist force into North Carolina six months before, originally commanded the corps. During the summer the men were sent north to support U.S. Army forces attempting to break stalemates in the Old Dominion. Ninth Corps soldiers would march and fight across some very famous battlegrounds for the rest of the war. The Ninth Corps' history illuminates the truth a veteran used to describe the important band: "a magnificent body of soldiers, who fought valiantly on many widely distant fields."[1]

Divisions were the largest units in the U.S. Army until March 1862, when the first five corps were organized. After some bureaucratic shifting, additional corps formed later in the summer, with the Ninth Corps created to provide Ambrose Burnside a larger command at a critical time. An infantry corps, created through grouping at least two divisions, could meld a large body of soldiers capable of independently attacking and defending until other supporting units arrived. With shifting of regiments and leadership a constant in Civil War armies, keeping track of numerous changes to an infantry corps can create a morass of data for historians. Thus, the plethora of unit histories published in the last half-century often focus on individual regiments or brigades, the building blocks of Civil War armies. The 21st Massachusetts, which gave extended and highly costly service in the Ninth Corps, is an example of one regiment. A brigade grouped together multiple regiments, while a division included more than one brigade.

This book is intended to present anew familiar engagements while granting the spotlight to some brave troops whose names have been largely forgotten. Although the regimental lineup of an infantry corps changed regularly, many regiments spent the bulk of the war with the Ninth Corps. The heart of the command included seven regiments that never left the outfit from the Carolina coast through the end of the war. These were the 21st Massachusetts, 8th Michigan, 79th New York, and the 45th, 50th, 51st, and 100th Pennsylvania. Some other regiments—such as the 6th New Hampshire and 51st New York—spent part of the war in other corps but were attached to the Ninth Corps for most major engagements. Even those regiments only temporarily in the command, such as a division of Ohioans in Maryland, contributed greatly and therefore must be given justice in telling the Ninth Corps' story.

Because the bulk of the Ninth Corps' service and combat losses occurred in the Eastern Theater, this book does not detail the year Burnside's Boys spent in the West. The Ninth Corps was far smaller then, even when taking a prominent role in the siege of Knoxville, Tennessee. Key points about Western campaigns are overviewed, but this book focuses on Virginia and Maryland battles, incredibly costly in terms of casualties to the Ninth Corps often including four divisions. The introduction discusses the months immediately preceding the official formation of the Ninth Corps. Nineteen regiments serving in either North Carolina or South Carolina formed the Ninth Corps under Burnside after the units were called to Virginia. Part One's focus will be on the organization of the Ninth Corps and two early engagements, Second Bull Run and the smaller yet very chaotic battle of Chantilly. The second part of this book covers two weeks of September 1862, from the reorganization of the Army of the Potomac through the evening of September 16. Part Three focuses on one day, the devastating battle along Antietam Creek. Next, two parts discuss the movement to Fredericksburg, the terrible battle there, and the year in the West. Parts Six and Seven detail the last year of the war, when the Ninth Corps sustained horrendous losses back in Virginia. A presentation of the postwar lives of fifteen Ninth Corps veterans concludes the book.

Introduction

Origins of a Command in the Carolinas

To successfully quell the rebellion, the United States had to control the coastline of the Confederacy. Extending from the mid-Atlantic to the western shore of the Gulf of Mexico, the Confederate States of America had widespread links to trade routes bringing arms and supplies from abroad. The Union's military planners were compelled to find a way to control the porous sounds and rivers forging the connection between Confederate land and foreign weaponry and markets. As part of the effort to crush Southern commerce, men who would become Ninth Corps soldiers in July 1862 spent months along the coasts of North and South Carolina as early as the summer of 1861.

The two states immediately south of Virginia included coastal areas central to the Union strategy of suppressing Confederate trade. The U.S. Navy's South Atlantic Blockading Squadron would be based at Port Royal Island, South Carolina, while North Carolina served as the primary focus of the North Atlantic Blockading Squadron. Due to the navy's overwhelming firepower, notable successes took place along the Carolina coast early in the war. Hatteras Inlet, which provided egress for ships from the Atlantic Ocean to inland North Carolina, became Union-held territory in August 1861. The victory at Hatteras was against what one naval officer deemed "the most convenient entrance for the distribution of supplies to the Confederate army in Virginia." Moreover, the state offered "ample cargoes for outward bound blockade-running vessels."[1]

Although the United States Navy played a key role in dominating the Confederacy's supply lifeline, men of the U.S. Army were needed to occupy extensive oceanic real estate. As summer turned to autumn in

1861, Thomas Sherman and Ambrose Burnside, the two generals forming coastal forces in the North, remained busy organizing regiments. The generals did not know the destinations for the separate missions. Such details would be worked out as volunteers were brought together from several Northern states. Eventually, Sherman's expedition would go to South Carolina, while Burnside's force would be known as the Department of North Carolina.

EARLY NINTH CORPS LEADERS

To provide necessary context to the creation of the Ninth Corps, profiles of seven officers who held senior rank by late summer 1861 are presented below.

Ambrose Burnside would be the first commander of the Ninth Corps. Born in Indiana in 1824, Burnside joined the West Point Class of 1847, where he came to know many men who would play a prominent role in the Civil War, including George McClellan. A strong friendship developed between the two cadets, which paid dividends for Burnside before and during the American rebellion. Deciding to craft a future outside the army, Burnside resigned his commission in 1853, then failed in business ventures, most notably as the inventor of a breech-loading rifle. As a means for his friend to avoid ruin, McClellan ensured Burnside found railroad employment. After the attack on Fort Sumter, Burnside received command of a ninety-day unit, the 1st Rhode Island, then competently led a brigade at First Bull Run. He returned to Rhode Island shortly after the battle because of his regiment's expired term of service. Burnside quickly found himself back in Washington as newly arrived army commander George McClellan found use for his friend. Burnside received the star of a brigadier general on August 6. The vision of Burnside leading an amphibious operation quickly jelled after a meeting between the two generals.[2]

Edward Ferrero, who, for well or ill, would have long affiliation with the Ninth Corps, was born in Spain to Italian parents in early 1831. Moving to New York while still young, Ferrero developed an interest in dance instruction, a career his father found in his new country. Although the younger Ferrero taught dance at West Point, he did not attend the

Returning to Rhode Island shortly after First Bull Run, then Colonel Ambrose Burnside sat in the middle of a group during a welcome home celebration. Isaac Rodman, doomed to die as a Ninth Corps general at Antietam, stands to Burnside's immediate left. LIBRARY OF CONGRESS

military academy. Time in the New York militia helped him gain military experience prior to the Civil War. Ferrero was the commanding officer of the 51st New York in the summer of 1861. He would take his men to North Carolina under Burnside. Early in the expedition, Ferrero's regiment was part of a brigade including two future units in the Ninth Corps: the 21st Massachusetts and the 51st Pennsylvania.[3]

John Hartranft possessed an unyielding drive to serve. A Pennsylvania native with a background in engineering and law, Hartranft led a militia regiment at the start of the Civil War. Taking his troops south, the soldiers' term of service expired just before First Bull Run. Hartranft was horrified when his men elected to head home just before a major engagement. Hartranft stayed with Irvin McDowell's army prior to the battle. His bravery on the field would earn him a Medal of Honor for voluntarily serving as a staff member who "participated in the battle after expiration of his term of service, distinguishing himself in rallying several regiments which had been thrown into confusion." By the Autumn of

1861, Hartranft commanded the 51st Pennsylvania, which he had ready to sail with Burnside.[4]

A future commander of the Ninth Corps, *John Parke* was a brigadier general prior to the departure of Burnside's expedition. His brigade would include the 8th Connecticut and 9th New York, both destined for arduous service as Ninth Corps regiments. Parke's early life showed great promise. A native of Pennsylvania, he was second out of forty-three in the West Point Class of 1849. Parke's army service before the Civil War was in military engineering, a common role for excellent students and leaders. The young officer's skills were in high demand. Parke surveyed the Iowa-Minnesota border and the Little Colorado River, and he was Secretary of the Board for the Improvement of Lake Harbors and Western Rivers. Another major part of Parke's work experience was railroad surveying. He was involved in sensitive assignments, including surveying the U.S.-Canadian border in the disputed area of Washington Territory. A Regular army captain in late summer 1861, Parke went east when the Civil War started.[5]

Jesse Reno, a native of predominantly Unionist western Virginia, was a graduate of West Point's Class of 1846, which would become perhaps the most famous in the history of the academy. Although a classmate of George McClellan, Reno was three-and-a-half years older than the future commander of the U.S. Army during the Civil War. Reno finished eighth in his class, six positions below McClellan, then served in several locations as an ordinance officer. Two brevets in Mexico demonstrated his sterling qualities as a soldier. He spent two years in the 1850s assigned to the Utah Territory, part of the federal government's effort to show its power in a jurisdiction that did not appreciate Washington's authority. Assigned to an arsenal in southern Alabama in early 1861, Reno's command was bloodlessly overrun by state forces, an unavoidable fate that did not diminish the potential superiors saw in the captain. By the start of the Civil War, Reno was at Fort Leavenworth, Kansas, another post under threat from secessionists.[6]

An original brigade commander in the North Carolina expedition, Reno's strong leadership led his troops to place great confidence in their general. Reno was

4

never forgetful of the wants of his command; always setting a high example in his honest soldierly nobility of speech and action and devoted courage. We soon learned to love and respect him for the truth of his manly character no less than we confided in his military discretion; cool cautious, and slow till the moment came to strike quick and hard, and then with his men, inspiring them with his own magnetic irresistible daring. A man without fear and without reproach![7]

With Quaker parents deeply devoted to their principles, **Isaac Rodman** was given the middle name of Peace. A native of Rhode Island born in 1822, Rodman lacked formal military training, but proved his worth as an infantry officer. Engaged in business pursuits and elective office, Rodman faithfully served the public. A member of the Rhode Island Senate when the Civil War started, Rodman took part in First Bull Run as a captain in the 2nd Rhode Island. The regiment suffered severely, with ninety-eight casualties, including four officers killed in action. By early October, Rodman earned promotion to colonel of the 4th Rhode Island. The men and their Quaker leader joined Parke's Brigade in the North Carolina expedition.[8]

Isaac Stevens, short in stature but filled with drive and energy, led an adventurous and impactful life before the Civil War. First in his class at West Point in 1839, Stevens, like Parke a decade later, found himself a military engineer assigned to a variety of projects, including work in the Pacific Northwest. Unlike Parke, Stevens did not remain in the military up to the Civil War. He received plaudits and a wound as a staff officer in the War with Mexico, then resigned his commission in 1853. He represented the People of Washington Territory for eight years, four as governor and two terms as delegate to the U.S. Congress. Generally sympathetic to Native peoples, Stevens was heavily involved in negotiating treaties with several tribes. He authored many published works, including his memoir of Mexican War service and reports on railroad surveying work. He became colonel of the 79th New York, known as the Highlanders due to the Scottish ancestry common throughout the regiment, at the end of July 1861. Stevens next earned brigade command in the Army of the Potomac before Sherman's expedition to South Carolina.

Then, Stevens became commander of the First Division of the Ninth Corps in July 1862.[9]

BACKGROUND OF FIVE REGIMENTS IN THE CAROLINA EXPEDITIONS

Twelve of Burnside's regiments and seven of Sherman's would constitute all of the original Ninth Corps in July 1862. Information on the formation of some original Ninth Corps regiments provides context to the history of the command.

Burnside's 21st Massachusetts included many men from Worcester, with other counties and Boston contributing to the unit's initial muster roll. Part of the war's second wave of army volunteers, the 21st began forming shortly after the disaster at First Bull Run on July 21. By the 26th of the month, more than 500 men from seven companies constituted the regiment. As the unit's historian proudly wrote, "early in August the regiment paraded with a full front of brave, patriotic, intelligent, and muscular men." Frustration with supply problems during the summer led to a potential rebellion against army bureaucracy. Writing to the state's adjutant general's office, an officer in the 21st declared, "*No more consolidated morning reports* can be made of this regiment until some blankets are sent out."[10]

The 8th Michigan, one regiment in the Ninth Corps from beginning to end, started to organize in the summer of 1861. Hailing from several of the state's counties and ordered to rendezvous in Grand Rapids, the regiment's first colonel was William Fenton. A New York native and graduate of the state's Hamilton College, Fenton spent four years as a merchantman. Rather than stick with a seafaring life, Fenton married in April 1835, then settled in Michigan. He would serve his new state in different civic capacities, including as mayor of Flint. Departing Detroit on September 27, 1861, Fenton commanded 915 men. The 8th Michigan, with much devoted service ahead, would arrive in Washington three days later.[11]

In late 1863, the 6th New Hampshire would be attached to the Twenty-third Corps for a short time. Nonetheless, the intrepid Granite State outfit would serve in the Ninth Corps for nearly all of the war. The 6th finished its organization in Autumn 1861, mustering in for three years. The farmers who contributed greatly to the ranks came from towns in the central and southern part of the state. The 6th's early officers proved how service in a state militia was not necessarily conducive to extensive knowledge of how to train and motivate volunteer soldiers. Cold weather was another aspect of the regiment's early days that left negative impressions on the new recruits. Simon Griffin, from Keene in southwest New Hampshire, became second in command as the 6th's lieutenant colonel. He would have long affiliation with the 6th, even after promotion to brigade command.

As the cold autumn became winter, the 6th was preparing for the inevitable trip to Washington. The men moved out on Christmas Day, with the regimental historian recalling how residents "gave us a parting cheer of encouragement." Additional praise from Granite Staters awaited from other municipalities, where the 6th received "hearty cheers" from "every manufacturing town through which we passed."[12]

Although the 45th Pennsylvania would be part of the Ninth Corps from the beginning, the unit did not join Sherman in South Carolina until near the end of 1861. Only five companies of the regiment were assembled in the Keystone State by the time Sherman's initial force departed Annapolis in October. Continued diligent work from company commanders and original Col. Thomas Welsh from Lancaster County brought all ten companies together on October 21. Gov. Andrew Curtin presented the men with a state flag on the following day. After a relatively short march to Maryland, the men served as guards to prevent violence during their neighboring state's autumn elections. They would depart via steamers on November 21, with Fort Monroe, Virginia, as their first destination.

In the history of the 45th Pennsylvania, one officer recalled how the time in Virginia "was of great use to the regiment in many ways," especially because measles had hit the unit the previous month. "The weather and climate were such that our men recovered in a remarkable degree," with plenty of time for the battalion drills so vital to the discipline and training of a new body of troops.[13] By early December, the regiment would arrive to augment Sherman's force in South Carolina.

Another regiment that would span the entire history of the Ninth Corps, the 50th Pennsylvania, formed under the oversight of Col. Benjamin Christ. Companies from the 50th came from several counties in southern and eastern Pennsylvania. Colonel Christ promised Governor Curtin the men of the 50th would not disrespect the trust confided in them. On the 50th's departure for destiny in early October, a Harrisburg paper suggested "no nobler or more enthusiastic set of men" ever left the state. They would arrive in time to be part of Sherman's initial expedition.[14]

BATTLE EXPERIENCE IN THE CAROLINAS

Ideas for controlling the coastal Carolinas occupied the mind of Maj. Gen. George McClellan, who had commanded what would be deemed the Army of the Potomac since late July 1861. McClellan's expectations of what Carolina expeditions were required to accomplish grew later in the year after he took on the additional role of general-in-chief, the highest-ranking officer in the U.S. Army. Realizing the war appeared destined for a long duration, McClellan understood how coastal operations were central to the entire war effort. Burnside's men held a key role in this vision.[15]

Near Hilton Head, South Carolina, members of the 50th Pennsylvania stood ready for action. LIBRARY OF CONGRESS

For several months, men of the future Ninth Corps witnessed a range of events in locations throughout eastern North and South Carolina. A series of engagements defined Burnside's force. His troops took control of Roanoke Island, New Bern, Fort Macon, and other areas. Across the first half of 1862, the soldiers also learned the importance of continued training, such as regimental and brigade drills. Patrolling defensive lines and excursions into the countryside consumed much time for the troops occupying important Confederate territory.

Burnside later suggested of the February 8 conquest of Roanoke Island, "The results of this important victory were great, particularly in inspiring the confidence of the country in the efficiency of their armies in the field." The timing certainly proved good. Two days after Roanoke Island, the U.S. Navy captured Elizabeth City, North Carolina, halfway between the island and the Confederate naval base at Norfolk, Virginia. In the west the same week, Ulysses S. Grant was quickly seizing ground in northern Tennessee, with Fort Henry captured and Fort Donelson about to fall. Nashville was doomed, just like the North Carolina Coast.[16]

Penitent survivors had gained some time to rest. Of Burnside's first victory, a Rhode Islander suggested, "Thank god my life was spared, and the Stars and Stripes were in triumph over Roanoke Island." He continued, "Burnside intends leaving here tomorrow or next day for *somewhere*." His prediction of the next movement's timing was off by weeks, but the exultant warrior knew he needed some rest. He concluded, "Love to all. Good night. I now will turn in, not having had much sleep for the past sixty hours for many reasons."[17] Nagging fatigue would become the lot of many Ninth Corps men for the rest of the war.

More than a month later at New Bern, thick fog diminished Burnside's ability to fully plan and prepare for the attack. As troops moved into place, Burnside recalled, "We were much nearer to the enemy than we expected, and were soon in contact with them." Reno's brigade benefited as they marched over land along a railroad bed, rather than through seemingly endless swamps.

In the vanguard of Reno's Brigade, which covered the left of Burnside's front, the 675 men in the 21st Massachusetts made first contact with the enemy. Lt. Col. William Clark commanded the Bay Staters.

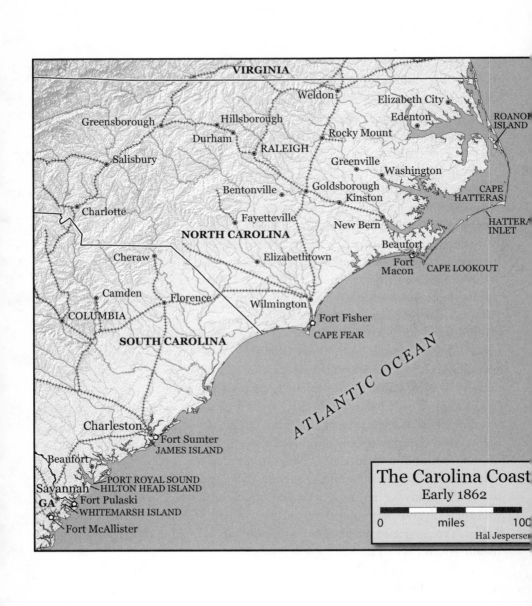

The Carolina Coast
Early 1862

0   miles   100

Hal Jesperse

VIRGINIA

Weldon

Greensborough   Hillsborough   Elizabeth City

Durham   Rocky Mount   Edenton   ROANOKE
                      ISLAND
Salisbury   RALEIGH

          Greenville
                   Washington
    Bentonville   Goldsborough
                Kinston   CAPE
                         HATTERAS
Charlotte   Fayetteville   New Bern   HATTERAS
    NORTH CAROLINA   INLET
                 Beaufort
Cheraw   Elizabethtown   Fort
                    Macon   CAPE LOOKOUT

Camden   Florence
             Wilmington
COLUMBIA

SOUTH CAROLINA   Fort Fisher
                   CAPE FEAR

ATLANTIC OCEAN

Charleston
   Fort Sumter
   JAMES ISLAND
Beaufort

Savannah   PORT ROYAL SOUND
        HILTON HEAD ISLAND
GA   Fort Pulaski
    WHITEMARSH ISLAND
Fort McAllister

One problem for the men across Burnside's command was the dampness leaving dozens in the regiment unable to fire their muskets. Moving ahead anyway, men in the 21st earned great respect from their commander. As Clark reported, "It is noteworthy evidence of the discipline and courage on the part of the men that more than 50 went into the battle having only their bayonets to work with."

General Reno was heavily involved in the movements of his brigade. The 51st Pennsylvania remained in a reserve position, due to the regiment's hard work the previous day helping to move cannons forward. They had practically no rest since arriving at their bivouac shortly before moving out for the assault. With the difficulty of an attack against strong fieldworks, Confederates were able to make their doomed stand costly to Burnside. Colonel Ferrero of the 51st New York noted the enemy troops returned fire with "great vigor, making sad havoc in our ranks."[18]

The right wing of the 21st Massachusetts reached the Confederate works before any other part of the attack. Retaining intense devotion to the cause and hearing friendly troops "heavily engaged" to his right, Reno, sword in hand, joined some of the first men of the 21st into the Confederate rifle pits, forcing out a North Carolina militia unit. Enough Southern troops were able to counterattack, however, so the Massachusetts soldiers were not able to maintain their advanced position for long. As more troops were added to the fray, "The battle now became general along our whole line," Reno reported, "and raged fiercely for about three and a half hours."[19]

Strong leadership from Isaac Rodman propelled the 4th Rhode Island into the Confederate defenses farther to the right. "Fourth Rhode Island, fall in," the Quaker general commanded. The attack by Rodman's men swung the tactical situation in favor of Burnside's troops. A man in the 4th serving on a naval vessel considered the Confederate fire "murderous," but Rodman's "grand charge" occurred at a critical time. With General Parke ordering support from the 8th Connecticut and 5th Rhode Island Battalion, the tide pushed Confederate forces back. Rodman's soldiers and the Connecticut troops placed national and state flags on the conquered works. "Thank God, the day is ours," Burnside said.[20]

The two sides sustained more than 1,000 casualties at the battle of New Bern, with the Confederates suffering 55 percent of the total. The strong showing from future Ninth Corps troops inflicted heartrending losses on the Confederates. An officer in the 33rd North Carolina, which endured half of the defenders killed in action, lamented, "Some of our bravest and best men found bloody graves in their first and only battle."[21]

Burnside wrote McClellan on March 15, the same day he was informed of McClellan losing his role as general-in-chief, retaining only his command of the Army of the Potomac. The note, sent shortly after Secretary of War Stanton expressed interest in Burnside coordinating with McClellan's army, announced the capture of New Bern and the planned attack on Fort Macon to the southeast. Burnside stressed his faith in "My dear Mac," and hopes for the future. Burnside was especially pleased with the quality of troops in his Department of North Carolina. He concluded the missive, "If I had 40,000 men like these, [I] could do almost anything." A similar sentiment was written to his troops as Burnside congratulated them on "their brilliant and hard-won victory." He noted, "With such soldiers, advance is victory."[22]

One state to the south, most weeks offered mundane work and limited fighting for soldiers in the South Carolina expedition. A wicked little battle occurred on an island in Georgia on April 16. The action resulted from the capture of Fort Pulaski by Union forces earlier in the month. Seven companies of the 8th Michigan embarked to escort engineers during a reconnaissance of Whitemarsh Island, immediately east of Savannah and 10 miles below the southern tip of Hilton Head. "I have for some time kept pickets and small scouting parties on Whitemarsh, knowing that the enemy occasionally visited it," reported Col. Marcellus Douglass of a Georgia regiment. The result led to what a Michigander labeled "a short but sharp conflict."[23]

In the early part of the engagement, small parties of men branched out across the island. Knowing the bulk of the regiment would rally near their disembarkation spot, the seven companies reunited in time to not get overwhelmed piecemeal. Certainly, the officers in these groups were learning a great deal about the need to concentrate forces. Some confusion existed early in the final engagement between the small contingents of enemy troops, as the advance company of the 8th Michigan fell back. The Georgians then were "pouring in upon us a steady and destructive fire," according to engineer James Wilson, although the Wolverine warriors were able to hold the Confederates in check. Colonel Fenton displayed excellent tactical judgment as he moved a company to the right in an attempt to hit the Georgians in their flank. Eventually, the Georgians fell back, and the isolated and endangered Michigan soldiers "gradually and very quietly under cover of night" were able to safely depart the island, with a return to their camps at Port Royal. The engineers reported a successful completion of their planned reconnaissance at the cost of ten dead and thirty-five wounded, well in excess of 10 percent of Fenton's engaged strength.[24]

Next to New Bern, the biggest fight for future Ninth Corps troops in the Carolinas occurred on James Island, immediately south of Charleston, South Carolina. An excellent Confederate position, known as Fort Lamar, stood near the small village of Secessionville. The most serious limiting factor to an assault on Fort Lamar was the fault of Mother Nature. A mile from the fort, the dry, expansive width of ground provided room for regiments to form. However, while nearing Fort Larmar, the ground became a bog and rather undulating. Moreover, as men moved east toward their target, the available space was considerably thinner, as if the Confederates intended to funnel Unionist lambs to the slaughter along the fort's walls.

The battle of Secessionville took place on June 16. The Wolverines of the 8th Michigan recorded 184 casualties, more than one-fourth of the entire Union loss during the battle. Among the regiment's suffering were sixty-one killed or mortally wounded. The Highlanders of the 79th New York were another regiment tested severely along the ramparts of Fort Lamar. As a brigade commander, Brig. Gen. Isaac Stevens led his former regiment and others during the horrible brawl.[25]

THE NINTH CORPS COALESCES

Creating Unionist enclaves along the Carolina coast, supporting naval efforts to suppress Confederate commerce, and simply occupying Southern ground were all important reasons for the expeditions to the

Carolinas. The largest prize of all remained Virginia. The need to protect Washington while also hoping to conquer the Confederate capital 100 miles away in Richmond placed the Old Dominion in the bull's-eye of Union war strategy. The main problem was the inability of Union field commanders, with considerably more soldiers than those in the Carolinas, to make lasting progress throughout Virginia. Thus sprang the movement of troops from other locations to the Confederacy's largest and most important scene of action.

For all his bluster and personal sense of destiny, George McClellan proved unable to make much of the Peninsula campaign he had conceived early in the war. This was an effort to strike Richmond from the east. By late June, McClellan's army was in full retreat after seeing the spires of Richmond. McClellan decided a retrograde from the Confederate capital was necessary after fierce counter blows by Robert E. Lee's Army of Northern Virginia. Known as the Seven Days, McClellan's loss of about 20 miles of real estate east of Richmond brought great concern to Washington's leadership, prompting the quest for additional troops.[26]

Ambrose Burnside played a central role in the drama. After consideration of the best approach for troop deployments, the president began the process culminating in the creation of the Ninth Corps. In his folksy style on June 28—in the midst of the Seven Days—Lincoln wrote Burnside, "I think you had better go, with any re-enforcements you can spare, to General McClellan." With McClellan's army in a better position by early July, Burnside had still not embarked his troops. Reaffirming the president's order, Secretary of War Stanton compelled the movement of Burnside's soldiers, with the troops under Reno and Parke heading to Virginia.[27]

Hosea Towne wrote of the effort to transfer much of Burnside's command north. Towne's 6th New Hampshire spent Independence Day "on board a nasty boat packed so thick that we could not all lie down at night." Leery of storms on the open water, Towne felt immense relief when his ship passed through Hatteras Inlet into the Atlantic. "We were pleased to see the sea as smooth as it was ever known to be," the Granite Stater wrote, "Perhaps this was a slight recompense for shaking us so severely when we came down last winter." The armada would arrive off Fort Monroe on July 7, with some troops waiting more than a day before going ashore.[28] Twelve future Ninth Corps regiments were out of North Carolina forever.

Burnside had a busy several weeks, with journeys to Washington where he joined discussions to craft a better strategic plan. The Army of the Potomac's repulse before Richmond certainly made Lincoln and Stanton lose further respect for McClellan's abilities. While in the capital, Burnside met with Henry Halleck, the new general-in-chief, and also spent time at McClellan's camps in June and July. Staff officer Daniel Read Larned, a staunch supporter of Burnside, wrote on July 7, "We shall undoubtedly see some pretty rough times now, but we are all in the best of spirits."[29]

Observant of both McClellan's needs and the perspective of the Lincoln administration, Burnside sent a cautionary note to the Army of the Potomac's commander in mid-July. Informing McClellan of his return to southeast Virginia after another trip to Washington, "Burn" wrote:

> *I've much to say to you, and am very anxious to see you. . . . The President has ordered me to remain here for the present, and when I asked him how long, he said 5 or 6 days. I don't know what it means; but I do know my dear Mac that you have lots of enemies, but you must keep cool; don't allow them to provoke you into a quarrel—you must come out all right.*[30]

Seven future Ninth Corps regiments from South Carolina were destined for Virginia. Stanton sent a short letter to Hilton Head on July 3 noting, "The condition of the Army under General McClellan requires that the whole available infantry forces of the Government should be immediately sent to his command on the James River." Maj. Gen. David Hunter, now in command in South Carolina, was required to dispatch "all the infantry force that can be spared" for McClellan's benefit. Two days prior, McClellan won a major defensive victory at Malvern Hill, but his position was still considered tenuous.[31]

Hunter moved to comply with Stanton's request, although he wondered about the fate of his department after losing so many troops. He originally promised ten regiments, but on July 11, he confirmed for

Stanton, "I send by General Stevens to Fort Monroe six regiments."
Hunter's promise of four more units included the hope that the additional troops would not be needed in Virginia. Hunter got his wish to
some extent, with the 45th Pennsylvania being the seventh and last of his
regiments ordered north. "We had very few sick and had lost scarcely any
of our number," the 45th's historian wrote to recall the good condition of
the unit when orders to head north were received.[32]

The obvious faith the Lincoln administration had in Burnside created the environment for the highly successful major general to command
more troops than the twelve regiments he brought from North Carolina.
Stanton used a July 15 order to Maj. Gen. John Dix, in command at Fort
Monroe, to effectuate the link between regiments from the two Carolina
expeditions. "Let General Hunter's troops be disembarked and placed
under the command of General Burnside," the secretary commanded.[33]

Even before the sea voyages north for the nineteen regiments,
McClellan envisioned how to use the additional manpower. President
Lincoln rejected McClellan's idea to move seven more regiments from
North Carolina to Virginia, which would have emptied New Bern of
Union troops. The general at least planned to use a different route, south
of the James River, an avenue meant to cut links between the seat of
Confederate government and the states below Virginia. The move would
bring victory to Union arms in under three years, but Lincoln seemed
chagrined enough by McClellan's failures to try other ideas. He even
created a new force, the Army of Virginia, under Maj. Gen. John Pope,
stationed well north of the Peninsula, along a line from the Shenandoah
Valley to Fredericksburg.

With unclear direction, Burnside moved his men to Newport News,
on the north bank of the James, across the Peninsula from Fort Monroe.
He would travel north on military and personal business for several days,
receiving an offer to take command of McClellan's army while in Washington later in the month. In turning down the promotion, Burnside
stressed his limited faith in his ability to wield such a large force. He
extolled McClellan, and also did not wish to hurt his old friend, who he
deemed a better general.[34]

Table Intro.1	The Original Ninth Corps and the Carolina Expeditions			
1st Division Brig. Gen. Isaac I. Stevens	1st Brigade Col. William Fenton	*8th MI*	*2nd Brigade, Sherman*	
		28th MA	Not brigaded, Sherman	
		50th PA	*2nd Brigade, Sherman*	
	2nd Brigade Col. Daniel Leasure	46th NY	1st Brigade, Sherman	
		79th NY	*2nd Brigade, Sherman*	
		45th PA	*Not brigaded, Sherman*	
		100th PA	*2nd Brigade, Sherman*	
2nd Division Brig. Gen. Jesse L. Reno	1st Brigade Col. James Nagle	2nd MD	1st Brig., 2nd Div., Burnside	
		6th NH	Williams Brigade, Burnside	
		48th PA	Williams Brigade, Burnside	
	2nd Brigade Col. Edward Ferrero	*21st MA*	*2nd Brigade, Burnside*	
		51st NY	2nd Brigade, Burnside	
		51st PA	*2nd Brigade, Burnside*	
3rd Division Brig. Gen. John G. Parke	1st Brigade Col. Rush Hawkins	9th NY	3rd Brigade, Burnside	
		89th NY	Williams Brigade, Burnside	
		103rd NY	1st Brig., 2nd Div., Burnside	
	2nd Brigade Col. Edward Harland	8th CT	1st Brig., 2nd Div., Burnside	
		11th CT	Williams Brigade, Burnside	
		4th RI	3rd Brigade, Burnside	

Frustrated in their effort to replace McClellan with the Eastern Theater's most successful general to date, the Lincoln administration decided to give Burnside a corps. On July 22, the day Burnside arrived in Washington, General Orders 84 created the Ninth Corps solely from the nineteen regiments that had spent many trying months in the Carolinas. Table Intro.1 shows the regimental lineup of the original Ninth Corps as they camped around Newport News. The last column lists the placement of the regiment in either Sherman's or Burnside's expeditions. Regiments joining Burnside in the spring have their division listed. Because a brigade was the largest organizational unit in the early months of either expedition, regiments that were part of the original waves of troops to the Carolinas have only their brigade noted. The seven regiments that would be in the Ninth Corps for its entire history are indicated in bold italics.[35]

PART ONE

The Chaos of a Virginia Summer

"It was sublime to witness, but awful to participate in."
—CAPT. THOMAS PARKER, 51ST PENNSYLVANIA

AT NEWPORT NEWS

"A BEAUTIFUL GRASSY PLAIN" GREETED THE 6TH NEW HAMPSHIRE around Newport News. Placed in a brigade with the 2nd Maryland and 48th Pennsylvania, the Granite Staters enjoyed many positive developments, albeit in a temporary location. Of the 6th Regiment's first night at their new camp along the James River, George Upton wrote, "I never slept better in my life." Later in the month he proclaimed to his wife, "With the help of God, we shall yet be victorious, and rebellion killed."[1]

A member of the 48th Pennsylvania gleefully wrote of ice cream and other refreshments, which augmented the soldiers' respite from marching and fighting. The happy and resting troops also had typical duties such as the invariable repetition of drill and serving on picket. The regimental historian recalled how proficient the 48th had become "in handling the musket," so drills and more formal parades for the dedicated soldiers "amounted to a poem," especially when visiting Northern ladies were observing.[2]

Colonel James Nagle of the 48th led the brigade of the three regiments. He had been serving as commanding officer of his regiment since October. Nagle had a wide range of military experience dating back to the Mexican War, where he led a Pennsylvania regiment. The native of Reading saw service in the state militia after Mexico and fought with a short-term Pennsylvania unit at First Bull Run. Returning home later in the summer, he found leadership of the 48th as his way back into the war at the age of forty.[3]

The other brigade in Reno's Division, under Edward Ferrero, included three strong regiments with service in North Carolina: the 21st Massachusetts and the "two 51sts" from New York and Pennsylvania. A Bay Stater recalled the pleasing oceanic breeze during the days of rest around Newport News. Fresh clams and boxes of treats from home further nourished the brigade. The historian of the 51st Pennsylvania recalled many games of baseball. Several officers "indulged in this game with right good zest." Colonel Hartranft was considered one of the regiment's best players.[4]

The Newport News camp gave two bakers in the 4th Rhode Island, part of Harland's Brigade in Parke's Third Division, a chance to practice their trade for the benefit of their comrades. A memoirist happily recalled, "There were two large, fourteen-foot brick ovens at the bakery, and two gangs of men to work them night and day." The double rations and extra 40 cents a day made the hot work worthwhile; the bakers were able to trade for additional food and other desirables. "We lived well, and were content with our lot," the talented chef remembered.[5]

The corps' First Division arrived on the Peninsula more than a week after Burnside's force. General Stevens wrote his wife to inform her that he slept for twenty hours during the trip from South Carolina to Virginia. The well-rested general must have been pleased as he surveyed the environs of Newport News. In a letter written at sea, William Lusk informed his mother of his happiness at being out of South Carolina, "Few of us regret to leave this unholy soil and wretchedly mismanaged department, where we have been sure only of mismanagement and disgrace." Those disgusted with the course of their war while in South Carolina discovered the delight of attaching themselves to a winner after the move north. As the historian of the 79th New York wrote, "The Highlanders were well pleased to serve under so distinguished a leader" as Ambrose Burnside.[6]

Earning the second star of a major general for his work in North Carolina, Ambrose Burnside became the first commander of the Ninth Corps in July 1862. LIBRARY OF CONGRESS

With all three divisions at hand, Burnside commanded about 13,000 men. Capt. Ralph Ely of the 8th Michigan recorded hard work for the troops fresh from the Palmetto State on July 20. The Wolverines quickly set up their new camp. Ely even commanded the regiment briefly.

Short in stature, but brave and highly respected, Isaac Stevens was the commander of the First Division, Ninth Corps until his death at Chantilly on September 1, 1862.
LIBRARY OF CONGRESS

Drills took up much time for Stevens's boys, just like their corps comrades. Colonel Fenton still led the First Brigade of the Division, with Daniel Leasure in charge of the Second Brigade, including the 46th and 79th New York alongside the 45th and 100th Pennsylvania.

Some bad blood emerged between the 46th and 79th New York while the men camped in Newport News. The German regiment included many members fond of wine, preferring the beverage to the whiskey common throughout many other regiments. When General Stevens ordered the stock of wine confiscated, then named members of the 79th to guard the alcohol, the 46th grew restive. Feelings became more disgusted the following morning, when only empty bottles remained. Perhaps this was an example of General Stevens playing favorites, with the division commander turning a blind eye as his original regiment consumed the wine. The spat was one reason for a change in organization. The two Empire State outfits would soon never serve in the same brigade again.[7]

Downtime around Newport News gave men the chance to ponder the big picture, with some starting to doubt the rumored expansion of the Union's war aims to include an end to slavery. General McClellan and many senior officers preferred to keep the fate of slavery peripheral to the immediate consideration of defeating Confederate armies. Although President Lincoln had yet to formally announce any bold effort, George Upton doubted his own resolve to keep fighting if the government added the abolition of slavery to war goals.

Aside from the military, we don't see much in the shape of humanity but Niggers, and the worst wish I have for anyone North is that all that think so much of them was out here to fight especially if they turn this warfare into fighting for the Niggers only. I came out here to help support the Constitution & Laws of the land, and for nothing else, and if it is turned into some other purpose—then those that do it may do the fighting.[8]

Regardless of a soldier's views of slaves and slavery, all could spend time dreaming of life before the war. Highlander Alexander Campbell felt the longing for home. He noted how the regiments were pleasantly situated, with water in bountiful supply. Campbell lamented the relatively low number of men present in the regiment, only about 400. Optimistically, he informed his wife that he would likely stay around Newport News for some time. "I have felt very Lon[e]ly all day," he concluded on July 20. Less than a week later, in response to his wife's plea, Campbell said he would not be able to make a quick trip home. He expressed a wish to see her and the boys, even for just two weeks, but furloughs were virtually unheard of, and recruiting duty was reserved for those of higher rank, or those who had been wounded.[9]

REBELLION IN THE RANKS

Downright insolence pervaded the 4th Rhode Island for several weeks. Problems began in June when Lt. Col. George Tew failed to gain the command of the regiment over an "outsider" from the 2nd Rhode Island, William Steere. Tew was very well liked by the regiment, and the men grumbled mightily through drills and their normal duties for a time. Steere confiscated liquor his soldiers had received in packages sent from home, then delayed pay for the men in an effort to control their negative impulses.

Tension remained at the start of August. As detailed by a regimental memoirist, one of Steere's attempts to address the regiment led to an ugly incident when a piece of firewood "scraped acquaintance with the side of his head." A central outcome of the strife was the court-martial of Pvt. Edwin Gallagher, Company E.

Gallagher was charged with violating two articles of war. Under the first charge, the private "did, by threats and boisterous language, create a sedition in the camp" of the regiment. Based on the four specifications under the second charge, Gallagher may very well have been the assailant of Steere in the incident involving the use of firewood as a club. The enlisted man was alleged to "seize or grasp" Lieutenant Colonel Steere "and attempt violence against his superior officer." In the only specification to which Gallagher pled guilty, the soldier also "did disobey the lawful commands of his superior officer, by continued disregard of orders to stop tumultuous noise and profanity." The final two specifications related to Gallagher's refusal to obey orders to return to his quarters and cease disrupting camp with his insolence and noise.

Found guilty on all charges and specifications, the court unanimously sentenced Gallagher, "To be shot until he be dead." Under military law, the court had no choice but to render the sentence. However, the recommendation for death was remitted as part of the process by which President Lincoln would review the matter. Gallagher may have considered himself fortunate that the founding father of the Ninth Corps, Ambrose Burnside, was leading the Army of the Potomac by the time the verdict was transmitted up the chain of command. Burnside echoed the request for reduction of the sentence for a soldier in an original Ninth Corps regiment. Instead, "the prisoner will be dishonorably discharged from the service, with a forfeiture of all pay."

The resistance from regimental malcontents calmed soon after the events leading to Gallagher's court-martial, with Steere still in command. Tew and thirteen other officers resigned later in the month. Steere's strong commitment to his men would be appreciated later in the summer, when he would be seriously wounded in Maryland.[10]

Even with some unhappiness, a general state of contentment prevailed. The victories in North Carolina marked Burnside's troops as special in the eyes of some other soldiers. As the historian of the 21st Massachusetts opined, "We were much pleased to find in what high regard General Burnside's men were held by their brother soldiers in Virginia." With the addition of Stevens's Division from South Carolina, he continued, "we felt that we had become a power in the centre of grand operations."[11] Soldierly success often pairs itself with danger, and the Ninth Corps would soon know plenty about how their reputation meant more active service.

MOVING FARTHER NORTH

As the troops rested around Newport News, the strategic situation in Virginia failed to offer clarity. McClellan kept his army protected around Harrison's Landing. Even a strong natural position at Malvern Hill—closer to Richmond—could not suit the cautious general. Meanwhile, John Pope's Army of Virginia started to assemble as a single force, although a division rested at Fredericksburg. Pope's arrogant demeanor and disrespect for some Eastern troops earned him few friends among his officers and the rank and file. Career soldiers across the U.S. Army, including McClellan and Burnside, strongly condemned Pope's ideas to live off the land and arrest Confederate citizens. Pope was certainly sure of himself, seeming to believe Robert E. Lee and his army could be pushed aside by sheer will. In a note to General Halleck on July 30, Pope's attempt at foresight proved utterly ridiculous. He reported the likely retreat of the Confederates to a line from Lynchburg to Danville, well west of Richmond and almost to the North Carolina border.[12] This would not be the first, last, or most devastating mistake John Pope made in the summer of 1862.

Burnside joined Halleck in a visit to Harrison's Landing late in July. The sense of stalemate on the Peninsula worried the Lincoln administration, especially with Lee starting to move his forces north to confront Pope. McClellan still dreamed of attaching Burnside's men and other troops to the Army of the Potomac for another shot at Richmond. In a one-on-one with his beleaguered and weary field commander, Halleck grew quite flustered. The Army of the Potomac was well southeast of Richmond and could not easily support Pope, who was under far more danger than anyone wearing the blue uniform of the U.S. Army realized. After McClellan sought troops in excess of his verbal agreement with Halleck, the fate of the Peninsula campaign was sealed. Because the move would further limit the means to support Pope, a western drive from south of the James was taken off the table. Halleck made some highly fateful decisions soon after returning to Washington.[13] The plans dramatically altered the trajectory of the Ninth Corps' summer. Relaxation along the James with pleasing summer breezes and plenty of bread would soon be a memory.

Orders officially terminating the Peninsula campaign began with a missive to Burnside, not McClellan. Halleck wired Newport News on August 1, "The troops of General Burnside's command will immediately embark for Aquia Creek, and on reaching that landing will take position near Fredericksburg; the movement to be made as rapidly as possible, and the destination to be concealed." The following afternoon, Burnside responded, "My troops are rapidly embarking," with a midnight departure planned. He also reminded Halleck of his corps' lack of wagons, ambulances, artillery, and cavalry, all left behind in the Carolinas. Halleck soon informed Pope of the initial effort to augment the Army of Virginia.[14]

On August 3 the Army of the Potomac was ordered to prepare for a sea voyage from Fort Monroe. "You will take immediate measures to effect this," Halleck demanded of the Peninsula evacuation. The following day, McClellan begged for a change to the order in a very long note to Halleck, predicting the evacuation of the Peninsula would bring a "fatal blow" to the war effort.[15]

Burnside rapidly took to the task of moving the Ninth Corps from Newport News to Aquia Landing, 10 miles north of Fredericksburg. While cruising up the river, Burnside's ship passed the boat carrying the 51st Pennsylvania, with the soldiers happy to see their corps commander. "Three cheers were given for him with a hearty good-will," the regiment's historian wrote.

Burnside arrived at Aquia on the evening of August 3 with some of the Ninth Corps. The rest of the troops arrived over the course of a few days, with Captain Ely reporting the 8th Michigan's disembarkation at Aquia on August 6. An officer in the 48th Pennsylvania absorbed the scenery on the train ride south to Falmouth, which reminded him of home. Sadly, a member of the regiment, perhaps overwhelmed with the stress of a soldiers' life, committed suicide during the steamer ride north.[16]

On the 4th, Halleck informed Pope of the delay in an advance of the Ninth Corps due to Burnside's lack of transportation, artillery, and cavalry. Pope's division at Fredericksburg could move west, at least, while Burnside occupied the area and protected the vital link with Aquia Landing. The presence of the Ninth Corps also guarded the region between Pope's army and Fredericksburg. Halleck compelled Pope to retain linkage with Burnside, showing obvious concern about the chance of Lee's army moving northeast to crush the separated Union commands.[17]

Men arriving around Falmouth soon found pleasures like those awaiting them a month before at Newport News. Fresh water appeared in abundance, and many wondered how they ever managed to stay hydrated and healthy from the fetid water they settled for in North

Carolina. The 6th New Hampshire's historian recalled the beautiful view in camp opposite Fredericksburg. The soldiers used subterfuge to feast on local delicacies. The Granite Staters possessed an abundance of counterfeit Confederate currency, thanks to a printer in Philadelphia. Ready to do more damage to the South, George Upton informed his wife of the expected move to augment a major attack. "I hope when they get the ball in motion, they wont[*sic*] let it stop till it gets into the Gulf of Mexico," Upton explained.[18]

Members of the 9th New York also enjoyed the scenery around Fredericksburg. "I do think that this country is the prettiest in the world," a memoirist penned. The spires of the city multiplied the charms of the vicinity. Hills dotted with tents did not detract from the location's attractions for the happy man. Like many of their comrades, the 9th New York had to send men out on picket duty, but the soldiers seemed much happier in Virginia than North Carolina.[19]

On August 8, Captain Ely took about one hundred men to relieve some of Pope's troops who had yet to march west. The Wolverines picked some blackberries, which undoubtedly proved a welcome treat. Hot weather prevailed as regiments alternated between duty on picket and rest in camp.[20]

Upset at the slow pace of troops moving off the Peninsula, Halleck wired McClellan on August 9. The stern rebuke Halleck penned offered proof "Mac" had failed to heed the advice of "Burn" to not make enemies in the Lincoln administration. With five full days elapsed since the order to remove his army from the Peninsula, McClellan's troops had yet to board a ship. Halleck scolded the Army of Potomac's commander.

> *I am of the opinion that the enemy is massing his forces in front of Genl Pope and Burnside and that he expects to crush them and move forward to the Potomac. You must send reinforcements instantly to Aquia Creek. Considering the amount of transportation at your disposal your delay is not satisfactory. You must move with all possible celerity.[21]*

The next day, McClellan showed the temperament of a spoiled child, and much worse. In a letter to his wife, the army commander noted, "I have a strong idea that Pope will be thrashed during the coming week—& very badly whipped he will be & ought to be—such a villain as he is ought to bring defeat upon any cause that employs him."[22] The only way Pope could lose would be through a military defeat costing thousands of Union casualties. McClellan's wish for such an outcome damages his historical reputation.

In contrast to his flustered friend, Ambrose Burnside had quickly moved his men to within supporting distance of Pope. Without a murmur, he then acted as an administrator for Pope, funneling troops west, even though Burnside was a senior major general to the Army of Virginia's commander. Burnside could have demanded command of Pope's army. Instead, a nineteenth-century writer lauded Burnside's "customary devotion to his country."[23]

TWO DIVISIONS TO THE RESCUE

A portion of Pope's army fought a bloody engagement at Cedar Mountain on August 9. Although the battle led to a Confederate withdrawal, the tussle unveiled the danger Pope faced from the bold Southern army, with Stonewall Jackson's men heavily involved in the fight. No one in the Unionist high command rested securely as Pope's men stood in central Virginia with Lee's army ready to brawl and knowing the divided nature of Union forces. A tense stalemate prevailed along Pope's line, which rested uncomfortably between the Rapidan and Rappahannock rivers, nearly 30 miles northwest of Fredericksburg. Pope had yet to gain reinforcements from Burnside or McClellan.

On August 9, Burnside gave an update to Halleck, noting the disappointing addition of only one regiment from South Carolina after four were expected. Hunter's decision to send a single regiment limited the manpower Burnside had when the Ninth Corps moved to help Pope. Based on intelligence he was gathering, Burnside kept Halleck's nerves on edge by suggesting Lee's force was likely on the hunt for Pope's army. Later in the day, Halleck replied, "I fear the enemy may attack Pope in large force. Be ready at a moment's notice to co-operate with him."[24]

The order sending the Ninth Corps forward arrived on August 12. Burnside was required to retain some troops to protect the region around Fredericksburg, a task given to Parke's Third Division. Then Burnside was ordered to "send the remainder to Pope's assistance by the road north of the Rapidan." Halleck requested frequent updates on the arrival of McClellan's troops finally getting ready to leave the Peninsula. Burnside himself stayed in Fredericksburg. Reno took charge of the two divisions heading west toward an unknown future attached to the Army of Virginia. Burnside sent some artillery and two companies of cavalry with Reno. Of his two divisions, Burnside promised they would arrive to assist Pope "as early as possible without breaking down the men."[25]

Reno, who had gained the second star of a major general earlier in the summer, commanded both his own division and the men under Stevens after the troops left Falmouth. The Ninth Corps had about 8,000 men across the two divisions for the march to join Pope. This would give the Army of Virginia close to 50,000 effectives before any of McClellan's men arrived. With continued hope for assistance from McClellan's army, the departure of the Ninth Corps was prudent, especially because the Army of Virginia was wedged between two rivers, something no textbook would suggest to a general.

Stevens's First Division included two artillery batteries, the 8th Massachusetts and Battery E, 2nd U.S. Earlier in the summer, the Massachusetts artillerists enlisted for only six months. Under the command of Capt. Asa Cook, the battery had quite an ordeal reaching Washington. Moving south via rail, a horrifying incident occurred south of Trenton, New Jersey. As the adjutant general was informed, "The train ran off the track and several of the forward cars were thrown into the canal." Cook's outfit lost two men and thirteen horses killed, with several reported injured, the costliest day of service the battery would suffer.[26]

A New Yorker, Lt. Samuel Benjamin, commanded the excellent 20-pound Parrott rifled cannons of Battery E. The unit had been attached to the same brigade as the 79th New York during First Bull Run. The Highlanders' historian noted the "mutual admiration" the two units reestablished. The cooperation included the occasional use of volunteers from the 79th to assist the battery. Benjamin, only twenty-three years old, graduated twelfth out of forty-five in the May 1861 class at West Point. Quickly promoted to first lieutenant, Benjamin and his battery spent several months in the defenses of Washington and on the Peninsula. A Highlander described Benjamin as "a skillful officer and perfect gentleman."[27]

The First Division's infantry consisted of three brigades, with only two regiments each. Benjamin Christ commanded the 8th Michigan and 50th Pennsylvania, while Colonel Leasure's two regiments were the 46th New York and his Roundheads of the 100th Pennsylvania. The 79th New York and 28th Massachusetts constituted the brigade of Col. Addison Farnsworth.[28]

Reno's Second Division retained the same organization under Nagle and Ferrero. The men in the 48th Pennsylvania gave up their "very pleasant and agreeable" posting in Fredericksburg to fall in for the march with their brigade comrades. As men from the regiment walked by on their way west from Falmouth, members of the 9th New York recalled the time they enjoyed with the Keystone Staters on Hatteras Island. To give their marching Pennsylvania pals a boost, "Our Regiment cheered them lustily as they passed," a 9th New York soldier wrote. The good wishes from fellow soldiers must have assisted the 48th's march, although one man recalled the unfortunate amount of mud encountered along the way. Additionally, the decision to not take tents left men exposed to night air that felt unexpectedly chilly. Evening thunderstorms added to the woe, with a Granite Stater suggesting, "Nothing will take the fun and vim out of a soldier quicker than rain and mud."[29]

To ensure a rapid march, General Stevens ordered his men to leave all surplus clothing and other equipment at their Fredericksburg camp. The division's first night on the trip found the men along Deep Run, which flows into the Rappahannock on the north side of the river. Thus, the first day's march amounted to roughly 13 miles. "Water very scarce," Capt. Horatio Belcher of the 8th Michigan wrote on the 14th. A detail walked 2 miles to find an excellent well capable of soothing hundreds of throats.

The next day, with Stevens's men moving before dawn, would see the division encamped around Rappahannock Station, an additional 18 miles. With Pope still on the other side of the Rappahannock, the men were required to head south, reaching Culpepper, then Racoon Ford on the Rapidan.[30] Reno's men then were the left flank of Pope's army.

Elements of the Ninth Corps started reaching Culpepper on the afternoon of August 14, with rain still a problem for men without adequate shelter. The start of the 15th "found all trying to dry themselves," a member of the 48th Pennsylvania recorded. One soldier in the state's 51st Regiment also remembered the rain, which seemed especially bad as the troops neared Pope's army. "It had rained nearly all day and the marching was most horrible," he recalled.[31]

Reno was under orders to establish the Ninth Corps north of the Rapidan between the roads around Raccoon and Somerville Fords, his right or center resting on Cedar Creek. The supply depot for Reno's men was Mitchell's Station on the Orange and Alexandria Railroad, about 2 miles north of the Rapidan and east of Cedar Mountain. On the 15th, Reno was ordered to maintain regular communication with the divisions of Irvin McDowell, about 2 miles west of the Ninth Corps.[32]

On August 14, the 8th Michigan suffered an unfortunate incident robbing the command of a brave, experienced, and excellent officer. Capt. Ralph Ely became the target of an unruly horse. The intrepid officer suffered notable internal injuries, including broken ribs, from the angered beast's kick. Confined to an ambulance for the rest of the day, Ely spent time in a Virginia hospital before being sent to Washington. He would be away from his men for a month.[33]

WORK FOR THE TROOPS AROUND FREDERICKSBURG

General Parke and his division remained near Fredericksburg into late August. Camp Parke, on a delightful hill north of the river, served as the 9th New York's home for a few weeks. The time allowed the men to reunite with a part of the regiment; Capt. Andrew Graham and about 100 men arrived after having remained on Roanoke Island. Members of the 9th benefited from some additional uniforms and equipment, which Graham's band brought north with them. Even Confederate residents enjoyed seeing the bright red and blue uniforms of the 9th New York while the men served on picket duty or paraded through Fredericksburg.

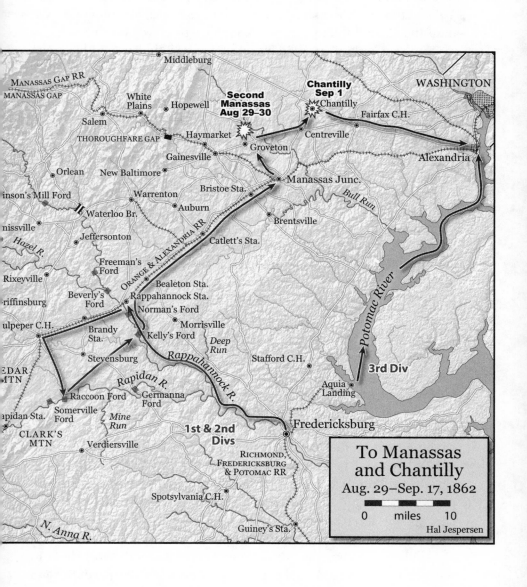

Map labels:

Middleburg

MANASSAS GAP RR
MANASSAS GAP

WASHINGTON

White Plains
Hopewell

Second Manassas Aug 29–30

Chantilly Sep 1
Chantilly

Fairfax C.H.

Salem

THOROUGHFARE GAP   Haymarket
Groveton
Centreville

Alexandria

Gainesville

Orlean   New Baltimore

inson's Mill Ford

Warrenton   Bristoe Sta.

Manassas Junc.

Bull Run

Auburn

Brentsville

Waterloo Br.

nissville

Hazel R.

Jeffersonton

ORANGE & ALEXANDRIA RR

Catlett's Sta.

Rixeyville

Freeman's Ford

Bealeton Sta.

iffinsburg

Beverly's Ford

Rappahannock Sta.

Norman's Ford

Potomac River

ulpeper C.H.   Brandy Sta.   Kelly's Ford   Morrisville

Deep Run

Stafford C.H.

Stevensburg

Rappahannock R.

EDAR MTN

Rapidan R.

Raccoon Ford   Germanna Ford

3rd Div

Somerville Ford

Aquia Landing

apidan Sta.

Mine Run

CLARK'S MTN   Verdiersville

1st & 2nd Divs

Fredericksburg

RICHMOND, FREDERICKSBURG & POTOMAC RR

Spotsylvania C.H.

N. Anna R.

Guiney's Sta.

To Manassas and Chantilly
Aug. 29–Sep. 17, 1862

0   miles   10

Hal Jespersen

Although the citizenry demonstrated "aversion" to the Union soldiers, "the Zouaves could extract a cheer as they passed," while, "the drum-major's attractive appearance rendered him conspicuously observed." On the 14th, a patrol from Company K found a group certainly unhappy to see the New Yorkers' splendid attire. Lt. George Herbert and his group of twenty-nine men captured thirteen Confederate soldiers, some equipment, and four horses.[34]

Taking some secessionist citizens' food created trouble for one soldier in the 89th New York. Sgt. Marvin Watrous of Company K had charges brought against him for killing some sheep. Burnside's direct intervention led to the dropping of the allegations, which appears surprising because of the general's aversion to damaging even disloyal citizens' property. Several men enjoyed the mutton feast made possible by pilfering the countryside, as Sgt. George Englis reported in a letter home on August 18. The pleasing and beautiful region around Fredericksburg was another aspect of the division's assignment Englis enjoyed.[35]

The 45th Pennsylvania was the only regiment in the First Division not sent to Pope with General Stevens. Instead, the men were employed in defending military infrastructure. The vital railroad connection between Aquia Creek and Brooks Station found protection from the 45th. The troops spread out to cover the tracks, with Companies I and K remaining at Aquia Creek. On August 14, Samuel Haynes noted, "We have the most comfortable camp," comparing the location favorably to Hilton Head, with the benefit of lower temperatures.[36]

Burnside used the Ninth Corps troops remaining in the area as his eyes and ears, ensuring fords on the Rappahannock close to Fredericksburg were guarded to prevent Confederate incursions. He was then required to head to Washington, leaving his duties at Fredericksburg with Parke. Prior to departing on the afternoon of August 14, Burnside provided details on some Army of the Potomac troops reaching Fredericksburg. He also reported on Reno's presence at Rappahannock Station, within supporting distance of Pope's army.[37]

William Lusk was one of the staff officers Burnside left behind to assist Parke. On August 19, he updated his mother about his duties and location, making note of the summer temperatures. "Here we are, occupying a fine house in the pleasant town of Fredericksburg," he noted, "with the thermometer standing ever so high in the shade." He witnessed the contempt many town residents had for the Union soldiers, concluding "a military occupation of a disaffected town is less pleasant than the tented field." Although concerned about Pope's orders potentially creating lax discipline as soldiers lived off the land, Lusk still viewed the Union cause as very powerful with "a great invincible army" that was "trusting in God and marching to victory."[38]

DEFENDING TWO RIVERS

William Lusk and millions of soldiers across the millennia have found trusting in their god easy, with military victory much harder to effectuate. Reno sensed the unease pervading his adoptive army. He wrote Burnside expressing a wish he remained back at Fredericksburg. Some soldiers matched such distraught feelings. A member of the 21st Massachusetts suggested men experienced great disquiet, "We soon began to wish that we had somebody besides General Pope at our head."

To give credit where due, Pope had not bungled irretrievably during the last several days. He would be neither the first nor the last Union general bested by Robert E. Lee and his devoted Southern warriors. Pope's army faced many limitations, including the lack of fresh cavalry, an absolute necessity for the support of Civil War infantry. Moreover, the inability to quickly unite all United States forces in Virginia worked against any positive result in August 1862. All was not lost for Pope, however, and the arrival of Reno's men improved the odds.[39] An analysis of the events across the two weeks between the arrival of Reno and the utter disaster at Second Bull Run must not bog down in the inevitability of Pope's ultimate defeat.

During the time spent between the rivers, Isaac Stevens certainly worked diligently. He used his sound appreciation for the impact topography has on military operations to accomplish the goal of watching the enemy. The First Division commander "always attached great importance to a thorough knowledge of the ground and seized every opportunity to gain it."[40]

The Second Division received artillery support for the river defense efforts. Pennsylvania's Independent Battery D, under the command of highly competent Capt. George Durell, previously served in Washington's defenses and then McDowell's command. The historian of the battery remembered the optimism the Keystone cannoneers expressed when attached to the Ninth Corps, just as two large armies maneuvered for a decisive collision. "Active service seemed to be in sight for the battery, which prospect nearly all the men appeared to welcome," he recalled.[41]

Pope still labored to find a way to grapple with Lee successfully. On August 17, he ordered cavalry forces south of the Rapidan. Reno had oversight of Brig. Gen. John Buford's brigade of cavalrymen, which crossed the river near the Ninth Corps. Also, south of the Rapidan, near Somerville Ford, part of the 2nd Maryland seized some Confederate prisoners and documents on Clark's Mountain after "a slight skirmish." A wonderful signal station and scouting location, the picturesque peak offered the chance to track enemy movements.[42]

The 2nd Maryland's bold effort ended on the 19th, a time when events had already started to overtake Pope. Three days before, Halleck had suggested Pope would be safer north of the Rappahannock. Lee was planning a major move against Pope's left, with orders issued for a significant effort on August 18. Snafus called off Lee's attack, but Pope finally saw the futility of holding ground between the Rapidan and Rappahannock. A retreat to the north was quickly ordered.[43]

"We marched all night and the next day," a Pennsylvanian wrote, before finding safety after crossing the river. Colonel Leasure remembered the nearly robotic nature of the soldiers as they made their way to their new position.

Marching thus, during those hours of darkness no word was spoken, and when the head of the column halted the whole column would sink as it were into the earth, and in a moment the officers and men of the line would be in a sound sleep; and when the head of the column moved, it seemed as though, without a word of command, the whole line rose and silently moved on.[44]

Historians rightfully acknowledge the necessity of the Unionist retrograde. Pope worked hard to make the retreat generally uneventful. The Army of Virginia stole a march on Lee, and Unionist forces were much better off as a result. In other good news, Halleck informed Pope of the projected arrival of the Fifth Corps, Army of the Potomac, at Aquia.[45]

One highly notable event the troops experienced at this time was the ordered departure of the musical bands accompanying many regiments. The historian of the Highlanders opined how the government no longer wished to pay and feed the band members, so they departed for home. The New Yorker lamented, "Our band had been our pride; none in the field could equal it, and its members, who were all professional musicians, were being constantly called on to instruct and drill the country bands who accompanied new regiments into the field."[46]

Protecting the area around Kelly's Ford on the Rappahannock became an important goal of the Ninth Corps. Possession of the excellent river crossing was central for the army's protection. Ninth Corps pickets had dangerous assignments while watching the ford, with several casualties sustained. As one member of the 50th Pennsylvania recalled, "Every day now seemed to have some slight skirmish in store for our forces." Some men even went beyond the river to engage Confederates in relatively small fights. Two members of the 51st Pennsylvania found themselves prisoners after Confederates captured them in a house near the river.[47]

Thwarted in the drive to overtake Pope's left, Lee began to see the virtue of moving beyond Pope's right flank to interrupt the Army of Virginia's supplies. With supporting troops coming from the east, Pope could not stretch too far to the west and north. Thus, Lee's boldness offered tremendous advantages to the Confederates. The stage was set for a Southern dash to the north, with devastating consequences for hundreds of men in the Ninth Corps.[48]

LEE OUTSMARTS POPE THROUGH MANEUVER

While so much was occurring to the northwest, Burnside kept busy. A visit with McClellan followed the short trip to Washington in the middle of August. Burnside also witnessed the ongoing evacuation of the Army of the Potomac from the Peninsula. Perhaps Burnside deserves credit for McClellan's improved drive to assist the war effort. When August 17 arrived, McClellan finally acted somewhat like a true team player. "I have seen Burnside," McClellan wrote Halleck, "Now that we are committed to the movement, you may be sure that it will be carried out without the delay of a moment." This, a soldier informed his boss, written two weeks after being ordered to evacuate the Peninsula. By August 20, McClellan requested promptness from his troops charged with assisting Pope's Army of Virginia.[49]

With the Ninth Corps in the field, a Highlander summed up the marching and countermarching that brought the men north of the Rappahannock, "The men thought they had covered sufficient ground for complaint." Reno led his division across the river first, with Stevens nearly a day behind. Later, in support of General Buford, Stevens joined a group of his men south of the river. The Highlanders and the 28th Massachusetts took a lead role in the engagement, which resulted in a few casualties.[50] Lee still plotted a move around Pope's right flank, hoping to force a Unionist pursuit.

Pope first knew of these strong enemy flanking efforts thanks to observation from McDowell's men late in the afternoon of August 21. Reno was informed to prepare to move half of the Ninth Corps toward the sounds of battle. The rest of Reno's force was to follow after Brig. Gen. John Reynolds and his division from the Peninsula arrived to take their place guarding the eastern flank of the army. At this time, now back at Falmouth, Burnside wired President Lincoln to inform him of the large number of boats visible south of Aquia, indicating that more of McClellan's army would be arriving for the overland march to Pope.[51]

Cavalry leader J. E. B. Stuart and Stonewall Jackson commanded successful forays around Pope. Thousands of enemy troops ended up behind the Army of Virginia, gaining some intelligence and capturing supplies, helping to feed the hungry Southerners. Lee's army was spread out across nearly 50 miles, but Pope failed to sever the connection anywhere. His best bet was to hold the eastern side of Thoroughfare Gap, 20 miles due north of Kelly's Ford. Pulling off such a move would have prevented timely support for Jackson from the rest of Lee's army, under James Longstreet.[52]

The opportunity lost created additional grounds for complaint from Ninth Corps men as they marched generally northwest along the river. A biographer of Pope suggests the decision to stay on the Rappahannock line for so long was justified as the location where Halleck expected to reinforce the Army of Virginia. Additionally, Halleck supported Pope's decision to stay put, even requesting he fight to remain on the river. The leading historian of the Second Bull Run campaign makes a better argument for Pope's earlier move north to confront the flanking enemy. Halleck cautioned Pope to withdraw if concerns grew about enemy movements to the army's rear. There existed no preemptory order for the Army of Virginia to remain glued to the line on the north side of the Rappahannock.[53] Moving the army north more quickly would have shown judiciousness, especially as a means to protect supplies and the territory west of Washington.

Lieutenant Benjamin made good use of his opportunity to show the prowess of his Regular army cannoneers as the Ninth Corps moved along the Rappahannock. During a midday break in the march on August 24, a group of Confederate horsemen with artillery appeared near the river. The enemy soldiers used shots from the big guns to bother the resting Unionists. Benjamin "very coolly and deliberately unlimbered and sighted one of his 20-pounders," a staff officer noted. Without much effort, Benjamin's battery hit the "annoying" Confederate cannon, prompting the enemy's withdrawal. Speaking of the strong Union presence greeting Lee's men at each Rappahannock ford during the previous few days, the historian of the 6th New Hampshire boasted, "he always found the Yankee there to dispute the passage."[54]

Excellent scenery added to the tolerable nature of the march on August 25, but concerns rose about the obvious signs of Lee's army being north of Pope. This was a vitally important day of the campaign, as Jackson clearly held dangerous ground north of the Unionists. Members of the Ninth Corps prepared for a change of direction after they reached the Orange and Alexandria Railroad. Marching along the tracks for many grueling miles, the troops marched northeast, in the direction of

Manassas Junction. The large Army of Virginia supply base there firmly rested in Stonewall Jackson's sights.[55]

HUNTING FOR AN OLD FRIEND

Jesse Reno and the immortal Stonewall Jackson had met twenty summers before when the two natives of Virginia entered West Point. Jackson, nine spots below Reno in class rank in 1846, was perhaps the most famous American soldier in the summer of 1862. With the turn toward Manassas, Reno and the Ninth Corps were a part of the force trying to find the wily Confederate. The task became more difficult with uncertainty prevailing about Jackson's true destination, especially after telegraph wires were cut, imposing silence between Pope's army and Washington. McClellan's welcome albeit late support faced an important limitation: Washington did not know the Army of Virginia's exact location.[56]

Simply reaching Warrenton Junction proved difficult for many soldiers. Captain Belcher of the 8th Michigan again noted the struggle to find good water. "Day very hot," he recorded on the 25th, "Over half the men fell out of the ranks on the march." Some needed the following morning to catch up with the regiment. A later countermarch, due to incorrect reports of enemy movements, proved taxing and frustrating for Reno's regiments. Continued exhaustion no doubt plagued many on the hunt for Jackson and his force of about 25,000 men.[57]

Varying reports regarding the location of Confederate forces made Pope very uncertain. He simply became ruled by events. Pope still held great faith in his ability to cause immense damage to Jackson's isolated command, especially if more elements of the Army of the Potomac joined him. Failing to prevent the advance of Longstreet's men through Thoroughfare Gap proved to be Pope's most fateful oversight during his short time as an army commander. He truly had the ability to destroy Jackson's force if Longstreet was prevented from connecting with Stonewall.[58]

The muddled situation meant more countermarching for Ninth Corps men. "Mortification," Captain Belcher wrote, prevailed when messengers brought word of Jackson's successful flank march, potentially placing Pope's entire command between wings of Lee's Confederates.

Intense rain added to the morose feeling among many in the Ninth Corps. Some men in the 48th Pennsylvania became prisoners during the day, thanks to the misdirection resulting from the baffled staff at Pope's headquarters. As a Bay Stater penned, the marching soldiers held "very little respect for the strategy of our commander."[59]

When isolated elements of the Army of the Potomac sustained dozens of casualties west of Washington, McClellan grew unenthused about sending more of his troops forward. William Franklin's Sixth Corps prepared to move west from Alexandria, but McClellan received permission to delay his advance until the Second Corps arrived from the Peninsula. McClellan also expressed concern about the security of Burnside's small command near Fredericksburg. He wrote Halleck multiple times on August 27, suggesting Burnside "would do better service in front of Washington." The idea was certainly true, but McClellan reverted to the type of behavior so evident in the slow transfer of his army north across the previous three weeks. He opined, "I still think that we should first provide for the immediate defence of Washington on both sides of the Potomac." McClellan added later, "I am not responsible for the past and cannot be for the future unless I receive authority to dispose of all the available troops according to my judgment." Here, McClellan acted out of greater concern for his personal reputation than his country. He already assumed the worst for Pope, ready to condemn him and tens of thousands of U.S. soldiers to their fate.[60]

Burnside diligently coordinated movements with Fitz John Porter, Fifth Corps commander. The possibility of threats to his position led Burnside to consider countermeasures. At 6:15 p.m. on August 27, he wired Halleck of plans to retain Falmouth "as long as possible, and then retreat to Aquia, holding that place, which I think will be comparatively easy with the aid of gunboats promised."[61]

Reno and the Ninth Corps had orders from Pope to "march at the earliest dawn of day" on August 28, "and if you are prompt and expeditious, we shall bag the whole crowd." The idea was for several parts of the army to trap Jackson, but Stonewall was too diligent to remain idle after capturing and enjoying so much Yankee food at Manassas Junction. He moved north of the Warrenton Turnpike, finding an unfinished railroad grade offering spectacular defensive possibilities.[62]

"His Unflinching Courage"

Reno, whose two divisions were near Greenwich, about 10 miles from Manassas Junction, wrote Irvin McDowell early on August 28. The day would take the two Ninth Corps divisions to the destroyed supply base. Pope's strategic stupor led to a belief that his army could easily defeat Jackson, still without support from the other half of the Confederate army. Stonewall Jackson eagerly awaited his chance to meet Pope, even with Longstreet a day away.[63]

Ninth Corps troops felt the inevitable pull of battle. Some were optimistic far beyond reality. Early on the 28th, a Bay Stater remembered hearing comrades suggest, "Jackson was surely bagged, and unless he surrendered would be cut to pieces within twenty-four hours." Yet, the desolation of Manassas must have smacked hope out of many soldiers. By the end of a weary day, where the Ninth Corps marched well to the east of Jackson's position, the same soldier noted how many were "sick at heart of General Pope and his strategy, which he had so bombastically told us was going to turn the tide of war in Virginia."[64]

Encamped near the First Bull Run battlefield, Ninth Corps troops could hear the sounds of a major fight to the west, which lasted until after dark. At Brawner Farm, six regiments under McDowell tangled with much of Jackson's entire command, and the Union troops proved very worthy of their immortal opponents. "We speculated together," the 6th New Hampshire historian wrote of his discussions with tentmates that evening, "about the result of the coming encounter" they knew would occur on the following day. Some were optimistic, others were expending what would be their last night alive.[65]

Orders for the following day articulated Pope's wildly incorrect view of McDowell having struck a retreating Jackson, with the Confederate supply trains and troops ripe for picking. Reno's men and other troops east of Jackson were ordered to march to Centreville on the 29th, away from the Confederates, where historians suggest Pope should have sent all of his troops. The retrograde, however damaging to the brash Pope's opposition to retreating, would have permitted a connection with the Army of the Potomac's Second and Sixth Corps amid strong fortifications.

A truly baffling aspect of Pope's plan for Reno on August 29 was the highly uncertain nature of the battle they would encounter. The commanding general offered little in the way of ideas on what part of Jackson's line Reno should strike. Pope lacked an understanding of the ground the men were charged with fighting on, certainly no recipe for success. "Push forward rapidly," Pope required, with Reno expected to head "toward any heavy firing you may hear."[66]

Pope's desire to strike Jackson overwhelmed any other sensible course his command could have pursued. As two Ninth Corps divisions prepared for what looked like a very active day, Colonel Leasure lost the services of more than 200 men, due to an order from headquarters. About half of the 46th New York would guard supply trains in the rear of the army, rather than face Stonewall along the unfinished railroad. Lt. Col. Joseph Gerhardt led the six companies guarding the wagons, while Col. Rudolph Rosa took the remaining four companies to battle.

Leasure held great confidence in the 650 soldiers remaining in his brigade. "They were men of iron," Leasure wrote. Due to the bountiful strength necessary for the difficult, hungry marches each day since leaving the Rappahannock, "weaker men had fallen out and gone to hospitals, or straggled in the rear."[67]

"Hot sun and dusty roads" hampered the march toward growing signs of battle. As each step moved men closer to fighting, "the contest seemed to increase in fury." The most difficult part of the march was the wounded men going to the rear of the Union lines. "This sight is one of the saddest in war experience," the 6th New Hampshire historian wrote. "The cannonading in the direction of Bull Run was growing heavier," a cannoneer recalled of the march from Centreville. With a rapid advance, the artillerists joined their infantry comrades, making their way to an engagement expected at any moment.[68]

Perhaps with the impact on charging Unionists fully in mind, Stonewall Jackson released some federal prisoners on the morning of the 29th. These men, captured over the previous days, had been granted furloughs. The move made sense for Jackson; he freed up some of his men who would otherwise have been guarding the captured troops. Members of the 21st Massachusetts received words of wisdom from the newly freed men, who were duty-bound to not take up arms until formally exchanged. Captain Belcher believed the furloughed prisoners totaled 600, while other sources lowered that number considerably.[69]

Many in the 79th New York waxed sentimental as they moved so close to where the regiment received its baptism of fire the previous summer. Several Highlanders pointed out landmarks they saw thirteen months before, when the war seemed destined for short duration. The seasoned veterans possessed the realism of how miserable the war had become. "Only by hard knocks and a great sacrifice of lives could a victory be obtained," the regiment's historian accurately wrote.[70]

Inspiring and bold leaders cannot whisk away the danger of battle, but they are able to motivate men with the power of their cause and the splendor of courage. Colonel Leasure was forever grateful for the presence of General Stevens on August 29. Stevens promised

that mine would be his fighting brigade that day and he should go in with me. I need hardly say that nothing in the wide world could have so conformed me to my most ardent wishes, and the eyes of the men lighted up with the enthusiasm which soldiers feel in the presence of a tried leader for they had learned to love the little smoke-visaged general, because his heart was with them, and they had witnessed his cool conduct in battle and knew his unflinching courage.[71]

All the men of the two divisions were exhausted and in danger as noon approached, but the morning had been especially hard on those having spent the overnight period on picket duty, like Companies A, D, F, and I of the 51st Pennsylvania. Enemy cannon fire, which included railroad iron cut into lengths approaching 2 feet, proved dangerous for the regiment before Stonewall's vaunted infantry were visible. With fixed bayonets, soldiers of the 51st went prone, serving as support for Durell's Battery.[72]

Earlier in the day, parts of Pope's army began assaulting Jackson. Because of the ridiculously unrealistic vision Pope had of Jackson's position and intentions, the attacks could not make a permanent dent in Stonewall's line. Even with some regiments well under the strength of a single company, the topography and woods masked Jackson's overall weakness.[73] The piecemeal assaults would continue in the afternoon, much to the detriment of the Ninth Corps.

"Brave and Highly Commendable"

An attack against Jackson's presumably unprotected right flank was central to Pope's thinking for August 29. As elements of his command fought in a disjointed fashion along the unfinished railroad, what Pope envisioned farther west included a major assault by Porter's Fifth Corps, with support from McDowell. Two horrendous fallacies completely mooted Pope's tactical vision. The arrival of Longstreet offered strong protection for Jackson's right and extended the Confederate line well to the south. Moreover, Pope's orders were so inadequate, any unbiased observer could easily conclude an attack by Porter on the 29th was not part of the commanding officer's plans. Pope even gave Porter an out to alter the order, as needed, or fall back completely.[74]

The first infantry engagement for the Ninth Corps at Second Bull Run epitomized the lack of clarity Pope had operated under for two weeks. Farnsworth's two regiments, the 79th New York and 28th Massachusetts, were called on to support units from different divisions, some of which had been engaged over the morning without gaining leverage against Jackson. As the day progressed, elements of Sigel's Corps were no longer on Farnsworth's right. Sporadic firing continued, with the historian of the Highlanders remembering the futility of the effort. The men could not see the Confederates, and soldiers aimed and fired at will but "at nothing in particular," with men falling all along the line.[75]

Fragmented assaults against Jackson continued. Other brigades, again without much support, attacked Jackson's center and left, with these strong efforts petering out by about 3:00 p.m. Then, the most sustained and damaging attack Ninth Corps men made at Second Bull Run brought Nagle's three regiments to and even partly beyond the unfinished railroad.[76]

Earlier in the day, the 6th New Hampshire rested well south of Jackson's position, but close enough to see the movement of troops and the intense, uncoordinated firefights. Col. Simon Griffin took time to point out some of the landmarks from First Bull Run while his men chomped on whatever food they still carried. The 6th's historian said the Granite Staters watched the battle while seeing wounded go to the rear. When the time to move out was ordered, the men dropped their knapsacks, with a few in the regiment left behind as guards. The knapsacks would be captured by victorious Confederates. The Granite Staters "did not care a fig for the knapsacks," the regimental historian declared, although "they did miss the contents very much."[77]

The 48th Pennsylvania rested for a time near their New Hampshire comrades. An officer in the 48th recalled witnessing the battle in front, with some men wondering why they remained idle well into the afternoon. Several soldiers seemed ready to fight, the officer remembered, "all were somewhat over-patriotic and zealous." He added, "It was provoking, too, to have to wait there looking on, for the firing was terrific, and the battle was raging furiously." Booming artillery made further impressions on the impatient troops, as the "sharp rattle" of muskets not far from the 48th's reserve position made the men realize they would soon be moving out.[78]

General Reno certainly seemed eager to become part of the fight. David Strother, a member of Pope's staff and Reno's fellow Virginia native, delivered orders to the Ninth Corps. The primary goal for the Second Division was to decrease threats to their own artillery from Confederate sharpshooters. Reno immediately got his men ready, and Strother was impressed with the "beautiful style" the soldiers showed as they headed out.[79]

A problem developed in the 48th Pennsylvania as they dealt with the woods and terrain closer to the unfinished railroad. One man in trouble as a result of the disconnected advance was Capt. Joseph Hoskings, leading Company F. He found himself in a hand-to-hand struggle with a Confederate officer after part of the 48th had drifted too far to the left. Hoskings was able to push his enemy down, but his determined opponent went for his own pistol. Just before Hoskings was about to lose his life, an infantryman from the 48th dispatched the Confederate with a shot to the head from a distance. Instead of being captured in the tumult, the isolated band of Keystone Staters soon linked up with their regiment. The number of years of life the Confederate lost cannot be known, but Hoskings had much to appreciate. More than a half-century after Second Bull Run, Hoskings still lived.[80]

Nagle's original battle line had the 6th New Hampshire on the left, and the 2nd Maryland on the right, with the 48th Pennsylvania in reserve. Movements of the two units created an opening in the middle, which the 48th rapidly moved into with precision. A fence line created an annoying barrier for the soldiers' march forward, but Nagle used the opportunity to organize his line and fix bayonets before moving closer to the Confederates. Facing northwest, the attackers were hindered a bit from the sinking sun. Some Union troops squinted due to the bright rays, while the Confederates clearly saw the advancing troops.[81]

"As soon as we got into the woods they commenced popping at us," Hosea Towne of the 6th New Hampshire wrote. "It was a terrible fight," he added, "the balls flew like hail stones and buzzed about our ears like bees." Towne's pal Henry McDonald, a Maine native, lost his life in the deadly chaos. "My particular friend was killed by my side," Towne continued, "We stood so near that the blood splattered my clothes." As "the ball passed through his head," Towne concluded of McDonald, "he did not speak or know anything" of his sad fate. Towne considered McDonald "a noble man, a kind friend, and a good soldier."[82]

The color guard of the 6th New Hampshire suffered early and often in the fight. Corp. John Stevens bravely took the colors after at least two flagbearers went down. Stevens pursued his duty even after being wounded twice. Knowing his injury was mortal, Stevens continued to fight. He was seen loading a musket before being killed. The regiment's historian added, "At the close of the fight Colonel Griffin brought off the colors, or what was left of them, for they were badly riddled by shot."[83]

Men fought with a wicked intensity on both sides, especially as Nagle's men pierced a part of the railroad grade. While facing Confederate fire, Nagle appreciated the mettle of his regiments. "All behaved nobly," he reported, "and deserve a great deal of credit for the manner in which they all came up to their work and drove the enemy from their intrenchments." The protective earth did not create a consistent defense across its entire width, which gave Pope's offensive moves on the 29th the possibility of making progress. A South Carolina brigade, fighting men on the left and front, in addition to Nagle's advance on their right, endured many difficult moments. The historian of the Palmetto men respectfully wrote of the Unionists, "The woods swarmed with them," and the boys in blue possessed "an energy never before witnessed by us." Both sides refused to give in for a time, leading to "a perfect death storm" for the brawling American warriors.[84]

At the main point of Nagle's attack, Confederate troops had to retreat slightly, which actually helped them gain additional defensive advantages from thick vegetation. "Our position was a good one for defense, and we were determined not to yield it unless the officers so ordered," a member of the 15th Alabama recalled. Like the South Carolinians farther to the left, the soldier certainly respected his Ninth Corps foes. Although the Southern fire proved staggering, the Union troops "did not lose hope nor cease their effort to break our line," adding many to the casualty lists on both sides. Of his three tough regiments, Nagle added, "It is impossible for me to particularize any for their conduct, as all, both officers and men, were equally brave."[85]

"The loss was very great on both sides," a Georgian fighting against Nagle remembered. The Confederates were "almost surrounded by Yankees," he wrote, "and we had a dreadful struggle in cutting our way out." As Confederate general Jubal Early recalled of the afternoon, "The battle was raging fiercely in our front."[86]

The tide turned against Nagle's men because of a furious flank attack from the west. Some Southerners were able to get partially behind the Unionists, creating a very difficult situation for Nagle. The brigade commander reported his men received fire "from concealed places, and particularly a heavy cross-fire from the left, which would have soon destroyed the whole command." As a member of the 48th Pennsylvania added, "the firing became hotter and hotter." Retreat was the only option.[87]

Fire from the west and rear proved devastating to the 6th New Hampshire companies on the regiment's left. "The dead and wounded

Col. James Nagle's men faced determined Confederate resistance on August 29, 1862, at Second Bull Run. LIBRARY OF CONGRESS

lay thickest at this point," the regimental historian wrote. The eastern part of the regiment still advanced some beyond the unfinished railroad, but Colonel Griffin knew the impossibility of prolonged resistance, so a retreat was ordered. Dozens of his men became prisoners during the Confederate counterattack.[88]

Some of Nagle's troops were able to fight back against the flank attack, but the war's history includes many stories where determined men were overwhelmed by troops attacking from a side or partially from the rear. As an officer in the 48th Pennsylvania suggested, "The contest was too unequal to last." Granite Stater George Upton informed his wife, "The Rebels fairly flanked our Brigade, and we was fortunate that [we] got out of it alive." Perhaps feeling embarrassed by the necessity, Upton added, "I ran for once for life & so did every man." Upton also wrote of two near misses. One bullet passed through a leg near the knee, then another nearly caused an injury to one of Upton's heels.

The New Hampshire and Pennsylvania troops recorded some confusion in their effort to escape the whirlwind. A New York officer from the Third Corps, bringing troops up on the right, found the Ninth Corps retreat destabilizing to his own line. He referred to Nagle's retrograde as "disgraceful," but how the retreat could have been made more efficient and less impactful on supporting troops is a question that will be forever unanswered.[89]

Theodore Nutting, a corporal in the 6th New Hampshire, kept his cap for many months as a way to remember nearly being killed along the Railroad Cut. He sent the damaged item home the following May, informing his family they would find interest in "my old Bull Run cap." The headgear proved "how near I came," Nutting added, to "being numbered among those who returned not from that ill-fated Battlefield." Believing the projectile creating two holes in the cap was caused by an errant comrade, Nutting noted how "the ball struck the side and passed through the top of the cap." Knowing the brutal dangers the regiment experienced at the battle, Nutting accepted the near-death experience caused by a friend. The act had been "done in the excitement of the hour," making the incident "careless and accidental."[90]

Times such as this could bring out greatness in men under intense pressure. Colonel Nagle, who would soon be a general, "was everywhere cheering on the men and barely escaped capture," a Keystone Stater noted. Lt. Col. Joshua Sigfried of the 48th Pennsylvania "was in the thickest of the fray, encouraging the men by actions, as well as words." Several junior officers also earned gratitude from their regiments with boldness and coolness during the difficult several minutes. Gen. Philip Kearny, a Third Corps division commander definitely did his part. With only one arm due to a wound in Mexico, Kearny rallied men on the right side of the retreat as his own troops were hurrying toward the unfinished railroad. With his trademark battlefield intensity, Kearny bellowed, "Fall in here, you sons of bitches, and I'll make major generals out of every one of you."[91] The times called for such desperate, thundering rhetoric.

Cannoneers in positions spread across the Unionist line to the south witnessed the "withering fire" Confederates unleashed against the attacking infantry units without the ability to know if their own guns could fire safely in response. The possibility of Union casualties from friendly fire was great. As federal forces retreated toward the supporting guns, the artillerists unleashed "a rapid fire of time-shell and shrapnel," with the shots flying over the heads of Pope's retreating soldiers.[92]

Nagle reported 518 casualties for the entire campaign, with the afternoon of August 29 creating the bulk of the losses. More than 180 of the casualties were captured or missing. The Confederate counterattack gave Jackson's troops the best chance to grab surrounded Unionists. The three regiments listed seventy-six killed in action. The 6th New Hampshire sustained thirty killed in what George Upton wrote was "a sad day to the N.H. 6th." Overall, Nagle's three regiments suffered one-third of the Ninth Corps' total casualties from their time with Pope's army, August 16 through September 2.[93]

Even with the horrendous suffering across all three regiments, certain elements of Nagle's command were especially hard hit. Of the twenty engaged officers in the 6th New Hampshire, five were killed, six wounded, and two were captured. Some in the 6th died later of their wounds, or never saw the regiment again after a medical discharge. Company E's Lt. George H. Muchmore, in his early thirties, died at a

Washington hospital two weeks after the battle. The two captured officers were adjutants, taken prisoner in their valiant efforts to deliver orders or rally the troops under fire.[94]

The difficult battle may not have offered much of redeeming value for Colonel Nagle, but he did receive the thanks of an officer in the 3rd Michigan, who appreciated the service from two men in the 48th Pennsylvania. Capt. Joseph Gilmour and Lt. William Cullen "rallied fighters until they had quite a company of them and united with my regiment," the Michigan officer thankfully wrote, "Their conduct was brave and highly commendable, and they were of much service."[95]

"NO SADDER NIGHT"

Leasure's men had a role in the day's fight. Earlier, General Stevens sent the small number of men, along with Benjamin's Battery, to the assistance of a division in Pope's First Corps. Later, as the swirling hell of the afternoon's attacks continued, the soldiers went farther to the right to assist General Kearny. Stevens, never afraid to join his men while under fire, advanced on the left of the large attack, an effort to roll up Jackson's eastern flank. Leasure first sent four companies ahead as skirmishers. Proud of their preparation, the colonel noted, "I had carefully trained my own regiment in marksmanship, and as many of them had been accustomed to the use of the squirrel-rifle before entering the service, they were easily converted into very effective sharp-shooters."

At first, Stevens grew anxious with what he deemed the slow pace of fire from Leasure's skirmishers. The colonel requested patience, and his men soon proved worthy of their commander's expectations. During the engagement, Leasure gained even more respect for Lieutenant Benjamin and his cannoneers, who provided vital support while under fire from enemy artillery. Leasure witnessed the gritty West Pointer "plying his 20-pounders as coolly as if he were practicing for fun." When dismounted, Benjamin needed a crutch due to a previous wound.[96]

When Leasure's infantry closed on the Confederates, they were exposed to intense fire along the line of the unfinished railroad "for fifteen minutes, which seem hours." A Pennsylvanian in Kearny's command deemed the horrific musketry "simply terrible." With the Unionists' flanks again in danger, there was no choice but to retreat.[97]

The brigade then took a position in battery support. Colonel Rosa suffered a wound in the action, as did Leasure. The brigade commander's day was not yet done. Trained as a surgeon, Leasure used his medical skills to assist injured soldiers. His compassionate work included treatment of Rosa, whose wound would lead to a discharge before the end of the year.[98]

Spending much of their day supporting artillery to the south of Pope's attacking columns, Ferrero's Brigade had plenty to worry about. Colonel Hartranft himself reportedly assisted Durell's Battery, the target of several Confederate guns. Hartranft requested his own soldiers stay protected by battlements, while the colonel manned the guns. Although there was a concern the position could be flanked, McDowell's men were close enough on the left to deter Confederate boldness.[99]

Ferrero's men had a tremendous view of the battlefield, with much heartbreak among the three regiments as they witnessed the charge of Nagle's men. The damage done to counterattacking Confederates by the line of artillery Ferrero supported warmed Unionist hearts, however. The day of surging concerns and emotions continued as sunset neared, with Ferrero's three regiments ordered forward into the line of woods close to the unfinished railroad. The soldiers continued to advance, "when General Reno ordered a halt, and dictated a hurried message for one of his staff to carry to General Pope." Reno clearly saw the futility of another unsupported charge as light waned. Before the staff officer went far, Reno decided to head to headquarters himself. Returning to Ferrero's line, Reno ordered the men to fall back. An appreciative regimental historian, clearly no fan of Pope, rejoiced. Reno was deemed "the true little soldier," thanks to the courage to suggest his army commander call off the day's attacks. Pope, a "reckless braggart," had agreed to end the efforts against Jackson, at least for the night. The 21st Massachusetts happily withdrew, luckily finding plenty to eat.[100]

Danger remained, especially for four companies of the 51st Pennsylvania sent forward on picket duty. Lt. Col. Thomas Bell led the advanced troops along the line all night. Bell was the type of leader armies needed, even if his manner may not have pleased all of his men. Not yet twenty-four years old on the North Carolina coast earlier in the year, Bell had threatened to shoot panicked troops at New Bern. Still, Bell had the respect of his soldiers, sharing risks and setting an example for others.[101]

Scenes and sounds of the immense human calamity filled the night for the Ninth Corps. The historian of the 6th New Hampshire, wounded during the afternoon, remembered the sheer grief. Of the regiment, he recalled, "No sadder night did it ever pass than that of August 29, 1862." Suffering more losses than any other day of the war, the 6th felt the profound cost, with nearly 200 casualties, "We had lost many of our best men, and their places could not easily be filled." As a 48th Pennsylvania officer sadly added, "One of the most melancholy features of the day was the roll-call at twilight that evening, and the noticing of the absentees."[102]

Pope had failed to concentrate his forces during the entire day. Stonewall Jackson faced great danger in his position, however strong the unfinished railroad appeared. The Unionist attacks never jelled into one solid mass hitting a single point with precision and unyielding force. General Stevens's son perfectly summed up the difference between the two commanding generals, "All that afternoon Lee was master of the situation."[103]

"WITH THE FURY OF DEMONS"

Longstreet's arrival on the afternoon of the 29th, along with Pope's inability to comprehend the intelligence he was receiving, portended disaster on August 30. Convinced Lee's army had begun a retreat back toward Thoroughfare Gap, Pope made plans for Porter's Fifth Corps to attack. With an unmistakable order, Porter attacked Jackson in the afternoon.

Ninth Corps men performed some routine duties on the morning of the 30th. Horatio Belcher, dutiful officer in the 8th Michigan, spent time with his pickets. Skirmishing and artillery duels, expected by any soldier on the field, did not seem to foreshadow unusual danger. By afternoon, more active work prevailed across several regiments. The most significant combat for the Ninth Corps brought further casualties to the Highlanders. A portion of the 79th New York advanced after pushing back Confederate pickets, then faced Jackson's main line, still concentrated along the unfinished railroad. Company commander John More and his 100 men felt the bitter storm from the defenders, with More falling seriously wounded. Surviving the injury and capture, the dedicated officer's time with the regiment was fortunately far from over. Perhaps one-third of More's intrepid band became casualties.[104]

A lull prevailed for a time. In Durell's Battery, one man recorded, "There seemed to be little disposition on the part of either side to attack." Ninth Corps men were called on to support Porter's early afternoon assault. The effort proved useless, although notable wounds occurred, including a serious injury to Colonel Farnsworth. He would never again lead men in battle.[105]

After Jackson's repulse of Porter, one of the most furious and successful attacks of the war began. Longstreet's unyielding columns started moving east, rolling up whatever federal forces stood in the way. As Unionists attempted to stem the rout in the undulating terrain south of the Ninth Corps' position, Reno worked to protect the inevitable retreat for whatever portions of Pope's command could survive the retrograde to Centreville, 5 miles away. Highly impressive defensive stands on Chinn Ridge and Henry House Hill, the scene of the Union disaster near Bull Run the previous summer, saved Pope.[106]

The retreat of Stevens's Division proved very arduous, with the final safety of the command in doubt. Across the entire day, about a dozen men from the 28th Massachusetts were killed in action. Corp. Michael Donnelly, a patriotic teamster in his mid-twenties, was one of those who died in the regiment on the 30th without having his body recovered. A part of the color guard, Donnelly was remembered fondly as a very kind person by his comrade John Ryan.[107]

Summing up the experience of many Ninth Corps troops as Longstreet's horde pushed ahead to the south, Captain Belcher wrote, "We barely escaped being flanked." The Highlanders and a supporting unit halted their retreat a few times to fire a volley at Jackson's men advancing from the unfinished railroad. A strong showing from Unionist artillery took additional steam out of Jackson's attempt to expand the withering Confederate assault.

Several men in the First Division fell in the retreat. The 50th Pennsylvania suffered twenty-four casualties on August 30, including six men captured and four enlisted men killed in action. Efforts to link more directly with troops on Henry House Hill did not succeed, so Stevens's depleted and weary line defended a position about a half-mile to the north.[108]

One of those lost in the 50th was Lt. Charles Kellogg, known as "Chas." Born the day after Christmas in 1836, Kellogg lost his life after being shot in the back on August 30. Transported to Alexandria, he died on September 1 at the Mansion House, a hotel used as a hospital. Temporarily buried at a Virginia cemetery the next day, the young officer's remains were later sent home to Bradford County, Pennsylvania. A lung hemorrhage was the official cause of death. Kellogg's death left both a widow and a child.[109]

As their retreat began, men in Reno's Division could still rely on an incredibly important constant: the example their general set. One soldier wrote of Reno, "Encouraged by his presence, as he sat fearless and calm upon his horse, the men coolly faced about under a really terrible fire of artillery and marched in perfect order to their new position." Nonetheless, Confederate progress seriously threatened the ability of Pope's men to retreat successfully. Ghoulish wounds awaited some men during the retreat; four members of the 21st Massachusetts were struck by the same piece of railroad iron fired from a Confederate cannon.

In the chaos and growing darkness on Henry House Hill, east of the main defensive line, and south of Stevens's troops, Reno's grit brought some semblance of order with the help of Ferrero's Brigade and William Graham's battery from the Artillery Reserve. The infantrymen spent most of the 30th relatively out of harm's way. Their role in the denouement would prove vital to the safe retreat of Pope's remaining forces. Grasping the importance of the moment, the historian of the 21st Massachusetts said the regiment possessed "a stern determination to show the Army of Virginia how they had learned to fight in North Carolina." Of the intensity of the fire across August 30, the historian of the 51st Pennsylvania would declare, "the roar of artillery and the rattle of musketry were beyond the power of description. It was sublime to witness, but awful to participate in."

As the inferno swirled around them, the three regiments, with their division commander near, fought with unmitigated ferocity. The brigade formed a semicircle in a central part of the hill, with Graham's cannons placed throughout. Reno supervised a strong alignment, a very necessary formation to check the Confederate advance coming from multiple directions. The crucial spot, generally free of natural obstructions, offered an excellent location to defend the army's retreat. The infantry's inspiration to hold out as long as necessary grew thanks to the dedicated Regular army cannoneers under Graham. As the historian of the 51st Pennsylvania wrote, the battery fired "all of its guns with the fury of demons."[110]

Graham's artillerists reciprocated the praise. In an article more than thirty years after the battle, a cannoneer wished to recognize Reno's men for their help, "honor given to whom honor is due," as he suggested. Knowing the infantry absorbed damage that protected the gun crews, the artillerist remembered firing at the Confederates about 600 feet away, "causing great destruction among them. The ground where they stood was strewn with their dead and dying." Lanterns were later needed so the cannoneers could see as Reno's men and Graham's Battery worked together very well, giving pause to worn-out Confederate warriors. Reno and Graham put up a splendid defense of the hill. The stanch Union soldiers stood long enough for darkness to compel very fatigued Confederates to see the necessity of stopping the attack.[111]

Although the day proved disastrous, in the waning minutes of August 30, Pope's command held a strong line, with flanks protected by Bull Run. Utter demoralization did not seize Pope's troops. The general suggested, "The withdrawal was made slowly, quietly, and in good order," due to the lack of further Confederate pursuit. Very much in need of a reliable presence, Pope added, "General Reno was instructed with his whole corps to cover the movements of the army toward Centreville." Pope would lash out at some subordinates, especially Porter, whose military future would be destroyed after a court-martial Pope initiated. Conversely, Pope had nothing but praise for Jesse Reno, the Ninth Corps' senior officer on the field.

He was always cheerful and ready; anxious to anticipate if possible, and prompt to execute with all his might, the orders he received. He was short in stature and upright in person, and with a face and manner so bright and engaging at all times, but most especially noticeable in the fury of battle, that it was both a pleasure and a comfort to see him . . . if he lacked one single element that goes to make a perfect soldier, certainly it was not discovered before his death.[112]

Conscientious Burnside, Peevish McClellan

Through the catastrophe of late August, Ambrose Burnside kept a watchful eye on the Rappahannock and Aquia. He drifted between optimism over the possibilities of Pope achieving a victory and his own isolated position around Fredericksburg. Burnside dutifully remained in contact with Washington and McClellan, who monitored the situation from Alexandria. McClellan's pettiness clearly impacted his judgment as Pope struggled to save his army near Bull Run.

Burnside actively forwarded information about what he had been hearing from Pope's army. Based on news from scouts, Burnside sent two messages before 9 a.m. on August 29 reporting extensive cannon fire from the battlefield near Manassas.[113] Plenty of time existed for more troops from the Army of the Potomac to arrive and assist Pope's army, but McClellan used any discretion he received from Lincoln or Halleck to withhold troops from Pope. Even before the start of the battle along Bull Run, McClellan kept worrying about phantom Confederate legions intent on taking Washington. His Sixth Corps lacked cannons and cavalry, so he did not press their advance. The troops could have proven decisive against the Confederates battling Pope, but McClellan dithered. One problem was certainly the dearth of emphatic orders from Halleck or Lincoln. Even when pushed more, however, McClellan acted on his clear preferences to maintain two of his corps closer to Washington and to see the defeat of Pope.[114]

News sent to McClellan did not paint a picture of massed Confederate forces between Washington and Manassas. Herman Haupt informed McClellan of the large amount of supplies sent to Pope in the overnight period into the morning of August 29, without Confederate forces disrupting the supply chain. Moreover, troops from the corps of Nathaniel Banks were protecting the vast stores arriving at Manassas Junction. McClellan should have realized the very minimal risk of sending so large a force as a corps to Pope. The indecisiveness of McClellan, Haupt wrote, amounted to "no suggestion of any relief for the army fighting in the field." The railroad man recalled his own state of "great dissatisfaction and uncertainty" due to McClellan's apparent lack of interest in supporting Pope.[115]

McClellan's caution included a great deal of illogical reasoning. He believed Lee had 120,000 men against Pope. If true, the best solution for the Union forces was to mass as many troops as possible. If Lee's huge army did exist, the enemy would have easily crushed Pope, then captured Washington by brushing aside McClellan's troops.

Burnside wired an interesting message early on August 30 that should have led his superiors to question the notion of the Confederates having a gigantic army in northern Virginia. Burnside reported zero enemy troops between Falmouth and Catlett's Station, not even 10 miles south of Pope's position. Ethan Rafuse, whose solid defense of McClellan's generalship deserves close study, renders a harsh judgment against McClellan on the issue. Rafuse agrees with other historians that McClellan failed to sufficiently support the Army of Virginia. The commander-in-chief himself was also very upset. President Lincoln, in summing up McClellan's actions during this most pressing moment of the war so far, remarked, "He has acted badly."[116]

Not worrying about his isolated position away from battle to the north, Burnside expressed a desire to serve in any capacity to help his country. Although his words were not accurate about the status of Pope's command, Burnside painted a true picture of his patriotism in an August 30 note to McClellan.

> *Your last dispatch indicates that we had rec'd orders to move from here, but we have rec'd no telegraph to that effect, and will as you directed remain here. We are jubilant over the success of Pope and hope to hear that he has completely routed the enemy.[117]*

Correspondence already discussed proves McClellan held no such desire for Pope's victory. Instead, McClellan remained a petulant officer more concerned about his own marginalized position away from battle while many in the Army of the Potomac were fighting. Perhaps Burnside's commitment to his country's victory, regardless of the general leading the troops, started the deterioration of the strong friendship between "My dear Mac" and "Burn." As the next three weeks would show, the relationship between the two men would never be the same after Second Bull Run. Burnside wanted Pope to destroy Lee, while McClellan silently wished for the destruction of the Army of Virginia.

"Our Cheerless Bivouac"

Less than three weeks had passed between the Ninth Corps' departure from Fredericksburg and the defeat at Second Bull Run. The men of the two divisions seemingly had endured years of privations during that short time. Rain in the early morning of August 31 epitomized the intense difficulty the soldiers faced in the second half of the month. As the 48th Pennsylvania's historian wrote, "We had sixteen successive days of hard campaigning on short rations, without tents, and had been living in the open since leaving Falmouth." The despondency of the defeat along Bull Run turned the men into "a pretty hard looking lot of soldiers."[118]

Much work remained for the Ninth Corps and the Army of Virginia. The gravest threat was the possible interposition of Lee's army between Pope and Washington. Lee likely would not have attacked Pope along the strong line of breastworks at Centreville. As Pope and others foresaw, Lee would attempt to move east after swinging around Pope's right flank. Time existed for Pope to retreat, or perhaps even attack. Halleck clearly favored some kind of Union offensive. Pope was slow to capitalize on the situation, generally remaining in place for much of the day on August 31.[119] The leader of the Army of Virginia was clearly a beaten man, his large ego crushed by his own incompetence.

At least men from the Ninth Corps could make use of a relatively inactive morning. As the 6th New Hampshire historian suggested, some hardtack and coffee could work wonders on famished and tired soldiers. Along with the wonderful sunshine, "new life" was put into the battered regiment. Sleep also helped, and many men had the chance for excellent slumber when Centreville was reached. Still, the unbearable conditions of the last few days foundered the hopes of many. Of the troops, a Keystone Stater suggested, "Their sufferings could not be half told if it were attempted." After all, as the 21st Massachusetts historian wrote, August 31 began "with nothing to eat when we arose from our cheerless bivouac, and no wood for fires."[120]

Much more had to be done, however, because the Confederates could still cause a great deal of trouble. Jackson's flanking move, even if slow, continued. Pope had to realize the Centreville defenses were no longer a tenable final fallback position. Movements on August 31 included an effort to better protect the area near Fairfax Court House, 7 miles east of Centreville's breastworks. General Reno suffered from illness, and he made Brigadier General Stevens the acting leader of both divisions, although Reno would be involved in the movements over the next two crucial days.[121]

With a mind full of pipe dreams, Pope tried to sound aggressive, but circumstances continued to overwhelm him. Halleck's thoughts about possibly counterattacking the Confederates went nowhere. He gave Pope the idea to continue the eastern retrograde. Ninth Corps men camped on the south side of Centreville to scout the Confederate position, perhaps figuring the army's inevitable retreat would need to start at any time. The early afternoon provided a chance for some men to eat and receive new clothing.[122]

On what would be the last morning of his life, Isaac Stevens received deeply mournful information about the state of his division. After a count of stacked muskets on September 1, Stevens had his son, one of his staff officers, compile the number of men ready for action. The 2,012 guns Hazard Stevens counted were almost exactly half of the troops who marched west from Falmouth on August 12. Later in the day, Lieutenant Benjamin recorded the bleak state of Stevens's mood, with the burdens of command showing on the respected general's face. The young cannoneer tried to bolster his chief's day by reminding him how revered Stevens was to the rank and file.[123]

Moving toward Ox Hill

The very fateful day of September 1, 1862, saw the Ninth Corps restarting the retreat of Pope's command. Pope viewed Reno's reliable men as key to figuring out Jackson's movements. Reno (or, more accurately, acting corps commander Stevens) "will notify those in his rear of his exact position and every step of his movement, and will ask support if he needs it," Pope directed. McDowell, already with orders to move to Fairfax Court House, was told to remain in contact with the Ninth Corps. The two divisions under Stevens acted as the vitally important link between safety to the east and the troops remaining in Centreville for a few hours. General Kearny had elements of the Third Corps in close support of Stevens.[124]

Conflicting orders in the early afternoon made some men wonder what their role would be on September 1. After the Ninth Corps was ordered to take the lead in the eastward moment, the men knew they could not stay around Centreville. The two Ninth Corps divisions needed to turn north before going too far east. The big left turn occurred after about 2 miles. Such a directional change was required because Stevens did not wish to meet Jackson where the roads the opposing forces marched on came together. Thus, he was right to seek Jackson's location when he did. The two divisions' march on the Warrenton Turnpike had included sounds of desultory firing to the left. The men "did not attach much importance to it as having anything to do with us," a Bay Stater recalled. "The day was gloomy, indicating rain," a Roundhead remembered. The heavens did not look better as the day progressed, but Stevens refused to let potential storms halt what he perceived as his mission, finding Stonewall Jackson and engaging him.[125]

Yet, Stevens erred in bringing on the battle of Chantilly. The need to figure out the location of Jackson's command did not require an attack by the Ninth Corps against Stonewall's more numerous troops. The necessity of protecting Pope's retreat, which would have enabled Union forces to mass themselves around Fairfax Court House, did not mean a battle had to be fought. Stevens acted as if a conflagration was necessary, for he clearly took the initiative against Confederate brigades posted south of the Little River Turnpike. Two modern books on the battle of Chantilly strongly support Stevens's aggressiveness while seeing no option but to attack. Another way did exist: simply watching Jackson while calling forward nearby supporting troops. Stevens deserves tributes and lamentations for his bravery and sacrifice on September 1, but he should not have attacked that afternoon. As Confederate Gen. James Longstreet wrote, "Stevens, appreciating the crisis as momentous, thought it necessary to follow the opportunity by aggressive battle."[126]

At first, some men did not know who the troops to their north were. Could the regiments just south of the Little River Turnpike and Ox Hill be friends? As a Roundhead noted, "The boys began a controversy whether they were Johnnies or Unionists." Stevens had to know most of Pope's command could support him if Jackson attacked from the Confederate position. By simply staying put after the Ninth Corps' march north from the Warrenton Turnpike, Stevens was not in danger, and neither was the line of troops heading to Fairfax Court House. Jackson possessed limited ability to damage the Unionist retrograde, and Stonewall knew as much. With Longstreet moving toward Jackson's command, Lee's chiefs were not looking to fight on September 1 if their flanking movement wallowed. Due to the slow progress Jackson had made in the last thirty-six hours, he understood how the dream of isolating and destroying Pope would not reach fruition.[127]

"OUTRIVALING PANDEMONIUM ITSELF"

Although Stevens had a good view of the ground between the opposing forces, he did not know the number of Confederates hiding in the woods. Nonetheless, the battle was on, with the three small brigades of the division in the lead marching at first with a front only one brigade wide. Stevens placed his Highlanders along with the 28th Massachusetts at the head of the infantry attack. Lt. Col. David Morrison, wounded at Secessionville, returned to duty in time for the battle. He commanded the brigade in place of the injured Addison Farnsworth. The 79th New York stood on the right of the brigade.[128]

Two of Morrison's companies were placed on skirmish duty, descending slightly at first in their move to the north. A company from the 28th Massachusetts also went forward in the brigade's initial line, as the troops began to draw enemy fire. Vegetation along a small brook inhibited the quick movement of troops in the lower ground between the Union and Confederate positions. Then, another rise greeted the attackers while Jackson's troops waited, with thick forest in their immediate rear. As Confederate skirmishers fell back, the Ninth Corps advanced to the area around a farmhouse and orchard. The men spread out across the field while under fire.[129]

Battery support included only Durell's and Benjamin's guns. The former unit "was hurried forward and entered the battle with the horses on full gallop," unlimbering near a field full of healthy corn. In contrast, the field to the right of the position was fallow. As the battery's historian wrote, "All the troops in the vicinity were soon engaged." Durell's men would be placed, with the assistance of General Reno, forward somewhat to support the infantry advance. Benjamin's guns remained to the right rear of the division's attack.[130]

Few fights in the Civil War were more confused as a result of the powerful thunderstorm that would rage during the battle of Chantilly. As the intensity of the engagement increased, so did the fury of Mother Nature, as if to tell erring mortals of the folly of their earthly disagreements. Yet, the dueling American warriors fighting near Ox Hill exceeded the cacophony of the storm. As a member of the 50th Pennsylvania remembered, "Rain descended in a deluge, the thunder was deafening, the lightning was blinding, yet these were surpassed by the more destructive fury and vengeance of the human combatants."[131]

The initial Unionist wave stalled. Multiple flag bearers in the 79th New York were down. William Lusk noted the desperate moment after General Stevens ordered him to the left of the line. The general, knowing his own son was among the wounded, then grabbed the regimental colors, imploring the men to charge. "My Highlanders, follow your general," were likely the last words Stevens would utter. A bullet entered his temple, causing instant fatal injury.[132]

Stevens's death occurred at a time when the Union assault found some momentum. The Louisianans in the front line of the Confederate defense started to give way under renewed pressure. Suddenly, the Ninth Corps men were upon their foes, with a fiendish round of hand-to-hand fighting. Thus far, as a member of the 28th Massachusetts noted, "Our regiment stood the severest fire that was witnessed." At the point of close quarters combat, his macabre recollection continued, "We ran through what we did not shoot. We bayoneted them. One man begged and got no mercy, a yankee ran him through. Thank God it was not an Irishman (that) did it."[133]

Jackson skillfully managed the evolving crisis, with large numbers of troops moving to the scene of greatest danger. One of the most important Confederate actions of the battle was the timely arrival and counterattack of a brigade under Lawrence Branch, a fiery secessionist and former member of the U.S. Congress. His North Carolinians offered crucial support to the endangered sector of the initial defensive line, "though heavily assailed in front and flank" by the Ninth Corps units trying to maintain their breakthrough.

Branch's men had not fared well fighting future Ninth Corps troops at the battle of New Bern. At Chantilly, the Tar Heels were able to gain revenge, although neither side seemed interested in abandoning the fight. As a member of the 33rd Tar Heel regiment wrote, "This was one of the severest engagements of the war." Also tussling with the Ninth Corps again, Gregg's South Carolinians proved crucial to Jackson's defensive plans. "The enemy, for a time, made a resolute resistance," a Confederate veteran of the brigade wrote, "and the firing was of the hottest." Gen. A. P. Hill praised his Unionist opponents at Chantilly, "The enemy obstinately contested the ground."[134]

The Confederates simply had more men to feed into the meat grinder. Starting the fight against the Ninth Corps in reserve, Jubal Early's Virginians divided somewhat near the Confederate center as the engagement intensified. The timely arrival of these reinforcements helped blunt the pressure Stevens's Division created.[135] The casualties mounted on both sides without much chance either force could gain a decisive advantage.

The lengthening of the attacking line increased the pressure the Ninth Corps could create. To the left of the 28th Massachusetts, the 50th Pennsylvania suffered seven killed in action and dozens wounded as the grisly, rainy battle continued. On the far left, the 6th New Hampshire assisted their Ninth Corps comrades. Hearing the natural forces unleashed from above, the regiment's historian remembered, "The artillery of the skies, chiming with that of the contending lines, contributed to the terrors of the strife." The presence of the New Hampshire men on the left likely stabilized the 50th Pennsylvania, which was having problems with the reorganized Confederate line. One determined Granite Stater reportedly fired 160 rounds of ammunition during the battle, using other muskets when his original weapon became too fouled to use.[136]

The 8th Michigan, the other regiment under Benjamin Christ, found difficult work in the fields and woods. Lieutenant Belcher remembered the intensity of the fight, even while being part of the division's later wave. The officer felt the impact of the pouring rain and very dark late afternoon, as if the sun had already set. Wolverines killed in action at Chantilly included Corp. Clark Hall and Pvt. Oliver Rhodes in Company D, as well as teenager Thomas Barnes in Company E. One soldier from the outfit was listed as missing in action, and therefore presumed dead. Sgt. Orville Wheelock perhaps suffered the most of those in the 8th Michigan. Remaining on the field for days with untreated injuries, he later had his left leg amputated. Wheelock died at an Alexandria hospital on September 9.[137]

Three regiments from Reno's Division stayed behind the main line. None of the units would be engaged much at Chantilly. The 51st Pennsylvania supported Durell's Battery, while the 2nd Maryland and 48th Pennsylvania were in reserve. Farther back from the main attack, men in these regiments had an unparalled view of the confused events. As an officer in the 48th wrote, the fight offered "a most indescribable scene, outrivaling pandemonium itself."[138]

The 21st Massachusetts and 51st New York comprised the far right of the Ninth Corps' line. They became caught in trying circumstances due to the premature darkness of the thunderstorm and the lack of communication between the disconnected regiments. Somewhere, brigade leadership was lacking. Instead of moving together in a line, the 51st New York advanced ahead of the Bay Staters. In the confusing conditions, the two regiments lost contact with each other, leading to very tense moments as the Unionists neared Confederate troops. Getting thoroughly soaked did not help the soldiers' spirits or ability to fire their muskets. Companies within the 21st began to drift apart, turning the line into a disorganized jumble of men. "The heavy rain and darkness made it impossible for us to feel sure about these men in our front," the 21st's historian wrote. Hoping they would not accidentally kill their comrades in the 51st New York, many Massachusetts men hesitated.

Trimble's Brigade, poised to take advantage of the Unionists' muddle, readied a greeting for Ferrero's disheveled line. The Confederates were in no better circumstances due to the weather and darkness, but they had the advantage of a strong defensive position. As an Alabamian recalled, the woods were "so thick that we could only see a few yards in front, but the hissing bullets from the enemy as they came rapping the bushes and trees, and occasionally hitting a man, was evidence to us that they were not far away."[139]

With the 51st New York drifting off to the right, the 21st Massachusetts completely lacked the ability to comprehend the danger facing the entire outfit. "While most of our poor fellows were standing with their guns at the shoulder, one of the deadliest volleys ever fired rolled upon us from our right and front," the regiment's historian lamented. With determination compelled by desperation, the 21st retaliated, although some men found their muskets could not create the spark to shoot back. Col. William Clark, seeing the impossibility of success under the conditions, ordered the regiment's withdrawal. Dozens of men, including the fatally wounded Lt. Col. Joseph Rice, were down with serious wounds.[140]

Supporting units from the Third Corps offered hope for greater success. In reality, the additional firepower did nothing but add to the casualty lists, the most famous of which was General Kearny, the second U.S. general killed at Chantilly. Kearny was attempting to rally parts of Reno's command, threatening the 79th New York with a blast of cannon fire if the Highlanders refused to charge, when he went forward on horseback, falling after a Confederate barrage. Robert E. Lee personally lamented the loss of Kearny, someone he had known for decades.[141]

Sporadic firing pierced the harsh evening as the rain abated. Very little had been gained for the approximately 1,000 casualties the two sides inflicted in the diabolical battle where nature and man both thundered with impunity. Perhaps the continued safety of Pope's retreat made

Chantilly a Union victory, but the best verdict possible is stalemate. The Confederates held the field, so they could not be blamed for feeling like victors.[142]

"I Have Lost My Good Friend"

Chantilly's misery deeply affected the Ninth Corps. Several regiments, especially the 21st Massachusetts, suffered considerably more than their corps comrades did at Second Bull Run. Officially logging 153 casualties during the entire campaign, with perhaps 90 percent of the losses on September 1, the Bay Staters were never the same after enduring the confused firestorm in the downpour at Chantilly. Much of the campaign's loss for the 50th Pennsylvania also occurred at Chantilly.[143]

For those well enough to walk away, clearing the battlefield and moving toward Fairfax Court House engendered many additional trials. Although Durell's Battery suffered no losses, the cannoneers witnessed their comrades "weary, wet, and hungry, many of them falling asleep in the pouring rain, unmindful of the pitiless storm." As the evening wore on "a piercing cold" made drenched soldiers suffer immediately subsequent to the unforgettable battle. "After marching all night," a Roundhead remembered, "daylight found us on the move," as the trek toward Alexandria continued. The troops, this veteran remembered, slogged along "footsore, almost naked, covered with dust, and having passed the hunger line in the long, long ago." The historian of the 51st Pennsylvania asserted a Ninth Corps soldier's condition could "be compared to that of a man being compelled to stand in cold water up to his chin for eight hours in succession."[144]

Alexander Campbell, seemingly destined for injury while still part of the 79th New York's color company, grew more despondent in the aftermath of the bloodletting near Ox Hill. Writing his wife on September 4 from a Washington hospital, the dour soldier provided information about his injury, a relatively minor bullet through the calf. Campbell luckily fled the field early, in time to board a wagon headed to Alexandria. Then he embarked on a steamer for the short ride to the capital. Miserable with the soldier's lot, Campbell added, "I have done my Last soldiring. I am tired of it any how it cant Last much Longer." He saw victory for one side or the other soon, and remarked of the Confederate army's rumored invasion of Maryland. "The south is fighting desperatly," he continued. The trials of the previous three weeks pummeled Campbell with unremitting fury. "I could not begin to tell you what we have came through since Leaving fredericksburgh," he intoned.[145]

Any Ninth Corps soldier had the right to feel utterly drained after the ordeal of being attached to Pope's army. The 6th New Hampshire's historian suggested the campaign concluding with the retreat to Washington's fortifications created "a fearful strain on our physical systems." From Chantilly to Fairfax Court House, the troops had to conquer "roads almost impassable" due to deep mud. Time allowed for a limited rest near Fairfax Court House before the retrograde had to continue.[146]

At 8 p.m. on the 2nd, General Reno informed McClellan of his divisions' march to within 3 miles of Alexandria. "They are very much worn out by the last 20 days marching," Reno's 1846 classmate read of the Ninth Corps, "I have lost heartily in the recent engagements." At Chantilly, especially, "our loss was severe."[147]

Because Lee turned north shortly after the battle and the Union army collected itself inside Washington's fortifications, many wounded at Chantilly from both armies remained on the field. Based on a report from the chaplain of the 21st Massachusetts, Reno penned a letter on September 3 to Confederate leadership in an effort to ease some suffering. He requested the right to send the chaplain and some medical personnel back to the battlefield "to bring away such of them as are able to be removed." The effort was certainly too late for those prostrate with wounds for nearly two full days.[148]

Positive developments on the 3rd provided a bit of reprieve from the disaster of the last week. As battery historian Charles Cuffel wrote, the weather was pleasant and food became more available. With a relative day of rest, the men were able to perform vital tasks like cleaning clothes and writing to loved ones. Men separated from their commands could use the day to reunite with their comrades and be thankful for enduring the horrible trial since leaving Fredericksburg, even without knowing when their next round of privations would start.[149]

"The whole corps mourned the loss of the brave and faithful Stevens," a Granite Stater wrote, "All who knew him loved him." Encomiums from regiments in Stevens's own division were even more fervent. The Highlanders wholeheartedly rejected Reno's order to bury Stevens on the field. Even Lieutenant Colonel Morrison bucked the Ninth Corps' senior officer. "Our men were very indignant at Reno's orders," the 79th's historian wrote. Adding to the poignancy of the regiment's sense of personal loss, he added, "After the war, the flag which he died to save was thoughtfully sent to General Stevens's family, by Colonel Morrison, and it is held by them as a most sacred relic."[150]

Hazard Stevens had the most to regret. At the moment of the general's death, his son/biographer suggested, "His noble, brave, and ardent spirit, freed at last from the petty jealousies of earth, had flown to its Creator."[151]

William Lusk felt Stevens would never receive sufficient credit from the country. Knowing the Ninth Corps division commander well, Lusk keenly informed his mother of the acute emotional pain resulting from Stevens's death.

> *I have lost my good friend, Genl Stevens, who has been sacrificed by little men who can poorly fill his place. Whenever anything desperate was to be performed, Stevens and Kearny were always selected, with this difference, though, that Stevens rarely was credited with what he did, while Kearny's praises were properly published.*[152]

MCCLELLAN AGAIN IN CONTROL

Halleck pressed Pope to ensure any Confederate flanking moves failed, while promising more assistance to the beleaguered Army of Virginia. "We are strengthening the line of defense as rapidly as possible," he wrote.[153] Any field commander reading those words from his boss had to understand the chance for an offensive was at an end. Pope could have retreated to the defenses of Washington days before, but then would have ceded command to McClellan, the senior major general.

Even before Pope finished his retreat, Halleck was communicating with McClellan in messages one would expect between a general-in-chief and the nation's senior field commander. At 1:30 a.m. on September 1, Halleck informed McClellan of Burnside's pending trip to augment the capital's defenses. Additionally, McClellan was told "to stop all retreating troops in line of works or where you can best establish an outer line of defense."[154] McClellan clearly was being handed overall control of the situation prior to a formal announcement from the government.

Early September led the Lincoln administration to realize McClellan offered the best chance to rally all the troops, including the Army of Virginia, the Ninth Corps, and McClellan's own army. September 2 proved to be the day when "My dear Mac" was informed of the government's renewed interest in his active services. Lincoln placed him in charge of all troops around the capital, including Pope's men as they reached the fortifications. Later in the day, McClellan went west to greet elements of Pope's retreating force. In Pope's presence, nearby soldiers began cheering lustily when they were informed of McClellan's control of the situation. The Union soldiers received a vital boost to their confidence simply knowing McClellan led them once more. By making himself visible to the troops, McClellan could inspire them.[155]

Lee had yet to make a bold move, so the capital's defenders might obtain a respite while McClellan restructured them around Washington. Any critic of McClellan must acknowledge his prowess as a motivator of soldiers and an organizer of an army. Perhaps Lincoln summed up the matter perfectly. Of McClellan, the president said, "If he can't fight himself, he excels in making others ready to fight." Later, on September 2 at a meeting of his cabinet, mostly a group of men who despised McClellan, Lincoln defended his decision to put McClellan in charge of Washington's defenses, "We must use the tools we have."[156]

Pope's obtuseness continued after his bosses had moved on with their stoic hope in McClellan. The Army of Virginia commander envisioned a revitalized attack with four corps, one under Reno. Pope's idea was ludicrous, especially because McDowell was suggested as another corps commander. The general with two failures at Bull Run requested to be relieved of his corps under Pope as McClellan regained control of all forces around Washington. Pope's ideas also left Burnside without a command. In reality, the Ninth Corps leader would be offered command of the rested Army of the Potomac to pursue the Confederates into Maryland. Unsurprisingly, "Burn" turned down the offer again while suggesting McClellan as the best possible commander for the moment. Pope was out, ordered to Minnesota to quell a Sioux uprising.[157]

From Aquia to Washington

Lincoln and Halleck knew Burnside's steady devotion to duty could be relied on during the crisis immediately after Second Bull Run. The catastrophic end of August led Halleck, the boss of all men in the United States Army, to see the necessity of bringing the rest of Burnside's soldiers closer to Washington. "You will embark your troops as rapidly as possible for Alexandria," Burnside had been ordered on August 31. His reply again typified Burnside's diligent devotion to his duty and country, "Dispatch received. All right."[158] Thus began the reunification of the Ninth Corps.

The trip from Falmouth to Aquia Landing proved enervating for Burnside and his seven regiments. Keenly interested in his soldiers' welfare, Burnside oversaw the departure from Falmouth, with the stress of the last several weeks evident. As one soldier wrote, "something of weariness could be detected in his usual elastic step." The decision to burn surplus stores unable to be transported led to billowing smoke from Fredericksburg. Burnside also made a decision he would rue before the next winter: bridges across the Rappahannock were destroyed as his command departed.

On the way to Aquia, a man in the 9th New York wrote of the march "over fearful roads deep in mud," with another Zouave remembering the "miserable" trek. Burnside, never a haughty senior officer, hopped out of his transportation multiple times to assist those stuck in the mud. By the time the men reached the landing, a lack of boats became another obstacle. As in North Carolina, small crafts were used to ferry men to larger vessels unable to move closer due to shallow water along the shore.

Burnside wired on September 1, "We are embarking as rapidly as possible. Is there anything now from Pope?" In another note, his superiors were informed, "Everything is progressing well." The general-in-chief replied to Burnside, "Pope still holds his own, but I fear will be obliged to fight again today. Hurry up your re-enforcements as rapidly as possible." Possessing commendable administrative talent, but not the lever of Archimedes, Burnside pressed for more boats, as well as protective warships at Aquia, on the evening of September 1.[159]

A waiting game prevailed on the 2nd. The navy provided gunboats, although a slow loading process prevailed. At 8:00 a.m., Burnside informed Halleck, "Nothing embarked since yesterday afternoon for want of transports. We have no coal for our tugs and lighters." The Ninth Corps leader then wondered if he should destroy wagons, other government property, and even the depot itself to hasten the movement. Halleck hoped a rear guard could protect Aquia but asked for the destruction of anything unable to make the trip up the Potomac. As if the words could literally make boats appear, Halleck ordered "Hasten forward the troops as rapidly as possible."[160]

By the morning of September 3, Burnside could report good news. Six regiments were about to board transports. Later in the morning, Burnside wired his decision to remain at Aquia until ordered north. By 5:30 p.m. he reported the departure of two artillery batteries.[161] Again, Burnside was proving his worth: steady progress against difficult logistical and transportation limitations, repeated contact with his superiors, and a drive to serve however his bosses requested.

Finally, nearly a week after the order to depart Fredericksburg, troops were ready to sail starting at about dusk on September 4. The 45th Pennsylvania, most familiar with the immediate area, stayed behind for two days to complete the destruction of surplus stores at the landing.[162] Burnside's sense of relief must have been exceedingly satisfying. But what would the future bring? The drive to serve and protect their country burned bright across Burnside's regiments. Still, the horrors in store over the next two weeks could likely not be envisioned.

Part Two

To the Mountain Gaps and Beyond

". . . having destroyed the advanced troops of the enemy."
–Col. Thomas Welsh, reporting on
the battle of South Mountain

Leadership Changes

The president and general-in-chief likely both assumed Burnside would revert to command of the Ninth Corps, but McClellan had other ideas. Just like in the Second Bull Run campaign, the Ninth Corps' senior officer would not directly command the outfit in Maryland. Wishing to boost his friend, even if Burnside's praise of Pope likely rankled, McClellan put Burnside in charge of a wing in the field army. The assignment included the reorganized Ninth Corps in addition to the First Corps, the former Third Corps under Pope. Fresh from his latest offer to take McClellan's job, Burnside's wing leadership put about 25,000 men under his authority, far more than the number he led to victories in North Carolina.

Burnside received warm applause and rousing cheers from the troops on September 5, as Capt. James Wren of the 48th Pennsylvania remembered. Perhaps the men figured Burnside, unlike Pope, would not squander lives with poor intelligence and plans divorced from reality. The troops knew a great deal about the cost of any military operation, successful or not, but the sense of being controlled by a feckless leader bothered them no longer.[1]

Reno's services were nearly lost to the Ninth Corps as the army reorganized around Washington. Joseph Hooker was slated to take over the Fifth Corps, as Halleck informed McClellan, while also saying Reno was being assigned to command the First Corps. McClellan wrote both Lincoln and Halleck to request a change to these orders. Although McClellan described himself as "an intimate friend and admirer of Reno," he suggested Hooker take the First Corps, with Reno staying as Ninth Corps commander. With some exaggeration not foreign to his character, McClellan opined, "to take Reno now is to break up Burnside's Corps."[2] The army commander got what he wanted, with Lincoln deferring to Halleck, who accepted McClellan's suggestions.

With Burnside taking command of an army wing, Maj. Gen. Jesse Reno fatefully led the Ninth Corps into Maryland in September 1862.
LIBRARY OF CONGRESS

While retaining Burnside and Reno as senior officers, the ascension of three new division commanders greatly changed corps leadership during the start of the campaign in Maryland. On the regimental level, four new units were spread across the Ninth Corps' three original divisions. Fresh from the North, the rookie regiments offered a large number of men with limited training. Some historians question the value of adding these relatively untrained units to a field army, but the crisis required such a move.[3] The Lincoln administration would not have felt sanguine for the capital's safety if nothing but untested troops remained in the fortifications while all the experienced soldiers took to the field. The four rookie regiments added to the Ninth Corps would serve nobly and suffer immensely in Maryland and beyond.

Orlando Willcox took charge of the First Division, due to the death of Isaac Stevens. Graduating ten spots higher than Burnside in West Point's Class of 1847, Willcox would not gain field experience in Mexico. A native of Detroit, Willcox resigned his U.S. Army commission in 1857, then returned to his home state to pursue a legal career while serving in the Michigan Militia. Taking the 1st Michigan to Washington in 1861, Willcox led the regiment at First Bull Run, then spent more than a year as a prisoner of war. He was exchanged in mid-August 1862, an exceedingly important time. Willcox enjoyed a very busy three weeks after gaining freedom. A dinner with President Lincoln was followed by a visit to his wife in Vermont, then a quick trip back to Michigan. Knowing so many high-ranking officers, including McClellan, Willcox easily found a position worthy of his star, having been promoted to brigadier general.[4]

Like Willcox, Second Division commander Samuel Sturgis was a West Point graduate who became a prisoner of war. Sturgis's career at the academy lacked Willcox's distinction. He graduated a year ahead of the First Division commander in the lowest quarter of the Class of 1846. Taken prisoner near Buena Vista during the War with Mexico, Sturgis would be released in just over a week. Later, Sturgis's army service included combat against Native tribes. At an Arkansas post when the state seceded, Sturgis took some men of his command to Kansas after others at the fort joined the South. He gained promotion to brigadier general in the same month as Burnside.[5]

Isaac Rodman became the leader of the Third Division, previously under John Parke. With several months of solid service during the war, Rodman gained the star of a brigadier general in late April 1862. Unfortunately, the insalubrious climate in North Carolina led to a serious bout with typhoid fever, prompting Rodman's return home for recuperation. He fatefully healed in time to respond to Burnside's request to rejoin the Ninth Corps on the eve of the new campaign. Parke would serve as chief of staff for the new wing commander.[6]

Jacob Cox, the youngest general in the Ninth Corps, had been wearing a star longer than any, including Burnside. Like George McClellan, Cox started the war as a general in the Ohio Militia. He joined the U.S. Army in May 1861, then had the good fortune to competently lead men under the supervision of McClellan in western Virginia later that year. Born in Canada to New York parents, Cox was not a West Pointer, rare in the leadership of the Army of the Potomac. He graduated from Ohio's Oberlin College in 1851, then worked as a teacher, lawyer, and state legislator.

Taking his Ohio division to Washington during the summer crisis of 1862, Cox quickly showed a penchant to serve without worrying much about his own advancement. Burnside exemplified those traits, and the two men formed a strong bond during their short time together. Immediately prior to being attached to the Ninth Corps, Cox held his men at the strategic point of Upton's Hill, Virginia, about 5 miles west of the White House in Washington. He regularly communicated with McClellan in early September, sending out cavalry on scouting expeditions and reporting the presence of dozens of stragglers from the defeated Army of Virginia. Not yet thirty-four years old, Cox was worthy of his station, and his Ohioans made a vital addition to the Ninth Corps.[7]

A TIME FOR REORGANIZATION AND REBIRTH

After the army's reorganization, the First Division would include two brigades with a total of eight regiments. At the start of the campaign, Colonel Christ's First Brigade included the 28th Massachusetts, 8th Michigan, the rookie 17th Michigan, 79th New York, and 50th Pennsylvania. Col. Thomas Welsh, original leader of the 45th Pennsylvania, took charge of the Second Brigade, with his own regiment joining with the 46th New York, still under Lt. Col. Joseph Gerhardt and the 100th Pennsylvania. The Roundheads started the campaign with Lt. Col. David A. Leckey as senior officer due to Leasure's Second Bull Run wound.

Eight regiments were also spread across the two brigades in Sturgis's Second Division. Both brigades included a new regiment. James Nagle added the rookie 9th New Hampshire to the three regiments he led at Second Bull Run. Ferrero's new regiment, the 35th Massachusetts, joined the brigade's existing three units, all under familiar leaders. Rodman's Third Division was also largely unchanged except for the addition of the 16th Connecticut, attached to Col. Edward Harland's Second Brigade.

A young and excellent officer Burnside deeply respected finally had a chance to lead a regiment into combat as part of the Ninth Corps. After missing the North Carolina coast, not for lack of trying on Burnside's part, Col. Henry Kingsbury was in command of the 11th Connecticut, still part of the Second Brigade, Third Division. After placement on the staff of Irvin McDowell, Kingsbury—a "magnificent soldier, disciplinarian, and daring officer"—gained a great deal of battle experience with McClellan on the Peninsula. Deeply admired by his West Point classmates and other members of the army, the young colonel respected the soldiers in the 11th and they returned the favor. Kingsbury's future seemed limitless.[8]

Cox's Ohioans were known as the Kanawha Division. Col. Eliakim Scammon headed the First Brigade, with the 12th, 23rd, and 30th Ohio, while Col. Augustus Moor commanded the 11th, 28th, and 36th Ohio in the Second Brigade. The division included two artillery batteries and three companies of cavalry. The most historically impactful regimental commander was Lt. Col. Rutherford B. Hayes, future president of the United States. Happy with the change of scenery, Hayes proudly noted what he deemed the high quality of the division's troops. Writing to his wife on August 30, Hayes boasted, "All of McClellan's army is near us, but we see nothing superior to General Cox's six Ohio regiments."[9]

Rookie regiments also offered much to their country. The 17th Michigan would prove a highly capable and bold outfit. Their colonel, William Withington, a Massachusetts native born in 1835, had earned captain's bars in the 1st Michigan. At First Bull Run, Withington remained on the field to rally his 1st Michigan after Orlando Willcox was wounded. Withington would be awarded the Medal of Honor for bravery during the July 1861 fiasco near Manassas. On his return to Michigan, Withington organized the 17th Regiment. In August, more than 1,000 soldiers departed the Wolverine State in time to reach Washington as the Second Bull Run crisis boiled over.[10]

David Lane, a diarist in the 17th Michigan, noted the wide array of careers and ages in the regiment. Some members were as young as sixteen. As expected in the nineteenth century, most of the recruits were farmers. Company E of Withington's unit included soldiers almost exclusively from the State Normal School in Ypsilanti. Regardless of their origins and careers, Lane continued, the patriotic Wolverines left behind all that was "dearer to them than life, sternly resolved to meet death on the field of battle, rather than suffer rebellion to triumph and the Nation be torn asunder."[11]

The assignment of the Granite Staters to the Ninth Corps gave Enoch Fellows a chance to reunite with other members of the South Carolina expedition. Fellows gained the colonelcy of the new regiment: one of five the state was required to raise under Lincoln's summer call for volunteers. Fellows had been recuperating at home after the tough service the 3rd New Hampshire experienced in South Carolina. Like the 17th Michigan, the 9th New Hampshire would include many men hardly able to afford a departure from their domestic chores and families, but the ranks were quickly filled. So determined was Ned Parsons to enlist, the sixteen-year-old lied about his age to gain a spot in the regiment. Franklin Taft, perhaps looking to avenge the death of his brother in the 2nd New Hampshire, also signed up, as did forty-one men who had been born outside the United States.[12]

Prior to leaving their home state, members of the regiment experienced problems with water and mud, bitter foes capable of causing much misery without inflicting wounds. Charles Dwight Chase, destined to die the following year very far from home, wrote his mother from camp in Concord on August 15. Although feeling "first rate," Chase hoped to receive a new flannel shirt and some towels in a package. The young soldier mentioned how several comrades were "digging a ditch around the tent to keep the water out."[13] Many are the trials and tribulations of a soldier.

On the trip south to Washington, the 9th New Hampshire was "greeted and honored in all the New England cities." Adjutant George Chandler also enjoyed the "perfect storm of enthusiasm and welcome" the people of Philadelphia offered. This contrasted sharply with the "solemn, subdued silence" the 9th received in Baltimore. On arrival in Washington, Chandler added, "It was a long hard ride, and we were glad to get to the end of it." Chandler grew very impressed with the defenses of Washington as the men camped just south of the Potomac River in Virginia. In a letter home, he suggested, "The whole country in this vicinity is laid out in earthworks and fortifications and rifle pits, and with proper resistance is unapproachable."[14]

The new soldiers had a fatiguing trek to reach the defenses on Arlington Heights, land that would soon become the nation's most famous cemetery. Charles Brigham, often known by his middle name of Lewis, informed his father of the horrible dust on the enervating late August day. "The sun was very hot with no wind," Mr. Brigham read, "A great many fell out with the heat and want of water." Foreboding sounds filled ears in the 9th New Hampshire as well, as part of the Ninth Corps, along with John Pope's army, fought for their lives 20 miles to the west near Bull Run. "I can hear the cannons roar as plain as day," Brigham informed his father.[15]

Several members of the Nashua Cornet Band had joined the 9th New Hampshire. The musicians were assigned to various companies of the new regiment, but they arranged to keep their designation as a band. As such, the band members found duty under the quartermaster's department for their brigade, assisting with a variety of tasks related to the supply for multiple regiments. The band would often play for officers or during dress parades. They also showed dedication to their fellow soldiers during battles, becoming stretcher bearers or hospital assistants.[16]

Soldiers in the new 35th Massachusetts started their permanent tenure in the Ninth Corps as the Antietam campaign began. Men from a single municipality often enlisted in such large numbers to fill an entire company with about one hundred men. A camp in Lynnfield provided the rallying point for those about to join the 35th, with companies that would become part of other new regiments also encamping in the town. The regiment's first colonel would be Edward Wild, a physician who had spent time in Europe treating casualties of the Crimean War. Wounded earlier in 1862 as an officer in the 1st Massachusetts, Wild never lost his drive to serve. The regiment's major, Sumner Carruth, was another Bay State native in the 1st Massachusetts wounded on the Peninsula.[17]

Wild found the rapid move from Massachusetts to Washington as less than desirable, although he understood "the demand for fresh troops." In a letter to Gov. John Andrew, Wild considered his men "quite *imperfectly* fitted out," with European rifles of "*very poor* quality and *dangerous* to handle." The colonel also informed Andrew of a few problems encountered in Philadelphia due to "a large number of drinking shops, which have been the pest to every regiment passing through." After finishing their first journey in late August, the 35th Massachusetts dug entrenchments along Arlington Heights, just across the Potomac from Washington.[18]

PERSEVERANCE PREVAILS IN THE NEW CAMPAIGN

Burnside's target for the first big march of the campaign was Leesborough, Maryland (now known as Wheaton), about 8 miles north of the camp made by Reno's first three divisions. After departing Upton's Hill on the evening of September 6, Hooker's First Corps and Cox's Kanawha Division had more than twice as far to reach Leesborough.[19]

Robert Hale Ives, Jr., a Rhode Islander on Rodman's staff, wrote of orders to march at 3 p.m. on September 6. The move was delayed so long that the young officer returned to downtown Washington, where he saw Chief of Staff Parke. The following day, troops in the three divisions with Reno were prepared to march in the morning, but hours of delays awaited prior to the start of the campaign.[20]

Hosea Towne penned a letter back to New Hampshire as the new campaign began. "I find myself safe and sound after many narrow escapes," the member of the 6th New Hampshire proclaimed. Reeling from the very difficult August, Towne discussed the loss of his knapsack, blanket, and change of clothes near Bull Run. "I never saw such a worn out set of men in my life," Towne continued.[21]

Reno's new regiments, not familiar with the grueling experience of military marching, must have felt every pound they carried. As Fisher Cleaveland, Company I of the 35th Massachusetts, informed his daughter, each soldier was essentially a beast of burden. With their large knapsack, blanket, and overcoat, the men also carried three days of rations and sixty rounds of ammunition. Adding a rifle of several pounds, the rookies worked hard, even though the day's distance was far from a record for Civil War troops. Heat zapped the strength of many. "We started with about 900 men," Cleaveland noted, "and when we camped we had not more than 300" due to the difficult conditions. Likewise, the 16th Connecticut endured "a terrible march" because of the "very hot and so dusty" conditions; simply seeing a few feet ahead became difficult.[22]

The 9th New Hampshire did not quite reach Leesborough on their first march. The men were a bit behind the rest of the corps, then they found the town to be about 3 miles farther north than expected. Very tired, they pressed on. "The day was hot, the dust deep," the regimental historian recorded. At a spot called Brightwood, the men benefited from a delightful grove of hardwoods. "The friendly and protecting trees," he continued, seemed to shield the rookie warriors during their rest. Another member of the regiment fondly recalled Brightwood. "How well I remembered that night," Daniel Hurd noted, "It seems to me I never have seen so bright moonlight," which helped him read a letter from home. The men would reach Leesborough the next morning. While watching thousands of soldiers march by, George Chandler noted, "All is uncertain."[23]

On the morning of September 8, Burnside reported the dilemma of men not being able to keep up, with the issue especially acute in Hooker's corps. The wing commander either did not know about or condoned the large number of rookie soldiers in the Ninth Corps who also found the march too taxing. Straggling issues became less acute soon enough.[24]

A dramatic and unfortunate confrontation between General Reno and Lieutenant Colonel Hayes occurred early in the march. Reno was unhappy when some cannoneers, with the help of soldiers in the 23rd

Ohio, took hay from a farmer to feed horses or make some bedding. Demanding to talk to a colonel, Reno was quickly met by Hayes, who defended his men. The future U.S. president said the Buckeye soldiers would pay for the materials, if required. Disrespectfully, Hayes asked Reno for his name, a query Hayes would have been better to avoid due to the two stars on each of Reno's shoulders. Hayes wrote of Reno putting a hand on his own pistol, an implied threat to the colonel. As discussed in a letter to his wife, Hayes regretted the incident, although he proudly stood up for his soldiers. Reno considered disciplinary action or even the arrest of Hayes, but nothing to that effect occurred, perhaps thanks to a conversation the corps commander had with Colonel Scammon, Hayes's immediate superior.[25]

Even in the immediate aftermath of Second Bull Run, mass gloom did not exist among units losing hundreds in action under Pope. Across McClellan's army and the Ninth Corps in particular, dejection did not sink Unionist hopes. Optimism bolstered the weary and defeated warriors. Hazard Stevens, who lost his brave father at Chantilly, wrote of the troops and Pope's debacle of a campaign, "That at the end of the battle there was disorder and demoralization among some commands it were idle to deny, but it has been grossly exaggerated."[26]

Soldiers in the Ninth Corps certainly might have looked sullen, horribly dirty, and too distressed for further trials. They had a right to feel downtrodden during their horrid summer. History simply does not support the idea of boys in blue being in worse physical or logistical shape than their victorious Confederate foes. As the historian of the 79th New York suggested,

Defeated in battle; wet through to the skin, and covered with mud from head to feet, we presented a rather demoralized appearance. But though defeated, we were by no means vanquished. We fought the Second Bull Run, but did not skedaddle. We were ready and willing to receive the enemy whenever he saw fit to advance.[27]

A Roundhead concurred with his Highlander comrade. The frazzled troops obviously would have preferred additional rest in Washington before another campaign, but when the necessity of countering Lee's invasion became evident, the soldiers mustered extra willpower and endurance. The 100th Pennsylvania man suggested the patriotic ranks in the Army of the Potomac "were ready for one more trial."[28]

Before the campaign began, perceptive soldiers in the Ninth Corps could detect how McClellan's leadership often inspired the troops. Henry Spooner, 4th Rhode Island, had a chance to rest on September 4 as he wrote his father from Washington, "Everyone seems to have the greatest confidence in McClellan and say he is the man for the time." Spooner continued, "if he has his own way all will be well."[29] Coming from an officer who never served under McClellan before the march into Maryland, Spooner's observations display the necessity of an army possessing a commanding officer who enjoyed the trust of his soldiers.

Hosea Towne noted the suffering of the last few weeks, creating a high level of despondency. "The soldiers are discouraged," the warrior wrote, "They see no prospect of peace or victory." Yet, Towne deemed himself "tough and hearty." Tens of thousands knew they needed rest, but they pushed on with the mission that had prompted them to enlist: defeat of the Confederacy. Even rookies endured when considering their important duties. "The boys are all well," Jabez Smith, 35th Massachusetts, wrote while resting a bit on September 8, following their first big day of marching.[30]

A factor in the soldiers' motivation was an array of tangible benefits accruing quickly while they marched through a pro-Union part of Maryland. The regimental historian of the 51st Pennsylvania remembered the vast, joyous reception bringing much comfort to men as Brookville was reached at about midday on September 9. "In passing through this section of country the troops were received with strong marks of kindness," including a great deal of food and drink. Additionally, chances existed "to wash their clothing and for a bath, a fine stream of water passing through the camp." In addition to army rations, "Fruit being in great plenty and fully ripe, the men did ample justice to it."[31]

Pleasing images from the Maryland countryside brought further motivation to the troops. Cox remembered the inspiration from an "evening march, under a brilliant moon, over a park-like landscape with alternations of groves and meadows which could not have been more beautifully composed by a master artist." The early trek in Maryland "remains in my memory as a page out of a lovely romance," the Ohio general added. Attractive farms unspoiled by war symbolized the hope the men had of a Union victory. Positive impressions from Maryland's natural beauty might not win battles, but the men certainly lessened the bitter memories from earlier in the year. Harvey Henderson, 89th New York, summed up his view of central Maryland in his diary, "The country is as fine as I ever saw."[32]

New men boosted many veteran soldiers. The 21st Massachusetts enjoyed the augmentation of Ferrero's Brigade by another Bay State outfit, the rookies of the 35th. Moreover, recruiting duty paid off; forty-five new soldiers joined the 21st on the eve of the Antietam campaign. The 51st Pennsylvania, another of Ferrero's units, reported "quite an acquisition to its ranks by the arrival of a large squad of new recruits from Camp Curtin." In Christ's Brigade, the 79th New York welcomed seventy recruits fresh from the Empire State. Any trepidation about the ability of untrained regiments to fight did not prevail. In the national crisis, more men were absolutely vital to success. As Charles Crofut, 89th New York, suggested to his sister on September 6, "It seems to me we have got troops enough in the field to whipp all Creation and [Stonewall] Jackson in the bargain."[33]

Corp. Frederick Pettit, a new soldier in the 100th Pennsylvania, started his march in Maryland a bit behind his Roundhead comrades. Although he grew concerned with the army's ability to win with the number of stragglers he had seen while marching north, Pettit grew very optimistic on reaching the assembled regiment still around Brookville on the evening of September 10. Pettit himself felt good after the early round of marching. Additionally, the 100th Pennsylvania's soldiers seemed ready to meet the enemy, even if the men did not yet know their destination.[34]

Men endured because of their strong devotion to the cause. Days of marching under warm conditions and plentiful dust tried many and proved too much for some. Nonetheless, even the newest soldiers who regretted missing their homes and families felt the pull of patriotism. As Fisher Cleaveland informed his son, "I should like to be at home if only for a few hours, but when it will be I do not know." He added, "At least I should try to do my duty to my Country first."[35]

The blazing sun added to the wretched trek "over the most execrable road I ever saw . . . and there was no relief from it," Henry Spooner wrote. Finally, at camp with his 4th Rhode Island after the tough march to Leesborough, Spooner noted the lack of wagons. Thus, "entirely without tents, officers and men were sheltering themselves as best they could from the heat of the sun under the shadow of their blankets and in little huts which they had built from the boughs of trees." Clearly accepting his fate out of national necessity, the difficult days brought "many drawbacks," Spooner concluded, "but it is not displeasing."[36]

Positive comments from senior officers buttressed a veteran regiment of solid discipline and immense fealty to the Union. Richard H. Morris, a young officer in the 9th New York, proudly wrote of how the regiment was praised by Ninth Corps generals during the laborious trek in Maryland. Writing his mother on September 10, Morris declared, "I can now say with certainty what has hitherto seemed like a boast, that your son is in the best regiment in the U.S. service. Burnside says so—Parke says so—Reno says so—everybody who has seen us says so and we know it." He added how Burnside did not see a single Zouave uniform in the lines of stragglers on the way north of Washington. With an expected battle looming, the positive impact of generals' approbation could not be denied, prompting the men to relish the thought of another brawl with the Confederates. As Morris wrote, "We expect to give a good account of ourselves when we meet them."[37]

Serious challenges remained, but neither Burnside's wing nor the whole army was weak, dispirited, or chronically undersupplied. The next two weeks would prove Northern soldiers' devotion to country and their ability to transcend enormous difficulty. One person deeply impressed with the Union army was James Longstreet, leading almost half of Lee's Confederates. The senior subordinate in the Army of Northern Virginia, Longstreet suggested the Unionists had fought very well in Pope's campaign, even if defeated at Second Bull Run and held in check at Chantilly. The men taking the field for the Union in Maryland remained a "formidable adversary, seasoned by many bloody fields," Longstreet correctly wrote.[38]

FINALLY TO FREDERICK

McClellan visited Burnside in Brookville on September 10. In providing an update to Halleck during the evening, the army commander reported the Ninth Corps was spread out between Damascus and Cracklinton. McClellan was clearly showing his preference for a leisurely march by writing, "I think there is little indication of the enemy's advancing either on Baltimore" or York, Pennsylvania.[39]

One could wonder if the friendship between McClellan and Burnside suffered further damage as a result of their conversation on September 10. By late morning of the next day, with an advance to Ridgeville postponed and during a heavy rain, Burnside was given orders for a westward scouting mission, which again echoed McClellan's cautious generalship. The division making the reconnaissance was certainly not asked to begin any type of offensive action. The idea was to hold a part of Parr Ridge for defensive purposes, rather than as a springboard for the advance of the whole army. Ridgeville was "an important point to hold," Burnside read, in case the Confederates moved east.[40]

By the evening of the 11th, Burnside had grown clearly exasperated with the pace of McClellan's advance. Reno had cavalry scouts within 2 miles of New Market without finding any Confederates. In an 8 p.m. message from his headquarters north of Damascus, the wing commander gave an accurate assessment of the situation followed by a somewhat disappointed conclusion. Burnside declared, "Everything would seem to indicate that the enemy has left this neighborhood, but in accordance with your directions I shall move carefully." Hooker and his First Corps were in supporting distance at Ridgeville. Lee's divided army, moving on Harpers Ferry or into northern Maryland, had started to abandon Frederick forty hours before.[41]

With men feeling the privations of a soldiers' life, the type of food available became a defining experience. The 35th Massachusetts' historian recalled efforts to experiment with the creation of sour apple sauce from the abundant trees along the march. Raw salt pork, bitter coffee, and hard bread became vital friends to the soldiers. Steps to supplement army fare deprived Old Line State birds of their existence. The historian continued, "Stray fowls were thrown into the pot and devoured almost before they could utter their last expiring clack." Other soldiers felt the necessity of nourishment due to the hot days and dusty roads.[42]

Even with the slow pace of McClellan's advance, his army was destined to reach Frederick. Cox's Division had the honor of entering the town at the front of the Ninth Corps. Frederick had just emerged rather unscathed from four days of Confederate occupation. Most Confederate troops were well on their way to other missions, especially the looming assault on Harpers Ferry. But danger remained, as an Ohio brigade commander found out the hard way.

Augustus Moor served under Cox as commander of the Second Brigade, Kanawha Division. Like thousands of devoted American patriots fighting for the Union, Moor had been born overseas, in the city of Leipzig, Saxony. He had experience in the Pennsylvania Militia and then as part of an Ohio regiment in the Mexican War. He was the original colonel of the 28th Ohio, serving in western Virginia from early in the war. Soon after crossing the Monocacy, he ran into trouble in the form of Confederate cavalry.[43]

A staff officer goaded Cox and then Moor, questioning why the Ohioans were failing to move swiftly into town. Moor took umbrage at what seemed like a criticism of his men. After moving forward, Moor and a small number of Unionists became prisoners.

Even if Moor did not welcome the tone of the staff officer, no order from Reno or Cox necessitated the zealous drive to move ahead in unknown territory without immediate help from a substantial force. Col. George Crook, 36th Ohio, became acting brigade commander after Moor's unfortunate capture. Charles Achuff, a young lieutenant from the 11th Ohio, fell under his dying horse during the brief melee, nearly being crushed. He would soon return to duty.[44]

The capture of Moor did not quell the Unionist tide, although much of the army remained east of the Monocacy as September 12 ended. Lieutenant Colonel Hayes recorded how the reception renewed the confidence of the men in his tired 23rd Ohio. Like earlier in the campaign, strong Unionist sentiments from locals steeled part of the Ninth Corps for future trials in Maryland. Hayes saw many "waving flags and clapping hands" among the citizenry. Prior to this triumphant stroll, the regiment lost many men who rested along the road near the town, saying they were unable to march farther. Yet, Hayes continued, the regiment's men were soon "hurrahing the ladies" when called to march into Frederick. In a letter to his wife the next day, Hayes credited Frederick's residents for the "magnificent and charming reception."[45]

Col. Hugh Ewing and his 30th Ohio also found much to pleasantly observe thanks to Frederick's "most extravagant" welcome. People in the town "shed tears of joy and gratitude," the regimental historian wrote, "and thanked and blessed us as long as we could hear their voices." Soldiers always could appreciate a hug and kiss from a thankful young lady, and some were reportedly held hostage by grateful Unionist residents who wished to provide a fine meal to the famished rescuers of the town. "Can the regiment ask greater acclamations at the hands of their countrymen," the historian wondered, "even at the deliverance of the Nation, than they received at Frederick City?"[46]

INTELLIGENCE COUP

"Burnside's entrance to Frederick exceeded all newspaper reports," Daniel Read Larned wrote, "Every one of the staff family wept." Flocking to a man with two stars on each shoulder, townspeople gave Burnside an "especially enthusiastic" welcome. With profuse cheers from pleased Marylanders, Burnside had to smile as "bouquets rained upon him." One suggested the departure of the Confederates and arrival of the Ninth Corps saved the town from "a great affliction," a bit of an exaggeration, because the Confederates were well behaved by the standard of historical invaders. Certainly correct, however, the same author noted forebodingly, "But there was little time for congratulations," because much hard and deadly work lay ahead.[47]

Ninth Corps units were spread out across Frederick as September 13 began. Capt. Ralph Ely found his way back to the 8th Michigan during the day. The previous month brought much pain and rest for the respected officer as he recuperated from an unhappy horse's kick. By the evening of the 12th, Ely arrived at New Market. He witnessed many troops passing on the National Road. His men were very glad to be reunited with their

A brigade commander at Fox's Gap, Hugh Ewing played a key role in the campaign from Washington to Antietam. LIBRARY OF CONGRESS

captain after Ely found their camp near Frederick, with cannon fire heard in the distance.[48]

"The people are very patriotic here we found," Burton Hine, 89th New York, penned in his diary after the regiment's evening arrival in Frederick. Hine must have really appreciated the warm greeting in the city, especially after sickness hindered him early in the campaign. "The ladies throw open their doors to us and give us water and things to eat and sung the Star Spangled Banner and several other songs," Hine continued. He concluded, "They say the rebels were ragged, lousy filthy and everything that is bad."[49]

The biggest move for Ninth Corps troops on the morning of the 13th was the support Rodman's Division provided cavalry west of Frederick. The two brigades acted independently of each other during the day and were not heavily engaged. The 4th Rhode Island's memoirist noted the "stout resistance" Confederate troops made at Middletown, but the location was occupied by Unionists that evening. Col. Harrison Fairchild's three New York regiments moved to the southwest, becoming part of an engagement near Jefferson. The troops were busy for several hours, "skirmishing for five miles," as one 9th New York man noted. The mission ended with the brigade's return march to Frederick "very tired from our severe day's labor," another member of the Zouaves remembered.[50]

With Lee's movements and numbers still somewhat uncertain, McClellan set up headquarters on the west side of town after his own triumphant parade in Frederick on September 13. The commanding general knew on the evening of the 12th that Jackson was heading to Harpers Ferry, but confusion still reigned during the next morning, especially because of Stonewall Jackson's indirect march to invest the federal garrison. The desire to assist Harpers Ferry predominated, as one of McClellan's staff officers recalled. In talking to Chief of Staff Marcy, he wrote, "great apprehensions" were felt about the garrison in the Virginia town. The idea to rescue Harpers Ferry was one constant preoccupation, with the intelligence picture changing mightily by early afternoon. McClellan went from timidity caused by lack of information to a degree of boldness granted by the biggest intelligence find of the war. Twelfth Corps troops not far from headquarters found a copy of Lee's orders dated September 9 outlining the Confederate army's movements, primarily with the purpose of capturing Harpers Ferry. McClellan had a copy of the order at about 2 p.m.[51]

In reaction to his knowledge of Confederate movements, McClellan would attempt to seize gaps in the South Mountain range as a means to divide the Confederate army. He placed the First Corps, still part of Burnside's wing, as the main force attacking Turner's Gap, a mile north of the Ninth Corps' target, Fox's Gap. William Franklin's Sixth Corps would assail Crampton's Gap, a key location from which to relieve the Harpers Ferry garrison.

Hooker's men had a long march to get to Turner's Gap, and—with good reason—some historians wonder why McClellan had the First Corps take such a lead role. After all, Edwin Sumner's wing, the Second and Twelfth Corps, had entered Frederick on the 13th after shorter marches than the First Corps, which remained east of the Monocacy that evening. McClellan simply did not wish Sumner, his most senior subordinate, to have a prominent role in the attacks along South Mountain.[52]

With a copy of Lee's plan, known as Special Orders 191, or "The Lost Order," McClellan knew a small command under Lafayette McLaws was on Maryland Heights as part of the force investing Harpers Ferry. McLaws was vital to Lee's conquest of the federal garrison. Yet, the two divisions on Maryland Heights were in grave danger from a bold Union drive; they could not cross the Potomac into Harpers Ferry if the Union troops in the town held out against Jackson's attack from the west. McClellan promised to save the garrison, but also felt somewhat powerless. The federal troops at Harpers Ferry numbered nearly 11,000, and a large quantity of supplies the Confederates undoubtedly wished to capture awaited Stonewall's conquerors.

Several hours before McClellan sent a complicated, long order to Franklin, the Sixth Corps commander indirectly appealed for more men. "I think from appearances that we may have a heavy fight to get the pass," Franklin had informed McClellan at 12:30 p.m.[53] Knowing Franklin's lack of initiative, McClellan should have used the diffidence communicated by the Sixth Corps commander to ensure a second corps was involved in the Crampton's Gap fight. With their forward deployment compared to the rest of McClellan's army, the Ninth Corps was the unit to spearhead the battle at Crampton's Gap, and Burnside was the general to command the vital attack. The Ninth Corps could have marched southwest from Frederick on the afternoon of the 13th, with a morning fight on September 14 at Crampton's Gap instead of Fox's Gap. Burnside would have remained a wing commander, directing Reno and Franklin's assault, ensuring more rapid success, the possible destruction of McLaws, and the salvation of the Harpers Ferry garrison.

Crampton's Gap, 5 miles south of Fox's Gap, held the key to attacking McLaws. An early history of the Army of the Potomac rightly suggested "McLaws would have been a sure prey to McClellan" if Unionists occupied Crampton's Gap.[54] Even if the army had moved more swiftly, the plan McClellan drafted to overwhelm McLaws lacked the firepower to readily seize Maryland Heights, capture McLaws, and rescue Harpers Ferry. In a long and complicated order sent at 6:20 p.m. on September 13, McClellan charged his friend Franklin with taking Maryland Heights through Crampton's Gap. Franklin would be supported by a Fourth Corps division that had been marching along the Potomac during the campaign. The three divisions were at rough numerical parity with McLaws, a state of affairs McClellan could have easily fixed by sending another corps to boost Franklin's numbers.

William Franklin proves to history that a man placing first in his West Point class may not have been put on earth to be a great soldier. Thanks to his friendship with McClellan, Franklin was given corps command on the Peninsula. Under McClellan's plan for September 14, after Franklin gained Crampton's Gap, "your duty will be first to cut off, destroy, or capture McLaws's command and relieve Colonel Miles," the commander at Harpers Ferry. Ordering such a grand action, the army commander concluded with words implying his grave doubts about the Sixth Corps' leader. McClellan awkwardly finished his note, "I ask of you, at this important moment, all your intellect and the utmost activity that a general can exercise."[55]

Franklin's short reply exhibits much about the corps commander's own sense of incapacity. At 10 p.m., Franklin plaintively acknowledged McClellan's crucial order by noting, "I understand them, and will do my best to carry them out." Franklin likely felt overwhelmed by his mission and could only promise his best. He could not rely on any direct oversight, had nothing close to overwhelming numbers, and knew McClellan had given the Sixth Corps the most important goal of the campaign thus far. The job was well beyond Franklin's talents.[56]

Using Burnside to command the Crampton's Gap attack would have given a more diligent commander experienced with independent operations the opportunity to wallop McLaws. Franklin would have taken a supporting role, rather than managing a vitally important mission with neither the confidence nor oversight of McClellan.

THE NINTH CORPS IN THE LEAD

McClellan used very general terms to update Halleck and President Lincoln at the end of a busy day. He wished his superiors to believe he was about to achieve a great victory against the Confederates, but he still lacked details and clarity, as the messages prove. To Halleck at 11 p.m., McClellan stressed the 120,000 Confederates he faced, ridiculously in excess of the enemy's strength. McClellan said the army would make "forced marches" to take advantage of the Lost Order's discovery. He noted the primary goal of saving Harpers Ferry, but how he could have done so while feeling heavily outgunned by Lee's army must have been a mystery to Halleck. McClellan again pleaded for more men, while predicting a "severe engagement" on the 14th.

At midnight, a message went to Lincoln. Painting a false picture for the commander in chief, McClellan promised "no time shall be lost." The "gross mistake" Lee made in dividing his force would lead the Confederate commander to be "severely punished" by the Army of the Potomac. "Will send you trophies," Lincoln was promised, "All well, and with God's blessing will accomplish it."[57]

On the afternoon of the 13th Cox had started toward Middletown, at about 3 p.m., six hours after Harland's Brigade went forward in support of cavalry. The divisions of Willcox and Sturgis followed. However, no other troops were moved west from Frederick during the day. Most surprisingly, the First Corps remained east of the Monocacy overnight. Although key support for the Ninth Corps at South Mountain, Hooker's three divisions could not arrive there until the afternoon of the 14th. The Ninth Corps was on its own in the struggle for Fox's Gap.[58]

Those wishing to give McClellan credit for great audacity on the afternoon of September 13 in light of the Lost Order's discovery must explain some vital facts. Although the movement of Cox's Division as a support for the cavalry reconnaissance is clear, this move may have been ordered before McClellan knew about the Lost Order. Moreover, Willcox was not ordered to support Cox, just to move in the direction of Middletown. This does not seem like a tremendous sign of courage and confidence from McClellan. After all, the army commander promised his bosses forced marches and trophies. If he truly meant that, why the Ninth Corps did not gain any direct support from Sumner's wing by evening remains a mystery.

Most perplexing of all, no orders were issued for a morning attack on the 14th, when the Ninth Corps had the responsibility to assail Fox's Gap. "The Kanawha Division made an easy march" to Middletown, Cox remembered, with the division headquarters established west of town. Yet, he again wondered why McClellan did so little. "There was certainly no time to lose," the Ohioan suggested, and he added how the Ninth Corps could have occupied "the top of South Mountain before dark." Mysteriously, "less than one full corps passed Catoctin Mountain that day or night, and when the leisurely movement of the 14th began," McClellan remained in Frederick until afternoon.[59] McClellan was acting like anything but an intrepid army commander. His lack of firm action proved he still had great doubts about what to do. Diffidence does not make for a great military leader.

Much debate has arisen about whether the movement west of three Ninth Corps divisions on September 13 was the result of McClellan's reading of Special Orders 191. Perhaps the advance of the First and Second divisions sprang from McClellan's intelligence coup, although the timing of the orders does not prove either side of the dispute correct. Sending only two divisions forward seems like great restraint in any case, as Cox suggested. McClellan wished to make his response to the Lost Order seem like a decisive moment, but he simply did not believe the informative find guaranteed him victory. McClellan was simply incapable of excellence if the slightest degree of inordinate risk appeared before him.

Regardless of McClellan's incomplete planning, men across units of the Ninth Corps began to sense the looming engagement. Even before leaving Frederick, the morning of the 13th had included "continuous cannonading," a "strong indication of an impending battle," as one of Durell's artillerists wrote. In a letter to an uncle, Lieutenant Colonel Hayes also noted the cannon fire on the 13th. Of the obvious fight not far away, Hayes showed respect for his foes. Although "filthy, lousy, and desperate," the Confederates were very worthy opponents, he wrote, and any fight "will be a most terrific thing." With cautious optimism, he continued, "I think we shall whip them, at any rate, but it is by no means a certainty." An officer in the 48th Pennsylvania understood the somber inevitability soldiers feel when battle beckons. By evening, "A bright full moon lighted the boys to bed that night—the last night some of the poor fellows were to have on earth."[60]

The new troops in the 9th New Hampshire would only arrive in Frederick during the morning of the 13th, with continued marching later in the day. Daniel Hurd recalled the difficult conditions over the last several days, including the numerous men who fell out of the ranks on the march. Due to the privations, the men rested well after they arrived in Frederick. "We had been on the march a week, and many, if not most of us," Hurd wrote, "had blistered feet, and you may be sure were glad when we camped for the night."[61]

Some enlistees in the new Granite State regiment attempted to lift spirits for those still in camp. Members of the Nashua Cornet Band, who had been ordered on September 10 to join their comrades in the 9th, found the regiment along the Monocacy. They tried to allay some of the stress and weariness of the march by playing a few pieces of music near Colonel Fellows's tent.[62]

"Take Them Anyhow"

McClellan sounded prepared for a fight in his notes to Washington and his communication with General Franklin. However, without orders to push Confederates to the west, generals in the Ninth Corps could not be blamed if they wondered what their men were to do in the morning. Like the day before, Cox credibly had planned an advance in support of cavalry. Starting the day west of Middletown, the Ohioans would not march far before reaching South Mountain, a range of peaks providing Lee an excellent rocky breastwork from which a relatively small force could delay the Unionists. Nonetheless, confidence infused the men of Scammon's Brigade. Sol Smith, a member of the 12th Ohio, recalled how his comrades looked forward to the possibility of easing the memory of Second Bull Run. Soldiers were "in the best of spirits and eager to meet the enemy," he suggested.[63]

Gen. D. H. Hill's five brigades were the only infantry immediately available to defend Fox's and Turner's Gaps. They had yet to fully assemble along the mountain crest. The Confederates needed to protect about 3 miles of the hilly and difficult ground. Hill's hasty deployment could take advantage of the lack of knowledge of the roads and ground instilling some caution in McClellan's advance. When the fight came, Hill's men had the chance to shine, aided by the superb defensive ground near the gaps.

By the time the final attack of the morning took place, the Ohioans under Cox would outnumber Samuel Garland's North Carolinians by about three men to one. Scammon's Brigade took the lead that morning, without such a heavy advantage of numbers. Garland, whose grandmother's mother was Frances Madison, sister of Founding Father James Madison, and his Tar Heels had a very difficult task. Natural and manmade obstructions offered the Confederates some solace, but the clear lack of aggression from McClellan perhaps was the best salve for Hill, Garland, and the small number of Southern defenders. As Cox remembered, "No battle was expected at Turner's Gap."[64]

Cox correctly decided the best approach to Turner's Gap, which the National Road bisected, was from the flank. As a result, Scammon's Brigade took roads to the left. They would make their fateful encounter with Garland's men below Fox's Gap, about a mile south of Turner's Gap. Crook's three regiments were in supporting distance, perhaps thirty minutes behind Scammon. Lieutenant Colonel Hayes and the 23rd Ohio were second in the brigade's line of march originally, but they were tasked with flanking the position below Fox's Gap. Ordered by Scammon to ascertain the force opposed to them, Hayes wondered what he should do if the Confederate infantry and cannons were too much for his regiment. "Take them anyhow," Scammon demanded. In thick forest and an understory seemingly impenetrable in places, skirmishers from the two sides had very limited knowledge of their opponents. Garland ordered the advance of the 5th North Carolina to support the Tar Heel skirmishers. Another North Carolinian observed, "Not till the lines seemed within a few yards of each other was the calm, radiant Sabbath morning broken by the crack of rifles."[65]

The only future president of the United States to command a regiment in the Antietam campaign showed highly commendable leadership on September 14. Needing to climb the hill and make the most progress possible against the difficult ground, Rutherford B. Hayes noted the appearance of some enemy troops. Understanding his orders to take charge of the important flanking maneuver, Hayes did not waver as some of his men began to fall. The regimental commander "ordered a charge, which his men, with a yell, made in gallant style." Maj. James Comly suggested the forward movement was executed "in as good order as possible through the thick woods into a corn-field." Extensive progress remained elusive, so Hayes decided on further boldness. The 23rd Ohio's second charge forced the Confederates back several yards, but their line remained intact and able to take advantage of some fencing.

Unfortunately, Hayes did not have the luxury of leading his men to additional glory. He suffered a wound above the left elbow as he ordered the second charge against the North Carolinians. At first behind his troops, a necessary shift in the regimental line meant Hayes was down between the two firing lines. Too weak to fall back without help, the colonel was rescued after his pleas for assistance from his Buckeyes.[66]

The bold 23rd Ohio continued to suffer in the confines of the forest and fields on South Mountain. Men fell during the charges and confused fighting against the 5th North Carolina. Pvt. Fitzerland Squires, Company K, suffered a mortal wound on the 14th. He left a twenty-one-year-old wife and two young children. Taken to Washington after the battle, Squires died nearly two weeks later. His one-year-old son Jefferson lived until 1950, never having known his father. Born in 1841, Thomas Wells was another member of Company K to lose his life as a result of a South Mountain wound.[67]

To the right, Scammon's other two regiments faced problems, especially from an artillery battery. Unionist cannoneers to the rear—

including Benjamin's excellent Regulars—assisted the infantry. Still Bondurant's Confederate guns flustered the 12th and 30th Ohio. A soldier in the latter regiment felt as if the gunners in the Southern battery were "hunting for us" with their shots. The enemy artillery did not remain long, but they certainly impacted the two Buckeye regiments, slowing Scammon's offensive punch.[68]

The roar of musketry filled the mountainside as Tar Heels in the state's 23rd Regiment caused further problems for Scammon. On both sides of the battle, getting a clear sense of the enemy's position proved difficult, with regimental leaders claiming progress in forcing the opposing troops back. Scammon reported his approbation regarding the strenuous work his units performed. The brigade commander wrote that the 30th Regiment "attacked vigorously," while the initial line of the 12th appeared "more like a charge than an advance of skirmishers." Overall, the 1,455 men in the three regiments impressed their commander, "In all of this I am happy to say there was no faltering."[69]

An unafraid officer losing his life during the battle was William Wirt Liggett, 12th Ohio. The officer "fell mortally wounded while fighting at the head of his company," Col. Carr White reported. Captain Liggett, an Ohio native born in 1835, held out for a few days, losing his life on September 20. He would be buried at Maplewood Cemetery in Ripley, Ohio.[70]

In maps of the battle, a fence appears along the Confederate line Garland worked so hard to maintain. Confederate troops remembered the fence looking much less impressive in reality. A member of the 23rd North Carolina classified the protective feature as a "tumbled down stone fence" and "more or less dismantled by time and was in places very low." Mother Nature did more to assist the Tar Heel defense against Scammon; the trees, rocks, and the hill itself proved a tremendous detriment to the Ninth Corps' morning attack.[71]

After progress moving closer to the Confederates, Scammon's 12th and 30th Regiments gained the assistance of close cannon support from two guns under young Lt. George Crome. This section of Capt. J. R. McMullin's 1st Ohio Light Artillery struggled just to reach a point higher on the mountainside to better support the infantry. Crews at the two guns, including some infantry volunteers, suffered severely. Crome himself sustained a mortal wound while working one of his guns. Colonel White of the 12th praised the "good service" of the big guns, even though Crome's effort—four rounds of double canister—was silenced by enemy sharpshooters posted in the thick woods to the west. McMullin expressed deep regret over the loss of Crome. "Yet," he concluded, "it is a consolation to his friends and companions in arms to know that he died at his post in the discharge of more than his duty."[72]

The inability to coordinate regimental movements due to the terrain and thick ground cover, as well as the absence of support, proved bothersome to Scammon's men and the Unionist cannoneers. The latter problem diminished when George Crook's men started to arrive. The best action Crook could take was to spread his regiments out, thereby lengthening the line of Cox's division and protecting the battered left of the 23rd Ohio. The 11th Ohio went to the assistance of the 23rd, with the newly arrived regiment becoming the left flank of Cox's Division. The 28th and 36th Ohio formed on the division's right, to the rear of the 30th Buckeyes. With more troops than Scammon, Crook's arrival would prove decisive to the morning fight below Fox's Gap.[73]

Morning Ends with Victory

Crook's 36th Regiment, largest in the division, included nearly 800 men. With buttressed flanks, Cox was ready for a major push with his entire command by about 11 a.m. With the 28th Ohio in a reserve position, the five charging Ohio regiments had plenty of muscle to push back the North Carolina brigade, who had lost Garland to a fatal wound during the morning.[74]

Thanks to the bitter work and sacrifice of Scammon's regiments and Crome's guns, Cox's line already had a respectable lodgment on the hillside. Crook's units did not have as far to go under fire compared to the First Brigade's men from earlier in the morning. As Crook himself recalled, "We lay down as close as we could get to the enemy without exposing ourselves." He believed the opposing lines were not more than 60 feet apart before the climactic charge of the late morning. When the bloody denouement arrived, Crook would witness a frenzy of combat including a large number of bayonet wounds. The sanguinary struggle between two armies of American warriors created a horrible human tragedy, albeit with the end result being a great victory for the Ninth Corps.[75]

Cox's strengthened left contributed to the division's renewed forward push. The 11th Ohio's presence solidified the western flank, and provided vital support to the 23rd Ohio, the most seriously damaged of Cox's six regiments. The 11th absorbed some damage after moving to assist their comrades in the 23rd. Lt. Col. Augustus Coleman commanded the 11th's right wing. The men were exposed to Confederate fire, "suffering heavily" in the opinion of Maj. Lyman Jackson. Virginia cavalry on the right of the North Carolinians inflicted some of the damage on the 11th Ohio. With Confederate bullets flying in from multiple sides, the unit's historian recalled, "our little Regiment received such a fire as clearly revealed the position of the enemy."[76]

With the 11th Ohio providing target practice for Tar Heels, the time for an overwhelming advance of the Kanawha Division had arrived. Sol Smith remembered the start of the attack, when Scammon, with "a voice of thunder" bellowed, "Charge bayonets!" The frustrated men from Scammon's Brigade, on the hill and under fire for two hours, brought fiendish intensity to their work. Several men wrote of the liberal use of the bayonet, with one soldier credited with dispatching three North Carolinians without firing a shot. Soldiers on both sides also turned their muskets into clubs due to the close quarters fighting along the dilapidated fence. As the unrelenting Buckeye wave pushed back the opposing troops, Sgt. Maj. Eugene Reynolds of the 23rd Ohio became a victim of the same gruesome tactics. The body of the twenty-year-old noncom was found near the farthest point of the regiment's advance. The intrepid soldier proved exceedingly worthy of the stripes he won at such a young age.[77]

Gaining leverage against the eastern portion of the Confederate line, Ohioans took control of the situation. Sol Smith wrote, "The rebel left was completely turned, and the glorious banner of the Republic once more victoriously baptised in blood." He added, "The Ohio and North Carolina regiments fought with a degree of desperation such as can scarcely be conceived."[78]

The doomed North Carolina line included men well versed in combat. They would endure even worse later in the war, but the debacle of September 14 was not the fault of those manning the decrepit fence. Even with the help of two more Tar Heel regiments, the men held a forlorn hope against the tide of determined Buckeyes. Yet, the Southern grit made Cox's five-regiment attack work for every inch. As a man in one of the newly arrived Confederate units wrote, "They opened upon us a heavy fire. Our men received them firmly, returning their fire with spirit." Under the pressure of the moment, another North Carolinian recalled, the 2nd North Carolina "fought in so many directions that no one knew which was front."[79]

Senior officers were quite pleased with the progress of the late morning attack. Respecting the enemy's "great obstinacy and boldness," Cox witnessed the amazing spirit of his division as the battle was won. Crook noted the continued advance of his men after the Confederates' fences and walls were conquered. Many enemy casualties, the Second Brigade commander wrote, were well to the rear of the first breach of the North Carolinian line.[80]

The 23rd North Carolina felt great pressure as the Kanawha Division advanced. The ferocious Ohioans forced a Confederate withdrawal "precipitate in the extreme," causing "great disorder" in the ranks of the Tar Heel outfit. The left of the regiment had several men captured by the charging Buckeyes. With mass confusion and desperation at the morning's climax, the 13th North Carolina faced similarly impossible circumstances while becoming nearly surrounded by regiments from both of Cox's brigades. A member of the Tar Heel regiment may have been a biased commentator, but he recalled the bitter morning with praise of the unit's will to resist the Buckeye wave. "Never was there a more stubborn contest," he suggested, adding that moment's desperation amounted to the most "heroic courage" shown during the war. The Tar Heels needed all the mettle they could muster. As the colonel who took brigade command after Garland fell reported, the attack of Cox's Division "was overpowering, and could not be resisted."[81]

Some Ohioans played a key role at South Mountain while in isolated spots. Leonidas Inscho, Company E, 12th Ohio, might easily have become separated from others in the thick forest. Inscho remained resolute in his duty, even after a hand injury. According to Inscho's Medal of Honor citation, "Alone and unaided and with his left hand disabled," the brave Buckeye "captured a Confederate captain and 4 men."[82]

Thanks to Inscho and 3,000 others, the Kanawha Division's short time in the Ninth Corps gave the command a very impressive laurel for posterity to respect. Unsupported by any other infantry and facing significant natural obstacles, the division proved worthy of the reputation men under Burnside won previously in 1862. With no clear guidance for continuing the attack, Cox rightfully gains support from historians for his decision to reorganize his lines and hold the bloody ground around Fox's Gap, rather than pursue the Confederates. With the unknown timing of support, rumors of Confederate reinforcements, and the continued mystery about the ground on the mountain, the time had arrived for rest and realignment. As Cox cogently explained, "Our own losses had not been trifling, and it seemed wise to contract our lines a little, so that we might have some reserve and hold the crest we had won till the rest of the Ninth Corps should arrive."[83]

PREPARING AN AFTERNOON ATTACK

The early afternoon brought a lull in the infantry fighting, although cannoneers on both sides remained busy. Skirmishers stood protected by trees in front of the line of regiments while artillery blasted the September air. Cox recalled, "The Confederate guns had so perfectly the range of the sloping fields about and behind us, that their canister shot made long furrows in the sod with a noise like the cutting of a melon rind."[84]

Anticipating help, Cox and his division had longer to wait than the Ohioans likely expected. Willcox's Division was the first to arrive, although delayed by an accidental detour on the north side of the National Road. A lack of guidance to Willcox on where Cox was deployed should be blamed on Burnside and Reno. They should have focused on ensuring the Ninth Corps reinforcements quickly found the right location. The First Division finally started filing into positions between Cox and the National Road by about 2 p.m. Sturgis moved up the Second Division, but the men did not arrive until about 3:30 p.m., a far cry from the forced marches McClellan promised to his bosses. Rodman's seven regiments reached the scene later. The day's slow start for the Ninth Corps epitomized the lack of urgency McClellan felt and the limited oversight he gave on the field.

With Confederate cannon fire on the minds of Ninth Corps officers below Fox's Gap, the proper placement of Union batteries to counter the threat became a central consideration of the afternoon. Capt. Asa Cook's Massachusetts battery worked hard to diminish the damage from Confederate artillerists. The Bay State cannoneers suffered five casualties on the day, the worst loss for the unit in a single engagement of the war, while Benjamin's guns were involved without sustaining any loss. One of Cook's pieces became disabled early in the afternoon. With further damage to the battery's supplies, "the men consequently fell back to the shelter in the woods until a later hour of the day," Cook reported.[85]

Two of Willcox's regiments, the 8th Michigan and 50th Pennsylvania, went to support Cox's right. After Willcox's two brigades finally arrived, the First Division commander struggled to find the proper alignment. Annoying Confederate cannons, the woods, and the topography contributed to Willcox's dilemma. The division formed on Cox's right, closer to the National Road, an excellent place for thousands of troops, but Willcox grew flustered with the enemy's cannon fire. Originally ordered by Reno to overlook the National Road, many of the troops faced north, with the division's line nearly at a right angle to the Ohioans. Rearrangement became necessary due to Confederate artillery. Doubts about the best position likely prevailed. A familiar face with a very large regiment arrived in time to boost Willcox's afternoon. William Withington's 17th Michigan buttressed the division's formation. Greeting his old friend and fellow former prisoner of the Confederacy, Willcox made plans that would dramatically alter the fate of the untested, yet deeply patriotic Wolverines.[86]

Before being called to move forward and complete arduous and deadly work against the enemy, the 17th Michigan would earn the praise of Willcox for helping to stem a panic. The problem was caused in part of the division due to the retrograde of horses and caissons from Cook's battery. Willcox became concerned about the disorder caused in his ranks, but he acted quickly to move the 79th New York and the 17th Michigan to face uphill along the Old Sharpsburg Road. "The Seventy-Ninth and Seventeenth here deserve credit for their coolness and firmness in rallying and changing front under a heavy fire," Willcox wrote.[87] The bold show by the two regiments helped reorganize those thrown into confusion by the retreating animals and equipment.

Strong leaders below the grade of division command steeled their men during the barrage of Confederate artillery. A member of the 45th Pennsylvania recalled the calming presence of Colonel Welsh. Although in charge of a brigade, Welsh stood with his original regiment during the early part of the division's time on South Mountain. "By a few cool assuring words," Colonel Welsh "soon allayed whatever excitement might have prevailed among the men" in the tense moments prior to moving out against the enemy.[88]

Many men from Sturgis's Division had no idea about the intensity of the morning on South Mountain. They had yet to reach the field into mid-afternoon. Daniel Hurd, 9th New Hampshire, wondered about the long delay during a short rest. "We had our breakfast and expected to start again soon," with sounds of artillery plainly audible. Until 2 p.m., rookies in the 35th Massachusetts "lounged idly about the bivouac looking curiously at the blue slopes of South Mountain to the west and little dreaming of the stern conflict its rough heights held for them." The lack of urgency in the high command painted an inaccurate picture for their troops. Finally, the Second Division was tasked with assisting Cox and Willcox. Orders for the move to the mountainside from one of McClellan's staff officers were based on the desire to support the imminent advance of the two Ninth Corps divisions under fire below the gap. As Sturgis went ahead, "His glittering columns could be seen for a mile, crawling up the winding road."[89]

Destined for a reserve position during the fight, Nagle's brigade included many men who spent the afternoon in a prone position below the summit. They could find some rest there while sensing the imperative need to hug the ground. As Hosea Towne recalled, "The balls passed over us enough to have killed us all had we stood up." In the division's other brigade, members of the 51st New York served nobly in dangerous roles. Orlando Caruana, who had carried off a wounded color sergeant at New Bern, volunteered with three others to find a spot to scope out the location of Confederate troops on September 14. "While so engaged," his Medal of Honor citation stated, Caruana "was fired upon and his three companions killed, but he escaped and rejoined his command in safety." The native of Malta, only eighteen years old, would live until 1917.[90]

Growing distressed from the unknowns of the afternoon as enemy cannon fire continued, Ninth Corps men below Fox's Gap knew their time for further efforts against the enemy would soon arrive. Cox, the general with the most experience on the hill that day, noted the plan for the final attack at Fox's Gap was "to advance the whole line, so as to complete the dislodgement of the enemy." With Confederate artillery a leading stressor since his arrival on the field, Willcox likely felt great relief with the attack order. As he reported, "I soon received orders from Generals Reno and McClellan, to silence the enemy's battery at all hazards."[91]

"THE 17TH IS DOING BULLY"

With their clean uniforms, not even three weeks removed from the Wolverine State, the 17th Michigan lacked experience. David Lane remembered his regiment filled with men who put their clean white gloves in their pockets. As duty called on South Mountain, he humorously recalled, "a wonder we did not put them on, so little know we of the etiquette of war." Regardless of their naivety, the 17th Michigan was picked to perform the very difficult task of getting around and behind the Confederate line on the right flank of the afternoon advance.[92] Willcox's decision and the insatiable tenacity of the regiment proved how callow soldiers can quickly achieve greatness.

The opening of the regiment's charge seemed to doom the 17th Michigan. Confederate cannons found their range as the Wolverines emerged into a clearing. With the intense artillery fire, men on the right of the regiment drifted left, potentially causing severe disruption as Wolverines crowded into the 45th Pennsylvania. Disaster was averted, and the 17th quickly rallied back to the right, with their flanking mission remaining a realistic possibility.[93]

Death's vicious reach still found many. Sgt. Eli Sears, Company K, took a wicked wound to the breast that exited his back early in the assault. After holding on for a few days, Sears, only twenty-three years old, lost his life on September 18. "Bitterly do I mourn his loss," David Lane wrote later in the month. "So kind, so thoughtful, always preferring another to himself," Lane honored his friend, "He died as heroes die." Many in the 17th would miss the courage of Sears, who Lane considered "the best, the most universally beloved of the regiment."

Seven other men in Company K were either killed during the battle or succumbed to injuries sustained on South Mountain. Although most were rather young, a private in his fifties was one of the fallen. Teenagers Edwin Ashley and Leonard Ives lost their lives in the company as did Owen Kehoe, fifty-two years old. The company's three other fatalities resulting from South Mountain were William Clay, George Henderson, and Daniel Tompkins.[94]

The personal tragedies of the rookie soldiers created a reputation the men would never relinquish. A young drummer, who moved forward rather than stay behind to assist wounded, was transported down the hill with a leg injury. He persisted in his belief in the 17th as his comrades faced Confederate cannons and muskets farther up the hill. Men from the 21st Massachusetts, far more familiar with the cost of war, received an update from the wounded lad. Rising up from his stretcher, the proud youth declared, "The 17th is doing bully!" Men in other regiments also received encouragement from the bloodied youngster as he was transported to a hospital.[95]

During their very difficult movement under fire, the 17th Michigan's soldiers likely cared nothing of the fame they were producing for themselves. Terror flew down the mountainside in the form of deadly Confederate metal. Sheer numbers proved vital to the regiment as their flanking force battled the tide. Perhaps more than 800 men reached the bullseye of the attack, to the left and slightly behind Confederates on the flank of Thomas Drayton's Brigade. The Georgians were in for a devastating greeting from the Wolverines under Colonel Withington.

Willcox watched as his friend Withington and a regiment with officers he personally knew reached such a crucial point. "The Seventeenth

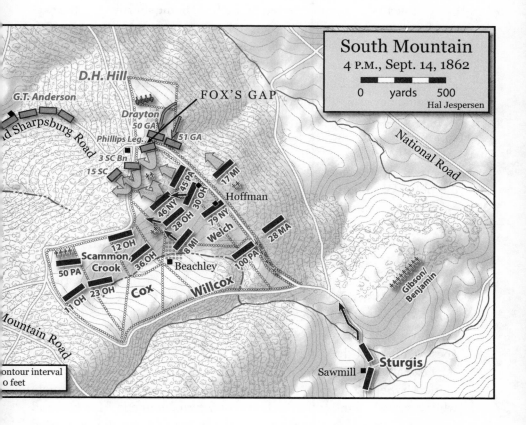

South Mountain
4 P.M., Sept. 14, 1862

0   yards   500

Hal Jespersen

D.H. Hill

FOX'S GAP

G.T. Anderson

Drayton
50 GA

Phillips Leg.

3 SC Bn

15 SC

51 GA

Old Sharpsburg Road

17 MI

Hoffman

45 PA

30 OH

46 NY

28 OH

79 NY

Welch

28 MA

National Road

12 OH

Scammon,
Crook

36 OH

8 MI

Beachley

100 PA

Gibson/
Benjamin

50 PA

23 OH

Cox

Willcox

11 OH

Mountain Road

Sawmill

Sturgis

contour interval
0 feet

Michigan rushed down into the hollow, faced to the left, leaped over a stone fence, and took them in flank," he remembered. The reopening of fire from Cook's battery assisted the effort to push the Confederates back. The additional cannon fire from Unionists took some pressure off of the charging infantry, as the Confederate artillerists renewed their duel with Cook and other cannons on the far right of the Ninth Corps' line.[96]

Colonel Withington received praise from home shortly after the battle of South Mountain. Having seen telegrams announcing how the 17th Michigan battled an entire Confederate brigade, the residents of Detroit felt tremendous pride in the regiment. One correspondent heard of "the glorious result" at South Mountain, and also expressed concern about the regiment's losses. "Would to God we could in any way alleviate your suffering—If we can either to yourself or your noble companions," he continued, "speak and I assure you of a hearty response." Another writer informed Withington, "Our city is wild with delight." Hearing also of a slight wound to the colonel, the letter continued, "God be praised that our noble Withington is not seriously injured."[97]

The glorious attack still devastated the new regiment. Withington's unit reported the second-highest number of casualties for a Ninth Corps regiment at South Mountain. Color bearer Felix Randall was killed while setting the Wolverines' pace. In all, twenty-six were killed in action and 106 wounded. Company K was certainly the hardest hit, with stories of great loss filtering back to Michigan. The death of Corp. George Myron Hawley evidently impacted the state's adjutant general's office in a special way. In the records of the regiment, the description of Hawley's end goes well beyond the common short and bureaucratic listings that seem impersonal. According to the list of Company E fatalities, Hawley "died gloriously Sept. 15th of a wound in the Pelvis received the day before while fearlessly fighting in the Battle of South Mountain." Hawley and four of his regimental comrades from the town of Napoleon were buried in a single grave at Oak Grove Cemetery.[98]

Some of the 17th Michigan's wounded who were doomed to die as a result of their gallant charge lingered far longer than the unfortunate Hawley. Pvt. Dan Hopkins, from the town of White Lake and twenty-five years old, was later transported to a hospital in Frederick for further medical treatment. He died on November 8. George Kirk in Company B lost his life in Frederick on the last day of September, while Jesse Kinyon, in Kirk's company, held out for three months, dying at a Washington hospital in mid-December.[99]

Comrades in the Ninth Corps deeply respected the 17th Michigan for the ferocity and determination of the charge up South Mountain. The historian of the 79th New York noted some early criticism lobbed at Colonel Ferrero for selecting the rookie Wolverines for the charge, "but the Michigan troops, wherever engaged, displayed a bravery that was seldom equaled and never surpassed." Pleased with his own 45th Pennsylvania, Colonel Welsh added that the 17th Michigan demonstrated "a bravery and constancy" highly admirable for new troops. General Willcox added a similar encomium, declaring his friend Colonel Withington and the 17th "performed a feat that may vie with any recorded in the annals of war." A Bay Stater suggested the "glorious charge" proved the Confederates "had been so unfortunate as to sting the muscular heroes of the 17th Michigan into madness for revenge," due to the cost the rookies sustained during their charge. In a short tribute to his Wolverine comrades, the 51st Pennsylvania's historian could be forgiven for mistaking the creature giving a nickname to the State of Michigan. Of the brave boys in the 17th Regiment, the Keystone Stater declared, "They fought like tigers."[100]

CHARGING TO WITHINGTON'S LEFT

For all of the patriotic grit in the 17th Michigan, the Wolverines did not conquer Fox's Gap by themselves. Other regiments in several brigades played a central role in the drama unfolding for the Ninth Corps that afternoon. The attack, which displayed excellent teamwork across Reno's command, benefited greatly from combat leaders capable of inspiring men and setting a highly commendable example.

The 45th Pennsylvania and 46th New York, both from Welsh's Brigade, led the charge on the left of and across the Old Sharpsburg Road from the 17th Michigan. With perhaps 700 men in the two regiments, the relatively small front line still inflicted a great deal of carnage on the Confederates posted in a sunken position along the road and protected by a stone wall. Moving up at double quick through a cornfield, with

The nephew of Pennsylvania's governor, Col. John Curtin fearlessly led the 45th Pennsylvania at South Mountain. Later, he would command a Ninth Corps brigade.
LIBRARY OF CONGRESS

Companies A and K forward as skirmishers, Lt. Col. John Curtin, only twenty-five years old and a nephew of Pennsylvania's governor, led the 45th Regiment. Originally a private in a Pennsylvania unit, Curtin had worked his way up through officer ranks to command the veterans in Welsh's original outfit. The 100th Pennsylvania's Roundheads trailed in support of the two-regiment front line.[101]

Soon after moving out, the line's advance encountered a fence in the cornfield not far from the Confederate defenders. Firing from the position proved a mistake for the Unionists, because the noise drew enemy cannon blasts. As a veteran of the 45th remembered, "Our officers were yelling at the top of their voices, 'Cease firing!'" The shouted orders did not stop all in the regiment from blasting away with their smoothbore muskets. The high-caliber weapons shot buck and ball, several projectiles leaving each musket with every shot. Confederates well protected by the stone wall took some casualties, but the need to get closer remained imperative for Welsh's line. "Forward to the fence" the brigade commander and Curtin ordered.[102]

While coming up through the corn, the 46th New York suffered severely from one cannon shot. Maj. Julius Parcus was the senior officer wounded in the explosion, while two men from the regiment were killed and several others injured. The wound led to the resignation of Parcus in early 1863. He was one of the unit's original captains.[103]

The engagement intensified as supporting units assisted Welsh's front line—and the 17th Michigan began their crucial move around Drayton's left. With the strong support, the 45th Pennsylvania, losing men rapidly, neared the Confederate line. Under intense pressure, "the enemy was driven in the wildest confusion," as Southern troops retreated, were overwhelmed, or fell dead and injured. A member of the 45th grimly added, "Our Harpers Ferry muskets with a good sized ball and three buckshot, at short range, had done fearful execution."

"Under a very heavy fire of musketry," Lieutenant Colonel Gerhardt reported, the 46th New York contributed to the rout. He thanked Ohioans for their assistance during the costly denouement against Drayton. Seeing his men making good decisions under fire, Gerhardt concluded, "Both officers and men behaved gallantly," using cover as much as

Samuel Sturgis led a division of the Ninth Corps throughout the campaign in Maryland. LIBRARY OF CONGRESS

possible to diminish losses. The dedicated Unionist wave, according to division commander Sturgis, pushed the Confederates "back with great slaughter."[104]

The 30th Ohio had an open view to the initial part of the attack before joining in on the left of the line. Of the fight, a Buckeye suggested, "there was one of the most stubborn musketry duels that I witnessed during the war." The regimental historian painted a clear picture of the action and gave his regimental comrades a share of credit for the seizure of Drayton's line.

> For forty-five minutes, a terrible storm of leaden hail swept across the field. The men exhausted their ammunition and fresh supplies were divided among them. In many instances, their arms became foul and were immediately exchanged for those of a fallen comrade. The glorious Thirtieth stood her ground like adamant, and when reinforcements arrived, the rebels had already withdrawn their battery, and the Brigade retreated even from their stone wall.[105]

General Cox praised the grim determination he witnessed from the Ninth Corps' left. "The advance was made with the utmost enthusiasm," he reported. He credited Willcox's regiments, which "gallantly overcame all obstacles," and there certainly were natural and man-made impediments to the successful attack. Across his view during the day, Cox observed, "everyone seemed stimulated by the determination not to be excelled in any soldierly quality."

Admiration for regiments from across the corps was not the only example of Cox's penchant to deliver credit where due, even to men not in his division. Lt. Horatio Belcher, 8th Michigan, earned special praise in Cox's report. Belcher assisted scores of men who had been thrown into confusion during the afternoon. The extreme amount of Confederate cannon fire and enemy skirmishers could cause men to become demoralized or disoriented on the mountainside. Belcher "rallied about 100 men and led them up to the front," Cox wrote in praise of the Wolverine. Placed in battery support, Belcher and his temporary command "performed their duty admirably."[106]

Below the hill on the right of the attack, artillery officers set excellent standards for their men to emulate. Durell's Battery found plenty of work as Sturgis and his division arrived, just as Willcox prepared his men to advance uphill. Racing ahead to find a position near the far right of the Ninth Corps, the Pennsylvania cannoneers dealt with heavy counterbattery fire, but completed good service in support of the unfolding infantry attack. Tree branches rained down on the men for a time, with a heavy branch falling on Captain Durell himself. Thankfully the admired artillerist's most serious injuries were bruises. He remained able to lead his men during the difficult moments, prepared to do his duty as the battery's senior officer.[107]

Drayton's Brigade withered severely as the bullseye of the Ninth Corps attack against Fox's Gap. Well over 600 casualties, with one-third killed or mortally wounded, devastated units in the command. Some historians criticize Drayton's leadership, but he performed as well as expected under the deluge.[108] The inability to coordinate support to the troubled line around the Wise Farm doomed Drayton and his men. The difficult ground and thick undergrowth meant any men defending the gap faced impossible odds. Historians should not be so swift as to lambast Drayton for being placed in a no-win position at a crucial time. As Colonel Welsh of Willcox's First Brigade reported of the doomed Confederate stand,

> *Our troops continued to advance, utterly regardless of the slaughter in their ranks, until, having destroyed the advanced troops of the enemy, he was compelled to give way and retreat with his artillery and infantry in great confusion.*[109]

"HELLO, SAM. I'M DEAD"

Like the Kanawha Division's attack in the morning, the Ninth Corps' momentum from the successful afternoon assault did not propel the regiments down the western side of the mountain or toward Turner's Gap, which Hooker's First Corps was assaulting. With regiments amassed around the Wise Farm and surrounding woods, Reno went forward to better understand the situation. He expressed regret for the halted charge and wished to see the ground better as daylight began to wane.

Units placed in reserve during the afternoon's brawl had been moving up the hillside to support tired comrades in other regiments. The 51st Pennsylvania, which spent the attack in support of Durell's cannons, headed toward Fox's Gap, then was placed on the right of the victorious line by Reno himself. Soon thereafter, the regimental historian recorded, "a most murderous fire of musketry" rained down from Confederates posted in the twilight. The firing induced rounds of shooting by several groups of soldiers, including the 35th Massachusetts, leading to friendly bullets hitting members of the 51st Pennsylvania. The bloodshed might have been worse if the 51st New York did not threaten to attack the erring 35th Regiment.[110]

Contemporary and modern writers have scorned the 35th Massachusetts for their tragic mistake at this difficult moment. Perhaps the rookies' overzealousness originated from their inexperience. Soldiers in the 35th had certainly witnessed enough in their climb up the hill under tense conditions for their emotions to boil over. As the state's adjutant general would learn, "We met a sad procession of stretchers with their bleeding burthens, and ambulances, bearing mutilated or inanimate forms." A wounded Unionist had also propelled the 35th forward by telling the new regiment, "Hurry up, boys, you will have a chance to flesh your bayonets today."

The great risks inherent in a military campaign grow with the inclusion of new troops, especially in the waning light at South Mountain on September 14. Colonel Wild's regiment was not to blame for being ordered to Washington in August or being added to the field army chasing the Confederates in Maryland. In a report home, Wild rightfully lamented the 35th's lack of proper drill. "They were ready to do anything they were ordered," he proffered, "if they only knew how to do it."[111] The colonel's faith in his men would be proven correct very soon.

General Reno became a victim of the evening's shooting. A bullet fired in the early stages of the confusion around the gap struck Reno in the chest. Taken downhill a short distance, then seeing his old friend Samuel Sturgis led Reno to reportedly declare, "Hello, Sam. I'm dead."

The general died not long after, near a majestic oak tree.[112] Having spent half his life in the army, Reno became the second Ninth Corps general to die in action in the first half of September.

Much ink spilled after the war regarding Reno's death, including who fired the fatal shot. The debate involved allegations of friendly or even unfriendly fire from Union troops. One soldier suggested a member of the 23rd Ohio intentionally killed Reno because of a concern about the possible court-martial of Lieutenant Colonel Hayes. An eyewitness in the 51st Pennsylvania countered that Reno was clearly hit in the front of his body from a bullet fired from above Fox's Gap. The general's location when wounded "was so near the brow of the hill, that it would have been impossible, from the nature of the ground, to have formed a line in his rear." Thus, it was "not at all likely that he was hit by one of our own men." Moreover, the 23rd Ohio was posted far to the left. Reno was clearly safe from a Buckeye looking to protect Hayes from a court-martial that was not going to happen in any case.[113]

What cannot be doubted was the great sense of loss many felt. One of those contributing perspective to the postwar debate about the details of Reno's demise opined, "The army never knew a braver nor more gallant officer than Major-General Jesse L. Reno." The 51st Pennsylvania's historian considered Reno "a gentleman, a friend and a soldier. His bravery had never been doubted, for it was of that cool, deliberate, but cautious character, that inspires an army to follow into the very jaws of death." The Highlanders' historian added, "His loss was deeply felt by us all," while the 21st Massachusetts' chronicler deemed Reno, "the soldier without spot or blemish."[114]

Senior officers, some of whom had known Reno for twenty years, expressed intense regret over his loss. The most profound words came from Burnside. In his campaign report, the wing commander wrote of "the deep sorrow which the death of the gallant Reno caused me." He expounded by noting "an intimate knowledge of his high and noble character had endeared him to me, as well as to all with whom we had served." Undoubtedly using words of firm conviction, Burnside concluded, "No more valuable life than his has been lost during this contest for our country's preservation."[115]

The Ninth Corps permanently lost the services of another officer near the time of Reno's fatal wound. Colonel Wild of the 35th Massachusetts suffered an injury costing him his left arm at the shoulder during the looming darkness, a very disorienting time in the thick and unknown woods. As the colonel himself informed Gov. John Andrew, the regiment's late afternoon advance at South Mountain was over "an extensive tract of forest, and a very rough ground indeed." Wild's second wound of the summer failed to knock the fighting spirit out of him. Although gone from the corps forever, he served in various commands for the remainder of the conflict.[116]

DEFENDING THE LEFT IN DARKNESS

Disoriented Confederate units failed to link with Drayton in the chaos of the moment on the afternoon of September 14. Different brigades eventually marched in several directions on the hill, never able to assist Drayton as the Ninth Corps pounced. Some of the Confederates did find Unionists to fight before the day ended. Gen. George B. Anderson, leading his brigade of North Carolinians, had a brief clash against the left flank of the Ninth Corps, generally Fairchild's New Yorkers and Clark's guns, with some support from a few other regiments. Fairchild had less than 1,000 men who had moved to their position earlier in the day in order to support Cox. Albeit brief, the combat with Anderson added to the human tragedy in the area below Fox's Gap.

The key part of the Unionist flank was a cornfield constituting the end of the line below the gap. Clark's guns and Fairchild's three regiments were concentrated in the field. Some historians believe the line started out generally straight, with a later shift forming an L along the road lining the cornfield. The colonel of the 4th North Carolina, marching in the direction of the 50th Pennsylvania, which had formed on Fairchild's right, painted a picture of the complicated nature of the move toward the unexpected Northerners. "Our progress was necessarily very slow," the Tar Heel officer remembered, "as the woods were very dense and the ground very rugged and mountainous." In the confused situation, only the 89th New York would record casualties among Fairchild's New Yorkers, likely due to both the growing darkness and the angle of Anderson's advance. The Confederates simply did not know where they were going or when, if ever, they would encounter the Ninth Corps that evening.[117]

Nonetheless, a member of the 50th Pennsylvania said the enemy made a "determined" move against the troops manning the position. Triple charges of canister from Clark's big guns, the Keystone Stater added, damaged the Confederate advance, as did "terrific fire from the infantry," especially because the combat was at relatively close range. Like two of Fairchild's regiments, the 50th unloaded on the attackers without reporting one man killed.[118]

Members of the 9th New York also participated in the rout of Anderson's Tar Heels. Richard Morris penned a letter in which he noted the Confederates "were met by such a heavy fire that they fell back in disorder." The Zouaves' historian remembered the Confederates "made an impetuous charge on the battery, yelling and discharging their muskets," but with the position of the Unionists, the enemy had no hope. Lauding his fellow New Yorkers in the 89th and 103rd regiments, the historian suggested movements and shooting across the brigade were "as coolly and methodically performed as though on drill in winter camp." Also thankful for supporting regiments to their right, a Zouave described the brigade's defense as a "wall" that "replied so violently that the surging tide rolled back with great loss."[119]

Serious wounds from the short night fight did not cost some men their lives immediately. Lewis Simpson, Company K, 89th New York, suffered an injury leading to the amputation of his left leg. Lingering for months, a second operation was required, essentially the removal of more of his leg, likely from infection. Discharged from a Frederick hospital in February 1863, Simpson continued to cling to life. He died on May 1, more than seven months after his horrible wound.[120]

Although the short burst of fire caused few Empire State casualties, soldiers still felt the loss of just one comrade. George Englis, 89th New York, mentioned the death of his friend and fellow Company K member Christopher Knight, one of only two in Fairchild's Brigade reported as killed in action at South Mountain. With a bullet wound to the heart, Knight, a Rhode Island native, was six weeks away from turning twenty-five years old. The payback had been fierce, however, even if Englis could not bear the loss of his friend. He counted twenty dead Confederates in front of the regimental line.[121]

Possession of the Somber Hillside

The 17th Michigan deserved the accolades they received as untried troops in a very difficult first battle. Yet, they did not sustain the most Ninth Corps casualties on South Mountain. Curtin's 45th Pennsylvania reported 134 losses, including forty-three killed or mortally wounded. Combined, the Wolverine rookies and Curtin's men suffered nearly 30 percent of the Ninth Corps' casualties on September 14.[122] The dramatic and taxing charge against Drayton proved to be highly decisive, instilling panic into the Confederate high command, especially as Hooker's overwhelming force to the north also pushed Southerners back.

Men from the 45th Pennsylvania would never be the same after their victory. "No member of the Forty-fifth need blush for having been at South Mountain," one soldier declared. In the regiment's bloodiest day, some of those killed at South Mountain were teenagers Henry Chambers and William Hunter, and Mifflin County native James Baird. Lt. William Grove had volunteered in April 1861, joining a ninety-day regiment. He reenlisted, then became an officer in the 45th. In his early twenties, Grove's wound on September 14 led to his death five days later. He now sleeps near many of his other comrades on the grounds of Antietam National Cemetery.[123]

Losses of dear compatriots reverberated among soldiers of the 45th Pennsylvania who had missed the battle. Lt. Samuel Haynes was too sick to depart with his regiment from Washington. He walked through Fox's Gap before catching up with his outfit along the Antietam on September 20. Haynes felt emotional devastation during his visit to comrades' graves.

I saw the place to-day where 28 were buried in a row on the battlefield. They are buried as nicely as possible and each grave is marked plainly with a headboard. Poor fellows! Dwight Smith and Jimmie Cole lie together and the first tears that have started from my eyes since my mother died fell on their graves. They were indeed the most intimate and truest friends I had in the army.[124]

The 23rd Ohio proved very worthy of praise. With 130 casualties, the most damaged Buckeye regiment at South Mountain barely trailed the 17th Michigan and 45th Pennsylvania in the casualty count. As a whole, the Kanawha boys sustained 40 percent of the Ninth Corps' loss on September 14.[125] They would not be in the command by the end of the month, but McClellan had made a strong decision to attach the Ohioans to the Ninth Corps. They proved vital to the goal of pushing Confederates off of South Mountain.

"Our valiant troops slept on the ground and on their arms," Sam Sturgis wrote, with the enemy "leaving his dead in ghastly numbers scattered on the field." During the night and the subsequent morning, members of the Ninth Corps examined various parts of the South Mountain killing ground, forever changed by what they saw, sometimes not believing their own senses.[126]

"All about us lay the dead and dying, while the groans and cries of the wounded sounded in our ears," the regimental historian of the Highlanders remembered. Falling temperatures and concerns about any nearby enemy troops prevented rapid provision of water and medical assistance to the wounded. On the following morning, members of the relatively unscathed 6th New Hampshire moved uphill. The regimental historian added, "The bodies were lying in all positions imaginable, and all were as black as a negro." George Upton of the regiment added, "I viewed *leisurely* the scenes of carnage & blood, but *pen* nor language of mine can express its horrors."[127]

After moving up the hill to support Cox's Ohioans, Henry Spooner of the 4th Rhode Island recalled, "I stumbled over 2 dead rebels and found another wounded through the thigh." Large numbers of Confederates "sometimes in heaps" were also seen, with Southern soldiers "nearly all shot through the head," Spooner added. While walking around the position of the 48th Pennsylvania after the battle, a sergeant reported finding 105 dead Confederates. An officer in the regiment added, "Sickening horrors and dreadful sights" dominated the mountainside. Another Keystone Stater remembered finding the road Drayton defended "full of dead rebels. They lay, actually two and three deep. One fellow hung upon the fence opposite, an arm and leg on either side, literally riddled with bullets."[128]

A 9th New York soldier summarized the post-battle sites he witnessed and heard about in a diary entry. "The Rebel dead are scattered about us," he wrote, "and there is every horrible proof that our foes fought for their splendid position here, with a dogged valor well worthy of a better cause." James Wren of the 48th Pennsylvania counted Confederate losses in a small area. One patch of 40 square feet included sixteen dead enemy troops. A New Hampshire man recorded seeing "the enemy's dead in every direction."[129]

Losses across the Ninth Corps included men from various states, walks of life, and age groups. George W. Gove, who had been born in March 1842, was one of the young men wounded at South Mountain. Born in Henniker, New Hampshire, the devoted citizen and patriot helped recruit Company G of the 9th New Hampshire while also attending to his study of the law in his hometown. He departed Concord as a sergeant, not even three weeks prior to the regiment's first battle below Fox's Gap. The shoulder wound Gove received confined him to a hospital in Keedysville, west of the gap, for the remaining four weeks of his life.

A biographical sketch of Gove's short existence demonstrates how the end of just one life in war—in a regiment suffering a relatively light twenty-nine total casualties—can mean an epic amount of loss for society. At a young age, Gove "exhibited a fondness for books," making him "so promising as a scholar." His devoted father worked hard to improve young Gove's chances in life, difficult due to the family's modest means. The "ever kind and genial" Gove became "well advanced in Latin and Greek" as a teenager. He also found military matters of interest. The likelihood of higher rank seemed quite promising had the youngster's life been spared.[130]

Holding on at the Keedysville hospital, Gove's willpower could not conquer the effects of his wound. He died on October 12, with his devastated father making the trip to Maryland to retrieve his son's remains. Buried at Henniker's Old Cemetery, Gove "was the first martyr of the town in the war." Friends remembered him as "ever kind and great," with many knowing "few of his associates if any had a brighter future before them." Instead, the sergeant's "disembodied spirit dwells free from the cares of the earth—in full communion with his maker."[131]

BURNSIDE AND McCLELLAN ON SEPTEMBER 14

The success on South Mountain for both corps in Burnside's wing did not mean the Army of the Potomac's high command functioned efficiently during the day. A wide range of problems were evident beyond McClellan's slow pace and uncertain generalship. The September 15 surrender of the Harpers Ferry garrison was something McClellan did not do enough to prevent. His missives to bosses about saving the garrison amounted to nothing but the unrealistic dream of a cautious general.

Burnside also lacked initiative. Perhaps sensing his waning influence with McClellan, Burnside did not push matters concerning the Ninth Corps. Due to poor planning, the First and Ninth Corps led the charge at South Mountain, although the two commands started the day on opposite sides of Frederick. Burnside did not see the need to coordinate the movements of the two corps. He would condemn Hooker in a report filed in early 1863. The wing commander had no complaints about alleged slowness with the First Corps' attack in his initial report penned two weeks after South Mountain. Burnside, not known for egotism or a vindictive streak, likely looked for someone to share the blame. His later charge of a slow attack by Hooker should not be taken seriously.[132]

September 14 was clearly not Burnside's best day as an army officer. The awesome firepower of the entire Ninth Corps did not assemble on South Mountain early enough. Cox was simply believing he was the lead infantry in a reconnaissance during the morning. He soon found himself stifled by a Confederate force able to compensate for a numerical disadvantage through good use of terrain around Fox's Gap. With two corps commanders under him and McClellan in charge of the entire army on the crucial day, Burnside may not have known his place. Wing commands could easily sow confusion. Reno's boldness immediately before his death contrasts with the tentativeness gripping the army's high command during the day. Neither Burnside nor Reno did enough to concentrate their forces quickly, even with the obvious Union victory.[133]

Pro-Burnside works written in the nineteenth century offer a more sympathetic view of the wing commander's actions. One author suggested Burnside managed the fight at South Mountain "with great skill, moving his troops with consummate promptness," a hagiographic conclusion. Another book found Burnside "moved his troops with great promptness, and carried a position which many had regarded as tenable."[134] In reality, Burnside lacked an understanding of McClellan's plans, clearly did not sense the need to reinforce Cox rapidly, and failed to ensure Willcox had the correct orders on where to send his troops initially. The general did excellent work in North Carolina and Virginia earlier in 1862, but South Mountain gives history a clear view into why Burnside turned down army command.

Yet, greater accountability for the incomplete victory of September 14 must rest higher in the chain of command. As the 9th New Hampshire's historian appropriately concluded, "If, through General McClellan's over-cautiousness, the golden opportunity was lost, then on his shoulders must rest the responsibility." McClellan's presence likely made Burnside show less initiative, simply because headquarters failed to place any sense of urgency in the movements of the two corps under the command of "Dear Burn." As Hartwig rightfully suggests, Burnside did not have the drive to extrapolate bold moves from limited orders. Instead, he acted within the confines of his instructions, failing to show initiative when great alacrity could have been recommended to a superior. McClellan minimized any credit his old friend would receive for the victory, including failing to even mention the wing commander in his evening dispatches to Washington announcing the success along South Mountain.[135]

A Confused and Slow Advance

"The troops behaved magnificently. They never fought better," McClellan informed Halleck in an evening message on the 14th. One man who likely concurred with McClellan's assessment of Unionist soldiers was Robert E. Lee, who initially moved to terminate his campaign in Maryland as a means to save his army. When wiring Halleck, McClellan did not yet know of Franklin's late but successful effort to take Crampton's

Gap, although the victory there neither saved the Harpers Ferry garrison nor trapped McLaws. When receiving the news of the planned surrender of the garrison the next morning, Lee quickly altered his retreat. His army would reassemble just east of the town of Sharpsburg, along a beautiful creek known as the Antietam. "I am hurrying up everything from the rear," McClellan informed Halleck, "to be prepared for any eventuality." Once again, promised alacrity from George McClellan did not translate into a swift strike at the retreating Confederates. September 15 would be a very confusing day, with the Ninth Corps' tepid movement causing further friction between Burnside and the army commander.[136]

McClellan's clear preference to marginalize Burnside became evident in a communication directly to Hooker on the evening of September 14. The First Corps commander, technically subordinate to wing commander Burnside, was informed of the Ninth Corps' success to the south around Fox's Gap. Additionally, a Second Corps division was being placed under Hooker. "Please hold your present position at all hazards," McClellan wrote, "Let me know at daybreak tomorrow morning the state of affairs in your vicinity, and whether you will need further re-enforcements." Hooker's independence was soon made official, with Burnside's wing abolished the following day, ostensibly on a temporary basis. Burnside was not told to revert to command of his old corps, a severe oversight of McClellan's that would bring havoc to army communications for days. Due to Reno's death, Cox had become Ninth Corps commander. Burnside was no longer a wing commander, but he did not take direct command of the Ninth Corps. He suddenly seemed like a useless appendage of the army bureaucracy, perhaps to McClellan's delight.[137] Such was the cost inflicted on a general who had the temerity to wish victory for John Pope just two weeks before.

Giving Hooker the key role in the pursuit of Lee's army, McClellan stayed back until the afternoon. In Durell's battery the morning after the big guns fired about 250 rounds of ammunition, food became an overarching necessity. Thanks to baggage wagons, "a good supply of black coffee, pork, and hard bread was served to men who had performed night duty." The ability of such victuals to revive tired soldiers should never be underestimated. After the 2nd Maryland gave the 48th Pennsylvania a chance to go down the hill for rest and food, the Keystone Staters could enjoy the contents of their haversacks. "A first rate's night sleep" also gave the survivors of South Mountain a refreshing start to another day.[138]

While looking for something to eat, the regimental historian of the 51st Pennsylvania doubted the conventional wisdom suggesting Union troops were better supplied and nourished than their Southern opponents. After examining many Confederate haversacks found on the field, he discovered "bread, rolls, biscuits and cakes" in abundance. He added, "Many famished Union soldiers have regaled themselves on the contents of a dead rebel's haversack." With the large number of deceased enemy soldiers nearby, many Unionists had better meals because of the successful attack at South Mountain.[139]

Tending to shattered bodies became a role for some men who had no training in medical matters. William Canfield, a member of the 9th New Hampshire who missed the previous day's battle due to sickness, and some of his comrades assisted at a hospital. "I had no thought of self now," Canfield wrote, "but bent all my energies to the task of caring for the wounded." Several actions, such as bringing water, washing wounds, or simply offering "words of comfort" made Canfield a credible battlefield nurse, even though he admitted, "We had no experience in such things, but did the best we could." The devoted healers undoubtedly provided noble service, but at the cost of further sickness for Canfield.[140]

On September 15, trouble for the Ninth Corps did not arrive as a result of the enemy. Instead, an anemic advance, far short of McClellan's expectations, greatly increased the ill will McClellan felt for "Dear Burn." At 8 a.m. on the 15th, the Ninth Corps was ordered to move through Fox's Gap, then toward Boonsboro after taking a right in Pleasant Valley, immediately west of South Mountain. Burnside was expected to be in regular contact with Hooker's advance on the Ninth Corps' right, as well as with Franklin's command to the south. The conquerors of Fox's Gap were to be "prepared to lend such assistance as may be necessary in either direction," or to cut off Lee's retreat, as circumstances dictated. The corps was expected to remain as aligned as possible with Hooker's advance. In another morning message, Burnside was told to keep baggage wagons out of the road to ensure rapid movements for Ninth Corps troops.[141]

The succor of Harpers Ferry should have been McClellan's over-riding priority. Burnside as a wing commander united with Franklin at Crampton's Gap twenty-four hours before was a far preferable outcome, as previously discussed. McClellan's lack of clarity on his intentions for Burnside's role immediately after South Mountain does not excuse the languid advance of the Ninth Corps on September 15. Burnside's histor-ically respected lack of ego did not prevail in the later part of the Antie-tam campaign. For once he appeared to put his own aggrandizement and authority above the good of his country.

An early missive to Burnside on September 15 began, "The General commanding directs you to advance with your whole corps" on Boons-boro straight from Fox's Gap. With the end of the wing command also directly stated in this message, headquarters implied Burnside should take direct command of the Ninth Corps. Another morning message to Burnside made celerity even more imperative. Elements of the Fifth Corps "will follow you on the same road, and be ready to support you," the note declared, "General McClellan desires to impress upon you the necessity for the utmost vigor in your pursuit." Yet, as men worked to energize their fatigued bodies and bury the dead around Fox's Gap, the Ninth Corps failed to move as McClellan expected. As the 35th Mas-sachusetts historian wrote, "The weather was fine and favorable," but no preparations were made for the Ninth Corps to advance.

Near noon, a Fifth Corps division arrived at Fox's Gap, unable to continue because the immobile Ninth Corps blocked the road. Quick communication from a Fifth Corps division commander to headquarters led to a 12:30 p.m. note to Burnside, telling him to let Porter's division take the lead in the advance, with the Ninth Corps to follow. A slow march by his command meant Burnside would take a minor role in any army activity on September 15. He would be in the rear of all troops that had been in the area of Turner's or Fox's Gap on the previous evening.[142]

Due to Franklin's skittish generalship, Burnside's slow movement of the Ninth Corps appeared likely to pay dividends during the afternoon. Even after the successful Confederate conquest of Harpers Ferry, con-cerns remained about any possible enemy designs on the Army of the Potomac's left flank and rear. Halleck certainly lost sleep over the prospect of Lee swinging around behind McClellan. Franklin reported a large Confederate force in the valley north of Maryland Heights, prompting headquarters to view Burnside's men as a possible reinforcement. Reports of a major enemy concentration were wildly inaccurate, but a 3:45 p.m. message went to Burnside suggesting the Ninth Corps should move south to Rohrersville and be in communication with Franklin. "If with your assistance he can defeat the enemy in front of him, join him at once," the order read. If the Sixth Corps commander did not need the help, "march direct to Sharpsburg and cooperate with us."

Circumstances changed in less than an hour. "The commanding general directs you to move your command at once to Sharpsburg," Burnside read, because a Unionist attack against Lee's stalwarts seemed likely. Prior to McClellan's mid-afternoon arrival along the Antietam, the commanding general received intelligence from subordinates about the Confederate force remaining in Maryland. Hooker's morning missives expressed the likelihood Lee intended to cross back into Virginia, but a dedicated albeit small Southern force stood defiantly at Sharpsburg. At 2:15 p.m., Hooker reported what he witnessed of the Confederate line. He believed the limited number of Union troops immediately available east of the Antietam was insufficient to attack. However, "Their position is not a formidable one," the First Corps leader suggested.[143]

The Ninth Corps began arriving late in the day, as the sun quickly fell in the western sky. About the time of McClellan's arrival around 3 p.m., Burnside and Cox, in advance of their four divisions, were part of the group of generals congregating near the bridge over the Antietam on the road from Boonsboro (known to history as the Middle Bridge). Cox recorded several positives about this meeting, including the amiable greeting Burnside received from his chief. McClellan also acted happy when introducing Cox to several Army of the Potomac senior officers. Even though a stranger to most at the meeting of generals, Cox felt welcome due to McClellan's friendly manner. The Ohioan recalled McClellan put Cox on "an easy footing" and "in a very agreeable and genial way."[144] Interestingly, reports of the meeting give no sign of a schism between "Dear Burn" and "Mac."

Troops continued to assemble, but no attack happened so late in the day. Regarding the Ninth Corps, McClellan brushed aside Burnside's comments when the men were ordered to move south about a mile to man the far left of the army. "He grumbled that his troops were fatigued, but I started him off anyhow," the army commander wrote of Burnside.[145] Even a quarter century later in posthumous memoirs, McClellan's great disappointment in his old friend remained obvious.

Several factors conspired to work against an attack on September 15. As a headquarters staff member suggested, "The tardiness of our troops prevented an engagement." Due to delays in troop movements and traffic jams on the road between Boonsboro and Antietam Creek, McClellan's army could not concentrate until late in the day. The line of troops were a disorganized mess and an insufficient understanding of fords capable of supporting troop crossings prevailed. McClellan had ordered quick action, and his subordinates did not live up to their high rank.[146]

Yet, once again, the army commander should not be excused from blame. If McClellan wished to attack Lee's line on the 15th, he would have done more far earlier in the day to push his forces and personally examine matters from east of the creek. Perhaps McClellan's restraint can be easily defended, but Lee's force still lacked the divisions involved in the Harpers Ferry operation. McClellan never had a better chance to destroy the Confederate army than in the afternoon of September 15. Considering the waning daylight, his limited knowledge of the ground, and the unknowns about Lee's numbers, McClellan was too cautious a general to take the risk.[147]

"WE CONFIDENTLY EXPECTED A BATTLE"

Perhaps September 16 offered a better chance for a major strike at Lee's divided army before Jackson's Harpers Ferry conquerors reunited with their fellow Confederates near the Antietam. Ninth Corps troops were gaining impressions of another big fight in Maryland. If they were able to read McClellan's missives to Halleck, imminent battle could be anticipated. At 7 a.m., a message went to the general-in-chief noting the lack of knowledge about enemy numbers and a persistent fog shrouding the landscape. Nonetheless, the plan was to "attack as soon as situation is developed," McClellan promised. "The time lost on account of the fog is being occupied in getting up supplies, for the want of which many of our men are suffering," he concluded.[148]

Ninth Corps men could appreciate the lack of battle so soon after South Mountain. The 21st Massachusetts historian recalled the "beautiful spot" of the regimental bivouac, not far from Antietam Creek. With all four divisions assembling in the vicinity of Rohrbach Bridge by the evening of September 16, a member of the 30th Ohio described how Confederate cannons posed a danger to regimental camps. Buckeye Corp. David Taylor died as a result of the artillery fire. Born in 1840 and a member of Company I, Taylor rests in Antietam National Cemetery, the future grounds of which were filled with Confederate cannons during Lee's bold final stand in Maryland.[149]

Without a heavy engagement, firing continued throughout September 16. As General Cox recalled, "It was hard to restrain our men from showing themselves on the crest of the long ridge in front of us." Confederate cannoneers replied to such sightings, leading to a response from big guns in the Ninth Corps. "We confidently expected a battle," Cox added, of the atmosphere along the Antietam.[150]

Regardless of the questionable calls Burnside had made in the previous few days, his personal courage could not be doubted. The senior Ninth Corps officer faced danger along with his men in the tense hours of September 16. Captain Wren of the 48th Pennsylvania penned his observations of Burnside's conduct, with the general showing pluck while letting his men know they were not alone. After two mules died from one Confederate shot, Burnside asked his men to bear the shortage of rations, for a strike at the enemy loomed. Giving three cheers to their chief, Wren reported, the men stood fast to their duty. Pickets stayed busy exchanging shots with the enemy until after dark.[151]

While McClellan visited the army's left to study the ground held by the Ninth Corps, his conversation with Burnside turned to the commander's budding attack plan. McClellan did not launch a major attack on the 16th, but rather formulated an idea and positioned troops for the following day. Clearly liking Hooker's aggressiveness, he put the First

Corps in the vanguard of the army. During the afternoon, Hooker's three divisions crossed the Antietam via the Upper Bridge and a nearby ford, more than 4 miles from the Rohrbach Bridge the Ninth Corps would make famous. In a conversation with Cox after McClellan departed, Burnside announced Hooker's men would lead the effort against Lee west of the Antietam. "Burnside's manner in speaking of this implied that he thought it was done at Hooker's solicitation," Cox suggested.

The most notable combat on September 16 came late in the afternoon, as darkness neared. Hooker's First Corps, with no infantry support, ran into some of Stonewall Jackson's men posted in advance of the main Confederate line north of town. McClellan's plan, communicated neither in written orders to his corps commanders nor at a conference of his generals, lacked concentrated power at any point. Without clear guidance, Union generals would have a difficult time turning Lee's last stand in Maryland into a decisive victory. Some historians point to a very logical conclusion from McClellan's unclear vision. He did not plan to overwhelm the Confederate army. Instead, he was content to simply see Lee re-cross the river into Virginia.[152]

A MORASS OF PLANNING ON SEPTEMBER 16

Many historians question the value of McClellan's order to move Hooker across the Antietam on September 16, suggesting the element of surprise vanished from the Unionist attack.[153] This overrated contention neglects a far bigger limitation of McClellan's planning. Two corps should have gone across the Antietam to the north earlier in the day, with another corps assigned to assist the Ninth Corps around Rohrbach Bridge and Snavely's Ford downstream. Surprise was not needed if four Union infantry corps assaulted Lee's northern and southern flanks early on September 17. The Confederates could have been overwhelmed under such an arrangement.

The Ninth Corps factored into McClellan's plans as the only corps assigned to the Union left. Far from Hooker, Burnside would become engaged, McClellan opined, at a time when the First Corps attack appeared to be making progress. Hooker promised a dawn fight to the north, but Burnside was not told to assault the bridge at such an early time.

Ethan Rafuse suggests only one corps could have attacked from the army's left flank, the area Burnside and Cox controlled. The ground Unionists would assault in the area around Rohrbach Bridge was certainly less conducive to a successful attack of more than one corps. Also, any advance across the terrain offered a diminished chance for spreading troops out and maneuvering easily compared to Hooker's flatter and more open sector. However, McClellan should have seen the necessity to augment Burnside's force. Such troops could have attacked more than just the bridge, thanks to fords along the creek.[154] Rafuse makes a highly credible analysis of the Antietam battlefield, but there is no reason to conclude an attack in the southern part of the field had to be limited to one corps.

In his memoirs, McClellan makes some reasonable arguments about why the Union's left should not have initiated the attack. The strong defensive ground in front of Burnside, and the nature of the ground on Hooker's portion of the field, made the Union right the preferable point for opening the attack. Nonetheless, McClellan's timidity prevented him from envisioning a far stronger left wing at Antietam capable of causing serious damage to Lee while Hooker's men drove the Confederates south. Without two corps attacking each Confederate flank, we have the battle of Antietam history knows very well, a tactical draw with the Army of the Potomac unable to take advantage of the number of troops better planning would have made available.

One reason McClellan spent time around the Ninth Corps on the 16th was to express concern about the posting of troops. Engineers on McClellan's staff worked with officers of the corps to implement McClellan's idea for Burnside's solo assault. McClellan's lack of vision in his battle plan strained logic. He correctly noted the strong defensive ground to the west of Rohrbach Bridge, but then permitted only one Union corps to strike the area. With a firm charge from their chief and definitive plans to use a second corps in the area, the engineers might have shaken off their languid pace to find Snavely's Ford and placed troops there. The Confederates would defend the same excellent ground, but 8,000 to 10,000 more Union troops would have been on the other side of the creek. Then, the final push would have had a better chance to encircle Lee's army before the Southerners could retreat across the Potomac's only usable ford.

McClellan very likely embellished his personal concerns on September 16 about a Confederate attack from Harpers Ferry hitting the Ninth Corps after Cox and his divisions moved west of the bridge.[155] The fear played out in a very devastating manner on September 17. Whatever McClellan ordered Burnside to do regarding troop dispositions the day before the battle, he failed to ensure any flank attack could be met by a sufficient number of his own troops. While trying to make himself seem prescient about protecting Burnside's left flank, McClellan's comments in his memoirs illustrate his inadequate battle plan and the failure to support Burnside.

Thus, McClellan repeated his primary tactical failure at South Mountain: concentration of most Union forces in one area while neglecting a crucial point of attack. At South Mountain, McClellan's drive to capture supplies supposedly around Boonsboro placed only one corps at Crampton's Gap. At Antietam, four corps—the First, Second, Sixth, and Twelfth—would eventually cross the Upper Bridge in an attempt to take Lee's army from the north, while one corps attacked the strongest Confederate position on the field.

In his campaign report, Burnside detailed the posting of troops by the evening of September 16. On the ridge east of the fateful bridge, Benjamin's six rifled guns unlimbered at a good spot. Lacking many other suitable locations for artillery positions, other Ninth Corps guns were posted on the east side of the hill, enjoying partial cover. Infantry formed behind Benjamin, with Crook's Ohioans nearest the Middle Bridge. Sturgis was in the rear of the Kanawha brigade. Rodman's Third Division formed to the left, with support from Hugh Ewing, commanding Scammon's Brigade. The three regiments were under Hugh Ewing of the 30th Ohio after Scammon moved up to command the division in place of Cox. Willcox's Division served as Burnside's reserve.

Rodman's seven regiments were in the best place to attempt a crossing early in the day, which could flank the defenders' position from the right rear. The division lacked a clear understanding about the ford's location, which cost much time during the battle. The unknowns about the landscape limited the ford's potential as a decisive location to cross the creek.[156] Lack of clarity on the fords below Rohrbach Bridge was a terrible oversight, perhaps the worst error made during the Army of the Potomac's preparations for battle along the Antietam. McClellan simply made poor use of the more than thirty-six hours between his arrival just east of the creek and Hooker's opening assault on the morning of September 17.

The muddled Ninth Corps command situation was difficult enough for Jacob Cox. The problem was not just the presence of Burnside, a superior officer who had no other troops to command other than the corps Cox ostensibly would control. The Ohioan also felt the additional negative effects of being a corps commander under the oversight of headquarters engineers. Cox was especially correct on these points. In his memoirs, he lamented,

> *To depend upon the general staff for this is to take away the vigor and spontaneity of the subordinate and make him perform his duty in a mechanical way. He should be told what is known of the enemy and his movements so as to be put upon his guard, and should then have freedom of judgment as to detail.*[157]

McClellan wasted time personally attending to part of the Ninth Corps' realignment on the morning of September 16, when he should have been getting two corps moving across the Upper Bridge. Even with the intervention of the army's senior officer, Burnside's troop placements did not happen quickly enough to please McClellan. Another message from headquarters blasted Burnside for failure to move with expected celerity. A time for the note was not given, but from the context, delivery may have occurred in the late evening of September 16 or in the overnight period. Whatever level of modesty governed Burnside's conduct, he must have been profoundly hurt by the words.

> *The general commanding has learned that, although your corps was ordered to be in a designated position at 12 m. [noon] to-day, at or near sunset only one division and four batteries had reached the ground intended for your troops.*

The general has also been advised that there was a delay of some four hours in the movement of your command yesterday. I am instructed to call upon you for explanations of these failures on your part to comply with the orders given you, and to add, in view of the important military operations now at hand, the commanding general cannot lightly regard such marked departure from the tenor of his instructions.

With McClellan in no hurry to attack, one wonders why he felt the need to excoriate Burnside for slowness for the second consecutive day. On Burnside's behalf, a staff officer reported back to army headquarters on the 17th, providing a summary of the previous day's efforts to align the Ninth Corps in accordance with McClellan's expectations. The message added, "General Burnside directs me to say that he is sorry to have received so severe a rebuke from the general commanding, and particularly sorry that the general commanding feels that his instructions have not been obeyed." Holding fast to Burnside's reputation as a dutiful subordinate, the message promised, "nothing can occur to prevent the general from continuing his hearty co-operation to the best of his ability in any movement the general commanding may direct."[158]

Historical evidence leaves a trail of legitimate questions about Burnside's decisions at key points during the Antietam campaign, far more so than his North Carolina expedition or during August in Virginia. McClellan's efforts were also far from perfection. Jacob Cox used one sentence to link the Army of the Potomac's senior officer with the course of events since Union troops started arriving at Antietam Creek on the afternoon of September 15. "The opportunity was still supremely favorable for McClellan, but prompt decision was not easy for him," wrote the Ninth Corps general who respected the army chief.[159] Like at South Mountain, McClellan would strike, albeit with poorly articulated plans and insufficient troops at the point of his attacks west of a tranquil Maryland stream. The lack of support would create immense difficulty for the heroic band of men resting near a bridge soon to bear the name of the Ninth Corps' most senior officer.

PART THREE

Glass in a Hailstorm:
The Battle of Antietam

"They started on their mission of death full of enthusiasm."
–BRIG. GEN. SAMUEL STURGIS

OPENING SCENES ALONG THE CREEK

THE NINTH CORPS HAD NEARLY 13,000 SOLDIERS PRESENT FOR DUTY at daylight on September 17, the moment when Hooker's First Corps began the slaughter 3 miles to the north, fighting to a bitter and bloody stalemate. Three additional infantry corps would be engaged to varying degrees in the northern part of the field through the morning and into the afternoon. The inability of McClellan to coordinate overwhelming force north of Sharpsburg displayed his lack of vision for the battle, and perhaps even his desire for a generally indecisive result followed by a Confederate retreat.[1]

The Ninth Corps started the day as they would finish it, alone. Jacob Cox remembered, "The men were astir at dawn, getting breakfast and preparing for a day of battle." The earliest sunlight illuminated some troop positions to Confederate infantry and cannoneers, resulting in desperate efforts to find cover, especially for elements of Rodman's Third Division. Three men from the 8th Connecticut were killed and four wounded by one cannon shot, some of the first of more than 2,300 casualties for the Ninth Corps during the day. Nearby, in Henry Spooner's Rhode Island company, two soldiers, "not ten feet from me were killed by the explosion of one shell." Well after dawn, enemy fire continued to create difficulties for the Unionists east of Rohrbach Bridge.[2]

Samuel Benjamin, whose Regular battery was positioned near the center of the corps, quickly sprang into action, providing another example of why the artillery officer garnered so much respect. "We opened fire early on a battery which was shelling General Rodman's division, soon silencing it," the young leader reported. Other Ninth Corps cannoneers began to respond during these opening salvos. Durell's Battery, joining the left of a line of big guns stretching north almost to the Middle Bridge, had the range to counteract the Confederate gunners. "The cannonading was very heavy," the battery historian remembered, with both sides employing artillery "with the utmost vigor."[3]

Relatively few of the corps' casualties on the day were caused by the early morning firing, but a member of the 9th New York recalled the difficult moments. Confederates fired whatever they could load into cannons.

And not content with sending one, they sent a whole cloud of them, and a beautiful range they had too. Every one of them exploded just as nicely as they could wish, squarely over our heads, shaking its fragments among us, leaving only a harmless cloud of smoke to roll peacefully away. . . . We finally got out of range into an open field and into something like shape, and then what do you think we got? No more use of grape and canister, but nothing less than stumps of railroad iron as long as my arm. If this was not adding insult to injury!

Another member of the regiment suggested the brilliant blue and red uniforms of the Zouaves assisted the Confederates with their artillery targeting. After the moves to avoid danger, the regiment finally could enjoy breakfast as they awaited orders. Colonel Fairchild reported thirty-six casualties across his three New York regiments as a result of the Confederate cannonade.[4]

An officer in the 48th Pennsylvania, Nagle's Brigade, remembered, "'Twas a fearful morning—fit harbinger of the bloody scenes to follow." A shot from one Confederate cannon nearly caused a terrible tragedy in the ranks of the 21st Massachusetts. The soldiers were on the northern part of the Ninth Corps line supporting Durell's Battery. One ball buried itself in the ground, then exploded near the 21st's color guard, prompting the unit historian to write, "We supposed that none of the guard had escaped without injury." Fortunately, all those near the regiment's colors "picked themselves up one after the other, entirely unhurt."[5]

Avoiding Confederate cannon fire and sharpshooters early in the morning would prove rather easy compared to the gamut of difficulties facing the Ninth Corps later in the day. Mother Nature provided the most obvious and formidable roadblock. The ground west of Rohrbach Bridge offered a wonderful defensive bulwark for the Confederates, what one Army of the Potomac historian called "a natural Gibraltar." Cox's observations also noted the potential of very few defenders successfully holding the excellent ground. All along the line, the heights that Confederates would defend commanded the ground the Ninth Corps had to traverse before crossing the bridge. Unionists charging from the south would expose their left flank to the enemy while trying to reach their target.[6]

Fences, rocks, and trees provided good cover for the Confederates, who showered the Ninth Corps advance with copious amounts of lead. Nonetheless, like so many of the Confederate regiments at Antietam, losses earlier in the summer significantly reduced manpower. Only about 300 Georgians in the 2nd and 20th Regiments manned the defensive line. They could use Unionist confusion and the blessings of nature to hold back an entire infantry corps for a time, but Lee could not augment the number of troops in the area. He took a division away from the job of protecting Snavely's Ford in order to support his weakening left and center north of town.[7]

AWAITING ORDERS

The damaged friendship between George McClellan and Ambrose Burnside weighed heavily on the fate of the Ninth Corps at Antietam. In his memoirs, filled with McClellan's self-laudatory judgments and scorn for those he deemed imperfect, the army commander wrote, "The attack on the right was to have been supported by an attack on the left." This gave Burnside's single corps the role of supporting the four corps eventually positioned north of town.[8] One need not be second in his West Point class to see the folly of McClellan's analysis. The Ninth Corps was ordered to attack alone against the most formidable ground Lee held at Sharpsburg. The soldiers in the four divisions would have enough problems simply crossing Antietam Creek, to say nothing of providing timely assistance to the bulk of the army miles away.

For the important role the Ninth Corps had in McClellan's mind, the troops spent plenty of time inactive while Hooker and Sumner's men fought for their lives north of town. A New Yorker lamented, "While a great battle was being fought on the right and in the centre of the army, the great force which composed the left wing remained inactive during the fore part of the day." The historical record supports the transmission of an order early in the morning to Burnside, perhaps about 7 a.m. to move his men closer to the Rohrbach Bridge, then await an order to attack. McClellan lied when he claimed the attack order followed at 8 a.m. The *Official Records* time the order at 9:10 a.m., with both Burnside and Cox suggesting 10 a.m. as the delivery time. The important command from headquarters should not have required fifty minutes for delivery, but even getting the message to Burnside at 9:30 a.m. is still ninety minutes later than McClellan's blatantly incorrect time. The attack order stated,

> *General Franklin's command is within one mile and a half of here. General McClellan desires you to open your attack. As soon as you shall have uncovered the upper Stone [Middle] bridge you will be supported, and if necessary, on your own line of attack. So far all is going well.*[9]

Several important points should be considered regarding the order. Why did McClellan inform Burnside of Franklin's approach? The Ninth Corps' attack apparently was to be timed with the arrival of fresh troops at the Middle Bridge. Such an idea made Burnside poor support for three corps already engaged north of town prior to Franklin's arrival. Incredibly concerned about possible Confederate counterattacks, McClellan waited until Franklin's men had nearly arrived before committing the Ninth

Corps to battle. McClellan wanted both the Fifth and Sixth Corps on or near the field before unleashing Burnside against Lee's strong right flank. The cautious commitment to battle always marking McClellan's generalship was obvious as he pondered his left flank at Antietam.[10]

Cox's review of McClellan's false charge of an 8 a.m. order deserves great respect. Cox brings clarity to the matter by cogently suggesting the wording of the order contradicts McClellan's later effort to blame Burnside. Cox's memoirs point out the tardiness of McClellan's attack order. "The manner in which we had waited, the free discussion of what was occurring under our eyes and our relation to it, the public receipt of the order by Burnside in the usual and business-like form," Cox suggested, "all forbid the supposition that this was any reiteration of a former order." Most fatal to McClellan's false aspersions on Burnside is the acknowledgment in the army commander's initial campaign report that Burnside received the attack order at 10 a.m.[11]

Moreover, McClellan's plan to reinforce the Ninth Corps was wholly inadequate and unrealistic. He likely conditioned Burnside's reinforcement on protection of the Middle Bridge to ensure the safety of the span that served as the heart of the Army of the Potomac's position east of Sharpsburg. McClellan's credible concern for defending the army's center became an overriding obsession. If the Sixth Corps was to be Burnside's support, the plan died due to McClellan's apprehension about the right flank, where the attack faltered after 35,000 men had advanced into the meat grinder. The bulk of Franklin's force went to the right, the fourth corps of the day committed north of town. A general as cautious as McClellan would never have stripped his center of Porter's Fifth Corps to supplement Burnside. There were no troops available to reinforce the Ninth Corps, at least in McClellan's mind. Even if some did exist, they could not rapidly help Burnside if trouble occurred after the Rohrbach Bridge was crossed. Thus, McClellan sent one corps against strong defensive ground, with the left flank of Burnside's attacking column unprotected.[12]

Regardless of the exact time Burnside received the attack order, or the mendacities McClellan penned to defend himself, Cox correctly noted the intensity of the moment when the Ninth Corps began to assault the bridge. The Ohioan declared, "It seems now very clear that about ten o'clock in the morning was the great crisis of the battle." Even with considerably more men, McClellan's force to the north had not significantly pushed back the Confederate left. A disastrous assault from a Second Corps division seriously hampered McClellan's hopes. Now he had one corps in position to try to punch through Lee's right, where few troops manned exceptionally good defensive ground.[13] The Ninth Corps' battle was about to begin in earnest.

THE SACRIFICE OF THE 11TH CONNECTICUT

A hodgepodge of units from across the Ninth Corps assembled east of Rohrbach Bridge as the first attack neared. Some Unionist outfits had pushed skirmishers forward earlier in the morning. As Confederate Gen. Robert Toombs admitted, the Ninth Corps men "drove in my pickets and advanced with heavy columns to attack my position on the bridge" before 8 a.m. After the corps moved forward in anticipation of the order to attack, the Second Division held the left of the initial line, with cannons from Benjamin and a section of Simmonds's Kentucky battery nearby. The organization of the Ninth Corps at Antietam is shown in table 3.1.

The two brigades under Sturgis faced relatively little danger, as their position was well southeast of the bridge, to the right of the Confederates on the other side of the creek. Crook's Brigade was in reserve on the right, with the 11th Connecticut from Rodman's Division constituting the bulk of the skirmish line after two companies of the 11th Ohio were engaged in the task earlier in the morning. Colonel Harland's other regiments moved south with the rest of Rodman's warriors as they prepared to seek out a ford to flank the Georgians. Ewing's Ohioans served as Rodman's support.[14]

Highly respected and full of an unbridled potential for greatness, Col. Henry Kingsbury prepared to move his 11th Connecticut forward. His regiment of nearly 450 men outnumbered the two Georgia units by perhaps 150 muskets, but the Connecticut soldiers faced daunting natural obstacles. Kingsbury divided the 11th into wings, with Lt. Col. Griffin Alexander Stedman, Jr. in charge of the right. Stedman was just over a year younger than Kingsbury. An 1859 graduate of Trinity College,

Table 3.1.   The Ninth Corps at the Battle of Antietam

Corps Commander—Brig. Gen. Jacob Cox

1st Division Brig. Gen. Orlando Willcox	2nd Division Brig. Gen. Samuel Sturgis
1st Brigade *Col. Benjamin Christ* 28th Massachusetts 17th Michigan 79th New York 50th Pennsylvania	*1st Brigade* *Brig. Gen. James Nagle* 2nd Maryland 6th New Hampshire 9th New Hampshire 48th Pennsylvania
2nd Brigade *Col. Thomas Welsh* 8th Michigan 46th New York 45th Pennsylvania 100th Pennsylvania	*2nd Brigade* *Brig. Gen. Edward Ferrero* 21st Massachusetts 35th Massachusetts 51st New York 51st Pennsylvania
	Artillery Pennsylvania Light, Battery D 4th United States, Battery E

3rd Division Brig. Gen. Isaac Rodman	4th Division Col. Eliakim Scammon
1st Brigade *Col. Harrison Fairchild* 9th New York 89th New York 103rd New York	*1st Brigade* *Col. Hugh Ewing* 12th Ohio 23rd Ohio 30th Ohio
2nd Brigade *Col. Edward Harland* 8th Connecticut 11th Connecticut 16th Connecticut 4th Rhode Island	*2nd Brigade* *Col. George Crook* 11th Ohio 28th Ohio 36th Ohio
Artillery 5th United States, Battery A	*Artillery* 1st Battery, Ohio Light Simmonds' Battery, Kentucky Light Artillery

Source: OR, Vol. 19, I, 177–78.

Stedman started his war experience as a captain in the 5th Connecticut. A lawyer by trade, Stedman quickly grew interested in learning how to be an excellent military leader. As one historian noted, the young officer "devoted himself with untiring energy to acquire a knowledge of his new calling." Major of the 11th by November 1861, he became lieutenant colonel of the regiment in June.[15]

Henry Benning, whose Confederates had been stopped by Ninth Corps men on Henry House Hill during the denouement at Second Manassas, felt incredibly isolated as the Union move toward the bridge portended disaster. Benning's 2nd and 20th Georgia "were left at the bridge without any artillery supports whatever." Also bereft of immediate infantry assistance, the combative Confederate officer had no "expectation of receiving any re-enforcements," because to get to Benning friendly infantry would be required to run the gauntlet of fire from the Union batteries east of the Antietam.[16] The small and devoted Peach Tree State warriors Benning commanded were all the colonel had on hand. For three hours, that would be enough.

The line of men from the Nutmeg State fanned out north and south of the bridge. Believing initiative could win the day, Capt. John Griswold, leading Company A north of the bridge, attempted to make progress with a bold dash into the creek. He died on the west bank as dozens in the 11th fell at a horrifying rate. Like so many in the war, Griswold was a great young patriot lost to his country far too soon. Only twenty-five years old when he died, he was born in Old Lyme, Connecticut. After graduating from Yale, Griswold spent time as a surveyor in Kansas, then sailed for the Pacific in early 1860, remaining far from home for six months. He returned to Connecticut from California at the start of the Civil War. An individual described Griswold's short military career by saying he "showed great boldness on the field of battle."[17]

Kingsbury would also fall, hit multiple times while leading the left of the regiment. One soldier recalled the strong leadership and compassionate oversight Kingsbury provided. The young colonel was "an officer greatly loved by all the division." With a keen interest in his soldiers' welfare, the appreciative Connecticut infantryman noted of Kingsbury, "He always took the trouble to find out and let the men know if there was time to make coffee at a rest."[18] Kingsbury's death was a tragic moment for many under his command.

Kingsbury's brother-in-law, Confederate Gen. David R. Jones, also suffered great emotional anguish. Troops under his command fired the shots taking Kingsbury's promising life. Jones and Kingsbury were not just related by marriage. The two men truly respected each other, even while serving on opposite sides of the nation's fratricide. Later in the day, after hearing the news of Kingsbury's mortal wound, Jones grew inconsolable. He resigned his commission soon after, dying in early 1863 from a heart ailment. The sisters married to either Jones or Kingsbury were nieces of former U.S. president Zachary Taylor. Three months after his death, Kingsbury's wife Evelyn gave birth to his only child.[19]

After expressing concern about the initial Unionist advance, Toombs reported his pleasure at the fate of Burnside's first effort. The 11th Connecticut "was repulsed with great slaughter." He was not exaggerating. Without being engaged later in the day, the 11th Connecticut sustained 139 casualties at Antietam, including forty-eight men killed or mortally wounded. Several of the lost warriors would ultimately be buried in Connecticut, while some, such as Company E's Benjamin Beach, rest at Antietam National Cemetery.[20]

CROOK'S BRIGADE BEFUDDLED

The lack of knowledge Ninth Corps officers had of their mission was obvious as the order to begin the attack percolated down the chain of command. George Crook recalled hearing firing in his front, but he knew virtually nothing about what was occurring. According to Cox, Crook's three Ohio regiments were "to march under cover of the Eleventh Connecticut, and attempt to carry the bridge by assault," with Sturgis in reserve. When informed of his mission, Crook asked a staff officer, "What bridge?" Some men in the ranks did not even know a creek divided the two opposing armies. Crook bitterly recalled in his memoirs how his men would be killed to discern the true extent and nature of their position more than thirty-six hours after Union troops first started arriving east of the creek.[21]

How much blame should Cox receive for the poor information made available to division and brigade commanders on September 17? The general's memoirs are not filled with the self-promotion common to some officers who served in the war. He did acknowledge the difficulty of seeing Burnside as the true commander of the Ninth Corps at Antietam. One cannot blame the Ohioan much for being concerned about the discordant command arrangement caused by Burnside's stringent belief in still being a wing commander, not the direct commander of the Ninth Corps. As a historian rightfully suggested, "With Burnside close to him," Cox "probably felt as if he were the mere tactical leader of the corps, not thinking for it, but simply seeing that it executed the orders which came to him from or through Burnside." Of the senior officer on the army's left, the same historian suggests, Burnside "had mistaken his vocation, and that it was a misfortune for the country that he was ever promoted beyond the rank of colonel." Perhaps these words are too harsh, but Burnside clearly did not do enough to understand the natural features in the area around Rohrbach Bridge.[22]

Wherever blame best lies, Cox's expectation of Crook leading the assault on the bridge failed to pan out. Crook, incredibly perplexed about his mission, assumed the opposite of Cox. Only after Sturgis's two brigades possessed the span did Crook report his own men were advancing to cross the bridge. This was one of the most notable and serious failures of communication between Ninth Corps officers this day. Instead of attacking as a brigade, the three Ohio regiments were a disjointed group unsure of their surroundings or how best to effectuate orders. The frustration of Maj. Lyman Jackson, 11th Ohio, is clearly discerned from his battle report, penned three days later. "I do not know the duty assigned," but he assumed the goal was to support the two companies of skirmishers sent forward early in the morning. Yet, Jackson felt the regiment's two wings worked "under conflicting orders," with the right moving toward the skirmish companies while the left headed in the direction of the Confederate defenses.

One problem with the brigade's attack was the mortal wounding of Lt. Col. Augustus Coleman, the competent and respected leader of the 11th Ohio. "In advance of his men, cheering them on, and closing up their broken ranks, he fell with his face to the foe," according to the regiment's history. A cadet at West Point who did not graduate, Coleman put aside his agricultural pursuits at the outbreak of war, organizing a company and earning the rank of captain. Coleman lost his life six weeks away from his thirty-third birthday, "his noblest monument is the affectionate remembrance of brave men." As Jackson lamented of his fallen boss, "no better, braver, truer officer ever served our country, and no regiment can feel a loss more severely."[23]

With so much confusion governing the moment, the Ohioans would not cross the creek via Rohrbach Bridge, contrary to the vision of Union generals. Crook found a ford north of the span. He reported the 28th Ohio was able to cross with water not quite knee deep. Crook's dispersed units did not gain the west side of the Antietam as a group. Perhaps distressed about the disorganized effort he had presided over during the morning, Crook admitted in his memoirs of the need to return east of the creek to call the 36th Ohio forward after the 28th crossed at the ford. Crook's brigade—sustaining only sixty-seven casualties all day, the lowest of any in the corps at Antietam—became a non-factor in the battle, without the ability to support the attack.[24]

"DON'T YOU UNDERSTAND THE ENGLISH LANGUAGE?"

With the inevitable advance of his division, Sam Sturgis knew some rearrangement of artillery would be necessary. As the general reported, his cannons were "placed in new positions, so as to aid in clearing the wood on the opposite bank, strongly occupied by the enemy." Big guns in the Ninth Corps helped the infantry advance, but the artillery's ability to inflict notable casualties on the Confederates was low. Colonel Benning's two scattered regiments only had the numbers to place a man about every 8 feet along the line.[25]

Brig. Gen. James Nagle took all four of his regiments into the fight as the vanguard of the division. The narrow valley offering access to the bridge required the troops to be fed in one at a time during the opening moments of the assault, but only because of the unimaginative deployment of the whole corps in the previous hours. If Sturgis had spread more of his men to the north under the protection of the topography, the next thirty minutes would have provided a better chance for a Union triumph. An attack from the east beginning out of the enemy's range and with protected flanks offered the possibility of a better outcome for the Ninth Corps.

The rough summer for Nagle's Brigade culminated in the intense difficulty the soldiers faced in the advance to the bridge. Nagle envisioned exactly what would happen to his men. As he reported, "From this strong position the enemy poured a terrific fire upon our infantry, which was replied to in a very spirited manner by all the regiments in my brigade." Based on the division's starting position well south of the bridge, most of the regiments had the unenviable task of exposing their left flank to Confederate fire during the charge toward the stone target spanning the Antietam.[26] Perhaps Nagle's survivors from Second Manassas thought they could never be in a worse fix, but the time under fire east of Rohrbach Bridge likely surpassed the summer's previous privations.

The 2nd Maryland, Lt. Col. Eugene Duryeé in command, led the way, with the 6th New Hampshire immediately behind. The second half of the brigade included the 9th New Hampshire followed by the 48th Pennsylvania. Theodore Dimon, acting surgeon for the Maryland regiment, observed Duryeé near the front of his men, with the colonel assisting in the removal of fences to facilitate his regiment's move forward. Men quickly began to fall due to the accurate fire of the concealed enemy on the west side of the creek. Regarding the difficulty and danger of the bold charge against the bridge, Dimon, in a letter to his wife the week following the battle, sadly noted, "These boys just stood to be shot down."[27]

Optimistically thinking the brigade could take the bridge and conquer the enemy on the other side, the regiments went ahead with fixed bayonets. Confederates quickly began inflicting damage on the column. Unionists retaliated, but the Georgians' altitude and cover ensured Nagle's first two regiments suffered severely. The historian of the 6th New Hampshire said the intensity of the shooting made Confederate rounds seemingly hit "every inch of ground over which our troops must march to reach the bridge." The Granite Stater described how "such sweeping destruction" could halt "the advancing column, but the men sheltered themselves behind logs, fences, and whatever other cover they could find, and bravely held the ground already gained."

Additional help from the brigade augmented Nagle's chance to make something of his orders. The 9th New Hampshire and 48th Pennsylvania boldly moved forward, at first posting themselves south of Nagle's other two regiments. A correspondent in the 9th informed a newspaper, "New Hampshire blood flowed freely in the contest," but the rookie troops "never flinched" and "stood before the awful carnage without one thought of yielding." One reason for the stout effort from the 9th New Hampshire may have been, as Daniel Hurd remembered, the Granite State rookies "knelt behind a rail fence, where we could rest our rifles and fire at the Rebels on the wooded bluff across the creek."[28]

A tough fighter from the 6th New Hampshire received some assistance from Capt. James Wren after the 48th Pennsylvania went forward. With forty cartridges left, the Granite Stater suffered a wound costing him a finger, making further firing difficult. Wren agreed to load and fire the weapon after the soldier bit the ends off of each cartridge. Dropping his sword and essentially becoming an enlisted man, Wren fired many rounds. After his original gun became too hot to hold, Wren picked up abandoned weapons nearby to continue expending the cartridges his brigade comrade had provided.[29]

The placement of Wren's regiment did not meet the expectation of General Sturgis, who grew incredibly agitated. Accosting Lt. Col. Joshua Sigfried, Sturgis's consternation came alive with a bellowed condemnation and question, "God damn you to hell, sir, don't you understand the English language?" Left with no option but to comply, Sigfried moved the regiment from what was the left of the bridge line, well below the bridge, to the north, offering greater support to the brigade.[30]

Starting out about a half-mile northeast of the bridge, then moving closer, Captain Clark's Battery E, 4th U.S. won the praise of Nagle. The battery's "excellent service" took some heat off the First Brigade. Clark was wounded multiple times during the day. First Lt. William Baker gave his life for his country while leading a section of Clark's battery. He was less than three weeks from his twenty-third birthday.[31]

Pvt. Charles Judkins, 9th New Hampshire, sustained a wound at Antietam. The photo includes a long saber bayonet used by the regiment. LIBRARY OF CONGRESS

In their second fight of the week and only a month removed from home, the 9th New Hampshire made a steadfast effort to contribute, suffering ten killed in action and fifty-nine total casualties. Even with their large number of men available compared to the veteran Ninth Corps regiments, the 9th New Hampshire possessed limited chances to seriously damage the hidden Georgians. They did not hold a position with the best angles to fire on their antagonists. When the bloodied 2nd Maryland and 6th New Hampshire tried again for the bridge, then fell back to the northeast, the 9th held their position south of the span, benefiting less than their comrades from protective topography. Of the horrible day, the 9th's George Tracy averred, "Oh that I may never need to witness such scenes again."[32]

With Colonel Fellows earning further plaudits from his men for bravery and excellent leadership, his second in command, Lt. Col. Herbert Titus, suffered a wound after becoming another officer who picked up a musket and joined the enlisted men. Titus served in the 2nd New Hampshire early in the war, working his way up the officer ranks. Elmer Bragg remembered, "The Lieut. Col. held up his mangled arm, as he was carried to the rear, and bade us stand at our post." Titus had much life ahead of him.[33]

One historian correctly suggested the 2nd Maryland "specially distinguished itself" on September 17. John T. Durham, not yet twenty years old, suffered his second wound of the summer while serving in Company A. The devoted patriot would muster out with the regiment in 1865, then live fifty-five more years. With fewer than 200 engaged, the 2nd Maryland suffered sixty-seven casualties at Antietam, including seventeen dead. Capt. Malcolm Wilson, Company F, was the outfit's one officer killed in action. A native of Lancaster County, Pennsylvania, Wilson was forty-three years old. Dr. Dimon wrote of Wilson being killed by a cannon shot, which took away the top of his head. As would be the case for regiments on both sides of the entire war, several of the 2nd Maryland's wounded would spend months in hospitals, then receive medical discharges.[34]

The target of Ninth Corps troops during the morning of September 17, 1862, Burnside's Bridge spanned Antietam Creek southeast of the town of Sharpsburg, Maryland. LIBRARY OF CONGRESS

CONQUERING THE BRIDGE

With the First Brigade's attack sputtering, Sturgis knew the time had arrived for Ferrero's men to advance. The division commander did not show any inclination to follow up on Ferrero's suggestion to use some potential crossing spots below the bridge, because his orders from Burnside focused on seizing the span itself. Ferrero suggested Nagle's men concentrate on the bridge because the Second Brigade suffered from fatigue and a lack of rations, but Sturgis rightfully insisted his other four regiments needed to move ahead. "Go on," he ordered Ferrero, with the colonel remembering his mission was "to move forward my brigade, and carry the bridge at all hazards." An officer in the 21st Massachusetts wrote of a detail added to Ferrero's orders. As the state's adjutant general was informed, "Our brigade was commanded to carry the bridge at all hazards at the point of the bayonet."[35]

The brigade commander's initial effort to move out failed to register with Col. Hartranft of the 51st Pennsylvania or Col. Robert Potter of the New York outfit. "The 51st to the front," Ferrero declared, but neither regiment's senior officer assumed the command was meant for their own men. Regardless of the army bureaucracy's potential error of placing regiments with identical numerical designation in the same brigade, Sturgis was immensely proud of his battle-hardened 51st regiments as confusion waned and the New York and Pennsylvania warriors went forward. "They started on their mission of death full of enthusiasm," the general reported. The 51st Pennsylvania's historian noted the men seemed especially motivated after hearing General Burnside's request for the two 51st's to lead the way. Ferrero's personal promise of renewed whiskey rations for the two regiments undoubtedly helped move the patriots toward the bridge.[36]

Despite the inefficient leadership and lack of communication that ruled the Ninth Corps' morning, trained and dedicated soldiers willingly confronted the possibility of maiming or death for the sake of their cause. One of Ferrero's staff officers saw the impact of what the whiskey promise and any other motivation had on the two regiments as they approached their destiny. Second Lt. John Hudson remembered how "the regimental officers moved without hesitation, and the men at once followed example."[37]

Learning from the exposed left flank danger that inhibited Nagle's initial assault, the two 51st's advanced on the bridge from a different direction, improving their chance of success. They moved north prior to their advance, first taking advantage of the twin knolls protecting the Ninth Corps position. The two regiments would then charge the bridge directly, without exposing their left. A stone wall gave the Pennsylvanians, who were in front, the chance to fire across the creek before the final rush to the bridge. Musketry from Ferrero's regiments and supporting Ninth Corps troops proved formative to the task of taking the bridge; Georgians began to fall back prior to the final assault. Out of respect for his Southern antagonists, the 51st Pennsylvania's historian noted how Benning's men "used every exertion known in military parlance to rid themselves of their now troublesome foe, but all in vain." By early afternoon, Benning suggested the lack of ammunition and massive length of the Union line doomed his regiments to retreat or capture.[38]

Men from other units wished history to know troops not in the "two 51st's" contributed to the lodgment made on the west side of the creek. The 21st Massachusetts noted their close position to the front part of Ferrero's attack. While attempting to inflict punishment on the creek's defenders, the Bay Staters had a hard time seeing what they were shooting at. With infantrymen firing about thirty rounds "into the wall of shining leaves" obscuring the Georgians, the shooting seemed futile. The 21st's historian was glad the Ninth Corps artillery helped out, but he noted the wounding of two members of the regiment from friendly canister fire.[39]

A prominent historian of the Antietam campaign suggests the 21st Massachusetts performed poorly at this decisive moment, but his criticism is unjust. The Bay Staters likely did waste some ammunition prior to the brigade's attack, but many men in the Ninth Corps who fired into the Georgians' natural redoubt took shots without seeing individual enemy soldiers.[40] Such exuberance from the Massachusetts regiment exposed some Confederate warriors who fired in return. Thus, there does not appear to be grounds for questioning the regiment's performance during the stressful moments.

As the historian of the 51st Pennsylvania declared, the result of the close firing between the opposing forces meant Ferrero's lead regiments "with heroic fortitude and a firmer resolution" knew "the bridge must and should be theirs." Yet, an impetus tide of Union blue did not sweep across the creek as the Maryland stream was conquered. Lieutenant Hudson remembered how tired all the troops felt from a difficult summer, making their success at the bridge look more like the triumph of a disorganized mob than a victorious infantry corps. The men were not going to recede without greater chance of additional victory, he suggested, but they also lacked a "bounding energy" as the Georgians fell back. Ferrero wrote of the 51st Pennsylvania being the first to successfully breach the Antietam, followed closely by Potter's New Yorkers.[41]

Pvt. John Thompson, Company B, 51st New York, was one of the nineteen in the regiment killed in action. The twenty-year-old bricklayer volunteered for war in the summer of 1861. His mother, who would die the next year, and sister relied on his small soldier's salary to help make ends meet. Thompson is buried near comrades in Antietam National Cemetery.[42]

VICTORY BRINGS A DEFENSIVE MINDSET

The object of the morning's fight came into the possession of Union forces by about 1 p.m. Men of the Ninth Corps likely felt a great sense of relief after the bridge was finally won, but the day's work could not be considered anywhere close to complete. An uphill fight of unknown intensity remained. The key was to concentrate men west of the bridge, seize Snavely's Ford to the southwest so Rodman's command could cross, and proceed toward Sharpsburg. A strong showing by the Ninth Corps would then force Lee back to his only escape route on the Potomac while a renewed Unionist attack from the north added to the chaos for Lee's men. On paper, the Ninth Corps could link up in one strong line to accomplish the smashing deed. As with any military action against hilly topography and dedicated enemy troops, ultimate victory was far more difficult than the designs of generals. The frustration and heartbreaking casualties of the morning were about to get much worse.

Relative quiet prevailed to the north by early afternoon as Burnside's Boys started to establish their bridgehead on the west bank of the Antietam. The time was right for the Ninth Corps to make a profound impact on the battle with a rapid advance northwest, up the slope between what would be forever known as Burnside's Bridge and the Town of Sharpsburg.

McClellan, his friendship with Burnside weakened, turned fatalistic about the hope for decisiveness from his left flank. No statement typifies such thinking more than what the army commander wrote in a letter to his wife before the end of September.

> *I ought to rap Burnside very severely & probably will—yet I hate to do it. He is very slow & not fit to command more than a regiment. If I rap him as he deserves he will be my mortal enemy hereafter—if I do not praise him as he thinks he deserves & as I know he does not, he will be at least a very lukewarm friend.*[43]

Not even two weeks after giving his former friend command of two infantry corps, McClellan claimed Burnside never should have received a general's star.

A defensive mindset governed the moment. Cox recalled, "Our first task was to prepare to hold the height we had gained against the return assault of the enemy which we expected," then "reply to the destructive fire from the enemy's abundant artillery."[44] The potential of McClellan's philosophy instilling caution into subordinates seems like a reasonable interpretation of Cox's words, even though McClellan, in a private letter to his wife, craved more offense at the time. At least the acting Ninth Corps commander addressed the issue honestly in his extensive postwar writings. Much to the detriment of the Union cause, the work of the Ninth Corps became languid at the crucial moment when a decisive victory may have been gained through greater alacrity.

As with other parts of the Ninth Corps, Rodman's Division had a frustrating morning of limited progress. Compared to their comrades engaged near Rohrbach Bridge, at least the part of Burnside's command searching for Snavely's Ford suffered minimal damage. But they did nothing meaningful to assist their comrades attempting to traverse the bridge. Rodman's division and Ewing's Ohioans started forming southwest of the bridge as the rest of the corps was spanning the Antietam.[45]

Tired troops, limited ammunition, enemy forces of unknown strength, and even the philosophical desire to defend a dearly bought bridge may be seen as justifications for a slow afternoon attack. But the Ninth Corps had not fought itself to complete fatigue across the entire command. Willcox's Division remained relatively rested, while Rodman's ford hunters would have possessed a good deal of ammunition.[46]

Did McClellan expect such a crushing blow from the Ninth Corps? He talked tough in the early afternoon, wishing Burnside to push on to seize Sharpsburg. However, McClellan made no effort to funnel fresh regiments or the cavalry reserve to Burnside's Bridge, as he had previously promised. The Ninth Corps still considerably outnumbered their Confederate foes south of town, but the terrain, by McClellan's own admission, presented difficulties. The need for reinforcements and better flank protection should have been patently obvious. McClellan failed to grasp the potential of the moment, so concerned as he was about the possibility of Confederate counterattacks. For all his complaints about

Burnside's torpor, McClellan's lack of a solidified plan should be seen as the most severe limitation on Union victory at Antietam.[47]

"ONE OF GOD'S NOBLEST WORKS"

In his report written less than a week after the battle, Cox noted his request to Burnside "that Willcox's Division, which had been held in reserve on the left bank, might be sent over and take its place on the right front." The idea of augmenting the number of troops and placing Sturgis in reserve was "immediately ordered" by Burnside, Cox added.[48] The moment illustrates the inefficiency caused by the untenable command arrangement on McClellan's left. A corps commander should never feel compelled to request from a superior a division of his own corps to assist with holding a position or bolstering an attack.

Shortly after the 51st Pennsylvania pierced the Antietam at the bridge, regiments that had experienced less enemy fire during the day joined their victorious comrades across the creek. Ferrero's rookies in the 35th Massachusetts were the next behind the Keystone and Empire State units, followed by the 21st Massachusetts. The 35th filed to the right and quickly formed a regimental line, looking uphill. Compared to other spots west of the bridge, a less severe incline greeted the 35th in their new position. The 21st Massachusetts remained closer to the bridge, with the 6th New Hampshire from Nagle's Brigade nearby. Crook's Ohioans were also on hand. Ewing remained to the south, still in a reserve position behind Rodman.[49]

Confederate cannon fire became a notable danger to the gathering Union line. As Sturgis reported, "Here the troops displayed their heroism more, if possible, than on any former occasion, for the enemy opened with canister and grape, shell and railroad iron, and the vehicles of destruction fell like hail among them." After the war, a soldier from the 89th New York remembered the array of metal fired from Confederate cannons. He proclaimed "the whole contents of a blacksmith's shop" must have been loaded into the enemy's big guns. Lt. James Baldwin, 35th Massachusetts was "badly hurt" at this time "by a bursting shell which tore away all the fleshy portion of his thigh for a length of fourteen inches."[50]

Smoke created by soldiers cooking coffee may have pinpointed the location of the Ninth Corps in repose west of the bridge. If so, men from the 51st Pennsylvania may have indirectly killed their second in command. As Lt. Col. Thomas Bell was walking his horse back down to the creek for some water, the young leader died after being hit by a piece of shell. Lieutenant Hudson remarked positively about Bell's military acumen, beloved personality, and kind manners. Bell's intention to see Union arms victorious dated back to his enlistment at the dawn of the war. Multiple examples of Bell's bravery led to praise from senior officers, including Burnside. Bell was even credited with saving the lives of seventeen Confederates captured west of the creek. Only twenty-four years old, Bell first thought his wound was not serious, but he died later in the day.

The regimental historian effusively penned his thoughts about Bell. "Few as good men as he and none better, fell during the whole rebellion," he suggested." Bell "was an exemplary Christian, a faithful friend, a strict disciplinarian, but not harsh, a thorough gentleman, a ripe scholar, a truly patriotic and brave soldier; in short he was one of God's noblest works." Lt. Jacob Gilbert Beaver and Davis Hunsicker were the regiment's other officers listed as killed during the battle.[51]

Whatever his shortcomings since South Mountain, Burnside did not remain away from danger. Some of McClellan's staff members suggested the senior officer on the army's left did not cross the bridge, but careful students of the Antietam campaign have questioned such accounts. Those doubting Burnside's personal courage in postwar letters to McClellan may have figured "My Dear Mac" wished to hear such statements. However, one newspaper artist drew Burnside holding the hill with some of his troops west of the bridge. Additionally, in a postwar article, Cox wrote, Burnside "took his share of personal peril" as barrages from Confederate big guns continued.[52]

In addition to men receiving some measure of refreshment and ammunition during the afternoon lull, a line for advance formed. On the right of Clark's Battery, the 100th Pennsylvania manned a skirmish line, with the Highlanders of the 79th New York extending well to the north, nearly reaching the left of Fifth Corps skirmishers who had crossed Antietam Creek at the Middle Bridge. The rest of Willcox's two brigades lined up behind the skirmishers, with Col. Thomas Welsh placing the 8th Michigan, 46th New York, and 45th Pennsylvania left of the Lower Bridge Road, which connected the Rohrbach (Burnside) Bridge to Sharpsburg. Christ's three regiments (28th Massachusetts, 50th Pennsylvania, and 17th Michigan) lined up behind the Highlanders to the right of the road. Although they had served on picket overnight, men in the 50th Pennsylvania seemed especially enthusiastic as time for the afternoon attack neared.[53]

Orlando Willcox's Division would be central to the history of the Ninth Corps.
LIBRARY OF CONGRESS

After their difficult morning, the 6th New Hampshire crossed the bridge under life-threatening Confederate artillery fire. The Granite State unit "received a storm of shot and shell from the enemy's batteries." Union cannoneers, like their infantry comrades, made their way west of the bridge. Durell's Battery was part of the Ninth Corps artillery contingent attempting to assist with protecting the bridgehead as plans for an advance of Burnside's infantry were formed. Captain Clark's gunners joined the cacophony. The artillerists replied to the Confederates while also being harassed by some Confederate infantry to the west. The Southern troops were likely Georgians under Toombs sent forward to support their exhausted comrades in the 2nd and 20th Regiments.[54]

The collection of Ninth Corps cannons and infantry had to be highly imposing to any observer. Several of the Confederate brigades facing the attack had suffered heavily on South Mountain. General Longstreet knew the decrepit condition of the Confederate army, but he also held a keen respect for the Southern soldiers being called to Herculean tasks around Sharpsburg. Of the effort to defeat the afternoon attack, Longstreet wrote, "Batteries from all parts of our field drove to General Lee, as well as detachments of infantry, including some with fresh wounds from the morning battle, but the battle moved bravely on."[55]

Leaving token personnel on the east side of Antietam Creek, the impressive array of Ninth Corps manpower was ready to continue their westward attack by 3 p.m. Burnside's report noted the goal of the afternoon was to "attack the town of Sharpsburg and the heights on the left." The men were inspired after their conquest of the bridge and the restful period prior to the next advance. As one historian noted, "The order to advance was received and obeyed by the troops with great enthusiasm. They pressed forward rapidly, cheering and exultant." Cox recorded more than 500 Ninth Corps casualties to seize Burnside's Bridge. The butcher's bill for the day was about to increase exponentially.[56]

ATTACK OF THE RIGHT FLANK

After two hours, Willcox seemed ready to move his eight veteran regiments forward on the northern part of the Ninth Corps line. In addition to two infantry brigades, Willcox had the benefit of a section of guns from his Massachusetts battery. The two cannons were under the command of 1st Lt. John Coffin. Notably older than most lieutenants on the field, Coffin was thirty-seven years old. Originally placed several hundred feet ahead of Willcox's soldiers, Coffin moved farther forward to support the advancing infantry, eventually firing canister rounds into the resolute and outnumbered Southerners.

As their Ninth Corps comrades to the south would experience, the rolling ground hindered the First Division's attack. Few parts of the earth were safe. "We were under fire from the moment a man appeared at the crest of the plateau or crossed the hollow," Willcox reported. He was pleased to know some artillery was with him as his division "gallantly advanced over the plateau toward Sharpsburg."[57]

The Roundheads on the skirmish line left of the Lower Bridge Road did their job well. Frederick Pettit remembered seeing groups of Confederate infantry and artillery, but the enemy skirmishers quickly ran. Pettit was another Ninth Corps soldier who recalled the railroad iron blasting from Confederate cannons. By running ahead to some haystacks, the men of the 100th Pennsylvania were able to target the bothersome artillerists, with the crews from one battery suffering due to the determined Pennsylvanians. Separated from his regiment, Pettit assisted his comrade Pvt. John P. Wilson, who had suffered a knee injury early in the fight, courtesy of Confederate buckshot.[58]

Confederates south of the Boonsboro Pike, on and near the future Antietam National Cemetery, had waited out a stressful morning and early afternoon. One Virginian remembered seeing an impressive array of troops for hours. Intense cannon fire, predominantly from Fifth Corps guns, proved loud and annoying. A South Carolinian, in an apple orchard near the Lower Bridge Road, complimented his Unionist foes for unleashing "the heaviest and most terrific artillery firing during the entire war." The shots did the defending infantry little harm. The men could not afford any casualties; the Virginians in Richard Garnett's entire brigade totaled less than 500 muskets. With cannoneers shooting canister at Willcox's men, a Virginian near the right flank of the thin line witnessed "the immense column of well-drilled infantry" approach. A "slow but steady tread" against Garnett meant trouble for the outgunned

Southerners. Although blasts from cannons inflicted casualties on Will-cox's two brigades, the attack continued.[59]

Although closer to the main body of Confederates, the scattered Highlanders on the skirmish line fared better than their comrades to the rear moving up in compact lines. As the regimental historian wrote, "We held on through the storm of deadly hail, our open order as skirmishers favoring us more than the troops in our rear, who suffered in a greater degree." The line halted about 300 yards from town, with some Regular army troops in the Fifth Corps joining the Highlanders to continue the skirmish fire, with much of the shooting directed at enemy artillerists.[60]

Southerners' fire counted against Welsh's Brigade. On Welsh's right, the 45th Pennsylvania moved forward near the Lower Bridge Road. "One of our best and noblest corporals," Thomas B. McWilliams, fell during the day in Company E. Immediately to the left, the 46th New York was annoyed by Confederates making good use of the terrain and stone walls. Still, several Ninth Corps soldiers from multiple regiments were able to grab enemy prisoners. Ralph Ely, 8th Michigan, near the right of Fairchild's New Yorkers, was one officer to record capturing some Confederates.[61]

Even with some success, an inability to retain proper alignment disrupted the attack's momentum. As the general reported, Christ's regiments made good progress, but soon found themselves ahead of their support, Crook's Ohioans. This created the unenviable situation where Christ's men experienced fire from multiple batteries and a line of Confederate infantry. Welsh's arrival on the left decreased the amount of lead exclusively targeting Christ's regiments. A bold advance from the 17th Michigan, the right of Christ's line, may have confused the enemy somewhat, but Willcox did not make a decisive breakthrough.

Coffin's immediate superior, battery commander Asa Cook, praised the lieutenant's work, the most difficult situation Ninth Corps cannoneers faced at Antietam. Placing his guns south of the Otto farmhouse, Coffin deserved "especial commendation" for his conduct, Cook penned. The lieutenant's "gallantry on all occasions during the day was worthy of the highest praise." After a slight change in the placement of his two guns, Coffin reported producing a "terrible effect upon the rebel lines."

His section held the ground until he ran out of ammunition. Willing to praise his own subordinates for their efforts, Coffin observed "the greatest bravery and coolness" of his gun crews.[62] The artillerists deserve great credit for their work supporting Willcox's infantry.

Willcox's right flank suffered the most. The 17th Michigan and 50th Pennsylvania combined for 155 casualties, nearly half of the losses across the division's eight regiments. Capt. James Ingham, thirty-five years old, was the only officer killed in action in the Keystone State outfit. The regimental historian included a remembrance from the chaplain, who was with Ingham when he died. "It was my painful duty to be Captain Ingham's attendant during his last moments," Chaplain Meredith noted, "His last audible words were 'Attention, Company! Aim, Fire!' and then his brave soul passed into the Great Beyond, where battle scenes are unknown." Four Company C men died fighting in the 50th Pennsylvania: Jeremiah Helms, Augustus Berger, Daniel McGlenn, and Richard Fahl. Helms, listed as a musician, was only seventeen years old.[63]

The utterly traumatizing whirlwind of war enveloping the 17th Michigan in mid-September continued west of the Antietam. The rookie unit's losses included eighteen killed in action, adding to the petrifying butcher's bill the outfit paid in its first campaign. Among the dead were Lewis Jones, Company B, a twenty-two-year-old "instantly killed" while in the act of reloading his musket. Diarist David Lane recalled how the regiment nearly advanced to the edge of Sharpsburg, but then withdrew due to lack of ammunition. Confederates still battered the regiment "with bursting shells and hurtling balls."[64]

FAIRCHILD'S CHARGE

The three New York regiments under Col. Harrison Fairchild constituted the heart of the Ninth Corps attack on the afternoon of September 17. Members of the 9th New York long recalled the stress and grandeur of the moment as the brigade prepared to move forward. The regiment's artillery company was able to find Confederate targets before the infantry charge, "though a rebel battery on the other side shelled us severely." The New Yorkers' cannon fire ended up burning alive some wounded Confederate skirmishers, who had been left behind on straw stacks prior to

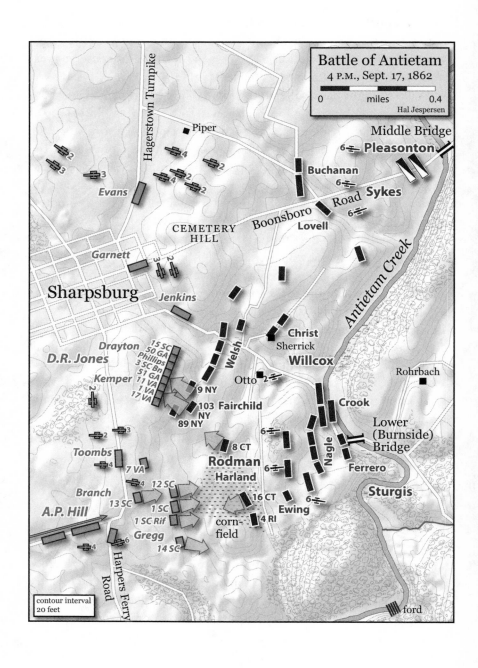

Battle of Antietam
4 P.M., Sept. 17, 1862

0   miles   0.4

Hal Jespersen

Middle Bridge

Pleasonton

Hagerstown Turnpike

Piper

Buchanan

Boonsboro   Road   Sykes

Lovell

Evans

CEMETERY HILL

Antietam Creek

Garnett

Sharpsburg

Jenkins

Welsh

Christ

Sherrick

Willcox

Rohrbach

D.R. Jones

Drayton

15 SC
50 GA
Phillips
3 SC Bn
51 GA
11 VA
1 VA
17 VA

Kemper

9 NY

Otto

Crook

103 NY

Fairchild

89 NY

Nagle

Lower (Burnside) Bridge

8 CT

Rodman

Ferrero

Harland

Toombs

7 VA

16 CT

Sturgis

Branch

12 SC

13 SC

1 SC

Ewing

4 RI

A.P. Hill

1 SC Rif

corn-field

Gregg

14 SC

Harpers Ferry Road

contour interval
20 feet

ford

These two Confederates likely perished from Ninth Corps bullets west of Antietam Creek. LIBRARY OF CONGRESS

a retreat back to the main Southern line. The enemy's big guns exacted their own damage on the New Yorkers, with one member of the Zouave outfit remembering the terror of Confederate shells "striking and bursting in the ranks." An officer noted how the enemy launched "missiles of almost every variety, from shrapnel to railroad iron." Colonel Fairchild complimented his men in his post-battle report, "Though the fire was severe, the brigade remained firm in its position for nearly an hour, until ordered to advance."[65]

Strong leadership can instill great courage into fighting men when the moment of an attack arrives. One member of the 9th New York was grateful for the commanding presence of Lt. Col. Edgar Kimball. A New Hampshire native and veteran of the Mexican War, Kimball, the regiment's original major, had seen many fights before the struggle along the Antietam. An appreciative enlisted man inspired by Kimball's obvious determination suggested the commanding officer was "firmly impressed with the presage that he would never be killed in battle." The prediction was true, but Kimball would not survive the war.[66]

Lt. Matthew Graham doubted Kimball's judgment as the time to move out approached.

I was lying on my back, supported on my elbows, watching the shells explode overhead and speculating as to how long I could hold up my finger before it would be shot off, for the very air seemed full of bullets, when the order to get up was given. I turned over quickly to look at Colonel Kimball, who had given the order, thinking he had become suddenly insane; never dreaming that he intended to advance in that fire, and firmly believing that the regiment would not last one minute after the men had got fairly on their feet.[67]

Cox's idea was for Rodman's Division to sweep forward, then wheel to the right, in an effort to retain a linkage with Willcox. Fairchild's units, which originally lined up on Willcox's left, should have had a relatively easy time making the connection, but the disjointed nature of the attack, partially due to the undulating terrain, made Cox's plan difficult to effectuate. As so often in the war, the vision of a general unfamiliar with the ground collided with the harsh reality of a battle's inherent unpredictability and chaos.[68]

Robert Bowne, a nineteen-year-old in the 89th New York, recalled the exhilarating moment when the attack opened, followed by the frenzied Confederate resistance. In a letter to a newspaper, the young warrior noted, "We sprang to our feet and with a cheer fixed bayonets and charged upon them, getting into the very outskirts of the village of Sharpsburg, the Rebels stubbornly disputing every inch of ground." On the left of Fairchild's advance, the 89th did not have the benefit of flank protection due to the wide gap opening up between Rodman's two brigades.[69]

The observant Zouave Charles Johnson formed indelible impressions of cannon balls flying in several directions. One seemed headed directly for the teenage warrior. "If it is true that you never see cannon balls except when they are coming toward you, I must have been in a fair way for eternity," he safely wrote in his memoirs. Not long after tracking multiple cannon shots, Johnson was moving forward with the regiment. His own first shot soon came, after observing a line of Confederate skirmishers. With a continued advance, "the fire seemed ten times hotter," Johnson recalled. Soon, he would be wounded in the hip.[70]

The 103rd New York, in the middle of Fairchild's line, was barely over half its potential strength during the charge. Three companies had remained on Hatteras, arriving in Washington on September 17. The charge still proved very costly to the 103rd, which recorded 117 total casualties, including twenty-four killed in action. Some of the soldiers losing their lives were Sgts. Henry Bergmann and Charles Biehl, and Pvts. Charles Brown and Gottlieb Newmann. Capt. William Brandt suffered a severe wound that would cost him his life in early 1863. Conrad Kroell, one of the many natives of Germany in the regiment, took a painful wound to the right groin. He then became a prisoner of war.[71]

Ground over which the men advanced under heavy fire included some level areas between increases of elevation. With losses mounting, the attackers pressed on. One 9th New York memoirist recorded how his regiment attempted to set an example of unyielding courage on the frightful field. After reaching a second rise, with crossfire and more Confederate cannons severely damaging the advance, the New Yorker suggested, "The Zouaves did not blench before this new destruction, but impetuously pressed onward." After a brief rest when another hill was surmounted, Lieutenant Colonel Kimball ordered a distinctive bugle call, attempting to not only rally the bloodied regiment, but to offer "a shout of defiance to the enemy." Knowing many comrades were down, the remaining soldiers gained "additional nerve to avenge them."[72]

Lieutenant Graham had spent his war as a sergeant and then officer in the 9th New York. He led men from Company H as horrendous Confederate fire blasted Fairchild's three regiments. While involved in the intense fratricide along the rolling Maryland landscape, he would be wounded, then return to his regiment for the duration of their service. Decades later, Graham wrote of the "frightful" loss across the regiment's line. When pondering the hellish sounds that afternoon, Graham's mind wandered back to an officer's words regarding one of the most famous engagements in European history. In a letter to Rush Hawkins in 1894, Graham recalled, "We could hear the crash of missiles through the ranks, and strange as it may seem, that sound brought like a flash to my mind a saying of Lannes, when describing the Battle of Austerlitz: 'I could hear the bones crash in my division like glass in a hailstorm.'"[73]

Color companies across the three regiments had a difficult time under withering Confederate fire. As Robert Bowne recalled, "Our colors went down six times, and as often were picked up again." The men made a strong testament to the importance of their battle standards. Bowne continued, "The blood of one of the Sergeants is still on our banner, or rather what used to be called a banner; it does not look much like one now, being all torn to shreds."[74]

The terrifying havoc and ghastly wounds failed to damper the courage of Capt. Adolphe Libaire, Company E, 9th New York. Only twenty-two years old and a native of France, Libaire joined the regiment as an officer in May 1861, proudly serving his adopted land. In the middle of great danger, Libaire demonstrated how a non-native American can serve the country with unrivaled devotion. His Medal of Honor citation reads, "In the advance on the enemy and after his color bearer and the entire color guard of 8 men had been shot down, this officer seized the regimental flag and with conspicuous gallantry carried it to the extreme front, urging the line forward."[75]

Almon Reed, a young private in the 89th, was one of many wounded men to somehow endure Fairchild's charge. In a letter to his parents, he recalled the sheer volume of Confederate fire, especially from artillery. Taking a shot to the calf, Reed fell near the enemy line. With action swirling around him for the next several minutes, Reed recalled, "I was left in the disputed ground in the cross fire." In addition to the danger of being stepped on by a charging friend or foe, Reed added, "I was almost buried with the dirt and small stone that had been thrown upon me by the shot which plowed the earth on every side" after Fairchild's men withdrew from the area.[76]

Part of Capt. David McIntosh's Confederate battery had moved up on the right of Kemper's troops while the New Yorkers advanced. One of the cannoneers remembered Fairchild's line pausing for a moment in a prone position in order to minimize the threat of the double canister rounds McIntosh was shooting. Union batteries were assisting the infantry by firing on the three Confederate guns, which inflicted some casualties. With battery horses falling, McIntosh ordered his men back as the tide of infantry grew too close. Although the guns were abandoned, they were never captured by Rodman's advance. After Fairchild's eastern retrograde, the determined South Carolina gunners were back at work.[77]

Fairchild's bold charge inflicted unspeakable suffering on his decimated regiments. As many in the 9th New York expected, they would set an example for other units to follow. The highly honorable Zouaves sustained 235 casualties during the battle, including forty-five killed in action and more than 170 wounded. Overall, 455 of Fairchild's men were hit during the charge, nearly half his command. One Confederate counted forty Union corpses near his cannons. John Bailey, 9th New Hampshire, praised the Zouaves for their charge and a "fearful loss," adding of the ground being "thickly dotted with their dead."[78]

In his battle report, Lieutenant Colonel Kimball estimated his men moved forward about 800 yards, nearly reaching the Harpers Ferry Road. Kimball witnessed one shell take down eight of his men, with a private losing his head to a cannonball. In addition to the great loss in the ranks, Kimball's horse was killed. With the order to withdraw, the regiment's commanding officer saw men with tears in their eyes "at the necessity which compelled them to leave the field they had so dearly won."[79]

Durell's cannoneers attempted to assist Fairchild. The battery's historian remembered, "This was the hardest fought action and was carried on at the shortest range of any in which the battery had been engaged." Isaiah Sellers, a teenage artillerist, suffered a serious wound during the action when a piece of case shot penetrated one of his lungs.[80]

The men of the 9th New York felt great pride despite the regiment's costly afternoon. "The Ninth surpassed itself, doing gloriously," one Zouave wrote.[81] Yet, the men could not rout the well-posted group of Confederates, two brigades amounting to less than 700 men. Even with the left of the 89th New York overlapping the flank of the 17th Virginia, the Southerners were not overwhelmed. Some Virginians even captured a color of the 103rd New York. The two diminished Confederate brigades finally yielded, but Fairchild's men were unable to seize the Harpers Ferry Road just below Sharpsburg. A catastrophe was beginning to shrivel up Rodman's other brigade farther to the south. When the wounded Almon Reed gazed left that afternoon, he remembered, "As soon as I was down, I could see A. P. Hill's division coming up on our left at right angles to our line."[82]

DISASTER ON THE LEFT

Before crossing the creek at Snavely's Ford, Edward Harland received unfortunate news regarding one of his regiments. The 11th Connecticut, severely damaged earlier in the day, would not participate in the afternoon attack. After sending an aide to call up the 11th Connecticut, the colonel was informed that the staff officer could not locate the unit, which had moved from its earlier position supporting a battery. Harland reported, "I saw nothing more of the Eleventh Regiment Connecticut Volunteers until about sunset, when I met the remnant of the regiment near the bridge."[83] The lack of one regiment, however depleted, deprived Harland of vital manpower as he prepared for the unknowns awaiting his men west of the Antietam.

The 8th Connecticut, under Lt. Col. Hiram Appelman, had moved forward earlier, on the left of Fairchild's advance. Appelman went down with his second wound of the war, the first being at the siege of Fort Macon. He would carry a bullet in his leg for the rest of his life, which ended in 1873 at the age of forty-eight. He was clearly devoted to the Union cause, having served early in the war, volunteering as a private.[84] Maj. John Ward took command of the beleaguered Nutmeg warriors.

Assisting Fairchild, the 8th Connecticut marked "every yard of advance with the blood of fallen men." Horace Williams, a member of Company A, remembered the intensity of the Confederate defense. "It was the hottest fire I was ever under, though I have been several times where we lost over half the company," he sadly wrote. Sgt. Whiting Wilcox, "brave and broad-shouldered," kept fighting even after wounds to the face. Williams saw Wilcox soon receive a fatal wound to the upper chest.[85]

Lt. Marvin Wait was the lone officer killed in the 8th Connecticut. He was only nineteen years old. Enlisting as a private, Wait worked his way up the ranks. During the hellfire of September 17, "Wait refused to go to the rear" after suffering an injury to his right arm. "Seizing his sword with his left hand," according to one source, Wait "encouraged his men to press on, until he fell riddled by bullets." Wait's tombstone, which stands in his hometown of Norwich, notes the teen officer fell "while gallantly leading his men," and, "He died with his young fame about him for a shroud."[86]

On the division's left flank, Harland's remaining two regiments marched into a buzz saw. Confused orders delayed the advance of the rookies of the 16th Connecticut and the 4th Rhode Island, General Rodman's old outfit. During efforts to quell the muddle and bring some order to the moribund attack, Rodman suffered a fatal chest wound. Six weeks after his fortieth birthday, Rodman died at a field hospital on September 30. With the earlier deaths of Stevens and Reno, the Ninth Corps gained the somber honor of being the only such command in all Union armies during the war with three dead generals in the same month due to battle wounds.[87]

As if the leadership vacuum caused by the loss of Rodman could not do enough to make for a chaotic situation, Harland's effort to lessen the calamity proved difficult after his horse went down. Now running around the battlefield, Harland knew severe problems were afoot. The arrival of A. P. Hill's division, marching against the exposed Unionist flank, boded a catastrophe. Harland's exhausting attempt to maintain a viable battle line faced serious problems due to the timely arrival of Hill's veterans. The first Confederate brigade on the scene was Maxcy Gregg's South Carolinians, worthy opponents the Ninth Corps faced at Second Bull Run and Chantilly.[88]

With some of his men likely wearing blue uniforms captured at Harpers Ferry, Hill relentlessly moved his brigades forward to the very tempting target of the Ninth Corps' unprotected southern flank. On lower ground, the 16th Connecticut and 4th Rhode Island entered a cornfield of 40 acres, many men unsuspecting the rout they were about to suffer. From a position 600 feet due west of Harland, the historian of Gregg's unit remembered, "the brigade was carried over one of the many steep hills that characterize that country, and arranged for battle." Even though Hill's attack would devastate Union plans for the afternoon's battle south of Sharpsburg, a difference of opinion prevailed among Gregg's officers about whether they were to begin offensive action immediately. Some regimental leaders suggested Hill preferred a more passive stance. To the misfortune of the New England men marching against Gregg, the Southerners quickly seized the initiative.

One of Gregg's regimental commanders praised his boss for sensing the opportunity to surprise the Ninth Corps. "Immediate and prompt measures were taken by Brigadier-General Gregg to engage the enemy, then so near us," the officer reported. The South Carolinians "commenced a deadly fire upon the enemy in the corn-field" and the surrounding undulating ground.[89]

With Company H of the 16th Connecticut out in an effort to detect any surprises, Harland ordered Col. Francis Beach to change the regiment's facing direction. Implementation of the order did not consistently occur across a command of 900 rookie troops. All might have been fine if the soldiers had had the luxury of time to prepare. As the 16th's regimental historian wrote, "The rustling of cornstalks warned us that the rebels were on us." The 4th Rhode Island had yet to come up on the left, leaving the inexperienced 16th Regiment vulnerable.

In the ensuing difficult few minutes, Colonel Beach worked hard to improve the chances for his men to fight back. With members of his regiment returning fire, Beach tried to stem the tide, although the effort would have proven highly difficult for a more experienced field officer leading well-trained soldiers. As one South Carolina officer reported, "We delivered a destructive volley" into the 16th Connecticut "before our presence seemed to be realized." Harland credited Beach with rallying his large force, even after initially falling back. Nonetheless, a tide of pandemonium overwhelmed the 16th Connecticut as "volley after volley in quick succession was hurled into our midst," the regiment's chronicler wrote. A veteran of the horror recalled how "officers and men fell around us by scores."[90]

Pvt. John Bingham, five weeks away from his eighteenth birthday, was one member of Company H to die in the battle. His remains now rest at First Church Cemetery in his hometown of East Haddam. Two of Bingham's brothers died later in the war, one at the notorious Andersonville prison.[91]

The 4th Rhode Island's advance proved too late to change the dynamics of the situation. Col. William Steere moved his men up near the left of the 16th Connecticut, but the Rhode Island regiment was "subjected to the fire of Rebel batteries, of which it was in full view." Steere still tried

Teenager John Bingham, 16th Connecticut, lost his life at Antietam.

to engender cooperation with the 16th, sending Lt. Col. Joseph Curtis to the right to suggest an uphill attack by the two regiments. Unfortunately, as Curtis reported, "the corn being very thick," he failed to make contact with Colonel Beach or others of authority. Thus, "I returned to tell the colonel that we must depend upon ourselves."[92]

Henry Spooner recalled, "The color bearer carried our flag up the hill to test them and was shot dead." The 4th Rhode Island was "giving and receiving a brisk fire," the captain continued, but lacked help, especially with their left flank unprotected. With hostile missiles arriving from three sides, Spooner judged the order to retreat "imperatively necessary." The Ocean Staters "retired scattering," he added, "to avoid as much as possible their fire." He concluded, "'Tis wonderful that so many escaped."[93]

With hopes rapidly dimming for anything positive for Harland's two left regiments, the Confederates made the most of their target shooting of New Englanders. "The firing during this period," as the historian of Gregg's troops proclaimed, "was as rapid as possible, and on our side unusually accurate." The cornfield, packed with inexperienced Connecticut soldiers who had an exposed flank for a time, became utter mayhem and carnage. The 16th's historian lamented, "The most helpless confusion ensued."[94]

An inability of Hill's brigades to form rapidly likely saved the Union division's seven regiments from even more damage. Nonetheless, the casualties were appalling. In his extensive study of corps strength at Antietam, Ezra Carman estimated Rodman had 2,791 men in action, with a combined loss of 1,077, including 220 killed outright. Although engaged strength and total losses vary by source, about four in every ten men under Rodman at Antietam became a casualty. Only one other federal division, Sedgwick's in the Second Corps, had a higher casualty percentage than Rodman's men on September 17.[95]

The heartbreaking numbers amounted to terrible human suffering. Harland's three Connecticut regiments accounted for more than one-fourth of the Ninth Corps' casualties at Antietam. In the 16th Connecticut, four officers were killed or mortally wounded, not even 10 percent of the rookie regiment's death toll for the short time they marched into the cornfield inferno. The four deceased officers were Capts. John Drake, Newton Manross, and Samuel Brown, as well as Lt. William Horton.

Manross had led a fascinating and impactful life of thirty-seven years. As a youngster, he became interested in books and a wide range of subjects. An 1850 graduate of Yale, Manross would earn a doctor of philosophy degree, then became a professor of chemistry and botany. His fascination with the world led to travels in Mexico and Central America. He died as the commander of Company K in the 16th Regiment.[96]

The modern historian taking the most detailed look at the 16th Connecticut concludes the unit failed to act with courage at Antietam.[97] This is an unfair charge. Simply volunteering in the summer of 1862 when the sheer misery of the war was well known was an act of great valor. Advancing into the unknown that late summer afternoon west of Antietam Creek proved the mettle of men who had not been trained sufficiently for the terror. The men who gave their blood and lives should not be blamed for their rush to war. As suggested previously, placing some new units in the field made sense early in the campaign. The unconscionable lack of flank protection for the Ninth Corps west of the creek explains the disaster, not the conduct of the 16th Connecticut. The cornfield undoubtedly inhibited order in the ranks, and the surprising brawl with truculent and dedicated Southerners did not help matters. Callow warriors about to be overwhelmed deserve no blame for the catastrophe. The most trained Unionist soldiers may have faced quick defeat if placed in the same circumstances.

CONFEDERATES PRESS THE QUESTION

With a boldness typical of Lee's soldiers, the brigades inflicting severe losses on the Ninth Corps after the arrival of Hill's Division attempted to press on. Hill had four more brigades arriving after Gregg's South Carolinians. As they spread out over the high ground along the Harpers Ferry Road, the temptation to throw Burnside's force back across the Antietam undoubtedly grew in the hearts of Confederate generals and privates alike. A Tennessean in James Archer's brigade recalled the Union cannon fire inflicting losses as the men lined up for what was hoped to be a decisive counterattack. Still, the proud Tennessee warrior saw Ninth Corps men fall "by the score before they got out of range."[98]

Harland's overmatched troops retired east while Hugh Ewing started bringing his three Ohio regiments into action. Due to the nature of the ground and the extended length of the Confederate advance, the Ohioans had a difficult mission; simply moving forward as a single line would have failed to protect their flanks sufficiently. As a means to defend against Confederates originally on their left, Col. Carr White of the 12th Ohio reported his men turned somewhat north after their westward advance. The vital movement was performed "under a shower of shell and canister that threatened the destruction of the regiment," White reported. The 12th may have faced great risk that afternoon, but White did not advance his troops nearly as far as the rest of the brigade.[99]

To White's immediate north, the 30th Ohio moved out "right down into the very jaws of death," one veteran noted. The move seemed to puzzle the Confederates for a moment, although the 30th had advanced into a horrible fix. As Maj. George Hildt wrote, "A withering fire was directed upon us from our left flank" after the Ohioans reached a stonewall on ground lower than the attacking Confederates. The Ohioans stood fast, firing a dozen rounds or more before the deteriorating situation showed Hildt the folly of further resistance. Four companies moved slightly to the north in an effort to link up with their comrades in the 23rd Ohio, but the six other companies remained along the wall, absorbing fire from multiple directions. The regiment's open left flank, due to the inadequate advance of the 12th Ohio, became an obvious target for Confederates.

A man in the 30th suggested the old smoothbore muskets the regiment used "were not very dangerous if you aimed at anything." Even if armed with better guns, the men confronted a brutal reality for several minutes. As the regimental historian sadly recalled, "The balls flew like hail through the corn and many a brave soldier fell." Hildt detailed a sad litany of officers and enlisted men wounded along the regiment's front, including Color Sgt. Nathan J. White. The twenty-five-year-old soldier "stood amidst the rain of bullets and defiantly waved the color toward the advancing enemy," Hildt wrote, "when he received a shot in the breast and fell dead." True to his trust to the last, the brave sergeant had won the honor of carrying the colors early in 1862, promoted from the rank of corporal. Admired by the whole regiment, White "was among the last to leave" the regiment's advanced position, leading to the tragic loss of his life. The sergeant was the first of three brothers to die in action in 1862.[100]

On the right of the brigade, the 23rd Ohio, under Maj. James Comly, solidified the ground Fairchild's New Yorkers used for their retreat. Comly reported relatively low casualties compared to South Mountain, but the 23rd's important role still cost the outfit nearly seventy men. Sgt. Joshua Armstrong, only nineteen years old, fell defending the regimental colors early in the advance. "The conduct of the officers and men was beyond praise," Comly suggested.[101]

ROOKIES NO MORE

Although each of Ferrero's four regiments—all held in reserve since the bridge crossing—advanced somewhat to buttress the Union line late in the afternoon, the 35th Massachusetts went forward slightly farther than their more experienced comrades. On the left of Crook's Ohioans, the 35th occupied dangerous ground as the sun quickly dipped in the western sky. General Cox ordered the advance of the 35th Regiment, which had about 800 men in line, larger than most Confederate brigades south of Sharpsburg. The purpose of the movement, one historian suggested, was "to interpose some force to prevent the enemy from falling upon the broken commands striving to retreat across the bridge." Regimental commander Sumner Carruth, "instructed *to hold the position while a man with a musket survived*," was eager to prove his soldiers' worth. The men moved forward after Carruth shouted, "Attention 35th!"

The regiment moved downhill, then found a rail fence of inconsistent quality between the Otto house and the 40-acre cornfield. The desperate moments gave no time to lament the imperfect protection. As cannon blasts and musket balls "swept like a hurricane" toward the 35th's rookie soldiers, Confederate infantry made good use of a stonewall in their late-day efforts against the Ninth Corps. Many in the 21st Massachusetts and the two 51sts had limited ammunition, but the large group in the 35th contributed to lessening the chaos created by the Confederate counter-attack. "Our first fire was a rattling volley," the regimental historian wrote,

"It was a steady roll of musketry." In a letter to his daughter, Fisher Cleaveland wrote of firing about forty rounds before being wounded "in the forefingers of my right hand." Although he would be out of action for a few weeks, Cleaveland happily noted the lack of any broken bones.[102]

Many of Cleaveland's comrades suffered a far worse fate. Capt. Albert Bartlett was killed outright at Antietam, while Capt. Horace Niles and Lt. William Palmer would later die of their injuries. Pvt. David Hinkley died on his forty-second birthday. The fervent patriot had been born in Maine the same year the new state joined the Union as a result of the Missouri Compromise. Alphonso Reed, only twenty-two years old, also lost his life on September 17. His two parents, granted lives seventy years longer than their son's, had more than forty years to grieve. Reed's tombstone denotes he was a "martyr to his country's honor."[103]

Table 3.2 illustrates the killed and wounded of the 35th Massachusetts by company. Many men across the regiment suffered serious wounds requiring months of convalescence. Several would receive discharges for Antietam injuries months after the battle, while others endured extended time in hospitals or back home before dying. Due to his Antietam wound, teenager Charles Dam of Company C lost his life in the last week of 1862 in his hometown of Chelsea. Joseph Ridlon, another Company C man and Chelsea resident but more than twice the age of Dam, spent five months attempting to return to duty, but received a disability discharge in late February 1863.[104]

Among the wounded in the 35th was their commanding officer, Sumner Carruth, the second time in 1862 he would be on a casualty list. Governor Andrew was informed Carruth was "shot through the neck, and obliged to retire." The dangerous injury nearly shredded the officer's jugular vein. The competent leader would not be out of action long.[105]

Capt. William S. King took command of the regiment after Carruth's injury. He set a strong example for the resolute Bay Staters on the firing line. King was soon wounded, shot several times, but took off the regimental colors due to the degree of loss in the 35th's color guard. Full of fight and determination to preserve the Union, King, a forty-three-year-old auctioneer from Roxbury, had plenty of war left in him after convalescence back home. Another captain, Tracy Cheever, doomed to

Table 3.2. Casualties by company in the 35th Massachusetts at Antietam

Company	Killed	Wounded	Missing	Total
A	1	10	0	11
B	5	25	2	32
C	6	22	0	28
D	1	8	0	9
E	3	20	0	23
F	4	7	3	14
G	9	36	2	47
H	3	15	9	27
I	4	14	0	18
K	14	31	0	45
Total	**50**	**188**	**16**	**254**

Source: This data, which has forty more casualties than the number reported in the *Official Records*, was extracted from the regimental roster in Adjutant General, *Massachusetts Soldiers, Sailors, and Marines in the Civil War*, Vol. III (Norwood: Norwood Press, 1932), 647–708.

a wound west of the creek and a long recovery, observed the work of his company while giving the men commands like "Pop away, boys." The 35th's battle line had plenty to shoot at, from enemy infantry along the distant stonewall, others to the left in the 40-acre cornfield, or Southern artillerists who were popping away themselves.[106]

The regimental historian detailed the gripping moments when the 35th Massachusetts endured shocking trials. As the late summer sun dipped lower in the sky, the writer painted scenes of Herculean difficulty and simple terror. "It was work in dead earnest and intensely exciting," he remembered, "there was not time for thought then—load and fire!—load and fire!"[107]

Like their corps comrades throughout the rolling ground west of the Antietam, the 35th Massachusetts retreated east after their brawl with Confederates. Rightfully so, much credit goes to Ferrero's "two 51sts" for seizing Burnside's Bridge in the early afternoon, but Sumner Carruth's 35th Massachusetts sustained significantly more loss on September 17 than the 51st New York and 51st Pennsylvania combined. The two experienced regiments did not contribute much to the afternoon attack with their slight advance on the left of the 35th. According to the adjutant general's roster, the rookies suffered fifty killed in action during the day, half of Ferrero's total across his four regiments. Almost two dozen additional members of the 35th would die of injuries from the fighting at Antietam. The brigade commander made a general statement about "the pride I feel in commanding such valiant soldiers as they have proved themselves," true for each of his four excellent regiments.[108] One wonders why Ferrero failed to specifically note the great sacrifice of the 35th Massachusetts. Counting South Mountain, the rookies suffered the most by far across the entire brigade.

The regimental historian of the 21st Massachusetts witnessed how the rookies "suffered terribly, but gallantly maintained their position." Due to their green status as soldiers, however, the historian lamented how the 35th's "officers and men were not so well skilled in taking all the care of themselves which the proper performance of their duty would permit." All great soldiers lacked experience at one point. Without a doubt, however, like the 17th Michigan at South Mountain, the 35th Massachusetts proved worthy of the Ninth Corps' reputation first demonstrated on the Carolina coast. No one could rightfully call the 35th Massachusetts rookies anymore. George Upton, a Granite Stater in Nagle's Brigade respectfully wrote, "The Mass. 35th was most *awfully* cut to pieces. I never s[aw] such a bloody set of men as they were when they came out of the fight."[109]

Two highly dedicated men from the 35th might confound those historians who question the employment of rookie troops. Marcus Haskell and Frank Whitman exhibited bravery bringing each a Medal of Honor. Teenager Haskell, "wounded and exposed to a heavy fire from the enemy, rescued a badly wounded comrade and succeeded in conveying him to a place of safety." In the overnight period, Whitman joined a small party from the regiment heading west to provide succor to the wounded during a time of bright moonlight. Whitman, one of the last to leave Company G's firing line in the late afternoon, informed some officers of the needs of those injured along the rail fence to the west. Cautioned to not go too far by pickets from the 51st Pennsylvania, Whitman went a greater distance than the officers who contributed to the errand of mercy. Lieutenant Hudson from Ferrero's staff recalled Whitman being "the most fearless of any & went further than any of us." In his citation for the nation's highest military award, Whitman was credited with "saving the lives of several of his comrades at the imminent risk of his own."[110]

Colonel Wild, out of action due to the wound received at South Mountain, showed a great deal of pride in an update to Governor Andrew. "Subjected to slaughtering crossfires," the 35th Massachusetts performed with "a steadfastness that veterans might be proud of." Wild added the regiment's "behavior was admirable throughout," especially considering the difficult ground and the relative lack of support. The proud colonel rightfully judged his men "magnificent" west of the Antietam.[111]

MCCLELLAN'S BROKEN PROMISES

As the Ninth Corps fell back from the intense yet disjointed battle west of the Antietam, Ambrose Burnside must have felt abandoned by his chief. Seven hours earlier, Burnside first read McClellan's 9:10 a.m. attack order. The army commander promised the Ninth Corps would be "supported, and if necessary, on your own line of attack" after the troops "uncovered" the Middle Bridge. Any officer with the order in hand could logically expect fresh supporting infantry in the vicinity of Rohrbach Bridge soon after the Ninth Corps crossed the span.

By early afternoon, McClellan hedged his bets on the battle's outcome in a wire to Washington.

We are in the midst of the most terrible battle of the war—perhaps of history. Thus far it looks well, but I have great odds against me. Hurry up all the troops possible. Our loss has been terrific, but we have gained much ground. I have thrown the mass of the army on the left flank. Burnside is now attacking the right, and I hold my small reserve, consisting of Porter's (Fifth) corps, ready to attack the center as soon as the flank movements are developed.[112]

Like many missives to superiors during his career, McClellan's note included factually true information under a veneer of illogic and falsehood. One may only guess how the modest and respectful Burnside might have reacted by 1 p.m. had he known the southern flank of the army was not yet "developed" to McClellan's satisfaction. With much of his entire corps, about 10,000 muskets, moving across the Antietam, Burnside had without question uncovered the Middle Bridge, the benchmark for McClellan's release of support to the Ninth Corps. The thousands of wounded Unionists who had been assailing Lee's left since dawn also may have wished to let their commander know of the "development" of the army's northern flank. As one Union veteran and historian of the campaign suggested of McClellan, "His orders were not well adapted to the success of his plan."[113]

Porter's infantry west of the Middle Bridge did very little to support Burnside's right flank in the afternoon. Clearly, the Ninth Corps' assault south of town was the only offensive McClellan had in mind.[114] So concerned about the viability of his army north of the Ninth Corps, McClellan assuaged his fears of defeat, rather than satisfy a promise to reinforce Burnside, the best chance for an afternoon victory at Sharpsburg.

Eager to defend Burnside's honor, staff officer Daniel Larned wrote of his discontent. "I find a bitter feeling against McClellan," he stated, "Had Burnside been reinforced at the hill, the whole rebel army could have been annihilated." Defeating an enemy to the point of complete obliteration was far harder than McClellan's critics surmised, although the incomplete nature of the victory rankled. "The disgust and surprise at Porter's men not being sent forward at that time is intense," Larned added. He opined the failure to sufficiently aid the Ninth Corps "seems like the intended sacrifice of Burnside."[115]

By the time the Ninth Corps went from nearly conquering Sharpsburg to falling back toward the bridge, McClellan's gloom prevailed. As Burnside noted in congressional testimony, "I had sent to General McClellan for re-enforcements, but received a message from him that he could not give me any, at the same time directing me to hold the bridge at all hazards." These words align with those witnessing McClellan's abject despondency at this point in the battle. Resorting to histrionics, the army commander informed a staff officer, "Tell General Burnside, that this is the battle of the war; he must hold his ground till dark, at any cost."

Before the officer's departure, McClellan bellowed, "Tell him also that if he cannot hold his ground, then the bridge, to the last man, always the bridge; if the bridge is lost, all is lost."[116]

HOLDING THE BRIDGE

With far less dramatic language, an early evening dispatch from headquarters repeated McClellan's vision. Chief of Staff Marcy informed Burnside, "whatever the result of your affair to-night may be, you must so guard the bridge with infantry and artillery as to make it impossible for the enemy to cross it." Five minutes later, after a report from Signal Corps staff, Burnside was informed of the likelihood of the enemy's withdrawal from Sharpsburg. Marcy pleaded, "Let the general know if the enemy is retreating, and he will push forward with the center."[117]

The time to strike Lee's center and left with the overwhelming, united force of multiple infantry corps and cavalry had passed several hours earlier. The Ninth Corps went from supporting the morning's main attack, to being promised supporting troops after taking the southern bridge, to being given nothing until the Confederates were retreating. Perhaps Burnside rolled his eyes when reading the determination of headquarters to support the Ninth Corps only if Lee was falling back, a far different standard than the promised reinforcements earlier in the day.

At twilight, Ninth Corps troops manned an exhausted and bloodied line which extended for hundreds of yards upstream and downstream of Burnside's (formerly Rohrbach's) Bridge. After suffering more than 1,500 casualties in the afternoon fiasco, the men transcended their utterly demoralizing day, the bloodiest of their existence thus far. Vital tasks remained for the men. As expected from the stalwart patriots filling the ranks of infantry regiments and artillery batteries, the Ninth Corps worked hard.

A teenager in the 23rd Ohio felt the pull of duty from behind the battle line. William McKinley, the second future president of the United States to enroll in the regiment, knew he must excel as a sergeant in the quartermaster's department. McKinley would be memorialized with the idea he never would have been a soldier in a different reality. Yet, at the dawn of the war, McKinley stood as "a lad who could not stay at home when he thought he was needed in the field." After the arduous fights along the Antietam, McKinley's duty made him a bundle of soldierly energy. He would quickly boost his comrades with sustenance.[118]

"As the day wore on," a biographer wrote, "it became evident to the young commissary, who was with the wagons two miles in the rear, that the men must be faint with hunger." After rounding up some stragglers, the nineteen-year-old on a mission headed out "over the intervening fields with two mule teams, drawing wagons loaded with rations and barrels of hot coffee." After the enervation necessary just to find his brigade, Ohioans by the hundreds cheered their guardian angel, Sergeant McKinley.[119]

The 6th New Hampshire, having gained some relative rest in the afternoon compared to their deadly morning on the other side of the bridge, was one of the regiments sent forward on picket during the evening. "When night came," the regimental historian opined, "neither army could claim a complete victory." The sentiment holds much truth, due to the sickening cost— 23,000 killed, wounded, and missing—but also because McClellan gained a limited amount despite his 12,000 casualties. Many, the Union commander included, assumed the battle would resume in the morning.[120]

Granite State comrades near the 6th Regiment spent the eerie overnight period likely flabbergasted by their first month of work for the United States. Col. Enoch Fellows and his 9th New Hampshire had not suffered like the three other new regiments during the Maryland campaign, but many men already had been lost to future service. Having endured extensive Confederate cannon fire from their reserve position during the afternoon, the rookie troops played a role in guarding the bridge bought, advanced from, and held with Ninth Corps blood.[121]

Like several companies across the corps, parts of the 48th Pennsylvania spent the evening and overnight period on a picket line. The darkness granted one Keystone State officer the chance to wax philosophical. What would the next day bring? How many would be dead the next day who had survived the unspeakable burden of September 17? A higher priority beckoned, thanks to another diligent soldier supplying imperative of sustenance. As the officer wrote, his contemplation of weighty questions quickly ended "by the appearance of Quartermaster-Sergeant Wagner, with a fine lot of boiled beef and fresh coffee."[122]

Regardless of his fall from grace in McClellan's eyes, Burnside had been active on the afternoon of September 17. Some soldiers witnessed his energetic efforts to support the attack. Lieutenant Benjamin reported being ordered by Burnside himself to target Confederate big guns and later fire blanks so the noise might make other enemy cannoneers fire on the Regular battery rather than Union infantry. Later in the day, he worked to ensure his men had the chance for a meal, even if many soldiers had a higher priority than nourishment as the most destructive day of their lives came to a close. Early on September 18, Capt. James Wren observed Burnside overseeing the arrival of fresh beef for his soldiers. Many men were so tired they had fallen asleep. Wren noted Burnside's tears after the general observed the extreme fatigue his men felt. "It is rest they want first," Burnside said.[123]

The Ninth Corps certainly deserved a respite. In the eighty-four-hour period beginning at mid-morning on South Mountain through the fight at Antietam, the command sustained more than 3,200 casualties. To veterans who had witnessed death for many months, the toll of their Maryland experience simply horrified. No one had yet witnessed losses of such a scale in so short a time. Due to a tough morning and even costlier afternoon, the Ninth Corps played a crucial role in what remains the bloodiest day in the history of the United States. As a 9th New York diarist accurately suggested of the hell experienced on September 17, 1862, "This day will be a famous one in the history of our country."[124]

COMMAND FAILURES

"Burnside had too much to do the day of the battle for the number of men he had at his command," Henry Spooner logically wrote in a letter near the end of September. Spooner incorrectly states the Ninth Corps was outnumbered on the southern part of the field, even after accounting for A. P. Hill's afternoon arrival. Nonetheless, Spooner was correct to suggest how the corps "was obliged to attack an enemy located in a very strong position."[125]

Regardless of the impressive valor across the Ninth Corps during the battle, several weaknesses marred the performance of army leadership. From Hooker's First Corps to the north down the Antietam to the Ninth Corps' sector of the field, senior officers lacked an understanding of the battle's goals and how bridges, the creek, and topography impacted the troops they would lead. The best example of this problem was George Crook's ignorance of the very existence of a bridge near his initial position. Across the whole day, Ninth Corps movements were fragmented as a result of the poor planning and lack of clarity between headquarters and Burnside's senior officers.

A primary criticism of how the Ninth Corps attacks unfolded was the inability to take advantage of numbers. On either side of the creek, the Ninth Corps was gifted with a heavy preponderance of troops against the defending Confederates. The key reason for the morning attack's inability to strike with overwhelming force was the abject failure to identify suitable fords to minimize casualties and quickly transport the command west of the Antietam. On their own initiative as the attack at the bridge moved forward, Crook's men found a crossing point north of Rohrbach Bridge, but they located the spot too late; the Ohioans were basically a non-factor before and immediately after the ford's discovery.[126]

Clearly, McClellan's staff officers failed to identify crossing points, especially the exact location of downstream Snavely's Ford. Moreover, the obviously inadequate communication between headquarters staff and Ninth Corps leadership hindered the effort to use fords to obviate the need for a costly attack against the bridge. McClellan's heart simply did not seem to be in the matter, even though he wasted his own time on September 16 directing placement of Burnside's troops.

Cox's discussion of the ford identification issue makes much sense.

Burnside's view of the matter was that the front attack at the bridge was so difficult that the passage by the ford below must be an important factor in the task; for if Rodman's division should succeed in getting across there, at the bend in the Antietam, he would come up in rear of Toombs, and either the whole of D. R. Jones's division would have to advance to meet Rodman, or Toombs must abandon the bridge.[127]

Burnside and Cox both knew a bridge assault would waste lives and time, yet they did not proactively work with McClellan's staff to the degree necessary to find proper fords. A major effort to carry Snavely's Ford early in the day offered the best opportunity for the Ninth Corps to overwhelm Confederates south of town and avoid extensive bloodshed in taking the bridge. The ford assault earlier in the day constitutes one of the great what-ifs of the battle of Antietam. At around 9 a.m., Lee called for a division to augment the Confederate line north of town. If Rodman attacked the ford at around 7 a.m., Walker's men would have stayed on the southern portion of the field, fulfilling McClellan's supposed goal of having the Ninth Corps be a diversion in favor of the attack from the north.

If the ford came into Rodman's possession hours earlier, Benning's small band protecting the bridge was doomed to capture. No general seemed to grasp the advantage of an early attack at Snavely's Ford. Perhaps Burnside and Cox's imperative view of the ford mission in reports and postwar writings is not hindsight. However, the failure to possess the ford earlier cost the Ninth Corps dearly.[128]

In his respected and credible postwar writings, Jacob Cox provides sound justifications for his actions leading the Ninth Corps on September 17. Any historian should understand the grounds for the Ohioan's diffident demeanor at Antietam. Burnside cast a long shadow. He clearly should have retaken the mantel of Ninth Corps commander after the dissolution of his wing command two days earlier. Cox was right to note the difficulty of an arrangement where Burnside still viewed himself as a wing commander, even with no other troops to command but the Ninth Corps. Nonetheless, Cox was the Ninth Corps leader during the battle. History must conclude Cox had some responsibility for the corps' severe shortfalls at Antietam, regardless of the objectionable command arrangement, how confusing the fighting became, or myriad other problems the soldiers faced on the army's left flank.

After accounting for the poor planning inhibiting the corps' work to conquer the bridge, the losses west of the bridge in the afternoon far exceeded the gallant morning effort to the east. There were several problems with how the generals organized and superintended the fight west of the Antietam. Colonel Fairchild had extremely reasonable grounds for complaint about a lack of support. His glorious charge had no chance to make a severe dent. As the colonel suggested, "The large force advancing on our left flank compelled us to retire from the position, which we could have held had we been properly supported."[129]

Isaac Rodman had his worst day in the war for reasons other than his mortal wounding. The general simply did not manage his troops well after they finally conquered Snavely's Ford. A modern historian suggests division command was beyond Rodman's talents, an excessively harsh judgment.[130] Rodman was a competent officer worthy of his station. Nonetheless, the Third Division essentially attacked in three waves, all unable to support each other sufficiently. In between Fairchild and Harland's two other regiments, the 8th Connecticut's lonely venture toward the Harpers Ferry Road epitomized the overall command failure impacting the army's left wing—limitations of men senior to Rodman. Helping force McIntosh's Battery back was all the 8th Connecticut could accomplish as a result of their poor position. The regiment's movements lacked a defined purpose linked to the advance of supporting troops.

On the corps' right flank, one can also wonder why the First Division could not make more of the opportunity to conquer Sharpsburg. Willcox's experienced regiments moved out valiantly. A significant missed opportunity was the paltry effort by Regular skirmishers and inconclusive cannon fire the Fifth Corps managed to Willcox's north. The possibility of a joint effort with Porter seems evident from an afternoon dispatch Cox sent to the Fifth Corps commander. As his own divisions were crossing the bridge, Cox informed Porter of efforts to strike Confederate infantry south of town with artillery. "We are advancing the Ninth Corps to Sharpsburg," Cox added, indirectly pleading for the help of the veteran troops Porter commanded. As the Ohioan suggested, "It was manifest the corps would, without re-enforcements, be unable to reach the village of Sharpsburg, since the movement could not be made to the right whilst the enemy exhibited such force in front of the extreme left."[131]

Without any help from other parts of the army, Cox made a sensible decision to recall the right of the attack as Hill's division started to roll up the southern flank. Willcox himself faltered during the assault. The undulating ground wreaked havoc on the maintenance of a solid, unyielding line of assaulting infantry. Willcox reported a lack of ammunition shortly before the division's retreat, but something seems missing from Willcox's leadership at Antietam. His eight regiments only sustained 337 casualties during the entire battle, and some of those were inflicted near the bridge before the two brigades advanced. Willcox did not achieve what he claimed in a letter to his wife on September 25, a "complete victory."[132] The division's commitment to the fight somehow seems insufficient. The eight regiments of the First Division only averaged forty-three casualties on the day, even though they were central to the planned conquest of Sharpsburg.

Poor results for the Kanawha Division west of the bridge ranks as one of the overlooked mysteries of the fight. As support for Willcox, Crook clearly did not do enough. The Ohioans might have stabilized Willcox's left after the withdrawal of Fairchild's New Yorkers. Crook's memoirs note the general's lack of faith in the attack plan. He even had the temerity to question Cox's vision for the battle. One wonders if Crook's heart simply was not in the fight this day. He makes several negative comments about his superiors during the Antietam campaign. An obvious lack of communication about his brigade's role hampered the chance for the excellent troops in the three regiments to contribute sufficiently.[133] Perhaps Crook felt his men were not going to be able to make much of an attack up the steep hills southwest of Sharpsburg. Without question, Crook failed west of Antietam Creek.

Crook's Ohio comrade, Col. Hugh Ewing, also did not have a good day leading a brigade. From McClellan down the chain of command to Ewing, no senior officer seemed concerned about the danger to the corps' left flank. Pushing uphill to Sharpsburg flirted with disaster without support on Rodman's left, something Ewing was perfectly situated to do. Instead of advancing on Harland's left, the Ohioans served as a reserve for the corps' southern wing. This was not necessary, since Sturgis's entire division was positioned to provide a backup to more advanced troops. Waiting to get into the fight until Harland was already defeated, Ewing contributed little to making the most of the moment, except for ensuring A. P. Hill's charging horde did not roll up Burnside's entire command.[134]

A significant Union cavalry presence rested around Middle Bridge most of September 17. At least a brigade of these troopers should have been on Rodman's left before the afternoon advance. Horsemen scouting the army's south flank could have made the difference by warning of Hill's approach and engaging the lead elements of the five brigades that had moved up from Harpers Ferry. Without the wallop Hill delivered to the Ninth Corps, Fairchild's New Yorkers and Willcox's entire division may have planted regimental and national colors in the center of Sharpsburg before dark.

With immense grit and patriotic drive, the Ninth Corps performed extremely difficult tasks in mid-September 1862. Fighting two major battles, the success at South Mountain and the bitter stalemate along Antietam Creek, the corps' infantrymen and cannoneers exhibited intrepid qualities, even with the numerous questionable decisions of their senior officers. Citizens of the North took notice. Colonel Withington of the 17th Michigan received a laudatory letter from a Wolverine State resident who heard about the sanguinary day of September 17. "It has given me great satisfaction to hear of the noble conduct of your Regiment in two of the most bloody and severe contests of this dreadful and unnatural war," the citizen wrote. With a lament, the writer continued, "I did not expect however that the stamina of the men would be so soon put to so severe a test." Turning positive about the outfit's budding legacy as a group of great soldiers, he added, "The shock has come and to their undying honor, they have met and sustained it with the heroic valor of veterans."[135]

PART FOUR

Autumn of Transition

*"Some have had no Blankets or overcoats since
the Battles in Maryland."*
–CAPT. BENJAMIN PRATT, 35TH MASSACHUSETTS

"OUR HEARTS WERE SORE AND SAD"

THE RELATIVELY QUIET SIX WEEKS the NINTH CORPS EXPERIENCED after the battle of Antietam began on the morning of September 18 with intense picket fire west of Burnside's Bridge. "At daylight," a 21st Massachusetts man wrote, "with stiff backs and limbs we reformed our line." He continued with the disappointment at seeing the Confederates clinging to their bloodied positions of the night before.[1]

Ralph Ely, 8th Michigan, wrote of the firing lasting all day, but a major engagement did not flare up. Another captain, James Wren of the 48th Pennsylvania, reported some intense rounds of firing as the warring American armies kept each other honest from opposite sides of a corn-field. Back on the east side of the creek, Durell's Battery gave both men and horses some good rest, with "no incident of note occurring." In the advanced line of the 21st Massachusetts, the day passed with "uncertain waiting" and "without anything of importance transpiring."[2]

Not all regiments manned the picket line across the whole day. The calm daylight illuminated a harsh reality for the rookies of the 35th Massachusetts. With well over 200 comrades wounded on the 17th, the Bay State soldiers faced deeply emotional hours and the unknowns of the new day. The regimental historian noted the small number of officers present.

"Only Captains Andrews and Lathrop and some half dozen lieutenants remained for duty with the regiment that morning." The three most damaged companies "each represented only by a small group of men," added to the pall near the Antietam.[3]

Melancholy filled many hearts in Harland's Brigade. The four New England regiments suffered well over 600 casualties, including 133 killed in action. Allowed to cross the Antietam on the evening of the 17th, the men returned to the 40-acre cornfield on the 18th. A memoirist in the 4th Rhode Island witnessed wretched sights. Dead Unionists had been stripped of clothes and shoes, items the Confederates severely needed. "We missed many cheerful faces from around the camp-fire," he wrote, "and our hearts were sore and sad for many a day after."[4]

Richard Morris, 9th New York, wrote of the tired nature of the men and the stressful hours of September 18. Morris noted, "I was under heavy fire four times on the 17th and was providentially preserved without a scratch and am ready for more." Still, he preferred slumber, "our days and nights having been confounded so much lately."[5]

Morris's wish for relaxation seemed destined to come true with McClellan in command. The general's messages to Halleck on the morning of September 18 offered this terse thought, "The battle will probably be renewed to-day." Instead of a promise to advance, McClellan asked for more troops. Halleck may not have been impressed with the dearth of details and the absence of a drive to win a larger victory, but the general-in-chief did request additional troops be sent to McClellan from Baltimore. He also asked the head of the Pennsylvania militia to give McClellan "all aid in your power."[6]

The very ferocity of the day reaffirmed McClellan's cautious approach to war. Regarding his decision to not renew the offensive, McClellan wrote of his study of the Confederate army and Lee's position. He also completed "a full and careful survey of the situation and condition of our army." McClellan then "concluded that success of an attack on the 18th was not certain."[7] The army did not assault the weakened Confederate line because McClellan could not guarantee victory beforehand. Such a banal determination deserves no detailed analysis because the lack of a perfect probability of victory has bedeviled military leaders throughout history. McClellan was too weak a leader to trust with winning the war.

Some men speculated why the attack did not resume. The lack of clarity led Oscar Robinson, 9th New Hampshire, to accurately inform his diary, "We have gained some ground but know not whether we have gained a decisive victory." A member of the 30th Ohio felt optimistic, even with the unspeakable horror of the previous day. "The troops were confident of victory, and awaited with impatience the renewal of the battle." The Highlanders' historian added, "The enemy could be distinctly seen occupying the position they held late the previous afternoon." Several in the regiment, "wondered why McClellan did not at once press forward and secure the fruits of the victory. . . . All day long we remained in a state of inactivity."[8]

Reasonable arguments for resting the army existed. Some men had not eaten much since South Mountain. Supplying the array of goods needed severely strained Union logistics. McClellan's lack of faith in many subordinates, including renewed doubts about Burnside, hampered any effort to make the army successful. Overall, the army retained faith in McClellan, but even admirers began to doubt his resolution to see the war through.[9]

Outright McClellan critics made their thoughts known in letters and diaries, with some Ninth Corps men flabbergasted by McClellan's lethargy. A soldier in the 9th New York penned frustrating words about the near rout of the Confederates on the 17th, with McClellan's irresolution lengthening the war. "Vigorous use of the bayonet would have routed or captured the whole force, and their army must have been destroyed," the Zouave suggested of the Confederate condition at the end of battle. Instead, "the cowardice or treachery of the commanding general permitted them to escape, and, so to speak, furnished the crutches with which they were to attempt a decent retreat."[10]

Lee soon used the metaphorical crutches McClellan provided. The Confederates withdrew from Sharpsburg by early morning on September 19. Like Orlando Willcox's letter to his wife, McClellan incorrectly informed Halleck, "We may safely claim a complete victory." Two hours later, McClellan added, "The enemy is driven back into Virginia.

Maryland and Pennsylvania are now safe."[11] There would be no continuation of the battle of Antietam.

In two letters shortly after the war's bloodiest day, George Rowell, Company C, 6th New Hampshire, expressed his weariness, as well as the possibility of additional fighting. He suggested the Confederates had been whipped "all to pieces." The Unionists had "kild a lot of rebels." Fellow Granite Stater James Lathe wrote similar ideas. With less than a week of combat under his belt, he declared, "I have seen all of war I ever wish to." Lathe continued, "The thing is indescribable." Yet, "I have no doubt that the bullets from my rifle have made some aches and pains."[12]

In late September, William Lusk, 79th New York, wrote a letter about his disappointment. Lusk illustrated why so many soldiers respected McClellan, even those seeing their chief's obvious limitations.

Ten days have gone since the battle, and yet there are no signs of bustle and busy preparation aiming at the destruction of our dirty foes on the other side of the river. . . . McClellan is cautious, and, without intending any disparagement, does not possess that lightning rapidity which characterized the "old Napoleon." Yet we of the Army are jealous of McClellan's reputation and fear the possibility of losing him . . . we believe him simply the best general we have got, and do not trust the judgment of old Abe in the selection of a new one.[13]

HEALERS AT WORK

Jabez Smith, 35th Massachusetts, missed the fight at Antietam due to sickness. He did receive news from the regiment, mainly about the large number of wounded men. There was pride and anguish in two short sentences he wrote to his parents on September 20. "We have made the Rebels skedaddle," he noted, "But with heavy loss."[14] Without question, the medical burden from the battle would be immense.

Mental and physical misery prevailed for the doctors and assistants in the hospitals around Sharpsburg. Dr. Dimon of the 2nd Maryland faithfully performed exhausting work from the start of the battle, followed by many days saving and healing lives. Starting at what was likely the J. F. Miller Farm, Dimon's efforts contributed to easing the suffering of many in the Ninth Corps. He reported the presence of a large contingent from the 35th Massachusetts.[15]

Compassionate comrades brought relief to some casualties. Still, as the historian of the battered 16th Connecticut found, "some of the badly wounded did not have any attention for several days." About twenty-five of the regiment's injured filled one barn, with "cries, groans, and entreaties" the only sounds. The strong spirits of some doomed to die brought solace to many, including those physically uninjured. Capt. Frederick Barber, Company H, had his right leg amputated, but retained a positive outlook. The regiment's historian added, "Barber lay in about the center of a barn, quiet, happy, and contented with his lot," as wounded comrades filled the floor around him.[16]

Members of the 9th New York returned to west of the Antietam on September 18, with some detailed to bury the dead. A hard campaign with unreliable food sources made immediate convalescence difficult for some injured men. As a Zouave memoirist suggested, "Many of the wounded were suffering far more than they otherwise would on account of their exhausted condition when they entered the fight, and many, no doubt, were dying for the same reason." As Harvey Henderson of the 89th New York lamented in his diary on the 19th, "What a terrible thing war is."[17]

Bullets inflicted death on some of those wishing to diminish human anguish in an enemy. Sgt. Alexander Prince, 48th Pennsylvania, fell while attempting to provide water to a wounded Confederate. An officer in the 48th recalled the fatal shot to the heart of the compassionate Prince. The officer continued, in the regimental history published in 1895, "His death-cry as he leaped in the air, and fell to rise no more, is still heard in the ear of imagination." The following day, James Wren, Prince's company commander, gave the sergeant's personal effects to his brother, who served in an artillery battery.[18]

On the morning of September 18, Dr. Dimon crossed the Antietam with supplies for his Marylanders. A keg of whiskey, which Dimon claimed was ammunition when General Nagle made an inquiry, was set up on a tree stump near the 2nd Maryland's skirmish line. As Dimon poured healthy doses, he gave the men an update on their wounded comrades east of the creek.

Dr. Dimon later provided Burnside an update about the skirmish line. Then, the surgeon returned to his charges. Dimon counted 147 wounded soldiers spread across three buildings in the days after the battle. Disgusted with some men failing to properly perform assigned hospital duties, Dimon ordered the culpable tied to an apple tree by the thumbs, with the guilty soldiers' toes barely touching the ground. The surgeon reported the positive effect of the punishment: smoother operation of his makeshift hospital.[19]

"YOUR PRECIOUS LIFE"

The sad yet inspirational story of twenty-five-year-old Robert Hale Ives, Jr., illustrates the human misery war inflicts. Ives, a youngster of much promise and privilege, started life in Providence, Rhode Island. His formative years were blessed by a deeply loving mother and father, who provided "every advantage which parental wisdom and care could supply," and "influences the most favorable for inspiring generous sentiments and developing high qualities of character." Graduating at the age of twenty from Brown University in his native city, Ives then traveled in Europe to expand his horizons. At the outbreak of civil war, personal and business duties retained Ives at home. He longed for being in the field, however. As the catastrophe in Virginia unfolded during the summer of 1862, Ives successfully attempted to become part of the army. His lieutenant's commission on General Rodman's staff, dated August 19, prompted Ives to prepare for the success he hoped for in the Union army. Although they had recently lost a daughter, Ives's parents approved of Robert's decision to take to the field.[20]

With a diligence typical of his life thus far, Ives quickly prepared for his trip to join Rodman's division. Writing a friend living in New York City, the new officer humorously asked for some important help. The August 23 letter began, "You know I am always bothering you one way or another without apologizing." Ives requested his friend visit the Colt factory at 240 Broadway to purchase pistol cartridges. "I think they come in packages of 12 cartridges each," Ives added.[21]

His trip south began on September 1. During his train ride to destiny, Ives likely passed through the same storm drenching Ninth Corps men at Chantilly. His diary's most notable wording for the first day of the trip was "very stormy night." Spending nearly half of September 2 in New York City, Ives departed for Washington at 6 p.m., arriving in the post–Bull Run chaos of the following morning. Heading to Willard's Hotel, Ives did not know of Rodman's whereabouts. Meeting the general on September 5, Ives was ordered to be at headquarters the following morning at 10 a.m.[22]

Ives advanced with the Third Division to Antietam Creek and beyond, facing unrivaled danger along Rodman's disjointed and unprepared line west of Burnside's Bridge on the afternoon of the 17th. The young officer assisted with the posting of the 4th Rhode Island, the southernmost regiment in the Army of the Potomac.[23] Disaster then struck the Ninth Corps in general and Ives personally.

At about the same time as Rodman's mortal injury, Ives was also hit, as was his doomed horse. The lieutenant's wound, which tore away skin and muscle around his right knee without breaking bones, must have caused waves of gripping pain. Even with an intact skeleton, Ives faced grave danger from infection of the large injury. The exact timing of his rescue on the field went unrecorded, but he likely did not receive medical care until September 18.[24]

With a strong will, Ives clung to life. News from Robert Hale Ives, Sr., who went to Maryland to care for his son, led another family member to write Lieutenant Ives with hope for a recovery from the horrible, agonizing wound. The September 23 letter noted,

> I have had such terrible visions of your sufferings. We knew the extreme danger which you had been in. Your horse shot under you. It is truly wonderful that you should have been in the severest battle of the whole war and yourself in the hardest fighting. . . . If I were sure that you were not suffering greatly, I should feel that the wound that brings you back is almost a blessing. Very thankful we do feel to the God of mercy who has preserved your precious life in so great peril.[25]

The Rhode Islander likely did not live to read his kinsman's letter. He died on September 27 at a Hagerstown hospital. One historian suggested, "His death was serene and beautiful; the fitting close of a young life modestly and religiously, yet bravely and heroically, given up for his country in the hour of her calamity and her greatest need." A cousin of the fallen Rhode Island officer summed up the family's feeling of utter loss. "It is overwhelming to us all," Anne Woods wrote, and "to me a profound grief—He was a true friend & one of the most attractive young men I ever saw. All hope, all crushed at a blow!!"[26]

Ives's memorialists articulated a plethora of praise and remembrance. A Brown University fraternity labeled Ives "one of its most highly esteemed graduate members." Another important organization to Ives, which had provided him riding experience and knowledge of military life back home, established "as a mark of respect to the memory of the deceased, the Corps will wear the usual badge of mourning for Thirty days."

One individual observed how the intelligent and wealthy Ives never attempted to flaunt his good name or notable means. Ives lived an unpretentious and happy life. As the memorialist recalled,

His tastes were quiet & refined, & his habits most strikingly domestic. It may be that his affections were naturally somewhat exclusive; but it seemed to me that his apparent reserve of manner & retiredness of habit, arose rather from a want of due appreciation of himself. His modesty was most genuine. Perhaps there is no trait in his character which his friends so touchingly & constantly recall as this.

Another tribute believed Ives's example would motivate others to sign up for the defense of the Union, even at great personal cost.

Only a month elapsed from the day of his departure from home to the day of his funeral. So brief was his campaign, so sad was its close. Yet not wholly sad. For his example will not be lost. It will call, it does call today, to young men of wealth and culture and refinement to be willing to make the same sacrifice which he has made. Few have so much to sacrifice as he. None can offer what they have more modestly or more generously.[27]

Like so many soldiers on both sides, a deep religious faith comforted Ives during his time on earth. He had been a strong supporter of St. Stephen's Church in Providence, the location of his memorial service before internment at the North Burial Ground. The completion of the church's new building had occurred earlier in the year. Ives had assisted with raising funds for its construction, where he was a "habitual worshipper and a devout communicant." As Ives neared death, he offered $5,000 for the retirement of debt the church accumulated during the construction process. The remaining $15,000 was quickly raised, with much of it undoubtedly given out of respect to the departed Union officer. Fittingly, a memorial window to Ives at St. Stephen's praises "his piety and worth, and benefactions for religion and his death for his country."[28]

"WE MUST HAVE SHOOK THE UNIVERSE"

Numbers quickly grew in the weeks following the battle of Antietam, with new regiments a key to the puzzle. Unlike the four rookie outfits experiencing the carnage of South Mountain and Antietam, some other new Ninth Corps units raised over the summer did not arrive before September's bloody toll.

The 36th Massachusetts reported for duty with the Ninth Corps after heading south from the Bay State on September 2. With a quota of 15,000 recruits, Massachusetts had quickly moved forward to fill necessary musters. The men were not far behind the Ninth Corps when the march in Maryland began, but they were too late to participate in South Mountain or Antietam.[29]

William Draper, a new captain of Company E, caught up to the 36th Massachusetts on their march in Maryland. He was impressed with the men, but also witnessed the need for further training. Observing the rookies soon after his arrival in camp on September 19, Draper remembered, "They had had almost no drill, and, with exceptions, did not know the manual of arms." Draper soon noted how Company B developed a reputation for being the best drilled part of the 36th, but he intended to make his own company the model for the regiment.[30]

The 20th Michigan also narrowly missed the horrible battles in Maryland. In the opening months of the war, Col. Byron Cutcheon, an educator-turned-officer, had taught some students rudimentary military maneuvers, even if the "soldiers" lacked equipment. In his autobiography, Cutcheon recalled, "I had organized the young men of my department in the school into a company and had drilled them in foot movements, though we had no arms." With requests from Washington for more regiments blaring loudly across the North over the summer, Cutcheon added, "It sounded the call of duty to me. I felt that the time for me to go had come."

Four of the 20th's ten companies originated in Washtenaw County, including the cities of Ypsilanti and Ann Arbor. Claudius Grant, thirty-one, graduate of the University of Michigan and principal of Ann Arbor's high school, organized Company D. Like Cutcheon, Grant's interaction with students on a daily basis proved vital to the state's recruitment efforts. As the regimental history noted of Grant, "His connection with the high school and the university made him familiar with many young men of a class very suitable for good leaders and non-commissioned officers."

Leaving Michigan in early September, the regiment arrived in Frederick by September 20, joining the Ninth Corps at Sharpsburg two days later. The next day, Grant recorded a walk over the battlefield. "Saw the graves of some poor fellows," he wrote. As they settled down into camp, the Michigan men improvised shelter with the use of cornstalks, because many of them did not have tents.[31]

Similar to other new regiments arriving after Antietam, the 10th and 11th New Hampshire provided the Ninth Corps with fresh troops from a state already represented in the command. Col. Walter Harriman took charge of the 11th Regiment, which would become a permanent Ninth Corps unit after time in Washington's defenses. Like their comrades in the 10th New Hampshire, Harriman's soldiers marched out of the national capital in time to reach the Ninth Corps' Maryland camps by early October.

Harriman had used riveting patriotic speeches in his effort to attract recruits, with the ranks filling rapidly. As the regimental history noted, "In eight days his regiment was filled to overflowing." By Thursday, September 11, the men were ready for their train ride to Washington, with

Harriman performing a marriage ceremony for one of his lieutenants, Joseph B. Clark, before departure.[32]

Crowds greeted the new soldiers through most of the major cities they traversed on their way to destiny in the army. Deeply memorable scenes awaited the 11th during their stop in Philadelphia. Capt. Sewell Tilton, leading Company B, wrote of a reception "of the most generous and enthusiastic character" from residents of the nation's first capital city. What he termed "a bountiful collation" awaited, thanks solely to "the liberality of the private citizens." Soloman Dodge of the regiment added, "The people of that city are the most enterprising and patriotic people that I ever saw."[33]

While waiting for the advance to the front, Sgt. Charlie Paige attended to a problem his spouse Millie was having back home. She clearly missed her husband, with Charlie writing on September 28, "I hope and pray that you may try each day to rely on Christ for support and comfort." After the march into Maryland, he felt the need to add, "I feel sad to think that you feel so bad and cry over your sadness. I wish you was as cheerful and resigned as I."[34]

Formed after an order from the state's governor in May 1862, the 7th Rhode Island took some time to organize, finally mustering in on September 6. Riding a steamer to New York City, the regiment boarded another ship for the continued journey south, where a boisterous greeting from Philadelphia's citizenry made a grand impression. After a less grateful crowd in Baltimore, the Rhode Islanders pressed forward to Washington. By the end of the month, the regiment went north again, through Baltimore in route to their assignment with the Ninth Corps.[35]

Col. Zenas Bliss took charge of the rookie Rhode Islanders. He graduated forty-first out of forty-six cadets in the West Point Class of 1854. Although his tenure at the Military Academy lacked overall distinction, Bliss would prove to be a great American soldier. In the eight years from graduation to leadership of the 7th Rhode Island, Bliss served at several forts in Texas. With the arrival of war in April 1861, Bliss left Fort Quitman for a march to San Antonio, where he was taken prisoner as a captain of the 8th U.S. Infantry. He spent nearly eleven months in captivity before being exchanged. For a few months, he led the 10th Rhode

Island, which saw no action. Bliss became colonel of the 7th Regiment on August 21, 1862.[36]

Across the entire Army of the Potomac, twenty recently organized regiments, totaling more than 18,000 soldiers, were added by early autumn.[37] These new units did much to augment troop strength, even with their inexperience. Great sacrifice in the rookie regiments of the Ninth Corps earlier in September proved untested troops could excel.

By early October, Burnside gained oversight of three corps—the Second and Twelfth in addition to the Ninth—with his headquarters at Harpers Ferry. Orlando Willcox became the head of the Ninth Corps. With a time of relative inactivity, wives of many senior officers visited. The new 36th Massachusetts likely gained respect from Willcox when the unit's glee club sang for Mrs. Willcox shortly after her arrival in camp, near the time her husband officially became corps commander.[38]

Col. Daniel Leasure, recovered from his Second Manassas wound, became First Division commander after Willcox's elevation. The division gained a third brigade, necessitated by troop losses and the addition of two of the rookie regiments. Lt. Col. David Morrison would command the First Brigade for much of October. In addition to his Highlanders from New York, the brigade included the 28th Massachusetts, as well as the 17th and 20th Michigan.[39]

The 8th Michigan remained a part of the Second Brigade, with Colonel Fenton back in command. He had returned to the army a week after the battle of Antietam, having spent time on recruiting duty. The regiment gained about thirty new members as a result of Fenton's work. For the early autumn, the brigade also included the 46th New York and 50th Pennsylvania. Into October, the men were assigned to picket duty along the Potomac near Point of Rocks, Maryland. The historian of the 50th recorded the pleasing food available. "We feasted on fresh fish," he wrote, "which were caught in great abundance."[40]

Thomas Welsh held the command of the new Third Brigade for part of October. In addition to the rookies of the 36th Massachusetts, the brigade included the battle-hardened 45th and 100th Pennsylvania. The historian of the 36th noted how the new Bay State warriors were "warmly attached" to their brigade comrades from their late September arrival onward.[41]

In the Second Division, Nagle and Ferrero led their brigades into autumn, with Colonel Bliss and the 7th Rhode Island joining Nagle, and the 11th New Hampshire becoming the fifth regiment under Ferrero. The new troops could learn much from the eight experienced and devoted veteran regiments in the division, still led by Sam Sturgis.

Due to the death of General Rodman, respected and competent John Parke took temporary command of his former division, but soon returned to his staff assignment. Brig. Gen. George Getty then became the new division commander. Getty led the brigades of Fairchild and Harland, with the 10th New Hampshire added to the former, and the new 21st Connecticut joining the other Nutmeg State units and the 4th Rhode Island under Harland.[42]

Jacob Cox's Ohioans headed back to western Virginia. The great courage and determination of Cox's six regiments in Maryland gave an exemplary illustration of Buckeye grit. Even with an uneven performance across the division's leadership, the two months the Ohioans spent in Virginia and Maryland provided a significant boost to the careers of the division's senior officers. Based on Burnside's endorsement, McClellan heartily recommended a major generalship for Cox, a promotion that quickly happened. A member of the 30th Ohio recalled the Antietam campaign's positive impact on senior officers. "That division started into the campaign with one Brigadier-General and six Colonels," he wrote, "and came out with one Major-General and four Brigadier-Generals." He concluded, "Some of the boys facetiously remarked that we must have shook the universe, to make the stars fall so thick."[43]

THE NINTH CORPS IN REPOSE

"I feel weak but am not sick," Jabez Smith of the 35th Massachusetts informed his parents on September 21. Many of his comrades across the Ninth Corps could write the same line shortly after Antietam. Along with most of the army, Smith and the rest of Burnside's Boys were not pressed into hard service, although marching was necessary to reach new campsites.[44]

Respected for his competence and hard work, John Parke held a variety of senior positions in the Ninth Corps. LIBRARY OF CONGRESS

After the undesirable duty of picket firing and burying the dead at Sharpsburg, the Ninth Corps went on a short journey, ending near the confluence of Antietam Creek and the Potomac River. The temporary camp, around the Antietam Iron Works, sat nearly 3 miles southwest of Burnside's Bridge. Drills and picket duty prevailed in the new location. Full of idealism as a new volunteer, a man in the 36th Massachusetts enjoyed the spot. "The tents of the men were soon up," he wrote, "and the camp-fires lighted. A more brilliant scene can hardly be imagined than that presented by these fields around us, illuminated by innumerable camp-fires."[45]

A New Hampshire rookie penned a letter home five days after the battle of Antietam. Destined to die of disease in a Washington hospital before the end of the year, Charles Wood, Company K of the 9th Regiment, discussed a variety of experiences known to troops in the field. "When we are lying in camp," Wood suggested, "it is the laziest life you can ever find if it happens so that you can get enough to eat which we do most of the time." While marching, however, especially for an extended period, life "begins to be rather hard." Wood continued, "It has been so hard that some that we thought was the toughest at home has been left behind." Then, when under fire,

> *you folks at home cant imagine anything about the risk a fellow hast to run in facing the cannons and muskets of these Rebs. I thought when I was at home I should like the idea of being in one fight, I have been in two and can truly say that I am perfectly satisfied.*[46]

Effects from wounds remained a primary aspect of many soldiers' lives. Capt. William Bolton, 51st Pennsylvania, had suffered a shot to the face at Antietam, breaking jaw bones and costing him some teeth. Bolton had a difficult recuperation, which included months back home. His journal includes daily references to his level of pain, which varied quite a bit within the same week. Frequent letters from members of the regiment did much to lift Bolton's mood.[47]

Late in the month, Rhode Islander Henry Spooner wrote his father about bullets that hit inanimate objects. His coat had holes from

Confederate fire, and Spooner seemed quite proud. He intended to send the coat home, requesting his parents safeguard the garment, "a trophy of the battle of Sharpsburg." Later in the year, he referred to the coat as "a relic" from the horrible fight. Spooner also noted a fellow officer's decision to mail home a sword damaged along the Antietam. Mr. Spooner read, "You had better get a sight of it if you want to appreciate the force of a minie ball."[48]

President Lincoln visited the army in early October, reviewing the Ninth Corps on the 3rd. Lincoln talked grand strategy with McClellan and toured the Antietam battlefield. Ninth Corps men had generally positive views of Lincoln's visit. The historian of the 21st Massachusetts called Lincoln's review, "One of the great incidents of our stay" in Maryland, while the 9th New Hampshire's chronicler recalled "the inspiring effect" of Lincoln's visit. Another wrote about the twenty-one-gun salute greeting Lincoln and the rousing cheers from soldiers across the Ninth Corps.

Lincoln's physical presence made an impression on many. David Lane of the 17th Michigan was pleasantly surprised during the commander in chief's review. "My curiosity was gratified by seeing a 'live President,'" Lane noted, "and above all, 'Old Abe.'" Pictures failed to portray the true dignity of the man, the soldier continued, "He looks much better than the likenesses we see of him—younger, and not so long and lank." Conversely, a captain in the 48th Pennsylvania suggested, "The thin, careworn appearance of the President is distinctly remembered—a marked change from a year before." George Chandler, 9th New Hampshire, recalled more of a languid Lincoln than the countenance of an immortal political leader. "Father Abraham passed close by us," the Granite State soldier noted, "and looks careworn and thin."[49]

Shortly after returning to Washington, Lincoln sought to move the army he had just visited. With no ambiguity about Washington's expectations, General Halleck intoned, "The President directs that you cross the Potomac and give battle to the enemy or drive him south. Your army must move now while the roads are good." If the army moved closer to Washington, Halleck promised 30,000 additional troops. Moving farther west into the Shenandoah Valley offered McClellan only up to 15,000 new troops.

As was so often the case when his bosses ordered something, McClellan did not become a bundle of powerful energy with his army. Dispatches demonstrated McClellan's lack of offensive drive, even though he promised a rapid advance in his reply to Halleck the morning after the order arrived. A key concern for McClellan was the relatively low number of troops fit for duty in many veteran regiments. Obviously concerned about the penchant for peevishness from the army commander, Halleck quickly directed, "The army must move, and the old regiments must remain in their crippled condition." Although he acknowledged limitations due to the army's weary state, McClellan's boss brusquely avoided any thought of compromise. "The country is becoming very impatient at the want of activity of your army, and we must push it on." Halleck continued, "After a hard march, one day is time enough to rest." Comparing the Army of the Potomac to the Confederates or European armies, the general-in-chief concluded the Unionist troops "are not sufficiently excercised to make them good and efficient soldiers."[50]

As McClellan fought with his superiors yet again, orders sent the Ninth Corps east a few miles into Pleasant Valley, an aptly named strip of land immediately west of South Mountain. The corps had first entered the valley on September 15 on the way to Sharpsburg.

Marching conditions proved enervating in the trek from Antietam Iron Works, even in early autumn. Granite Stater George Rowell noted the imperfect road, adding to the "tough march through the hot sun." David Lane recorded, "There was not even a whispering breeze to cool our throbbing brows." Yet, the Wolverine enjoyed simply being on the move. "The order to march is always welcome to me. I hate the monotony of camp life," he wrote, "We want to finish up our work and go home to our families." The hard work provided a fantastic benefit when the march was over. As John Bailey of the Nashua Cornet Band recalled, "Here, a beautiful panorama presented itself." Another New Hampshire kid referred to the valley as "a very pretty place."[51]

The Ninth Corps had 15,679 troops present for duty and thirty-five pieces of artillery on October 10. The protection of Potomac fords became an important role for Burnside's large command of three corps, but most days well into October included mainly light duties. A Ninth

Corps brigade was as far east as Frederick during the middle of October. They were part of the hunt for J. E. B. Stuart's very active cavalry, which completed a successful raid into Pennsylvania, much to McClellan's embarrassment. The inability to prevent the complete ride around McClellan's entire army led to a further reduction in Lincoln's moribund faith in his army commander.[52]

Men made the most of their extended period of relative inactivity. In addition to regular duties, soldiers wondered what the future might hold. Harvest season created a pleasurable treat for many, as the historian of Durell's Battery remembered, "Apples were plentiful in the surrounding country, and a gnawing appetite for apple dumplings seemed to have become epidemic in camp." With some additional work, men went to a mill for some flour, bought sugar for 11 cents a pound, and purchased condensed milk from sutlers.[53]

Cannoneers did not possess a monopoly on baking a good apple dumpling. An officer in the 48th Pennsylvania commented on the soldiers' appreciation for the special treat, which "became a staple dish." Natural pleasantries, the officer continued, included "the blessing of the most charming weather for the most of the stay" in Pleasant Valley. The Keystone warrior summed up the valley by calling their temporary home "a lovely piece of country indeed."[54]

Hosea Towne enjoyed the "excellent barns" he saw in Pleasant Valley, with additional signs of highly productive farmland. He was not as efficient at picking apples as some of his Ninth Corps comrades, however. Towne detailed the expenses a soldier sometimes accrued to augment army rations. Even if only adding a slight amount to his food supply, Towne felt blessed. "I paid 38 cents a peck for some ordinary pie apples," Towne wrote, "and if you could see me eating them with a slice of cheese for which I paid 25 cents a pound, you would find me enjoying myself as you would a turkey dinner."[55]

Rookie troops in the 20th Michigan found many pleasing aspects to their first few weeks as part of the Ninth Corps. While in Pleasant Valley with their division, the Wolverines found "plenty of excellent water from abundant springs" on the east side of South Mountain. This contrasted with what another officer described as the "yellowish mud hue" of the best water found shortly after the battle of Antietam. As an added bonus, the men were "surrounded by scenery that could not well be surpassed." Later in the month, a march south took the 20th to Noland's Ferry on the Potomac, about 12 miles from Harpers Ferry. At the new site, the men built "a pleasant and attractive camp in a fine grove."[56]

A new soldier in the 11th New Hampshire informed his wife and children about some of the difficulties he was encountering. In three October letters home, Benjamin Nelson clearly regretted his enlistment over the summer. He merely wished for "two potatoes a day on a piece of bread," which would be preferable to the available army fare. Fortunately, he had no problems with lice yet, "but I expect to every day." Although seeing some improvements in his existence, Nelson still considered his circumstances as "poor." He was feeling somewhat content with the relative lack of hard work and limited marching. Yet, "I should like to come home if I could, but I cannot." In an effort to diminish the family's amount of concern with his litany of problems, Nelson concluded a letter with "you must not worry about me."[57]

Sickness remained a dire foe, with men complaining of poor health even while receiving food and enjoying the surroundings in Pleasant Valley. John Wilcox, 9th New Hampshire, used diary entries to convey his condition. On the 19th, Wilcox added, "Sick all day, as usual." Another Granite Stater, Henry Muchmore of the 11th New Hampshire, was finding how hard life as a soldier could be. Still in Pleasant Valley late in the month, Muchmore wrote a friend, "I have been unwell most of the time since we got to Washington." Optimistic about getting better, Muchmore also noted how frequent meetings and prayer events with the excellent regimental chaplain could help lift spirits.[58]

At the same time, soldiers had been observing and thinking about the dramatic reduction in several regiments. In the 17th Michigan, still not even sixty days separated from home, stark evidence of the terrible September was clear. David Lane wrote, "This splendid regiment that left Detroit two months ago nearly one thousand strong, mustered today, at inspection, two hundred and fifty-six men fit for duty." In addition, "There are more sick than well, the result of insufficient supplies," and lack of attention to the needs of men by officers.[59]

Although in the army only a short time, the philosopher-historian of
the 7th Rhode Island sensed the strong friendships budding and growing
around camp. Although the men had yet to see a battle, "It has become
evident that the sharing of common dangers and privations establishes
more cordial relations between men than common occupations and
pleasures." Men with rude or unpleasant personalities "were melted into
sympathy at once" if a comrade became ill.[60]

FINALLY BACK TO VIRGINIA

As his men idled away October, McClellan remained under orders to
confront the Confederates. He still had the temerity to ask Halleck on
October 21 if Lincoln's order to move remained operative. Offering no
ambiguity, Halleck informed McClellan of the continued expectation,
communicated fifteen days previously, that the Army of the Potomac
seek out Robert E. Lee's soldiers. "The President does not expect impos-
sibilities, but he is very anxious that all this good weather should not be
wasted in inactivity," Halleck stated. McClellan promised swift action,
which for him meant the passage of four more days before an advance.[61]

When the mighty host began to move, neither the army nor the
Ninth Corps marched as one united whole. Per an order from headquarters, Burnside sent some troops to bridges over the Potomac on the
morning of October 26. A portion of the Ninth Corps would be one of
the first parts of the army to breach the Potomac line for the return trip
to the Confederacy. Nearby, a division from the defenses of Washington
temporarily assigned to the Twelfth Corps teamed up with the army's
vanguard. By evening, elements of the Ninth Corps across multiple
divisions camped south of the Potomac near Lovettsville. Aware of the
move some troops had been making, Adj. George Chandler, 9th New
Hampshire, wrote proudly on the 25th, "The number of troops between
here and the Potomac is immense."[62]

The rest of the army would follow over the next few days. Demonstrating the idealism of rookie soldiers, the 11th New Hampshire historian wrote, "The men hailed with delight the order, which came on
Saturday, October 25, to be ready to march the following morning." The
rookies and some others in the Ninth Corps did not start marching until

about midday on the 27th. Something other than a move to a new camp-site became evident as Ferrero's Brigade went to Knoxville, Maryland, then Berlin, near bridges spanning the army's namesake river.[63]

Colonel Bowman, 36th Massachusetts, reported some negative aspects of the trek to new camps. The state's adjutant general was informed of "a very tedious march, during which it had rained all day." Nonetheless, plenty of optimism existed across the temporary camps and marching Ninth Corps brigades. William Lusk, eager to let his mother know the positives of a new campaign, set the tone for the entire Ninth Corps. "Let us pray for success—and hope," he wrote, "All the time I lay in camp I did not feel well." Yet, on the opening march, with cold and rain his enemy, Lusk proclaimed, "I lost all my ill-feelings, and, after a night's sleep, am in better condition than I have been in for weeks." Not far away, with freezing temperatures descending on the 21st Massa-chusetts in Lovettsville, the men retained a healthy dose of inspiration, because "we had good fires, and were not uncomfortable," even without tents on the morning of October 28.[64]

The Army of the Potomac presented a formidable front across Northern Virginia as October ended. McClellan spread forces far enough to occupy Leesburg by the end of the 28th, with more troops crossing farther upstream under Burnside's watchful eye. Near noon on the 29th, Lincoln showed no signs of distress about the tardy advance. A thankful president wrote McClellan, "I am much pleased with the movement of the army." The makings of another grand campaign were evident. Unfor-tunately, McClellan's overestimation of Confederate strength continued, as did his arguments with his bosses.[65]

"There is a grand and great forward movement in progress," Charles Paige of the 11th New Hampshire informed his wife as November opened. The month started with fine weather and nearly all of the Army of the Potomac back in the Confederacy. Some portions of the Ninth Corps had already spent time on the sacred soil of Old Virginia. Four full days at a camp in Wheatland brought a happy break for the brigades still reeling from the difficulties of South Mountain and Antietam. James Wren, 48th Pennsylvania, fondly recalled a goose supper on the last night of October.[66]

Soldiers in Sturgis's Division enjoyed the temporary period of quiet and relaxation. Near Vestal's Gap, the 21st Massachusetts guarded the northern opening in the mountain range. "Our army showed a glorious strength in the open country near us," the regimental historian noted, with the veteran and rookie troops "perfectly in hand" and "in admirable discipline and spirits." Charles Paige happily recalled how the early November days brought "good times foraging and living high."[67]

The sounds of war remained audible. As the historian of the 16th Connecticut remembered, the regiment's November 1 trek, which ended in Wheatland, had included the sound of firing in front. "Orders were given to be ready to march at a moment's notice," the Nutmeg soldier wrote. General Willcox expected either a major battle soon or the creation of winter quarters.[68] The men were certainly in a good spot for a prolonged camp, but McClellan had promises to keep.

On the second day of the month, the Ninth Corps marched about 20 miles. The ordeal was not tantamount to what the 20th Michigan historian suggested, "the general advance on Richmond," but the army was moving well. The Ninth Corps marched in three lines, with Getty's Third Division in the middle of the powerful conglomeration of troops. Sturgis's men were the farthest west of the corps' advance, with acting division commander Daniel Leasure taking his brigades south on the left of Willcox. The town of Union, Virginia, stood as the projected middle of three divisions after the march. A division from the defenses of Washington joined the Ninth Corps for a portion of the campaign.[69]

One of McClellan's concerns for the day was the fate of Snicker's Gap, a bit west of the Ninth Corps. The gap was another spot from which Confederates could strike the right flank of the Unionist advance. By evening, the gap was in McClellan's hands, with Lincoln notified of the achievement. Whatever goals for a swift movement McClellan had communicated to his superiors, Lee, like usual, possessed far more alacrity. Detecting the threat, the Confederate commander moved the corps of James Longstreet to Culpepper, southwest of McClellan. Ever confident in his troops, Lee kept Stonewall Jackson's half of the Southern force west of the mountains.[70]

The great autumn conditions began to fade as wind and cold became more noticeable on November 3. Captain Wren reported the unwelcome appearance of mud, something likely to bring the best laid plans of a Civil War army to a screeching halt. No matter what the climatic reality, Lee had blocked a rapid advance south, meaning McClellan's idea for an offensive toward Culpepper became stillborn. A leader as skittish as McClellan would never become bold with the possibility of Stonewall Jackson crossing the Blue Ridge to smash the Unionist right flank.

On November 3, based on an order from McClellan's headquarters, the Ninth Corps received a new division commander. Daniel Leasure returned to his brigade after Brig. Gen. William Burns took over the First Division. Burns began his military career at West Point, graduating in the lower half of Burnside's class. A typical career in the peacetime army was replaced by intense action from early in the Civil War. Serving with McClellan in western Virginia, Burns would then suffer multiple injuries during the Peninsula Campaign, one in battle and the other from a fall off his mount. After convalescence, Burns would begin his short tenure with the Ninth Corps.[71]

Skirmishing during the week led to few casualties, but the men on the march knew danger invariably circled the lives of soldiers. The historian of the 6th New Hampshire had a chance to find humor among the peril. Sometimes the risks did not come from the enemy, or even a fellow human being. During some action near the Rappahannock at Warrenton Springs,

> *the army mules, as a rule did not take to the music of screeching and bursting shells, and when these were dropping among them, it was more than the drivers could do to keep the animals in position. Brake or bit could not hold them. To see the teamsters in a bad fix always made the boys laugh, for they seemed to think the drivers were men who did not wish to go into battle, and so got positions as mule-drivers. Still, the drivers were in nearly as much danger from the heels of their mules as the other boys were from shot and shell.[72]*

Mother Nature refused to relent in her dominion over armies. As snow fell during one evening, a very interesting incident occurred in Ferrero's Brigade. The circumstance offered a rare occasion when someone of a lesser rank could overrule a general. Brigade Surgeon Cutter confronted Ferrero as the men were within a few miles of the Rappahannock. At about 10 p.m., Cutter "forbid" Ferrero from continuing the march, based on the remembrance of the 51st Pennsylvania's historian. Ferrero said he must proceed to the river with his men, but "Dr. Cutter replied that he was responsible for the health of the brigade," and therefore "protested against making the men ford a river in the midst of such a stormy night." Cutter added he would happily welcome a court-martial to redeem his authority as brigade surgeon, prompting Ferrero to relent. The troops soon bivouacked under the protection of some woods. In Nagle's Brigade, John Bailey of the 9th New Hampshire recalled, "We built large fires by the roadside and tried to get warm."[73]

"OUR HISTORIES ARE IDENTICAL"

Before the end of November 6, Burnside's Boys would reach the Rappahannock, near Waterloo, as snow whitened the ground. Some soldiers reported water freezing in their canteens, with Henry Spooner in the 4th Rhode Island feeling the "'balmy' Southern breeze" on the coldest day of the regiment's history thus far. A man from northern New England began to wonder if they had been magically transported back home. The historian of the 6th New Hampshire recorded the exclamation of a comrade waking up others the next morning after seeing the snow, "Get up—get up quick! By George, we're in old New Hampshire."[74]

The white precipitation likely caused some consternation for Brig. Gen. Catharinus Buckingham, who had departed Washington for the Army of the Potomac with vital orders. He first visited Burnside, then the two men went south together for a chat with McClellan. The orders Buckingham carried relieved McClellan of his command, then placed Burnside in charge. Resisting the call to duty now seemed unpatriotic, so Burnside accepted. As was his usual practice, he had no intention of hurting McClellan and preferred to not take charge of the entire army.

McClellan cordially accommodated his dismissal, a move he undoubtedly expected.[75]

A Twelfth Corps man wrote about what many soldiers thought of Lincoln's change in army leadership. "General McClellan's suspension from command does not go down well in the army," the Delaware warrior suggested. The president's decision did create some ill will in McClellan's command, but some historians make too much of the issue. There were no mass resignations by officers.[76] Lincoln cannot be blamed for giving up on McClellan. Under the U.S. Constitution, no army commander can expect to long endure without the confidence of his civilian bosses.

The new commanding general's first statement to his army was vintage Burnside. The bulk of General Orders No. 1 declared,

> *Having been a sharer of the privations and a witness of the bravery of the old Army of the Potomac in the Maryland campaign, and fully identified with them in their feeling of respect and esteem for General McClellan, entertained through a long and most friendly association with him, I feel that it is not as a stranger that I assume their command.*
>
> *To the Ninth Corps, so long and intimately associated with me, I need say nothing; our histories are identical.*
>
> *With diffidence for myself, but with a proud confidence in the unswerving loyalty and determination of the gallant army now intrusted to my care, I accept its control, with the steadfast assurance that the just cause must prevail.*[77]

In an effort to support Burnside, General Willcox ordered prayer and divine services across the Ninth Corps. Lt. Samuel Haynes, 45th Pennsylvania, noted the extensive amount of discussion among soldiers as a result of the command change. He felt Burnside "has the confidence of all the officers and men with whom he has already come in contact and he has prestige bright, beside his bald head, checkered shirt and bobtailed horse, to carry him through the great tribulation." George Englis, 89th New York, wrote home on the subject, echoing Haynes's ideas and optimism.[78]

Burnside's first days of command starkly illustrated the logistical limitations he inherited. As a Massachusetts man noted of November 8, "The vanguard of the army seemed to have outmarched the supply trains." Fresh beef was available to many in the Ninth Corps, but the lack of bread created discontent. With the troops generally immobile for a few days, another Bay Stater in the Ninth Corps deemed their camp "Hunger Hallow." Roundhead Frederick Pettit wrote on the 8th of the successful foraging efforts of famished troops who readily confiscated the livestock of several secessionists. A corps comrade from Rhode Island spoke for many by noting, "Those who have never suffered day after day the pangs of hunger know little of the value that is set upon food of any kind and in any condition."[79]

The Ninth Corps was now part of the army's Right Grand Division, grouped with the Second Corps. Edwin Sumner commanded the two corps. Based on returns from November 10, Willcox's Ninth Corps had 14,223 men present and equipped, as well as thirty-six pieces of artillery. The corps had the fewest men and big guns of any in the army that Burnside had with him. Including the Twelfth Corps, which was in reserve at Harpers Ferry, divisions unattached to any corps, and cavalry, Burnside had slightly more than 130,000 soldiers ready for battle. The defenses of Washington added 80,000 more present and equipped troops.[80] The Unionist horde in Virginia and around the capital were an immensely powerful force. How could they be used effectively?

Troops remained mostly in camps as Burnside studied the possibilities for the army's advance. Sometimes elements of the Ninth Corps only moved in response to false alarms, prompting a hungry return to camp. "The weather is quite pleasant," Sewell Tilton of the 11th New Hampshire informed his diary on November 9. The next day, he reported continued cannon firing from various directions, giving a level of eeriness to Unionist lives. "We are liable to be called on to move again at any time," the captain concluded.[81]

By November 12, troops headed for White Sulphur Springs (near the current town of Remington), another spot with a ford on the Rappahannock. The march began before daylight, with the ford reached within a few hours. The area was close to the same spot many of the men used while along the river back in August. Enemy troops had recently set fire to the bridge over the river. On the corps' autumn arrival at the spot, a Pennsylvanian recalled the bridge "being completely demolished," with "charred logs" having fallen into the river.[82]

Capt. George Durell and his Battery D, Pennsylvania Light Artillery, moved along the river road in the rear of Sturgis's Division and supply wagons. Soon, guns were booming. Teamwork across batteries assisted Durell. Capt. Jacob Roemer's big guns and Sam Benjamin's artillerists joined the fray. The help was very welcome. As Durell reported, "The battery was exposed to a very heavy fire for over an hour, holding their position until the train had passed."[83]

Concerns about the ability to check Confederate probes were dispatched up the chain of command. From a signal station, Willcox informed Burnside's headquarters (through Chief of Staff John Parke), "Ferrero reports the enemy as driving in our pickets." Sturgis's staff had also let Ninth Corps leadership know "a section of artillery and three squadrons of cavalry are advancing toward Warrenton Springs." Sturgis proved capable of meeting the need for swift action. Later in the day, he informed Willcox, "I have now no fear of my position."[84]

OPPOSITE FREDERICKSBURG

During the march south, George Chandler, adjutant of the 9th New Hampshire, had much on his mind. "I don't *hanker* for another fight," he informed his mother, "Still I look at it rather more as a matter of business than at first." Like many of his Ninth Corps comrades, the soldier showed great concern about supply problems. "We have been so far in advance of our teams," he penned, "as to be obliged to bivouac at night without tents." His "pretty tough life" included rumors that Colonel Fellows would take a leave of absence or resign. "Should he do so," Chandler noted, "I should much regret it." Fellows elected to resign his commission.[85]

By a different fate, another Ninth Corps outfit lost its leader. Lt. Col. Sumner Carruth, 35th Massachusetts, who suffered a wound at Antietam like dozens of his men, went forward across the Rappahannock in the search of a meal. Hunger and a quest for some supplies may have motivated Carruth, but the decision to separate himself from his regiment was a poor one. After cavalrymen breached the Ninth Corps picket line, a Confederate patrol captured Carruth and another officer. Whisked off to a Confederate prison, Carruth would be absent from the army until exchanged months later.[86]

Some officers grew distraught after false information spread about the incident. The injured Colonel Wild and Company F's Capt. Benjamin F. Pratt, in command of the picket detail of the 35th, both wrote home to clarify the record. "This incident, which has been badly misrepresented in the newspapers," Wild suggested, "I mention for the sake of relieving from odium those two officers, to whom I attach no blame."

The unfortunate incident received "so many contradicting reports and misrepresentations," Pratt declared, "They went there without doubt for a good dinner." On the contrary, Pratt knew the homeowner who still lived in the house. Although "a radical secessionist," the resident proved quite kind during the company's three days of duty in the vicinity. "I was the last one that spoke with Col. Carruth before he crossed," Pratt added. Soon after the colonel's capture, Confederate cavalry "came near down to the Bridge, drove in our Cavalry Pickets, and then went back."

If any positive outcome resulted from the mid-November episode, Pratt extolled the conduct of Maj. Sidney Willard, who took charge of the 35th Massachusetts during the cannon firing and exchange of musketry along the river. "Under fire for the first time," Pratt wrote of Willard, the major "proved himself to be a Cool, Brave man, and a good officer." Wild also knew of Willard's virtues, reporting to the state's adjutant general of the major's "coolness" and "good management."[87]

By November 16, the cold marching proved difficult and long. Samuel Haynes penned a letter about the improved supply situation, although he had worried about the "lamentably short" amount of food. The normally dreaded hardtack cracker grew in esteem across Ninth Corps camps. Few soldiers adored the unpalpable sustenance, but "tack" as Haynes called it, proved much beloved at this time. The corps marched beyond the Orange and Alexandria Railroad late in the day, covering about 15 miles. Arriving near Warrenton Station in the evening, George Upton, 6th New Hampshire, wrote his wife, "With the exception of a cold I never was better in my life." Unfortunately, he added, "it is a hard business to camp out this time of year."[88]

Edwin Sumner's two corps were the first to reach Falmouth, opposite Fredericksburg on the north side of the Rappahannock. In camp shortly before arrival on November 18, John Bailey, the New Hampshire musician attached to Nagle's Brigade, was very happy, "Our whole corps camping on one field. Weather delightful." Shortly before transferring out of the Ninth Corps, John Ryan and the 28th Massachusetts enjoyed the beautiful view of Fredericksburg as the grand division began forming on the other side of the river. The most indelible feature of the landscape, on the far side of town, was the fine defensive terrain Confederates would control for weeks.[89]

The necessary work of patrolling the river fell to veterans and rookies alike. The 51st Pennsylvania was responsible for three-quarters of a mile of riverfront, starting at Falmouth. The "very stormy and cold" weather made the necessary chore regrettable. When off duty, the Keystone Staters would frequently visit sutlers, who lived up to their reputation for low-quality goods at high prices.[90]

On November 20, the Roundheads were ordered to begin work on an important task. The wagon road from Belle Plain, east of Falmouth on the south bank of Potomac Creek, was vital for transporting supplies. After reporting to General Willcox, the hardy men of the 100th Pennsylvania moved out to work on repairing the road. Unfortunately, rain soured the mood of those in the work crew. Putting up tents and finding hay to cover the ground lessened the level of saturation around camp. During the subsequent days, the 100th Pennsylvania busily tried to cover the muddy road with brush and whatever else was available. The Roundheads returned to their old camp on Sunday the 23rd.[91]

Unionists in any threatening number could not move across the river into Fredericksburg without pontoon bridges, still an elusive commodity for Burnside. The army commander waited for the engineers and all their necessary accoutrements as November's final week started. General-in-chief Halleck wrote Burnside on the 23rd, opining that less senior officers had not moved fast enough. He suggested Burnside could hold others to account for any future delays in delivery of the vital pontoon trains. Undoubtedly obsessed with his own feelings of inadequacy at leading the army, Burnside still could not shake problems beyond his control. The army bureaucracy had failed him.[92]

Stalemate along the Rappahannock was not the only irritating constant in the lives of the Ninth Corps. Mud lasted for days on end after the frequent bouts of rain or snow that quickly melted. Capt. Ralph Ely, 8th Michigan, noted an inspection of the Ninth Corps by General Sumner. The event was conducted on November 26, the day before Thanksgiving. A Massachusetts man lamented the experience, writing, "It had rained the night before, and it was somewhat uncomfortable standing three hours in the mud and water waiting for the appearance of the general."[93]

A member of the 4th Rhode Island devoted an entire paragraph in his memoir to recollections of the mud around Falmouth.

Virginia mud has this peculiarity: that when wet it assumes a paste-like consistency, and sticks to the feet like glue; hence, when one set his foot down into it, it would cling tenaciously to his shoes, so that at times while lifting the foot to take another step the shoe would be left behind, firmly imbedded in the mud, thus making travel extremely difficult, and sometimes quite impossible.[94]

Thanksgiving Day brought some positives for men across the Ninth Corps. In one important area, the weather showed signs of improvement. "Many were the efforts which the men made to prepare from army stores a suitable feast for the day," the 36th Massachusetts historian remembered. At this time, the regiment received orders to relocate its camp. The better site, only a few hundred feet away in a forest of young softwoods, proved far more pleasing than the previous location.[95]

Cannoneers in Roemer's Battery, stationed near a relatively thin part of the river, kept a careful watch for possible Confederate incursions. Roemer recalled the daily rotation of infantry support, as well as continual efforts to strengthen the embrasures, vital protection against Confederate artillery. Much labor would be needed across the weeks around Fredericksburg, with men cutting and moving a great deal of wood to serve as protection for men and cannons. An order on November 30 led to the use of about a dozen cords of wood to augment Roemer's shield against enemy fire.[96]

Some Unionist interaction with Confederates did not portend such danger. With so many troops from both armies within sight of the Rappahannock, a certain amount of fraternization was inevitable. Shouting across the river to joke with each other became common. An officer in the 48th Pennsylvania recalled one such interchange. "How did you like Bull Run," a Confederate hollered. "Better bury your dead at South Mountain," a Unionist replied. The Confederate, a member of the Louisiana Tigers, later suggested they would capture President Lincoln, then make him a prisoner in Richmond. Of the Tigers, the Pennsylvanian countered, "There's none of them left—the last died running."[97]

Camped in a relatively isolated spot closer to the riverfront than most other regiments in the Ninth Corps, many members of the 21st Massachusetts participated in the jocularity with the Confederates. As with the remembrance of the Pennsylvania officer, the Bay Stater noted how frequently the Southern troops mentioned their great successes in the battles along Bull Run. When reminded of the Union victories in September, a Confederate might respond, "Too many Yankees in Maryland to the acre." A Southern Irishman could express his disappointment with Emerald Isle natives in blue by declaring he never thought an Irishman could fight against liberty.[98] From a state firmly opposed to slavery, perhaps a Massachusetts man in the Ninth Corps responded with nothing but an ironic smile.

ARRIVAL OF NEW REGIMENTS

By early December, the Ninth Corps completed another realignment after the departure of the 28th Massachusetts and the addition of several other regiments. The 29th Massachusetts swapped positions with the 28th, which became part of the famous Irish Brigade of the Second Corps. When added to Willcox's regiments, the 29th was under the command of Lt. Col. Joseph Barnes.[99]

Lt. Augustus Ayling recorded his early impressions of the regimental swap. Hearing the news of how his 29th Massachusetts would move to the Ninth Corps, Ayling favored the change. The non-Irish soldiers in the regiment felt like oddballs in the Irish Brigade. When considering the campsite around their new comrades in Willcox's Division, however, Ayling preferred his previous location. Initially, many men in the 29th thought brigade commander Col. Benjamin Christ was being sacrilegious, but they changed their mind when they learned his last name was pronounced, "Krist."[100]

Another solid group of Michigan men, the state's 2nd Regiment, had been part of the Ninth Corps since mid-November. The battle-hardened regiment was led by Orlando Poe, who graduated sixth out of forty-nine in the West Point Class of 1856. He then spent more than four years as a lake surveyor. Rising quickly during the first year of the Civil War, Poe held staff commands in the Department of the Ohio and under General McClellan. The Wolverines found much service on the Peninsula, with Poe earning Third Corps brigade command during the summer of 1862. After time in the Washington defenses, the young officer took his regiment into Virginia. Soon, Poe would lead the entire First Brigade, First Division.[101]

Several officers of the 2nd Michigan grew very concerned about a rumor regarding consolidation of their regiment with the 8th Michigan. Fears grew when orders transferring Poe's regiment to the Ninth Corps were announced. Some bad blood developed between Poe and his junior officers when several men thought Poe would not be concerned about the fate of the 2nd Michigan if he received the star of a brigadier general. A potential rebellion of officers against Poe did not boil over, no arrests occurred, and the two regiments were never consolidated.[102]

With multiple Ninth Corps regiments from the state already, the 13th New Hampshire would join the Third Division in December. The regiment departed the state capital of Concord in early October and was then posted in northern Virginia for several weeks. Confident in the regiment, Alonzo Pierce informed a brother on October 10, "The soldiers are determined to do their duty come what may." A part of the soldier's confidence was the large number of regiments posted around Washington. Later in the month Pierce reported how some of his comrades lacked his own faith in the future, with six deserting.

During the regiment's trek to join the Ninth Corps' Third Division, Pierce wrote of six hard days prior to arrival at Aquia Creek. He quickly learned how difficult weather sometimes compounds the miseries of army life. While on the move to Fredericksburg, Pierce noted, "The supply wagons got stuck in the mud and it took ten or a dozen men and as many mules to get them out." With snow followed by warmer temperatures, the muddy fate seemed likely to continue. Pierce added, "We have lived on raw pork and hardtack all the week except what we stole from the rebels."[103]

The 12th Rhode Island, a nine-month regiment, joined Nagle's Brigade. The regiment's short service began in Providence. The troops mustered in on October 13, with Col. George Browne in command. For their first night with the Ninth Corps, the rookies of the 12th Regiment camped alongside new brigade comrades in the 7th Rhode Island. The spot became known as "Camp Smoke" due to the necessity of using wet wood to build fires.[104]

DECEMBER DOLDRUMS

Jabez Smith, who had struggled with sickness since joining the 35th Massachusetts, started another month in a hospital. He remained away from his comrades while convalescing in Washington, struggling with the limitations of his health and the dearth of war news. Like so many other soldiers in camps or hospitals, Smith also despaired about the lack of family updates due to slow mail or those at home not writing enough. The prospect of another battle he would miss occupied some of Smith's thoughts, as well. "I expect they are going to have an aufle battle before long," he accurately predicted to his parents on December 1. Like many soldiers with nagging illness, Smith would sit out a significant part of the war.[105]

By early December, the conditions began to wear on the tired and cold troops at the front. Benjamin Pratt, 35th Massachusetts, informed the Bay State adjutant general, "We had a hard march from Pleasant Valley to this place." Across the wretched weeks, "a great many of the men came in Barefoot. Some have had no Blankets and overcoats since the Battles in Maryland." The overarching devotion to the higher cause pushed the soldiers, not even four months out of Boston, to continue. As Pratt concluded, men in the regiment "are ready to march on to Richmond whenever ordered. And we all hope to be there soon."[106]

Drills filled much time for soldiers across Willcox's three divisions. The 29th Massachusetts performed several typical duties in the opening third of December. The soldiers were assigned to police a campsite, with some men also on picket duty. Capt. James Wren and the 48th Pennsylvania experienced hours of work almost daily in the practice of soldierly maneuvers and marching. In addition to the company drill Wren would lead as an officer, regimental drills were also practiced. Wren noted four hours of drill a day was required for experienced troops, with new soldiers enduring five hours. General Nagle announced the resumption of brigade drill as December started, "much to the disgust of all hands interested," another officer in the 48th suggested.[107]

The inability to complete pontoon bridges near Fredericksburg severely hampered Burnside. Lincoln did not wish to wait indefinitely, regardless of the difficulties a lack of sufficient bridge material posed. The president attempted to balance the competing needs of the army and country by trying to not force Burnside into something rash. The army commander received promises of support from many of his senior officers, including Right Grand Division commander Edwin Sumner, although dissension among generals cast a pall of negativity over the eastern side of the Rappahannock.[108]

Meanwhile, George Rowell, 6th New Hampshire, felt colder temperatures and longed for many items from home. He outlined his requests in an early December letter. Undershirts, stockings, and drawers were the clothes immediately on Rowell's mind. He then turned to a range of eatables, with six pies and several loaves of bread topping the list. He continued, "And put two lbs of butter in and some cheese, and ¼ lbs of green tea and a lot of dried apples and a dozen or two of fried cakes, and a small baked chicken if you can." Many other soldiers around Falmouth likely had similar visions of packages from home.[109]

Picket duty, an ongoing necessity with the enemy just across the river, required teamwork between regiments. James Wren commanded 150 men of the 48th Pennsylvania who kept an eye on the Rappahannock.

Members of the 46th New York joined the line on Wren's left. The cold night late on December 7 was difficult, leading to some frozen boots. Ears battered by the temperatures also dampened Wren's mood. The next morning, he again visited picket posts. Using his spyglass while mounted, Wren could see Confederates eying him. Perhaps an unwritten rule of peace between enemy pickets protected Wren.[110]

Army leadership attempted to lessen problems with the wintry feel by getting the troops to construct small dwellings from plentiful forests. A Pennsylvania infantryman wrote of the order for log home construction creating "a slaughter of the woods." Like men throughout the army, cannoneers in Durell's Battery passed the day on the 7th building better accommodations. The orders "came none too soon," the artillerists' historian wrote, "for cold weather and snow soon followed, and the men were poorly clad." Clothing and shoes in terrible condition added to the woe of camp life for the battery, as well as other men in the Ninth Corps. As Benjamin Nelson, 11th New Hampshire, wrote, "I am not very smart. I have got cold and have felt rather shiftless for a week." Observing the frozen ground and rough time for the men, Nelson concluded, "It is as cold here as it is in new hampshire."[111]

Even after the orders to improve camp sites, the army would not remain stationary. December 10 brought preparations for a move. Ralph Ely in the 8th Michigan and some regimental historians recorded troops drawing sixty rounds of ammunition each. By the morning of the 11th, rumors of battle were replaced by more obvious signs of imminent trouble. As the 21st Connecticut historian recalled, "The roar of cannon rang out among the hills and valleys, rousing us from our slumbers, as the very earth trembled and shook."[112]

Assisting Engineers

The number of troops Burnside had for the looming battle gave the Army of the Potomac a notable advantage against Lee's Confederates. Based on returns from December 10, the three Unionist grand divisions had slightly more than 120,000 men present and equipped. Sumner's force, including the Second and Ninth Corps, had the lowest of the three grand divisions, with nearly 25,000 officers and men, as well as ninety pieces of artillery, many of which were on Stafford Heights. The impressive position for big guns east of the river could mightily augment an infantry attack. Burnside's army spread out from Fredericksburg to the south for about 3 miles.[113]

Work at the river began for some in the Ninth Corps on the evening of December 10. "The night was bitter cold," Robert Bowne informed a newspaper back home, as the 89th New York worked with engineers at one of the bridges being built on the southern end of the main part of Fredericksburg. This was the central of six bridges the Army of the Potomac would construct prior to the battle. Col. Harrison Fairchild, who led a brigade at Antietam, now held the command of only the 89th.

Protected early by darkness and fog, bridge building began on December 11. Bowne wrote of the central bridge being about half finished at daylight, a point when cannon blasts and Confederate fire created an unholy cacophony. George Englis noted the intense level of musketry aimed at the Unionists trying to span the Rappahannock. Even with the help of the 46th New York on their right, Fairchild's regiment could not provide sufficient covering fire against the concealed Confederate infantrymen. As Brig. Gen. George Getty reported, the Confederates created excellent shooting locations behind stone walls and inside buildings on the other side of the river. Noting several attempts to complete the bridge, Getty continued, "in each case the workmen were repulsed with loss."[114]

The same fate met Unionist efforts to construct two bridges upstream, while spans south of Fredericksburg proceeded without notable problems due to the more isolated crossing site. Parts of the Second Corps fought determined Confederates during the morning. On request, Getty received hearty support from dozens of Ninth Corps volunteers in the 8th Connecticut, who sustained slight loss attempting to protect bridge builders to the north.[115]

By mid-afternoon, with the sun already low in the western sky, General Burnside had endured enough of the Confederate sniping. Speaking with Colonel Fairchild directly, the army commander wished to ensure better progress completing bridges. Fairchild's subsequent order sent four detachments of twenty-five men each across the river in different boats. They were "to land, charge, and take a given point." The colonel noted his wishes were "promptly obeyed and most gallantly executed." Sixty-five Confederates, including four officers, became prisoners of the Ninth Corps. The 89th New York, with ten casualties during the day, then reunited and held their new position until the central bridge was finished.[116]

SACKING FREDERICKSBURG

Small groups of Confederate infantry put up a ferocious fight in parts of town to delay Burnside's advance. As the initial resistance ended later on December 11, the conquest of the Fredericksburg riverfront gave the Unionists the opportunity to widen their occupation of the city. The relatively warm overnight temperatures created a great deal of fog by morning. More troops then crossed the Rappahannock, although a good deal of Burnside's force remained east of the river. Nonetheless, a New Hampshire man penned in his diary later on the 12th, "The city is full of troops."[117]

During their crossing of the bridge, warriors in the 15th Connecticut, which had arrived at Falmouth and joined Harland's brigade earlier in December, faced Confederate projectiles for the first time. Three casualties were sustained, including one soldier who would die of his wound. After reaching the city, the scene of desolation made an impression on the regimental historian. "Here nothing was lacking to add to the destruction of war," he remembered. Houses were "riddled with shot, or opened by exploding shell, blackened and burned."[118]

The historian of the 51st Pennsylvania recalled the immense noise. With the long arm of both armies blasting away, "the earth quaked for miles around as if convulsed by some hidden spasm of nature in the very centre of its rotundity." The "terrific" rates of fire remained a prominent memory for other Ninth Corps men, with one writing of the destruction balls created in the city itself. Random blasts brought danger to the Unionist infantry, even from cannons in Burnside's army.[119]

During the stressful hours, soldiers turned against Fredericksburg, stealing or destroying in a disgraceful orgy of pillaging. Perhaps the ruin wrought from the deafening cannons lessened the qualms of some troops; more smashed furniture and broken glass seemed inconsequential. As a modern history of the 9th New Hampshire suggested, the level of contempt even restrained soldiers felt sprang from either a hatred for Fredericksburg or the inexorable tendency of a mob to satisfy its own cravings. A member of the regiment wrote home after the battle, remembering the enjoyment of the troops, perhaps with a somewhat guilty conscience. George Chandler noted, "I wish Uncle could have gone with us into Fredericksburg. It would have astonished him and I fear gratified him to see the havoc our boys made. I have a few trinkets as memorials of the place which I hope to get home sometime."[120]

Whatever the personal justifications, the willful sacking of Fredericksburg dishonored the Northern cause. Some in the 35th Massachusetts danced in the streets while wearing women's clothes. The regimental historian wrote of the Bay Staters "cutting a swell appearance and exciting much mirth." With cannons remaining hot, he added, "It was a sickening mixture of death and frivolity."[121]

Tobacco became a prized capture. After a large quantity was located, regimental teams worked to seize as much of the free treat as possible. "Each soldier boasts his several pounds flinched from the enemy," Ocean State officer Henry Spooner wrote of the tobacco harvest. "The houses were literally sacked, and soldiers lounged on sofas and cushions," he added. Additionally, Unionists "drummed out patriotic tunes from pianos which had long been devoted to secession's strains alone."[122]

Spooner was undoubtedly not the only officer whose complacency failed to check the army's breakdown in discipline. Unrestrained soldiers did not seem disturbed as men destroyed the contents of homes or headed east with stolen goods in hopes of getting back to camp with whatever of value. One problem inhibiting a headquarters response to the sacking of Fredericksburg was the capture of a provost marshal patrol on the north side of town. Perhaps the overwhelmed law enforcement apparatus of the army could not have kept up with the debauchery anyway.[123]

A Granite Stater saw Fredericksburg trapped "in the midst of a mighty whirlwind." If the outnumbered Confederates were shaking during the advance of Burnside's army into Fredericksburg, the Southerners may have just been feeling the cold. They held too strong a position to pine for a different circumstance. With excellent terrain advantages, the Southerners possessed seemingly infinite confidence. One highly accurate Confederate officer, who would die in the looming battle, had written his thoughts in a late November letter. Pondering the inevitable Union advance, he asserted, "Never was an army more ready to meet a foe than ours is. In my opinion, he comes to his doom."[124]

PART FIVE

Fredericksburg and the West

"If properly supported, good results might have been attained."
–COL. ANDREW DERROM, 25TH NEW JERSEY

PROBLEMS FROM THE BEGINNING

FOG SHROUDED NINTH CORPS SOLDIERS AFTER WHATEVER FITFUL sleep they could manage at the start of December 13, 1862. Organized movement of troops waited until after 9 a.m., a point when fog started to decrease. Of the stupendous noise from cannon fire and musketry during the morning, Charles Paige, 11th New Hampshire, recalled, "It was terribly awful, and yet wonderfully exhilarating." Also part of Sturgis's division, the 21st Massachusetts had an important task after arriving on the western edge of town to support pickets from George Getty's Third Division. As the regimental historian wrote, "Unfortunate in their miserable gray overcoats," the Bay Staters "were compelled to take them off and store them in one of the houses for fear of being mistaken for rebels by our artillery men."[1]

Nagging doubts natural to Ambrose Burnside may have been no more prominent across his life than on this pivotal morning. After weeks of waiting for the arrival of bridging material, Burnside was about to launch his first major attack as an army commander. The battle of Fredericksburg would be one of the most lopsided Union defeats of the war, creating cascades of negative effects for Burnside personally and his army. The looming Unionist assault was an exceedingly difficult one, primarily due to the brilliance of Robert E. Lee in managing an exceptionally good defensive position.

Burnside's exhausted state of mind, inexperience as an army commander, and lack of personal confidence contributed to his failure to articulate clear and tenable orders for the army's attack across a wide front. Confused orders and insufficient leadership on the army's left led to a poorly managed battle for two divisions of the First Corps. Wing commander William Franklin lacked the boldness necessary to implement the overwhelming attack Burnside may have envisioned on the left. Franklin's cautiousness prompted an unsuccessful effort against Stonewall Jackson in which the First Corps suffered 3,300 casualties.[2]

The Right Grand Division's battle opposite Fredericksburg then became the key to Union planning. Major General Sumner, a subordinate devoted to Burnside, was ordered to seize the heights Confederates occupied so ominously, including the stone wall lining Marye's Heights. The Ninth Corps stood to the left of Darius Couch's Second Corps, with the two brigades under Sam Sturgis closest to Couch's men. George Getty's Third Division was immediately to the south, with William Burns's First Division farther down the line, his left nearly linked with Franklin's right. Orlando Willcox summed up the cramped position and role of the Ninth Corps. "The troops of this command," he reported, "occupied the center, which I understood it my duty to hold, and at the same time to afford support to the attacks which Generals Franklin and Couch were to make."[3] The Ninth Corps held a poor position to meet the role Willcox understood for his three divisions. Only three brigades would assist the Second Corps, while no meaningful Ninth Corps support went to Franklin. The looming afternoon disaster would add more than 1,300 casualties to the Ninth Corps' 1862 butcher's bill.

"THE INCARNATE SPIRIT OF WAR"
The Second Corps suffered staggering losses in a short time while trying to force the Confederates out of the formidable Marye's Heights line. Sturgis, "observing the disaster," ordered Ferrero's brigade to assist Couch at 12:30 p.m. The 51st New York, earlier assigned to support artillery, remained near the division's Regular army battery, which due to Capt.

Joseph Clark's wounds, was under the command of Lt. George Dicken-son.[4] The sad fate of the battery would epitomize the day's result for the Ninth Corps and Burnside's army as a whole.

Posted on a rise in town to the left of the Second Corps, Dickenson and his men felt intense Confederate pressure, quickly sustaining thir-teen casualties. In his early twenties, Lieutenant Dickenson would lose his life on the field. Second Lt. John Egan then took the reins of the battery, which had been under fire since "before the first piece was in position." Enemy musketry from various directions targeted the battery. An observant infantryman noticed a sergeant "with blood flowing from a wound in his head, encouraging his men and directing their aim." With the intense incoming bombardment, Egan reported, "Twice all the can-noneers were driven from their pieces." The battery was withdrawn from the field after thirty minutes, with Sturgis supporting Egan's order that brought the surviving artillerists out of the nightmare.[5]

As Ferrero moved out, the division commander wrote, "The fire of artillery and musketry which the enemy now concentrated upon the Second Brigade was terrific, but they stood manfully up to their work." Two days before, Ferrero had crossed the Rappahannock with 1,930 men. Their numbers quickly withered in the late autumn afternoon as Confed-erates happily viewed another Unionist line attempting the impossible. Prior to the charge, Ferrero formed his brigade into two lines of battle. The regiments "advanced under a terrific fire of shell and musketry," Fer-rero wrote, "never halting until we arrived in short range of the enemy." Ferrero was happy to note the eventual assistance from the 51st New York, which moved up into the maelstrom. The Empire Staters "advanced in gallant style," Ferrero recalled, "losing terribly while marching alone over this deadly plain."[6]

Confederate muskets and artillery inflicted an immense amount of human suffering in Ferrero's regiments. Maj. Sidney Willard took the 35th Massachusetts toward the stone wall. "Forward boys," he shouted, with his sword pointing the way. "Dress on the colors; and remember your glory at Antietam." As a history in the records of the state adjutant general noted, Willard "seemed like the incarnate Spirit of War." The stellar officer had not yet "advanced ten paces" before being "smitten by the leaden death-messenger and carried from the field to die."[7]

Ferrero's other Bay State regiment faced withering Southern lead, as well. While still trying to clear the town to reach the field beyond, losses mounted for the 21st Massachusetts. The original color sergeant fell, with the sacred banner grabbed by Thomas Plunkett. Continuing on his new mission of guiding the regiment, an exploding artillery shell cost the brave Plunkett parts of both arms. With more than two decades of life remaining, Plunkett would receive the Medal of Honor for his difficult moments. Regarding the conduct of the entire regiment, the adjutant general was informed, "it is superfluous to state that both officers and men behaved like veterans."[8]

Maj. Sidney Willard died while leading the 35th Massachusetts against the excellent Confederate defensive position west of Fredericksburg. LIBRARY OF CONGRESS

At the cost of both arms, the brave Thomas Plunkett would receive a Medal of Honor for leading the 21st Massachusetts in the charge against Marye's Heights. LIBRARY OF CONGRESS

Prior to the arrival of the 21st Massachusetts, Colonel Hartranft and the 51st Pennsylvania constituted the brigade's left. The colonel, per his historical reputation, inspired his men by exposing himself to danger before the advance began. With Ferrero imploring the 51st forward, Hartranft quickly responded. The regimental historian grew mystified "how under the sun even one man reached alive the position assigned." Capt. Ferdinand Bell of Company B, "as fearless as he was gentle," lost his life during the charge. Fencing inhibited Hartranft's effort to move his unit to the apex of the advance as "the men of the 51st were falling at every step."[9]

The 11th New Hampshire, to Hartranft's right, suffered more than any Ninth Corps regiment at Fredericksburg. Colonel Harriman shouted, "Attention 11th," to order his men forward, prompting Charlie Paige to remember, "We all knew what he had got to do. I made up my mind for the worst." The regiment pressed on, prompting a frazzled Granite Stater to lament, "Not a damned one of us will be left to tell the story!" As the regimental historian responded, "I had to laugh, in all the fury of the battle; things looked, however, as if he was about right." Confederate missiles continued to scream down from Marye's Heights "with deadly effect."[10]

Blasting away with their muskets even while facing impossible odds, the rookies in the 11th New Hampshire seemed boxed in. William Fish wrote of the imperative to go prone. "We lay on the ground for a few hours just as close as we could get our faces to the ground to escape the storm of bullets which were flying over us." Even with comrades still being injured, Fish added, "It seems almost a miracle how we escaped so well as we did." Fish's letter about the battle was written nearly two weeks later from a Washington hospital. He was not wounded by Confederate fire but suffered a serious injury to his ankle as the regiment fell back under the cover of darkness.[11]

Harriman did not blame his men for seeking relative safety by hugging the ground. In his report, the colonel praised the 11th for displaying "heroic bravery and unflinching firmness." Harriman added that some members of his command fired 200 rounds during the afternoon, with sporadic shots made as darkness began to rule the maudlin slope below the Confederate position. "Under for that long period the most terrific shower of iron hail," Harriman concluded, the regiment did not "swerve a single hair." Ferrero echoed Harriman's positive comments. The new regiment, the proud general opined, "marched up as bravely and fought as valiantly as the veterans of the brigade."[12]

NAGLE JOINS IN

After seeing the difficulties Ferrero's regiments tackled, General Sturgis knew more men from his division would be necessary. Brig. Gen. James

Nagle's six regiments, a mix of experienced units and those new to the army, received the call to advance at about the time the brigade commander nearly met his demise. As an officer in the 48th Pennsylvania remembered, Nagle and some subordinates were near a brick stable when a cannon ball "struck the building penetrating both walls." The Confederate ordinance exited the stable "just above the heads of the General and staff," leaving the men covered by dust and nearly injured by flying bricks.[13]

With the 48th Pennsylvania held in reserve for the moment, Nagle moved his five other regiments toward the Confederates. The units were required to pass along and across railroad tracks soon after reaching the edge of Fredericksburg's streets. At the point where the brigade reached the deep cut of the railroad, Lt. Col. John Babbitt, 9th New Hampshire, found the regiment subjected to "a galling enfilading fire from the enemy's artillery." Although admitting to the "considerable confusion" caused as a result, Babbitt reported his regiment found an adequate position from which to blaze away at Marye's Heights. The Granite Staters then stood for the seemingly countless minutes before dark as ammunition dwindled and men fell.[14]

A great young leader in the 9th New Hampshire performed well at the perilous moment. Capt. John Cooper, only twenty-one years old, retook command of Company K earlier in the morning, having completed his convalescence from a wound at Antietam. Mature well beyond his years after losing both parents early in life, Cooper wished to share the dangers of those under his command. "Loved by his men most cordially," Cooper performed "good service" while on the field below the Confederate position.[15]

On Nagle's right flank, the brigade's other New Hampshire outfit shined again under highly difficult circumstances. Simon Griffin and his 6th Regiment faced the leaden storm with the experience and perspective of great veterans. Four days after the battle, George Upton informed his wife, "On going in to the fight we were subjected to the cross fires of the enemy's Batteries on the heights beyond." Due to the appalling level of human suffering, "The carnage was exceedingly awful. We are pretty much reduced, and we conclude that about two fights more will finish us."[16]

"When we were about half way across the field," the 6th's historian remembered, "a shell exploded right in the midst of Company K, killing two men outright, wounding some, and knocking others out of line." Already moving at double quick, others in the 6th did not halt after the fatal missile arrived. Like so many other troops at Fredericksburg, the attacking Unionists went prone to find some protection from the rising ground. "There," the historian added, "if we lifted so much as a hand, it was sure to be hit."[17]

On Griffin's left, members of the 7th Rhode Island moved ahead into their first battle. Col. Zenas Bliss quickly lost senior officers. Lt. Col. Welcome Sayles, killed instantly when hit by a shell, had been assigned control of the regiment's right half. Bliss was "sprinkled from head to foot" with blood and lung material due to Sayles's devastating injury. Major Jacob Babbitt, fifty-three years old, also fell. He would cling to life for ten days, dying at an Alexandria, Virginia, hospital. In his last letter home, Babbitt wrote, "Should it be my lot to fall, know that it was in defense of our beloved Constitution."[18]

With his adjutant also down, Bliss delivered the necessity of strong leadership. As his men found whatever shield they could from the lay of the land, Bliss displayed great courage at a time of terrible danger. The colonel's Medal of Honor citation notes how Bliss "rose to his feet, advanced in front of the line, and himself fired several shots at the enemy at short range, being fully exposed to their fire at the time."[19]

John F. Austin, another member of the regiment wounded soon after moving forward, barely escaped with his life. Writing a sister from a Washington hospital on December 17, Austin noted, "I am as well as could be expected after being wounded. My head is not very bad as the ball did not go through very deep." Austin survived his convalescence after receiving a medical discharge. He would join the Rhode Island Militia as an officer in September 1863.[20]

To the south, the 12th Rhode Island also endured Confederate hell-fire. The regiment's advance was halted as the men dropped to the ground in an effort to avoid cannon blasts and musketry. After the prone respite, the new soldiers continued into the havoc of Southern fire. Men hoping to find cover in the indentation of the railroad cut grew despondent when a Confederate cannon fired straight down the trench. Escaping that new danger, the men continued on, knowing they could not find a safe square inch on the field below Marye's Heights. As a veteran of the 12th wrote, "If ever I prayed in good earnest it was while I was running the gauntlet of those rebel rifle pits."[21]

Lt. Oscar Lapham, in Company B, felt utterly forlorn as he rose up from the railroad cut.

When my head passed above the top of that bank it seemed to me there was a perfect hurricane of lead howling, screeching and hissing through the air. The ground was strewn with dead and wounded and debris of all sorts—haversacks, knapsacks, canteens and broken muskets. It seemed to me, as I stood up, that the air above my head was thick enough with lead to cut my finger off if I had held it up.[22]

Like with Bliss and the 7th Rhode Island, the 12th's leader, Col. George Browne, lost some of his senior officers, creating command difficulties in the rookie regiment. Nagle reported how the new outfit experienced "some little difficulty" moving ahead and aligning. Nonetheless, the brigade commander suggested Browne "is entitled to much praise for his personal conduct." Browne suggested the 2nd Maryland's fragmented advance hindered his own troops, creating "considerable disorder" among soldiers of the two regiments.[23]

With Nagle's left wing on the southern edge of Sumner's attack, much of the rest of the Right Grand Division melded together in the killing ground between town and Marye's Heights. Regiments from Sturgis's two brigades tried to sustain some measure of pressure on the Confederate line, with little effect. Any thoughts of trying to flank the right end of the Confederate line were stillborn due to the unremitting enemy fire.[24]

As the division's lone reserve, members of the 48th Pennsylvania listened and watched as the dreadful afternoon unfolded. Observing the path of Confederate shells was one way to pass the difficult moments. Soon after moving forward at about 2:30 p.m., the regiment attracted a great deal of Southern attention, what an officer considered "a terrible storm of deadly missiles." The randomness of where cannon balls and musketry fell was another aspect of the fight the officer recalled so well. One individual could be completely unharmed by an exploding shell, while another a short distance away could be covered in dirt, marked by powder, or left to die.[25]

Each company of the regiment detached a small number of members, those considered the best shots, to target Confederate cannoneers. Some level of revenge could be gained this way, as enemy artillerists fell on occasion. Northern lives may very well have been saved by the use of the 48th's most accurate marksmen. Nonetheless, the Unionists could not do enough as firing continued and daylight began to wane. The intensity of the noise and the glut of Confederate fire made for a harrowing ordeal even for the day's survivors. As the regimental historian of the 48th recalled, "Every faculty was absorbed in our work."[26]

"They cut us up dreadfully," Pennsylvanian Henry Heisler informed his sister. Discussing the fate of a soldier in his company, Heisler added, "One of them had his whole head shot off by a shell." Escaping the horrors of the field below the Confederate position was a highly dangerous idea while daylight lasted. Staying prone even after an individual's ammunition ran out was the best option. General Sturgis himself knew as much. He would not start to withdraw his division until relief arrived well after dark. Even with the lack of progress, Sturgis was grateful for the courage so many of his soldiers exhibited, "Every man fought as if the fate of the day depended upon his own individual exertion."[27]

HAWKINS MAKES AN EFFORT

Willcox's men were not done with charges against Marye's Heights. The third part of the Ninth Corps' support of the main attack began at 5 p.m. Willcox ordered one brigade of the Third Division to move forward, with the other brigade behind in support. Rush Hawkins's Brigade would be the division's lead. The men would be engaged on the southern end of the main Confederate position along Marye's Heights, near the spot of the farthest advance of Nagle's left. The field below the wall, already filled with fallen Unionists from Sumner's two corps, had additional space to accommodate the late-day bloodletting.[28]

New Yorker Rush Hawkins led his brigade in the last charge of Ninth Corps units at Fredericksburg. LIBRARY OF CONGRESS

Earlier in the day, the unfortunate cost of friendly fire became a notable memory for many in Getty's two brigades. Union cannons firing from the east side of the Rappahannock occasionally blasted ordinance that would fall short. Capt. Henry Hoyt, 8th Connecticut, reported the "severe ranking fire" the regiment endured due to errant Unionist shells. Maj. Martin Buffum of the 4th Rhode Island lamented, "Several of the men were wounded by shells fired from one of our own batteries across the river, very many of which exploded in our immediate vicinity."[29]

The railroad cut, lateness of the day, undulating ground, and mud limited the utility of an attack from one more brigade. An officer in the 13th New Hampshire wondered if any plan had been realistically developed. He suggested, "The Union Generals could not have known and really did not know the extreme difficulties of this assault." General Willcox optimistically believed a further effort near the southern end of Marye's Heights might make the difference. He hoped "to draw off some portion of the enemy's troops from our right, and, possibly, to find a weak point in his lines, and effect a lodgment." Evidence points toward Willcox making his own decision to move Getty's division ahead; army headquarters does not seem to have required the attack.[30]

The corps commander's optimism seemed buttressed by a false report about Second Corps troops breaching part of the stone wall. William Marvel, the most diligent student on headquarters-corps communication at the battle of Fredericksburg, believes Willcox reported the Second Corps' success to Burnside at 3:25 p.m., although the note is timed an hour later in the *Official Records*. The positive report from the right, however erroneous, likely played a major role in Willcox's decision to order Hawkins forward.[31]

Overly sanguine generals were not the only problem Hawkins and his regiments faced. Hazel Run confined the assault to a narrow strip of land not conducive to successful offensive operations. Tired Confederates remained determined to resist, making the Unionist plan less of a sure thing than those wearing stars may have assumed. The effort had to be attempted, per orders, so Hawkins began to move out. Knowing how darkness would likely save lives, an officer in the 13th New Hampshire,

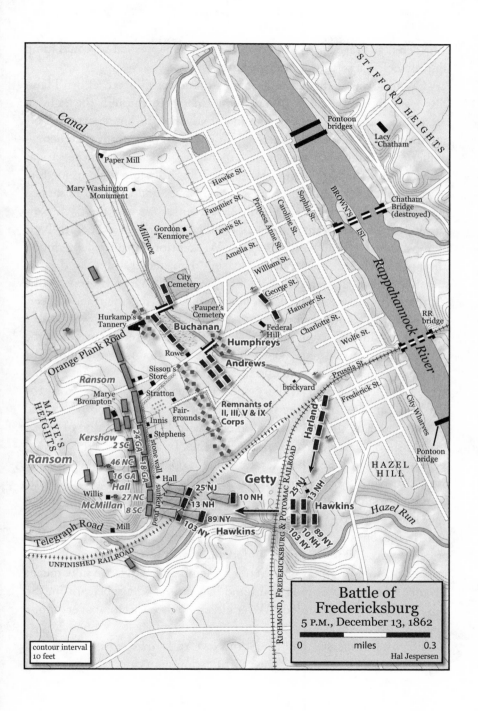

STAFFORD HEIGHTS

Canal

Paper Mill

Mary Washington
Monument

Gordon
"Kenmore"

Millrace

Hawke St.

Fauquier St.

Lewis St.

Amelia St.

Princess Anne St.

Caroline St.

Sophia St.

William St.

George St.

Hanover St.

Charlotte St.

Wolfe St.

Pontoon
bridges

Lacy
"Chatham"

BROWN'S ISL.

Chatham
Bridge
(destroyed)

Rappahannock River

RR
bridge

City
Cemetery

Orange Plank Road

Hurkamp's
Tannery

Pauper's
Cemetery

Buchanan

Rowe

Sisson's
Store

Humphreys

Andrews

Federal
Hill

brickyard

Prussia St.

Frederick St.

City Wharves

Ransom

Marye
"Brompton"

Stratton

Innis

Fair-
grounds

Remnants of
II, III, V & IX
Corps

Harland

Hazel Hill

Pontoon
bridge

MARYE'S
HEIGHTS

Kershaw

2 SC

24 GA

18 GA

Stephens

stone wall

sunken road

Hall

25 NJ

13 NH

10 NH

Getty

25 NJ

13 NH

Hawkins

Ransom

46 NC

16 GA

Hall

Willis

27 NC

McMillan

8 SC

89 NY

103 NY   Hawkins

Hawkins

103 NY

10 NH

89 NY

Hazel Run

Telegraph Road

Mill

UNFINISHED RAILROAD

RICHMOND, FREDERICKSBURG & POTOMAC RAILROAD

**Battle of
Fredericksburg**
5 P.M., December 13, 1862

0   miles   0.3

Hal Jespersen

contour interval
10 feet

considered as brave a man as any in the regiment, wished he could jump up to knock the setting sun down faster.[32]

Confusion would rule the brigade's noble yet doomed effort. Hawkins tried to ensure his regiments could navigate through the railroad cut, crossing diagonally along the line of advance. In his report, the colonel noted how his troops "received an enfilading fire from the enemy's artillery and infantry." Some redressing of the lines became necessary as soldiers in blue fell while others struggled mightily just to continue forward. Lieutenant Thompson suggested how mud and the ground sapped the power from both his own 13th New Hampshire and the 25th New Jersey. The Garden State regiment's line had fractured, so the 13th New Hampshire moved up to fill the gap. "We kept on in spite of the mud," Thompson wrote, although the soggy soil "damaged, if it did not destroy, the effective power of both regiments." Still, Col. Aaron Stevens of the 13th was impressed with his regiment, musing, "the men and officers advanced firmly and steadily."[33]

Col. Andrew Derrom, leading the 25th New Jersey, reported on the soldiers' ability to advance, albeit haltingly and against great odds. The day simply could not be won due to "a heavy fire in front" and "enfilading fire on the left flank of artillery and musketry." Friendly fire from the rear also detracted from the brigade's offensive power. Shooting ceased for a time during the desperate moments, with Derrom writing of only a level of shooting expected from a picket line. In addition to the obvious terrain advantages the Confederates enjoyed, Derrom could not even see the 103rd New York, a regiment the 25th was supposed to advance with. "If properly supported," Derrom wrote of the attack, "good results might have been attained."[34]

Thompson shared Derrom's sense of helplessness, even after the brigade moved closer to the Confederates on the southern end of the stone wall. The young Granite Stater remembered, "Advance now means advance to a grave, or upon scant and bad rations in a rebel prison." So close to the enemy, he added, "We could easily throw a stone over among them."[35]

Harvey Henderson and the 89th New York marched in the second line of Hawkins's regiments. The mortification men can feel while under fire was succinctly noted in Henderson's diary. "It looked like certain death," he wrote. Leading the 89th forward, Harrison Fairchild, quite familiar with forlorn attacks after Antietam, reported on the problematic afternoon. Quickly seeing the impossibility of a good outcome, Fairchild witnessed "great confusion" in the 13th New Hampshire, the regiment to his immediate front. Fairchild could not stem "an immediate panic and stampede" of his soldiers.[36]

Darkness brought a sense of awe to a member of the 9th New York, watching the conflagration from his regiment's reserve position. "At this time the grandest scene of the battle was to be witnessed," he remembered, "The fire on both sides was still kept up, and the air was brightly illuminated with a grand pyrotechnic display." Eventually, a New Hampshire soldier added, "night mercifully draws her mantle of darkness on the horrible scenes below."[37]

George Getty's two brigades suffered 296 killed, wounded, and missing. The eighty-five casualties in the 25th New Jersey—more than one in four men lost in the attack—topped the division. Derrom's Company A included five killed or mortally wounded, most of those in the 25th who died as a direct result of the battle. As with other regiments across the war, many men wounded in action would never return to the field. Some New Jerseymen with amputated limbs lingered in hospitals well into 1863 before receiving medical discharges.[38]

Although part of Getty's reserve and only suffering sixteen casualties, the 4th Rhode Island lost their commanding officer. Lt. Col. Joseph Curtis, only twenty-six years old, "fell dead from his horse" after "a fragment from a shell had struck just below his eye and passed up into his brain," according to Lt. Henry Spooner. He continued, "I was just behind him when he fell, and immediately dismounting to assist him, I found him perfectly motionless and dead." Curtis would be buried at North Burial Ground in Providence.[39]

TERRIBLE LOSSES IN THREE NEW REGIMENTS

As some Ninth Corps men tried to use darkness to escape their position close to the Confederate line, many others stayed at the spot of their farthest advance near Marye's Heights. Lieutenant Spooner noted how soldiers laid on their arms overnight. He was quite thankful for the rise of ground protecting his 4th Rhode Island. "It is only surprising that no more were killed," he mused in a letter home.[40]

Three regiments never under fire before—the 11th New Hampshire, and 7th and 12th Rhode Island—accounted for one-third of the Ninth Corps' killed in action at Fredericksburg. Col. Walter Harriman's 11th New Hampshire topped the Ninth Corps butcher's bill. The 195 casualties in the regiment included nineteen killed and twenty-five captured or missing. Nagle's two Rhode Island regiments constituted the bulk of the loss in the brigade. Zenas Bliss's 7th Regiment suffered 158 killed, wounded, and missing, with the 12th Rhode Island losing a total of 108.[41]

After a request from division surgeon Calvin Cutter, members of the 9th New Hampshire band assisted with medical care as much as possible. Their first mission led to the clearing of four houses and a church. Not long after, "The surgeons began to cut and slash," John Bailey wrote in his diary, "many limbs being no doubt needlessly lost" due to the volume of wounded troops. While "gaining nothing," so many Northern soldiers suffered. Nonetheless, Cutter's devotion to the troops cannot be denied. As General Ferrero reported, Cutter fell from his horse on December 13, but still "was unremitting in his attentions to the wounded, and was of invaluable service."[42]

Having seen so many men hit did not diminish Charlie Paige's firm faith. "I know God was near me," the 11th New Hampshire man wrote to his wife, "I felt no fear worth naming." When a sergeant in the regiment needed transportation to a hospital, Paige and four others carried him back toward town. Another bullet hit the unfortunate casualty. The ball traveled from his left shoulder, exiting on the right side. After shells wounded two of those moving the sergeant, Paige wrote of being "truly thankful" for reaching the hospital at about 10 p.m.[43]

Part of Hawkins's brigade, the 10th New Hampshire experienced their first enemy fire at Fredericksburg, three months after leaving home. Col. Aaron Stevens provided a list of casualties from the regiment's difficult December afternoon. Even with forty killed or wounded, the 10th was fortunate, Stevens suggested. In an early January letter, he wrote, "I have reason to thank God . . . for his preservation of my officers and men and myself."[44]

Far fewer members of the Ninth Corps would have survived Fredericksburg if Major General Burnside pursued an idea he conceived after the bitter repulse of the Right Grand Division. The army commander wished to personally lead the Ninth Corps in a charge up the hill to Marye's Heights on December 14. Edwin Sumner receives much credit from history for dissuading his chief from such a reckless action.[45]

Orlando Willcox's confidence in further attacks on December 13 waned considerably as he took up his pen after the battle. In a letter to his wife on December 16, the Ninth Corps leader opined, "I can truly say the failure of our bold, impracticable attempt upon the enemy's fortified lines was not unexpected." The time of year, condition of the ground, and overall dynamics of charging Marye's Heights operated against success, Willcox continued. He remained a firm believer in ultimate Union victory, just not under such trying conditions.[46]

OPTIMISM AND DESPAIR ALONG THE RAPPAHANNOCK

"The firing was very heavy yesterday and the conflict exceedingly severe," Lt. Henry Spooner informed his parents on December 14. Adding further truth, Spooner lamented, "The enemy's position is very strong, and when they will be forced from it is dubious." A Confederate artillery officer, witness to the immense slaughter below Marye's Heights correctly pegged Fredericksburg as "the simplest and easiest won battle of the war." Elmer Bragg, 9th New Hampshire, observed, "The customary quiet has settled down again upon the army and things again appear as before the battle, except for our diminished ranks, which tells its own mournful tale."[47]

Those unscarred by visible wounds below Marye's Heights had to endure the difficulties of military life after a bitter battlefield defeat. Troops did not start to recross the Rappahannock until December 15. Soon, the stark reality of a humiliating loss at the hands of Confederates filled minds and hearts. Jerry Smith, 51st New York, likely summed up the mentality of many as he wrote of the meteorological facts prevailing as the season changed. "Cold, raw weather most of the time," he reported home on December 20. Nonetheless, damaged morale did not doom either the Ninth Corps or the army to a feckless future, with men across Burnside's command not giving up.[48]

Valorous troops could still rest with a certain level of contentment, even though Fredericksburg was a costly disaster. As the Massachusetts adjutant general was informed soon after the battle, "This being the eighth general engagement in which the 21st Mass. Vols. has acted an important part during the past year, it is superfluous to state that both officers and men behaved like veterans." The general was also informed, "it is but just to add that the reputation won by the 2nd brigade under the gallant and lamented Reno was worthily sustained at the battle of Fredericksburg."[49]

In the 9th New Hampshire, George Henry Chandler captured such sentiment, a mix of the maudlin and hopeful. In letters written before 1863 began, Chandler knew the defeat at Fredericksburg "must be a serious blow to the Union cause," adding "the slaughter was immense." As with many in the Ninth Corps after Second Bull Run, however, Chandler called on an inner strength to persevere. "You may consider me as comfortable and happy," he noted on Christmas Day, "not admiring this style of life, but willing to stand my hand and abide the end." Simple pleasures could help men feel better. On New Year's Day, another New Hampshire soldier complained about the dearth of good news, but "it is not bad lying in camp beside a good fire."[50]

Friendly competitions around regimental campsites were a way to discover some winter joy. John Bailey, 9th New Hampshire, found the work to construct huts fascinating to observe. In his diary on December 20, he noted, "The boys all busy in completing their houses, each trying to outdo the other in style and finish." Chimney creation was another necessity as cold weather persisted, although sometimes men would struggle mightily to build sufficient draft to ensure what Bailey humorously called "our mansions" could remain smokeless.[51]

Through the storm clouds of disaster, David Lane, 17th Michigan, believed the army could find a victorious path eventually. Better leadership was the key.

Surely we have made blunders, but will we not profit by them? We are learning the art of war—time is required to change a citizen into a soldier. Our officers are being weighed—the light weights cast aside or relegated to their class—and the good work will go on until one is found of size and weight to cope with Lee. 'Tis said, "Great generals are born, not made."[52]

Highlander William Lusk, who pined for the return of McClellan and had very little faith in the Lincoln administration, detailed his morose mindset in several letters later in December. Even as he described the lack of planning before the battle of Fredericksburg and the difficulty in seeing any good from defeat, he pinpointed ways soldiers could move on. "I am determined to be good-humored in bidding farewell to the old year," even though 1862 brought "so many disasters," Lusk informed his sister. Members of the acclaimed 79th New York "mean to celebrate the New Year," with turkey, ham, bread, and punch. Corps commander Willcox stopped by the Highlanders' January 1 festivities.[53]

Time for fun prevailed because President Lincoln canceled an advance Burnside wished to make on December 30. Two Sixth Corps generals who doubted Burnside's abilities had visited Washington to express their views. This led Lincoln to wire Army of the Potomac headquarters, prohibiting a major move until Burnside could discuss matters. Burnside promised to see Lincoln the following day, a meeting at which the president informed Burnside of doubts from his own generals. Smarting from the incident and without clear guidance from Washington, Burnside returned to his ragged army near Fredericksburg.[54]

Ninth Corps men began the year continuing to work at staying warm, while also serving on picket duty. Moving water and wood became a cumbersome necessity. Those keeping an eye on the Rappahannock had a chance to converse with friendly Confederates, which was common while also contrary to orders. "A series of pleasant days" warmed spirits, even with frosty nights. Notable changes in temperature created an enemy those in the Army of the Potomac would know throughout their service: Virginia mud. As the historian of the 29th Massachusetts remembered, "the ground was like a quagmire, and the roads almost impassable."[55]

Men in the Third Division experienced a reorganization on January 5. A third brigade was formed by moving two regiments from each of the original brigades. The 21st Connecticut, 13th New Hampshire, 25th New Jersey, and 4th Rhode Island constituted the new brigade. As the senior colonel, Arthur Dutton of the 21st Connecticut assumed command. A memoirist from the Ocean State regiment noted his satisfaction with the change. Lieutenant Spooner, also of the 4th Rhode Island, had the added joy of an excellent new horse, purchased from the regimental chaplain, who was heading home. Spooner happily declared he now possessed "the *fastest* horse in the regiment."[56]

The next day brought a review of the Ninth Corps by Generals Burnside, Sumner, and Willcox. The "cold and wet" conditions produced "rather a tame affair," but likely gave Burnside a boost when seeing his former command. As Willcox reported, the weather did not hamper hearty cheers from Ninth Corps men on seeing Burnside. To Lieutenant Thompson of the 13th New Hampshire, the greeting Willcox's divisions gave the army commander seemed less rousing. The young junior officer detected "stern determination rather than enthusiasm" in the army.[57]

Hamilton Dunlap, 100th Pennsylvania, informed his sister of the friendly Confederates that could be met at a watering location both sides used. Trying to be respectful of orders against such fraternization, Dunlap refrained from meeting his enemy. "We were so close," however, "I could hit one with a stone."[58]

Sickness plagued many regiments, as officers and surgeons worked to improve conditions. The move to Getty's new Third Brigade came at a time of terrible health problems for members of the 21st Connecticut, with the regiment's historian remembering twenty soldiers buried in the month after Fredericksburg. A change to higher ground seemed to lessen the danger from disease, with the regimental surgeon gaining credit for saving lives.[59]

Later in January, Theodore Nutting wrote his mother and sister. The 6th New Hampshire man felt despondent. "I am discouraged and have about given up the idea of ever getting out of this hellish war," which "has lasted long enough." Casting about for blame, Nutting added, "Curses on the leaders and instigators of this unholy and bloody war, I say." Another soldier not keen on emancipation, Nutting went so far as to request money that he might use after deserting. "I want the money in case of emergency," the bitter soldier concluded, "for fighting for Niggers is played out with me."[60]

Fresh from picket duty on January 11, Charles Dwight Chase informed his father of the very disagreeable weather as a rapid freeze followed rain. The soggy and cold duty zapped the young soldier's energy. A member of the 9th New Hampshire, Chase wrote in hopes of a good pair of boots, which would have made the duty somewhat bearable. "This Southern mud," he added, "and water to stand in all night is not very agreable, I assure you."[61]

The elements were about to make life even worse for the army and Burnside himself. The two biggest developments for Union arms in Virginia during the second half of January were what history calls "The Mud March," as well as the end of Burnside's command of the Army of the Potomac. By the time both the Lincoln administration and the army were ready to move, Mother Nature forced a bitter end to Burnside's plans. Ninth Corps troops stayed in camps as part of the force directly across from Fredericksburg, so the men did not experience the seemingly infinite mud that plagued the march. Soon after beginning, Burnside's last advance as commander of the Army of the Potomac left tens of thousands of soldiers horribly dejected, while dozens of men, horses, and mules died from the harsh weather and soil seemingly able to swallow living things at will.[62]

With continued spats among headquarters and senior generals, Burnside's frustrations reached their apex. He demanded the dismissal of several of his generals, or the acceptance of his resignation. President Lincoln took the latter course, quickly offering army command to Burnside's nemesis Joe Hooker. Regarding Burnside's fall, William Lusk summed up the thinking of many, "If Burnside was not a Napoleon, he was a first-rate soldier, and in a subordinate position can do splendid service to the country."[63]

Burnside used a general order to offer his farewell to the Army of the Potomac. Putting aside his ego, something Burnside did better than most senior generals during the war, he requested the troops show devotion to their new commander. Burnside added, "In taking an affectionate leave of the entire army, from which he separates with so much regret, he may be pardoned if he bids an especial farewell to his long-tried associates of the Ninth Corps."[64]

NEWPORT NEWS AGAIN

As the army changed commanders, dull life continued for Ninth Corps soldiers. Drill, staying warm, and trying to lift spirits however possible occupied a great deal of time. The 21st Massachusetts historian noted the Bay Staters were part of the army's extensive picket detail on January 28, with fresh snow falling. Soldiers watching the river had a chance to see Confederates engage in snowball fights. The next day, men in the 21st worked hard to increase the regiment's amount of firewood. Of the vital need for biomass, the historian wrote, "The supply has been very short for some weeks, and the men have dug up every stump near the camp."[65]

Hooker immediately took steps to improve the lot of his soldiers. By early February, David Lane reported, "We are building a huge oven, large enough to supply our brigade with soft bread." Additionally, the 35th Massachusetts historian remarked how the improved weather boded well for the future. At the start of February, "the weather became milder for several days; the influence of spring was soon felt, hope revived with the season." He also pointed to administrative improvements Hooker made as a means to support the troops. Along with fresh bread, vegetables could easily please a soldier.[66]

Command shuffles brought change to the Ninth Corps. More senior generals took short-term command. John Sedgwick and William Smith held the highest spot in the corps for part of the winter, with Orlando Willcox returning to leadership of the First Division. He did not seem dejected about his demotion. Willcox wrote about being on good terms with Hooker.[67]

Nothing brightened the life of Ninth Corps men over the winter more than orders to change their location. On January 31, Halleck ordered Hooker to move the entire corps to Fort Monroe. The Ninth Corps' immediate future was more time at Newport News, a place where so many pleasing memories were made over the summer.[68] Then, the wonderful location served as a transition point from the Carolina Coast to Second Bull Run and the Antietam campaign. Where their next assignment would send them remained a mystery.

Recollections and letters of the time at Newport News unsurprisingly noted the greatness of the spot, especially compared to the cramped and muddy camps around Falmouth. The 21st Massachusetts historian happily wrote of Newport News as "still a beautiful place for a camp, and our line of new tents, a mile and a half long, made a very impressive show." Charlie Paige, 11th New Hampshire, was thrilled. "This is a beautiful place," Paige wrote home, "It is level for miles and no Virginia mud either." Charles Brigham, of the state's 9th Regiment and fresh from four months in a hospital, described the new camp as "a nice sandy place in sight of the James River." He enjoyed living in a hut of pine logs, what he called a "tip top shanty." A pleasant sea breeze added to the positive mood.[69]

On February 25, many soldiers benefited from increased morale due to a grand review of the Ninth Corps. Charles Brigham estimated 17,000 men were part of the big event. "You could not see either end," he wrote, "nothing could be seen but artillery and infantry." A Massachusetts officer thought the review might not have been enough to justify the extensive amount of drill occurring across regiments in recent days. He felt a new campaign was in the offing, but still, no one could pin down a location for the next adventure. Mysteries about the future did not hamper soldiers who enjoyed the fine, sunny day that blessed "the finest review we have yet seen," according to a New Hampshire officer.[70]

With Burnside on leave, Orlando Willcox noted the rumors floating around Newport News. Willcox correctly expected the command would remain linked to Burnside. For the moment, the men fell under Maj. Gen. John Dix, head of the Department of Virginia. Like so many of his soldiers, Willcox did not let questions about the future cloud the present. He informed his wife of the sublime nature of regimental camps at

Newport News. Dix, meanwhile, wondered if Burnside would supplant him as commander of the department, which was based at Ft. Monroe.[71]

Orders resolving the mystery of the Ninth Corps' new assignment began with an early March letter from Horatio Wright, in charge of the Department of the Ohio, to the governor of Kentucky. The state held prominence in Union war planning. Wright, responsible for organizing Kentucky's defense from his headquarters in Cincinnati, agreed with the governor on "the necessity of further forces" to shield Kentucky from Confederate invasion. Although Wright believed some troops could come from Kentucky itself, additional men "must be sent from other departments." Wright also suggested a more senior officer should take command of the department. Fresh from leave, Burnside seemed an obvious choice. On March 16, Halleck ordered Burnside to take two divisions to Cincinnati, then immediately assume command of the Department of the Ohio.

In orders the next day, Burnside placed Maj. Gen. John Parke in command of the portion of the Ninth Corps heading west. The plan originally had the Second and Third divisions prepare for the long journey, with Willcox's division staying put. However, Getty's men would be the division remaining at Newport News, but only for a short time. The regiments received orders to augment the siege force around Suffolk, Virginia, south of the James River, starting in early March. Of the Third Division's infantry regiments, only the 4th Rhode Island would serve in the Ninth Corps again.[72]

TO KENTUCKY

Parke's two divisions did not head for Cincinnati at the same time. Willcox's men departed first, with the troops breaking camp at Newport News on March 19. Via steamer, the brigades ventured to Baltimore, where railroad transportation awaited. Of the train journey, David Lane, 17th Michigan, wrote, "We were three days and three nights on the cars, winding around or darting through the rocky barriers that opposed us." A Highlander recalled, "We were as comfortable as our cramped quarters admitted" during the long journey. Riding through more than twenty mountain tunnels was a treat for the soldiers, a Roundhead wrote his family. The division started arriving near Burnside's headquarters early in the morning of March 27.[73]

Sam Sturgis and his Second Division had begun vacating their Newport News camps on March 25. An overnight stay in Baltimore was necessary due to the lack of railroad cars. An officer in the 51st Pennsylvania noted how the city's residents, although known for secessionist proclivities, were happy to see the 2nd Maryland among the soldiers waiting for their turn to ride toward the setting sun.[74]

Even if the mode of transportation was not eminently comfortable, men in the division—like Willcox's regiments—found much to remember about the trek to Cincinnati. Meals from appreciative citizens in cities and towns helped instill a great sense of happiness in the traveling soldiers. Charles Brigham, 9th New Hampshire, wrote of the "nice supper" in Pittsburgh, with "a dinner of the best kind" awaiting the men in Cincinnati.[75]

The Ninth Corps began moving west at nearly the same time General-in-chief Halleck sent a long message to Burnside about the goals for the Department of the Ohio. The message, sent on March 23, included work for the Ninth Corps and other troops that would soon be organized into the Twenty-third Corps. Without turning his ideas into stringent orders, Halleck suggested Burnside focus on relief for the Unionist region of East Tennessee, occupation of mountain gaps between that region and Kentucky, and dispersing forces across Central Kentucky. Halleck noted the department's difficult mission, but Burnside's devotion to his duties helped the general comprehend how to defend the large patch of geography for which he was responsible.[76]

Putting great energy into his assignment, Burnside likely grew gleeful after being informed the Ninth Corps was heading west. He dispatched numerous messages daily through March, ordering brigade commanders to ensure sufficient ammunition for their men, and sending a note to recently promoted Brig Gen. Thomas Welsh, to head to Cincinnati to rejoin his troops. The dedicated officer was spending some time at home on leave. Later in the spring, Welsh would command the First Division after Willcox was given command of a military district under Burnside.

"I will help all I can," Burnside wrote Halleck on March 30. He also used the note to express his hope that the Third Division of the Ninth Corps could be sent to Kentucky. The dream would not be realized. Logistical challenges in Burnside's department limited the ability to sustain offensive drives against Confederate territory. Just two divisions of the Ninth Corps helped provide relief to both Burnside and his bosses about the state's safety.[77]

After their great trek to the Bluegrass State, Ninth Corps men found little risk from enemy forces. As the Massachusetts adjutant general was informed, from the perspective of the 35th Regiment, the time in Kentucky brought "considerable marching," but "nothing of importance occurred." Troops were posted in different areas to respect Washington's desire for the protection of Central Kentucky.[78]

Spread out across several locations as spring continued, Ninth Corps soldiers marched a great deal without notable sightings of enemy troops. Burnside's Boys found Kentucky very pleasing and quite beautiful. Jerry Smith, 51st New York, was so smitten he mused, "I think if I live to get out of this, I will come out here and settle down." "This is a fine country," New Hampshire's Theodore Nutting wrote home, "and we have many Union friends among the Citizens." Another Granite Stater joyously declared, "We have been making ourselves quite comfortable here," seeing landscapes "as fertile as a garden." He was adoring "the finest part of creation I have ever seen." Growing up in a state filled with natural beauty, the compliments New Hampshire men gave Kentucky ring quite loudly. George Rowell, 6th New Hampshire, called the region around Lexington, "the handsomest Country that ever I put my eyes on." Soon, the Second Division would march to Lancaster, 30 miles due south of Lexington. To the west, the First Division camped near Lebanon, Kentucky.[79]

Quite busy managing his department, Burnside still had a particular interest in the Ninth Corps. On April 26, he wrote the governor of New York with a special request regarding the 51st Regiment. "As this is one of our best regiments and has seen very hard service," Burnside wrote, "it is very desirable that its ranks should be filled up." Of special concern to Burnside were the thirteen officer vacancies.[80]

Burnside still assumed East Tennessee would be the next major destination for his troops, grouped as the Army of the Ohio. With regiments camped across cities and towns in Kentucky, a surprising twist awaited the Ninth Corps.[81] Parke's two divisions would instead witness the denouement of a seminal campaign of the war. The heat and humidity of Mississippi beckoned.

VICKSBURG AND JACKSON

Vicksburg had vexed Union political and military leadership for a year. The city sat on a high bluff overlooking the Mississippi River. As the Ninth Corps headed south in June, Maj. Gen. Ulysses S. Grant's forces had been mired in a siege for a month, quite costly in terms of casualties. Even if the final outcome was likely going to be a Unionist victory against the surrounded town short on supplies, the army wanted Grant to have more men at his disposal.[82]

As constantly occurred in Civil War armies, reorganization was ongoing for the Ninth Corps during the year in the West. Five regiments sent to Kentucky in the spring did not venture to Vicksburg. Both the 27th New Jersey and 12th Rhode Island went home to muster out after their nine-month enlistments. Three Second Division regiments remained in Kentucky: 2nd Maryland, 21st Massachusetts, and 48th Pennsylvania. This trio of units, all of which would rejoin the Ninth Corps, temporarily became part of Burnside's Twenty-third Corps.[83]

Logistical magic occurred to move the two divisions to Vicksburg. The troops reached Cairo, Illinois, meeting place of the Ohio and Mississippi Rivers, for a steamer ride south. Landing in Memphis for a short stop, the Ninth Corps reached the Louisiana shore across from Vicksburg on June 14 as protective gunboats eyed the Mississippi's banks. The troops then began crossing the river into the Union position around Vicksburg.[84]

Memories of an unbearable Southern summer remained indelible for Ninth Corps men. Soldiers experienced what a New Hampshire man called "beastly" weather. One major side effect of the hot conditions was insalubrious water, if any could be found at all. Discovering better camps became a necessity, which led to changes in location as June unfolded.

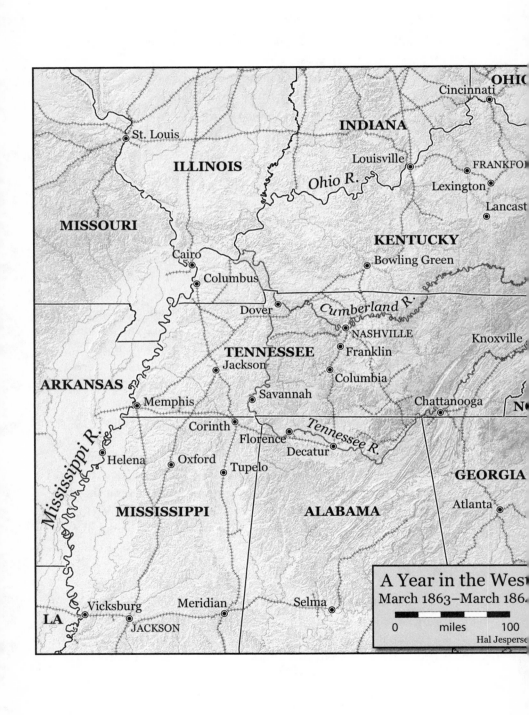

OHIO

Cincinnati

INDIANA

St. Louis

ILLINOIS

Louisville

FRANKFORT

Ohio R.

Lexington

Lancast

MISSOURI

KENTUCKY

Cairo

Bowling Green

Columbus

Dover

Cumberland R.

Knoxville

NASHVILLE

TENNESSEE

Franklin

Jackson

Columbia

ARKANSAS

Savannah

Chattanooga

N

Memphis

Corinth

Tennessee R.

Florence

Mississippi R.

Decatur

Helena

Oxford

Tupelo

GEORGIA

Atlanta

MISSISSIPPI

ALABAMA

Vicksburg

Meridian

Selma

LA

JACKSON

A Year in the West
March 1863–March 1864

0   miles   100

Hal Jesperse

Even with the dangers to health from the dry and hot conditions, soldiers still made the best of their situation. As the 51st Pennsylvania's historian remembered, "insects of all descriptions" plagued lives, but the troops "gather daily large quantities of blackberries, and also a fruit resembling very close to what we call at home mountain cherries." Giving credit where due, the Keystone Stater pronounced the Mississippi fruits "vastly superior."[85]

After moving camps multiple times north of the doomed city, Parke's men would not take a major military role as the siege unfolded. Digging entrenchments and protective structures took much time, as heat and humidity continued. Sporadic skirmishing, rather than organized attacks, constituted the extent of Ninth Corps combat operations. Milldale, north of Vicksburg, would be the camp of longest duration for Parke's troops before they moved farther east.[86]

On July 4, the day after the Army of the Potomac's major victory at Gettysburg, Confederate forces around Vicksburg surrendered. Grant's weary but determined army then occupied a Southern citadel sitting above the country's mightiest river. Of the city, George Rowell, serving as a hospital steward in Nagle's brigade, informed his parents, "It is a hard looking place," with the inhabitants "fairly starved out." The best fare for residents was mule meat, with no bread in sight.[87]

As a fresh force, having spent less than three weeks in the trenches, the Ninth Corps became part of the field army sent east to Jackson. Grant had been concerned about possible Confederate reinforcements coming from that direction. Although limited potential existed for Confederates to threaten Grant's mighty force around Vicksburg, Parke and his men would factor into the conquest of a Confederate state capital.[88]

Marching conditions were exceedingly difficult. Highlander Henry Heffron recalled his travails in a letter. The excursion to Jackson included "five days hard marching with hardly any water." Desperate for some hydration, he continued, "I actually drank water on that march that a thirsty mule could not be encouraged to touch."[89]

Like many soldiers, David Lane used humor as an effort to accept his fate in a July 5 letter.

No doubt our northern friends think they have seen dusty roads, but if they could have seen us yesterday or today, they would have thought the dustiest time they ever saw was clean and airy in comparison. The road, and two or three rods on either side, was beaten into the finest powder, and the feet of men and horses caused it to rise in sooty clouds, which enveloped us in their stifling, smothering folds. There was no breeze to carry it away—no possibility of avoiding it.[90]

"The heat was so intense that quite a number were overcome by it," Granite Stater John Bailey wrote in his diary. Some men went straight into the Big Black River, which the Ninth Corps crossed on July 7, without removing clothes. In his regimental history, Col. Byron Cutcheon of the 20th Michigan remembered temperatures that exceeded 100 degrees at points during the trek to Jackson. This could prompt surgeons to order marches halted until later in the day. A torrential downpour further hindered the soldiers' easterly journey, however welcome the cooler water could feel. The next day, men would end up thirsty due to the scorching sun.[91]

By July 10, the Ninth Corps reached the outskirts of Mississippi's capital. "This day was extremely hot," Sumner Carruth would report to the Massachusetts adjutant general. Many men would drop from heat stroke as the tension increased due to the likelihood of a major engagement. Regiments would support each other on the skirmish line for a few days, then rotate out for a day or two of rest. As in Vicksburg, regiments went to work digging rifle pits and preparing for a larger fight, with regular skirmish fire continuing.[92]

An attack would not be needed to conquer Jackson. Confederates evacuated the city during the overnight period of July 16–17. "The rebs set fire to a lot of commissaries stores and a whole square of buildings which were on fire," as Ninth Corps men moved in, New Hampshire's William Fish wrote. Additionally, Unionists "picked up a lot of their deserters who had managed to get left behind." A South Carolinian praised Henry Heffron for the 79th New York's gallantry more than a year previous. Heffron proudly wrote, "He complimented us in the highest terms, and said we were better known in the South than any other regiment in the federal army" due to the intensity of the Highlanders' attack at Secessionville.[93]

After a short occupation of Jackson, Parke's two divisions returned to Vicksburg. Colonel Cutcheon classified the first day's march west "as trying as any the regiment ever made." The Massachusetts adjutant general was informed of the harsh conditions endured before the troops reached their former camp at Milldale. The trip was considered "the hardest four days of marching the 9th A[rmy]C[orps] has yet seen." Parke's brigades covered about 50 miles on the return to Vicksburg, with Simon Griffin remembering the "fearful ordeal for the men," in which "some died on the road."[94]

Mississippi would soon be a memory to the men of Parke's command. On the last day of the very busy and difficult month of July 1863, Grant informed Parke of the Ninth Corps' imminent return to Burnside's department. As quickly as transportation permitted, the troops would move up to Cairo, Illinois, to await further orders. Grant, eager to note the important contributions others made to his own success, praised the Ninth Corps for "valuable services in the campaign just closed." "The endurance, valor, and general good conduct" of Parke's men "are admired by all," Grant added. Parke was then instructed to have "Vicksburg" and "Jackson" added to regimental and battery flags.[95]

REDEEMING KNOXVILLE

Encomiums from General Grant may have lifted Ninth Corps spirits, but disease and lasting illness permanently impacted regiments across Parke's command. As the historian of the 36th Massachusetts remembered, "Every day the effect of the southern campaign was shown in the increasing number of the sick." General Welsh died in Cincinnati later in August. The competent and respected officer was struck hard by malaria, with many others facing "fearful" sickness.[96]

The most significant military service the Ninth Corps performed while in the West was the defense and eventual salvation of Knoxville, Tennessee. Still a priority for Washington officials and General Burnside, protection of the Unionist city and region of East Tennessee grew in importance as Confederates threatened the area. Southern success at

Plagued by malaria contracted in Mississippi, Brig. Gen. Thomas Welsh, a Ninth Corps division commander, died in Cincinnati in August 1863. LIBRARY OF CONGRESS

the battle of Chickamauga in September heightened the dangers facing Chattanooga and Knoxville. After returning from Vicksburg, the reorganized Ninth Corps again became half of the Army of the Ohio, sent to East Tennessee at the critical moment. Burnside took command of the small army in the field.[97]

Strong Unionist sentiment among residents provided Burnside important information about the difficult topography and Confederate forces. Loyalist irregulars also hindered Confederate movements when the fate of Knoxville was still uncertain. Even as Burnside and the Army of the Ohio approached Knoxville, they faced difficult supply issues and the possibility of slim reinforcements should Southern forces decide to mount an attack against the city. Pressing on, Burnside's army dedicated themselves to protecting the Unionist residents. As Robert Jameson, surgeon in the 29th Massachusetts, observed, loyal United States citizens around Knoxville had been suffering from "Jeff Davis Despotism," a reference to the Confederate president.[98]

General-in-chief Halleck deprecated Burnside's abilities and willingness to fight in a missive to Major General Grant, in charge of all army operations in the area. As was his style, Grant had more optimism, offering Burnside assistance and the calm competence so often lacking in Union generals during the war.[99]

Lt. Gen. James Longstreet led his corps against Burnside. A significant battle in the East Tennessee drama occurred on November 16 at Campbell's Station, less than 20 miles west of downtown Knoxville. Regardless of concerns Washington may have held about Burnside, he maneuvered his men well, reaching a crucial crossroads before the Confederates. Pressed hard, Burnside held his command together while starting a retrograde east. Early on the morning of the 17th, Burnside wired President Lincoln, "We have resisted his advance steadily, repulsing every attack, holding on till our position was turned by superior numbers, and then retiring in good order."[100]

Burnside and the Ninth Corps would then head to Knoxville, preparing to hold out as long as possible against Longstreet. Fort Sanders, standing north of the Tennessee River, proved central to the defense of the city. Although an imperfect military bastion, scaling the high fort would prove very difficult. Rifle pits outside the fort offered excellent positions for Unionists. Ninth Corps troops truly shined during the siege of Knoxville. Still not yet twenty-four years old, cannoneer Lt. Samuel Benjamin held an important leadership position atop the fort, proving his indispensable abilities yet again. Burnside praised the young artillerist multiple times in his campaign report.[101]

Less than 4,500 men were present for duty in the Ninth Corps on November 20. The small command stood paramount in the defeat inflicted on Longstreet when Confederates assaulted Fort Sanders on the morning of November 29. The brunt of the attack hit the spot Lieutenant Benjamin wished, the northwest salient. The intensity of the violence and the close quarters fighting lived on in Ninth Corps memories. Surgeon Robert Jameson said the piles of Confederate dead after the battle were "the awfulest sight I ever beheld."[102]

Bravery was not in short supply. Sgt. Francis Judge, 79th New York, earned a Medal of Honor after a flag of the 51st Georgia was planted on the works of Fort Sanders. Judge then "leaped from his position of safety, sprang upon the parapet, and in the face of a concentrated fire seized the flag and returned with it in safety to the fort." Nearby, as Lieutenant Benjamin reported, "I put my pistol within 6 inches of a rebel's face and pulled the trigger three times. They were on the exterior crest of the parapet all the time."[103]

The successful repulse of Longstreet's attack did not end concerns about the Unionists' ability to hold Knoxville. A letter David Lane wrote on November 30 included hopes that General Grant would successfully bolster the Ninth Corps with supplies and men, because "we are on the verge of starvation."

The defeat of the Confederates was the subject of a long letter William Fish wrote in December. "Thank the Lord I have passed through the dangers and hardships of the past 19 days," he proclaimed, "Knoxville is strongly fortified by nature and art." During a truce, burial details went to work. The determined opponents "traded, joked together, caught chicken together, and bid each other goodbye," Fish penned. He pondered the bizarre sight of men shooting at each other one day, then shaking hands the next.[104]

TO ANNAPOLIS AGAIN

Longstreet pulled back from Knoxville in early December. A winter of adversity for the Ninth Corps followed salvation of the city. With supplies nearly out, the troops found little edible to take along for the march north to a month-long encampment near Blain's Crossroads. On arrival, a member of the 45th Pennsylvania recalled how soldiers were compelled to use "the country as our principal commissary." Most members of the brave regiment reenlisted on the first day of the new year. With so many deciding to devote three more years or the duration of the war to the army, the regiment's veteran volunteers earned the right to a furlough of thirty days. The 21st Massachusetts, 8th Michigan, 100th Pennsylvania, and most other Ninth Corps regiments formed in 1861 reenlisted as the new year began. A soldier electing to muster out after only three years still had time to serve. Without the right to a furlough but only required to remain in the army a few more months, about sixty Wolverines from the 8th Regiment joined the 20th Michigan for the rest of their war.[105]

Men electing to not reenlist, or those in newer regiments not yet done with their first tour of duty, focused on surviving the winter. Charles Paige, 11th New Hampshire, noted, "as a substitute for good food, parched corn, or corn otherwise prepared does very well." He mused how hard tack, "when we could get it was dainty food, so was one half pound of flour or cob meal." The 36th Massachusetts's historian wrote of the difficulties in staying supplied in East Tennessee. "Foraging parties were sent out on every hand, but the natives generally 'were plumb out,'" offering very little to hungry soldiers.[106]

David Lane remained in Knoxville, tending to wounded at a hospital. He took care of several comrades in the dedicated and brave 17th Michigan. Lane had plenty to do in his role as nurse. "I have many strong attachments here, and cannot well forsake them to return to the regiment." Lane would remain in Knoxville until the beginning of spring.[107]

Although cold days could sting in the mountains of East Tennessee, an order dispatched on January 12, 1864, demonstrated how the army bureaucracy viewed the Ninth Corps as an important tool for winning the war. Preparations for the next campaign were at the heart of the order, which sent Burnside to New York City for the purpose of recruiting more men. Washington's expressly stated goal was to increase the corps' strength to 50,000 men. The idea would prove rather quixotic, but, as expected from a devoted patriot, Burnside promptly moved to implement the order. As in early 1862, the ultimate location for his troops had yet to be determined.[108]

Into the new year, conditions around Blain's Crossroads remained "deplorable in the extreme," as the 48th Pennsylvania's historian opined.

Lack of good food stood as only one of the miseries. The Keystone Stater recalled the dearth of proper clothing, including shoes. Footgear would often be nothing more than "raw beef-hides, when obtainable, cut into moccasin form and tied with strips of the same." Patriots persevered, as great soldiers did so often during the war.[109]

Change existed as a constant in January. With so few troops due to furloughs, the two-division alignment was reduced to one for a time. Maj. Gen. John Parke, who had served as Burnside's chief of staff in the Army of the Ohio, returned to Ninth Corps command in late January. Robert Potter, originally of the 51st New York, had led the corps since August, then headed to New York for recruiting work when Parke returned. The diminutive command moved closer to Knoxville later in the month, with some skirmishing occurring along the route. Food scarcity continued, with Sewell Tilton, a New Hampshire soldier, writing, "We marched without breakfast" as the trek south began.[110]

With the dull weeks of dreary winter fading away, Ninth Corps troops began the journey back east thanks to a series of orders from the War Department. Special Orders 110, dated March 8, announced Annapolis, Maryland, "as a depot and rendezvous" for the Ninth Corps. Burnside was then ordered to "immediately arrange for the care, control, and instruction" of his command. Six days later, Lt. Gen. Ulysses S. Grant, the army's new general-in-chief, informed Burnside that the Ninth Corps around Knoxville would soon depart Tennessee for Annapolis.[111] The future still a mystery, Burnside's Boys at least had a new destination. They did not know that the war would be over in thirteen months. Although the troops expected sacrifice, the cost of victory would utterly stun the most prepared patriot.

PART SIX

Hellish Spring

*"It is utterly impossible to convey to you
an accurate idea of what this campaign is."*
—DANIEL READ LARNED, NINTH CORPS STAFF MEMBER

"ACTION IS WHAT WE WANT"

The Ninth Corps amounted to a dramatically different organization by the start of May 1864. Many regiments with long service under Burnside joined new units from across the Union. As time in Annapolis wound down, the Ninth Corps was once again comprised of four divisions, one of which included African American enlisted men. When the time came to move back to Virginia, Burnside had nearly 20,000 soldiers present for duty, with thousands more on the way, on detached service, or sick.[1]

Prior to the spring campaign, a fundraising committee helped add 180 soldiers to the 46th, 51st, and 79th New York Regiments. Some letters from the field later in the year thanked the group for their patriotic drive. By the end of August, the 51st Regiment, which had remained in Kentucky during the East Tennessee campaign, would gain 564 of the 667 men raised through the committee's work.[2]

Other veteran regiments added men through new enlistments. The 6th New Hampshire, which also remained in Kentucky rather than head to Knoxville, included 500 soldiers by the start of what history calls Grant's Overland campaign. The regimental historian had a mixed verdict on the new soldiers. Although some proved excellent men, several of the rookies would desert before the 6th even left Kentucky. Overall, "a large majority of them were worthless," the frustrated veteran asserted. Nonetheless, the drill and training taking place in Annapolis brought the regiment "up to a high standard, both as to numbers and effectiveness."[3]

By the time the corps crossed the Rapidan in early May, every brigade included regiments new to the Ninth Corps. Only three months after his twenty-eighth birthday, Brig. Gen. Thomas Stevenson commanded Burnside's First Division. Stevenson had joined the Massachusetts militia early in life. He rose to the rank of major, then became colonel of the 24th Massachusetts, an original part of Burnside's North Carolina expedition. Remaining on the coast after the original Ninth Corps regiments departed for Virginia, Stevenson showed great promise, wearing a brigadier's star before turning twenty-seven. His life in the Ninth Corps would be tragically brief.[4]

Distinguished colonels led Stevenson's two brigades. Sumner Carruth's six regiments were his 35th Massachusetts, along with the 56th, 57th, and 59th Bay State infantry, all of which were raised in a major Massachusetts recruiting effort that had started in 1863. Two seasoned U.S. Army regiments, the 4th and 10th, rounded out Sumner's Brigade. Daniel Leasure's three regiments were the 3rd Maryland, 21st Massachusetts, and his reliable Roundheads, the 100th Pennsylvania.

The state labeled the new Massachusetts regiments as "veteran" outfits, with each unit ideally stocked with a majority of soldiers who had served at least nine months earlier in the war. Formation of the regiments proceeded slowly. Although in his early twenties, Stephen Minot Weld earned the lieutenant colonelcy in the 56th Massachusetts. As months passed, he doubted if the regiment would ever exist due to the low number of interested men. "Recruiting, or rather attempts at it," Weld lamented, had "been going on for three weeks at least" before a single enlistee showed up. By the end of the year, the 56th only mustered four companies. The full regiment departed for Annapolis in March.[5]

Unable to reach the 50 percent veteran threshold, the 57th Massachusetts still filled quickly, training at Camp Wool in Worcester. Benefiting greatly from the patriotism of non-native Americans, more than 20 percent of soldiers in the unit were born in either Ireland or England. In

Brig. Gen. Thomas Stevenson would be another Ninth Corps general to lose his life in the Civil War. He was killed near the Ni River as Burnside moved toward Spotsylvania Court House. LIBRARY OF CONGRESS

Many Civil War soldiers were very young, including this recruit in the new 56th Massachusetts. LIBRARY OF CONGRESS

total, almost one in four members of the 57th had been born outside the United States.[6]

A determination to serve burned brightly among Carruth's command. From Annapolis in April, Lt. Ward Frothingham, 59th Massachusetts, witnessed a series of speeches from members of the Maryland legislature. He was pleased with the strong nationalistic sentiments among the orators. However, Frothingham craved more tangible progress in the war. "The time for talking is over, and has been for some time," he proclaimed, "Action is what we want."[7]

Rolling out with Stevenson's Division, the 14th Massachusetts Battery had departed home in early April with 142 enlisted men and five officers. Receiving their big guns and horses shortly before leaving Annapolis, the new outfit headed toward destiny. Including many men devoted to their task, the battery also mustered some who quickly dodged their new responsibilities. Six recruits of the battery would desert prior to reaching Virginia.[8]

Brig. Gen. Robert Potter's Second Division continued the trend of veteran and rookie regiments under strong leadership. Zenas Bliss's guidance blessed the 36th and 58th Massachusetts, 51st New York, 45th and 48th Pennsylvania, and 7th Rhode Island. The Bay Staters of the 36th Regiment included the contingent from the 29th Massachusetts who elected to not reenlist. On furlough back home at the start of the campaign, the veterans of the 29th who would serve through the war would return to their regiment in early June.[9]

Simon Griffin's six-regiment brigade included representation from the three northern New England states. Maine's last two infantry regiments of the war, the 31st and 32nd, joined another new command, the 17th Vermont, as well as the established Granite Staters in the 6th, 9th, and 11th Regiments. Many of the Green Mountain boys had previous experience in the army. They would go to Virginia under Lt. Col. Charles Cummings, a trained physician, who had served in state's 16th Infantry, a First Corps regiment heavily engaged in the defense against Pickett's Charge at Gettysburg.[10]

"We are having pretty good times now," Pvt. William Elmore Howard wrote from the 17th Vermont's camp in Burlington on April 12. Four days later, the confident twenty-year-old warrior added, "I am tough and hearty." In Washington by late April, Corp. James Pollard noted the regiment's four hours of daily drill. On the 25th, Pollard wrote of being "under marching orders with 90 rounds of cartridges."[11] Like so many of their idealistic comrades, Howard soon needed all his grit, and Pollard would quickly find use for his ammunition.

Table 6.1. The Ninth Corps near the Start of the Overland Campaign

Corps Commander—Maj. Gen. Ambrose E. Burnside

1st Division Brig. Gen. Thomas G. Stevenson	2nd Division Brig. Gen. Robert B. Potter
1st Brigade *Col. Sumner Carruth* 35th Massachusetts 56th Massachusetts 57th Massachusetts 59th Massachusetts 4th United States 10th United States	*1st Brigade* *Col. Zenas R. Bliss* 36th Massachusetts 58th Massachusetts 51st New York 45th Pennsylvania 48th Pennsylvania 7th Rhode Island
2nd Brigade *Col. Daniel Leasure* 3rd Maryland 21st Massachusetts 100th Pennsylvania	*2nd Brigade* *Col. Simon G. Griffin* 31st Maine 32nd Maine 6th New Hampshire 9th New Hampshire 11th New Hampshire 17th Vermont
Artillery Maine Light, 2nd Battery (B) Massachusetts Light, 14th Battery	*Artillery* Massachusetts Light, 11th Battery New York Light, 19th Battery

3rd Division Brig. Gen. Orlando B. Willcox	4th Division Brig. Gen. Edward Ferrero
1st Brigade *Col. John F. Hartranft* 2nd Michigan 8th Michigan 17th Michigan 27th Michigan 109th New York 51st Pennsylvania	*1st Brigade* *Col. Joshua K. Sigfried* 27th U.S. Colored Troops 30th U.S. Colored Troops 39th U.S. Colored Troops 43rd U.S. Colored Troops
2nd Brigade *Col. Benjamin C. Christ* 1st Michigan Sharpshooters 20th Michigan 79th New York 60th Ohio 50th Pennsylvania	*2nd Brigade* *Col. Henry G. Thomas* 19th U.S. Colored Troops 23rd U.S. Colored Troops 31st U.S. Colored Troops
Artillery Maine Light, 7th Battery (G) New York Light, 34th Battery	
	Provisional Brigade *Col. Elisha G. Marshall* 24th New York Calvary (dismounted) 14th New York Heavy Artillery 2nd Pennsylvania Provisional Heavy Artillery

Source: *OR*, Vol. 36, I, 113–14.

As illustrated in table 6.1, Orlando Willcox returned to Virginia leading the Third Division. Veteran colonels John Hartranft and Benjamin Christ commanded Willcox's two brigades. Six of the division's eleven regiments hailed from Willcox's home state of Michigan, all but one experienced in the Ninth Corps. Hartranft's 51st Pennsylvania and 109th New York joined the 2nd, 8th, 17th, and 27th Wolverine infantry. New to Burnside was the 1st Michigan Sharpshooters, which had spent eighteen months guarding an armory back home and Confederate prisoners in Chicago. Christ's four other regiments were the 20th Michigan, David Morrison's Highlanders, the new 60th Ohio, and the dedicated and experienced 50th Pennsylvania.[12]

Charles Hodskin, a member of the 2nd Michigan, wrote about the Ninth Corps' departure from Annapolis and march through Washington. On Sunday, April 24, Hodskin noted the difficult march in rain. While traversing the national capital the following day, Hodskin wrote of the Ninth Corps being "reviewed by the President from the balcony of the Willard Hotel." Burnside stood by the president during the festive moment.[13]

The 109th New York under Hartranft had spent eighteen months as railroad guards near Washington. Known as the Binghamton Regiment after the city of their organization, the 109th had an excellent commander, Col. Benjamin Tracy. Destined for long service to his country, Tracy had been born in Tioga County in 1830. A lawyer and active Republican before the war, Tracy had led the 109th since its formation in August 1862. He would not command the regiment long, but his positive example shined brightly.[14]

Brig. Gen. Edward Ferrero commanded the Fourth Division, which would eventually total nine regiments of United States Colored Troops (USCT). Those favoring the enlistment of African American soldiers had tread an arduous path from the opening of the war. President Lincoln rejected the idea early on, concerned about the response from the slave states remaining in the Union. A deeply skeptical public also played a role in the political decision to hold off on formation of units where Black men could fight for their country. Federal legislation in 1862 started the sea change, as did Lincoln's Emancipation Proclamation. As a seemingly endless war dragged on, the necessity of utilizing a great manpower resource—men of color wishing to defeat a slave power—led to the enlistment of African Americans.[15]

In August 1863, President Lincoln, at his witty best, tried to dispel doubts in the minds of some white soldiers who had written him, suggesting they had no interest in fighting to free slaves. The "unconditional Union men" told Lincoln they would happily save their dishonored flag, fired on by rebellious Southerners. The Union alone, Lincoln countered, now seemed an insufficient justification for fighting due to the example so many African Americans set by enrolling in the army.

You say you will not fight to free negroes. Some of them seem willing to fight for you; but, no matter. Fight you, then, exclusively to save the Union. I issued the proclamation on purpose to aid you in saving the Union. Whenever you shall have conquered all resistance to the Union, if I shall urge you to continue fighting, it will be an apt time, then, for you to declare you will not fight to free negroes.[16]

Epitomizing the imperfect nation he wished to save, Hosea Towne, 6th New Hampshire, observed regiments of the Fourth Division in Annapolis. Even with harsh language, Towne saw the benefit of calling on a large pool of men, especially because of his state's poor recruitment effort.

There are two or more negro Regts here which make rather a shady appearance, but I have no objection to their doing the fighting. The more they put in the better if it is a nigger war. Let the niggers fight. New Hampshire is disgracing herself in the way they take to fill their quotas. If they cannot send decent men to the army they better send none.[17]

With the revolution in thinking in the government and the hearts of many Americans, members of the 19th, 23rd, 27th, 30th, 31st, 39th, and 43rd USCT headed toward destiny in the Ninth Corps. The regiments had been recruited in several states. Soon, the 28th and 29th USCT would join the division. Sgt. Benjamin F. Trail, a member of the 28th, wrote home on May 2, noting his recent departure from Indianapolis with twenty other soldiers and two officers. "Cheered by the citizens" of Pittsburgh on the way east, the devoted band spent most of a day in Baltimore, receiving a great meal while awaiting transportation to Washington. After the last part of their ride, Trail and the others were sent to the Virginia side of the Potomac, "more than glad" to find their regiment at Camp Casey in Arlington.

Trail was moved by the beauty he saw, including the winding Potomac River that formed the boundary between the seat of the United States government and the Confederacy. The immense unfinished dome of the U.S. Capitol made Trail feel very optimistic. The large number of troops heading south to fight for the Union gave Trail, who was born in 1840, a vision of the likely fate of the regiment. Unlike the other three divisions of the Ninth Corps, Ferrero's men would not be put into battle immediately, although their time would arrive.[18]

White officers led USCT companies and regiments. Capt. Albert Rogall, an experienced leader with hard service at the battle of Shiloh and other locations in the West, had joined the 27th USCT at a camp in Ohio. He noted many difficulties in the early part of the division's service. The rapid, rainy journey from Annapolis and disrespect from some residents while the men marched through Washington were just two of the issues. In early May, Rogall noted several times the poor state of supply, mainly a lack of food. He also grew maudlin when seeing how the war had so devastated the beautiful country in central Virginia.[19]

Another Fourth Division officer focused on the bright side. Twenty-five-year-old Capt. Alfred Dodge, who led Company F of the 39th Regiment, had previous service in the 10th Vermont. As a Ninth Corps man near Manassas Junction in early May 1864, Dodge wrote home expressing a great sense of pride in his mission, "I like my situation much and my health is just as good as I can ask for." He continued, "The men are obedient and seem to place all confidence in their officers and I will not ask for any better set to be in command of."[20]

SPANNING THE RAPIDAN

Due to the slow pace of recruitment, several of the Ninth Corps' new regiments lacked the full complement of ten companies. Finally marching in
Christ's Brigade in early May, the 1st Michigan Sharpshooters had toiled
in noncombat roles for months at barely over half strength. Likewise, the
58th Massachusetts departed home with only eight companies. Company K would not join the outfit until near the end of the year. The War
Department did not allow a colonel to command smaller organizations,
which limited some excellent officers, such as Francis Randall of the 17th
Vermont, to additional recruiting duty back home.[21]

The start of the campaign created an awkward command situation. Army of the Potomac commander George G. Meade had
Grant, his superior officer, in the field with him, while Burnside was
senior to Meade as a major general. The touchy matter led Grant
to keep the Ninth Corps outside of Meade's control. As Burnside
wrote of the arrangement, "The corps acted as a separate army, under
my immediate command, reporting direct to the headquarters of
Lieutenant-General Grant."[22] Thus, Meade directed three corps with
Grant looking over his shoulder, while Burnside's movements were coordinated by Grant, who acted as a middleman between the Ninth Corps
and the Army of the Potomac.

As Burnside's Boys moved south, they were assigned the task of
guarding supply wagons. The role did not seem glamorous, but the
importance of the work could not be denied. The Army of the Potomac
numbered nearly 120,000 men. Simply feeding such large numbers
placed great demands on logistical staff. Fears of Confederate raids left
some men trigger happy while keeping an eye on their surroundings
during the evening of April 30. Robert Allen, a hospital steward who was
part of the 22nd New York Cavalry, attached to the Ninth Corps early in
the campaign, joked, "Pickets sent out, who were soon firing at stumps
and bushes, as green pickets always do."[23]

With Meade's three corps farther south, some Ninth Corps men
worried about the possibility of being forgotten. Harlan Closson, 3rd
Vermont Light Artillery, lamented the long rainy marches while bringing up the rear of the Union's mightiest army. A cold wind added to the

cannoneer's foul mood. "Quite a disappointment," he mused, "We would have been glad to have had an opportunity to do our part when the great armies meet."[24]

Veterans likely fretted less about not being in the lead, especially because they knew the necessity of protecting supplies. "We are scattered," David Lane, 17th Michigan, wrote of the entire Ninth Corps at the start of May, "All the way from Centerville to Warrenton." The devoted Wolverine continued, "Our work is an important one" because the army's continued supply was "dependent on our vigilance and energy." Although restless and ready to move forward, Lane remained focused on the immediate mission, however unglamourous.[25]

Daniel Larned, still a member of Burnside's staff, noted how quickly a new campaign altered an individual's exterior.

> *It is very strange how soon camp life changes the whole appearance of a person. A week ago we were all in good clothes, clean faces, and fair skins. Now we are in camp browned and burned as if we had been through a dozen campaigns already. We are in for all the "luxuries of war."*

Optimism pervaded. Larned added, "Our troops are all in good condition, and we are ready for whatever comes." A cavalryman assigned to Burnside's headquarters witnessed the euphoric mindset. "It is known that our road is onward to Richmond, and I can't but think it must fall under such Armies as are now performing opporations against it."[26]

A major fight was brewing, with plenty of action likely for all of Grant's minions. The Union's commanding general certainly was not forgetting the Ninth Corps. Grant was in regular contact with Burnside as a southerly march continued. When Grant wrote on May 3 that "rations, forage, ordnance and medical stores" must be the limit of what the Ninth Corps carried in wagons, Burnside knew his men were being sent forward with a combat role. The next target for the Ninth Corps was Germanna Ford on the Rapidan. Grant required Burnside to make "forced marches" to reach the ford, located about 4 miles northwest of a place called Wilderness Tavern.[27]

Grant commended the Ninth Corps in his memoirs for the command's very trying, rapid trek from Annapolis. On a day of intense battle for Meade's three corps, Stevenson's Division, the first Ninth Corps infantry south of the river, began traversing Germanna Ford early on the morning of May 5. After crossing later, 9th New Hampshire musician Lewis Simonds penned in his diary, "can hear the musketry very plain where we lay." Capt. Adelbert Twitchell, an experienced cannoneer commanding the 7th Maine Battery, informed the state adjutant general of the "sharp skirmishing four miles in advance tonight." After Meade's large engagement with Lee on May 5, Twitchell accurately predicted more fighting.[28]

TO BATTLE ON MAY 6

Across miles of inhospitable forest and undergrowth, the Army of the Potomac fought without connecting in the Wilderness. The Sixth Corps supported the Fifth along the Orange Turnpike. To the southeast, the Second Corps held an isolated position along the Orange Plank Road. On battle maps and in the minds of army leaders, the Ninth Corps could easily bolster either wing of Meade's force. However, the forest and thick undergrowth frustrated Burnside's effort. The ground made artillery next to useless as senior officers and men in the ranks could not clearly see the enemy. As expected from such disadvantages, the Ninth Corps had a limited impact after crossing the Rapidan.

The 51st Pennsylvania, Hartranft's Brigade, began May 6 on picket duty. Starting about 4 a.m., the tired Keystone Staters gained what qualified as good rest, about two hours in reserve, before activity began in earnest in Ninth Corps camps. The initial advance of Potter's and Willcox's Divisions, ordered by Grant at 6:20 a.m., would be to the southwest, in the direction of Parker's Store, with the intent to link with the Fifth Corps. After a short time in reserve, Stevenson's men were sent to support Hancock's Second Corps to the south, near the intersection of the Brock Road and Orange Plank Road. Stevenson started moving toward Hancock at about 7 a.m., arriving an hour later.[29]

As Burnside's Boys prepared to move deeper into the Wilderness, the Ninth Corps was not the imposing force implied on orders of battle.

Having the Fourth Division guarding supplies was merely one problem. By the time three Ninth Corps divisions began moving forward, some regiments were missing from their brigades. The 7th Rhode Island had remained behind protecting trains, while the 60th Ohio would not rejoin Christ's Brigade until after the battle. Likewise, Griffin's men went ahead without the 9th New Hampshire or the 32nd Maine. The soldiers were also exceedingly tired after marches far longer than those undertaken by other elements of the army over the previous ten days.[30]

Potter and Willcox began their trek shortly after a counterattack from Longstreet started pushing back Hancock's command to Burnside's left. Perhaps as much as the dark forest and tangled undergrowth, the Ninth Corps' relative lack of firepower hampered any support Burnside could provide. Criticism about an anemic attack on May 6 would be lobbed at Burnside, with some merit. However, staffers serving both Grant and Meade who were with Burnside at the time did not view an attack as likely to poke through Confederate defenses to the south of the Fifth Corps. Even if Burnside grew bold, one wonders how Ninth Corps flanks could have been protected with an advance all the way to Parker's Store, which Meade falsely reported Burnside as reaching. Nonetheless, pro-McClellan elements remaining in the army, along with generations of historians were convinced of Burnside's inherent lack of offensive spirit. A modern biographer of Hancock suggested neither the Ninth Corps nor Burnside himself should have been seen as worthy of their Confederate opponents in the Wilderness.[31] This is an especially ridiculous conclusion, because Burnside trounced Longstreet six months before in Tennessee, while Hancock barely held on in the Wilderness.

Regardless of the pontifications of anti-Burnside historians, positive signs occurred early in the advance on May 6, with the 6th New Hampshire serving as the vanguard for Potter's Division. The regimental historian noted how Confederate skirmishers fell back as the Granite Staters advanced. The officer leading the 6th's skirmishers expressed concern about a possible Confederate trap, leading to caution in senior officers. Halts were made, giving Confederate cannoneers a chance to shell Potter's men "to our great discomfort," the 6th New Hampshire historian recalled.[32]

Confederate infantry added to the unpleasant moments along the road to Parker's Store. Colonel Griffin moved more of his regiments forward, forming a battle line. Bliss's brigade moved to the left, with "quite brisk" fire developing. Men from Company K, 45th Pennsylvania, screened Bliss's advance. As William Roberts of the company recalled, "The first man I saw fall was Simon Sanders," two men away on the left. Ordered to check on the fallen soldier, Roberts discovered "a bullet had pierced his heart, killing him instantly." Soon, Roberts himself would be hit. The Confederate ball would cost him an arm. Before the end of the day, 140 members of the 45th Pennsylvania would be casualties.[33]

The advance had pushed close to the Chewning Farm and the Confederate rear. General Potter had arrayed his force to make the most of the situation. With Griffin's men "warmly engaged," as the 36th Massachusetts historian wrote, the situation seemed propitious for a concerted attack. Perhaps more could have been done if Burnside had moved with celerity, or his troops did not stop for breakfast in their trek to the southwest. Later in the morning, the expanding Confederate defensive line instilled further doubt in Unionist minds.[34]

Willcox's troops helped extend the Ninth Corps' line to the north, with the goal to link with Warren's Fifth Corps. Several men in the two brigades would be captured during the morning, including some Native Americans from a company in the 1st Michigan Sharpshooters, under enemy fire for the first time. A North Carolinian wrote with interest after the war of finding Bibles in the Ojibwa language among the captured Wolverines. As a result of the tense hours, Col. Byron Cutcheon, 20th Michigan, remembered feeling as if "we were not to attack, but to hold that line."[35]

One of those hit early in the fight was William Hill, recently promoted to lieutenant in the 50th Pennsylvania. A member of Company C wrote of Hill calling the troops to attention before the move toward the west. Hill died about thirty minutes after being wounded, one of twelve killed in action in the regiment on May 6. Hill's wife Mary, who would live nearly sixty more years, received a pension of $8 a month after her husband's death.[36]

The concerted effort by Longstreet to the south brought a change in orders. Burnside's new goal was to assist Hancock's beleaguered divisions. With some of Willcox's men remaining behind to keep an eye on Confederates to the west, the rest of the Ninth Corps were tasked with saving the Second Corps.[37]

STEVENSON ASSISTS HANCOCK

Headquarters expressed impatience with Burnside in the 11:45 a.m. order that repurposed the Ninth Corps. "Push in with all vigor" to attack the enemy in front of Hancock, chief of staff John Rawlins demanded. The Second Corps commander "has been expecting you for the last three hours." After turning to the southeast, thousands of troops from the Ninth Corps found more unforgiving ground between the road to Parker's Store and Hancock's line. General Potter reported severe problems from the "dense wood" and "almost impenetrable undergrowth" while advancing without even the modicum of trails. Finally able to reform a line after crossing an enervating mile, Potter found himself "entirely unable to see anything" due to the seemingly endless biomass. With some of the forest on fire, smoke added to the difficulty.[38]

Stevenson's two brigades had been under Hancock's control since 8 a.m. Three days before, roll calls across Sumner Carruth's six regiments found more than 3,200 men present for duty, nearly 75 percent of which were in the three new Massachusetts regiments. The 300 officers and soldiers in the 35th Massachusetts would be one of several Ninth Corps regiments missing the battle while guarding supplies. With the veterans of the 21st Massachusetts barely totaling 200 men, Leasure's three veteran regiments likely appeared about the size of one of the three new Bay State regiments under Carruth.[39]

An American warrior as determined and valiant as any produced from the nation's bloodiest conflict moved out as part of Carruth's Brigade. Col. William Francis Bartlett, not yet twenty-four years old, led the 57th Massachusetts. Three years before, while a junior at Harvard, Bartlett enlisted as a private in the 20th Massachusetts while having as his main interests "billiards, suppers, college clubs, and the society of young ladies." The following year on the Peninsula, Captain Bartlett lost his left leg near Yorktown. During time with another Massachusetts regiment in Louisiana, Bartlett suffered his second combat injury. Still burning to fight, he became colonel of the 57th in time to head south from Boston in April 1864.

Keeping control of his horse with only one leg seemed to pose a challenge for Bartlett. He penned in his journal on May 4, "Thrown twice. Not hurt." The following day, predicting battle that seemed to draw Bartlett like a magnet, he added, "I hope I may get through, but hardly expect it. His will be done."[40]

In another new regiment, Stephen Minot Weld, 56th Massachusetts, recalled the moment, suggesting "the musketry firing was fearful. It was one continual roll, at long intervals broken by the loud booming of cannon." As Stevenson's two brigades arrived, Leasure's regiments moved south, while Carruth went west on the Plank Road. The brigade would soon move to the right of the road.[41]

Confusion reigned across Hancock's area of responsibility. Carruth's regiments took part in a morning attack, which brought no advantages to any of the beleaguered Unionists under Hancock. Bartlett and his 57th Massachusetts stood at the center of the vortex. The brave colonel had to withdraw from the field after his third combat injury of the war, a head wound suffered at about 11 a.m. In his diary the young leader wrote of his first night in a hospital, "Lay there among the wounded and dying till night," when he was placed in an ambulance.[42]

Bartlett's men fell by the score. The 57th Massachusetts would suffer horrendous casualties in the Wilderness, 15 percent of the entire Ninth Corps' loss in early May's carnage. At the time, 245 were listed as killed, wounded, missing, or captured. A twentieth-century regimental history upped the total to 262, close to 50 percent of those at the battle. The highest-ranking fatality was Capt. Joseph Gird, commander of Company B. The Louisiana native's memorial stone in Worcester Rural Cemetery notes, "He sleeps where he fell." More than ninety men from the regiment were either killed outright or mortally wounded on May 6.[43]

Several members of the 57th would never see the regiment again due to subsequent medical discharges. George Woods, a private in Company G, informed the adjutant general, "It will be some time before I get well," with a right hand "perfectly useless." A medical discharge in June ended Woods' military career.[44]

Death claimed many men in the 57th who were originally listed as missing. An eyewitness account corrected the status of Charles Knox to killed with a bullet to the forehead, while William Peabody and George Emerson would die over the summer in Andersonville prison.[45] Clearly, the willingness of Ninth Corps men to sacrifice cannot be doubted.

An officer since early in the war, Col. Charles Griswold, 56th Massachusetts, was another man to fall. Capt. Zabdiel Adams remembered, "Our brave colonel stood at the right of the line, firing his revolver." Soon after learning of Griswold's demise, Adams continued, "the thing began to look bad for us" as Confederates swarmed north of the Plank Road. Adams himself was soon hit.

Stephen Weld became the twenty-two-year-old commander of the regiment after Griswold's wound. Weld felt a great sense of loss when the colonel died, which he considered "a sad blow, as I was very fond of him." Continuing, Weld lamented, "He was extremely brave and behaved like a gallant soldier. He was shot through the jugular vein while holding the colors, which were covered with his blood."[46]

With a stalemate prevailing later in the morning, Leasure's three veteran regiments held an excellent position to fulfill a mission Hancock wished completed. Suffering from the same problems as all other leaders in the Wilderness, Hancock could not see far into the miasma of forest. Leasure's units were ordered to advance into the woods, then move north across the entire front of Hancock's line. Although Leasure did not encounter Confederates in significant numbers, the historian of the 21st Massachusetts was quite pleased with the "beautiful steady charge" of Leasure's "little brigade." The proud Bay Stater elevated the importance of the effort, essentially suggesting the action forced back Confederates. Also praising Leasure's action, one of Grant's staffers suggested the men completed a mission of "striking brilliancy."[47]

After their move north across Hancock's line, Leasure's men were placed in reserve. Thus, the three regiments were not routed by another of Longstreet's assaults before midday. Like many attacks begun in dense

Col. Charles Griswold, 56th Massachusetts, suffered fatal injuries at the Wilderness, May 6, 1864. LIBRARY OF CONGRESS

woods, the Confederate effort eventually sputtered, partially because of the nearly mortal wounding of Longstreet by friendly fire.[48]

"ALL THE ENEMY SEEM TO HAVE GONE TO FIGHT BURNSIDE"

By early afternoon, the armies returned to the impasse that prevailed prior to Longstreet's flank attack. Most of Potter's and Willcox's soldiers had begun pouring into their new position nearer Hancock as General Lee attempted to find the right combination of units to assail his Northern foes. At 2 p.m., a headquarters staff member wrote Meade of the lack of activity on Hancock's line along Brock Road. "All the enemy seem to have gone to fight Burnside," Meade was informed.[49]

The line Potter and Willcox formed west of Hancock and north of the Plank Road initially included three brigades. Colonel Christ remained near the Chewning farm until afternoon. The brigades of Griffin, Bliss, and Hartranft had a chance to make a tremendous impact. General Potter seemed ready for a fight, even after the draining march to his new position. Unfortunately, the nature of the ground remained a significant obstacle. "I reformed as quickly as possible and moved to the attack," Potter reported, "being entirely unable to see anything from the thickness of the wood." Horace Porter, from Grant's headquarters, noted how Burnside stopped for lunch before the advance was completed. Porter also witnessed the terrible difficulty Potter found in the terrain. Troops were "struggling through underbrush and swamps," leading to "futile" efforts to retain alignment.[50]

Not knowing of the wound costing Lee his best corps commander, David Lane observed how the Ninth Corps would soon be "face to face with our old acquaintance, Longstreet." Bliss placed his regiments west of Griffin's for the inevitably disjointed attack that would follow. Hartranft was able to support Potter to the right rear. As lines were being formed, Col. Constant Luce, 17th Michigan, reported, "We did not discover the enemy until the firing commenced." This short burst of shooting presaged the main event.[51]

When the two divisions attacked around 2 p.m., the propitious nature of Burnside's timing nearly caused a disaster for Confederates, men in three brigades under Abner Perrin, Col. William Perry, and Gen.

Edward Perry. William Oates, leading two Alabama regiments, remembered the Confederates preparing to launch their own attack. Instead,

> *almost simultaneously my skirmishers were fired upon by troops of*
> *Burnside's corps, which lay in a ravine to our left. . . . On came a long*
> *line and opened a heavy fire on my command, caught Colonel Perry in*
> *the act of changing front with the other regiments of the brigade, and*
> *struck General Perry's brigade squarely in the flank and decimated it*
> *at once.*[52]

Col. William Perry remembered, "Nothing was left us but an inglorious retreat, executed in the shortest possible time and without regard to order."[53]

Like every other initial success either side enjoyed in the Wilderness, Burnside's attack sputtered. Colonel Luce reported Ninth Corps men moving into parts of the Confederate lines, but "our troops were compelled to fall back." In the advance of Griffin's New Englanders, Walter Harriman and his 11th New Hampshire experienced "murderous fire, the bullets raining upon the men like hailstones." Lt. Col. Moses Collins suffered a fatal head wound, another soldier in the regiment lost to his country forever. A deeply respected lawyer in his community of Exeter, Collins's death "will carry sorrow to many hearts," a newspaper bewailed.[54]

The 11th's advance exposed the unit's flanks. Eleven men from Harriman's regiment would be captured, including the colonel himself. Harriman successfully dropped his sword on the ground before Confederates could make the ceremonial demand for the weapon. A New Hampshire man picked up his colonel's sword, keeping the prize in Union hands. More than four months later, Harriman would be exchanged.[55]

Lt. Col. Charles Cummings sustained a bloody injury while on a knee smoking his pipe and directing the fire of his men. Using his medical training, Cummings detailed his wound in a letter to his wife. The Confederate ball *struck me on the right side of my head. . . . It cut a hole . . . about two and a half inches long in my scalp. . . . [I]t bled with such profuseness from the breaking of a branch of the temporal artery that I concluded to go to the rear thinking I might faint if I remain or if repulsed I should fall into the hands of the rebels.*[56]

In Bliss's brigade, the 36th Massachusetts lined up with the 51st New York on the left and John Curtin's 45th Pennsylvania to the right. After a Confederate volley, the line adjusted slightly, then pressed on, with the regiments breaching part of the enemy line. Nonetheless, "the foeman was worthy of our steel," the 36th's historian suggested. Encountering problems, the 51st New York could not keep up the pace, exposing the interior portion of Bliss's line to Confederates. Again, Unionists were forced to fall back.[57]

Confederates were not content to merely inflict losses. The Southerners made a counter charge, adding to the chaos of the moment among Potter and Willcox's troops. The pressure led to more Northerners being taken prisoner, and additional casualties. At a time for strong leaders to shine, Col. Benjamin Tracy rallied broken troops, proving worthy of a Medal of Honor. His citation declared, Tracy, "seized the colors and led the regiment when other regiments had retired and then reformed his line and held it."[58]

Colonel Hartranft's boldness also steadied the line. As expected from their conduct in previous campaigns, the 17th Michigan was especially prominent during the moment. Colonel Luce recalled, "My regiment arose at the time and gave three cheers and opened upon the enemy," which led to a Confederate retrograde.[59]

The afternoon quickly proved costly to both sides. Col. Frank Graves, leading the 8th Michigan, fell near the enemy's works. An officer in the regiment from the beginning, Graves epitomized the type of leader Michigan produced during the war. Hartranft felt deep respect for the "gallant style" of Graves's leadership. Due to the chaos that day, the colonel's body was never recovered.[60]

As both sides attempted to find advantages, Christ's Brigade arrived. "Go in and give them hell," Christ demanded of his men. Colonel

Cutcheon remembered how the 50th Pennsylvania "received a very heavy fire at point blank range," very likely the reason why the Keystone Staters sustained well over half of the brigade's loss in the battle, seventy-one out of 112 casualties. The 50th's historian saw a purpose to the regiment's sacrifice by declaring, "Our presence had the effect of infusing new energy into the disordered and broken ranks."[61]

The bold counterattack had been led by Confederate reinforcements. As Col. William Perry remembered, the Southerners went straight for Burnside's troops, then "swept them away like chaff."[62] Nonetheless, the impossibility of a significant breakthrough of Ninth Corps lines became evident. The fates of war once again dictated that fighting in the Wilderness could lead to horrible casualties without an appreciable change to the tactical situation.

The day proved too much for Zenas Bliss, who was struck down by hunger, exhaustion, and the effects of the heat. The 7th Rhode Island historian wrote of the excellent brigade commander as he went to the hospital later in the day, that Bliss "had not eaten anything for three days," but would not leave the field.[63]

GETTING OUT OF THE WILDERNESS

Sanguinary combat without decisive result would continue in the Wilderness. A final attack, which began in the late afternoon, brought further bloodletting. With so many commanders befuddled by the thick woods, smoke, and burning biomass, army headquarters could be expected to be even more blind to developments. Meade envisioned a 6 p.m. attack that would finally overpower Lee's minions. The army commander wrote to Hancock, the combined might of the Second and Ninth Corps "will, I think, overthrow the enemy."

Even with supporting troops from three other corps, Hancock was in no position to advance. He informed Meade of the "partially disorganized condition" of the Brock Road front. Hancock asked Meade for more information about his vision for the assault, closing with the query, "Will you indicate a front?"[64]

Capt. Josiah Jones and his company in the 6th New Hampshire were south of the Ninth Corps line as the attack began. The entire division "had a hard fight," Jones reported, with confused forays shedding more blood without lines changing to any notable degree. David Lane, seemed fatalistic as he recalled the late afternoon effort, "The order was promptly obeyed, but the Rebels were strongly entrenched, and we could not dislodge them." Colonel Perry was a Confederate happy to see the languid pace of another Unionist assault. "Considering their numbers," Perry opined, "their effort has always seemed to me a feeble one."[65]

An especial horror about the Wilderness was the fires that consumed some wounded men. Those casualties avoiding incineration faced an abyss of unknowns. Stephen Brown, 17th Vermont, used a gun strap around his shoulder above a serious wound, which "prevented a fatal hemorrhage," but did not obviate an evening amputation. On the way to Fredericksburg in an ambulance, he said, "I never saw a medical attendant," while two passengers died.[66]

Worried parents could contact a state adjutant general in hope of some update. William Flanagan would send a July 4 letter hoping for news about William, Jr., a member of the 57th Massachusetts wounded two months earlier. "He wrote me that he was badly wounded and was left four days on the field without any care," the father plaintively wrote. The unfortunate soldier had sent a May 17 letter, noting he was in a Fredericksburg hospital. Mr. Flanagan had heard no more news. His son had perished from his injuries.[67]

Only eleven days after leaving Boston, the 59th Massachusetts tasted battle for the first time in the Wilderness. State records show the 59th lost twelve killed in action on May 6, with thirty-eight more wounded or missing. Due to a gunshot wound to the thorax, Swinton Dunlop, a native of Scotland, was one of those killed in action. His cousin James, a lieutenant, recruited Swinton into the regiment.[68]

FIGHTING FOR THE NI RIVER

Life moved on for the bloodied regiments of the Ninth Corps. A Vermonter summed up May 7 in his diary by noting, "We lay in line of battle." Grant had no interest in more pointless fighting, so he crafted a plan to keep moving south, hoping to beat Lee to Spotsylvania Court House. The Ninth Corps began moving out on May 8. Taking a break at

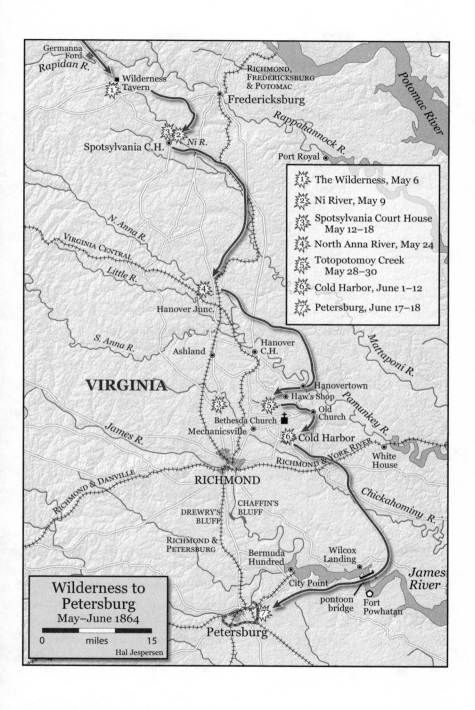

Germanna Ford
Rapidan R.
Wilderness Tavern
☼1☼

RICHMOND, FREDERICKSBURG & POTOMAC
Fredericksburg

Rappahannock R.

Potomac River

☼3☼ ☼2☼
Spotsylvania C.H.   Ni R.

Port Royal

N. Anna R.

VIRGINIA CENTRAL

Little R.

☼4☼

Hanover Junc.

S. Anna R.

VIRGINIA

Ashland

Hanover C.H.

Mattaponi R.

Hanovertown
Haw's Shop
☼5☼
Old Church
Bethesda Church
Mechanicsville
☼3☼
☼6☼ Cold Harbor

Pamunkey R.

RICHMOND & YORK RIVER
RICHMOND & DANVILLE
James R.
RICHMOND

White House

Chickahominy R.

CHAFFIN'S BLUFF
DREWRY'S BLUFF

RICHMOND & PETERSBURG

Bermuda Hundred

Wilcox Landing

City Point

pontoon bridge
Fort Powhatan

James River

☼7☼
Petersburg

☼1☼ The Wilderness, May 6

☼2☼ Ni River, May 9

☼3☼ Spotsylvania Court House May 12–18

☼4☼ North Anna River, May 24

☼5☼ Totopotomoy Creek May 28–30

☼6☼ Cold Harbor, June 1–12

☼7☼ Petersburg, June 17–18

Wilderness to Petersburg
May–June 1864

0   miles   15

Hal Jespersen

Chancellorsville, the men would be the left of Grant's advance. Ordered to ensure his troops had five days of rations, Burnside was also informed of the major effort to move wounded men to Fredericksburg.[69]

Clogged roads and roving Confederate cavalry created dangers for those left behind to tend to wounded comrades. Like his time in Knoxville, David Lane, 17th Michigan, served as a hospital staff member in the aftermath of the Wilderness. He would be taken prisoner soon after the battle, as the Ninth Corps moved out.[70]

A bit north of the Ni River,[71] the road between Fredericksburg and Spotsylvania curves southwest. As troops neared the river, deployments for a fight began. With token Confederate resistance, time near the crossing did not cost the Ninth Corps many casualties. As tough fighting occurred to the west for the Fifth Corps, however, Grant lost the opportunity for a decisive Unionist breakthrough.

Due to the stiff Confederate resistance in the center of Grant's advance, headquarters infused caution into Burnside, with the imperative of safeguarding the Ninth Corps wagon train noted in multiple messages on May 8. "The greatest vigilance should be exercised in the protection of these trains and the keeping of them well up," chief of staff John Rawlins directed at 12:45 p.m. The Ninth Corps was also required to stop at "Gate," assumed to be a house on the north side of the Ni along the Fredericksburg Road. Alacrity and a swift attack at Spotsylvania were not part of the immediate plan, but the expectation was to move beyond the Ni the following day. On roads crowded with wagons, the march on May 9 was started early, with men moving at 3 a.m.[72]

Willcox's Division took the lead, with Stevenson slated to start thirty minutes later. Because of the poor maps, Willcox neared the Ni, believing the Gayle House was the "Gate" in his orders. Instead, the Third Division was well south of the stopping point Grant intended. Thus, at 8:45 a.m., headquarters requested an advance toward Spotsylvania starting from "Gate." Ninety minutes earlier, Willcox was notably farther south, in sight of Confederate pickets at the river. Grant must have been surprised to hear that Willcox was in contact with the enemy while isolated from Meade's three corps. Although Willcox overestimated Confederate strength, the Ninth Corps was being more aggressive than Grant wished his left flank to be.[73]

Without orders, Willcox kept moving, sending Christ's troops south beyond the river after chasing away Confederate skirmishers. With some men carrying a musket for the first time that morning, the 60th Ohio took the lead, performing well enough in their initial engagement. Confederate pressure pushed back the left of Christ's advance, surprising the 1st Michigan Sharpshooters. Other elements of the brigade rallied, with especially strong service from the 50th Pennsylvania. The regiment would lose five killed in action, with dozens wounded, the bulk of Willcox's loss for the day.[74]

Capt. Samuel Schwenk of the 50th Pennsylvania received praise after the fight. Lt. Col. Byron Cutcheon reported "that the bravery of one man was most conspicuous," lessening dangers to the advance. Schwenk ordered a bayonet charge from the four right companies of the regiment after the left side of the 50th was pushed back. Further boldness from the 79th New York and 17th Michigan at the crucial moment helped stabilize the situation, leading to Willcox's lodgment south of the Ni.[75]

Schwenk had turned twenty-two years old the day before his valiant action. An original officer in the 50th Pennsylvania, his competence and courage led to multiple battle wounds and promotions across the war. He would remain a fixture in the regiment until the end, receiving the brevet of a brigadier general in 1865.[76]

More troops from the Ninth Corps augmented the position on both sides of the Ni. Even if the men moved farther south than Grant's intention, they were not in serious danger from Lee's army, spread out for several miles along an east–west line near Spotsylvania. The most eminent modern historian of the Overland campaign chastised Willcox for not making more of the situation.[77] This criticism seems out of place, because the Ninth Corps was actually farther south than Grant thought. Being closer than all other parts of Meade's army to the ultimate goal of the Court House does not seem like a bad result. A dash for Spotsylvania by the Ninth Corps, again with great unknowns and the coordination problems that plagued the army in the Wilderness, seemed too much to ask.

Some bad blood was created in the Ninth Corps on May 9. Willcox extolled the 60th Ohio in a note, while the 1st Michigan Sharpshooters received a mild rebuke. The modern historian of the Sharpshooters overplays Willcox's reaction. Calling the division commander's immediate response to the fighting on May 9 an "official censure" goes too far. Willcox's criticism of the sharpshooters was not echoed in his campaign report or memoirs; the general did not condemn any of his men. Rather, Willcox stated his division "repulsed repeated assaults of the enemy." Later, he proclaimed, "I never felt more pride in any battle or of any troops than of those of Ny River, Virginia, May 9, 1864."[78]

"MEN WENT DOWN ON THE RIGHT AND LEFT"

General Thomas Stevenson's death on May 10 brought change and sorrow to the Ninth Corps. Resting along the Ni soon after his division came up, a bullet "struck his head and he fell over, instantly killed," a Roundhead remembered. "We met with a severe misfortune," Burnside wrote, when a Confederate found his mark in another Ninth Corps general. The "brave and efficient solider," Burnside continued, had rendered commendable service since early in the war. Stevenson's younger brother Robert, who would earn a general's brevet in 1865, outlived Thomas by sixty-four years.[79]

After hearing news of Stevenson's death, Daniel Larned grew melancholy. The pace and horrors of the new campaign melded with the loss of a respected general to wallop the young staff officer. "We are all very sad," he observed, "Never does home and friends seem so dear to me as when surrounded by these terrible scenes."[80]

The inexorable southerly move of Grant's four corps continued. After further maneuvering and some fierce combat to the west of the Ninth Corps, plans for a major attack were formulated, with the advance expected near dawn on May 12. The Ninth Corps would charge across difficult ground, then into strong entrenchments while also protecting the Unionist left flank. With the Second Corps to the north, Grant directed Burnside to launch "a vigorous attack." Grant demanded, "You will move against the enemy with your entire force promptly and with all possible vigor" starting at 4 a.m. Both the Fifth and Sixth Corps would be standing by on Hancock's right to support the attack.[81]

Burnside's troops spread out to the south of the Second Corps. The Ninth Corps commander misinterpreted Grant's orders, originally believing the Ninth Corps was being asked to head directly for Spotsylvania Court House. Such a move would inhibit a connection between Burnside and Hancock, something no corps commander should look to do. A continuous line between corps offered the best chance to avoid a counterattack against an exposed Union flank. Cyrus Comstock, one of Grant's staff officers corrected the error during a discussion with Burnside. Although Burnside would be annoyed by Comstock's oversight, the staffer's presence offered necessary clarity on a key matter.[82]

Potter's Division prepared to be the vanguard, with Griffin's New Englanders holding the line on Hancock's left. Working against difficult terrain again, albeit not as wooded as the Wilderness, eerie early light mixed with fog made the advance bothersome and highly memorable. Dampness caused an especially dangerous condition for some: muskets that failed to fire. Nonetheless, Griffin's men possessed a good deal of confidence. Oscar Robinson believed the 9th New Hampshire was "never under better discipline" than before the May 12 attack.[83]

In the advance of the main Confederate position stood the brigade of James Lane's experienced and tough North Carolinians. "In the best of spirits, the brigade welcomed the furious assault with prolonged cheers and death dealing volleys," Lane opined in a postwar article.[84]

Difficult circumstances beyond Confederate fire hindered Griffin's men. The historian of the 32nd Maine remembered, "In the uncertain light of early dawn, amid the drifting mists, and along the dusky forest-paths, they plunged and struggled through swamps and ditches, across morasses, and over tangle underbrush and slashing." Nonetheless, the Unionists won the opening round. "On we went driving the rebel skirmishers before us," a 6th New Hampshire man recalled. Elements of Hancock's Second Corps, crashing through Confederate resistance to the north, ended up assisting Griffin's Brigade.[85]

James Pollard, 17th Vermont, updated his diary after the memorable day. "This morning we advanced on the rebs and drove them." Pollard recalled firing 24 rounds. Giving himself great credit, then realizing he may have taken an inordinate amount, Pollard believed he "killed 6 rebel colour bearers before I was wounded, that is, they fell when I fired."[86]

George Chandler was another New Englander down with an early morning wound. In a letter the following day, the 9th New Hampshire man wrote, "The ball entered my right thigh and passed directly through, but fortunately did not enter the bone." He hoped his family would not be alarmed, because he did not view the wound as serious. Chandler expected to be in Washington soon, and then home after a discharge. Still in Fredericksburg four days later, Chandler added, "Do not grieve about me, I am among kind friends."[87]

"Men went down on the right and left," a Maine soldier wrote, "but the colors never wavered, and the brigade pushed on undauntedly." Lane's men buckled, leading to the capture of some Carolinians and two cannons. Relying on the experience and grit of his troops, the skillful Lane refused to fold. "I never saw such heroism as was then displayed, both by officers and men," a North Carolinian remembered. Lane competently moved most of his regiments slightly back, with the 37th North Carolina remaining on the right. This regiment was then able to pour a withering flank fire into the Unionists.[88]

Robert E. Lee and his determined army quelled the disaster with a bold stroke from the Confederate reserve. The counterattack arrived without mercy. As Oscar Robinson, 9th New Hampshire, remembered,

The hitherto rattling fire from the enemy now came with a crash, and the enemy before unseen now appeared directly in our front and to our left with less than a hundred paces, advancing in no less than three lines of battle. We could plainly distinguish countenances and count every star upon their hated banner. . . . To remain longer was annihilation.[89]

Surveying the scene, Colonel Griffin saw the northern part of the Confederate charge forcing back Hancock's men, placing great stress on his own brigade's right. Men fell regularly, but without breaking the spirit of a regiment. Destined to suffer one hundred casualties, the 11th New

The brigade of Simon Griffin suffered immensely in the last year of the war. Corp. Alvin Williams, 11th New Hampshire, would lose his life to wounds at Spotsylvania. LIBRARY OF CONGRESS

Hampshire "stood like a wall of adamant," the unit's historian wrote, "The surviving men quailed not." But the inevitability of a retrograde quickly became real. One 9th New Hampshire man recollected how the Confederates "gave us a volley lengthwise which sent us staggering back to the woods." Another Granite State officer recalled being "under a severe fire in front and on flank."[90]

One regimental historian described Potter's attack as en echelon, which means Griffin's soldiers advanced first, followed by John Curtin and the First Brigade. Curtin substituted for Zenas Bliss, who suffered from a painful ankle injury. Curtin was charged with connecting with Griffin's left after the New Englanders linked with Hancock.[91] Ensuring the vital bond was established and retained across three brigades of two different corps would have been highly challenging under any circumstances.

The moment found Robert Potter, as good a division commander as the Ninth Corps ever knew, unable to dictate events. By 5 a.m., with Griffin fully engaged and Curtin trying to provide support, Potter reported, "The engagement had become very hot." After Griffin's original advance faced the brutal Confederate counter charge, Potter simply could not sweep deep into the enemy position. Neither side gained an advantage, while Potter's Division lost hundreds of men.[92]

Capt. Amos Buffum, leading the left of the 36th Massachusetts, moved his part of the line forward within close proximity of the enemy. As the outfit's historian recalled, Confederates then unleashed "a murderous volley, which will never be forgotten by any who survived it." The men deeply appreciated Buffum's "splendid coolness and courage" as he avoided being hit while ordering the Bay Staters to return fire. With two brothers killed in action earlier in the war, Buffum would survive, for now.[93]

Frederick Pettit, 100th Pennsylvania, suggested the lack of a second wave spelled doom for the effort to seize Spotsylvania Court House. The Confederate entrenchments were too strong to take and hold without more support. Charge and counter charge for several more hours failed to alter the stalemate.[94] The lack of detailed descriptions of the fighting by several members of the First Division known for excellent diaries and letters points to a lackluster effort, insufficiently coordinated with Potter.

With regiments still north of the Ni River early in the morning, Willcox was not given a role in the opening attack on May 12. If the Ninth Corps charged at dawn with three divisions and more urgency, the Confederate right might have given way. Gordon Rhea correctly concludes Burnside's attack on May 12 was "feeble and inept," especially because Grant's order to quickly push forward the entire Ninth Corps was not implemented.[95] Along with the dearth of flank protection, the failure to move Willcox up to participate in the early morning attack defined the Ninth Corps' experience at Spotsylvania.

PROBLEMS ON THE LEFT FLANK

Grant sent nervous missives across the morning, suggesting headquarters had lost patience with Burnside. At 10 a.m., Grant wrote Comstock, "Tell Burnside to push hard with everything he can bring into the fight." Twenty minutes later, Grant ordered Burnside to move a division to the right to assist the Second Corps, then, "push the attack with the balance as vigorously as possible." Implying a doubt about Burnside's will, Grant concluded, "See that your orders are executed."[96] Although the move of a Ninth Corps division to Hancock's aid was countermanded, Grant seemed irresponsibly unconcerned about Robert E. Lee's penchant to launch flank attacks.

As at Antietam, the southern terminus of Burnside's line was also the end of the entire Union army. One problem not completely in Burnside's control was the lack of support south of the Ninth Corps position. With Grant's staffer Comstock taking such a prominent role directing Burnside's choices on May 12, one wonders why headquarters did not offer support for the Ninth Corps' left prior to the attack. Soon, dozens of Ninth Corps men would become prisoners or lose their lives. Even with Grant's immortal status, he proved unable to coordinate the Ninth Corps with the Army of the Potomac. The task simply seemed too difficult for anyone.

Willcox was ordered to attack at 2 p.m. The Third Division commander placed the 7th Maine Battery on the right front of his line, with Roemer's New York cannoneers in the rear. Then, Willcox "reported to General Burnside that I expected an attempt of the enemy to attack and turn my left." Sam Benjamin, chief of the division's artillery, brought up more batteries to shore up the line.[97]

The two brigades under Willcox moved west toward the Confederate works at about the same time a duo of enemy brigades moved through woods below the exposed southern end of the Ninth Corps. The inevitable clash became a confused seesaw affair perfectly summed up by Willcox, "The captors of one moment being prisoner of the next."[98]

Bravery and competence from Roemer's Battery led Willcox to give special credit to the New Yorkers. Roemer, who was exceedingly busy on May 12, recalled the effect his battery's fire had on the brigades attempting to overwhelm the southern flank. The charging Confederates, Roemer remembered, were "presenting their left flank to the Battery, and gave us a chance to send our shots directly lengthwise of their line." Roemer added, "The effect was terrible." Sam Benjamin was so pleased, the division's artillery chief said, "Roemer it was a God-send that you were here."[99]

Friendly cannons could only do so much. The 51st Pennsylvania found circumstances so difficult that the close-quarters fighting led to the capture of the regiment's flags and several prisoners. As the unit's historian lamented, "The loss of the colors chagrined the men tenfold more than the loss of their comrades, for by some it was looked upon as a most damning disgrace." The moment's horror could not be denied. As the Keystone Stater added, "It seems almost a miracle that any man escaped death or capture." Men from the 50th Pennsylvania reported similar circumstances. The unit's historian wrote, "A most desperate hand to hand conflict took place. The bayonet and butt end of the muskets were freely used."[100]

Capt. George Bisbing, leading Company I of the 51st suffered two wounds on May 12. A hand injury in the morning failed to worry the dedicated officer much. At around 2 p.m., Bisbing sustained a staggering hit from a Confederate musket, with the ball entering his right side and exiting the left. Bisbing's life ended in a Washington hospital one month later. A veteran of the Mexican War, Bisbing had won a highly esteemed place in the hearts of men in the 51st Pennsylvania. A newspaper tribute deemed Bisbing "a matchless soldier" and "model citizen."[101]

Attempting to thwart Lee's flank attack led to danger for hundreds of devoted Ninth Corps soldiers. About 200 men from the 2nd Michigan served as the infantry support for several cannons on the flank. The determined Wolverines only suffered a dozen casualties, but they were in the center of the tempest. Determined to conquer the force he faced, Lane witnessed the impact of Ninth Corps artillery against his 37th North Carolina. "I have never seen a regiment advance more beautifully than it did in the face of such a murderous fire," the brigade commander suggested. One member of the Tar Heel regiment called the blasts of cannon fire a "sudden and bloody surprise."[102]

Lane also recalled with great respect the resistance of the Ninth Corps men ready to die to defeat the Confederate advance. "The enemy's artillerists fought with great gallantry," the Southern brigade commander wrote, "some being shot down while serving their pieces after a part of the battery had fallen into our hands." Capt. William Rogers, 19th New York Battery, reported how the fire from Lane's North Carolinians "soon killed or disabled nearly all of my cannoneers." Thanks to his drivers and volunteer members from the 2nd Michigan, canister fire continued against the Confederates.[103]

William Humphrey, leading the 2nd Michigan at the start of the day, was called to take command of Christ's Brigade. Capt. James Farrand, who had been born in London, England, in 1830, gained leadership of the 2nd. Determined to save his adoptive country, Farrand fell while moving his regiment against the flank attack.[104]

Other Wolverines sacrificed to push back the enemy. A different Confederate brigade hit the 17th Michigan as Hartranft's line was stuck between attacking to the west and defending against Confederates to the south. The left ends of the two opposing brigades became intermingled, "which resulted in the loss and gain of some prisoners," Hartranft reported. The 17th Michigan had one color fall into Confederate hands. Colonel Luce wrote of being knocked to the ground by a shell, with a dying Unionist crashing on top of him. The regiment lost a large number of prisoners but a Confederate general was also whisked away as a captive of the Ninth Corps. Neither army could gain an advantage as American warriors fell on both sides.[105]

Farther north, the First Division did not make much headway. Lt. Col. Stephen Weld wrote of the intense Confederate fire as the 56th Massachusetts moved out. While neither side accomplished much, he continued, "We had brisk skirmishing all day." The one hundred casualties in the 58th Massachusetts included Capt. William Harley and F. Gilbert Ogden, the regimental adjutant, "both young men of more than ordinary ability and promise."[106]

As the endless day droned on, troops remaining in line did not wish to give up the fight. Lt. Col. Isaac Catlin, leading the 109th New York, pleaded with Willcox,

> *General: Will you send us re-enforcements immediately, or give us an order to withdraw. Major Moody and Captain Schwenk with detachments of the Twenty-seventh and Twentieth Michigan and Fiftieth Pennsylvania and a portion of my regiment are here. They will be captured, I am afraid, but we will hold as long as possible.*[107]

"IN THE MIDST OF LIFE WE ARE IN DEATH"

About 400 Ninth Corps men were captured or missing as a result of the May 12 fighting. A quarter of those soldiers were in the 50th Pennsylvania, with the regimental history needing three pages to list all of the prisoners. To add to their costly May, the 50th had twenty killed as a result of the Spotsylvania bloodbath. Company G accounted for six of those, including Corp. Thomas Gillet, who was buried at the new Arlington National Cemetery. Another lost in the company, teenager James Stroud, would leave a mother who had four decades of life left to grieve. One of Stroud's siblings lived until 1941.[108]

The appalling weather added to the intense memories that day. The historian of the 32nd Maine recalled, "They fought on in the midst of the pouring showers as unconcernedly as if they were unconscious of any other emotion than the fierce excitement of battle." The continued firing along Griffin's front lasted until night, completing a horribly tough day for the northern New Englanders. Darkness led to the building of more entrenchments, with "but little sleep" possible in the rain.[109]

James Stetson was another 57th Massachusetts man to die in May. Stetson lied about his age, enabling him to sign up at seventeen without parental consent. The teenage warrior lost the lower third of his right leg from a bullet wound on May 12. "In the midst of life we are in death," Mrs. Stetson was informed from Emory Hospital in Washington on May 30. The original amputation likely grew infected, leading to further fruitless surgery. James died "from the effects of an amputation of his right thigh." The surgeon concluded, "Allow me to assure you that he received the best care that this hospital could afford."[110]

Burnside undoubtedly mourned the intense cost of May 12. Due to an injury to one of the great Ninth Corps men the war produced, the major general had a profound reason to feel impacted. Sam Benjamin remained conspicuous during the harrowing day, especially while his cannons were nearly overrun by Lee's flank attack. A nasty neck wound, which easily might have killed the excellent artillerist, was not enough for Benjamin to leave the field immediately. However, May 12 was his last day on a field of battle. Although the Medal of Honor was rare even for the bravest of deeds, Benjamin would receive the highest military award for "particularly distinguished services as an artillery officer" across his entire three years of service.[111]

Spotsylvania saw the end of the war for an original Ninth Corps regiment. The 79th New York, one day away from leaving the army after three years of service, was not with their brigade on May 12. The Highlanders served as the provost guard for the Ninth Corps, destined to oversee the dozens of Confederate prisoners captured during the day. The brave veterans then left for home. After suffering a hand wound on May 9, Col. David Morrison mustered out with his men at the end of the month. Morrison received a brigadier general brevet the following year.[112]

Burnside labeled the battle of May 12 "a most fearful conflict," with a "very doubtful" outcome. After desultory firing across the lines for a few days, Daniel Larned questioned the validity of Northern newspaper reports calling the previous week a great victory. Instead, the campaign seemed to grind on without progress. "The enemy is very obstinate and determined," he proclaimed, "and shows no signs of retreat." His words could also sum up an indecisive fight on May 18. The following day,

Burnside's lines shifted slightly, but the men would not begin to move out until May 21. Since leaving the Wilderness two weeks before, the Ninth Corps had sustained more than 3,000 casualties, with Meade's three corps losing 15,000 more. Unbowed, Grant once again tried to steal a march on Lee to press the Confederates closer to their capital.

Grant hoped his troops departing Spotsylvania would find an opportunity to strike a major blow at a divided portion of Lee's force. Gordon Rhea points to Stanard's Mill as one such possibility. In his examination of the day, Rhea shows the difficulty historians sometimes have in assigning blame for a failed tactical plan. He suggests Burnside exhibited "timidity" at Stanard's Mill. At the same time, Rhea said Burnside's decision to not attack seems understandable. Grant's highly discretionary orders for the day make Rhea's latter determination a correct conclusion.[113]

The next major action of the campaign would occur along the banks of the North Anna River, 25 miles from downtown Richmond. Newly promoted to brigadier general, John Hartranft studied the Confederate defensive position along the North Anna after arriving on the morning of May 24. General Lee posted his troops in "a natural fortification, being very rocky and abrupt, covered with heavy timber and thick underbrush." Southerners worked to improve the already impressive natural defenses along the river, with Confederate troops and artillerists keeping fords under a watchful eye. Two days of fighting would begin on May 23, Burnside's fortieth birthday. Grant's orders for the 24th called for the Ninth Corps to either support Hancock at Chesterfield Bridge, the left of the army, or cross the North Anna at Ox Ford, about a mile to the west.[114]

Because some men not keeping up on the march became prisoners, army headquarters had grown concerned about straggling in the Second Division. Potter reminded his men of penalties for falling behind. An evening order on May 23 declared,

The disgraceful laxity of all officers of the division in the matter of straggling has called forth the severest animadversions at the headquarters of the army. All brigade and regimental commanders will detail a sufficient rear guard to prevent all straggling, who will use their bayonets freely, and if necessary, shoot any straggler.

Only soldiers with a written determination of disability from a medical officer would be allowed to not march behind their regiments. Potter would also recommend for dismissal any officer absent without permission.[115]

CRITTENDEN'S FOLLY

May 24 brought the official integration of the Ninth Corps into the Army of the Potomac. Grant accomplished the needed cohesion with Special Orders 25. The purpose of having Burnside report directly to Meade was to "secure the greatest attainable unanimity in co-operative movements" as well as bring "greater efficiency in the administration of the army." Dutiful Burnside informed his superior Meade, "I have the honor to report to you with the Ninth Army Corps."[116]

On the same day, Burnside's trio of divisions approached three different crossing points on the North Anna. Potter served as Hancock's immediate support to the east. At the center of the army at Ox Ford, cannoneers were especially busy in Willcox's Division, the only troops directly under Burnside's control during the North Anna operations. Roemer's Battery blasted the Confederate works south of the river with nearly 500 rounds on May 24. Nearby infantrymen stayed busy when not on picket. With 200 comrades, Charles Hodskin, 2nd Michigan, worked hard on fatigue duty, likely focused on the improvement of fieldworks near Ox Ford. Hodskin wrote of the day being "the hardest time that I ever had on duty."[117]

Casualties would be suffered across the entire line, with the First Division's effort being the costliest. The two brigades crossed the river at Quarles Mill, more than a mile west of Willcox. The 35th Massachusetts historian recalled the North Anna's "picturesque" qualities. Moving a brigade to the south side proved slow because the river was "deep for fording" and "full of rocks."[118]

The flanking move was intended to swing to the east after crossing the river, then strike the western portion of the Confederate line near Ox Ford. New leadership oversaw the effort. Maj. Gen. Thomas Crittenden had directed the First Division since soon after Stevenson's death, with Brig. Gen. James Ledlie commanding the First Brigade. Crittenden would be in the Ninth Corps for less than a month, while Ledlie's disastrous service would last longer.[119] May 24 offered some illustration of the generals' command deficiencies.

Crittenden failed to move his entire division in a timely manner to assail the Confederate flank. One Bay Stater suggested the division commander's intention was to move the Second Brigade up to initiate the attack, with Ledlie in reserve. Instead, Ledlie's regiments went forward alone. A Confederate whirlwind soon encircled them.[120]

Serving as the brigade's picket line, the 35th Massachusetts spanned out with their left flank near the river. Nine companies covered the brigade's advance, with Company G in reserve. Admiring the way the Bay Staters formed a skirmish line and advanced, the regimental historian boasted, "The boys dashed ahead in the spirited way an old soldier loves to see." The work to push Confederate pickets back did not seem difficult, especially with the excellent marksmen in the 13th Pennsylvania Reserves, Fifth Corps, to the right of the 35th.

Compared to their easy advance against Southern pickets, the Unionists grew far less sanguine after seeing the main Confederate position. Even if the northern portion of Lee's line facing Ox Ford had the best defensive prospects, Confederate engineers and exhausting labor made the west wing of the formation a mighty breastwork. Witnessing much of what the Bay State skirmishers of the 35th Regiment saw, the historian of the 13th Reserves lamented, "Rarely has such a check-mate been given." Stymied in position before Ledlie's other regiments joined in, several men in the 35th Massachusetts became prisoners.[121]

John Anderson, an officer in the 57th Massachusetts served as the messenger between Ledlie and the division commander, who remained at the ford. Ledlie requested three more regiments from Crittenden. The additional troops had yet to reach the ford, so no help was available. Crittenden's first inclination was to prohibit an attack, but he called the messenger back to demand instead Ledlie use the "utmost caution." Attacking a strong defensive position without support seemed like a losing proposition. Crittenden declared, "I am afraid it will be a failure."

Anderson suggested Ledlie did not seem interested in Crittenden's perspective. Rather, the general appeared drunk, yet ready to make a name for himself. Ledlie's regiments were already within easy range of the enemy. As one report noted, "The Rebels opened a terrible fire of grape and canister." This caused an adjustment of the brigade in an effort to decrease the risk of damage from the murderous cannon fire. Confederate muskets then joined the fray. "The action was hot for an hour or two," the 35th Massachusetts historian recalled, "without material change on either side" as ammunition supplies dwindled along Ledlie's line.[122]

To make matters worse, a thunderstorm began in the early evening. Some Southern troops poured over their works to blast the Unionist right and front. Still leading the 56th Massachusetts, Stephen Weld had a bullet tear through his coat without inflicting an injury. Weld estimated the farthest advance of the brigade was 100 yards from the excellent Confederate works.[123]

Like Edward Wild and Sumner Carruth, Charles Chandler's Civil War began as a member of the 1st Massachusetts Infantry. Three years after first departing for war, Chandler found himself in charge of the 57th Massachusetts south of the North Anna on May 24. The rapidly deteriorating situation added to the new regiment's very damaging month. In his mid-twenties, Chandler attempted to assist color sergeant Leopold Karpeles after the brave native of Bohemia was wounded. Endeavoring to keep pushing ahead, Karpeles, who would receive the Medal of Honor for his courage this month, eventually relinquished his banner, then moved to the rear. Soon thereafter, Chandler had an arm blown off, along with other wounds.[124]

Capt. Albert Prescott and two privates went to the mortally wounded Chandler's assistance. "But the rebels pressed hard," a newspaper story recorded, leading Chandler to request his men save themselves. Much affected by the severe injury to a highly respected officer, Prescott and Chandler said goodbye. The captain later suggested "that he had almost rather have been shot himself than be obliged to leave him."[125]

Ledlie's attack cost the Ninth Corps more than two dozen dead, and about 200 additional casualties, including fifty prisoners. Observers south of the river and later historians spare no scorn for Ledlie, while Crittenden receives hardly any rebuke. Ledlie deserves the opprobrium, but Crittenden had the chance to either delay Ledlie's advance until the arrival of the division's other brigade or to peremptorily order Ledlie to not attack. He did neither, which was in line with his reputation for incompetence. One observer of Union generals believed Crittenden, who had no combat experience before the war, lacked the leadership and willpower to form "an opinion of his own," while also failing to take "any responsibility that he could possibly avoid." The thoughts related to Chickamauga, but certainly apply to the North Anna as well.[126]

Crittenden had few admirers among those with whom he served. His enemies, which included Secretary of War Stanton, ensured he was forced out of the Western Theater after Chickamauga. He was then given his Ninth Corps division, mainly due to political necessities. From a famous Kentucky family, Crittenden had to be given a job, resulting in dreadful consequences to the patriots in Ledlie's Brigade on the North Anna. Rhea notes how Ledlie did not receive a rebuke from his immediate superior after the battle. Perhaps that truth prevailed because Crittenden knew of his own failures on May 24.[127]

The day after the North Anna fight, Crittenden's pettiness and idiocy were obvious. Informed of being placed under Fifth Corps leader Gouverneur Warren, junior to Crittenden as a major general, the Kentuckian wrote Burnside. Although suggesting he would "cheerfully" obey Warren, Crittenden added, "I do not think that I ought to be placed in this position," proposing that Ledlie take over the division. Not known for a focus on his image, Burnside tried to heal Crittenden's bruised ego. "I fully appreciate your feelings," the corps commander noted, "but under all circumstances I would as a friend advise you to remain where you are." Burnside offered to query Grant about Crittenden's removal but thought such a step unwise. The corps commander concluded, "You know I would not advise you to do anything that would not, in my opinion, result in good to you."[128]

Unable to recross the river in a downpour, the division started constructing breastworks to hold off a possible Confederate counterattack. With such an impressive position and not feeling well, Lee did not grow aggressive in the dark. The 21st Massachusetts historian saw the "painfully evident" excellence of the Confederate defensive position at the North Anna. He continued, "The more it was reconnoitered during the next two days, the worse it looked."[129]

"A Braver Man Never Lived"

Potter's men crossed Chesterfield Bridge on May 24, an act trying the nerves of thousands. Capt. Percy Daniels, 7th Rhode Island, witnessed "heavy fire" screaming in from Confederate artillery as Curtin's Brigade traversed the river. Mixing with the enemy's missiles, the intense thunderstorm so noticeable to Ledlie's troops to the west produced "a scene of gloom if not terror," as the 58th Massachusetts advanced.[130]

The witty historian of the 6th New Hampshire used memorable words to describe the march to the south side of the river. "We were in plain sight of the enemy as we crossed, and they amused themselves by sending shell down among us from a battery just above the bridge." The troops bore the ordeal "with as much grace as we could," he continued, because Potter was in no position to retaliate against the higher and well protected Southerners.[131]

Potter's right rested on a bluff in the river as his men built earthworks while still harassed by Confederate fire. Lined up against Lee's eastern flank, northern New England men attempted to endure the bitter stalemate along the North Anna. Like the rest of the army, Griffin's men were becoming experts in the construction of entrenchments. Lt. Col. Charles Cummings, 17th Vermont, noted how his men "immediately proceeded to intrench ourselves" after spanning the bridge. The work of building protective structures led to a good position for defense, a Maine man opined, although they were "hastily constructed."[132]

Neither side seemed interested in a full-scale assault on the other's defensive bulwarks. Testing the enemy became important, however, especially as Grant planned another disengagement from Lee's line, followed by a flanking march around the Confederate right. This led to some intense work for Griffin's men on the evening of the 26th. Signs of a fight were obvious to a Maine man, who wrote, "The enemy in our front became more active and annoying." As the 6th New Hampshire's historian added, the Confederates were "disposed to be troublesome."[133]

General Potter reported his men "drove back the whole line of the enemy's skirmishers," allowing the division to move somewhat closer to Lee's works. With the imminent recrossing of the river, any short occupation of the ground was not worth the cost. George Upton witnessed the death of Lt. Col. Henry Pearson, an original captain in the 6th New Hampshire. Attempting to gain a better view of the enemy, Pearson was hit as soon as he raised his glass. Upton lamented how the brave and respected officer sustained injuries to his left hand and head, "letting out his brains." Upton continued, Pearson's "loss is deeply felt . . . many an eye unused to tears was wet upon that day, and in a time like this, he is a great loss to the country."[134]

"It was a sad night for the Sixth Regiment," the unit's historian wrote. Pearson certainly justified Potter's praise as "a very fine officer." Pearson joined the army in time to be at First Bull Run. Returning home, he led efforts to recruit the 6th New Hampshire, becoming a captain at age twenty-one, then lieutenant colonel before his twenty-third birthday. Pearson rests in Grave 4,103, Fredericksburg National Cemetery. As his comrade Hosea Towne wrote of the special officer, "a braver man never lived."[135]

DIFFICULT END TO A WEARISOME MONTH

Troops began pulling out of the North Anna line during the evening of May 26. Still in close contact with Confederates, Potter's men sensed the danger while preparing to evacuate. By 9 p.m. some Southerners moved forward to interfere with the withdrawal. "The firing was so heavy," the 7th Rhode Island historian suggested, the aggressive Confederates likely had "occupied our picket line." After relief from the Second Corps, Potter's Division began their trek away from the North Anna.[136]

To the west, Crittenden faced danger from intense rainfall. Stephen Weld said the darkness and precipitation made the recrossing of the North Anna quite difficult. "It rained heavily," the young officer remembered, "so that the river rose and almost washed the bridge away." After safely reaching the north bank, the excellent troops had to first march northwest, the opposite direction of Grant's new move, to cover the Fifth Corps' crossing at Jericho Ford.[137]

Burnside skillfully managed the reunification of his corps in the difficult conditions. As the three divisions headed toward the Pamunkey River, Willcox led the advance, with Potter in the middle, and Crittenden in the rear. Detached from their brigade, the 35th Massachusetts supported First Division engineers, a very important and honorable assignment. Repairing roads and building foot bridges decreased the wear on soldiers' feet, making the march easier. The work could be "hard and often perilous," but the regiment would be held back from fighting during their assignment. As Fisher Cleaveland of the 35th wrote in early June, "We do not expect to go into a battle unless the whole Corps has to go in and we are necessary to win the day."[138]

Very difficult conditions prevailed on the march. Starting out before noon on May 27, men would never forget the next enervating thirty-six hours. As Percy Daniels reported, the 7th Rhode Island crossed the Pamunkey River near the end of May 28 after covering 31 miles with only five hours total rest across the previous day-and-a-half.[139]

A member of the 2nd New York Mounted Rifles, a regiment serving for a time in the Ninth Corps as dismounted troops, remembered the disheartening trek.

> *Our march, this day, was dreadful, the heat tropical, the dust, as fine as flour and nearly a foot deep; thousands of men keeping as well closed up as possible to prevent straggling, while the road all along was strewed with carcasses of horses and mules, causing an insufferable stench. . . . To stop was impossible, a rear guard and a cavalry patrol forced up the stragglers.*[140]

Faron Anderson and comrades in the 2nd Michigan, Hartanft's Brigade, found good things to eat while resting near an abandoned house close to the river. Anderson described how soldiers "took everything that they could lay their hands on." He continued, "You had ought to have seen the things fly," with pigs, chickens, potatoes, and ripe cherries meriting special mention. In hopes of keeping his brother from enlisting, teenager Anderson described the difficult march from the North Anna. "Some of the men layed down and died," he wrote, with those still ambulatory "all dust" and suffering from blistered feet.[141]

William Randall, a 1st Michigan Sharpshooter temporarily with the ambulance corps, remembered how several horses could not keep going during the difficult trek to the Pamunkey. Randall's own horse, in addition to a sergeant's, were placed in front of wagons to fill in for spent equines. While walking, Randall wrote, "Gen'l Burnside and Staff passed by." Taking quick action due to the condition of the train, Burnside ordered Orlando Willcox to detail an officer with thirty soldiers to help keep the wagons moving. Randall continued, "Horses could drag the wagons along on the level but the men pushed the wagons up the hills."[142]

Ninth Corps cannoneers pressed on as well. Capt. Jacob Roemer recalled soldiers and equines "thoroughly worn out," with supplies of rations and forage unsatisfying, thoughts echoed by Adelbert Twitchell, 7th Maine Battery. After crossing the river, Burnside's Boys took up a temporary position near Hanovertown. Experienced in the ways of war over the last few weeks, artillerists and their nearby comrades began the construction of breastworks on May 29.[143]

Burnside's three divisions acted as Grant's reserve. May returns for the Army of the Potomac showed nearly 130,000 present troops, of which Burnside commanded 23,071 soldiers and forty-eight cannons. No decisive victory had been won, but Grant and Meade were only 10 miles northeast of Richmond with a firm supply line.[144] In less than a month, great sacrifice of lives had placed the Union horde 50 miles southeast of the Rapidan crossings used to initiate the battle of the Wilderness.

Frederick Petit, a veteran of hard service since South Mountain, considered the trek from the North Anna to the Pamunkey the hardest in the history of the 100th Pennsylvania. Burnside's tired soldiers had done their part to meet Grant's goal of a wide maneuver to the southeast to box Lee's army into a position backed up to the Confederate capital. Unionist supplies would flow via ships from White House Landing on the Pamunkey. Additionally, by moving so far east of Richmond, Grant could be easily reinforced by troops from the Army of the James, which had wasted nearly a month with limited progress after advancing up the Peninsula. Soon the Eighteenth Corps, which included several regiments that had been detached from Burnside in early 1863, would become part of the Army of the Potomac.[145]

Trying to make the most of the bogs and topography, troops changed positions multiple times before May ended. Moving early on the 29th, the men got to work creating more breastworks at their new position.

Probes of the Confederate lines were conducted during the day. Further battle was inevitable. Yet, the hard work to create entrenchments often did not seem worth the time, with additional position changes on May 30. Willcox's men were on Potter's left. To Willcox's right was a division of the Fifth Corps.[146]

The fight to successfully take the assigned position did not rank high in notable engagements of the war, but good teamwork among Ninth Corps brigades and other elements of the army made the operation a success. Most notably, Curtin's Brigade connected with Hancock's left a half-mile south of Totopotomoy Creek. The cost was relatively light in what a regimental historian called a day of "sharp skirmishing," rather than battle. Nonetheless, the costs of war became evident as some brave patriots would never be able to return to the army. An example was John Urie, a teenager in the 1st Michigan Sharpshooters. Taking a ball in the left thigh, Urie would be medically discharged from service.[147]

No historian will argue that Ambrose Burnside was the war's best general. However, some who have earned great respect across decades detract from their otherwise solid scholarship to mock and disrespect Burnside's accomplishments. Gordon Rhea referred to Burnside as the "portly" leader of the Ninth Corps who lacked "clairvoyance and the split-second timing of an acrobat," creating less chance of success on May 30.[148] Of course, perfect timing and the ability to predict the future were not present in any general in military history on all days. May 1864 was not the greatest month for any military leader in American history, including General Grant. With the unforgiving ground, need for long marches, and nonstop work for many soldiers, Rhea should have given Burnside more credit for his leadership in late May, which helped the Union cause as an unforgiving spring continued.

BLOODY TRANSITION TO JUNE

As Col. William Hurey, 2nd Michigan, reported of May 31, "We advanced our line nearly half a mile to a position covering the Shady Grove road," and began to construct new breastworks. Even in a reserve position, Crittenden's men faced danger as they were tasked with holding lines, or advancing to recently vacated positions. By the end of the day

Burnside wrote, "Several detached lines of skirmish pits were carried, and our people took position close up to the enemy's main line."[149]

Orders did not call for a general engagement. On the last day of May, the 45th Pennsylvania "kept on skirmishing all afternoon." A Company G soldier, Sgt. Thomas Davies, who had recently turned twenty-one, took a spent ball to the chin during the advance, his second of what would be three war wounds. Calling the dent made "his dimple," Davies served as an example of an immensely dedicated patriot who was rewarded with a long life. He lived until early 1929.[150]

General Grant never contented himself with having a good line of battle firmly entrenched against Confederate attacks. Advancing his men continued to be the goal in hopes of perhaps forcing Lee's army against the Chickahominy River, not much more than 5 miles from the center of Richmond. A good deal of confusion existed as headquarters moved troops around, which may have surprised an adjacent brigade of a different corps. This was especially true after the Sixth Corps vacated its line to move more than 2 miles. Difficult topography, being in close contact with the enemy, and the tired nature of everyone made communication breakdowns inevitable. Burnside remained very busy during the day trying to retain linkages with other parts of the army.[151]

The exchange of skirmish fire on May 31 cost the 48th Pennsylvania a splendid leader. Maj. Joseph Gilmour took a bullet in the left leg while overseeing the construction of rifle pits. Amputation later in the day, followed by evacuation to a Washington hospital, accomplished little. Gilmour died on June 9, three weeks short of his thirtieth birthday. The regimental historian praised Gilmour, originally the captain of Company H, as "an excellent officer, quiet, unassuming, and as brave as man could be; a perfect soldier." General Potter memorialized Gilmour as "invaluable."[152]

More extensive fighting was destined for the start of June. A "Provisional Brigade" under Burnside had a role in the looming drama. These troops were engaged to a limited extent at Spotsylvania on May 12, serving to the left rear of Willcox during the Confederate counterattack. Assigned to the First Division, the assorted units were commanded by Col. Elisha Marshall, an 1850 graduate of West Point. He led the 14th

New York Heavy Artillery into the Overland campaign. In addition, Marshall's Brigade included unmounted New York cavalry and the 2nd Pennsylvania Provisional Heavy Artillery.[153]

Heavy artillery regiments, often referred to as "Heavies," were not intended to become infantry. Manpower necessities compelled such use of the garrison troops in the field. Rumors of the government's interest in converting Heavies to infantry did exist as the units were recruited. One announcement denied that the government would take such an action. "Those who know, assert that there is not the least foundation for such a rumor," a New York newspaper inaccurately printed. Instead, "The men are enlisted for Heavy Artillery and cannot be transferred to any other branch of the service without their consent. Government would not dare to perpetrate an act of fraud such as a change of this kind would be."[154] In the name of saving one united nation, the federal government would indeed put muskets in the hands of a large number of heavy artillerymen, turning the guardians of forts and cannons around Washington into combat soldiers.

As a result, thousands of men believing their war would consist of light duty prepared for their first major combat. After some additional shuffling of troops, the Ninth Corps was positioned between the Second and Fifth Corps by the afternoon of June 1. The army's location was in an area known as Cold Harbor. Burnside's southern terminus, the left of Crittenden's Division, was at the center of the army. To the south, the left of the Sixth Corps rested a short distance from the Chickahominy, 7 miles from the desk of Jefferson Davis, president of the Confederacy.[155]

"DETERMINED COURAGE AND RESISTANCE"
Oscar Robinson, 9th New Hampshire, was flabbergasted on June 1. "My greatest surprise and *wonder*," the warrior announced, "is that I am alive. I am *grateful* and feeling dependence upon my merciful creator and preserver."[156] Many comrades along the Army of the Potomac's Cold Harbor line likely felt the same way. Men in the trenches would receive no relief as the new month brought a cascade of dangers.

June began somewhat quietly. The 35th Massachusetts assisted with the construction of new entrenchments forming a right angle in

Crittenden's line along Shady Grove Road, near Bethesda Church. The 35th's historian called the formation "an odd piece of engineering."[157] Creation of the angled front on the left of the Ninth Corps likely resulted from an interest in flank protection, due to the more active nature of the fighting to the south, lines the Fifth Corps held. Crittenden's men were posted along Beaver Dam Creek and a spot dubbed Magnolia Swamp.

Senior generals continued to coordinate necessary shifts in troops. John Gibbon's Division of the Second Corps stood to the right of Burnside's line, next to Potter's two brigades. Hancock and Burnside corresponded during the late morning and early afternoon in an effort to prevent any dangerous gaps from opening. As was his penchant, Burnside offered to help in whatever way possible. Also required to connect with the right of the Fifth Corps, the Ninth Corps leader promised "to keep a close connection with Gibbon in any event." Although still not able to attack without causing a general engagement, Burnside concluded, "Should Gibbon require any assistance, I shall be glad to give him all in my power."[158]

Stephen Weld, 56th Massachusetts, did not like his regiment's position. Crittenden's two brigades "occupy a very unpleasant place," because "a cloud of dust envelopes us night and day." Coincidentally, Lee was planning to assail the area. The North Carolinians of Col. Risden Bennett's Brigade attempted to surprise Crittenden's Division, with some partial success. To the south, troops in John Gordon's Division took part in the short Confederate offensive.[159]

Tar Heels smacked into Marshall's Provisional Brigade, with the 14th New York Heavy Artillery especially in danger along Shady Grove Road. Several men fell, including John Gainer and George Hilts, both of whom would die of wounds. Two of the captured Heavies, Lorenzo Newton and George Van Sant, would die in July at Andersonville Prison, Georgia.[160]

Disruption of the brigade's line caused a great deal of concern across the Ninth Corps. Men from the 35th Massachusetts, who were at work on nearby entrenchments, did not have their muskets handy, but they made an effort to reach their weapons, "which caused considerable confusion," the regimental historian remembered. The Bay Stater gave credit to Ninth Corps artillerymen, who "most ably" worked their guns during the panic.[161]

General Willcox sent supporting troops to help hold back the Confederates to his left. The 51st Pennsylvania and 60th Ohio, a regiment from each of Willcox's two brigades, provided timely assistance that helped stem the tide. Darkness did not aid the Confederates either. As one member of the 14th North Carolina mused, "We drove him, and but for the fall of darkness we might have scored a great success."[162]

William Randall had a good view of the fight from behind Crittenden's line. He may have agreed with the Confederate who thought darkness saved the Ninth Corps' left. The enemy "came very near breaking the lines," Randall wrote shortly after the war. As with the 35th Massachusetts historian, Randall noted the importance Unionist cannon fire played during the evening fight.[163]

Willcox's two regiments contributed to the eventual Confederate repulse as men fired "volley after volley into the enemy." Scorn existed for the Heavies and Crittenden's men in general as a result of the line's disruption. General Hartranft believed no fight was evident in Crittenden's command that evening. An officer in the 51st Pennsylvania wrote that the First Division failed to make any resistance to the attack. The regiment's historian also suggested the entire First Division "fell back without firing a single shot." The Keystone Staters likely exaggerated the lack of will in Crittenden's men.[164]

Ledlie's campaign report does not mention his brigade's participation in the evening fight of June 1, perhaps because he regretted a poor showing from his troops. General comments about how two particular regiments assisted during the campaign pointed to valiant conduct that likely stabilized the situation during the Confederate attack. The 4th and 10th United States Infantry, professional soldiers temporarily part of the Ninth Corps, would depart Burnside's command for the Fifth Corps later in June. Ledlie extolled the Regular troops.

The Fourth and Tenth Regiments of U.S. Infantry have borne a conspicuous part, and the determined courage and resistance of the officers and men of these regiments deserve especial mention. Though few in number, and most of the time commanded by lieutenants, their marked bravery and intrepidity calls for the highest encomiums of praise.[165]

"THE GENERAL WAS TRUE TO HIS WORD"

Skirmish firing continued along the rest of the Ninth Corps line. Potter's men stood bravely to the task, with northern New Englanders giving and receiving fire on June 1. Cannon blasts kept both sides poised for the possibility of more intense service. The new soldiers of the 32nd Maine were learning much while still losing men. The regimental historian lamented the randomness of wounds and death as the men stood ready at all times of the day. Late in the evening, Confederates "concluded to try us on," he wrote, as the Mainers "gave the rebs a reception which drove them into their entrenchments again."[166]

With June 1 passing by, Grant grew more impatient. Hopes for lasting achievements to the south led to the overnight movement of the Second Corps from the army's right to the left. Hancock's departure made the Ninth Corps the northern end of the army on June 2.[167] Such a circumstance likely made those doubting Crittenden's Division feel even more leery, because no supporting troops were on the right flank of Burnside's corps. The next two days would bring the worst difficulties of the army's time at Cold Harbor.

Since May 5, Confederates inflicted nearly 5,000 casualties on the Ninth Corps. The incredibly difficult march to the Pamunkey, the shifts in position south of the river, and the steady rate of firing at Cold Harbor wore heavily on Burnside's Boys. Stephen Weld wrote his father about the intensity of the previous month.

Our men are pretty well used up by this campaign. Officers as well as men need rest, and I hope we shall get it before long. A great many of the men are without shoes, and most all of them are in rags. . . . We shall have some pretty hard fighting before we get Richmond. . . . I never knew before what campaigning was. I think, though, that all this army have a pretty fair idea of it now. We have had to march all day and night, ford rivers, bivouac without blankets or any covering during rain and sunshine, and a good part of the time have been half starved. I know that no one staying at home can have any idea what this army has been through.[168]

Neither army would receive the rest or supplies Weld hoped for. The centrality of religious faith served as a rock to many soldiers in what had likely been the most difficult month in their lives. A penitent Frederick Petit, 100th Pennsylvania, mulled the subject in a June 1 letter. He declared, "Through the watchful care of Him who never sleepeth my life and health has been preserved." Moses Whitehill, 17th Vermont, expressed similar feelings in his letters during the spring of 1864. By late May he informed his brother, also a soldier, "Providence has seen fit to spare my life."[169]

Letters from home could bring smiles to worn-out warriors. After receiving a late May missive, devoted Burnside staffer Daniel Larned expressed great happiness. Before reading about news from home, "I was more depressed than any time since the commencement of the siege of Knoxville," Larned wrote. Steady determination kept men in the ranks and willing to sacrifice for their country. After surviving the first month of the campaign, Samuel Haynes, 45th Pennsylvania, pondered the future, seeing the death of the Confederacy requiring great cost. He believed "this campaign is destined to be the death blow of the Rebellion and also the death blow to many thousands of brave men."[170]

Strong leadership often proved decisive, the reason so many men stood by their colors. The historian of the 6th New Hampshire remembered an important moment when the troops were posted near Bethesda Church. Recently promoted to brigadier general, Simon Griffin went to his former regiment, requesting two companies of skirmishers.

Almost every man in the regiment stepped forward, and he had to pick his men himself. He did so, saying, "I will not ask you to go any farther than I will go with you." The men selected went cheerfully to their dangerous duty, and the general was true to his word.[171]

"FIGHTING FIERCELY AND EFFECTIVELY"

All the fortitude, faith, and stamina soldiers possessed had to remain close at hand as the Cold Harbor segment of the Overland campaign reached a bloody conclusion. Burnside had a difficult time on June 2 simply arranging his troops after what to him was the surprising departure of Hancock's entire line. Tempers flared as Meade suggested the Ninth Corps had been informed of the move of the Second Corps. The army commander agreed to allow Burnside's change of position, with the expectation that connection with the Fifth Corps would not be abandoned.[172]

An army mired in egos as much as the swamps east of Richmond had a difficult time aligning to promote both offensive and defensive possibilities. Gouverneur Warren, a highly proficient military engineer masquerading as a competent corps commander, grew upset with Burnside's initial arrangements. Immediately south of the Ninth Corps, Warren wrote Burnside at 7 a.m., "In order to open roads to our left and to develop the enemy's position I have had to extend my line from your left upward of 4 miles." Warren felt the need to pull back his Fifth Corps in order to protect himself or lend support in case the Ninth Corps needed help. Burnside was not even aware of where to find Warren as confusion ruled Meade's army again. In response, Burnside received a 9:15 a.m. directive to "move simultaneously with General Warren so as to keep massed in rear of his right," and be prepared for any contingency. Crittenden's beleaguered brigades screened the southeasterly move of Burnside's two other divisions.[173]

An enemy always in the mood to fight caused great chaos after Potter and Willcox moved the bulk of their brigades toward Bethesda Church. By early afternoon, Burnside was ready for Crittenden to march down Shady Grove Road to reunite the three divisions. An attack from several Confederate brigades again attempted to surprise the Ninth Corps. Without much effort, Confederate troops made Crittenden look like an unprepared general.[174]

Fortunately, a small group of soldiers under Potter and Willcox had yet to move. They offered excellent support to the beleaguered First Division. A dismounted rifleman from New York, part of Curtin's command, penned a vivid portrait of the afternoon fight. The regiment had been divided to perform picket duties, with one group posted on the road. "About this time a thunder storm, with a heavy shower, came on," he wrote. Then, "just as it ceased we formed on the road, and expected to continue the march, when we heard a rattle of musketry from our rear."[175]

The 20th Michigan, Christ's Brigade, was another outfit ready to assist Crittenden's star-crossed men. "Our pickets were attacked before we deployed," Claudius Grant wrote in his diary. Isolated for a time, Colonel Cutcheon reported the 20th stood, then fell back to a line of rifle pits, where they gained the support of Marshall's men on the left. After less than stellar support from the 14th Heavies, the 24th New York dismounted cavalry assisted Cutcheon. During their stand, the 20th Michigan suffered thirty-five casualties.[176]

Other Ninth Corps men under assault assisted with the final repulse of the Confederates. The determined veterans of the 21st Massachusetts, suffering worse than Cutcheon's unit, provided a vital level of tenacity on Crittenden's left. The regiment's historian discussed the Bay Staters' central role in the drama. "The determined and skillful courage with which the 21st met and checked the advance of the rebels cannot be praised too highly," he suggested. As the men "fell slowly back fighting fiercely and effectively," troops from both the Fifth and Ninth Corps evacuated to new postings. Among those killed or mortally wounded during the afternoon were thirteen soldiers of the 21st.[177]

No Ninth Corps regiment suffered more on June 2 than the Round-heads, the reliable soldiers of the 100th Pennsylvania. Dozens of men fell in the successful resistance to the Confederate tide. Frederick Pettit, whose service to history would be immense due to his bravery and cogent letters, received a severe hit to the left arm. The brave warrior was away from his regiment for five weeks.[178]

"THE LOSS OF SO MANY FINE FELLOWS"

Flustered by a month of stalemate when attacking the smaller Confederate army, Grant planned a major strike against Lee's right flank after Hancock's corps moved south. With the attack not launched until early on June 3, Southern warriors had time to improve the entrenchments already guaranteed to make any fight costly. Instead of bringing a day of triumph against Lee's determined warriors, the attacks ended as a great disappointment to Grant.[179]

Perhaps the sad outcome for Union arms was preordained, due to the great level of fatigue across the army. Confederates endured the same problems, but notable gains from concerted assaults against incredibly strong defensive positions were highly unlikely. The 36th Massachusetts historian summed up the condition of Curtin's Brigade, "The night was stormy and intensely dark," he wrote, with the troops having "no shelter," with "much discomfort" inhibiting sleep. Due to the rain, Ninth Corps men were "most uncomfortable," an officer in the 48th Pennsylvania remembered. He witnessed men "drying their blankets and clothing before wood fires" early in the day.[180] The drenched warriors had endured so much across the previous five weeks.

Unionists struck Confederate lines across a curving front of 6 miles, with the Ninth Corps generally facing north. Potter opened the ball just after dawn. Curtin's exhausted brigade moved forward with the support of Griffin's men. A North Carolinian facing Potter noted the benefits and difficulties of the Unionists having a body of woods on their part of the field. The Tar Heel remembered, "The enemy were enabled to make near approaches in our front," but "we could hear distinctly the orders given by their officers." Another Tar Heel on the Confederate army's left pronounced June 3, "perhaps the hardest day" of his regiment's existence, being without food while either shooting at Burnside's men or working to improve breastworks.[181]

The swamp around Matadequin Creek made navigating a battle line impossible. Nonetheless, John Curtin, as diligent a combat leader as any who served in the Ninth Corps, stood ready to send his men against the difficult topography. The 7th Rhode Island historian described the scene, "Forward was the word from Colonel Curtin, and forward we went." Across the brigade, some men foundered in "mud and water half way up to the knees," while also driving Southern pickets.[182]

If the muck failed to break the Ninth Corps, Confederate fire had a better chance. On the left of Curtin's advance, the 36th Massachusetts had returned from detached service working on entrenchments just in time to augment the brigade's effort. "As we neared the woods," the regiment's historian remembered, "a withering volley swept the line." This opening fire inflicted a mortal wound on Color Sgt. Adams French, Company D, who had proudly stood at his post for the entire campaign. A corporal captured the falling colors before they hit the ground, as "a galling fire" from the Confederates continued.[183]

Keystone Stater Bob Reid bemoaned, "In no engagement of the 48th did they expend more ammunition than this." He also recalled the bursting of Unionist cannon shells among Curtin's soldiers, necessitating a change of position to ensure the balls traveled a greater distance to their intended Confederate targets.[184]

Familiar with terrible suffering, the 45th Pennsylvania had the most difficult experience of any in the Ninth Corps around Cold Harbor. Charging into "a murderous fire of musketry and grape and canister," the veterans "never wavered," Eugene Beauge wrote. Charley Terbell took a bullet to the knee that had just passed entirely through the body of a comrade on the 45th's line. Living a decade into the next century, Terbell talked of the wound bothering him until the end of his life. As the excellent soldiers continued their doomed advance, the 45th Pennsylvania received an order to halt and construct more earthworks. "There," Beauge added, "keeping close to the ground for protection, what was left of the Forty-fifth held their part of the advance line under fire all day."

The 45th Pennsylvania once again exhibited immortal courage. Due to the nature of the difficult ground, Companies G and H were confined to a ravine that unfortunately stretched at a right angle to the Confederates. This allowed for exceedingly accurate fire against the confined duo of companies. First Lt. George Scudder, temporarily leading Company H, died on the field, while the commander of Company G, Lt. John Gelbaugh, took a nasty wound. Several men who joined the regiment in recent weeks also went down. In total, more than half of those in the 45th Pennsylvania fell that day, with forty-one killed or mortally wounded. The regiment suffered 181 casualties around Cold Harbor, more than 10 percent of Burnside's entire loss from June 2 through the 15th. After South Mountain, June 3, 1864, was the bloodiest day in the 45th Pennsylvania's service.[185]

Much of the damage inflicted on Curtin came from the brigade of John Cooke, a highly capable officer. A veteran in one of Cooke's regiments noted how the repulse of Burnside brought tributes to the North Carolinians from the Richmond *Examiner*, "which was said to have praise only for Virginians." The brigade worked well with other Confederate troops near Bethesda Church, leading to the failure of any Ninth Corps effort. The 7th Rhode Island's historian remarked on the accuracy of his opponents when he surmised, "It was as impossible for a man to expose himself without being hit as it is to go into a rainstorm and not get wet."[186]

Willcox advanced Hartranft's Brigade to the left of Curtin. The goal for the move included the recapturing of the works Marshall's men vacated the previous evening. That portion of the assignment seemed easy enough, but the rest of the day did not alter the status quo on the northern portion of the battlefront. Confederates to the left halted Hartranft's further progress, leading his men to begin constructing protective earthworks. As so many reported during the campaign, bayonets, tin cups, or even hands were used for the necessary digging.[187]

Assuming the center of Hartranft's front line, the 27th Michigan suffered the most across the brigade. Col. Edwin Schall, 51st Pennsylvania, died from a bullet to the neck during the charge. He went to war with a three-month regiment in 1861, then served as an officer in the 51st for the rest of his life. Several of his brothers also served in the distinguished regiment. Greatly saddened by the loss of his friend Schall, Maj. William Bolton assumed command.[188]

Ninth Corps artillerists were able to find good angles to augment the June 3 attack. Jacob Roemer reported firing 228 rounds across the day. By midday, the cannons were repositioned to support an expected afternoon charge. By the time the Ninth Corps was set to renew the attack, the battle's afternoon phase was canceled by a disappointed Union headquarters.

Never without danger, skirmish duty led to the death of Capt. William R. Ham, 32nd Maine. Ham, in his mid-thirties, sustained the wound "while deploying his company." He died early the following morning. Praised as "a good officer and brave soldier," Ham's loss "is deeply felt and regretted by the whole command," the state's adjutant general was informed.[189]

Harsh realities struck Lt. Col. John Whiton, 58th Massachusetts, as a result of the June 3 carnage. He wrote of losing three friends, including captains Thomas McFarland and Charles Upham. "All three were buried in coffins and laid side by side." Whiton bemoaned, "Alas, sad it was for me when this next day I went to the regiment and *felt* the loss of so many fine fellows."[190]

Maj. Barnabas Ewer was another valued officer in the 58th to fall on June 3. Well into his fifties, Ewer earned much respect in his oversight of the regiment. With enough sorrow in his life after the death of two spouses in earlier decades, Ewer felt great pain from his own wound, as well as the casualties his men suffered. When a surgeon informed Ewer of his inevitable death, "Not a sign of fear was visible on his countenance." The regimental historian deemed Ewer a "universal favorite," adding, "never did I hear him spoken of save with feelings of the deepest respect and admiration." The 58th Massachusetts sustained the second most casualties of any Ninth Corps regiment from June 2 through the 15th.[191]

"WE ARE WILLING TO DIG"

Burnside's Boys had a rough day on June 3, but they accounted for only 800 of the nearly 6,000 casualties in the Army of the Potomac. The day exemplified the bitter equilibrium the two armies had retained across the previous month. Burnside likely saw the futility of further combat around Cold Harbor, but he worked with other generals in an attempt to make something of the sacrifice. June 3 was the last of the grand attacks in the area, although the men stayed somewhat in place for more than a week.[192]

Burnside wrote headquarters of the problem evacuating all of the Ninth Corps' wounded, due to the paucity of wagons, as well as a concern about Confederate raids to the east of Bethesda Church. He also wished to ensure the Fifth Corps would stay in place to the Ninth Corps' left as a means to protect those trying to evacuate injured men.[193]

Members of the 9th New Hampshire knew the pain of lost comrades and the wicked sights awaiting them on June 4. As one Granite Stater noted, "It was a pretty hard looking sight" to examine the battlefield. In the battered 45th Pennsylvania, men tried to find some normalcy while rotating on and off picket duty. Anything to keep from reliving the horrors of the campaign would have been good for Samuel Haynes. "I dread to speak of the casualties," he sadly penned. Also in early June, an officer in the 50th Pennsylvania reported home, "We have been under fire every day since the 6th of May."[194]

George Upton, 6th New Hampshire, accepted his lot. Missing sleep and feeling the last week in particular, Upton agreed with the necessity of entrenching at a new position. He wrote on June 5, "As this mode of doing things saves lives, we are willing to dig." Defeating the Confederacy, he added, will be "a long job, as such things cannot be hurried." During his 44th day since departing Annapolis, Upton kept looking to the bright side. "We are in better trim for active operations, than the day we started, as we are hardened into it," he wrote, "The army is also in excellent spirits."[195]

Pondering the previous few weeks, Daniel Larned expressed many emotions in a letter while the troops remained around Bethesda Church. "Hard fighting for our old corps" prevailed for two days, the staff officer averred, with field headquarters "in full view of the battle field" and thus "constantly under fire." Later, Larned referred to the Confederates as "spiteful and very determined." Boots and spurs remained on whenever sleep was attempted, due to the expectation of attack at any time. Even with his close position to the front, Larned added, "It is utterly impossible to convey to you an accurate idea of what this campaign is."[196]

Working to best solidify the army's position meant continued shifting of troops. By June 5, Ninth Corps men moved to the southwest, aligning with the Eighteenth Corps on the left. Constant vigilance against Confederate probes or larger attacks remained imperative. Charles Hodskin wrote of the changing position while also seeing and hearing "constant skirmishing in our front" and "shots flying over pretty fast." Diligent pickets in both armies led to minor advances without any appreciable advantage gained.[197]

Additions to casualty lists inevitably resulted from the two armies' proximity and the continuous need to keep watch for enemy movements. As Granite Stater Sewell Tilton wrote on June 7, pickets were "saucy as ever, keeping us continually on alert." Two days later, Aaron Dickinson,

6th New Hampshire, died after a "shot through the brain," Hosea Towne wrote. Dickinson had exhibited some disciplinary problems early in the war; he was stripped of his corporal's stripes in February 1862. Wounded at Fredericksburg, he was discharged, then reenlisted in early 1864.[198]

A larger movement of the Army of the Potomac remained on General Grant's mind. In a missive to Chief of Staff Halleck, Grant mentioned the idea of shifting the army farther to the south, crossing the James River as a way to still menace the Confederate capital while leaving other options open. Grant believed Lee's men would not resort to offensive operations. Rather, standing behind strong entrenchments offered the Southern army the best chance to resist without the major losses guaranteed from storming Union earthworks. After a very bloody month, Grant knew destroying the Army of Northern Virginia could no longer be his primary goal. Rather, the target would become Confederate logistical and supply routes, making Petersburg, 20 miles south of Richmond, a sensible destination.[199]

Several changes to the organization of the Ninth Corps took place before the army departed Cold Harbor. With Crittenden out, James Ledlie became First Division commander, a tragic and fateful change. Col. Jacob Gould, 59th Massachusetts ascended to brigade leadership. For a short time, Ebenezer Peirce, 29th Massachusetts, took command of Ledlie's other brigade. A general in the Massachusetts militia at the start of the war, Peirce lost an arm on the Peninsula in 1862. He had short assignments as a Ninth Corps brigade commander during the year in the west.[200]

The 179th New York joined Peirce's Brigade on June 11. Five weeks earlier, only three companies of the new regiment had traveled to Washington. Three more joined by the time the outfit was officially attached to the Ninth Corps.[201]

Two new units from Wisconsin joined Hartranft's tired veterans. The 37th and 38th Infantry had been raised in the Badger State earlier in 1864. Samuel Harriman, a captain in another Wisconsin regiment, took the lead in raising the 37th. By mid-May, eight companies had assembled in northern Virginia for training under the lieutenant colonel, with Harriman back home to recruit. While the Ninth Corps was fighting at Cold

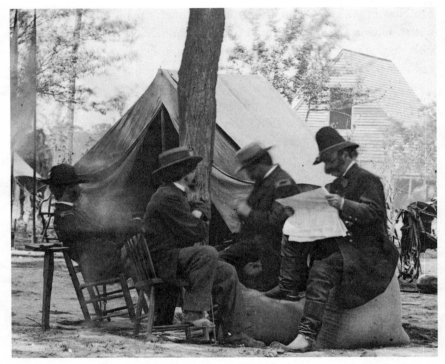

With stalemate ruling the Cold Harbor front, Ninth Corps commander Ambrose Burnside had time to read a newspaper during the second week of June 1864.
LIBRARY OF CONGRESS

Harbor, the 37th arrived along the Pamunkey. Seven hours of picket duty constituted their initial service with the Ninth Corps.[202]

After "very pleasant" marching and the steamer ride up the Pamunkey, the 38th Wisconsin officially joined the Ninth Corps on June 10, shortly before the 37th. Not knowing the sheer horror of the war they were joining, a member of the 38th wrote of the unit's mindset during the preparations to move to the front, "Nothing could exceed the enthusiastic readiness of the officers and men to enter on the campaign then opening for them." Like many other units joining the Army of the Potomac that spring, the 38th did not have a full complement of companies on leaving their home state. Only four companies of the 38th had mustered into federal service when the departure for war arrived.[203]

PUSHING TO PETERSBURG

On the last day at Cold Harbor, Jacob Roemer and his cannoneers in the 34th New York Battery had fun at the expense of their foes. The artillerists had picked up twenty-seven unexploded fused shells in recent days. As Roemer reported, the battery "refixed them, and sent them back from whence they came." Roemer's cannons fired sixty-four rounds the day before, with June 12 bringing fifty-three more shots.[204]

After typical activities along the battleline for days, the Ninth Corps started to move out near dark on June 12, heading east. The troops gave up less than ideal bivouac and battle locations for a long and difficult march. By daylight the next morning, Cold Harbor could be seen as a distant and unpleasant memory. The soldiers' course curved south before reaching the Chickahominy River. As the 7th Rhode Island historian gleefully penned, the 13 hard miles "changed our resting-place from a wide waste of drifting sand to a bright green valley, between whose shaded hills flowed a tiny stream."[205]

Still working hard assisting engineers, the 35th Massachusetts did their part by improving roads and expediting the movement of wagons. Swampy ground around the Chickahominy flustered the Bay Staters. The regimental historian described the soupy mess as "extensive and wild and intricate beyond description."[206]

Inevitable traffic jams made June 13 a frustrating day. The next morning, the Ninth Corps crossed the Chickahominy, then proceeded toward an even bigger target, the James. Ferrero's Division was nearing a reunification with Burnside. For now, the regiments of U.S. Colored Troops headed farther to the east as part of their continuing mission to guard supplies.[207]

Resting between two rivers, Ninth Corps troops had made a very impressive march of more than 50 miles in forty-eight hours. The men then received nearly a full day of rest. Lt. Col. Stephen Weld, 56th Massachusetts, noted his campsite, the property of John Tyler, former president of the United States and member of the Confederate Congress. The contradiction in the recently deceased politician likely did not occupy Weld's mind. The young officer had to satiate a much more important necessity. As he wrote in his diary, "I do not think I was ever so hungry in my life." Thanks to some of his troops who wished to assist their commander, Weld feasted on a broiled quail that evening.[208]

The Sixth Corps traversed the James ahead of Burnside's divisions. Spanning the river had been possible due to the diligent work of engineers who had quickly constructed a pontoon bridge more than 2,000 feet long. Ninth Corps troops started crossing on the evening of June 15. After the fateful moment, Lt. Col. Cummings, 17th Vermont, happily wrote his wife. He referred to the region as "delightful. You would enjoy travelling through it in peaceful times & I think you would like such a spot as this plantation."

The ominous reality of war remained, with an engagement soon likely for the weary soldiers. A forced march of more than 20 miles was immediately started. As Meade commanded in an army circular, the Ninth Corps was to move quickly west, then "take a position on the left of the Second Corps." With Benjamin Butler's Army of the James engaged with Petersburg's defenders, Charles Hodskin knew what the future held. He jotted in his diary, "There is heavy cannonading in the direction of Butler."[209]

Burnside was originally ordered to issue four days of rations to each soldier before crossing the river. When delays kept supply wagons away from the Ninth Corps, headquarters insisted Burnside start moving. Burnside replied that the rations were being allotted before he received the new order to move on. He seemed satisfied that the provision of food had proceeded well enough before the order to move to the west.[210]

Some still went hungry. Pushed to the brink for weeks, soldiers in the Ninth Corps would long recall the march from the James River to the trenches of Petersburg. A member of the 2nd Pennsylvania Provisional Heavy Artillery remembered "the sun being broiling hot, dust very thick, with no rations and very little water." A Granite Stater wrote, "The men fell out badly." Some "straggled in the rear for miles." The 29th Massachusetts historian lamented, "Many men of the regiment—and of all the regiments—had been left on the road in an exhausted condition, so that when our lines were formed on the night of this day, the corps was but a skeleton compared to its former strength." Another veteran corroborated the diminished numbers after the "distressing forced march," leaving "very attenuated" lines of infantry on arrival before Petersburg. Only three enlisted men were present in Company A, 21st Massachusetts.[211]

Despite human endurance already strained to the limit and diminished ranks due to straggling, headquarters insisted on an attack soon after Burnside's regiments arrived and manned the position east of the Confederate trenches. A late-morning directive pointed toward a planned attack at 6 p.m.

With the wearied nature of the entire Union army and the lack of communication prevailing since the Rapidan was crossed more than a month before, the evening's effort did not amount to anything beyond skirmishing. Hancock reported to headquarters, "I do not think the men attack with persistence; they appear to be wearied." Burnside added, "nothing of importance occurred in our front." Additional entrenching at least improved the line, offering protection against Confederate bullets and shells.[212]

"No Severer Loss"

Although the Fifth Corps was moving toward Burnside's left, the Ninth Corps planned the early morning attack of June 17 as the army's southern flank, with Potter's brigades forming two lines. Griffin's men aimed for the Shand House, while Curtin's troops on the left had a Confederate battery in their sights. In an effort to facilitate surprise and increase the force of the troops arriving at the defensive works, Potter reported, "Canteens and cups were packed in haversacks to prevent noise, and orders were given to rely upon the bayonet, and not fire a shot." With some of his troops in reserve, Potter's soldiers went forward at dawn, about 3:15 a.m.[213]

The first line of Griffin's force, from right to left, included the 17th Vermont, 11th New Hampshire, and 32nd Maine. Charles Cummings only had 135 men in the Green Mountain regiment. The attack was not an uninterrupted rush by troops charging at full speed. Rather, as Cummings noted, his men first had to march up a steep hill, then surmount earthworks protecting Unionist skirmishers. After dealing with those obstacles, Cummings wrote, "I reformed my line and gave the order to charge." He was impressed as his small band "rushed impetuously forward." The speed of the victory pleased Cummings even more. "In less time than I can write this," he reported, "we had captured 2 cannon, a caisson, 6 horses, 70 prisoners," and the colors and adjutant of a Tennessee regiment. New Hampshire soldier Ransom Sargent believed the number of Confederates still asleep when the attack hit greatly lowered the loss in Griffin's Brigade.[214]

The historian of the 32nd Maine described the impact of the sudden attack on the Confederates around the Shand House. "In the same instant that they became aware of the column charging down upon them out of the darkness, they were struck and swept away by the momentum of its swift advance." Chronicling the 11th New Hampshire, another veteran suggested the "stealthy, quick step" of the northern New Englanders served to overwhelm the initial enemy line. With some bias, he added, "It was one of the finest assaults of the whole war."[215]

Lt. Orlando Wales Dimick, 11th New Hampshire, undoubtedly wished for a better end result for himself. In charge of the regiment's two left companies, Dimick grew confused due to the lack of daylight. He approached what he thought was a squad of his unit. Instead, "I had made a serious mistake and found myself in the presence of a half dozen of the enemy." Too isolated to be rescued, Dimick added, "I was a prisoner and a more depressing feeling I have never experienced." He felt the "terrible weight" of his error.[216]

Not yet eighteen years old, Reuben Vining was the only member of the 32nd Maine killed during the attack. One month earlier, Vining's older brother died of wounds sustained at Spotsylvania while serving in another Maine regiment. In his report, Cummings noted the death of First Lt. Guy Guyer, who fell early in the charge with a bullet to the breast. Guyer was remembered as "one of the most gallant and faithful officers in the regiment."[217]

Not all of Curtin's Brigade went forward on Potter's left. Taking a leading part in the effort, the 36th Massachusetts had a key role in the assault against Battery 15. As the regiment's historian wrote, "None who participated in that attack will fail to remember the morning of the 17th of June while life shall last." Considered as brilliant a fight as the Bay Staters ever participated in, "it was one of the saddest days of our history," with a notable victory "purchased at a heavy cost," including seven killed or mortally wounded. Less than one hundred soldiers were part of the 36th's attack; many of the troops had either yet to catch up after the long march from Cold Harbor or were confined to hospitals.[218]

Capt. Otis Holmes quickly fell as the 36th darted toward the Confederate works. Of the devoted patriot, the regiment's historian stated the unit,

> *sustained no severer loss during its term of service. Few men possessed in so marked and special degree the respect and affection of his men. Strong and vigorous in body and mind; a brave, fearless soldier; a cool, sagacious advisor; careful and prudent of his men, he was a noble specimen of manhood, and an ideal soldier. . . . The entire regiment had learned to love and esteem him, and his untimely death was mourned by all who knew him.[219]*

Even with the losses of leaders like Holmes, "Our victory was very complete," boasted the historian of the 48th Pennsylvania. Perhaps 600 Confederates were captured. Burnside was quite pleased with the result, suggesting, "Potter dashed forward in most gallant style." With Southern backs now even closer to Petersburg, pickets from Potter's advanced position moved up to challenge the new Confederate line.[220]

In a rare moment of praise for the Ninth Corps, George Meade grew ecstatic after hearing news of Griffin's success. At 7 a.m., headquarters informed Burnside, "It affords me great satisfaction to congratulate you and your gallant corps on the successful assault made this morning." Meade noted "the wearied condition of your men" while lauding the "highly creditable" behavior during Griffin's dawn foray. Headquarters also implied the need for further efforts to attack the enemy, as Lee's army had yet to fully arrive below Petersburg. Perhaps trying to assuage Burnside's concern about the unprotected left flank of the Ninth Corps, Meade added that Warren was being ordered to post the Fifth Corps to the south.[221]

Men involved in the attack had a right to feel a sense of accomplishment. As the state's adjutant general was informed, the 31st Maine participated in "a most splendid charge." However, failures of coordination doomed the effort to what a modern historian labels a "facile" attack. The lack of an even better outcome rests with a variety of causes, including confusion about the line of advance for Willcox's Division and the difficult ground over the area of Ledlie's advance. The inability to make more of Potter's hard work and the sacrifice of his men stands out as an important communications failure of headquarters and Ninth Corps leadership. The problem was not as serious as at Antietam, but the tremendous loss later in the day can be traced to the incomplete dawn attack Potter directed so well.[222]

WILLCOX'S TRAGIC EFFORT

Instead of a full-scale blow with three divisions, the Ninth Corps opened its participation in the siege of Petersburg with uncoordinated efforts from each division. The costliest of the assaults occurred in the afternoon of June 17 as Orlando Willcox moved his regiments into the fray. With optimism, then great sadness, Charles Hodskin, 2nd Michigan, perfectly summed up what was the bloodiest day in the history of his regiment. "The spires of Petersburg are visible," the Wolverine scribbled, "We have had hard fighting & our Regt have lost a great many men."[223]

The catastrophe for Hartranft's Brigade unfolded under the watchful eye of an engineer respected by contemporaries and most historians. Second in the 1851 West Point class, James St. Clair Morton served competently in several commands earlier in the war. He became chief engineer of the Ninth Corps at Spotsylvania. Considered an energetic and reliable analyzer of terrain, Morton's skills utterly failed as Willcox's men moved out.[224]

Advancing at about 2 p.m. from their position occupying the Confederate earthworks Griffin seized earlier in the day, Hartranft's poor guidance from Morton led the regiments across the new Southern line, rather than directly into the works. The 2nd Michigan lined up facing north, at a right angle to the rest of Hartranft's command. The brigade's other regiments curved north as part of Morton's direction, allowing the enemy to easily enfilade the doomed Unionist soldiers. As Col. William Humphrey of the 2nd Michigan reported, "By some error, the lines were not formed correctly," with the troops offering their flank to the enemy.[225]

The afternoon saw the first men killed in action in the two new Wisconsin regiments, both in the front of Hartranft's main line. Staring at the impressive new Confederate defenses, the historian of the 37th Wisconsin remembered "the hot bright sun almost blinding us and heating the dry sand under our feet," nearly enough to cause blisters without moving. Then, a "wild, loud cheer" opened the charge. Dust and smoke quickly started to obscure Hartranft's target as the Confederate defenders fired at the brigade. Soon, the men were "shattered and broken," the dejected Badger exclaimed.[226]

Soldiers suffering from the poorly planned attack included Pvt. Sanford Rogers and Sgt. Lyman Heath, both of the 2nd Michigan. Taking a bullet to the right leg above the knee, Rogers held on for more than a month. He lost his life on July 30 in New York City. Only twenty-one years old, Rogers was buried at Cypress Hills National Cemetery in Brooklyn. Sustaining a similar injury during the doomed charge, Heath would have his right leg amputated in July. He died at a Washington hospital two days before Rogers, with burial at Arlington National Cemetery.[227]

Orlando Willcox suggested a dearth of proper artillery support vexed the attack. Truth likely exists in the general's statement. However, the terribly bad direction from Morton caused the greatest problem. As Willcox himself admitted, "Hartranft's left struck the enemy's pits, but melted away in a moment." The withered left companies of the advance, Willcox added, lost seventy-seven out of ninety-five men.[228]

With hundreds falling in a few minutes, among those destined to die was Morton himself. He would posthumously receive promotion to brigadier general for formulating such a ridiculous course for the attack. A Wisconsin soldier may have lacked a West Point education, but he clearly saw a much better reality than Morton's plan. Instead of being exposed to a murderous fire on the left flank, the Badger opined, "Had we but been allowed to go right ahead, we should have taken the whole and suffered much less loss than we did." Colonel Humphrey grasped the sacrifice better than anyone. With 310 men present for duty at the start of the day, the attack left 188 casualties in his 2nd Michigan, including nineteen killed, losses the officer correctly deemed "exceedingly severe."[229]

Christ's regiments moved up as Hartranft's men continued their drift toward the Second Corps' left. Soldiers in the Second Brigade suffered, as well, but not to the extent of Hartranft's losses. Exemplifying the Army of the Potomac's attacks since the Wilderness, Christ's effort faltered due to unmerciful topography. Perhaps confused by Hartranft's sudden curving charge, not all regiments under Christ went toward the Confederate works. The 50th Pennsylvania reached the westernmost point of the attack. As the regimental historian recalled, the 50th's soldiers received orders "to hold its position at all hazards."[230]

Recently transferred from Marshall's Brigade, the 24th New York Cavalry continued to serve dismounted during the early part of the Petersburg siege. Capt. Calvin Burch, Company G, fell mortally wounded during the day. His widow received a glowing tribute from another officer. Burch died that morning,

calmly and quietly, surrounded by weeping and loving friends, breathing out his life cheerfully, with the noble consciousness that he met his death in the front fighting for and upholding the glorious flag of his country. Yesterday afternoon he led his company on a fierce charge, when they were met by a cross or enfilading fire, which nearly cut the entire regiment in pieces. Many brave officers fell, but your husband received a bullet in the lungs, which could not be traced out; of this he died this morning, regretted by all who had the pleasure and honor of his acquaintance, and worshipped by his entire company, who cannot be consoled at their irretrievable loss.[231]

Burch had enlisted in early 1864, part of the surge in recruitment during the winter before the Overland campaign. The lamented patriot, still not thirty years old, rests at Woodlawn Cemetery, Oswego, New York.[232]

"I Should Have Preferred Charges against Him"

With the Roundheads manning the skirmish line for the First Division, General Ledlie's men prepared to see if a third attack from Burnside's Boys could sufficiently rattle the Confederate line. With two brigades in front and the two heavy artillery units of the Third Brigade in support, the observant historian of the 21st Massachusetts described the opening of Ledlie's advance. The regiments went forward "fearlessly over the bodies of a thousand of their comrades in the 2d and 3d divisions, who had fallen in the two previous attacks."[233]

The First Brigade only included the three new Massachusetts regiments. Lt. Col. Joseph Barnes, 29th Massachusetts, commanded the Second Brigade in the place of Colonel Peirce. Hoping for the shock value of a rapid charge, Ledlie ordered his men to not fire before reaching the Confederate works. His men then attacked "at a run over the entire distance with steadiness and bravery." The initial Unionist burst showed promise, with hand-to-hand fighting after Ninth Corps men reached the ditch serving as a Southern earthwork. "Too much praise cannot be accorded the men making this charge," Ledlie reported.[234]

With a shot to the head, Capt. Charles Goss, leading Company C, 21st Massachusetts, was killed early in the attack. Praised as a "conscientious, brave, and faithful officer," Goss held the respect of the entire regiment. A lieutenant at Antietam, a painful thigh wound did not hold Goss back from further service. The charge of June 17 "the last of his twenty battles," the outfit's historian remembered, saw Goss once again head "to the front with a noble enthusiasm."[235]

Leading the 57th Massachusetts, Lt. Col. Julius Tucker, not yet twenty-three years old, was another officer taking a devastating wound to the head. With the bullet entering the left side of his face, Tucker was assumed to be instantly killed. Taken to the rear, he held on. The Confederate bullet took away eleven teeth, some bones, and vision in the left eye. The young hero would die soon after the war, buried in his hometown of Charlton.[236]

Major Levant Rhines and his 1st Michigan Sharpshooters found themselves in a tough spot in the disorganized firefight. Although not part of Ledlie's Division, Rhines moved up to support the evening attack. During their bold action on Ledlie's left, the Wolverines took dozens of Confederate prisoners, but the Southern warriors captured and hustled out nearly eighty sharpshooters to prison camps. Rhines was mortally wounded during his daring effort. A New York native and descendant of Mayflower passengers, Rhines was thirty-two years old. He would be buried at Chapel Cemetery, Sandstone, Michigan.[237]

The two regiments of Heavies endured difficult hours as part of the June 17 assault. Color Sgt. John D. Wareing, 2nd Pennsylvania Provisional, fell very early in the attack, losing a leg to grape shot. Pressing on, the men were ordered to "double quick," increasing their rate of advance. Further progress drew "a heavy fire of grape, canister and musketry" as deaths and wounds quickly added up. Less than a third of the original membership of the unit answered the following morning's roll call.[238]

Only their brigade comrades in the 14th New York Heavy Artillery had a worse day than the Pennsylvania Heavies. Sustaining nearly 250 casualties, the Empire State soldiers charged into a Confederate whirlwind. "Our regiment behaved splendidly," a young officer wrote the following day. Those killed in action included teenagers like Edward Adams and William Allen, as well as older soldiers like Myron Brown and Harrison Carey, both in their thirties. More than seventy men were killed in action across the duo of heavy artillery regiments. Between the 15th and 30th of June, Burnside's two regiments of Heavies sustained one in six Ninth Corps casualties.[239]

The highest-ranking loss from Ledlie's Third Brigade was Maj. Job Hedges, commanding the 14th Heavies. Not yet thirty years old, Hedges had enlisted more than two years before. Taking a leading role in recruiting, Hedges rose quickly. From regimental adjutant as a lieutenant, he was a major by early 1864. Hedges was considered "a noble officer." All of the regiment, a newspaper report proclaimed, "regret the death of their beloved commander." As he bravely led his men on June 17, Hedges "was literally riddled with bullets."[240]

Nothing permanent resulted from the charge, other than lost and mangled lives. Holding the advanced Confederate line for a time, a lack of ammunition rendered Ledlie's attackers vulnerable. Barnes reported 10 p.m. as the time a retreat became necessary due to threats from rallying Confederates. With only seventy-five men that day, the 29th Massachusetts lost twenty-nine during the action.[241]

Stephen Weld grew enraged when he looked for assistance from General Ledlie during the evening. Again accused of drunkenness, Ledlie seems not to have played much of a factor in the attack. Weld penned a very unflattering picture of Ledlie's behavior, suggesting the division commander seemed uninterested in the fate of his men. Unfortunately, Weld did not take the step any regimental commander had a right to do under the circumstances: arrest Ledlie. Feeling diffident due to his youth, Weld failed to take such a bold yet justified step. In his postwar writings, Weld looked back with regret over his inaction. "If I had been older and had more sense," he lamented, "I should have preferred charges against him."[242]

ENDING A FRIGHTFUL SEVEN WEEKS

The following day led to another attack that did not dent the will or earthworks of the Southern warriors determined to keep Grant's minions out of Petersburg. Thus began a vicious stalemate that would last until the fall of the city in early April 1865. With progress seemingly impossible against strong Confederate earthworks, Theodore Nutting, 6th New Hampshire, would inform his family on June 19, "How much longer this fearful and terrific contest is going to last God only knows. I hope not long."[243]

Only forty-five days passed between Burnside's crossing of the Rapidan and the conclusion of the opening phase of the Petersburg siege on June 18. In that time, 65,000 casualties were inflicted on Grant's force, with more than 9,000 killed, wounded, missing, or captured in the Ninth Corps. Although the Army of Northern Virginia absorbed a similar percentage loss, General Lee and the Confederates seemed closer to exhausting the Union army and reducing the North's will to fight than Grant was at subduing the South.[244]

The three weeks from the arrival at Cold Harbor through June 18 were an especially costly time for Burnside's Boys. In addition to the battle wounds of the first twelve days of June, nearly 3,000 casualties were suffered from the crossing of the James to the end of the month, with most of those occurring in the first two days in front of Petersburg. At the end of the month, Burnside only had 15,290 soldiers present and equipped, a ghastly number compared to the excess of 20,000 with him two months before. The loss grows worse when considering the reinforcements added to the command after the battle of the Wilderness.[245]

Neither side showed much of an interest in giving up, so death and all the realities of war would persist. For much of the rest of the Ninth Corps' service, time alternated between duty on the front line or in reserve. As William King, 17th Vermont, wrote in late June, "We have to lay in the breastwork two days in the burning sun within shouting distance" of the enemy, "and then we are relieved and fall back in the rear in the woods and stay there two days." Regardless of their location, King bemoaned, "The heat is too much for our boys." Another worry, bad water, led to the use of quinine in the whiskey ration of the 2nd Pennsylvania Provisional Heavies, an effort to decrease sickness from fetid hydration.[246]

Two major developments, the arrival of Ferrero's Division and the beginning of the Petersburg Mine, closed out June for the Ninth Corps. On the 20th, as Ferrero reported, "by command of Major General Burnside, the division was placed in the second line of works." Earlier in the month, word that the African American soldiers would finally receive a chance for military duty suited Alfred Dodge, 39th USCT. "We are to take the field," he scribbled. The danger perpetually linked to a soldier's destiny became evident early on. By the end of June, the division recorded nine casualties, including two killed in action as the seemingly impregnable Petersburg trenches were improved each day.[247]

The standoff created when two enemy armies build extensive earthworks did not suit an inventive officer and his men. Lt. Col. Henry Pleasants, 48th Pennsylvania, pondered an idea as the siege settled in with the start of summer. Commanding a strong and experienced regiment including many coal miners, Pleasants visualized a major surprise capable of not only denting a portion of the Confederate defenses but also bringing a decisive Union victory. As Burnside wrote in his campaign report, "On the 26th of June a letter was received from General Potter, stating that he believed a mine could be run under the enemy's works." In the early phase of the Petersburg doldrums, the sad legacy of the Crater began.[248]

PART SEVEN

Slow Victory around Petersburg

"The severities of the campaign have reduced my men rapidly."
–CAPT. ADELBERT TWITCHELL, 7TH MAINE BATTERY

SETTLING IN TO THE SIEGE

COMPARED TO THE FRENZIED ACTIVITY SINCE EARLY MAY, THE PERIOD immediately after the attacks of June 18 began six weeks without major combat or horrid marches. The relative reprieve made each day meld into the next, possibly creating boredom for soldiers. As General Potter wrote, "nothing very marked occurred" from June 19 through July 29, a time period almost as long as the crossing of the Rapidan through the opening fights near Petersburg.[1]

Life was still quite difficult. Continued danger from the enemy kept Ninth Corps soldiers on edge. After forty-eight hours of rest, the 50th Pennsylvania returned to the front on June 21. "We were constantly under fire," the outfit's historian recalled, "and it was never safe for anyone to show his head above the breast-works." Even with "utmost caution," the experienced outfit suffered eight killed and eleven wounded while serving on the picket line through July 29. For the entire month of July, other than the battle of the Crater on the 30th, Burnside's four divisions sustained nearly 700 casualties.[2]

One of many Ninth Corps men to lose his life was Lt. Hiram Little, 11th New Hampshire. Esteemed as "an officer of signal bravery, whose dry wit every Eleventh man can recall," Little held his rank since the summer of 1862. As the regiment's Walter Pingree remembered,

Confederates were taking "shots at us all the time" after the initial attacks at Petersburg. Little was hit in the neck on June 20. He would die on the Fourth of July. The grieving Mrs. Little gave up life two months later.[3]

Albert Rogall, 27th USCT, wished to face more danger. On June 22, he opined, "Our colored division is an unnecessary expense to the government," due to the lack of action. He also learned to respect his Confederate foes, who he deemed as quite brave, albeit for an unworthy cause. The next day, "bullets were exchanged with full cordial[i]ty." Continuing to be plagued by sickness, Rogall's health did not improve, partly due to the scent and sight of freshly killed cattle.[4]

Josiah Jones, 6th New Hampshire, shared Rogall's maudlin mindset. After seeing a friend shot in the face early in the siege, Jones was pressed by the "very hot and dusty" time on duty. The army "seems to be no nearer the end than when we left the Rapidan," he wrote. Henry Muchmore, another New Hampshire man, held more optimism. "I have seen 50 dead rebs in 10 rods square," he observed, "I think we shall conquer in the end but it may not be this year."[5]

Alfred Dodge, 39th USCT, continued to hope. "I always make up my mind to be contented," the Vermonter proclaimed in July. He retained fond visions of home and wished for a visit back to the Green Mountains. "Not that I am homesick," he wrote, "but that it would be a little more agreeable than to hear the crack of a reb shell every five minutes."[6]

Improving already strong earthworks filled some days in the summer sun. The construction of a log home near General Potter's headquarters was a notable achievement recorded by Peleg Jones, 7th Rhode Island. In both old and new regiments, a hauntingly small number of men were able to perform duties. With long service in the Ninth Corps, the 21st Massachusetts had only 110 men present on June 20. Across the next six weeks, the small and dedicated band would sustain fourteen casualties.[7]

Not all moments were bad. Although soldiers had to risk Confederate fire to enjoy a sweet treat, members of the 45th Pennsylvania charged an ice house in early July. Within sight of Confederate pickets, one Keystone Stater recalled, "The boys took chances and frequently brought chunks of ice into camp," part of the recipe for some wonderful lemonade. Assistance from organizations such as the Christian Commission and the Sanitary Commission augmented diets with pickles, apples, and a variety of vegetables. "As the season advanced," however, "we suffered much from heat," something that would plague Ninth Corps men all summer.[8]

With lines close, New Hampshire soldier George Codman enjoyed friendly meetings with Confederates. Members of the two armies were "getting to be the best of friends," Codman wrote on July 17. He also noted the usual routine of two days at the front, followed by two days behind the lines. While resting, Codman listed some good food he savored: ham, potatoes, coffee, and milk. A happy surprise arrived as he relished "tomatoes by just opening a can." Later in the month, Codman's brigade comrade Albert Raymond, 17th Vermont, echoed the positives. He praised the "tip top" rations, which sometimes included turnips or cabbages. "We are well cared for as soldier boys," Raymond added.[9]

BUILDING THE MINE

Working underground, crews from the 48th Pennsylvania escaped the drudgery of trench life and the dangers of picket duty. The mining operation lifted morale throughout the regiment, even with the intense labor required from digging, moving earth, and eventually filling the mine with gunpowder. The two leading figures of the effort, Lt. Col. Henry Pleasants and Sgt. Henry Reese were both serving their adopted country. Thirty-one years old in 1864, the commanding officer began life in Argentina, with an American father who met his wife while on business. Reese, four years the junior of his colonel, had been born in Wales. He quickly became the key figure at the mine, spending nearly every hour of each day overseeing the difficult project while Pleasants used his engineering skills to boost the mine's chance of success.

Early on, several challenges became evident. Those expanding the length of the shaft through intense digging faced exceedingly tough physical labor. The experienced miners knew the traditional pick would not work in the cramped confines of a tunnel far shorter than the average man. This led to blacksmiths transforming standard army picks into a straight tool, a stronger, better instrument than bayonets. In total, Pleasants estimated his work crews knocked down and removed more than

18,000 cubic feet of earth to create a shaft 511 feet long, as well as two lateral galleries of nearly 40 feet each.

Peppered with questions from engineers at army headquarters, Pleasants had to take time away from his oversight role while trying to please superiors. In one answer, Pleasants wrote, "The mining has been carried on without interruption since it was begun—There are 210 men employed every 24 hours, but only two can mine at a time at the extremity of the work." Most other soldiers hauled out earth in hardtack boxes.[10]

In two areas crucial to a successful mine, Pleasants displayed shrewdness Meade's engineers believed he lacked. Framing proved vital to keep the shaft from crumbling under the weight of the earth above. A nearly catastrophic collapse occurred on July 2. Ventilation, necessary to ensure men deeper into the mine could breathe, required the introduction of fresh air and the draft of a fire to exhaust stale air and gases. What Pleasants deemed the "wild enthusiasm" for the project across the regiment allowed for steady progress. "Work on the shaft went on day and night," the proud colonel remembered.[11]

Scientific knowledge and engineering skill informed Pleasants of the requisite length of the shaft. He requested a theodolite, an instrument used in surveying, to assist with the calculations. Army headquarters failed to provide the vital tool. Pleasants believed the bureaucratic wall was due to the "deliberate indifference" of General Meade and his chief engineer James Duane. Fortunately, "Old Burnside came nobly to my rescue," Pleasants wrote. The corps commander informed Washington of the need for a theodolite, which was quickly made available. Of the tool's importance, Pleasants remembered, "If it had been of solid gold set with diamonds, it could not have been more precious to me." Using clandestine means to keep his mathematical observations veiled from Confederates, Pleasants' engineering acumen led to wonderfully accurate measurements.[12]

Even a curmudgeon like Meade wished to praise the work of the 48th Pennsylvania. In early August, Pleasants and all in the regiment gained encomiums for "skill displayed in laying out" and building the mine. "Great credit" went to the Keystone Staters for their "willing endurance" and "extraordinary labor and fatigue." So much went right from the initial idea of the mine to the completion of the back-breaking labor during the third week of July. The rest of the Crater drama would prove quite tragic, for a wide variety of reasons.[13]

AN ARRAY OF HINDRANCES

Praise for the mine days after its explosion did not mean army headquarters had enthusiastically given the work a green light from the beginning. While soldiers from the 48th Pennsylvania invested immense time and toil in the project, Meade and others held extensive doubts about the viability of the mine and the subsequent infantry attack. Without strong support from senior leaders, the whole endeavor possessed little chance to dramatically alter the tactical situation south of Petersburg. The effort seemed doomed from the start.

A central weakness was the ground targeted for attack. Even Burnside, testifying in August before the court of inquiry examining the disastrous hours following the mine explosion, questioned the location of the offensive his troops led. "The principal obstacle," Burnside suggested, "was the presence of the enemy to our right and left, which enabled them, the moment our troops attempted to advance to the top of the crest, to give them a fire in the rear." Meade expounded during his testimony:

> I never considered that the location of General Burnside's mine was a proper one, because, from what I could ascertain of the position of the enemy's works and lines erected at that time, the position against which he operated was not a suitable one in which to assault the enemy's lines, as it was commanded on both flanks and taken in reverse by their position on the Jerusalem plank road and their works opposite the Hare house.[14]

Thus, two of the most senior major generals in the Union armies during the Civil War—even with the bitterness between them—agreed on a central problem. Meade and Burnside did not like the position for the designated attack. The miners of the 48th Pennsylvania should not be blamed for picking the site. Rather, superior officers failed to harness their drive in a place more conducive to victory.

Meade's most dastardly act was the rejection of Burnside's attack plan. Burnside's initial idea put Ferrero's Fourth Division at the vanguard against the main Southern position, a place often called Cemetery Hill. Logical reasons to give the lead to USCT regiments included their relative state of rest; the troops had not endured the horrendous fighting from the Wilderness through the opening of the Petersburg siege. Also, the potential shock value of 4,000 African Americans pushing beyond the Crater immediately after the explosion could not be denied.[15]

Meade did not like the idea of inexperienced troops opening the post-explosion moment. After further discussion with Burnside, Meade promised to let General Grant have the final say. Less than twenty-four hours before the ordered detonation, the word was handed down: Burnside's white troops, not Ferrero's USCT regiments, must lead the charge. Both Meade and Grant believed the Northern public would act with revulsion if the attack failed while inflicting high casualties on African Americans. After presiding over three months of military operations that had resulted in 70,000 casualties to Northern white men, Grant and Meade suddenly grew concerned about appearing callous by risking 4,000 non-white lives. The fight following the explosion was guaranteed to harm many individuals, North and South, white and Black. Dictating which divisions could attack lessened the chance of a productive assault. Burnside was not at his best when bristling under poor decisions of superiors. Meade's micromanagement permanently severed any chance for a positive relationship between himself and his most experienced corps commander. Ironically, Ferrero's African American soldiers still suffered the most casualties of any Union division during the sad day.[16]

Having USCT units lead did not guarantee success. Yet, the men had earned an important combat role. Because Meade decided to overrule Burnside's decision on which division should initiate the attack, the army commander held far more responsibility for any failure than Meade had the moral courage to assume.[17]

Another ridiculous bit of micromanagement was the reduction in the amount of gunpowder allowed to create the explosion. Pleasants, an experienced mining engineer, wished for 12,000 pounds. Meade refused, so Pleasants settled for 8,000 pounds. A stronger blast likely would have created a crater with smoother sides and less depth, advantageous to any troops who ended up in the hole. Even with less powder, some of Ledlie's troops were hit by debris as a result of the explosion, but a larger blast was still preferable for the shock value and greater damage done to the Confederate defenses.[18]

Meade and Duane mocked the entire project. In letters between the two officers, both referred to "Burnside's Mine," perhaps a conscious effort to deflect blame from themselves if the plan failed. Duane was right on a key point Meade would utterly fail to make real: Burnside must gain sufficient support from other parts of the army after the explosion. Although Fifth Corps commander Warren issued orders for his men to prepare to support Burnside, his innate caution and lack of a team mentality with his brother officers would be one reason for the catastrophe to come.[19]

Despite the plethora of challenges, Pleasants, his regiment, and Ninth Corps leaders succeeded. Not quite certain of the army's plan for his brainchild, Pleasants pondered the project in a letter to his uncle. "I have worked harder of late with body and brain than I ever did in my life before," the exhausted miner wrote. The "gigantic work" faced opposition from those with biases due to their Regular army backgrounds and over-all lack of respect for the Ninth Corps. Yet, Pleasants continued, "Old Burnside stood by me." Pleasants felt uneasy about sending "several men with my own hand at one blow into eternity, but I believe I am doing right."[20] Sadly, the Herculean work to build the mine led to the bloodiest day Ninth Corps men would ever face.

"A Regular Pennsylvania Blow Up"

George Upton, 6th New Hampshire, wrote dozens of letters home during his war service. Doomed to die soon after the mine explosion, Upton's final letter includes examples of the racism, fatalism, and devotion to the Union he exhibited during his service.

I don't feel much like rushing up to their fortifications, but I always go when duty calls, and whenever ordered, even if it be to the cannon's mouth. I do not pretend to have more courage than many other soldiers

but I should hate to be called a coward. . . . It seems there has been a
trial on the part of some to see if peace could not be attained by the
use of the Pen, but the Nigger knocked it all in the head, so we must
continue with the sword and bayonet.[21]

Details vary to some extent, but the general facts about the mine explosion can be easily distilled. At what Colonel Pleasants recorded as 4:44 a.m. on July 30, 1864, 4 tons of gunpowder ignited, creating a large hole in the Confederate lines. Stressful moments had occurred starting at 3:30 A.M., the time ordered for detonation. Imperfect fuses caused the delay, leading an impatient Grant and Meade to order a highly reckless infantry assault before the mine finally lit up, an attack the explosion thankfully made moot.[22]

When the mine detonated, dozens of Confederates were instantly killed, some buried feet below the ground, others torn to shreds or thrown a considerable distance. As one Confederate officer wrote, those on duty at the battery immediately above the fired powder were "over-whelmed." Multiple companies of a South Carolina infantry brigade suffered severely from the convulsion. In a short account, a New Hampshire soldier in the Tenth Corps indelibly remembered, "It made the ground shake like *an earthquake.*"[23]

Ninth Corps troops felt the greatest shock from the culminating seconds of the mine project. Although Stephen Weld wrote of a surprisingly muffled sound from the blast, he declared, "The explosion was the grandest spectacle I ever saw." Quivering earth constituted the first sign of Pleasants's success. Then, Weld added, "I looked up and saw a huge mass of earth and flame rising some 50 or 60 feet in the air, almost slowly and majestically, as if a volcano had just opened." Smoke quickly escaped from the entire perimeter of the large hole.[24]

Proud of the handiwork of his regiment, George Heisler had expected the mine to produce "a regular Pennsylvania blow up." At the moment of destiny, Heisler saw "a fine explosion" sending Confederates flying in all directions, including into the Ninth Corps lines. The 48th Pennsylvania then sat out the battle, serving as a rear guard, assisting with the necessary task of sending stragglers forward.[25]

Another soldier described the "grand sight" at the moment of det-onation, followed by a "column of fire and smoke with cannon, horses, men and earth co-mingled therewith," something "never to be forgotten by those who saw it." A Vermonter echoed the memory of a convulsed earth covering the surrounding landscape with an array of organic and inorganic matter. "A shapeless mass" falling down created "a frightful shower of mangled corpses, severed limbs, and decapitated trunks."[26]

Many cannons opened immediately after the mine rocked the dawn. Jacob Roemer wrote of 200 big guns "causing the very earth to tremble with their thunder." Capt. Frank Kenfield, 17th Vermont, expressed an appreciation for what the artillery barrage might do for the brigades about to move forward, "It seemed as if Hell was let loose for our benefit."[27]

BURNSIDE'S FATAL ERRORS

Meade's distrust of Burnside did not cloud the army commander's vision for the infantry attack. After the mine explosion, Meade's order required the Ninth Corps to "immediately move rapidly upon the breach, seize the crest in the rear, and effect a lodgment there." The key to the day, Meade correctly surmised, would be a swift advance deep into the Confederate position. The Eighteenth Corps and Warren's Fifth Corps were to protect Burnside's flanks as the attack began. In addition to supporting artillery, Meade necessitated "promptitude, rapidity of execution, and cordial co-operation," three characteristics severely wanting across his army since the Wilderness.[28]

Burnside's most serious mistakes of the war occurred after receiving the July 29 attack order. The decision on which troops would lead the Ninth Corps toward Cemetery Hill nagged, but only for a short time. Historians lambast Burnside for allowing chance to make the choice. Ledlie, Potter, and Willcox drew lots for the "honor" of being the initial Ninth Corps men into the breach. Through this haphazard process, General Ledlie's First Division became the vanguard.[29]

Then, further disaster awaited due to Burnside's inattention to vital details. As he ordered, Ledlie was to immediately "move his division forward as directed by verbal orders this day, and if possible, crown the crest at the point known as Cemetery Hill, occupying, if possible, the cemetery."

These were not the words with which to launch an overwhelming attack of an entire infantry corps. Meade compelled Burnside to swiftly attack Cemetery Hill. Burnside cast doubt over the whole enterprise by using the phrase "if possible" twice in his short command to Ledlie. The grand assault appears discretionary under Burnside's wording, even though Ledlie claimed in his report that his two brigades were ordered to assault Cemetery Hill.[30]

In Burnside's written order, Willcox would protect the left of the main advance. Potter's two brigades were to move up to the north of Ledlie, the Ninth Corps' right flank. Ferrero's orders called for an advance after Ledlie moved beyond the breach, which would make room for the USCT regiments to augment the investment of Cemetery Hill.[31]

Burnside's written order to his division commanders clearly lacked the sense of urgency Meade had communicated earlier in the day. Whatever Meade's faults, his order pointed the Ninth Corps in the right direction: Move rapidly beyond the Crater to Cemetery Hill. In conversations and written orders to his division commanders, Burnside failed to plant the necessity of a speedy conquest of Confederate lines hundreds of feet west of the Crater. In essence, Burnside gave the weakest division commander in the history of the Ninth Corps the option of attacking beyond the limits of the Crater. Burnside was clearly doomed as an army officer if the attack failed.

"A Hopelessly Disordered Mass"

Elisha Marshall's Second Brigade began the Ninth Corps attack. With no pressing orders from their brigade commander or Ledlie, the regiments did not move forward together as a brigade should. To start the advance, Lt. Col. Benjamin Barney demanded, "Forward, Second Heavies" from his Pennsylvanians. The large group of soldiers who enlisted to man mortars and cannons around the national capital then became the lead in the charge after the mine explosion.

Regiments under Marshall essentially acted as three distinct groups, with only Barney's band continuing the attack army headquarters envisioned. Unsupported in the effort to advance, the 2nd Pennsylvania Provisional Heavy Artillery could not press on much beyond the Crater.

The 14th New York Heavies grew interested in salvaging Confederate cannons partially buried or thrown outward by the blast of gunpowder Pleasants had unleashed. Even with reportedly light enemy fire initially, neither the 179th New York nor 3rd Maryland pressed the advantage in the direction of Cemetery Hill. Leadership seemed nonexistent.[32]

Witnessing the farce of an attack thus far, the 35th Massachusetts, still acting as engineers, brought up the rear of the division. The unit's historian penned his observations of the bizarre moment. "Within the crater our troops were cheering loudly and celebrating the success of their assault," he wrote, "but making no motion in a body to secure the ridge of the hill." Unable to alter the facts of the moment, the engineers got to work turning around entrenchments recently in the possession of the Confederates. This allowed use of the protective features by Unionists who would face toward Cemetery Hill.[33]

Burnside wrote of the exceedingly difficult ground Ledlie confronted. "The brigade advanced rapidly to the fort that had been mined," Burnside noted, "now a crater of large proportions and an obstacle of great formidableness." The size of the Crater was estimated as 150 feet long, 60 feet wide, and at least 25 feet deep. Terrain did not improve beyond the big hole. Burnside lamented the huge clumps of clay torn out of the earth as a result of the explosion. The Confederate position beyond included bombproofs, pits, traverses, and undulations, "forming a labyrinth as difficult of passage as the crater itself." Spreading troops out and keeping good formations beyond the Crater would prove impossible, especially if the men were under fire. Burnside condoned his soldiers' efforts to seek shelter from the crater and trenches, even though his order was to assault the hill beyond.[34]

At a time when regiments needed strong, active leadership, the division commander evacuated to a bombproof in the rear. A physician testified to giving Ledlie a requested "stimulant" of rum. Not interested in disparaging subordinates to save himself, Burnside labeled Ledlie as "quite sick" during the day, likely unable to walk from division headquarters to the Crater.[35] With his health so poor, and apparently hit by a spent ball, Ledlie should have relinquished command.

General Bartlett's men advanced with their leader and his peg leg trying to make the most of the moment. Proud of his inexorable devotion to duty, Bartlett remembered, "I got up to the enemy's works about as soon as anyone." Nonetheless, he lacked the power, mobility, and perhaps even the skill to manage his brigade. Confusion prevailed.[36]

The moment proved especially tragic because the disorganized Confederates were not yet putting up a stout resistance. Missing strong leadership, the historian of the 21st Massachusetts whimsically mused, "Oh, for an hour of General Reno, then!" Instead, "a hopelessly disordered mass of our men" foundered in the Crater and nearby entrenchments. Regardless of his reported determination to conquer Cemetery Hill, Ledlie acted on the discretionary wording of Burnside's orders. The First Division did not make an impact. An eminently probative sentence about the moment's dismal leadership came from another Bay Stater: "Where great danger is involved," John Anderson argued, "a timid commander is always sure to take advantage of any implied doubt" regarding what an order says.[37]

POTTER AND WILLCOX QUICKLY STALL

As a result of the feeble effort from Ledlie and the aftermath of the explosion itself, supporting troops faced the morass around the Crater. General Potter summed up the situation his Second Brigade encountered.

> *As soon as General Griffin found that the division of General Ledlie was in the mine, he advanced his skirmishers, and followed with his brigade. The smoke which arose from the explosion, and the immense cloud of dust which hung over the place, made it almost impossible to see anything, and to some extent some of the leading regiments of his troops and those of General Ledlie's division got mixed up.*[38]

Griffin had placed his first wave under the command of Col. Daniel White. The three regiments, 31st Maine, 9th New Hampshire, and 2nd Maryland, quickly seized some Confederate entrenchments on Burnside's right, proving able also to repel a small counterattack. White informed Griffin of his limited success, then added, "Quite a force of

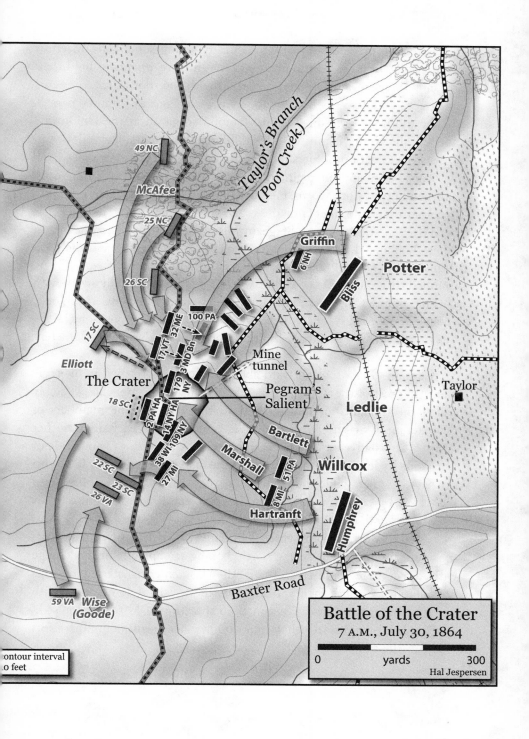

49 NC

McAfee

25 NC

26 SC

17 SC

Elliott

The Crater

18 SC

2 PA HA

14 NY HA

38 WI 109 NY

27 MI

22 SC

23 SC

26 VA

32 ME

100 PA

17 VT

3 MD Bn

179 NY

Taylor's Branch (Poor Creek)

Griffin

6 NH

Bliss

Potter

Mine tunnel

Pegram's Salient

Bartlett

Marshall

51 PA

8 MI

Hartranft

Ledlie

Willcox

Taylor

Humphrey

59 VA **Wise (Goode)**

Baxter Road

Battle of the Crater
7 A.M., July 30, 1864

0   yards   300

Hal Jespersen

ontour interval
0 feet

rebels remain on our right." Optimistically seeing some forward effort from Ledlie, in reply Griffin requested the three regiments to hold their ground. The general promptly moved up with the four other regiments in his brigade. Except for casualties, little changed as minutes passed. As the morning wore on, a North Carolinian gazed at the Union line north of the Crater, counting sixteen different regimental flags aligned in breastworks the Southerners once occupied.[39]

Zenas Bliss and his regiments followed Griffin on the right. Newly returned to the Ninth Corps, members of the 4th Rhode Island promptly "received the compliments of the rebels in the shape of a shrapnel that burst over us, striking down Sergeant Jillson, color-bearer, and one or two others." Behind the Ocean Staters, Capt. Theodore Gregg and the 45th Pennsylvania encountered "a severe fire from the enemy's works." The confined space north of the Crater, Gregg added "was literally swept with canister, grape, and musketry." Bliss's units faced additional roadblocks because some men from Ledlie's Division had taken up positions in the trench north of the Crater.[40] The time for an easy advance to Cemetery Hill had passed.

Captain Gregg took forward about half of the 210 men in his regiment. The rest of the 45th remained behind in Union trenches. Quickly seeing the difficulty of moving beyond the Crater, some members of the veteran outfit suffered horribly. As Captain Rees Richards, another Ninth Corps native of Wales, remembered, "A shell tore away one side of Theodore Eyde's face; also his eye. I immediately wrapped his face with my handkerchief, while the wounded part was yet clean and bloodless." He suffered greatly in military hospitals before a discharge eight months after his wound. Eyde lived until 1890.[41]

Trying to regain some type of initiative, Bliss had three regiments move up the trench line to the north, hoping to supplement this charge with three more regiments. The 58th Massachusetts started on this mission with Gregg's men and the 4th Rhode Island as support. With brevity, Maj. James Bucklin summed up the effort: "We were repulsed." A regimental memoirist echoed his commander's sentiment. The effort brought "the hottest fire we ever experienced."[42]

To the south of the Crater, Willcox's advance of one brigade sputtered. Quite critical of how the morning had unfolded, Willcox could do little but send his regiments "pell mell into the crater" due to the lack of support on his own left, where the Fifth Corps was positioned. Accepting his own share of the blame, Willcox admitted that he misunderstood Burnside's orders. Believing his role was to charge into the Crater itself, Willcox later considered his own analysis of the attack plan an absurdity.[43]

Like Potter's regiments, soldiers in the Third Division needed no time to realize the enemy had started to recover from the shock of the mine explosion. With Hartranft's Brigade in front, Willcox reported, Confederates "now concentrated so heavy a fire upon the point that our troops, in seeking temporary shelter, became still more mixed with each other and with the First Division." What Willcox termed the "regimental cohesion" of his advance withered. Part of the problem may have resulted when Hartranft ordered some of his men to help the 14th Heavies with the rescue of Confederate cannons buried by the detritus of the Crater explosion.[44] No general in the vicinity seemed focused on Cemetery Hill.

A Badger in the beleaguered 37th Wisconsin called the Crater and surrounding terrain "a perfect slaughter house." The regiment would suffer nearly one-third of the casualties in the entire brigade on July 30, including thirty-four killed in action. Still with only five companies, the 38th Wisconsin joined their comrades under fire. The 38th lost nine killed after exposure to galling fire on the flanks. "Every officer and soldier distinguished himself" during the day, Lt. Col. Colwert Pier reported.[45]

By the time William Humphrey headed out, the cramped condition in the Crater aggravated men from three divisions. Bitterness among Humphrey's units began when several individuals, including the brigade commander, vilified the 46th New York, which broke in sheer desperation. Humphrey deemed the unit's failure "causeless." Capt. Alphons Serviere defended his men in the 46th. He ordered the retrograde, claiming his regiment followed brigade comrades already moving away from a wall of Confederate missiles.[46]

Humphrey accomplished little for the rest of the day. His men sustained the lowest loss of Burnside's eight brigades, only 216 casualties.

The 50th Pennsylvania's historian deemed the Confederate fire "a most remarkable shower of shot and shell."[47]

"EVERY MINUTE IS MOST PRECIOUS"

With a level of patience earning him the nickname "Snapping Turtle," George Meade's consternation grew exponentially as the hazy sun illuminated scenes of a disjointed battle. At 5:40 a.m., the army commander asked Burnside, "What news from your assaulting column? Please report frequently." Such a message was justified because Meade's attack order was not being carried out. Burnside's reply set in motion a long series of communications poisonous to the Meade-Burnside relationship and deeply destructive to Burnside himself.

"We have the enemy's first line and occupy the breach," the corps commander nonchalantly stated. "I shall endeavor to push forward to the crest as rapidly as possible." Already feeling some despair, Meade's headquarters directed another note to Burnside. Chief of staff Humphreys lamented news that "your troops are halting at the works where the mine exploded." The Ninth Corps must "be pushed forward to the crest," Humphreys directed. "Call on General Ord to move forward his troops at once."[48]

Ord's Eighteenth Corps, positioned to the Ninth Corps' right, was certainly seen as central to the support of Burnside. Ord incorrectly believed Burnside was in charge of all tactical arrangements on July 30, giving the Ninth Corps leader authority Meade never granted. In early July, Meade had made very clear prior to any attack that Burnside could not direct overall operations or issue commands to other generals. Per Meade's dictate, Burnside was not the morning's overseer.[49]

At 6 a.m. Ord received an order to "at once move forward your corps" to take Cemetery Hill in a move independent of Burnside. Showing a horrid lack of imagination two hours later, Ord informed Meade that the area around the Crater "is already full of men," making an advance "impossible by reason of the topography, to charge in the manner you indicate." A pet of Grant from the West, Ord assumed the Crater and the surrounding ground were the only place he could attack.[50] Clearly, Burnside was not the only corps commander to lack vigor on July 30.

On the left of the Ninth Corps, Warren and his Fifth Corps held promise as further support to Burnside. Even before headquarters made an inquiry of Ord's status, Humphreys asked Warren about conditions in front of the Fifth Corps. The chief of staff concluded his note to Warren, "If there is apparently an opportunity to carry their works, take advantage of it and push forward your troops." Granting Warren any discretionary latitude to attack meant no attack would occur.[51]

Meade could not understand why Burnside could make so little of the attack. "Our chance is now," Meade asserted in a 6 a.m. missive. "Push your men forward at all hazards (white and black), and don't lose time in making formations, but rush for the crest." Ten minutes later a reply informed Meade of the order to all four division commanders to continue the attack. "It would be well," Burnside interjected, "if Warren could do something constructive." Without promising anything from the Fifth Corps, Meade responded forty minutes later, "Every minute is most precious," words a plaintive parent might use to spur a child to obedience.

Palpable bitterness grew between Meade and Burnside. "I am doing all in my power," Burnside claimed, "It is hard work, but we hope to accomplish it," the defeated corps commander averred. Unsurprisingly, Meade reacted like a bursting volcano: "What do you mean by hard work to take the crest?" The army commander became irate over the presumption Burnside had officers who refused to obey the founding father of the Ninth Corps. Feeling great umbrage, Burnside doomed his career with the conclusion of his 7:35 a.m. message: "Were it not insubordinate I would say that the latter remark of your note was unofficerlike and ungentlemanly."[52]

"TILL WE SEE WHAT THE EGYPTIANS CAN DO FOR US"

Perhaps the Fourth Division offered hope to salvage the day. Edward Ferrero's nine units of United States Colored Troops, some still without the full complement of ten companies, lined up early in the morning behind Willcox's men. At first hesitant to join the jumble of troops around the Crater, Ferrero received an urgent order from Burnside to seek an advantage in the confused situation. As they worked to organize their troops for a renewal of the attack, Elisha Marshall and General

Bartlett saw the two USCT brigades moving toward the Crater. The duo of officers decided to hold off on pressing forward, per Marshall's language, "till we see what the Egyptians can do for us."[53]

An officer in the 9th New Hampshire lauded how the Fourth Division troops were "cheering wildly" during the opening of their charge. Andrew Humphreys also praised the effort of the division. Even as impossible ground created great havoc in regimental alignments, Humphreys respected the "alacrity" of the soldiers, although the cramped confines of the Crater seemed to swallow up many men.[54]

With so many of the African American troops going into the Crater already packed with white comrades, time for bold leadership arrived. Ferrero, spending a good deal of the battle with Ledlie in a bombproof to the east, was not the leader to create hope from the tumult. One who tried mightily was Col. Delevan Bates, 30th USCT, a twenty-four-year-old New York farmer. In the vanguard of his brigade and taking troops to the right, around the position of some Second Division soldiers, Bates looked for an opening. As another officer in the 30th remembered, "We climbed over the rebel breastwork toward our line and ran along just outside of the abatis." Soldiers from several USCT regiments were part of this bold display of martial American courage.[55]

With the original color bearer of the 30th USCT wounded, Bates was trying to find a way to assault Confederate positions and ultimately Cemetery Hill. While a mortal wound struck down his second in command, Bates would receive a Medal of Honor for "gallantry in action where he fell, shot through the face, at the head of his regiment." As the chaplain of the 43rd USCT observed, black noncommissioned officers exhibited commendable bravery after their white officers fell.[56]

The charge that would net the USCT about 200 South Carolina prisoners began with an excellent showing of ardor from the 43rd USCT. Lt. Col. Henry Seymour Hall, who would lose his right arm in the fight, noted his Black and white soldiers charged "with resistless valor . . . using saber, pistol and bayonet with the most terrible deadly effect."[57]

Col. Joshua Sigfried felt thankfulness for "the great exertions of the officers and heroic determination of the men." His brigade's progress was, however, limited due to the crowded nature of the Crater and the

Confederate resistance. After their move to the right, the 30th and 43rd USCT were separated from the rest of Sigfried's command. Fortunately, Col. Henry Thomas had his five USCT regiments in line with Sigfried's left. The moment was as close as any Ninth Corps units got to creating a long line of troops arrayed against the enemy. Sigfried lamented how the formation was "very much exposed to the fire of the enemy" for "at least an hour."[58]

Officers and men quickly fell, with Col. Henry Thomas seeing Lt. Christopher Pennell "riddled through and through" with bullets as the twenty-one-year-old held his sword and the brigade guidon aloft. The youngster, Thomas reported, performed "everything an officer could do to lead on the men." Pennell's bold example may have inspired USCT soldiers to stand tall in conquered Confederate works, but Thomas remembered that "half the few who came out of the works were shot."[59]

The 23rd USCT, which suffered by far the most casualties of any regiment on July 30, sustained seventy-four killed in action. Capt. Frank Holsinger recalled, "The volley my company received decimated its ranks considerably." More than one-third of the regiment's loss would be missing men and officers, several of whom were likely killed after being captured, based on various reports of the savagery many saw that day.[60]

Colonel Cleaveland Campbell, heading the 23rd USCT, fell along with so many of his soldiers. With experience in both infantry and cavalry regiments earlier in the war, Campbell was a seasoned veteran well before his thirtieth birthday. Death from pneumonia nearly a year later would claim Campbell, three months after he received a brevet star as a brigadier general. He rose from the rank of private across a short but glorious military life. In remembering several of his officers who fell, Thomas wrote, "Such men cannot easily be replaced, nor the void they leave in our hearts readily filled."[61]

Colonel John Armstrong Bross, leading the 29th USCT, made himself conspicuous as his beleaguered African American troops looked to conquer. Near the farthest point of advance, Bross became another great and optimistic leader of African American soldiers to die for the Union and freedom. General Ferrero notified Bross's brother of the colonel's tragic end. "He was a thorough gentleman, a good soldier, and a brave officer." The colonel's honorable leadership inspired "each and every one to do all, and to dare all, for the benefit of his country, and the suppression of this unholy rebellion."[62]

CONFEDERATE REVENGE

Horrendous casualties in the USCT regiments could not compensate for some ground gained, about 200 prisoners taken, or the relatively small number of killed and wounded enemy troops. A wicked Confederate counterattack would end Ninth Corps efforts during the day. Knowing they were key to the defense of the important city of Petersburg, Confederate warriors faced the Ninth Corps with a grim determination. The sight of African Americans with muskets heightened the will to resist. Hearing shouts of "no quarter" from USCT soldiers, many Confederates prepared for a horrendous fight. "To be captured by the negro troops meant death not only to ourselves but, it appeared, to the helpless women and children in Petersburg," one North Carolinian remembered.[63]

The drive of USCT members to kill Rebel prisoners stemmed in part from reports of Fort Pillow, where dozens of African American soldiers were slaughtered earlier in the year in Tennessee. "Remember Fort Pillow," a sentiment that would naturally animate a member of the USCT, likely led to the murder of some Confederate prisoners near the Crater.[64]

Confederate law threatened the enslavement of any captured USCT soldier and capital punishment for white officers leading African Americans troops. One New Hampshire soldier suggested, "The sight of the colored troops seemed to intensify the enemy's rage against their assailants, and every available weapon was turned upon them."[65]

As William Mahone's Confederate Division advanced, Ferrero's two brigades moved back toward the Crater and deeper into Union lines. One USCT officer labeled Mahone's effort "a terrific counter-charge," in which "we were routed," prompting a Unionist retreat. Devastating casualty rates across the USCT units occurred because "the air was full of bullets and men were dropping all around." As a Virginian happily observed, "I saw the back of more Yankee soldiers than my eyes had ever before beheld."[66]

The Crater became a rallying point, however impossible the position seemed as a defensive bastion. Nothing good for Burnside's Boys could occur in the cramped confines of the hole as Unionists from several Ninth Corps regiments tried to endure. If no racial overtones permeated the gruesome atmosphere, horrible wounds and extensive hand-to-hand fighting was going to prevail, especially after Ferrero's retrograde. With their saber bayonets, essentially swords taken off muskets, Oscar Robinson, 9th New Hampshire, noted the regiment's effort to protect themselves.[67]

Colonel Sigfried extolled 1st Lt. James O'Brien for "the most heroic courage and daring," while "standing on the summit of the crater cheering the men on amidst a terrific fire of shot and shell." Sam Haynes, 45th Pennsylvania, witnessed Capt. Theodore Gregg nearly lose his life with a gun pointed at his head. Unimpressed with the idea of surrender, Gregg took the Confederate's pistol, then ran him through with his sword. Gregg then moved on with the sword remaining in the unfortunate Southerner. "The fighting was hand to hand," Haynes added, "and beats anything I ever saw, heard, or read of."[68]

At 9 a.m. Burnside reported to Meade of the retirement of Ninth Corps and supporting Eighteenth Corps troops. Many of Burnside's Boys still held the Crater and nearby ground. "I think now is the time to put in the Fifth Corps promptly," Burnside suggested. With no succor from the cowardly Warren, the situation was dismal. Forty-five minutes after Burnside's plea for help, the Ninth Corps was directed to retreat. Meade updated the order at 10 a.m., granting Burnside discretion on the timing of the day's final retrograde.[69]

One of the brave Americans doomed to capture and death in a Confederate prison was Sgt. Maj. Benjamin Trail, 28th USCT. He had optimistically written home about the beauty of the national capital and the large number of Americans fighting to save the Union. Trail's young life ended in November 1864. He rests at Danville National Cemetery, Virginia.[70]

Some white soldiers grew afraid of being taken captive with USCT members. As Solomon Oakley, 109th New York, wrote,

It worried me that I would be taken Prisoner and probably would have been had I not have been afraid of being captured by the Rebels on account of being found with Negro Soldiers . . . the thought of Fort Pillow was too fresh in mind. So, Capt. Evans and I held a counsel of war and determined to evacuate, the Regt had all left us but one man, and so we ran the gauntlet. We had to run over an open field . . . exposed to a fire upon both flanks from rebel sharpshooters. I think that while I was making this distance not less than 200 rifle shots were fired at me.[71]

TWENTY MEDALS OF HONOR

An attack that stalled soon after Ledlie's supposed charge, or repulsed warriors running for their lives later in the morning, did not mean Ninth Corps courage took the day off at the Crater. Twenty Medals of Honor and nearly 3,500 casualties made July 30, 1864, very memorable for all parts of the command.

Although engaged for nearly three fewer hours than the three white divisions, the Fourth Division suffered significantly more casualties than any other. Moreover, a much higher percentage loss prevailed for the Fourth Division. Ferrero only had one in five soldiers under Burnside, but USCT soldiers accounted for two in five Ninth Corps casualties on July 30. As Col. Henry Thomas suggested, "Whether we fought well or not, the scores of our dead lying as thick as if mowed down by the hand of some mighty reaper and the terrible loss of officers can best attest."[72]

With the most casualties and greatest success of the four divisions, only three of the twenty Medal of Honor winners at the Crater came from Ferrero's USCT regiments. Sgt. Decatur Dorsey, born into slavery in Maryland in 1836, would be the only African American to be awarded the nation's highest military honor for that day. In the 39th USCT, Dorsey "planted his colors on the Confederate works in advance of his regiment, and when the regiment was driven back to the Union works, he carried the colors there and bravely rallied the men."[73]

Medals of Honor went to men in seven of Burnside's brigades. Six of the twenty awardees had been born outside of the United States. Exhibiting great courage across 1864, Abraham Cohn, 6th New Hampshire, would be one of four soldiers in Griffin's Brigade to receive a Medal of Honor for the Crater. A Jewish immigrant from Prussia, Cohn's citation notes his bravery at both the Wilderness and the Crater. On July 30, he "bravely and coolly carried orders to the advanced line under severe fire."[74]

Nathaniel Gwynne, the youngest of the twenty awardees, joined the dismounted 13th Ohio Cavalry after being born in the state fifteen summers before. Not yet officially mustered, Gwynne persisted in his wish to join the charge of Hartranft's Brigade on July 30. The young hero suffered a serious wound that would cost Gwynne his left arm.[75]

Medals of Honor would not recognize the bravery of all men. Pvt. Lewis Martin, Company E, 29th USCT, epitomized American bravery at the Crater and after. Due to shell and gunshot wounds, Martin would lose most of his right arm and his left foot on July 30. Great pain from broken bones in his shoulder hounded Martin as well. Deemed "totally disabled" at a Washington, DC, hospital in late 1865, Martin lived a very difficult life as a result of his sacrifice. More than eleven years after the Crater, Martin at least "walks very comfortably" thanks to an "artificial foot." The necessity of aid from another person meant Martin's life would be defined by his dependence on others.

Vigorous in earlier years, by his early forties, Martin weighed only 155 pounds, well below his heft while in the army. Regular medical examinations noted his continued eligibility for a monthly federal pension, which went from $24 to $72 later in Martin's life. The difficulty he faced included pain in his limbs and "nervous and physical systems" well into the 1880s.[76]

In Disaster's Wake

The Ninth Corps would never be the same after the Crater. On July 20, Burnside reported 15,272 men present and equipped. On July 31, only 10,700 such soldiers were available, a decrease of nearly 30 percent. Trying to understand why the attack failed, Jerry Smith, 51st New York, penned a letter on August 5. "If they had kept the colored troops out, it would have been a victory, & a big one, too," Smith pointedly and incorrectly declared. Yet, he tried to be fair, using the language of the day. "The darkies wasn't so much to blame," Smith added, "it was the officers that led them in. The officers were drunk."[77]

Simon Griffin would be another who suggested the bottle might have negatively impacted Ninth Corps fortunes at the Crater. In his reminiscences, he referred to the First Division commander as "Judas Ledlie" and "a poor drunken imbecile." Ledlie's drunkenness, witnessed by some earlier in the war, does not have such strong support in the evidence of July 30. Excellent historian Earl Hess notes the lack of proof.[78]

Some Ninth Corps soldiers wished to inform others of the courage USCT troops displayed. With abrasive language, Samuel Haynes at least linked all Ninth Corps men together with his thoughts. "They all fought as men never fought before in the war, niggers and all," he opined, "Every man who was in the fight bears testimony to splendid conduct of the darky troops."[79]

Numbers support Haynes and those impressed with USCT units. Across Burnside's command, the two most damaged regiments were in the Fourth Division. The 23rd USCT sustained 310 casualties, one in eight of Burnside's losses. With 200 casualties, the 30th USCT paid dearly for their prominent position west of the Crater. Nearly 600 of Burnside's lost were captured or missing in Ferrero's Division alone. Of that number, the total of African American prisoners who were murdered can never be known.[80]

Of the six white brigades, Griffin's men suffered the most. "Genl Griffin cried like a child to see his old Brigade so used up," George Codman noted, "It is enough to make any one cry to see the places that used to be filled with familiar faces." The 11th New Hampshire sent 128 into the battle, with only sixty-three returning. As the 6th New Hampshire historian observed, "Our hearts were all very sad that night at the loss of so many brave fellows, with so little to show for the heavy cost."[81]

Maine's adjutant general was informed that the 31st Regiment included only two officers and fifty-three enlisted men present for duty on August 1. Nearly ten times that many troops in the outfit were sick or wounded. Five officers in the 31st suffered death at the Crater. Echoing such sadness, Moses Whitehill, 17th Vermont, informed his brother, "We stand now but a hanfull of men before the enemy." Six of the regiment's officers would die due to Crater wounds.[82]

Like 300 of their men, General Bartlett and Colonel Marshall became prisoners after Confederates forced the surrender of troops in the Crater. Grim determination remained for those who survived in the First Division's ranks. The historian of the 21st Massachusetts noted the sadness over the loss of Capt. William Clark, who had been paralyzed after a bullet in the spine on July 30. Transported home, Clark died in mid-August, "an officer of strong character" and courage who had sustained his first major wound at Chantilly nearly two years before.[83]

Colonel J. Parker Gould was another Bay Stater struck down with a mortal wound at the Crater. With previous experience with the 13th Massachusetts, Gould led the 59th Regiment. He would lose a leg prior to the end of his life on August 21 in a Philadelphia hospital. Memorialized as "a brave and capable officer," Gould, forty-two years old, rests in his hometown of Stoneham.[84]

"READY TO AWAIT THE VERDICT OF TIME"

Burnside quickly found himself in trouble far deeper than the Crater's 25 feet. He faced two major threats to his career. First, Burnside's failure to keep headquarters regularly updated on July 30 formed the basis for a possible court-martial. Second, the Crater court of inquiry was charged with determining fault for the catastrophe.[85]

Officers who reported to Meade constituted the court of inquiry. As Richard Slotkin cogently established, Burnside held the losing hand before such a tainted tribunal, but that does not mean he lacked some reasonable arguments. Trying to find a body of judges not biased by who their boss was, Burnside wrote Secretary of War Stanton in early August. Respectful of the court, which was headed by Second Corps commander Winfield Scott Hancock, Burnside rightfully pleaded, "I beg to submit that it should be composed of officers who do not belong to this army." He added that the court's bias in Meade's favor should be obvious. Stanton tersely denied Burnside's request. Nonetheless, the dutiful corps commander remained "ready to await the verdict of time."[86]

James Ledlie was the court of inquiry's most notable missing witness. Clearly having no future in the army, Ledlie was stripped of division command in early August, never to resume field duty. He would resign his commission in January.[87]

Meade, who presented a long list of evidence as the court's first witness, never felt positive about the entire mining operation. With the field unsuitable for an infantry assault, Meade owned the attack of his army. Instead, he told the court, "I cannot be held responsible for the failure which afterward resulted."[88] This served as Meade's command to his inferiors: They must blame someone else.

Early in the proceedings, he claimed, "I had a full appreciation of the difficulties that were to be encountered in Burnside's attack." A moment later, Meade opined, "I never considered that the location of General Burnside's mine was a proper one." Meade also suggested he opposed use of the Fourth Division to open the attack, yet his view was not "that the colored troops were inferior to his best troops."

Meade was correct to suggest the best approach for the Ninth Corps was a rapid, unrelenting attack designed to occupy Cemetery Hill. Yet, his lack of faith in the operation was obvious with how quickly he gave up the idea of using supporting troops on Burnside's flanks. He let the court know, "if we could not carry the crest promptly by a *coup de main*," he would order a withdrawal "as quickly and safely as possible." Meade averred "nothing but murder" would occur if the Ninth Corps failed in the rush to Cemetery Hill. To counter such defeatism, Burnside suggested to the court, "I did not think that we had fought long enough that day."[89]

Perspectives of other officers proved very interesting. Some committed to the truth were not in the Ninth Corps and therefore less likely to be seen as biased in Burnside's favor. Even among Burnside's corps, credible thoughts about reasons for failure on July 30 were elucidated.

The first officer to testify after Meade and Burnside was Major Duane, the army's chief engineer. By indirectly questioning the site of the attack, Duane did no favors to Meade, even if the court did not see failures higher than Burnside. "I do not think that there was any reasonable chance of success," Duane said. On the same day, fatalistic Fifth Corps commander Warren grumbled of the attack, "I never saw sufficient good reasons why it should succeed."[90] With Duane's lack of interest in helping Colonel Pleasants build the mine, and Warren's inability to do anything substantial on July 30, their pessimism was unworthy of army officers who were key to success.

Near the opening of Robert Potter's testimony, the Second Division commander answered a question about why the attack failed. First, Ledlie did not "carry out the orders to advance through the enemy's line and seize the hill." Next, "no attempt was made at a diversion at any other part of the line" after the opening charge foundered. Finally, Potter suggested, the initial arrangement of troops was imperfect. Potter said Burnside requested his views on the advisability of withdrawal by the late morning of the attack. "I told him," Potter testified, "we could hold the position, but unless something was going to be done there was no use in it."[91]

General Ferrero agreed with Potter on key points. Demonstrating the bad blood among division commanders, Ferrero pointed to Ledlie's failure "to go forward immediately after the explosion." Moreover, the explosion created a hole inimical to rapid military movements. Ferrero was then asked his expectation if the Fourth Division was allowed to open the infantry attack. Showing great confidence in the USCT, Ferrero responded, "I have not the slightest doubt from the manner in which they went in, under very heavy fire, that had they gone in in the first instance, when the fire was comparatively light, but that they would have carried the crest of Cemetery Hill beyond a doubt."

Orlando Willcox bolstered the view that Ledlie's inadequacies doomed the day. He added, "The troops that went in support of the leading division should have gone in almost simultaneously with it, and should have gone to the right and left avoiding the Crater." Burnside essentially received blame from his Third Division commander for the lack of urgency after the explosion. However, Willcox's key point reflected poorly on Meade, "The attention of the enemy was not attracted to any other point than the crater." Simon Griffin echoed that sentiment.[92]

Brig. Gen. Adelbert Ames, Eighteenth Corps division commander, offered several cogent points. Highlighting Meade's failure of leadership, Ames said no effective use was made of the Eighteenth Corps. "At no time were my troops farther advanced than the woods in rear of our own works," Ames testified. He suggested "a clear head" was needed to direct operations. Only Meade, by the army commander's orders to Burnside, had the right to assume such power over multiple corps. Ames observed how one officer's management efforts "might have corrected a great many of the faults that then existed." Instead, "everybody appeared to be acting for himself."

Ames withered Meade's view that he could not be responsible for the ineffectual attack. Near the end of his time before the court, Ames condensed this view into an indictment of Meade, without using the army commander's name.

> *I don't see how ordinary troops, with good commanders and one head to direct, could have possibly failed under the circumstances. It was necessary that some one person should be present to direct the various movements and make them one operation. If there had been perhaps the result would have been different.*[93]

BURNSIDE'S DEPARTURE

On the seventeenth day of the court's work, findings were issued. "The operation was one of time," the court wrote, with the inability to make something of the attack the entire fault of Ninth Corps leaders, not Meade. Burnside "failed to obey the orders of the commanding general" in several key respects, including the formation of the attacking column, not preparing the area in front by removing enough abatis and obstructions, and not using engineer troops effectively as a way to remove further physical hindrances to the attack. The central finding against Burnside was "neglecting to execute" Meade's vision. The Ninth Corps failed to quickly move against Cemetery Hill, which certainly doomed Burnside.

Ledlie received opprobrium for "neglect of duty," while Ferrero was castigated for neither forming nor moving the Fourth Division timely. Both generals certainly should not have spent the bulk of the battle in a bombproof, although the court did not say they were drunk. For unknown reasons, the court found enough facts to blame Zenas Bliss. Not in an advanced enough position to "see what was going on," as the court wrote, Bliss was no more negligent than many other generals that day, including Meade. Finally, the Third Division's poor performance was placed at Willcox's feet, "The court is not satisfied that General Willcox's division made efforts commensurate with the occasion." Judging from existing primary sources and casualty returns, the finding against Willcox makes more sense than any other conclusion the biased body presented.[94]

A reading of the court's transcript shows a great deal of criticism levied at Meade by indirection thanks to officers like Adelbert Ames, men courageous enough to report the truth. Additionally, a congressional investigation cast doubt on Meade's leadership during the Crater tragedy.[95] Meade should have resigned as a result of July 30. This offered him the honorable way out of a situation he had not enjoyed since the crossing of the Rapidan three months before. Instead of early retirement, Meade would command the Army of the Potomac for the rest of the war.

Burnside departed the army shortly after his testimony. Placed on leave for twenty days but not court-martialed, he never returned to the field. John Parke, Burnside's trusted chief of staff who missed the Crater fight, became Ninth Corps commander. Except for brief periods, he would hold the post for the rest of the war.[96]

In his campaign report, Burnside cast no notable blame on subordinates. Having endured thus far "this most trying campaign," Burnside thanked his officers, who were worthy of "a nation's gratitude" for "heroic courage and firmness on the field." In presenting Ninth Corps casualty data, Burnside listed 12,440 killed, wounded, and missing since crossing the Rapidan.

Burnside gave the Fourth Division especial plaudits because of "its faithful and courageous deportment" while marching and in action. With language laudatory for his time but awkward to twenty-first-century minds, Burnside added that the conduct of the division "has given great hope for the future elevation and usefulness of the colored race."[97]

Burnside deserved some blame for the failure at the Crater. He did not ensure the attack moved rapidly to Cemetery Hill. Although history deems the Ninth Corps commander a man of relatively small ego, Burnside still had a keen sense of honor. Working under Meade in the Army of the Potomac struck too deep at Burnside's self-respect. His best periods of military service occurred in North Carolina and East Tennessee, successful operations in which Burnside acted as an independent commander; his bosses were nowhere in sight during either campaign. When placed under direct supervision of another general, Burnside grew less imaginative and deeply hurt at crucial times when not getting his way. Burnside simply may have been more focused on his own interests than previous generations of historians have deduced. He very much wished the Union cause to succeed, but the founding father of the Ninth Corps lacked the wide range of skills necessary to be a consistently great general.

DIFFICULTIES OF THE SEASON

After what he deemed the "great slaughter" of July 30, Josiah Jones, 6th New Hampshire, wrote of friendly meetings with Confederates during the truce of August 1. "We mingled with the rebels," Jones reported, "the officers of each side talking together and the men exchanging coffee for tobacco." He enjoyed the "very pleasant interview" with his enemies.[98]

Revelry mixed with unfortunate necessity during the day. The reprieve from fighting provided time to bury the dead and bring in the small number of wounded who could finally receive medical care. By late morning, Burnside informed headquarters that 220 men had been buried, most of them from Ferrero's Division. As General Potter reported, the four-hour truce was informally extended because the burial trench was incomplete. A Rhode Islander found the work deplorable, "The bodies were swelling from the heat of the sun to an immense size, and were filled with maggots and flies." Additionally, "Men were torn into all shapes, and the crater was filled with bodies lying in heaps."[99]

Following the burial detail, August brought a return to life in the trenches. After nearly a week of rest, the 51st Pennsylvania stood in their old lines, finding unremitting danger. As the regimental historian remembered, "The shelling and firing was as severe as before, and a man had to move about very cautiously." Confederates had built a new fort to the right of the Keystone Staters, which subjected anyone making himself visible to a lethal crossfire. As a New Hampshire officer added, "Our corps has been the only one under constant fire."[100]

After writing Maine's adjutant general in late July about the lack of promotion opportunities, Adelbert Twitchell, 7th Battery, told a more serious tale of woe in another letter. "The severities of the campaign have reduced my men rapidly," Twitchell lamented. After arriving in Petersburg, the battery had been "put in position at the front, and kept in position forty-seven consecutive days up to Aug. 4th," which "bore upon the men severely." Ten days of rest then lightened the burdens the brave Mainers had faced for so long.[101]

General Potter reported on the important work of improving fortifications and the abatis designed to inhibit an advancing enemy. What the 21st Massachusetts historian dubbed "wearisome and perilous duty" remained for many months, offset by some rest, however fitful. Corporal Richard Loomis, a hardened veteran of the 21st Regiment, suffered a serious wound from a sharpshooter on August 8. Having joined the war in the early months, the brave veteran lived until 1906.[102]

As Ledlie departed, the First Division received a new commander. A New York native, Julius White had served alongside the Ninth Corps

Even as they worked hard to keep soldiers fed each day, members of the quartermaster department of the First Division, Ninth Corps, had time for this photo in August 1864. LIBRARY OF CONGRESS

in the Knoxville campaign while leading a division in the Twenty-third Corps. He also had experience as a Ninth Corps division commander and chief of staff for short periods over the summer. Not considered a great leader by some historians, White's seniority led to his promotion. He offered good experience throughout the difficult summer of 1864, showing strong skills during his first battle under Parke. White would remain as First Division commander for only three months.[103]

With rotation to the rear lines infrequent in some cases, lack of rest plagued the Ninth Corps. Alfred Dodge, a USCT officer lucky to survive the Crater without being captured, spent ten consecutive days at the front. By the second half of August, he could expound, "My health is as good as ever and would be a little better if the rebs did not make so much noise in the night." Sometimes barrages of Southern artillery would begin around midnight. Frequent rains helped to lower the heat but made trench life or marching more enervating.[104]

In his last day of service to the Ninth Corps, Ambrose Burnside likely caused George Meade's temper to flare yet again. On August 13, Burnside wrote headquarters regarding the difficulty of supplying men for ordered duties. With 2,200 soldiers on work details the previous day, Burnside objected to the request for 400 additional men, beyond the 1,000 already scheduled for work that evening. "The corps is not in condition to furnish such large details," Burnside declared. Chief of Staff Humphreys wrote back that afternoon, outlining the need for the soldiers to improve protective works. Not content to let the matter go, Burnside wrote again, giving the number of men from the different divisions who were already occupied with fatigue duty. Tersely, Humphreys replied, "the additional requisition of 400 men must be furnished."[105] Losing yet another dispute, Burnside went on leave later in the day, never again to command troops in the field.

Flies and mosquitoes became unwelcome guests in the trenches, with men struggling to find any kind of happiness. A whiskey ration could assist with raising morale, if only for a short time. As the historian of Durell's Battery wrote of the ability to imbibe, "Whether it was intended to kill malaria germs or infuse courage in the timid was not learned."

Disappointingly, "the treatment was not continued long enough to produce any positive results."[106]

"A Braver, Truer, and Nobler Soldier Never Lived"

Battle, rather than the invariable skirmishing and other physical labor, called the Ninth Corps once again, even with the limitations on maneuver inherent in a military siege. The first major fight after the Crater involved supporting the Fifth Corps in an advance to the west, part of Grant's goal of attacking Confederate supply lines. Warren was ordered "to make a lodgment upon the Weldon Railroad," which would cut a Confederate rail line from North Carolina. The action was also intended to conduct reconnaissance of the enemy's position and defensive works. Parke's tasks included direct support to the Fifth Corps, while also occupying Warren's old position. Potter's and Ferrero's troops assumed the latter role, unengaged in the looming fight.[107]

Situated along Weldon Railroad about 10 miles south of Petersburg, the main action would take place on August 19 around Globe Tavern, which gave the battle its name. Finding another area of difficult topography and wet soil, elements of the Fifth Corps ran into trouble. Willcox's brigades, in the advance of the Ninth Corps, moved to support one of the engaged divisions. On reaching the field, Willcox's troops received several hours of rest. "The men were in the best of spirits," a Keystone Stater recollected, after receiving fresh bread and pork before battle.

By the time of the near disaster for the Fifth Corps, the day was already into late afternoon. Of the direction given General Hartranft as to the best place for his men to advance, Willcox wrote, "I ordered him to go in where the fire was the heaviest." Colonel William Humphrey followed with another brigade of infantry, which was sent to the left of the Union position.[108]

Yet to be given the official rebuke from the Crater court of inquiry, the brigade performed noble service, placing luster back into the reputation of original Ninth Corps units such as the 51st Pennsylvania and 8th Michigan. Moving into some woods, the northern flank of Hartranft's line included the 37th and 38th Wisconsin, and 13th Ohio dismounted cavalry. The left half of the brigade, the 27th Michigan, 109th New York,

51st Pennsylvania, and 8th Michigan, advanced into a more open field. These four units were first engaged, followed by the Badgers and Buckeyes. Of the right of his line, Hartranft reported, the three regiments "soon met the enemy also advancing."[109]

The 51st Pennsylvania seemed motivated this day. As the historian reported, "The loss in the 51st was very heavy." Finding his beloved mount Gimlet difficult to manage on the field, regimental commander Lane Hart led his men on foot. Another enlistee from the summer of 1861, Hart rose steadily through the officer ranks. He had been a captain five weeks before assuming command of his regiment. While inspiring his troops, the twenty-six-year-old fell with a very nasty wound. A shell passed through both thighs. Considered hopeless, heroic fortitude gave Lane far more life. He lived until 1924.[110]

Farther to the left, another officer of stellar reputation and great courage fell. Horatio Belcher lost his life from his third wound of the war. "I am pained to mention" Belcher's demise, Hartranft reported. With a wound at Bethesda Church ten weeks earlier, Belcher refused to be away from his duties. Of Belcher, Hartranft concluded, "A braver, truer, and nobler soldier never lived."[111]

Even with an effective strength of barely 1,000 men, the arrival of White's First Division stabilized different parts of the Union line. Except for the 100th Pennsylvania, Lt. Col. Joseph Barnes moved forward with a brigade full of Massachusetts soldiers. The 21st Massachusetts took part in the battle with only three companies, all that remained of the valiant outfit after more than 140 men departed for home at the end of their term of service.[112]

The historian of the 29th Massachusetts noted the division's advance "in the midst of a blinding rain-storm," simultaneous to "a fierce assault upon the right flank" by a Confederate division. With some of Warren's men disorganized, the situation "threatened a serious disaster."[113]

Under the command of Capt. Orange Sampson, thirty years old, the three companies of the 21st Massachusetts entered the fray. "Still a hard hitter in battle," the unit's historian proclaimed, Bay Staters and Roundheads served nobly in support of Warren's pressed troops. General White, with his links to the Ninth Corps from the previous year, implored his troops to remember their pluck at Campbell's Station in Tennessee. The historian of the 35th Massachusetts remembered "the boys cheered vociferously" after White's oratory, "It was the most inspiriting scene for many a day." Meeting Mahone's determined troops, Unionists were ordered to fire low. "The carnage was deadly," the scribe of the 35th Regiment wrote, with a Roundhead remembering his comrades giving Confederates "the point of the bayonet."[114]

Leading White's other brigade, Lt. Col. Gilbert Robinson witnessed his command "utterly routing" Mahone. Robinson was especially pleased with the conduct of New York's 14th Heavies, "the first and longest engaged of any regiment in my command." The 2nd Pennsylvania Provisional received additional encomiums from Robinson. As had held true for weeks, the Heavies in the Ninth Corps suffered extensively. The two units would sustain nearly one in five of Parke's losses during the battle.[115]

The 50th Pennsylvania brought additional luster to their excellent reputation. Assisting with the recapture of rifle pits the Fifth Corps had abandoned, the Keystone Staters won the day after "a desperate hand-to-hand struggle." Sgt. Charles Brown received a Medal of Honor for grabbing the colors of the 47th Virginia, with the Unionists also capturing a hefty lot of prisoners. Eight killed in the regiment increased the war's grisly toll inflicted on the 50th Pennsylvania.[116]

Both Parke and White were pleased with the conduct of the two divisions involved at Globe Tavern. Parke correctly suggested his troops "arrived most opportunely" to salvage Warren's effort. White reported, "Both officers and men behaved throughout the engagement with great steadiness and gallantry." With nearly 600 casualties, the Ninth Corps did far more to assist the Fifth Corps than Warren had the leadership and courage to offer at the Crater. As Hamilton Dunlap, 100th Pennsylvania, cogently wrote of the day, the Ninth Corps "arrived in time to save their bacon."[117]

"An Unlucky Friday for Us"

With the success of the move to the Weldon Railroad, the Ninth Corps stretched four divisions from near Globe Tavern east to the Jerusalem Plank Road, with the Second Corps to the right. The area became the

Ninth Corps' home for more than a month. In a reserve position on August 22, Theodore Nutting, 6th New Hampshire, expressed an eagerness for any orders to move. "Three months and five days and I will be once more a free man," Nutting added, "We have much fighting to do, but I stand just as good a chance as any one so I will hope for the best." He would die a Confederate prisoner later in the year.[118]

Sickly Albert Rogall continued with his very bleak mindset. The USCT officer went to a hospital on August 21, staying in multiple locations across several days. He held immense scorn for the army's medical facilities, suggesting criminals received better care than the nation's soldiers. At City Point Hospital, located at a primary Union supply depot, Rogall found circumstances even worse. By early September, he noted the only significant aspect of his existence was being attacked by lice.[119]

Confederates showed determination to reopen the Weldon Railroad, so the western portion of the Ninth Corps position remained active. As Salmon Gates, 17th Vermont, wrote at the end of August, "The Rebels have made 4 strong efforts to retake the road but failed every time, and we are inclined to think they cannot take it," because "strong hands and willing hearts" manned the impressive Unionist defensive positions. Even with the horrible loss the regiment suffered, Gates expressed a firm determination to ensure victory.[120]

A reorganization of the Ninth Corps occurred as August ended. Meade requested Parke attempt to consolidate his command, with Parke agreeing to roughly equalize the number of troops across the three white divisions. Additionally, some units, such as the 2nd Pennsylvania Provisional Heavy Artillery would be transferred out of the Ninth Corps. Due to the consolidation and lack of experienced senior officers, Simon Griffin would enter battle by the end of September with a brigade of ten regiments.[121]

Fisher Cleaveland, 35th Massachusetts, felt fine on duty with his comrades. Time on picket was the most notable work during September. The intrepid soldier was pleased to return a letter to his daughter after he received two from her. Cleaveland expressed happiness about the lack of firing in front of his brigade, a rarity over the previous four months. A fatherly instinct burned bright, for Cleaveland frequently offered advice to his daughter, who was a school teacher. "Try to have the scholars learn as fast as you can," he suggested, "and try to make them understand what they learn for if teaching children is worth anything it is worth doing well."[122]

Having joined the Ninth Corps in June, the dismounted soldiers of the 13th Ohio Cavalry likely pined for their mounts and attachment to a cavalry command. Stuck with their fate as summer continued, the regimental historian noted the variety of labor the Buckeyes had much experience performing. "Building heavy breastworks, cutting down trees in front of works, doing picket duty, with an occasional skirmish with the enemy" defined life. Through the end of summer, as the 29th Massachusetts historian recorded, "everything remained in the same condition," with the exception of the continual upgrades to Ninth Corps fortifications.[123]

Rumors of another large fight floated around camps. The strong leadership of Lt. Col. Charles Cummings, 17th Vermont, prepared his tough warriors for another bout with the Confederates. As he wrote to his wife on September 30, the last day of his life, "Fighting in this vicinity cannot be much longer delayed. All the signs of the times indicate a determination on the part of Gen. Grant to make an early onset for the possession of the rebel capital."[124]

September 30 would be a dark day for Parke's command. Once again in support of the Fifth Corps, two divisions moved west of the Weldon Railroad. This time, saving the incompetent Warren cost the Ninth Corps dozens more killed and wounded, as well as about 700 soldiers captured. The day proved the notion that strong leaders sometimes falter. With the Second Division routed and on the brink of disaster, Robert Potter, Simon Griffin, and John Curtin, three of the best senior leaders the Ninth Corps ever knew, all performed poorly.

Grant hoped to force Confederate troops to protect railroad lines and Petersburg itself. Seeking some level of clarity about the exact aim, Meade replied in the evening of September 27, "I can send two divisions of the Ninth Corps to-morrow beyond our left and beyond where Warren was the other day." Orders on the 28th began the movement for Willcox and Potter.

On September 30, Warren assigned the Ninth Corps divisions to protect his left. He reported the heavy woods in front inhibited his own view of the ground, but, if Parke so desired, Warren said Willcox and Potter could advance. A Fifth Corps division then swiftly captured a Confederate fort. This good news, even with the forested shroud so inimical to good military intelligence, led Grant to his usual aggressiveness. "I can't help believing that the enemy are prepared to leave Petersburg if forced a little," Grant erroneously suggested to Meade.[125]

Weather conditions to start what would be known as the battle of Poplar Grove Church could have made men cast aside concerns of looming chaos and death. As the 36th Massachusetts historian remembered, "a day of perfect autumnal beauty" dawned. Parke's instructions from headquarters stressed the need to remain linked to the Fifth Corps on the right while moving in a northwesterly direction. "Try to open a route across the swamp to vicinity of Miss Pegram's," Parke was told. The Pegram house stood less than 2 miles west of the Weldon Railroad and halfway between the Squirrel Level Road and Boydton Plank Road.

Colonel Curtin sent the 7th Rhode Island out "to cut a road through the swamp." Other Ninth Corps men advanced with relative ease for a time. Continuing to the northwest, the troops traversed "a narrow belt of timber and came to a large opening in which stood the Pegram House." Hartranft's men then formed a right angle to protect the left flank of the advance. Per Parke's order, Potter quickly moved to attack, which initiated the catastrophe.[126]

In the advance to the Pegram House, Griffin's and Curtin's brigades occupied positions on either side of a Fifth Corps division. Potter's two brigades then moved together with the goal to reach the Boydton Plank Road. With some Confederate skirmishers visible, Potter ordered Griffin to support his own brigade's skirmishers "with a line of two or three regiments, and follow with the rest of the column." Experienced troops and indications "that the enemy had mostly withdrawn," gave Potter confidence, even with the lack of flank support as the two brigades moved out.

Griffin's Brigade was led by skirmishers from the 2nd New York Mounted Rifles, misnamed because of being dismounted. The second line included all three of Griffin's New Hampshire units, as well as the 2nd Maryland. None of these commands had a large number of men. On the right of the third line, the 17th Vermont had the two Maine regiments on their left, as well as the 56th Massachusetts and 179th New York. Even a strong commander like Simon Griffin would have a difficult time controlling and leading ten regiments in such a situation. Suddenly, as Griffin reported, "we met the enemy also advancing, with a line of battle stronger than our own, and overlapping us on both flanks." Potter noted enemy troops moving in a way that could cut off his brigades. Southern warriors also appeared likely to cleave the two Ninth Corps brigades apart. To make matters worse, Potter wrote, "the enemy now advanced a considerable force to my left, attacking impetuously."[127] Table 7.1 shows the organizations of Potter's large division.

Table 7.1. The Large Brigades of the Second Division at Poplar Grove Church, September 30, 1864

Division Commander—Brig. Gen. Robert Potter	
1st Brigade Col. John Curtin	2nd Brigade Brig. Gen. Simon Griffin
21st Massachusetts (3 Companies)	31st Maine
	32nd Maine
35th Massachusetts	2nd Maryland
36th Massachusetts	56th Massachusetts
58th Massachusetts	6th New Hampshire
51st New York	9th New Hampshire
45th Pennsylvania	11th New Hampshire
48th Pennsylvania	2nd NY Mounted Rifles
4th Rhode Island	(dismounted)
7th Rhode Island	179th New York
	17th Vermont

Source: OR, Vol. 42, I, 142.

The historian of the 32nd Maine remembered Confederates attacking "with irresistible force, throwing the entire Second division into confusion by the sudden and vigorous attack, in front and flank." Having been called forward to join the skirmishers, New Hampshire troops fought tenaciously as "rifles flashed almost in the faces of the advancing foe." Yet, the Confederate tide could not be resisted for long. One Tar Heel suggested the Confederates launched "a sharp and spirited attack."[128]

After advancing beyond flank support, Granite Staters in the 6th Regiment found themselves in a very tough spot. A portion of the unit marched through an enclosed part of a farm. With the sudden advance of the enemy, many became trapped, unable to climb over the high fence walls. The regimental historian, one of the dozens captured that day, wrote of being "penned up and surrounded by swarms of yelling rebels." In addition to dozens wounded, Griffin lost more than 400 soldiers to capture.[129]

Nearly twice as many prisoners were taken from Curtin's command on the left. Before the wicked charge of Confederates, Curtin was able to align with Griffin. The main command difficulty may have been the large number of units each senior officer oversaw, with Curtin taking nine. Surveying the scene after encountering Confederate pickets, Curtin witnessed his right units becoming engaged, but "I could discover no enemy in my front and to the left." As with Griffin's advance, circumstances changed quickly. Summing up the new reality before Curtin's line, a Keystone Stater suggested, "It was an unlucky Friday for us."[130]

Per Curtin's report, "desperate fighting ensued." Confederate cavalry unleashed the biggest surprise of the day on the brigade's left. In a few moments, the bulk of the 35th Massachusetts, 51st New York, and 45th Pennsylvania fell into Confederate hands. With 350 going into the fight, only sixteen in the 51st escaped. Despite a higher percentage able to flee, the 45th still lost 185 of 230 men.[131]

In a reserve position, the 48th Pennsylvania's Henry Pleasants grew quite distraught at the number of Ninth Corps troops retreating into his line. As Captain Bosbyshell remembered, Pleasants "with drawn sword slashed to the right and left amongst them with the strength of an athlete, staying the flight effectually anywhere near his sweeping sabre. Many a sore head and stinging rib resulted from the blows well laid on by him." Col. Percy Daniels and elements of the 7th Rhode Island proved valuable in reorganizing panicked units.[132]

The most credit for salvaging the day goes to General Hartranft, leading a brigade in Willcox's Division. Like the senior officers under Potter, the wooded terrain had prevented Hartranft from gaining a full view of the field. The retreat of the 35th and 36th Massachusetts was his first sign of problems. In addition to the collapse of Potter, Hartranft reported, "the skirmish line which I had established across the swamp to the westward, now on my left flank, had been driven in." The 2nd and 20th Michigan were first ordered to fall back, followed by the rest of Hartranft's troops. A solid defensive line, with the expected orders to dig in and build breastworks, brought a successful end to an enervating day, what Josiah Jones, 6th New Hampshire, called "an ill conducted affair."[133]

"AMONG THE GLORIOUS MARTYRS TO NATIONAL AND HUMAN LIBERTY"

With brevity and truth, New Hampshire soldier Lewis Simonds filled pages of an 1864 diary. Of September 30, he wrote, "Had a very heavy battle today." Nearly 1,300 Ninth Corps soldiers became prisoners as a result of the fight at Poplar Springs Church, close to 75 percent of Parke's casualties.[134]

Sgt. Hiram Drown, 6th New Hampshire, was mortally wounded on September 30. "Among those of our best men killed," the regimental historian wrote, Drown was a "fine fellow." He held a powerful claim to his comrades' respect, having "always been full of life and fun," while enlivening "the spirits of the other men when they were becoming discouraged." Drown rests with so many other Civil War veterans at Arlington National Cemetery.[135]

Sixteen of Parke's officers were killed or mortally wounded during the battle, bringing further leadership drain to the Ninth Corps. The 21st Massachusetts lost Capt. Orange Sampson, who had enlisted as a private in the first month of the war. Joining his new regiment later in 1861, Sampson tread the difficult path of the 21st for more than three years. Another highly competent young officer, Sampson rests at Norwich Bridge Cemetery, Huntington, Massachusetts.[136]

The 58th Massachusetts, Curtin's Brigade, lost two officers, Capt. Charles Johnson and Lt. John Fiske. Of the captain, who died a Confederate prisoner, the regimental historian suggested, "He was in every respect worthy of the title of a soldier and gentleman." Ambrose Burnside might have known Johnson, who logged 1861 service in the 1st Rhode Island. Fiske was a veteran of the 35th Massachusetts. He had been wounded at Spotsylvania while an officer in his second regiment.[137]

Three lost officers in the 17th Vermont included Parke's highest-ranking fatality during the fight, Lt. Col. Charles Cummings. Confederates interred the regimental commander on ground they temporarily retained. Soon after, Ninth Corps men located Cummings's burial site. Simon Griffin sent a letter to Cummings's widow. "Would to God that I could soften the terrible blow," the brigade commander mourned, "Your husband has given his life to his country." At the front of his Green Mountain troops, Griffin praised Cummings as "a brave and gallant officer." He concluded, "Please accept my deepest sympathy in this heart-rending affliction."

The colonel's brother wrote Mrs. Cummings with additional support. "Anything which I am able to do for the family of my deceased brother both for his sake and for their own I shall be glad to do," he promised. "As the elder brother, he was the leader," the letter continued. "Gifted with a versatile genius," the colonel "contributed largely to the defense of those principles of civil liberty which underlie our institutions as a nation and which, at first assailed by pen and voice, are now assaulted by physical force."

Newspapers focused on many of Cummings's virtues. One suggested the colonel's last words, "Save the Flag, boys," should be the clarion call for all patriots. With a strong will to fight the Rebellion, Cummings's last command was "a fit emblem to embalm a soldier's grave." Another paper printed additional laudatory words. The departed officer's name "will forever be written among the glorious martyrs to national and human liberty."[138]

"BEAN SOUP OR WHATEVER"

The immediate priority for the Ninth Corps was the retention of ground gained before the repulse of September 30. "We can hold our own, and that is about all," Josiah Jones wrote in early October. With strong earthworks along their new line near the Pegram house, Ninth Corps men withstood Confederate attacks while dealing with intense rains. The demoralized dismounted troopers of the 13th Ohio Cavalry in Willcox's First Brigade were "thoroughly soaked, and besmeared with mud from the clay in the trenches."[139]

Seeing the dilapidated condition of his regiments, Robert Potter turned his attention to bureaucratic matters. In his October 20 report, Potter called for "a reorganization of the division, which, in its present condition, is inefficient. Regiments should be consolidated into battalions, and these battalions grouped into regiments, and new officers appointed." No such changes occurred through the rest of the year. The Ninth Corps retained three divisions, with Potter's two brigades still including a large number of regiments.[140]

The next engagement for Parke's Boys would be around Hatcher's Run late in the month. Few benefits accrued to the Unionists who were again attempting to pierce the Boydton Plank Road. The effort cost the army more than 1,700 casualties in what Charles Rundlett deemed "a continual roar all night." Parke's divisions suffered only 150 combat losses, a majority of which were in Ferrero's USCT regiments.[141]

For months, many soldiers expressed views on the pending national election, which pitted President Abraham Lincoln against former Army of the Potomac commander, Democrat George McClellan. Perhaps hoping for strong support from soldiers who cheered him so often in 1862, McClellan attempted to unseat the president who fired him two years before. "Little Mac" ran a very interesting campaign, in direct opposition to the peace plank in his party's platform.

Ninth Corps troops, never McClellan's strongest backers, saw through the subterfuge. "Peace resolutions don't go down with soldiers," George Codman opined. Even without calling for an end to the war, in contrast to the party that nominated him, McClellan was "played out," Codman added. Vermonter Eldin Hartshorn was another to question McClellan's acceptance of the Democratic nomination. Of the peace platform, Hartshorn averred, "If the Democratic Party are going into the canvas with such sentiments they will be defeated and driven out of sight."[142]

Those opposed to Abraham Lincoln's war goals were often called Copperheads. Before McClellan was nominated, soldiers expressed dismay at the peace goal of McClellan's party. "*We want peace*," Hamilton Dunlap, 100th Pennsylvania, explained in August, "but we want an *honorable* peace, and Abe is the man to bring that around." Expounding,

Dunlap promised his brother, "If you vote the copperhead ticket I will give you a pair of black eyes when I come home."[143]

Charles Rundlett, 11th New Hampshire, deemed Lincoln's reelection inevitable. Most soldiers would back the president, he wrote, "There is no possible doubt of it." Although not originally committed to emancipation, Ransom Sargent, another in the 11th Regiment, supported Lincoln.

If you remember two years ago we were fighting to restore the [union] as it was, but now it is entirely different. Slavery must be abolished and when the southern people get tired of fighting or whipped out, they can come back and have a permanent peace which it would be impossible to have with slavery existing. . . . Lincoln has been tried and found well capable of conducting the national affairs under very trying circumstances.[144]

In late October, a member of the 179th New York thought Meade might be making decisions about the army in an effort to boost McClellan's chances. "I of course, do not believe that Gen. Meade wishes our army to suffer defeat in order that McClellan might gain votes by it, but I write this to let you know how little favor Meade is regarded in this part, at least, of the army."[145]

The tide of good war news from other theaters seemed destined to sweep away McClellan's chances, something the votes of soldiers made possible. Lincoln won nationally, and among those in McClellan's former army. In the 32nd Maine, of the ninety-nine votes cast, Lincoln earned sixty-eight. The 51st Pennsylvania gave Lincoln a 253–145 tally against McClellan. The thinned ranks of the 6th New Hampshire voted 100–18 for Lincoln.[146]

Trench doldrums continued in November, offset by the euphoria of Lincoln's reelection. A major movement of the Ninth Corps occurred late in the month. Heading back east, several brigades filled in old Second Corps trenches, while others camped farther south, some stationed not far from the Crater. A member of the weary 45th Pennsylvania said many troops enjoyed being near their lines of last summer. Because of the time of year, however, soldiers had to get busy to stay warm. As the Keystone

Stater continued, "It took us several days to put our new quarters in shape to suit us," including the construction of chimneys. Mud was used to fill cracks in shanties.[147]

Soldiers began to see a realistic path to winning the war. One sure sign of progress was the growing number of Confederate deserters. As Brig. Gen. Simon Griffin wrote, the Southern troops giving up were "frequently half starved and hopeless," while testifying to the lack of supplies in Confederate camps. Griffin concluded, "The end seemed not far away." Talking to an enemy soldier who fled his post, the 35th Massachusetts' historian remembered the Confederate hoped Unionists would hang his own president, Jefferson Davis, "but let 'Bob' Lee off, for he was a good fellow."[148]

With the normal dangers from picket duty, the Ninth Corps sustained eighteen men killed across December, with ninety-two more wounded. However, numbers in the expanding Union force around Petersburg illustrated the increased chances of an eventual triumph. At the end of October, the Ninth Corps had nearly 16,000 present and equipped, with Meade's army fielding 57,000. When 1864 ended, the Army of the Potomac fielded 74,000 present and equipped troops. With a much smaller manpower pool, the South could not match the North's ability to rebuild battered armies.[149]

Military justice sometimes dropped the Union force by more than one in a day. A dual execution took place on December 10. The 7th Rhode Island's historian wrote of the deaths of two soldiers from the 179th New York, who "were hung for desertion," which was not the extent of their crime. The Ocean State scribe added the condemned "had been recognized among a lot of rebel prisoners captured by their own regiment." The crowd witnessing the executions included those compelled to watch, as well as a large group of the curious. After their grim deaths, the traitors were deemed "companions in life, dishonor, treachery and misfortune" who remain next to each other "in leveled unknown graves."[150]

Work crews performed different tasks to improve field fortifications and lives. Charles Rundlett, 11th New Hampshire, helped build an impressive structure, writing on December 4 about a mess hall which stood 250 feet long. "I shall get to be quite a carpenter if we keep on building," the proud Granite Stater wrote.[151]

Additions or subtractions of units in Parke's command took place across the last quarter of the year. A major change was the move of Ferrero's troops to the Army of the James. Damaged greatly at the Crater, the USCT regiments had certainly earned respect from their comrades. As the historian of the 11th New Hampshire suggested, "It is but justice to say that these troops had done bravely whenever an opportunity was given them to perform any service."[152]

To replace the numbers lost by the change, John Hartranft was given divisional command of six regiments from Pennsylvania. The 200th, 208th, and 209th regiments joined the First Brigade, with the 205th, 207th, and 211th in another brigade. A history of the units proudly noted the "husky, healthy lot of young men" in Hartranft's division. Some of the troops had served in the Army of the James before joining Parke.[153]

Regiments finally receiving the full complement of ten companies brought hundreds into the Ninth Corps. The 58th Massachusetts, one of many units in need of an infusion of soldiers, added its final two companies by December. On his way to the trenches as a member of Company K, Charles Read viewed the massive Unionist headquarters and supply depot at City Point on the James. He informed his brother that the area was "the damdist place I ever saw." Unfortunately, the company had temporary quarters "worse than my hog pen," Read added. "The first night we slept on a Pile of Bricks," with "a corpse all boxed up ready to send home." The following day was "rainy like the Devil," the hungry Read lamented. One of his first meals amounted to "Bean Soup or whatever." The travails of the young patriot offered an introduction to the life of a Civil War soldier.[154]

The few remaining in the three companies of the 21st Massachusetts lost their separate identity near the end of the year. The men at least remained part of a Bay State outfit after being attached to the 36th Massachusetts. "Its veteran members were naturally averse to the change," the 36th's historian noted. The decision compacted companies in the 36th from ten to only seven, which was another source of hurt feelings. Yet, the historian continued, "Military necessity is regardless of sentiment, and the change was peacefully made," with the members of the 21st "pleasantly received."[155]

Parke's two Maine regiments consolidated due to the massive reduction in officers and men in the battered outfits. By December, two companies of the 32nd Maine had no officers, while most others had only one. Even more pressing, he continued, "a small and feeble remnant" of the one thousand enlistees from early in the year remained. After just eight months of service, 80 percent of the regiment was no longer present.[156]

With the year winding down and feeling unwell for days, John Andrews, a twenty-two-year-old in the 179th New York, apologized to his father for a lack of letters. "My bones have ached, my head has ached," Andrews complained, with a lack of appetite and a generally languid feeling. If the war could not end in the spring, "I hope the slaughter of next summer's campaign will not be as great as last summer's was," he added. Concerned about the war taking one of his brothers, Andrews pleaded, "Don't let Homer enlist. I would rather hear that you had lost every dollar you are worth than hear that he had enlisted."[157]

Bombproofs, like this one used by the 7th Maine Battery, became vital to protecting lives across the nearly ten months of the Petersburg siege. LIBRARY OF CONGRESS

Surgeon Robert Jameson, 29th Massachusetts, described his home in a December letter.

> *It is what is called a "bomb-proof" made of very large logs. The roof being of the same material. Earth is thrown up all around on the outside to the depth of several feet and the same on the top. The name of course suggests its use. It is to protect us from the shells. . . . In some places along this front the pickets are not more than 20 paces from each other.*[158]

Some soldiers enjoyed a fine Christmas. Ward Frothingham, 59th Massachusetts, shared roast turkey, cranberry sauce, and peas with comrades. "The church bells are ringing for worship in Petersburg, the spires of which are in plain sight," he wrote home. Another Ninth Corps man to witness enemies deserting, Frothingham added, the surrendering Confederates "seem much pleased to find themselves safe and sound in the land of freedom."[159]

"A Memento of This Cursed Rebellion"

On the first day of 1865, Oscar Robinson, 9th New Hampshire, looked back on the previous year as a time of "suffering and death" interspersed with "triumph and victory." Happy to remain unwounded and well, the penitent Granite warrior added, "God has been *very merciful* to me." Robinson noted how warmth quickly returns to melt snow.[160]

Potter's troops manned the southern end of the Ninth Corps line. Describing his location close to Fort Sedgwick, Charles Nye, 7th Rhode Island, informed a friend, "We are camped at a Fort called Fort Hell by the Soldiers and it is the roughest hole that I ever got in." One reason for the fort's name was the intensity of Confederate fire, partly due to the proximity of the combatants. "Our picket lines are so close together in some places that they can throw crackers over at each other," Nye added.[161]

As the month advanced, Andrew Fitch grew quite acquainted with the racket of two armies during a siege. A surgeon from the 79th New York who stayed with the army into the new year, Fitch wrote, "There is firing every day between our batteries and those of the rebels but very little damage is done." He noted the daily casualties from musketry fire along the trenches, as well. At least a good house kept Fitch warm.[162]

Many lives focused on the necessity of firewood, even if winter was not terribly cold in central Virginia. A story of partnership between picket details from enemy armies found its way to the historian of the 36th Massachusetts. A work party of six from the regiment went toward a large tree with axes. They were met by a Confederate tree-chopping detail. The enemies decided "both parties should assist in cutting it down, and then divide it as equally as possible. . . . That night the blaze of the little fires in the rear of each picket line added to the comfort of the men."[163]

Byron Cutcheon, spending some time as a brigade commander, remembered January as "an entirely uneventful period." Two major aspects of life from the previous weeks remained: "The usual artillery duels and picket firing continued, and desertions from the enemy became frequent." In Cutcheon's command, Sam Schwenk, discharged in October due to a Cold Harbor wound, returned to the 50th Pennsylvania. Commissioned a major in February, Schwenk led the experienced regiment.[164]

Rain posed problems, as Albert Raymond of the 17th Vermont reported on January 10. "It is mashing the plastering off from our Houses," he wrote. Bad weather might be offset by news from home or other battlefronts where the final success of Union arms seemed assured. The historian of the 37th Wisconsin felt the ranks were filled with confident soldiers sensing victory. With "the net closing tighter and closer around rebeldom," he suggested, "the prospect of a speedy return to our homes" made winter's gloom bearable.[165]

Charles Read sent a January 22 letter requesting some treats due to his lack of pay. "Go to all the boys and pass your hat around and see if you can't get a chew of tobacco for your only Kin for I am hard up and can't get paid," he requested. Others at home "have a polite invitation to help fill up the box," Read added, with cider, milk, or cherries requested. Even with Read's plea to send the box via express, spoilage of such packages was quite common during the war. By early February, Read wrote, "I still bear you in mind while sitting in my Bomb Proof beside a good fire and all alone." He may very well have received a package from home, because

Read noted a bounty of cherries was being consumed while he warmed up. "I wish I was with you," he added.[166]

The randomness of death could shock soldiers. Samuel Waldron, 20th Michigan, died from a shot to the head. His younger brother lost his life in action along the North Anna. A week after Samuel died, James Norton, 6th New Hampshire, moved forward on picket duty. As comrade Edmund Brown wrote of Norton's gruesome injury, "The bullet went in to his mouth and came out on the back of his neck."[167]

A Maine soldier was executed in February. Reporting the incident on the 10th, Ransom Sargent wrote, "Today we had to go and see another man shot." He considered his doomed comrade "about the worst looking person I ever saw." Having deserted, the coward hid in a cave near the Appomattox River, engaging in theft to survive. Then, as Sargent wrote, the Mainer "murdered 3 full of something to eat," adding, "I guess he deserved death if anyone ever did." Nonetheless, Sargent did not enjoy having to witness an execution.[168]

Looking to break some monotony, Lt. Col. Thomas Hight, 31st Maine, sent a humorous present to the state's adjutant general in February. "I have the honor to send you a miniature mortar," Hight declared, "made from rebel bullets fired into Fort Sedgwick." The industrious Pine Tree State troops viewed the relic "as a memento of this cursed rebellion, which we are in hopes will soon be crushed."[169]

A potential weak spot in Ninth Corps lines drew the attention of army headquarters. With members of the 8th Michigan on duty, two Confederate deserters had passed through the picket line on the night of February 12. In a note to Major General Parke, chief of staff Alexander Webb reported the Confederates had been detained by cavalry in the rear, rather than Ninth Corps soldiers closer to the front. The issue prompted multiple messages. Colonel Samuel Harriman proclaimed, "That portion of our line is enfiladed by the enemy's fire," a difficult spot to continually monitor. Harriman indicated his frequent visits to the picket line, as well as instructions to officers. He classed the passage of two Confederates as "a humiliating fact," but concluded, "I cannot discover that there has been any neglect of duty on the part of the officers and men on my picket line."

Of the evening in question, Lt. William Clifford wrote, "I visited the different posts every hour and sometimes twice," finding the men doing their jobs and "nothing unusual." He added, "The night was extremely cold." In defense of his men, another officer declared with certainty, "the pickets of the Eighth Michigan Volunteers do their duty well."[170]

Danger lurked for soldiers regardless of their experience level. Across January and February, Parke's regiments suffered eighteen killed in action, with dozens wounded. Still, through these cold weeks, the Ninth Corps gained manpower. Nearly 19,000 men were present for duty at the end of February, with minimal organizational change to Parke's command. With so many new soldiers augmenting Union armies, experienced Ninth Corps men tried to teach rookies the sundry aspects of soldiering. In the 45th Pennsylvania, "it took a lot of hard work and patience" to ensure their callow comrades knew what "we all had to learn in order to be good for anything as soldiers."[171]

Target: Fort Stedman

A summary of Ninth Corps activities across the first twenty-four days of March notes, "Nothing unusual occurred along the lines of the corps." That fact changed dramatically before daylight on March 25. Named after a former Ninth Corps officer, Fort Stedman was built slightly more than a mile northeast of the Crater. Wishing to shock a portion of the Union line, General Lee approved an attack against the fort. The site for the charge appears to have been selected because of the proximity of Fort Stedman to the Confederate works, a distance of only about 450 feet.[172]

Potter's men, stationed on Parke's left, did not take part in the fight. Willcox's First Division was responsible for the fort north to the Appomattox River. Damaged over the course of the siege and as a result of settling ground during the winter, one Unionist wrote the fort's "nearness to the enemy prevented even the slightest repairs except in the most stealthy manner."[173]

Confederate troops targeted Fort Stedman and nearby lines in three waves. First, as a Southern division commander remembered, "a storming party consisting of fifty picked men carrying axes" were to clear away abatis and other obstructions. Following closely, 100 selected infantrymen

Fort Stedman stood about a mile northeast of the Crater. This photo shows a portion of the fort soon after the war. LIBRARY OF CONGRESS

"on whose courage and coolness we could confidently rely" constituted the second line, followed by the rest of three divisions under corps commander John Gordon. Due to the darkness, an attacking soldier wrapped a white cloth around his left arm to be more easily identified by comrades. Looking east shortly before the attack began, a North Carolina officer remembered, "There was absolutely no sign of life along the enemy's lines."[174]

Napoleon Bonaparte McLaughlen, a forty-one-year-old Vermont native, commanded the Ninth Corps brigade around Fort Stedman. A member of the U.S. Army in the 1850s without time at West Point, McLaughlen started the war as a second lieutenant, rising to leadership of the 1st Massachusetts in October 1862. At some very bloody fields before mustering out in May 1864, McLaughlen quickly returned to action as colonel of the 57th Massachusetts, winning a brevet star at Poplar Springs Church.[175] A respected and experienced soldier with time as an acting division commander, McLaughlen offered excellent credentials to the Ninth Corps and the Union cause as spring arrived in 1865.

Part of the 14th New York Heavy Artillery stood at Fort Haskell, about 1,000 feet south of Stedman. Four additional regiments were part of McLaughlen's Brigade. To the right of Fort Haskell, the Roundheads of the 100th Pennsylvania guarded Battery 12. The 29th Massachusetts stood near Battery 11, immediately to the left of Fort Stedman. The 57th and 59th Massachusetts, with the small 3rd Maryland, were nearby.[176]

Spread across the main line, a portion of the 14th Heavies garrisoned Fort Stedman. They did not need long to realize something other than their winter routine was unfolding early on March 25. Maj. George Randall reported two days later, "At 3 a.m. the officers of my command were informed by a sergeant of the picket that the enemy were advancing on our works." Failing in these early efforts, the Confederates then unleashed their full attack. "They moved with such rapidity," an officer overseeing the picket line remembered, "many of the pickets did not have a chance to reload their pieces." Randall added, "I ordered my men to use their bayonets and the butts of their muskets, which they did most gallantly."[177]

As the 29th Massachusetts historian remembered, "the entire storming party effected a wide breach in the works," including infiltrating the rear sally port of Fort Stedman. Capt. John Deane of the 29th reported, "Before our men had time to man the works the enemy entered our camp at the north front." Three companies of the experienced unit were captured. A "desperate encounter" occurred as other members of the 29th fought, but, as Deane wrote, "most of our men were taken prisoners."[178]

As a New Yorker suggested of the pre-dawn clash inside the fort, "The resistance our men made was creditable, but entirely unavailing." Time for a struggle was limited as the 29th Massachusetts tried to stem the Confederate tide. A Third Division staff officer praised the Bay Staters for their effort. "The regiment displayed staying qualities of a high order" during "a very severe struggle." Some in the regiment escaped captivity, finding comrades in Fort Haskell. Roundheads thwarted the attack, but most of the regiment also ended up using Fort Haskell as a gathering point.[179]

The early morning's drubbing surprised many officers and soldiers, but men quickly rallied. Capt. Joseph Carter, 3rd Maryland, "finding the enemy advancing in the rear of our works," had a skirmish line move forward, with the rest of his command in support. As overwhelmed Roundheads retreated south and Confederates looked for more success, Carter reported, "our skirmish line checked their farther advance." The highest-ranking Ninth Corps fatality on the morning was Lt. Col. Joseph Pentecost, leading the Roundheads in a counter charge.[180]

As the brigade's only reserve regiment, the 59th Massachusetts had an important role as the momentum began to shift. At first ordered to defend Battery 11, Maj. Ezra Gould had his men head to Fort Haskell, which he deemed "the only tenable and defensible part of the brigade line." Fire from remnants of Ninth Corps units brought further halts to the Confederate attack.[181] More reinforcements were on the way.

Artillery had a prominent role as the dark chaos gave way to daylight. Maj. Jacob Roemer, still providing competent leadership to the 34th New York Battery, saw the enemy's advancing lines, now only about four hundred yards distant from the Union lines. Roemer suffered an injury during the morning, with Pvt. Michael Fogarty earning his commander's praise for taking charge of one cannon. Overall, the battery would fire 370 rounds on March 25.[182]

At Fort Friend, northeast of Fort Stedman, Joseph Jones and his 11th Massachusetts Battery "promptly manned his guns upon the first alarm," according to Ninth Corps artillery chief John Tidball. As light increased, firing from the battery hit distant Confederates. Additionally, Tidball noted the 11th Battery used canister fire against troops who tried to attack Union artillery.[183]

Leading Willcox's Second Brigade, Col. Ralph Ely, a tested and excellent officer, had his men in action to the north of Fort Stedman. Ordering the 50th Pennsylvania to quickly move from a reserve position 2 miles away, Ely also had fifty members of the 1st Michigan Sharpshooters advance, serving as skirmishers in the direction of Fort Stedman.

The 2nd Michigan was posted on Ely's left. Under attack early in the morning, Capt. John Boughton reported, "It was too dark to see well." In face of the difficulties, the Wolverines held on. Nearly captured, Boughton ordered musketry fire against the charging enemy, allowing many in the regiment to escape the Confederate wave. Finding some shelter at

Battery 9, the experienced regiment contributed to the fire Ely's men sent into the Confederate left.[184]

As one veteran opined, the Southerners "were now in a position from which they could not easily extricate themselves. By an unexpected movement they had thrust their head of column through our line, but had succeeded in occupying only a small portion of it." John Hartranft seemed eager to reverse the morning's outcome. Spread out during the overnight period, Hartranft could not immediately form the six new regiments for a concentrated counterattack. Ordered to support Willcox, Hartranft quickly worked to retake the Fort Stedman line.[185]

Opening the Third Division's contribution to the day, the 200th Pennsylvania's initial move accomplished little except a good deal of damage to the regiment. Closer to the Confederate breakthrough, another effort gave the 200th some leverage, but the foothold could not be maintained. Linkage with the 209th Pennsylvania, in addition to Ely's assistance and artillery at Battery 9, brought pressure against Gordon's Confederates.[186]

Following three failed attempts to seize Fort Haskell, Southern troops began to see the impossibility of making more out of the day. Yet, as a division commander suggested, "General Gordon seemed loth to give up his cherished plans." Both sides fired at each other for a time without a change to the situation. With an attack order timed at 7:30 a.m., Hartranft prepared for the decisive push.[187]

Forming a circular line, regiments from two divisions moved out, easily routing the Confederates. In addition to bearing the brunt of the united line of Ninth Corps units, the wounded leader of the 57th North Carolina witnessed his men enduring "murderous cross fire" in their effort to return to the Confederate line west of Fort Stedman. Not much longer than thirty minutes after the counterattack opened, Parke wired headquarters of the victory, with original lines of the morning reestablished.[188]

"A LITTLE RUMPUS UP THE LINE THIS MORNING"

Some gave Hartranft and his regiments most of the credit for restoring the Union lines on March 25. Willcox endured the more difficult part of the morning, simply holding on against the pre-dawn onslaught.

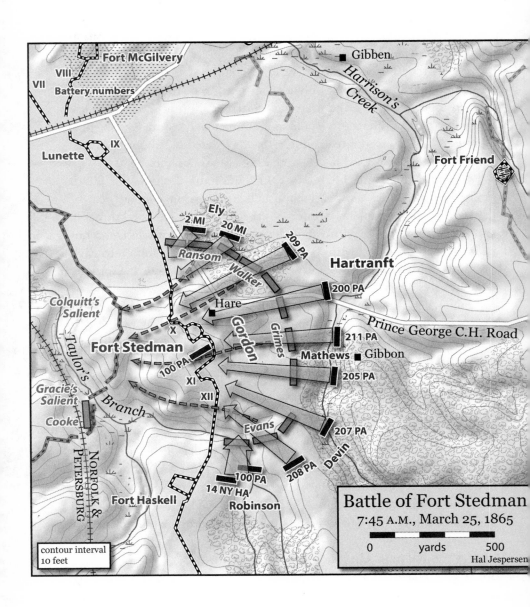

Battle of Fort Stedman

7:45 A.M., March 25, 1865

0   yards   500

Hal Jespersen

contour interval
10 feet

Fort McGilvery

VIII

VII

Battery numbers

Gibben

Harrison's
Creek

Lunette

IX

Fort Friend

2 MI

Ely

20 MI

Ransom

Walker

209 PA

Hartranft

200 PA

Hare

Gordon

Grimes

Prince George C.H. Road

Colquitt's
Salient

X

Fort Stedman

211 PA

Mathews

Gibbon

Taylor's

100 PA

XI

205 PA

Gracie's
Salient

Branch

XII

Evans

207 PA

Cooke

Devin

NORFOLK & PETERSBURG

100 PA

208 PA

14 NY HA

Fort Haskell

Robinson

Sustaining two-and-a-half times Hartranft's casualties, McLaughlen's Brigade was paramount in the day's salvation. Moreover, the final assault included regiments from both divisions, so Hartranft should not be solely lauded for the outcome.[189]

Regardless of the debate among old soldiers, the defense of the Fort Stedman line could be seen as the best example of Ninth Corps teamwork across the whole war. Two divisions, with perhaps the best artillery support that men under Burnside or Parke ever knew, worked very well together to plug a hole in the line, inflicting a large number of casualties and capturing 2,200 Southern warriors. By late morning, the Confederate disaster brought further optimism to Union troops that the war was nearly over.[190]

At City Point, President Lincoln had been visiting General Grant. With a son as a staff officer, Lincoln wrote Secretary of War Stanton, "Robert just now tells there was a little rumpus up the line this morning, ending about where it began." With a witty mind, Lincoln had summed up the Fort Stedman action, which, like so many other fights large and small in the previous 11 months, inflicted a great deal of suffering without changing much about the immediate situation. As Samuel Emerson, 18th New Hampshire, wrote in his diary on March 25, "Today has been a day of blood."[191]

General Tidball correctly stated, "The artillery upon the whole line was most skillfully and judiciously managed." Sustaining 110 casualties across all batteries, the day brought a great deal of sacrifice to the cannoneers. The highest-ranking artillerist to die was Lt. Ephraim Nye, 14th Massachusetts Battery. When a Confederate demanded he surrender, Nye refused to do so, costing him his life.[192]

The actions of the 14th New York Heavies at Fort Stedman once again proved those signing up for relatively easy garrison duty could become excellent infantry troops. They suffered a dozen killed in action, forty-five wounded and more than 200 captured, including General McLaughlen. "Beset on all sides and hemmed in," one writer described, the Heavies "from one bombproof to the other contested hotly every inch of ground." They sustained nearly 25 percent of Parke's loss on the day, more casualties than Hartranft's entire division.[193]

With gallantry on display across the morning, six soldiers were awarded the Medal of Honor for Fort Stedman. In addition to capturing the flag of a Virginia regiment, Joseph Carter, 3rd Maryland, escaped captivity on March 25, then brought in some Confederate prisoners. One of three members of the 29th Massachusetts to earn the medal, Maj. John Deane, "observing an abandoned gun within Fort Haskell, called for volunteers, and under a heavy fire, worked the gun until the enemy's advancing line was routed." Charles Pinkham, 57th Massachusetts, captured the battle flag of the 57th North Carolina, then "saved his own colors by tearing them from the staff while the enemy was in the camp."[194]

NEARING THE FINAL ASSAULT

Oscar Robinson observed the "miserably clad" Confederates taken prisoner on the 25th. "You need not be surprised to hear of a big move any day," he wrote home, "Everything is working gloriously." The devout warrior continued, "Let us have faith in God," who would "bring that long prayed for peace at no distant day."[195]

Attacking Fort Stedman proved to be the last offensive gasp of the dying Army of Northern Virginia. With so many troops lost forever and continued supply problems, a North Carolinian deemed the Southern force "a wounded lion at bay." A Badger in the Ninth Corps wrote that the days after Fort Stedman "passed in an uneasy, ominous state of comparative quiet, the lull that always precedes a storm of any kind."[196]

Before the Fort Stedman attack, General Grant believed Confederate weakness justified further efforts to overwhelm Lee's soldiers. Later in March, while other elements of the Union force moved west of Hatcher's Run, Parke prepared his three divisions for an inevitable battle. Prior to the overwhelming moment, extra vigilance was ordered along the line. Based on a message from army headquarters, Ninth Corps men doubled the number of trench guards on March 28, while also ordered to be ready for an imminent charge. Perhaps these directives would have been less onerous if the weather was better. Nathaniel Talbot, 58th Massachusetts, wrote at the end of the month, "It rained again this morning." Cooler and windy weather followed.[197]

On April 1, some Union troops routed Confederates at Five Forks, 16 miles to Parke's west. This sealed the doom of Lee's right flank. Parke's task was to crush resistance along his front. Given command of City Point on the James, the Ninth Corps leader had access to nearly 2,000 supporting troops, which boosted Parke's manpower to more than 19,000 soldiers.[198]

Terminating at the Appomattox River, Willcox's tested First Division held the northern end of the entire army. Well to the left, 1 mile south of the Crater, Robert Potter's two brigades had Hartranft's Division in support around Fort Sedgwick. Intense rounds of artillery sounded late in the evening. After a break of about three hours, the furious missiles flew again from the lines of both armies. Of the barrages immediately before the main infantry attack, Ninth Corps artillery chief John Tidball reported, "It is probable that never since the invention of gunpowder has such a cannonade taken place."[199]

Central to the unfolding conquest of Petersburg, Simon Griffin's brigade included 3,500 men. The experienced general had orders to begin an attack at dawn on April 2 but grew surprised six hours prior when told to assault the Confederate picket line immediately. Moving out in the dark, elements of the brigade seized about a mile of enemy trenches as well as 250 Southerners. By 3 a.m., Griffin was then informed the attack from his original line had not been postponed. Hurriedly returning to their original position, the brigade then prepared for the main event.[200]

The Jerusalem Plank Road bisected the Confederate ground targeted for the attack, with the seizure of Fort Mahone a central goal for the Unionists. Thomas Beals commanded three companies of the 31st Maine, which served as Potter's spearhead. In a conversation with Griffin shortly before the fateful moment, Beals was told to charge up the road until reaching the line of Confederate obstructions. The three companies would help pioneers remove impediments to the attack, then assist Griffin in the assault. Beals remembered, "Few of us expected to emerge alive from this affair."[201]

"All I Ask Is For You to Follow Me"

Behind the trio of companies under Beals, Griffin positioned regiments one after the other. This decision likely related to a concern about the "very rough ground" his men had to conquer. The 179th New York led the brigade, followed by the other companies in the 31st Maine. The 6th New Hampshire stood next, with the small 2nd Maryland and 17th Vermont. The new 186th New York made up the last of Griffin's regiments. Left behind to garrison the Union entrenchments, the 9th and 11th New Hampshire would be part of Parke's large reserve.[202]

In an effort to draw Confederates from Potter's front, Willcox's thin line created a distraction. With some of his men moving forward before the end of April 1, hundreds of soldiers from Samuel Harriman's First Brigade augmented the picket line. Harriman said the large picket force then "commenced firing in volleys, accompanied by cheers." After this good work, five of Harriman's regiments went to the left to supplement Potter's dawn charge. Harriman's regiments stood near the Third Division on arrival near Fort Sedgwick.[203]

Knowing the moment was nearing, Captain Beals attempted to motivate the attack's forlorn hope, his three Maine companies. "You all know the place we are to attack," he remembered saying, "All I ask is for you to follow me." Navigating across the ground in the dark proved a chore, but the Pine Tree Staters soon arrived at a Union picket post. The next goal was the Confederates' initial position. Beals wrote, "Without a stop we made for it at the double-quick. The Rebel pickets opened fire just as we were going over their pits."[204]

Lt. Albert Alexander, 211th Pennsylvania, led a group of pioneers forward on the right, with a mission similar to that of Beals. Taking plenty of axes and spades, the Keystone Staters would destroy impediments to advance. Losing his life on the important effort, Alexander deserved "more credit than I can here ascribe him," brigade commander Joseph Mathews reported.[205]

Hartranft's Pennsylvanians lined up on the Jerusalem Plank Road. Selecting four regiments as a reserve, including two from Harriman's Brigade, Hartranft used the 207th Pennsylvania and 38th Wisconsin in his front line. The men moved out in the faint light, Hartranft proudly writing how seven regiments began the attack "in the most handsome and gallant manner."[206]

Griffin's brigade was not far behind the three Maine companies. The level of conquest early in the assault impressed eyewitnesses. The 179th New York performed well, gaining parts of the Confederate line, as Hartranft's men were expanding their breach to the right. Entering a small battery near Fort Mahone, the 6th New Hampshire soon had possession of some big guns. Turning the cannons on the main Confederate line, the dedicated soldiers starting firing. "Though quite effective," the unit's historian remembered, he admitted to a rate of fire that was "a little slow."[207]

Even with their waning fortune, Confederates put up tough resistance, most effective on Potter's left. The defenders used the protective improvements made during the previous months. An officer in the 43rd North Carolina described fighting that pressed Potter's force. Defenders battled "at close quarters, driving them from traverse to traverse, sometimes in a hand-to-hand fight." Recapturing parts of the line, then able to return to Fort Mahone while seizing Ninth Corps prisoners, Confederates were determined to resist.[208]

Potter became one of the day's casualties, prompting Griffin to take command of the two brigades. Curtin's men also encountered trouble. The advance was not one bold rush, with some men going prone for a time. Charles Read took a piece of Confederate shell. As he wrote later in the month, "I have been in one good fight and got a wound in the hip, but I was not running." Instead, "I was lying down behind some dirt and firing at them Rebs, and a shell burst over me." One of the projectiles "came down and struck me right on the hip, and I tell you it made me sing."[209]

Those lost in Curtin's Brigade included Col. George Gowen, commander of the 48th Pennsylvania, who helped tear away abatis during the initial charge. Early on, cannon fire hit Gowen "carrying away the half of his face, killing him instantly." Considered "one gallantly beloved," an officer suggested of Gowen, "all who knew his splendid worth and promising future were grieved."[210]

Up the line, men across Hartranft's advance also felt the fury of the embattled Confederates. The 38th Wisconsin historian wrote, "The enemy is awake now, and fully realizes the danger that is coming." With a line of readied muskets, the Southerners "trained upon our column," sending "a storm of death." Hearing and seeing the same opposing troops, Colonel Mathews reported, "A murderous fire of grape, canister, and shell from the enemy had thus far met us at every step."[211]

Headquarters did not order further attacks along the Ninth Corps front. Parke still made timely use of his reserve regiments to sustain the day's gains. Additionally, a brigade of reinforcements from the Sixth Corps buttressed Hartranft's left. Griffin also gained the services of several regiments in what was deemed an Independent Brigade, under Parke's direct control from their City Point base.[212]

The Ninth Corps advance, along with other breaks in the lines, led Confederates to abandon Petersburg that evening. As the 38th Wisconsin's historian illustrated, "All night the troops lay in the captured works and witnessed the conflagration caused by the cotton and tobacco burnt by the enemy to prevent its falling into our hands." He also saw "stupendous columns of fire" falling back to earth, blowing up magazines in the city. Confederate boats set ablaze on the Appomattox added to the feeling that the siege of Petersburg seemed over.[213]

After a harrowing day, the clock would strike midnight to begin April 3, 1865. The last day of combat for the Ninth Corps had ended. Griffin's Brigade sustained the most casualties under Parke on April 2. Finally, 11 bloody months ended for the 17th Vermont. Fifteen members of the regiment were mortally wounded in their last charge. One of the Green Mountain men to lose his life was Cassius Ellsworth, shot in the left leg. The field amputation led to a transfer to a hospital in Alexandria, where Ellsworth died in mid-May. He would be like one in eight of his comrades who enlisted in the regiment, killed or mortally wounded in action.

Griffin wrote that his brigade lost 742 men in about fifteen minutes. Parke's total casualties in the previous few days exceeded 1,700, including 255 killed in action, a hefty toll for the final round of combat for a storied infantry corps. Across 1865, the Ninth Corps suffered nearly 3,000 casualties, most of those occurring in their final nine days of active operations.[214]

Conclusion: The Fate of Heroes

Ninth Corps men pushed into Petersburg on April 3. Elements of Willcox's Division planted flags on the courthouse and other buildings. Col. Ralph Ely accepted the surrender of the city, with some troops assisting to extinguish fires. Willcox's men garrisoned the streets. Finding a jail full of people, "mainly negroes," as Byron Cutcheon noted, troops from his 20th Michigan "broke the locks on the doors and let out all the inmates," taking no worry about the type of crime for which they were confined.[1]

The rest of the Ninth Corps followed the Sixth Corps out of Petersburg. Parke reported camping about 10 miles from the conquered city on the night of April 3. Five days later, Hartranft's men reached Nottoway Court House, nearly 40 miles west of Petersburg. Parke's troops were then spread out in a line stretching from Farmville, northwest of Nottoway Court House, most of the way back to Petersburg.[2]

Stephen Minot Weld, a prisoner since the Crater, returned to the 56th Massachusetts on April 4. After being paroled, he had been home since late 1864. Formally exchanged with a Confederate officer, Weld reached Nottaway Court House on April 7. He wrote home the next day regarding the loss of a treasured horse. Like so many fine animals during the war, the equine could not hold up to the strain of constant work. "I feel quite badly at losing her," Weld concluded.[3]

Several miles beyond the western terminus of the Ninth Corps, Lee surrendered the Army of Northern Virginia on April 9. When news of the end arrived, an Ocean State veteran happily wrote, "The enthusiasm was immense," prompting "cheer upon cheer." On that day, the 51st Pennsylvania spread out 2 miles to keep an eye on railroad tracks. Cars full of Confederate prisoners moved along frequently.[4]

William T. Sherman's Union army was still hunting Confederates in North Carolina. Simon Griffin wrote of the possibility that the Ninth Corps would head back to where the war began for so many of the men. Instead, they waited in central Virginia for several days. William Boston, 20th Michigan, recorded the sad news of President Lincoln's assassination, as well as the dull life of a postwar soldier. The march back to Petersburg began on April 20. The last major move for the Ninth Corps included time on the water, with the trip around Fortress Monroe likely bringing back three-year-old memories for the most experienced veterans. By the 27th, many Ninth Corps men were in Alexandria. The 29th Massachusetts, assigned as provost guard for Willcox's Division, camped in Washington.[5]

For some reason, the army moved more men to Virginia. Sick at home, William King, 17th Vermont, was abruptly recalled to his unit. "It seems that don't now one done care whether a man is sick or not," he wrote his wife before leaving Vermont on April 5. In May, King contracted smallpox, dying at an Alexandria hospital. The widow received a letter from a surgeon, "He was conscious of approaching death—said he was going home—that he should like to see his little boy before he died."[6]

Four weeks after the conquest of Petersburg, Charles Read wrote friends from Alexandria. With the Confederates defeated, soldiers still had to persevere against another old foe: rain. Read heard "the fellows holler in the night" due to the downpours, which inundated several tents. Of his fate as a soldier, Read seemed fatalistic; the timing of the return home would be decided elsewhere. "I am about as bad as a fish with a hook in his mouth," he bemused, "pulled around until someone takes me off the hook."[7]

John Barber, 7th Rhode Island, wondered about the purpose of keeping so many soldiers in the ranks. By mid-May, while stationed in Alexandria, he wrote home, "We are still lying here doing nothing." Soldiers without an enemy, men across the Ninth Corps engaged in typical chores. As the regimental history of the 45th Pennsylvania noted,

"Dress parades, battalion and company drills, inspections, reviews and so forth were kept up right along to remind us that we still belonged to Uncle Sam."[8]

Ninth Corps men remained for the Grand Review, a two-day parade through Washington in late May. The final march for Burnside's Boys proved quite memorable, with exceptionally good weather. A proud Pennsylvanian recalled, "The military display was something to be remembered a life time." Happy to see his former colonel a brevet major general, the 6th New Hampshire's historian witnessed Simon Griffin and his horse "covered with wreaths and garlands of flowers presented by the ladies and other admiring friends."[9]

Regiments finally went home, sometimes weeks after the Grand Review. Three hundred and fifty men in the 58th Massachusetts headed to Boston on July 15. Did the men feel that fifteen years or only the actual fifteen months had passed since the opening of their campaigning life? With the 56th and 57th Bay State regiments, the survivors in the 58th had endured the impossible. The three outfits combined for 466 killed or mortally wounded from the Wilderness through early April 1865, nearly 15 percent of those who enlisted.[10]

Seven other units joined the 57th Massachusetts in the group of Ninth Corps regiments with at least two hundred members killed or mortally wounded in action. With costly service that began in South Carolina, the 45th Pennsylvania topped the list with 227 soldiers losing their lives to battle wounds. The distinguished unit's costliest day occurred at South Mountain, followed closely by the brave assault near Cold Harbor. The 14th New York Heavy Artillery was the Ninth Corps unit second in the number of soldiers' lives lost in battle.[11]

Survivors found a way to move on and build lives that would never be the same. *William Bartlett* remained a prisoner for months after the Crater. He returned to field duty, receiving a brevet major generalship in March 1865. Bartlett lived in the South for a time, managing Tredegar Iron Works in Richmond. Only thirty-six years old, Bartlett's life ended from tuberculosis near the end of 1876. Born the year of her father's death, Edith Bartlett, the last of the general's four children, lived until 1959.[12]

Postwar life for *Samuel Benjamin* proved far too short. Remaining a soldier after convalescence from his Spotsylvania wound, Benjamin taught math at West Point for a year before heading to California. Other assignments included Washington, DC, and Arizona. He rose to become an assistant adjutant general, dying at the age of forty-seven in New York.[13]

Ambrose Burnside, the Founding Father of the Ninth Corps, pursued business interests and politics after resigning his army commission in early 1865. His most notable postwar achievements were winning elective offices in Rhode Island. He served as governor for two years, then later as a United States senator. Burnside died of a heart attack in Providence while a member of the Senate. Buried in the capital of the Ocean State, Burnside was fifty-seven.[14]

Decatur Dorsey got married in Baltimore soon after his 39th United States Colored Troops mustered out. Living in New Jersey in his later years, Dorsey felt many aches and pains from his military experience. Without receiving financial assistance from the government he saved, Dorsey was plagued by malaria and typhoid. Close to the end of his life, a notary public supported Dorsey's claim for an invalid pension by writing the American hero was "reputable and entitled to credit." Dorsey died in Hoboken on July 11, 1891. His widow, with limited means, applied for a pension soon after Dorsey's death. The only African American Medal of Honor recipient at the Crater, Dorsey rests at Flower Hill Cemetery, North Bergen, New Jersey.[15]

Taking division command in the Army of the James near the end of 1864, *Edward Ferrero* escaped notable damage to his career after the Crater, gaining a major general brevet. He left the army in August 1865, returning to a life as dancing instructor and ballroom manager. Ferrero received more historical respect for his nonmilitary activities than his long time with the Ninth Corps. At the age of sixty-eight, he died in New York City near the end of the nineteenth century.[16]

Simon Griffin spent life in Texas and back in his beloved New Hampshire. The excellent military leader authored books about two towns in the Granite State. He also spent multiple terms in the New Hampshire legislature. Griffin died in Keene at the age of seventy-seven on January 14, 1902.[17]

Without a great historical reputation, Edward Ferrero would receive the brevet rank of major general. He returned to his career as a dance instructor after the Civil War. LIBRARY OF CONGRESS

John Hartranft served as the warden overseeing those detained for the assassination of President Lincoln. Hartranft spent six years as governor of Pennsylvania. He was also active in the Grand Army of the Republic, a fraternal organization of Civil War veterans. For much of the first half of the 1880s, Hartranft was the collector at the Port of Philadelphia while also holding the rank of major general in Pennsylvania's militia. Hartranft died at the age of fifty-eight.[18]

Samuel Haynes, an officer in the 45th Pennsylvania, found work in the railroad industry. Living in Oil City, Pennsylvania, for the last two decades of his life, Haynes, like many of his fellow veterans, served his community, sometimes in elective capacity. A churchgoer and Mason, Haynes earned the status as "one of the most upright men" in his town. He died of cancer in 1899, aged sixty-seven.[19]

As with many survivors of the Civil War, existence proved difficult for *Daniel Leasure*. His Roundhead son lost his life at the Crater. Although limited as a physician because of the pains from Civil War service, Leasure worked in the medical field in Pittsburgh, Pennsylvania. Losing a wife in 1867, Leasure remarried in 1870, then moved to Minnesota. In 1882, the dedicated patriot finally received a small pension, based on his Second Bull Run wound. When Leasure died soon after, his widow excoriated the army bureaucracy for being so slow to recognize the brave officer's plight. Mrs. Leasure received a full widow's pension, but not until Congress acted in 1890.[20]

Robert Potter rebounded from his wound on April 2, 1865, his third of the war. Gaining a major generalship, the widower remarried later in the year, leaving the army in January 1866. He briefly held command of a military district of two Northern states, then labored greatly for three years while presiding over the bankruptcy of a railroad. Spending four years in England, the Civil War hero enjoyed "following the hounds and maintaining, by his generous hospitality, the credit of his native land and of a true American gentleman." Returning to the United States in 1873, Potter could sometimes be found in the national capital, keeping his congressman brother company. While enjoying a budding social life, Potter still suffered greatly from wounds. A bust in Albany lists the twenty-seven engagements Potter participated in, nearly a complete albeit short history of the Ninth Corps. He died in early 1887, not yet fifty-eight years old.[21]

Oscar Robinson provided gifts to posterity with his extensive writings while in the 9th New Hampshire. Delaying his schooling to enlist, Robinson graduated from Dartmouth College in 1869. Then moving to Albany, New York, Robinson became a respected educator, rising to principal of Albany High School from 1886 until his death in 1911. At a service to honor their dedicated leader, one person described Robinson as "Teacher and Friend." Honoring his commitment to the Union and teaching, a memorialist said of Robinson, "Not a man in this city has had the opportunity to do so much that would tell on the character and love of country. And no man could have served his generation to better purpose."[22]

Samuel Sturgis stayed in the Western Theater after the Ninth Corps returned east in 1864. Sturgis became colonel of the 7th United States Cavalry in 1869, spending years on the Great Plains. Fate was kind by placing Sturgis on recruiting duty in St. Louis when his second-in-command, Lt. Col. George Armstrong Custer, took the regiment to Little Big Horn in June 1876. Serving in the army for another decade, Sturgis died in 1879 in St. Paul, Minnesota.[23]

Before mustering out in July 1865, *Stephen Minot Weld* served as a brigade commander in Washington. He became a brevet brigadier general the next year, not yet twenty-four years old. Weld struggled financially in the aftermath of his father's death in 1867. He transcended difficulties, becoming quite wealthy as a textile manufacturer. A widower in 1898, Weld remarried in 1904. An interest in plants led to Weld's leadership of the Massachusetts Horticultural Society. Later residing in Florida, Weld died in 1920.[24]

With great personal courage, *Edward Wild* assisted with the recruitment of United States Colored Troops after he recuperated from his South Mountain wound. Taking the field, Wild continued with his firm devotion to ending slavery and saving the Union. He led a brigade and division in the Army of the James, leaving the military in 1866. Possessed with a keen interest in travel, Wild became a silver miner in North and South America. Aged sixty-six, he died and was buried in Columbia in 1891.[25]

Orlando Willcox never built a stellar historical reputation through long service to the Ninth Corps. Remaining in the army, Willcox held some administrative posts, as well as leadership of infantry regiments when he reverted to the permanent rank of colonel. He retired less than a year after receiving promotion to brigadier general in 1886. Willcox moved to Canada, then used a pseudonym to publish several novels. He died in 1907 at the age of eighty-four.[26]

Notes

Preface

1. H. R. Norton, "The Ninth Corps," *National Tribune*, March 3, 1904; Oscar Robinson Papers, Dartmouth College; William F. Fox, *Regimental Losses in the American Civil War, 1861–1865* (Albany, NY: Brandow Printing Company, 1889), 81.

Introduction

1. Ivan Musicant, *Divided Waters: The Naval History of the Civil War* (Edison, NJ: Castle Books, 2000), 76–89; Daniel Ammen, *The Navy in the Civil War, Vol. 2—The Atlantic Coast* (New York, NY: Charles Scribner's Sons, 1883), vi–vii, 163. Brig. Gen. Thomas Sherman was not related to the more famous William T. Sherman.
2. William Marvel, *Burnside* (Chapel Hill: University of North Carolina Press, 1991), 3–32.
3. Ezra J. Warner, *Generals in Blue: Lives of the Union Commanders* (Baton Rouge: Louisiana State University Press, 1992), 150–51; John H. Eicher and David J. Eicher, *Civil War High Commands* (Stanford: Stanford University Press, 2001), 233.
4. *Public Services of Brvt. Maj. Gen. John F. Hartranft, Union Candidate for Auditor General* (Norristown, PA: Wills, Fredell & Jenkins, 1865), 1–5.
5. George W. Cullum, *Biographical Register of the Officers and Graduates of the U.S. Military Academy at West Point, N. Y.*, Vol. 2 (Boston, MA: Houghton, Mifflin and Company, 1891), 370–71; Warner, *Generals in Blue*, 359–60.
6. William F. McConnell, *Remember Reno: A Biography of Major General Jesse Lee Reno* (Shippensburg, PA: White Mane Publishing, 1996), 4–41; Warner, *Generals in Blue*, 394–95; Eicher and Eicher, *High Commands*, 449.
7. Charles F. Walcott, *History of the Twenty-First Regiment Massachusetts Volunteers in the War for the Preservation of the Union* (Boston, MA: Houghton, Mifflin and Company, 1882), 17.
8. Warner, *Generals in Blue*, 409; U.S. War Department, *The War of the Rebellion: A Compilation of the Official Records of the Union and Confederate Armies*, 128 vols. (Washington: U.S. Gov't Printing Office, 1880–1901), Vol. 2, 387, 400.
9. Warner, *Generals in Blue*, 475; Eicher and Eicher, *High Commands*, 510; Cullum, *Biographical Register, Vol. 1*, 729–32; David A. Welker, *Tempest at Ox Hill: The Battle of Chantilly* (Cambridge, MA: Da Capo Press, 2002), 60–75.

10. Walcott, *History of the Twenty-First Regiment*, 1–2; 21st Massachusetts Regimental Correspondence, Massachusetts State Archives, Boston.

11. Wells B. Fox, *What I Remember of the Great Rebellion* (Lansing, MI: Darius D. Thorp, 1892), 13–16; https://www.findagrave.com/memorial/30028530/william-m_-fenton; George M. Blackburn, ed., *The Diary of Captain Ralph Ely of the Eighth Michigan Infantry* (Mount Pleasant: Central Michigan University Press, 1965), 15–19.

12. Lyman Jackson, *History of the Sixth New Hampshire Regiment in the War for the Union* (Concord, NH: Republican Press Association, 1891), 1–13.

13. Allen D. Albert, ed., *History of the Forty-Fifth Regiment Pennsylvania Veteran Volunteer Infantry, 1861–1865* (Williamsport, PA: Grit Publishing Company, 1912), 13–22.

14. Lewis Crater, *History of the Fiftieth Regiment, Penna. Vet. Vols., 1861–1865* (Reading, PA: Coleman Printing House, 1884), 3–4.

15. *OR*, Vol. 5, 35.

16. Marvel, *Burnside*, 59; Walcott, *History of the Twenty-First*, 35–36; Thomas H. Parker, *History of the 51st Regiment of P. V and V. V.* (Philadelphia, PA: King & Baird, 1869), 78–79; *OR*, Vol. 9, 74, 80; Marvel, *Burnside*, 60–61; Matthew J. Graham, *The Ninth Regiment New York Volunteers (Hawkins Zouaves)* (New York: F. P. Coby, 1900), 147–48; Ambrose E. Burnside, "The Burnside Expedition," *Personal Narratives of the Events in the War of the Rebellion, Being Papers Read before the Rhode Island Soldiers and Sailors Historical Society*, No. 6, 2nd Series (Providence, RI: N. Bangs Williams & Company, 1882), 26; Musicant, *Divided Waters*, 130–33; Julia Jenkins Morton, *Trusting to Luck: Ambrose E. Burnside and the American Civil War*, PhD dissertation, Kent State University, August 1992, 167–88.

17. William Stillwell Chace Papers, Rhode Island Historical Society.

18. Burnside, "The Burnside Expedition," 28; *OR*, Vol. 9, 221, 224, 229.

19. McConnell, *Remember Reno*, 51; *OR*, Vol. 9, 221; Marvel, *Burnside*, 73.

20. George H. Allen, *Forty-Six Months with the Fourth R. I. Volunteers in the War of 1861 to 1865* (Providence, RI: J. A. & R. A. Reid, 1887), 93–94; *OR*, Vol. 9, 238; Augustus Woodbury, *Major General Ambrose E. Burnside and the Ninth Corps* (Providence, RI: Sidney S. Rider and Brother, 1867), 57–65.

21. *OR*, Vol. 9, 247; Walter Clark, ed., *Histories of the Several Regiments and Battalions from North Carolina in the Great War, 1861–'65*, II (Goldsboro, NC: Nash Brothers, 1901), 544.

22. Reel 18, McClellan Papers, Library of Congress; *OR*, Vol. 9, 207.

23. *OR*, Vol. 14, 9–10; Fox, *What I Remember*, 18.

24. Blackburn, ed., *The Diary*, 34–35; *OR*, Vol. 14, 6–9.

25. Patrick Brennan, *Secessionville: Assault on Charleston* (Campbell, CA: Savas Publishing Company, 1996); Fox, *Regimental Losses*, 386; Hazard Stevens, *The Life of Isaac Ingalls Stevens*, Vol. II (Boston, MA: Houghton, Mifflin and Company, 1900), 399–415.

26. Brian K. Burton, *Extraordinary Circumstances: The Seven Days Battles* (Bloomington: Indiana University Press, 2001).

27. *OR*, Vol. 9, 404–10, and Vol. 11, III, 290.

28. Hosea Towne Papers, New Hampshire Historical Society.

29. *OR*, Vol. 9, 398–99; Reels 24 and 25, McClellan Papers, LOC; Marvel, *Burnside*, 92–93, 99; Daniel Read Larned Papers, LOC.

30. Reel 29, McClellan Papers, LOC.

31. Reel 3, Edwin McMasters Stanton Papers, LOC.

32. *OR*, Vol 14, 363; Albert, *History of the Forty-Fifth*, 33.

33. *OR*, Vol 11, III, 322.

34. Woodbury, *Burnside and the Ninth Corps*, 101–3.

35. Marvel, *Burnside*, 98–100; Stephen W. Sears, ed., *The Civil War Papers of George B. McClellan: Selected Correspondence* (Cambridge, MA: Da Capo Press, 1992), 361–62; Roy P. Basler, *The Collected Works of Abraham Lincoln*, Vol. V (New Brunswick, NJ: Rutgers University Press, 1953), 334; *OR*, Vol 11, III, 333.

PART ONE

1. Jackson, *History of the Sixth*, 59; George Upton Papers, NHHS.

2. Oliver Christian Bosbyshell, *The 48th in the War* (Philadelphia: Avil Printing Company, 1895), 52–53.

3. Warner, *Generals in Blue*, 339–40; Eicher and Eicher, *High Commands*, 403.

4. James Madison Stone, *Personal Recollections of the Civil War* (Boston: self-published, 1918), 53; Parker, *History of the 51st*, 186–88.

5. Allen, *Forty-Six Months*, 123–24.

6. Stevens, *The Life*, 422–23; Wiliam Lusk, *War Letters of William Thompson Lusk* (New York: self-published, 1906), 163; William Todd, *The Seventy-Ninth Highlanders: New York Volunteers in the War of the Rebellion* (Albany: Brandow, Barton & Co., 1886), 176.

7. Blackburn, *The Diary*, 39; Sandy Barnard, ed., *Campaigning with the Irish Brigade: Pvt. John Ryan, 28th Massachusetts* (Terre Haute, IN: AST Press, Terre, 2001), 52; Ernest Mettendorf, *Between Triumph and Disaster: The History of the 46th New York Infantry, 1861–1865* (Eden, NY: self-published, 2012), 7, 20–21.

8. Upton Papers, NHHS.

9. Campbell Family Papers, South Carolina Department of Archives and History.

10. Allen, *Forty-Six Months*, 124–29; General Orders No. 6, January 6, 1863, Court Martial of Pvt. Edwin Gallagher, 4th Rhode Island records, RIHS; https://www.findagrave.com/memorial/12087501/william-henry_peck-steere.

11. Walcott, *History of the Twenty-First*, 123.

12. Peter Cozzens, *General John Pope: A Life for the Nation* (Urbana: University of Illinois Press, 2000), 83–88; *OR*, Vol. 12, III, 521.

13. Marvel, *Burnside*, 99–100; Stephen W. Sears, *George B. McClellan: The Young Napoleon* (Cambridge: Da Capo Press, 1999), 239–42; Stephen W. Sears, *To the Gates of Richmond: The Peninsula Campaign* (Boston: Houghton Mifflin, 1992), 351–53; Morton, *Trusting to Luck*, 245–46.

14. *OR*, Vol. 11, I, 76–77 and Vol. 12, III, 523–24.

15. *OR*, Vol. 11, I, 80–81; Sears, *Civil War Papers*, 383–85.

16. *OR*, Vol. 12, III, 528–29; Blackburn, *The Diary*, 40; Samuel P. Bates, *A Brief History of the One Hundredth Regiment* (New Castle, PA: W. B. Thomas, 1884), 10; Bosbyshell,

The 48th, 56; Joseph Gould, *The Story of the Forty-Eighth* (Slocum Company, 1908), 62; Parker, *History of the 51st*, 191.

17. *OR*, Vol. 12, III, 531–32, 547; Woodbury, *Burnside and the Ninth Corps*, 105.

18. Stone, *Personal Recollections*, 54; Jackson, *History of the Sixth*, 63; Upton Letters, NHHS.

19. Charles F. Johnson, *The Long Roll* (East Aurora, NY: Roycrofters, 1911), 170.

20. Blackburn, *The Diary*, 40–41.

21. Reel 29, McClellan Papers, LOC.

22. Sears, *Civil War Papers*, 389.

23. Ben Perley Poore, *The Life and Public Services of Ambrose E. Burnside, Soldier—Citizen—Statesman* (Providence: J. A. & R. A. Reid, 1882), 155.

24. Cozzens, *General John Pope*, 93–97; John J. Hennessy, *Return to Bull Run: The Campaign and Battle of Second Manassas* (New York: Simon & Schuster, 1993), 27–30; Edwin C. Fishel, *The Secret War for the Union: The Untold Story of Military Intelligence in the Civil War* (Boston: Houghton Mifflin, 1996), 188–89; *OR*, Vol. 12, III, 553–54.

25. *OR*, Vol. 12, III, 565–66.

26. 8th Massachusetts Battery correspondence, MSA.

27. Todd, *The Seventy-Ninth*, 182–83; Cullum, *Biographical Register*, Vol. II, 781.

28. Stevens, *The Life*, 425; Eicher and Eicher, *High Commands*, 231.

29. Bosbyshell, *The 48th*, 57; Johnson, *The Long Roll*, 171; Gould, *The Story*, 62–63; Jackson, *History of the Sixth*, 65.

30. Mettendorf, *Between Triumph and Disaster*, 22; Belcher Diary, McCreery-Fenton family papers, Bentley Historical Library, University of Michigan; *OR*, Vol. 12, II, 545.

31. Bosbyshell, *The 48th*, 59; Parker, *History of the 51st*, 201.

32. *OR*, Vol. 12, III, 572, 574.

33. Blackburn, *The Diary*, 40–42.

34. J. H. E. Whitney, *The Hawkins Zouaves: Their Battles and Marches* (New York: self-published, 1866), 120–22; Graham, *The Ninth Regiment*, 244–46.

35. Eileen Mae Knapp Patch, ed., *This from George: The Civil War Letters of Sergeant George Magusta Englis* (Binghamton: Broome County Historical Society, 2001), 37–38.

36. Albert, ed., *History of the Forty-Fifth*, 251.

37. *OR*, Vol. 12, III, 568–69, 572; Marvel, *Burnside*, 103–4.

38. Lusk, *War Letters*, 176–78.

39. Walcott, *History of the Twenty-First*, 128; McConnell, *Remember Reno*, 59; Hennessy, *Return to Bull Run*, 34–42; Fishel, *The Secret War*, 194, 207–8.

40. Stevens, *The Life*, 427.

41. Charles A. Cuffel, *History of Durell's Battery in the Civil War, Independent Battery D, Pennsylvania Volunteer Artillery* (Philadelphia: Craig, Finely, and Co., 1903), 53.

42. *OR*, Vol. 12, III, 589–90, and II, 544; Edward G. Longacre, *General John Buford: A Military Biography* (Cambridge: Da Capo Press, 1995), 93–94.

43. *OR*, Vol. 12, III, 576; Hennessy, *Return to Bull Run*, 42–44.

44. Gould, *The Story*, 63; Daniel Leasure, "Personal Observations and Experiences in the Pope Campaign in Virginia," Military Order of the Loyal Legion of the United

States, Minnesota Commandery, *Glimpses of the Nation's Struggle* (St. Paul: St. Paul Book and Stationary Company, 1887), 144.

45. Cozzens, *General John Pope*, 100–2; Hennessy, *Return to Bull Run*, 51–54; *OR*, Vol. 12, III, 591–93.

46. Todd, *The Seventy-Ninth*, 185.

47. Jackson, *History of the Sixth*, 66–67; Crater, *History of the Fiftieth*, 25; Gould, *The Story*, 63; Walcott, *History of the Twenty-First*, 131–34; Parker, *History of the 51st*, 202–3.

48. Hennessy, *Return to Bull Run*, 56–70.

49. Marvel, *Burnside*, 104–6; *OR*, Vol. 12, III, 590, 593–94, 606.

50. *OR*, Vol. 12, III, 602–3, 609–10; Todd, *The Seventy-Ninth*, 186–87; Stevens, *The Life*, 428; Longacre, *General John Buford*, 95–96.

51. *OR*, Vol. 12, III, 611–13.

52. Hennessy, *Return to Bull Run*, 92–95.

53. Curt Anders, *Henry Halleck's War: A Fresh Look at Lincoln's Controversial General-in-Chief* (Carmel, IN: Guild Press, 2000), 177–79, 181; Cozzens, *General John Pope*, 103–4; Hennessy, *Return to Bull Run*, 107–11.

54. Stevens, *The Life*, 430; Jackson, *History of the Sixth*, 68–69; Bosbyshell, *The 48th*, 62–63; Mettendorf, *Between Triumph and Disaster*, 23–24; Belcher Diary, UM; Leasure, "Personal Observations," 145.

55. Walcott, *History of the Twenty-First*, 139–40.

56. Cullum, *Biographical Register*, Vol. II, 262, 268; *OR*, Vol. 12, III, 665; Hennessy, *Return to Bull Run*, 100–101.

57. Belcher Diary, UM.

58. Cozzens, *General John Pope*, 111–26; Hennessy, *Return to Bull Run*, 117–18; Anders, *Halleck's War*, 193–200.

59. Jackson, *History of the Sixth*, 69–70; Belcher Diary, UM; Gould, *The Story*, 65–66; Bosbyshell, *The 48th*, 64; Walcott, *History of the Twenty-First*, 140.

60. James I. Robertson, Jr., *Stonewall Jackson: The Man, the Soldier, the Legend* (New York: Macmillan Publishing, 1997), 554–57; Reel 30, McClellan Papers, LOC; Herman Haupt, *Reminiscences of General Herman Haupt* (Milwaukee: Wright & Joys, 1901), 99–100.

61. *OR*, Vol. 12, III, 699–703.

62. *OR*, Vol. 12, III, 704; Hennessy, *Return to Bull Run*, 135–37; McConnell, *Remember Reno*, 60–61; Fishel, *The Secret War*, 199–202.

63. *OR*, Vol. 12, II, 70–72, and III, 717; Hennessy, *Return to Bull Run*, 161–64; Cozzens, *General John Pope*, 128–32; Robertson, Jr., *Stonewall*, 559–61.

64. Walcott, *History of the Twenty-First*, 141.

65. Bates, *A Brief History*, 11; Belcher Diary, UM; Todd, *The Seventy-Ninth*, 191; Parker, *History of the 51st*, 210; Stevens, *The Life of Isaac Ingalls Stevens*, 441–42; Robertson, Jr., *Stonewall*, 561–63; Jackson, *History of the Sixth*, 71–72.

66. *OR*, Vol. 12, II, 74–76; Hennessy, *Return to Bull Run*, 195–96; Cozzens, *General John Pope*, 138–40.

67. Leasure, "Personal Observations," 150; Mettendorf, *Between Triumph and Disaster*, 25.

68. Jackson, *History of the Sixth*, 77–78; Cuffel, *History*, 64.

69. Walcott, *History of the Twenty-First*, 141–42; Stone, *Personal Recollections*, 64; Belcher Diary, UM.

70. Todd, *The Seventy-Ninth*, 197; Hennessy, *Return to Bull Run*, 243–44.

71. Leasure, "Personal Observations," 151.

72. Parker, *History of the 51st*, 210–11.

73. Robertson, Jr., *Stonewall*, 564–66.

74. Hennessy, *Return to Bull Run*, 224–39; Cozzens, *General John Pope*, 138–45; Fishel, *The Secret War*, 200–204.

75. Todd, *The Seventy-Ninth*, 199.

76. William Mark McKnight, *Blue Bonnets O'er the Border: The 79th New York Cameron Highlanders* (Shippensburg, PA: White Mane Books, 1998), 65–66; OR, Vol. 12, II, 261–62; Hennessy, *Return to Bull Run*, 244–58.

77. Jackson, *History of the Sixth*, 78–79.

78. Bosbyshell, *The 48th*, 65.

79. Cecil D. Eby, Jr., ed., *A Virginia Yankee in the Civil War: The Diaries of David Hunter Strother* (Chapel Hill: University of North Carolina Press, 1961), 93.

80. Gould, *The Story*, 65–66; https://www.findagrave.com/memorial/60397372/joseph -h_-hoskings.

81. Jackson, *History of the Sixth*, 80; Hennessy, *Return to Bull Run*, 259–60.

82. Towne Papers, NHHS; Augustus D. Ayling, *Revised Register of the Soldiers and Sailors of New Hampshire in the War of the Rebellion, 1861–1866* (Concord: Ira C. Evans, 1895), 322.

83. Jackson, *History of the Sixth*, 90.

84. OR, Vol. 12, II, 545; James Fitz James Caldwell, *The History of a Brigade of South Carolinians* (Bedford, MA: Applewood Books, 1866), 35–36.

85. W. A. McClendon, *Recollections of War Times* (Montgomery: Paragon Press, 1909), 111–12; OR, Vol. 12, II, 545.

86. G. W. Nichols, *A Soldier's Story of His Regiment* (privately printed, 1898), 49; Jubal Anderson Early, *Autobiographical Sketch and Narrative of the War between the States* (Philadelphia: J. B. Lippincott, 1912), 124.

87. OR, Vol. 12, II, 545; Gould, *The Story*, 66–67.

88. Jackson, *History of the Sixth*, 80–81.

89. Bosbyshell, *The 48th*, 66–67; Upton Letters, NHHS; OR, Vol. 12, II, 545.

90. Theodore Nutting Papers, NHHS.

91. Bosbyshell, *The 48th*, 67; Hennessy, *Return to Bull Run*, 267.

92. Cuffel, *History*, 64.

93. OR, Vol. 12, II, 261–62; Upton Letters, NHHS.

94. Jackson, *History of the Sixth*, 82–83; https://www.findagrave.com/memorial/1825 3949/george-h_-muchmore.

95. Gould, *The Story*, 68.

96. Stevens, *The Life*, 457–58; Mettendorf, *Between Triumph and Disaster*, 28–29; Leasure, "Personal Observations," 154–56.

97. Stevens, *The Life*, 458; Gilbert Adams Hays, *Under the Red Patch: Story of the Sixty Third Regiment Pennsylvania Volunteers, 1861–1864* (Pittsburgh: Regimental Association, 1908), 150–51; Bates, *A Brief History*, 13–14.

98. Mettendorf, *Between Triumph and Disaster*, 29–30; https://dmna.ny.gov/historic/reghist/civil/rosters/Infantry/46th_Infantry_CW_Roster.pdf.

99. Parker, *History of the 51st*, 210–12.

100. Walcott, *History of the Twenty-First*, 143–45; Stone, *Personal Recollections*, 65–66.

101. https://www.findagrave.com/memorial/8560061/thomas-sloan-bell.

102. Mettendorf, *Between Triumph and Disaster*, 30; Jackson, *History of the Sixth*, 83–84; Bosbyshell, *The 48th*, 67.

103. Stevens, *The Life*, 461.

104. Belcher Diary, UM; Todd, *The Seventy-Ninth*, 201–2; Stevens, *The Life*, 462; Hennessy, *Return to Bull Run*, 321–22; https://dmna.ny.gov/historic/reghist/civil/rosters/Infantry/79th_Infantry_CW_Roster.pdf.

105. Cuffel, *History*, 65; Eicher and Eicher, *High Commands*, 231.

106. Hennessy, *Return to Bull Run*, 362–406; Scott C. Patchan, *Second Manassas: Longstreet's Attack and the Struggle for Chinn Ridge* (Washington: Potomac Books, 2011), 18–83.

107. https://www.findagrave.com/memorial/94439850/michael-j-donnelly; Barnard, ed., *Campaigning*, 55–56.

108. Belcher Diary, UM; Crater, *History of the Fiftieth*, 27–28; Todd, *The Seventy-Ninth*, 203–5; Stevens, *The Life*, 470–74.

109. https://www.findagrave.com/memorial/134134346/charles-henry-kellogg.

110. Ira B. Goodrich, "Second Bull Run," *National Tribune*, May 4, 1893; Walcott, *History of the Twenty-First*, 147; Patchan, *Second Manassas*, 102–6; Hennessy, *Return to Bull Run*, 421–23; Parker, *History of the 51st*, 214–15.

111. Thomas T. Cooney, "Sykes' Regulars," *National Tribune*, February 9, 1893; *OR*, Vol. 12, II, 584.

112. *OR*, Vol. 12, II, 43; John Pope, "The Second Battle of Bull Run," *Battles and Leaders of the Civil War*, Vol. 2 (New York: Century Company, 1888), 474–75.

113. Marvel, *Burnside*, 107–8; *OR*, Vol. 12, III, 730–33.

114. Anders, *Henry Halleck's War*, 200–5, 210–17; *OR*, Vol. 12, III, 744–45.

115. Reel 30, McClellan Papers, LOC; Haupt, *Reminiscences*, 98–99.

116. Reel 30, McClellan Papers, LOC; Ethan Rafuse, *McClellan's War: The Failure of Moderation in the Struggle for the Union* (Bloomington: Indiana University Press, 2005), 259–72; Sears, *George B. McClellan*, 250–57; Sears, *Civil War Papers*, 420.

117. In the *Official Records*, Burnside's note shows Halleck as the recipient. The original telegram, however, where Burnside hopes for Pope's great victory, is clearly addressed to McClellan. *OR*, Vol. 12, III, 757–60; Reel 30, McClellan Papers, LOC.

118. Gould, *The Story*, 68.

119. Welker, *Tempest*, 81–107; Paul Taylor, *He Hath Loosed the Fateful Lightning: The Battle of Ox Hill (Chantilly), September 1, 1862* (Shippensburg: White Mane Books, 2003), 36–46; Hennessy, *Return to Bull Run*, 439–51.

120. Jackson, *History of the Sixth*, 87; Todd, *The Seventy-Ninth*, 208; Cuffel, *History*, 67; Parker, *History of the 51st*, 218; Walcott, *History of the Twenty-First*, 151.

121. McConnell, *Remember Reno*, 65–66; Walter H. Hebert, *Fighting Joe Hooker* (Lincoln: University of Nebraska Press, 1999), 125–26.

122. Cozzens, *General John Pope*, 187–89; *OR*, Vol. 12, III, 785; Anders, *Henry Halleck's War*, 244; Jackson, *History of the Sixth*, 87; Walcott, *History of the Twenty-First*, 152.

123. Stevens, *The Life*, 478–79.

124. *OR*, Vol. 12, II, 85.

125. Walcott, *History of the Twenty-First*, 161–62; William H. Huffman, "A Roundhead Who Was with Pope's Army at Chantilly," *National Tribune*, April 13, 1899.

126. Taylor, *Fateful Lightning*, 51; Welker, *Tempest*, 141–42; General James Longstreet, *From Manassas to Appomattox* (New York: Da Capo Press, 1992), 193.

127. Huffman, "A Roundhead"; Hennessy, *Return to Bull Run*, 448–50; Robertson, Jr., *Stonewall*, 579–80.

128. Todd, *The Seventy-Ninth*, 212.

129. Taylor, *Fateful Lightning*, 52; Welker, *Tempest*, 139–43; Todd, *The Seventy-Ninth*, 216–18.

130. Cuffel, *History*, 68; Welker, *Tempest*, 150.

131. Barnard, ed., *Campaigning*, 58; Crater, *History of the Fiftieth*, 29.

132. Lusk, *War Letters*, 180.

133. McKnight, *Blue Bonnets*, 69–71; Welker, *Tempest*, 159–62; https://www.28thmass.org/letters.htm.

134. Robertson, Jr., *Stonewall*, 580; Clark, ed., *Histories of the Several Regiments*, Vol. II, 31, 552; Caldwell, *The History*, 39; *OR*, Vol. 12, II, 672.

135. Early, *Autobiographical Sketch*, 129–31.

136. Crater, *History of the Fiftieth*, 29–30; Jackson, *History of the Sixth*, 87–88.

137. Belcher Diary, UM; 8th Michigan Regimental Records, https://michiganology.org/civil-war; https://www.findagrave.com/memorial/3257526/orville-c-wheelock.

138. Parker, *History of the 51st*, 220; Gould, *The Story*, 74–75; Bosbyshell, *The 48th*, 70.

139. McClendon, *Recollections*, 123–24.

140. Stone, *Personal Recollections*, 72–73; Walcott, *History of the Twenty-First*, 162–64; Welker, *Tempest*, 164–67; Taylor, *Fateful Lightning*, 72–76; Stevens, *The Life*, 489; https://www.findagrave.com/memorial/40347035/joseph-parker-rice.

141. Todd, *The Seventy-Ninth*, 221–22; William C. Oates, *The War between the Union and the Confederacy and Its Lost Opportunities* (New York: Neale Publishing Company, 1905), 151–52.

142. McConnell, *Remember Reno*, 68; Hennessy, *Return to Bull Run*, 450.

143. *OR*, Vol. 12, II, 261–62.

144. Cuffel, *History*, 69; Parker, *History of the 51st*, 220–21; Huffman, "A Roundhead."

145. Campbell Family Papers, SCDAH.

146. Jackson, *History of the Sixth*, 90; Parker, *History of the 51st*, 221; Bosbyshell, *The 48th*, 71.

147. Reel 30, McClellan Papers, LOC.

148. *OR*, Vol. 51, I, 782.

149. Cuffel, *History*, 69.

150. Todd, *The Seventy-Ninth*, 224.

151. Stevens, *The Life*, 486.

152. Lusk, *War Letters*, 180.

153. John W. Shildt, *The Ninth Corps at Antietam* (Gaithersburg, MD: Olde Soldier Books, 1998), 20; *OR*, Vol. 12, II, 82.

154. Reel 30, McClellan Papers, LOC.

155. D. Scott Hartwig, *To Antietam Creek: The Maryland Campaign of September 1862* (Baltimore: Johns Hopkins University Press, 2012), 43–45; Rafuse, *McClellan's War*, 273–74.

156. Sears, *George B. McClellan*, 259–62; Joseph Pierro, ed., *The Maryland Campaign of September 1862: Ezra A. Carman's Definitive Study of the Union and Confederate Armies at Antietam* (New York: Routledge, 2008), 60–64; William Roscoe Thayer, *The Life and Letters of John Hay*, Vol. I (London: Constable & Co., 1915), 129; Stephen W. Sears, *Lincoln's Lieutenants: The High Command of the Army of the Potomac* (Boston: Mariner Books, 2017), 339–42; Richard Slotkin, *The Long Road to Antietam: How the Civil War Became a Revolution* (New York: Liveright Publishing, 2012), 128–36; Anders, *Henry Halleck's War*, 248; Cozzens, *General John Pope*, 193–95; Welker, *Tempest*, 223–25; Taylor, *Fateful Lightning*, 119–22.

157. *OR*, Vol. 12, III, 808–12; Sears, *Lincoln's Lieutenants*, 344; Cozzens, *General John Pope*, 196–201.

158. *OR*, Vol. 12, III, 774.

159. Marvel, *Burnside*, 108–9; Allen, *Forty-Six Months*, 130; Poore, *Life and Public Services*, 157–58; Richard Morris Letters, https://dmna.ny.gov/historic/reghist/civil/infantry/9thInf/9thInf_Letters_Morris.pdf; Johnson, *The Long Roll*, 177; Reel 30, McClellan Papers, LOC.

160. *OR*, Vol. 12, III, 793–94, 799–800.

161. Reel 30, McClellan Papers, LOC.

162. Albert, ed., *History of the Forty-Fifth*, 47, 195.

PART TWO

1. John Michael Priest, *Captain James Wren's Civil War Diary: From New Bern to Fredericksburg* (New York: Berkley Books, 1990), 77; Bosbyshell, *The 48th*, 72.

2. Marvel, *Burnside*, 110–11; Hartwig, *To Antietam Creek*, 131–32; Reel 31, McClellan Papers, LOC; *OR*, Vol. 19, II, 188–90.

3. For a general overview of the summer's recruits in the Antietam Campaign, see D. Scott Hartwig, "Who Would Not Be a Soldier: The Volunteers of '62 in the Maryland Campaign," in Gary W. Gallagher, ed., *The Antietam Campaign* (Chapel Hill: University of North Carolina Press, 1999), 143–68.

4. Eicher and Eicher, *High Commands*, 570; Warner, *Generals in Blue*, 558–59; Robert Garth Scott, ed., *Forgotten Valor: The Memoirs, Journals, and Civil War Letters of Orlando B. Willcox* (Kent, OH: Kent State University Press, 1999), 345–51. The most extensive discussion of Willcox's life before the Civil War is found in the first half of Scott's

work, an excellent and vitally important book to understanding the history and personalities of the Ninth Corps.

5. Cullum, *Biographical Register*, Vol. 2, 278–79; Warner, *Generals in Blue*, 486–87.

6. Marvel, *Burnside*, 111–12; Warner, *Generals in Blue*, 409.

7. Jacob Dolson Cox, *Military Reminiscences of the Civil War, Volume I, April 1861—November 1863* (New York: Charles Scribner's Sons, 1900), 225–47, 263–65; Reels 30 and 31, McClellan Papers, LOC.

8. Walter J. Yates, ed., *Souvenir of Excursion to Antietam and Dedication of Monuments* (New London: E. E. Darrow, 1894), 40; Shildt, *The Ninth Corps*, 46.

9. Cox, *Military Reminiscences*, 225–26; Charles Richard Williams, ed., *Diary and Letters of Rutherford Birchard Hayes*, Vol. II, 1861–1865 (New York: Kraus Reprint Co., 1971), 333.

10. Eicher and Eicher, *High Commands*, 578.

11. David Lane, *A Soldier's Diary: The Story of a Volunteer* (self-published, 1905), 5–6.

12. William Marvel, *Race of the Soil: The Ninth New Hampshire Regiment in the Civil War* (Wilmington, NC: Broadfoot Publishing Company, 1988), 1–10.

13. Chase Family Papers, NHHS.

14. George Henry Chandler Papers, NHHS; George B. Tracy Papers, Library of Virginia, Richmond; Marvel, *Race*, 18–19.

15. Brigham Family Papers, NHHS.

16. John Batchelder Bailey Papers, NHHS.

17. Regimental Association, *History of the Thirty-Fifth Regiment Massachusetts Volunteers, 1862–1865* (Boston: Mills, Knight & Co., 1884), 2–9; Eicher and Eicher, *High Commands*, 166, 568.

18. 35th Massachusetts Regimental Correspondence, Massachusetts State Archives, Boston.

19. John W. Schildt, *Roads to Antietam* (Shippensburg, PA: Burd Street Press, 1997), 24; Bradley M. Gottfried, *The Maps of Antietam: An Atlas of the Antietam (Sharpsburg) Campaign, Including the Battle of South Mountain, September 2–20, 1862* (New York: Savas Beatie, 2013), 6–9.

20. Diary of Robert Hale Ives, Jr., Box 5 folder 3, Ives-Gammell-Safe Papers, RIHS.

21. Towne Papers, NHHS.

22. Fisher A. Cleaveland Papers, Duke; B. F. Blakeslee, *History of the Sixteenth Connecticut Volunteers* (Hartford: Case, Lockwood & Brainard, 1875), 8; Lesley J. Gordon, *A Broken Regiment: The 16th Connecticut's Civil War* (Baton Rouge: LSU Press, 2014), 28.

23. Edward O. Lord, *History of the Ninth Regiment, New Hampshire Volunteers in the War of the Rebellion* (Concord: Republican Press, 1895), 42–43; Marvel, *Race*, 27–28; Daniel Emerson Hurd, "My Experiences in the Civil War," 3; Brigham Family Papers, NHHS; 9th New Hampshire Regimental File, Anitietam National Battlefield; Chandler Papers, NHHS.

24. Reel 31, McClellan Papers, LOC; Pierro, ed., *The Maryland Campaign*, 83.

25. McConnell, *Remember Reno*, 71–73; Charles Richard Williams, ed., *Diary and Letters of Rutherford Birchard Hayes*, Vol. II, 346–49.

26. Stevens, *Life of Stevens*, 476.

27. Todd, *The Seventy-Ninth*, 211–12.

28. Huffman, "A Roundhead."

29. Henry Spooner Papers, RIHS.

30. Towne Papers, NHHS; Jabez Smith Letters, Auburn University.

31. Parker, *History of the 51st*, 223.

32. Cox, *Military Reminiscences*, 266; Cuffel, *History*, 71; Harvey Henderson Diaries, New York State Library.

33. Walcott, *History of the Twenty-First*, 186; Parker, *History of the 51st*, 222; Todd, *The Seventy-Ninth*, 226–27; Crofut-Humiston Family Papers, LVA.

34. William Gilfillan Gavin, ed., *Infantryman Pettit: The Civil War Letters of Corporal Frederick Pettit* (New York: Avon Books, 1990), 6–10.

35. Cleaveland Papers, Duke.

36. Spooner Papers, RIHS.

37. Richard Henry Morris Letters, https://dmna.ny.gov/historic/reghist/civil/infantry/9thInf/9thInfMain.htm.

38. Longstreet, *From Manassas*, 200.

39. *OR*, Vol. 19, II, 234; Pierro, ed., *The Maryland Campaign*, 87.

40. *OR*, Vol. 51, 809; Brigham Family Papers, NHHS.

41. Reel 31, McClellan Papers, LOC.

42. Regimental Association, *History of the Thirty-Fifth*, 23; Allen, *Forty-Six Months*, 139.

43. Eicher and Eicher, *High Commands*, 394.

44. Hartwig, *To Antietam Creek*, 198–99; Cox, *Military Reminiscences*, 271–73; J. H. Horton and Soloman Teverbaugh, *A History of the Eleventh Regiment (Ohio Volunteer Infantry)* (Dayton: W. J. Shuey, 1866), 68–70.

45. Williams, ed., *Diary and Letters*, 352.

46. Henry R. Brinkerhoff, *History of the Thirtieth Regiment Ohio Volunteer Infantry* (Columbus: James W. Osgood, 1863), 40–41.

47. Larned Papers, LOC; Poore, *Life and Public Services*, 163–64; Woodbury, *Burnside and the Ninth Corps*, 121; Marvel, *Burnside*, 115; Reel 31, McClellan Papers, LOC.

48. Gene M. Thorp and Alexander B. Rossino, *The Tale Untwisted: George McClellan and the Discovery of Lee's Lost Orders, September 13, 1862* (El Dorado Hills, CA: Savas Beatie, 2019), 9; Blackburn, ed., *The Diary*, 41–42.

49. 89th New York Regimental File, ANBL.

50. Allen, *Forty-Six Months*, 140; Morris Letters, https://dmna.ny.gov/historic/reghist/civil/infantry/9thInf/9thInfMain.htm; Johnson, *The Long Roll*, 182–84; *OR*, Vol. 19, I, 449–50.

51. James Harrison Wilson Papers, Delaware State Archives, Dover; Eby, Jr., ed., *A Virginia Yankee*, 106; Reel 31, McClellan Papers, LOC; Thorp and Rossino, *The Tale Untwisted*, 22–24.

52. Hartwig, *To Antietam Creek*, 284–92.

53. Reel 31, McClellan Papers, LOC; Donald R. Jermann, *Antietam: The Lost Order* (Gretna, LA: Pelican Publishing, 2006), 151–55.

54. J. H. Stine, *History of the Army of the Potomac* (Washington: Gibson Bros, 1893), 177.

55. Warner, *Generals in Blue*, 159; Brian Matthew Jordan, *Unholy Sabbath: The Battle of South Mountain in History and Memory* (New York: Savas Beatie, 2012), 98–100.

56. Reel 31, McClellan Papers, LOC; Timothy J. Reese, *Sealed with Their Lives: Battle of Crampton's Gap* (Baltimore: Butternut and Blue, 1999), 16; Timothy J. Reese, *High Water Mark: The 1862 Maryland Campaign in Strategic Perspective* (Baltimore: Butternut and Blue, 2004), 24–31; Benjamin Franklin Cooling, *Counter-Thrust: From the Peninsula to the Antietam* (Lincoln: University of Nebraska Press, 2007), 205–6.

57. *OR*, Vol. 19, II, 281–82; Jermann, *Antietam*, 155–59; Fishel, *Secret War*, 224–25.

58. John Michael Priest, *Before Antietam: The Battle for South Mountain* (Shippensburg: White Mane Publishing, 1992), 123–25; Thorp and Rossino, *The Tale Untwisted*, 25–27.

59. *OR*, Vol. 51, 827–28; Cox, *Military Reminiscences*, 274–77; Shildt, *The Ninth Corps*, 79.

60. Cuffel, *History*, 72; Williams, ed., *Diary and Letters*, 353; Bosbyshell, *The 48th*, 74.

61. Hurd, "My Experiences," 3; Brigham Family Papers, NHHS.

62. Bailey Papers, NHHS.

63. Sol. R. Smith, "South Mountain, *National Tribune*, January 17, 1895.

64. Hartwig, *To Antietam Creek*, 306–8; Eicher and Eicher, *High Commands*, 249; Jacob D. Cox, "Forcing Fox's Gap and Turner's Gap," *Battles and Leaders of the Civil War*, Vol. 2 (New York: The Century Company, 1884), 585.

65. Cox, *Military Reminiscences*, 280–81; Williams, ed., *Diary and Letters*, 355; *OR*, Vol. 19, I, 1040; Clark, ed., *Histories of the Several Regiments*, Vol. II, 220.

66. Priest, *Before Antietam*, 137; Charles Richard Williams, *The Life of Rutherford Birchard Hayes, Nineteenth President of the United States*, Vol. I (Boston: Houghton Mifflin, 1914), 198–200; *OR*, Vol. 19, I, 467; Hartwig, *To Antietam Creek*, 315–17; Jordan, *Unholy Sabbath*, 128–32; Williams, ed., *Diary and Letters*, 355–57.

67. https://www.findagrave.com/memorial/35809862/fitzerland-squires; https://www.findagrave.com/memorial/38438333/thomas-gallaudet-wells.

68. Brinkerhoff, *History*, 41.

69. *OR*, Vol. 19, I, 461–62.

70. https://www.findagrave.com/memorial/26564697/william-wirt-liggett; *OR*, Vol. 19, I, 465.

71. Clark, ed., *Histories of the Several Regiments*, Vol. II, 220.

72. Hartwig, *To Antietam Creek*, 305, 308; Brinkerhoff, *History*, 41–42; Priest, *Before Antietam*, 147–48; Jordan, *Unholy Sabbath*, 132; Shildt, *The Ninth Corps*, 78; *OR*, Vol. 19, I, 464.

73. Jordan, *Unholy Sabbath*, 141; Priest, *Before Antietam*, 145–47; *OR*, Vol. 19, I, 459, 471.

74. Hartwig, *To Antietam Creek*, 322–23.

75. Martin F. Schmitt, ed., *General George Crook: His Autobiography* (Norman: University of Oklahoma Press, 1946), 96.

76. *OR*, Vol. 19, I, 472; Gottfried, *Maps of Antietam*, 32–33; Horton and Teverbaugh, *A History*, 71.

77. https://www.findagrave.com/memorial/18513646/eugene-lauson-reynolds; Jordan, *Unholy Sabbath*, 142; Morris Letters, https://dmna.ny.gov/historic/reghist/civil/infantry/9thInf/9thInfMain.htm; Hartwig, *To Antietam Creek*, 324; Schmitt, ed., *General George Crook*, 96.

78. Smith, "South Mountain."

79. Clark, ed., *Histories of the Several Regiments*, Vol. I, 166, 245.

80. *OR*, Vol. 19, I, 459, 462; Schmitt, ed., *General George Crook*, 96.

81. Clark, ed., *Histories of the Several Regiments*, Vol. I, 695, and Vol. II, 221; *OR*, Vol. 19, I, 1042.

82. http://www.cmohs.org/recipient-detail/681/inscho-leonidas-h.php.

83. Hartwig, *To Antietam Creek*, 329–30; John David Hoptak, *The Battle of South Mountain* (Charleston: History Press, 2011), 60–62; Cox, "Forcing Fox's Gap," 587; Cox, *Military Reminiscences*, 285.

84. Cox, *Military Reminiscences*, 287.

85. James L. Bowen, *Massachusetts in the War, 1861–1865* (Springfield: Clark W. Bryan, 1889), 828; *OR*, Vol. 19, I, 433–36.

86. Pierro, ed., *The Maryland Campaign*, 150–51; Hoptak, *The Battle*, 67–70; Scott, ed., *Forgotten Valor*, 353–54.

87. *OR*, Vol. 19, I, 428.

88. Albert, ed., *History of the Forty-Fifth*, 51–52.

89. Hurd, "My Experiences," 3–4; Bowen, *Massachusetts*, 528; Eby, Jr., ed., *A Virginia Yankee*, 106.

90. Towne Papers, NHHS; Tracy Papers, LVA; http://www.cmohs.org/recipient-detail/232/caruana-orlando-e.php; https://dmna.ny.gov/historic/reghist/civil/infantry/51stInf/51stInf_Article_Caruana.pdf.

91. Cox, "Forcing Fox's Gap," 588–89; *OR*, Vol. 19, I, 428.

92. Lane, *A Soldier's Diary*, 11.

93. Gottfried, *Maps of Antietam*, 44–45.

94. Lane, *A Soldier's Diary*, 12; 17th Michigan Regimental Records, https://michiganology.org/civil-war.

95. Walcott, *History of the Twenty-First*, 189; Marvel, *Race*, 39.

96. *OR*, Vol. 19, I, 429.

97. William Herbert Withington Papers, Bentley Library, University of Michigan.

98. 17th Michigan Regimental Records, https://michiganology.org/civil-war; https://www.findagrave.com/memorial/8495052/george-myron-hawley.

99. 17th Michigan Regimental Records, https://michiganology.org/civil-war.

100. Todd, *The Seventy-Ninth*, 233; *OR*, Vol. 19, I, 429, 440; Walcott, *History of the Twenty-First*, 189; Parker, *History of the 51st*, 225.

101. Eicher and Eicher, *High Commands*, 194; Gottfried, *Maps of Antietam*, 42–45.

102. Albert, ed., *History of the Forty-Fifth*, 52–53.

103. Mettendorf, *Between Triumph and Disaster*, 32–33; https://dmna.ny.gov/historic/reghist/civil/rosters/Infantry/46th_Infantry_CW_Roster.pdf.

104. Samuel P. Bates, *History of Pennsylvania Volunteers, 1861–5*, Vol. I (Harrisburg: B. Singerly, 1869), 1060; Albert, ed., *History of the Forty-Fifth*, 55; *OR*, Vol. 19, I, 442, 443.

105. J. E. Walton, "Some Reminiscences of the Battle of Antietam," *National Tribune*, December 31, 1885; Brinkerhoff, *History*, 43.

106. *OR*, Vol. 19, I, 460–61.

107. Cuffel, *History*, 73.

108. Hoptak, *The Battle*, 77–78; Hartwig, *To Antietam Creek*, 359.

109. *OR*, Vol. 19, I, 440.

110. Parker, *History of the 51st*, 225–27.

111. 35th Massachusetts Regimental Correspondence, MSA.

112. McConnell, *Remember Reno*, 81–82; Marvel, *Burnside*, 122.

113. A. H. Wood, "How Reno Fell," *National Tribune*, July 26, 1883; Robert West, "Reno's Death," *National Tribune*, August 9, 1883; A. B. Crummel, "Reno's Death," *National Tribune*, August 23, 1883; McConnell, *Remember Reno*, 83–87.

114. A. H. Wood, "How Reno Fell"; Parker, *History of the 51st*, 227; Todd, *The Seventy-Ninth*, 235; Walcott, *History of the Twenty-First*, 190; Ronald G. Watson, ed., *From Ashby to Andersonville: The Civil War Diary and Reminiscences of George A. Hitchcock* (Campbell, CA: Savas Publishing, 1997), 19.

115. *OR*, Vol. 19, I, 418; Shildt, *The Ninth Corps*, 89. Burnside echoed the sentiments in his report in General Orders 17, which officially announced Reno's death to the Ninth Corps. The order was published at *OR*, Vol. 19, I, 423.

116. 35th Massachusetts Regimental Correspondence, MSA; Eicher and Eicher, *High Commands*, 568.

117. Priest, *Before Antietam*, 208–12; Clark, ed., *Histories of the Several Regiments*, Vol. I, 245; *OR*, Vol. 19, I, 187.

118. Crater, *History of the Fiftieth*, 34.

119. Morris Letters, https://dmna.ny.gov/historic/reghist/civil/infantry/9thInf/9thInf Main.htm; Graham, *The Ninth Regiment*, 271–72; Whitney, *The Hawkins Zouaves*, 132; Harvey Henderson Diaries, NYSL.

120. https://steunenberg.blogspot.com/2011/05; Patch, ed., *This from George*, 47; https://dmna.ny.gov/historic/reghist/civil/infantry/89thInf/89thInfMain.htm.

121. Patch, ed., *This from George*, 39; https://www.findagrave.com/memorial/33233453 /christopher-leonard-knight.

122. *OR*, Vol. 19, I, 186–87.

123. Albert, ed., *History of the Forty-Fifth*, 55, 58; Fox, *Regimental Losses*, 265; https:// www.findagrave.com/memorial/30632149/william-p_-grove.

124. Albert, ed., *History of the Forty-Fifth*, 251; https://www.findagrave.com/memorial /25112407/samuel-haynes.

125. *OR*, Vol. 19, I, 187.

126. *OR*, Vol. 19, I, 443.

127. Todd, *The Seventy-Ninth*, 235; Jackson, *History of the Sixth*, 99–100; Upton Letters, NHHS.

128. Spooner Papers, RIHS; Bosbyshell, *The 48th*, 77; Gould, *The Story*, 78; Barnard, ed., *Campaigning*, 58–59.

129. Johnson, *The Long Roll*, 186; Priest, *Civil War Diary*, 85–86; Bailey Papers, NHHS; William Marvel, *Lincoln's Darkest Year: The War in 1862* (New York: Houghton Mifflin, 2008), 199–201.

130. Biography of George W. Gove, undated, NHHS; *OR*, Vol. 19, II, 186.

131. https://www.findagrave.com/memorial/125187502/george-w-gove; Biography of Gove, NHHS.

132. Jordan, *Unholy Sabbath*, 200–202; Hebert, *Fighting Joe*, 136.

133. Sears, *George B. McClellan*, 287–88; Shildt, *The Ninth Corps*, 79.

134. Woodbury, *Burnside and the Ninth Corps*, 127; Poore, *Life and Public Services*, 167–68.

135. Lord, *History of the Ninth*, 68; Hartwig, *To Antietam Creek*, 330–33, 373; Marvel, *Burnside*, 122–23.

136. *OR*, Vol. 19, II, 289; Hoptak, *The Battle*, 169–82; Joseph L. Harsh, *Taken at the Flood: Robert E. Lee and Confederate Strategy in the Maryland Campaign of 1862* (Kent, OH: Kent State University Press, 1999), 298–329.

137. *OR*, Vol. 51, 831, and Vol. 19, II, 297; Stephen W. Sears, *Landscape Turned Red: The Battle of Antietam* (Boston: Houghton Mifflin, 1983), 150–55, 170–71.

138. Cuffel, *History*, 75–76; Bosbyshell, *The 48th*, 76–77.

139. Parker, *History of the 51st*, 229.

140. William A. Canfield, *A History of Army Experience* (Manchester: C. F. Livingston, 1869), 14–15.

141. Rafuse, *McClellan's War*, 300–304.

142. J. Stuart Richards, *A History of Company C, 50th Pennsylvania Veteran Volunteer Infantry Regiment: From the Camp, the Battlefield, and the Prison Pen* (Charleston, SC: History Press, 2006), 56; Regimental Association, *History of the Thirty-Fifth*, 35; *OR*, Vol. 51, 837, and Vol. 19, II, 295; Ethan S. Rafuse, "'Poor Burn?': The Antietam Conspiracy That Wasn't," *Civil War History*, Vol. 54, Number 2, June 2008, 159–62.

143. *OR*, Vol. 51, 837–38; Reel 31, McClellan Papers, LOC.

144. Jacob Cox, "The Battle of Antietam," *Battles and Leaders of the Civil War*, Vol. 2 (New York: Century Company, 1884), 630.

145. George B. McClellan, *McClellan's Own Story* (New York: Charles L. Webster, 1887), 586.

146. Wilson Papers, DSA.

147. Stine, *History*, 187–88; Cooling, *Counter-Thrust*, 224–27.

148. *OR*, Vol. 19, II, 307–8.

149. Walcott, *History of the Twenty-First*, 194; Brinkerhoff, *History*, 44; https://www.findagrave.com/memorial/24994465/david-taylor.

150. Cuffel, *History*, 77; Cox, *Military Reminiscences*, 304; Cox, "The Battle," 631.

151. Committee on Regimental History, *History*, 61; Priest, *Civil War Diary*, 88.

152. Cooling, *Counter-Thrust*, 227–33; Pierro, ed., *The Maryland Campaign*, 186–88; Ted Alexander, *The Battle of Antietam: The Bloodiest Day* (Charleston, SC: History Press, 2011), 55; Sears, *Landscape*, 169–79; Uzal W. Ent, *The Pennsylvania Reserves in the Civil War* (Jefferson, NC: McFarland and Company, 2014), 144–47.

153. Pierro, ed., *The Maryland Campaign*, 209; Sears, *Landscape*, 176–77; Hartwig, *To Antietam Creek*, 630–31.

154. Rafuse, *McClellan's War*, 309.

155. McClellan, *McClellan's Own Story*, 588–89.

156. Marvel, *Burnside*, 128–31; Cox, "The Battle," 632–33; Rafuse, *McClellan's War*, 311–12; *OR*, Vol. 19, I, 418–19; Hartwig, *To Antietam Creek*, 609–13.

157. Cox, *Military Reminiscences*, 304.

158. *OR*, Vol. 19, II, 308, 314; Pierro, ed., *The Maryland Campaign*, 329–30; Sears, *Lincoln's Lieutenants*, 376–77.

159. Cox, *Military Reminiscences*, 303. For a credible modern defense of McClellan's choices during the period between South Mountain and through the Battle of Antietam, see Steven R. Stotelmyer, *Too Useful to Sacrifice: Reconsidering George B. McClellan's Generalship in the Maryland Campaign from South Mountain to Antietam* (El Dorado Hills: Savas Beatie, 2019).

PART THREE

1. Reel 32, McClellan Papers, LOC; Pierro, ed., *The Maryland Campaign*, 202–5; Sears, *George B. McClellan*, 298.

2. Cox, "The Battle," 633; Blakeslee, *History*, 13; W. A. Croffut and John M. Morris, *The Military and Civil History of Connecticut during the War of 1861–65* (New York: Ledyard Bill, 1868), 265; Spooner Papers, RIHS; Jennie Porter Arnold, "At Antietam," *National Tribune*, October 18, 1888; *OR*, Vol. 19, I, 455–56.

3. *OR*, Vol. 19, I, 418–19, 423–24, 436; Cuffel, *History*, 77–78.

4. Johnson, *The Long Roll*, 189–90; Whitney, *The Hawkins Zouaves*, 137–38; *OR*, Vol. 19, I, 450.

5. Bosbyshell, *The 48th*, 76; Walcott, *History of the Twenty-First*, 199.

6. Stine, *History*, 217; *OR*, Vol. 19, I, 424; Marvel, *Burnside*, 132–34.

7. Phillip Thomas Tucker, *Burnside's Bridge: The Climactic Struggle of the 2nd and 20th Georgia at Antietam Creek* (Mechanicsburg: Stackpole Books, 2000), 49–52; Harsh, *Taken at the Flood*, 401–2; Sears, *Landscape*, 260–61.

8. McClellan, *McClellan's Own Story*, 602.

9. Whitney, *The Hawkins Zouaves*, 139; Marvel, *Burnside*, 132; *OR*, Vol. 19, I, 63, 419, and Vol. 51, 844.

10. Morton, *Trusting to Luck*, 284–90.

11. Cox, *Military Reminiscences*, 334–35; *OR*, Vol. 19, I, 31.

12. Sears, *Landscape*, 353–57.

13. Cox, *Military Reminiscences*, 335; Rafuse, *McClellan's War*, 315–19; Sears, *Lincoln's Lieutenants*, 399–401.

14. *OR*, Vol. 19, I, 452, 890; Marvel, *Race*, 54; Horton and Teverbaugh, *A History*, 74–75; Gottfried, *Maps of Antietam*, 202–5.

15. *Commemorative Biographical Record of Hartford County, Connecticut* (Chicago: J. H. Beers & Co., 1901), 65; Eicher and Eicher, *High Commands*, 506.

16. *OR*, Vol. 51, 162.

17. https://www.findagrave.com/memorial/19842613/john-griswold; John Banks, *Connecticut Yankees at Antietam* (Charleston, SC: History Press, 2013), 152–55.

18. Horace N. Williams, "Rodman's Brigade at Antietam," *National Tribune*, December 9, 1886.

19. John Michael Priest, *Antietam: The Soldiers' Battle* (New York: Oxford University Press, 1989), 218–20, 308; Eicher and Eicher, *High Commands*, 323–24; https://www.findagrave.com/memorial/70183432/henry-walter-kingsbury.

20. *OR*, Vol. 19, I, 197, 890; Fox, *Regimental Losses*, 181; https://www.findagrave.com/memorial/39812947/benjamin-j_-beach.

21. *OR*, Vol. 19, I, 424; Schmitt, ed., *General George Crook*, 97; Tucker, *Burnside's Bridge*, 89–94.

22. Francis Winthrop Palfrey, *The Antietam and Fredericksburg* (New York: Charles Scribner's Sons, 1912), 117.

23. Horton and Teverbaugh, *A History*, 75; https://www.findagrave.com/memorial/1476 6700/augustus-henry-coleman; *OR*, Vol. 19, I, 471–73.

24. Schmitt, ed., *General George Crook*, 98; Gottfried, *Maps of Antietam*, 206–7; *OR*, Vol. 19, I, 198; Pierro, ed., *The Maryland Campaign*, 333–34.

25. *OR*, Vol. 19, I, 444.

26. *OR*, Vol. 19, I, 446.

27. James I. Robertson, Jr., ed., "A Federal Surgeon at Sharpsburg," *Civil War History*, Vol. 6, Number 2, June 1960, 140–41, 150.

28. Priest, *Antietam*, 222–25; Pierro, ed., *The Maryland Campaign*, 334–35; Stine, *History*, 218; Jackson, *History of the Sixth*, 103–4; Lord, *History of the Ninth*, 109–10; Hurd, "My Experience," 4.

29. Priest, ed., *Civil War Diary*, 89.

30. Priest, *Antietam*, 229; Gottfried, *Maps of Antietam*, 208–9.

31. *OR*, Vol. 19, I, 447; https://www.findagrave.com/memorial/27681856/william -lawrence-baker.

32. Marvel, *Race*, 55–56; *OR*, Vol. 19, I, 197; Tracy Papers, LVA.

33. Lord, *History of the Ninth*, 110; Eicher and Eicher, *High Commands*, 531–32; Elmer Bragg Papers, Dartmouth.

34. Wilmer, Jarrett, and Vernon, *History and Roster of Maryland Volunteers, War of 1861–5*, Vol. I (Baltimore: Guggenheimer, Weil, Co., 1898), 71, 75–76, 79; Priest, *Antietam*, 340; Tucker, *Burnside's Bridge*, 98–104; https://www.findagrave.com/memorial/190803598 /john-t-durham; *OR*, Vol. 19, I, 197; https://www.findagrave.com/memorial/31851494 /malcolm-wilson; Robertson, Jr., "A Federal Surgeon," 143–44.

35. Priest, ed., "Tired Soldiers Don't Go Very Fast," *Civil War Times Illustrated*, Jan./Feb. 1992, Vol. 30, #6, 37; *OR*, Vol. 19, I, 448.

36. *OR*, Vol. 19, I, 444; Parker, *History of the 51st*, 230–32; Sears, *Landscape*, 265; Shildt, *The Ninth Corps*, 107.

37. Priest, ed., "Tired Soldiers," 39.

38. *OR*, Vol. 19, I, 444; Gottfried, *Maps of Antietam*, 210–11; Parker, *History of the 51st*, 233; H. L. Benning, "Notes by General H. L. Benning on the Battle of Sharpsburg," *Southern Historical Society Papers*, Vol. XVI, 393; Richard Slotkin, *The Long Road*

to Antietam: How the Civil War Became a Revolution (New York: Liveright Publishing, 2012), 316–17.

39. Walcott, *History of the Twenty-First*, 200.

40. Priest, *Antietam*, 232–34; Priest, ed., "Tired Soldiers," 38.

41. Parker, *History of the 51st*, 234; Priest, ed., "Tired Soldiers," 39; *OR*, Vol. 19, I, 448.

42. *OR*, Vol. 19, I, 197; https://www.findagrave.com/memorial/16147667/john -thompson.

43. Sears, *Civil War Papers*, 486.

44. Cox, "The Battle," 653.

45. Gottfried, *Maps of Antietam*, 214–15.

46. Pierro, ed., *The Maryland Campaign*, 333, 338–39; Marvel, *Burnside*, 137–39.

47. Sears, *George B. McClellan*, 314–16; Rafuse, *McClellan's War*, 321–26; Harsh, *Taken at the Flood*, 413–14; Pierro, ed., *The Maryland Campaign*, 359–60; Sears, *Landscape*, 267–68, 276–79; Slotkin, *The Long Road*, 318–19, 322–25.

48. *OR*, Vol. 19, I, 425.

49. Regimental Association, *History of the Thirty-Fifth*, 41–42; Watson, ed., *From Ashby*, 22; *OR*, Vol. 19, I, 448.

50. *OR*, Vol. 19, I, 444; "Commodore," "The Funny Side of Army Life," *National Tribune*, April 25, 1889; 35th Massachusetts regimental correspondence, MSA.

51. Parker, *History of the 51st*, 236–37; Priest, ed., "Tired Soldiers," 39–40; Priest, *Antietam*, 243–46; https://www.findagrave.com/memorial/8560061/thomas-sloan-bell; *OR*, Vol. 19, I, 202; https://www.findagrave.com/memorial/125087352/jacob-gilbert-beaver.

52. Cox, "The Battle," 653–54; Marvel, *Burnside*, 139, 447; Fletcher Pratt, *Civil War in Pictures* (Garden City, NY: Garden City Books, 1955), 69–71.

53. *OR*, Vol. 19, I, 430; Gottfried, *Maps of Antietam*, 216–17; Richards, *A History*, 60.

54. Jackson, *History of the Sixth*, 106; Cuffel, *History*, 81–83; Tucker, *Burnside's Bridge*, 139–40.

55. Longstreet, *From Manassas*, 261.

56. *OR*, Vol. 19, I, 420; Woodbury, *Burnside and the Ninth Corps*, 146; Cox, *Reminiscences*, 344.

57. https://www.findagrave.com/memorial/31206924/john-norton-coffin; *OR*, Vol. 19, I, 430.

58. Gavin, ed., *Infantryman Pettit*, 10–11.

59. William N. Wood, *Reminiscences of Big I* (Charlottesville: Michie Company, 1909), 54–55; Frank Mixson, *Reminiscences of a Private* (Columbia: State Company, 1910), 29.

60. Todd, *The Seventy-Ninth*, 242–43; Gottfried, *Maps of Antietam*, 222–27.

61. Albert, ed., *History of the Forty-Fifth*, 216; Mettendorf, *Between Triumph and Disaster*, 34; Blackburn, ed., *The Diary*, 43.

62. *OR*, Vol. 19, I, 430, 434–35.

63. *OR*, Vol. 19, I, 196; https://www.findagrave.com/memorial/46362018/james-b -ingham; Crater, *History of the Fiftieth*, 35–36; https://www.findagrave.com/memorial /73448529/jeremiah-helms.

64. 17th Michigan Regimental Records, https://michiganology.org/civil-war; Lane, *A Soldier's Diary*, 12–13.

65. Morris Letters, https://dmna.ny.gov/historic/reghist/civil/infantry/9thInf/9thInf Main.htm; Whitney, *The Hawkins Zouaves*, 140–42; Graham, *The Ninth Regiment*, 292; *OR*, Vol. 19, I, 451.

66. Whitney, *The Hawkins Zouaves*, 143.

67. Graham, *The Ninth Regiment*, 293.

68. *OR*, Vol. 19, I, 425–26.

69. https://dmna.ny.gov/historic/reghist/civil/infantry/89thInf/89thInfCWN.htm.

70. Johnson, *The Long Roll*, 192–93.

71. Orville Samuel Kimball, *History and Personal Sketches of Company I, 103 N. Y. S. V, 1862–1864* (Elmira: Facts Printing Co., 1900), 25; *OR*, Vol. 19, I, 197; https://dmna. ny.gov/historic/reghist/civil/rosters/Infantry/103rd_Infantry_CW_Roster.pdf; 103rd New York Regimental File, ANBL.

72. Whitney, *The Hawkins Zouaves*, 144–45.

73. https://dmna.ny.gov/historic/reghist/civil/rosters/Infantry/9th_Infantry_CW _Roster.pdf; Graham, *The Ninth Regiment*, 294.

74. https://dmna.ny.gov/historic/reghist/civil/infantry/89thInf/89thInfCWN.htm.

75. https://www.findagrave.com/memorial/8219078; http://www.cmohs.org/recipient -detail/803/libaire-adolphe.php; Priest, *Antietam*, 263–64.

76. 89th New York Regimental File, ABNL.

77. J. L. Napier, "M'Intosh's Battery at Sharpsburg," *Confederate Veteran*, Vol. 19, Sept. 1911, 429; Priest, *Antietam*, 262–63.

78. *OR*, Vol. 19, I, 197; Caldwell, *The History*, 47; Sears, *Landscape*, 282–84; Bailey Papers, NHHS.

79. 9th New York Regimental File, ANBL.

80. Cuffel, *History*, 83; https://www.findagrave.com/memorial/29345779/isaiah-j _-sellers.

81. Morris Letters, https://dmna.ny.gov/historic/reghist/civil/infantry/9thInf/9thInf Main.htm.

82. *OR*, Vol. 19, I, 904; Gottfried, *Maps of Antietam*, 222–27; 89th New York Regimental File, ANBL.

83. *OR*, Vol. 19, I, 453.

84. https://www.findagrave.com/memorial/58768905/hiram-appelman.

85. Croffut and Morris, *The Military and Civil History*, 271–72; Williams, "Rodman's Brigade"; Adjutant Generals Office, *Record of Service of Connecticut Men in the Army and Navy of the United States during the War of the Rebellion* (Hartford: Case, Lockwood & Brainard Company, 1889), 327.

86. Adjutant Generals Office, *Record of Service*, 327; https://www.findagrave.com /memorial/80232736/marvin-wait; Banks, *Connecticut*, 21–25, 106–9, 113–15.

87. Marvel, *Burnside*, 143; https://www.findagrave.com/memorial/5896745/isaac-peace -rodman. Brevet promotions to brigadier general do not count for purposes of this anal- ysis. For example, three Second Corps colonels who were later awarded a posthumous star died in July 1863 of wounds received at Gettysburg. In September 1862, Stevens, Reno, and Rodman all had the stars of generals on their shoulder epaulets at the time of their fatal wound. The Ninth Corps being the only such command with three gener-

als killed in action in the same month from battle wounds was confirmed through use of various Civil War reference sources, including Eicher and Eicher, *High Commands,* and Frederick Phisterer, *Statistical Record of the Armies of the United States* (New York: Charles Scribner's Sons, 1883), 318–20.

88. Priest, *Antietam*, 265.

89. Caldwell, *The History*, 45; *OR*, Vol. 19, I, 992.

90. Lesley J. Gordon, "All Who Went into That Battle Were Heroes: Remembering the 16th Regiment Connecticut Volunteers at Antietam," in *The Antietam Campaign,* Gary Gallagher, ed. (Kent: Kent State University Press, 1989), 174–76; Gordon, *A Broken Regiment*, 31–36; *OR*, Vol. 19, I, 993–94; Blakeslee, *History*, 15–16; *OR*, Vol. 19, I, 453–54; Arnold, "At Antietam"; Gottfried, *Maps of Antietam*, 224–25; Sears, *Lincoln's Lieutenants*, 407–8.

91. https://www.findagrave.com/memorial/84993034/john-fuller-bingham; Banks, *Connecticut*, 41–46.

92. *OR*, Vol. 19, I, 456–57.

93. Spooner Papers, RIHS.

94. Caldwell, *The History*, 46; Blakeslee, *History*, 16.

95. Pierro, ed., *The Maryland Campaign*, 458; Priest, *Antietam*, 335–36, 340–41.

96. Banks, *Connecticut*, 18–19, 85–92, 116–20; https://www.findagrave.com/memorial /17080464/newton-spalding-manross; Gordon, *A Broken Regiment*, 46.

97. Gordon, "All Who Went," 179–87.

98. Felix Motlow, "Campaigns in Northern Virginia," *Confederate Veteran*, Vol. 2, Sept. 1894, 310.

99. *OR*, Vol. 19, I, 466.

100. J. E. Walton, "Some Reminiscences of the Battle of Antietam," *National Tribune,* December 31, 1885; *OR*, Vol. 19, I, 470; Brinkerhoff, *History*, 46–47; https://www .findagrave.com/memorial/73829891/nathan-j_-white.

101. *OR*, Vol. 19, I, 467; Priest, *Antietam*, 280–83; Gottfried, *Maps of Antietam*, 230–33; Pierro, ed., *The Maryland Campaign*, 353–56.

102. Regimental Association, *History of the Thirty-Fifth*, 45–47; 35th Massachusetts Regimental Correspondence, MSA; Priest, *Antietam*, 283–87; Bowen, *Massachusetts*, 529; Cleaveland Papers, Duke.

103. *OR*, Vol. 19, I, 201, 203; https://www.findagrave.com/memorial/101847715 /david-robinson-hinkley; https://www.findagrave.com/memorial/102510340/alphonso -prentiss-reed.

104. Adjutant General, *Massachusetts Soldiers, Sailors, and Marines in the Civil War,* Vol. III (Norwood: Norwood Press, 1932), 661, 664.

105. Eicher and Eicher, *High Commands*, 166.

106. 35th Massachusetts Regimental Correspondence, MSA; Eicher and Eicher, *High Commands*, 166; https://www.findagrave.com/memorial/121810870/william-sterling -king; Adjutant General, *Massachusetts Soldiers*, 660, 705.

107. Regimental Association, *History of the Thirty-Fifth*, 47–48.

108. Adjutant General, *Massachusetts Soldiers*, III, 645; *OR*, Vol. 19, I, 197, 449.

109. Walcott, *History of the Twenty-First*, 203; Priest, *Antietam*, 300; Upton Letters, NHHS.

110. https://www.findagrave.com/memorial/8148396/marcus-m_-haskell; Priest, *Antietam*, 303; Regimental Association, *History of the Thirty-Fifth*, 51–52; Priest, ed., "Tired Soldiers," 41; http://www.cmohs.org/recipient-detail/1472/whitman-frank-m.php.

111. 35th Massachusetts Regimental Correspondence, MSA.

112. *OR*, Vol. 19, II, 312.

113. Palfrey, *The Antietam*, 119.

114. Marvel, *Burnside*, 141–42; Rafuse, *McClellan's War*, 318–22; A. Wilson Greene, "I Fought the Battle Splendidly," in *Antietam: Essays on the 1862 Maryland Campaign* (Kent: Kent State University Press, 1989), Gallagher, ed., 71–75, 77.

115. Larned Papers, LOC.

116. House of Representatives, 37th Congress, 3rd Session, *Report of the Joint Committee on the Conduct of the War*, Part I (Washington: GPO, 1863), 641; Poore, *Life and Public Services*, 172, 174; Sears, *George B. McClellan*, 316–17; Slotkin, *The Long Road*, 333–34; Greene, "I Fought the Battle Splendidly," 76–78.

117. *OR*, Vol. 51, 844.

118. *William McKinley: Memorial Address Delivered by John Hay, Secretary of State, in the Hall of the House of Representatives, February 27th, 1902* (Lexington, KY: Transylvania Press, 1902).

119. Charles S. Olcott, *William McKinley*, Vol. 1 (Boston: Houghton Mifflin, 1916), 37–38; Pierro, ed., *The Maryland Campaign*, 358.

120. Jackson, *History of the Sixth*, 107; Palfrey, *The Antietam*, 119.

121. Marvel, *Race*, 60–62; Lord, *History of the Ninth*, 117–19.

122. Bosbyshell, *The 48th*, 82.

123. Johnson, *The Long Roll*, 196; *OR*, Vol. 19, I, 436; Priest, ed., *Civil War Diary*, 92–93; Priest, *Antietam*, 301–4.

124. Johnson, *The Long Roll*, 188.

125. Spooner Papers, RIHS.

126. Morton, *Trusting to Luck*, 291.

127. Cox, "The Battle," 650.

128. Marvel, *Burnside*, 149–50.

129. *OR*, Vol. 19, I, 451.

130. Slotkin, *The Long Road*, 325–27.

131. *OR*, Vol. 19, I, 426, and II, 315.

132. Pierro, ed., *The Maryland Campaign*, 357–58; Scott, ed., *Forgotten Valor*, 366.

133. Schmitt, ed., *General George Crook*, 97–99; Rafuse, "Poor Burn?," 170–71.

134. Palfrey, *The Antietam*, 118–19; Rafuse, "Poor Burn?," 172–73.

135. Withington Papers, Bentley Library, UM.

PART FOUR

1. *OR*, Vol. 19, I, 447; Walcott, *History of the Twenty-First*, 204–5.

2. Blackburn, ed., *The Diary*, 43; Priest, ed., *Civil War Diary*, 93, 95; Cuffel, *History*, 83–84; Walcott, *History of the Twenty-First*, 205.

3. Regimental Association, *History of the Thirty-Fifth*, 52; https://www.findagrave.com/memorial/31450857/charles-frederick-williams; 35th Massachusetts Regimental Correspondence, MSA.

4. *OR*, Vol. 19, I, 197; Allen, *Forty-Six Months*, 147–48.

5. Morris Letters, https://dmna.ny.gov/historic/reghist/civil/infantry/9thInf/9thInf_Letters_Morris.pdf.

6. *OR*, Vol. 19, II, 322, 326–27.

7. McClellan, *McClellan's Own Story*, 618.

8. Robinson Papers, Dartmouth; Brinkerhoff, *History*, 47; Marvel, *Race*, 62; Todd, *The Seventy-Ninth*, 243–44.

9. Rafuse, *McClellan's War*, 327–30; Sears, *Landscape*, 298–303; Sears, *Lincoln's Lieutenants*, 411–19; Slotkin, *The Long Road*, 344–52; Brooks D. Simpson, "General McClellan's Bodyguard: The Army of the Potomac After Antietam," in *Antietam: Essays*, Gallagher, ed., 44–63; John C. Waugh, *Lincoln and McClellan: The Troubled Partnership between a President and His General* (New York: Palgrave Macmillan, 2010), 157–61; Marvel, *Burnside*, 145–49.

10. Whitney, *The Hawkins Zouaves*, 151.

11. *OR*, Vol. 19, II, 330.

12. George H. P. Rowell Papers, NHHS, Concord, NH; Letter extracts from James W. Lathe, Dartmouth.

13. Lusk, *War Letters*, 214.

14. Smith Letters, Auburn.

15. Robertson, Jr., "A Federal Surgeon," 145–46.

16. Blakeslee, *History*, 19–21; https://www.findagrave.com/memorial/43396809/frederick-martiner-barber; Gordon, *A Broken Regiment*, 44–51.

17. Whitney, *The Hawkins Zouaves*, 151; Henderson Diaries, NYSL.

18. Bosbyshell, *The 48th*, 82; Priest, ed., *Civil War Diary*, 95; https://48thpennsylvania.blogspot.com/2008/09.

19. Robertson, Jr., "A Federal Surgeon," 146–49; Schildt, *The Ninth Corps*, 124–26.

20. John Russell Bartlett, *Memoirs of the Rhode Island Officers Who Were Engaged in the Service of Their Country during the Great Rebellion of the South* (Providence: Sidney S. Rider & Brother, 1867), 350–52.

21. Robert Hale Ives, Jr., Correspondence, Box 4, folder 12, Ives-Gammell-Safe Papers, RIHS.

22. Diary of Ives, Jr., Box 5, folder 3, Ives-Gammell-Safe Papers, RIHS.

23. *OR*, Vol. 19, I, 455–56.

24. Herreshoff-Lewis Family Papers, RIHS; Bartlett, *Memoirs*, 354.

25. Robert Hale Ives, Jr. Correspondence, Box 4, folder 12, Ives-Gammell-Safe Papers, RIHS.

26. Bartlett, *Memoirs*, 356; Herreshoff-Lewis Family Papers, RIHS.

27. Memorials to Robert Hale Ives, Jr., Box 5, folder 5, Ives-Gammell-Safe Papers, RIHS.

28. https://www.findagrave.com/memorial/21290853/robert-hale-ives; https://www.sstephens.org/history; Bartlett, *Memoirs*, 356.

29. Committee of the Regiment, *History of the Thirty-Sixth Regiment Massachusetts Volunteers, 1862–1865* (Boston: Rockwell and Churchill, 1884), 1–5, 12–14; 36th Massachusetts Regimental Correspondence, MSA.

30. William F. Draper, *Recollections of a Varied Career* (Boston: Little, Brown, and Company, 1909), 84–85.

31. Byron Cutcheon, *The Story of the Twentieth Michigan Infantry* (Lansing: Robert Smith Printing Co., 1904), 11, 15, 31–32; 1862 Diary, Claudius Buchanan Grant Papers, UM; Byron Mac Cutcheon Autobiography, UM.

32. Leander W. Cogswell, *A History of the Eleventh New Hampshire Regiment Volunteer Infantry in the Rebellion War, 1861–1865* (Concord: Republican Press Association, 1891), 3–4, 14–15; Amos Hadley, *Life of Walter Harriman, With Selections from His Speeches and Writings* (Boston: Houghton, Mifflin and Company, 1888), 107–17.

33. Sewell D. Tilton Papers, NHHS; Dodge Family Papers, NHHS; Charles Paige Collection, Folder 20, NHHS.

34. Cogswell, *A History*, 18–19.

35. William P. Hopkins, *The Seventh Regiment Rhode Island Volunteers in the Civil War, 1862–1865* (Providence: Snow & Farmham, 1903), 5–12, 17.

36. Cullom, *Biographical Register*, II, 599–600.

37. *OR*, Vol. 19, II, 368–69.

38. Marvel, *Burnside*, 155; Eicher and Eicher, *High Commands*, 570; Scott, ed., *Forgotten Valor*, 371; Larned Papers, LOC.

39. Mettendorf, *Between Triumph and Disaster*, 35–36.

40. Blackburn, ed., *The Diary*, 43; Crater, *History of the Fiftieth*, 37.

41. Committee of the Regiment, *History of the Thirty-Sixth*, 15.

42. Eicher and Eicher, *High Commands*, 252; Cullom, *Biographical Register*, II, 27, 33, 40–42.

43. Reel 33, McClellan Papers, LOC; Walton, "Some Reminiscences."

44. Smith Letters, Auburn.

45. *OR*, Vol. 19, I, 432–33; Whitney, *Hawkins Zouaves*, 154; Todd, *The Seventy-Ninth*, 246–47; Barnard, ed., *Campaigning*, 63; Cogswell, *A History*, 20; Committee of the Regiment, *History of the Thirty-Sixth*, 16.

46. https://www.findagrave.com/memorial/137551839/charles-a-wood; Wood Letter, 9th New Hampshire Regimental File, ANBL.

47. Richard Sauers, ed., *The Civil War Journal of Colonel Bolton, 51st Pennsylvania* (Conshohocken, PA: Combined Publishing, 2000), 86, 90–95.

48. Spooner Papers, RIHS.

49. Marvel, *Burnside*, 155; Blackburn, ed., *The Diary*, 44; Committee of the Regiment, *History of the Thirty-Sixth*, 16; Waugh, *Lincoln and McClellan*, 167; Walcott, *History of the Twenty-First*, 213; Lord, *History of the Ninth*, 148; Lane, *A Soldier's Diary*, 14; Bosbyshell, *The 48th*, 84; Chandler Papers, NHHS.

50. Sears, *Lincoln's Lieutenants*, 426–27; Waugh, *Lincoln and McClellan*, 167–74; Rafuse, *McClellan's War*, 346–50; *OR*, Vol. 19, I, 72, and II, 394–95.

51. Rowell Papers, NHHS; Lane, *A Soldier's Diary*, 15; Draper, *Recollections*, 88–89; Bailey Papers, NHHS; John E. Wilcox Diary, NHHS.

52. *OR*, Vol. 19, II, 410, 424, 454; Blackburn, ed., *The Diary*, 44; Rafuse, *McClellan's War*, 349–52.

53. Cuffel, *History*, 86, 88.

54. Bosbyshell, *The 48th*, 85–86.

55. Towne Papers, NHHS.

56. Cutcheon, *The Story*, 33; Spooner Papers, RIHS.

57. Benjamin Nelson Letters, Mike Pride Collection, Folder 14, NHHS.

58. Wilcox Diary, NHHS; Henry S. Muchmore Correspondence, NHHS.

59. Lane, *A Soldier's Diary*, 20.

60. Hopkins, *The Seventh Regiment*, 23.

61. *OR*, Vol. 19, I, 81, and Vol. 19, II, 464.

62. *OR*, Vol. 19, II, 433, 484, 494–95; Blackburn, ed., *The Diary*, 45; Bradley Gottfried, *The Maps of Fredericksburg* (El Dorado Hills: Savas Beatie, 2018), 12–13; Allen, *Forty-Six Months*, 150; Chandler Papers, NHHS.

63. Cogswell, *A History*, 20; Hadley, *Life*, 119–20; Parker, *History of the 51st*, 251; Marvel, *Burnside*, 156–57.

64. 36th Massachusetts Regimental Correspondence, MSA; Lusk, *War Letters*, 223; Walcott, *History of the Twenty-First*, 215.

65. Scott, ed., *Forgotten Valor*, 375; *OR*, Vol. 19, II, 504; Sears, *George B. McClellan*, 335–37; Rafuse, *McClellan's War*, 364–70; Waugh, *Lincoln and McClellan*, 174–75.

66. Paige Collection, Folder 23, NHHS; Priest, ed., *Civil War Diary*, 105–7.

67. Walcott, *History of the Twenty-First*, 215–16; Charles C. Paige, *Story of the Experiences of Lieut. Charles C. Paige in the Civil War of 1861–5* (Franklin, NH: Journal-Transcript Press, 1906), 26.

68. Blakeslee, *History*, 23; Scott, ed., *Forgotten Valor*, 376.

69. *OR*, Vol. 51, 914–15, 920–21.

70. Cutcheon, *The Story*, 34; Marvel, *Burnside*, 157; *OR*, Vol. 19, II, 532; Rafuse, *McClellan's War*, 369–73; Bradley M. Gottfried, *The Maps of Fredericksburg*, 14–15; Waugh, *Lincoln and McClellan*, 178.

71. Reel 34, McClellan Papers, LOC; Eicher and Eicher, *High Commands*, 155.

72. Jackson, *History of the Sixth*, 118.

73. Barnard, ed., *Campaigning*, 64; Parker, *History of the 51st*, 252–53; Bailey Papers, NHHS.

74. Priest, *Civil War Diary*, 108–9; Regimental Association, *History of the Thirty-Fifth*, 62; Spooner Papers, RIHS; Jackson, *History of the Sixth*, 126.

75. Waugh, *Lincoln and McClellan*, 179–82; Rafuse, *McClellan's War*, 375–76; Marvel, *Burnside*, 159–60.

76. John V. Harrington Papers, Delaware State Archives; Marvel, *Burnside*, 162; Jeffry D. Wert, *The Sword of Lincoln: The Army of the Potomac* (New York: Simon & Schuster, 2005), 180; Sears, *Lincoln's Lieutenants*, 435–36; Rafuse, *McClellan's War*, 376–79.

77. *OR*, Vol. 19, II, 557.

78. Scott, ed., *Forgotten Valor*, 378; Priest, *Civil War Diary*, 109; Albert, ed., *History of the Forty-Fifth*, 253; Patch, ed., *This from George*, 56.

79. Regimental Association, *History of the Thirty-Fifth*, 64; Committee of the Regiment, *History of the Thirty-Sixth*, 23; Gavin, ed., *Infantryman Pettit*, 32; Allen, *Forty-Six Months*, 152.

80. *OR*, Vol. 19, II, 569.

81. Todd, *The Seventy-Ninth*, 252–53; Crater, *History of the Fiftieth*, 39; Gottfried, *The Maps of Fredericksburg*, 20–23; Tilton Papers, NHHS.

82. Blackburn, ed., *The Diary*, 46; Walcott, *History of the Twenty-First*, 226; Parker, *History of the 51st*, 255.

83. *OR*, Vol. 21, 3, 5; Scott, ed., *Forgotten Valor*, 380–81.

84. *OR*, Vol. 19, II, 576–77.

85. Chandler Papers, NHHS; Marvel, *Race*, 86.

86. Regimental Association, *History of the Thirty-Fifth*, 67; Eicher and Eicher, *High Commands*, 166.

87. 35th Massachusetts Regimental Correspondence, MSA.

88. Albert, ed., *History of the Forty-Fifth*, 253; Allen, *Forty-Six Months*, 153; Gottfried, *The Maps of Fredericksburg*, 26–29; Upton Letters, NHHS.

89. Bailey Papers, NHHS; Barnard, ed., *Campaigning*, 65; Todd, *The Seventy-Ninth*, 255–56.

90. Parker, *History of the 51st*, 260–61.

91. Gavin, ed., *Infantryman Pettit*, 35.

92. *OR*, Vol. 21, 792–95; Marvel, *Burnside*, 166–68.

93. Blackburn, ed., *The Diary*, 46–47; Committee of the Regiment, *History of the Thirty-Sixth*, 24.

94. Allen, *Forty-Six Months*, 156.

95. Committee of the Regiment, *History of the Thirty-Sixth*, 24–25.

96. L. A. Furney, ed., *Reminiscences of the War of the Rebellion, 1861–1865, By Bvt. Maj. Jacob Roemer* (Flushing, NY: Estate of Jacob Roemer, 1897), 92–93.

97. Bosbyshell, *The 48th*, 93.

98. Cuffel, *History*, 100; Hopkins, *The Seventh Regiment*, 34; Walcott, *History of the Twenty-First*, 230; George C. Rable, *Fredericksburg! Fredericksburg!* (Chapel Hill: University of North Carolina Press, 2002), 146–47.

99. William H. Osborne, *The History of the Twenty-Ninth Regiment of Massachusetts Volunteer Infantry in the Late War of the Rebellion* (Boston: Albert J. Wright, 1877), 8, 13–14, 184–90.

100. Charles F. Herberger, ed., *A Yankee at Arms: The Diary of Lieutenant Augustus D. Ayling, 29th Massachusetts Volunteers* (Knoxville: University of Tennessee Press, 1999), 79–80.

101. Cullom, *Biographical Register*, II, 643; Eicher and Eicher, *High Commands*, 432.

102. Stephen W. Sears, ed., *For Country, Cause and Leader: The Civil War Journal of Charles B. Haydon* (New York: Ticknor & Fields, 1993), 289–90.

103. Alonzo Pierce Papers, NHHS.

104. J. W. Grant, *The Flying Regiment: Journal of the Campaign of the 12th Regt. Rhode Island Volunteers* (Providence: Sidney S. Rider, 1865), 5–44.

105. Smith Letters, Auburn.

106. Gordon, *A Broken Regiment*, 57–59; 35th Massachusetts Regimental Correspondence, MSA.

107. Herberger, ed., *A Yankee*, 80; Priest, ed., *Civil War Diary*, 117; Bosbyshell, *The 48th*, 93.

108. Marvel, *Burnside*, 168–72; Sears, *Lincoln's Lieutenants*, 448–50.

109. Rowell Papers, NHHS.

110. Priest, ed., *Civil War Diary*, 118.

111. Bosbyshell, *The 48th*, 94; Cuffel, *History*, 103; Sears, ed., *For Country*, 295; Sauers, ed., *The Civil War Journal*, 99; Priest, ed., *Civil War Diary*, 118–19; Nelson Letters, Folder 14, Mike Pride Collection, NHHS.

112. Sears, ed., *For Country*, 295; Blackburn, ed., *The Diary*, 47; Walcott, *History of the Twenty-First*, 236; Members of the Regiment, *The Story*, 58.

113. *OR*, Vol. 21, 1121.

114. https://museum.dmna.ny.gov/unit-history/infantry-1/89th-infantry-regiment -veteran; Patch, ed., *This from George*, 59; *OR*, Vol. 21, 315, 331, 345–46; Mettendorf, *Between Triumph and Disaster*, 38–39.

115. *OR*, Vol. 21, 349. Citing other sources, Rable, *Fredericksburg!*, 159, and O'Reilly, *The Fredericksburg Campaign*, 75–76, suggest the 8th Connecticut suffered a high casualty rate during their short time at a northern bridge guarding the engineers, but the regiment only sustained three total casualties across several days at Fredericksburg. *OR*, Vol. 21, 133.

116. *OR*, Vol. 21, 335, 346; Gottfried, *The Maps of Fredericksburg*, 60–65.

117. Rable, *Fredericksburg!*, 160–73; Francis Augustin O'Reilly, *The Fredericksburg Campaign: Winter War on the Rappahannock* (Baton Rouge: Louisiana State University Press, 2003), 97–101; S. Millett Thompson, *History of the Thirteenth Regiment of New Hampshire Volunteer Infantry in the War of the Rebellion, 1861–1865* (Boston: Houghton, Mifflin and Company, 1888), 41.

118. Sheldon B. Thorpe, *The History of the Fifteenth Connecticut Volunteers in the War for the Defense of the Union* (New Haven: Price, Lee & Adkins Co., 1893), 34.

119. Parker, *History of the 51st*, 257; Albert, ed., *History of the Forty-Fifth*, 253–54.

120. Marvel, *Race*, 95; Chandler Papers, NHHS.

121. Regimental Association, *History of the Thirty-Fifth*, 82.

122. Allen, *Forty-Six Months*, 164; Spooner Papers, RIHS.

123. Ransom F. Sargent Civil War Papers, Dartmouth; Rable, *Fredericksburg!*, 177–84; O'Reilly, *The Fredericksburg Campaign*, 118–26.

124. Thompson, *History*, 45; Thomas Read Rootes Cobb Papers, Duke.

PART FIVE

1. Paige, *Story*, 31; *OR*, Vol. 21, 325; Walcott, *History of the Twenty-First*, 240.

2. Marvel, *Burnside*, 162–89; Sears, *Lincoln's Lieutenants*, 456–59; Darin Wipperman, *First for the Union: Life and Death in a Civil War Army Corps from Antietam to Gettysburg* (Guilford, CT: Stackpole Books, 2000), 99–103; Ent, *Pennsylvania Reserves*, 172–82.

3. Sears, *Lincoln's Lieutenants*, 459–62; O'Reilly, *The Fredericksburg Campaign*, 247–49; Rable, *Fredericksburg!*, 218–26; Gottfried, *The Maps of Fredericksburg*, 78–79; OR, Vol. 21, 311.

4. *OR*, Vol. 21, 316.

5. https://southfromthenorthwoods.blogspot.com/2014/05; *OR*, Vol. 21, 318–19; Gould, *The Story*, 99; O'Reilly, *The Fredericksburg Campaign*, 294.

6. *OR*, Vol. 21, 316, 325–26.

7. 35th Massachusetts Regimental Correspondence, MSA.

8. https://www.findagrave.com/memorial/8201770/thomas-plunkett; 21st Massachusetts Regimental Correspondence, MSA.

9. Parker, *History of the 51st*, 269–71. Bell had experience in the state militia and the first infantry regiment his state would raise in the Civil War. Buried in his hometown of Easton, Bell was thirty-one years old; https://www.findagrave.com/memorial/151891667/ferdinand-w.-bell.

10. Paige Collection, Folder 23, NHHS; Hadley, *Life*, 129.

11. William W. Fish Correspondence, NHHS.

12. *OR*, Vol. 21, 329.

13. Bosbyshell, *The 48th*, 97.

14. *OR*, Vol. 21, 321–22.

15. https://www.findagrave.com/memorial/171302363/john-b-cooper; *OR*, Vol. 21, 322.

16. Upton Letters, NHHS.

17. Jackson, *History of the Sixth*, 127.

18. Hopkins, *The Seventh*, 44–45; https://www.findagrave.com/memorial/13021396/jacob-babbitt.

19. *OR*, Vol. 21, 323; https://www.cmohs.org/recipients/zenas-r-bliss.

20. John F. Austin Papers, RIHS.

21. Grant, *The Flying Regiment*, 48–52; George Waters Diman, *Autobiography and Sketches of My Travels by Sea and Land* (Bristol: Bristol Phoenix, 1896), 50.

22. Oscar Lapham, "Recollections of Service in the Twelfth Regiment, R. I. Volunteers," *Personal Narratives of the Events in the War of the Rebellion*, Third Series, No. 11 (Providence: Rhode Island Soldiers and Sailors Historical Society, 1885), 28–32.

23. *OR*, Vol. 21, 320, 324.

24. Gottfried, *The Maps of Fredericksburg*, 192–97.

25. Bosbyshell, *The 48th*, 97.

26. Gould, *The Story*, 100.

27. Henry Heisler Papers, LOC; *OR*, Vol. 21, 316.

28. Gottfried, *The Maps of Fredericksburg*, 230–31.

29. *OR*, Vol. 21, 332, 349, 352–53; Spooner Papers, RIHS; Whitney, *The Hawkins Zouaves*, 167; O'Reilly, *The Fredericksburg Campaign*, 413.

30. Thompson, *History*, 55; *OR*, Vol. 21, 312; Marvel, *Burnside*, 195.

31. *OR*, Vol. 21, 119; William Marvel, "The Making of a Myth: Ambrose E. Burnside and the Union High Command at Fredericksburg," in *The Fredericksburg Campaign:*

Decision on the Rappahannock, Gary W. Gallagher, ed. (Chapel Hill: University of North Carolina Press, 1995), 19–20.

32. Thompson, *History*, 50.

33. *OR*, Vol. 21, 336, 338; Thompson, *History*, 58.

34. *OR*, Vol. 21, 343–44.

35. Thompson, *History*, 59.

36. Henderson diaries, NYSL; *OR*, Vol. 21, 346.

37. Whitney, *The Hawkins Zouaves*, 168; Lord, *History of the Ninth*, 192.

38. *OR*, Vol. 21, 133; https://historicalpubs.njstatelib.org/searchable_publications/civil war/NJCWn819.

39. Spooner Papers, RIHS; https://www.findagrave.com/memorial/10309851/joseph -bridgham-curtis.

40. Spooner Papers, RIHS.

41. *OR*, Vol. 21, 132.

42. Bailey Papers, NHHS; *OR*, Vol. 21, 326.

43. Paige Collection, Folder 23, NHHS.

44. Aaron Stevens Papers, NHHS.

45. Scott, ed., *Forgotten Valor*, 404–5; Marvel, *Burnside*, 196–98; Rable, *Fredericksburg!*, 269–72; O'Reilly, *The Fredericksburg Campaign*, 431–40; Wert, *The Sword*, 202–3.

46. Scott, ed., *Forgotten Valor*, 403–4.

47. Spooner Papers, RIHS; Robert Stiles, *Four Years under Marse Robert* (New York: Neale Publishing Company, 1903), 132; Bragg Papers, Dartmouth.

48. Marvel, *Burnside*, 200; Jerry Smith Papers, NYSL; A. Wilson Greene, "Morale, Maneuver, and Mud: The Army of the Potomac, December 16, 1862–January 26, 1863," in *The Fredericksburg Campaign: Decision on the Rappahannock*, Gary W. Gallagher, ed., 171–217.

49. 21st Massachusetts Regimental Correspondence, MSA.

50. Chandler Papers, NHHS; Wilcox Diary, NHHS.

51. Bailey Papers, NHHS.

52. Lane, *A Soldier's Diary*, 24.

53. Lusk, *War Letters*, 262; Scott, *Forgotten Valor*, 408.

54. *OR*, Vol. 21, 900; Marvel, *Burnside*, 209–12; Sears, *Lincoln's Lieutenants*, 471–76.

55. Bosbyshell, *The 48th*, 100–101; Jackson, *History of the Sixth*, 131; Committee of the Regiment, *History of the Thirty-Sixth*, 29–30; Osborne, *The History*, 212.

56. Thompson, *History*, 96–97; Allen, *Forty-Six Months*, 183; Spooner Papers, RIHS.

57. Walcott, *History of the Twenty-First*, 258; Hopkins, *The Seventh*, 54; Scott, ed., *Forgotten Valor*, 410; Thompson, *History*, 96–97.

58. Dunlap Family Papers, LVA.

59. Sears, *Lincoln's Lieutenants*, 475–76; Rable, *Fredericksburg!*, 357–58; Members of the Regiment, *The Story of the Twenty-First Regiment Connecticut Volunteer Infantry during the Civil War, 1861–1865* (Middletown: Stewart Printing, 1900), 92–93.

60. Nutting Papers, NHHS.

61. Chase Family Papers, NHHS.

62. Marvel, *Burnside*, 212–14; Scott, ed., *Forgotten Valor*, 414; Rable, *Fredericksburg!*, 411–19; Thompson, *History*, 100–102; Sears, ed., *For Country*, 307–38; Bosbyshell, *The 48th*, 101–2.
63. Lusk, *War Letters*, 275.
64. *OR*, Vol. 21, 1005.
65. Walcott, *History of the Twenty-First*, 262.
66. Wipperman, *First*, 135–37; Lane, *A Soldier's Diary*, 28; Regimental Association, *History of the Thirty-Fifth*, 103.
67. Scott, ed., *Forgotten Valor*, 416–17.
68. *OR*, Vol. 25, 12.
69. Walcott, *History of the Twenty-First*, 263; Paige Collection, Folder 26, NHHS; Brigham Family Papers, NHHS; Smith Papers, NYSL.
70. Brigham Family Papers, NHHS; Herberger, ed., *A Yankee*, 101; Thompson, *History*, 114.
71. Scott, ed., *Forgotten Valor*, 417–18.
72. *OR*, Vol. 23, II, 104–5, 142–43, 147, 149–50; Patch, ed., *This from George*, 73.
73. Lane, *A Soldier's Diary*, 36; Todd, *The Seventy-Ninth*, 277; Gavin, ed., *Infantryman*, 64–66.
74. Sauers, ed., *The Civil War Journal*, 110–11.
75. Brigham Family Papers, NHHS.
76. *OR*, Vol. 23, II, 162–64.
77. Burnside Letterbooks, Vol. 6, RIHS; William Marvel, *The Great Task Remaining: The Third Year of Lincoln's War* (Boston: Houghton Mifflin Harcourt, 2010), 49–51; Eicher and Eicher, *High Commands*, 560, 570.
78. 35th Massachusetts Regimental Correspondence, MSA.
79. Gavin, ed., *Infantryman*, 67–86; Todd, *The Seventy-Ninth*, 281–83; Smith Papers, NYSL; Nutting Papers, NHHS; Chandler Papers, NHHS; Rowell Papers, NHHS; Brigham Family Papers, NHHS.
80. Burnside Letterbooks, Vol. 6, RIHS.
81. Burnside Letterbooks, Vol. 6, RIHS.
82. Ronald C. White, *American Ulysses: A Life of Ulysses S. Grant* (New York: Random House, 2016), 244–83; Warren E. Grabau, *Ninety-Eight Days: A Geographer's View of the Vicksburg Campaign* (Knoxville: University of Tennessee Press, 2000), 51–418.
83. Watson, ed., *From Ashby*, 102.
84. Jackson, *History of the Sixth*, 168–69.
85. Bailey Papers, NHHS; Marvel, *The Great Task*, 102; Parker, *History of the 51st*, 323.
86. Cutcheon, *The Story*, 57–58; Crater, *History*, 40–41.
87. Rowell Papers, NHHS.
88. Marvel, *The Great Task*, 150.
89. Henry Heffron Papers, NYSL.
90. Lane, *A Soldier's Diary*, 63.
91. Bailey Papers, NHHS; Cutcheon, *The Story*, 58; Committee of the Regiment, *History of the Thirty-Sixth*, 59–60.

92. 35th Massachusetts Regimental Correspondence, MSA; Parker, *History of the 51st*, 349–51; Tracy Papers, LVA.

93. Jackson, *History of the Sixth*, 185–89; Fish Correspondence, NHHS; Heffron Papers, NYSL.

94. Cutcheon, *The Story*, 62; 35th Massachusetts Regimental Correspondence, MSA; *Recollections of Simon Goodell Griffin*, Rauner Library, Dartmouth.

95. *OR*, Vol. 24, III, 565–66.

96. Committee of the Regiment, *History of the Thirty-Sixth*, 76; https://www.finda grave.com/memorial/5897126/thomas-welsh; https://sites.google.com/site/general welsh/lastcampaign; *Recollections*, Dartmouth.

97. Marvel, *Burnside*, 264–95; Terry Faulkner and Charles H. Faulkner, *Rediscovering Fort Sanders: The American Civil War and Its Impact on Knoxville's Cultural Landscape* (Knoxville: University of Tennessee Press, 2020), 31–54; Earl J. Hess, *The Knoxville Campaign: Burnside and Longstreet in East Tennessee* (Knoxville: University of Tennessee Press, 2012), 1–19.

98. Noel C. Fisher, *War at Every Door: Partisan Politics and Guerrilla Violence in East Tennessee, 1860–1869* (Chapel Hill: University of North Carolina Press, 1997), 78–82; Marvel, *Burnside*, 264–98; Robert Jameson Papers, LOC.

99. White, *American Ulysses*, 302.

100. *OR*, Vol. 31, I, 268.

101. Faulkner and Faulkner, *Rediscovering*, 74–83; *OR*, Vol. 31, I, 276–78.

102. Hess, *The Knoxville Campaign*, 151–68; Faulkner and Faulkner, *Rediscovering*, 135–44; Marvel, *The Great Task*, 232–34; Jameson Papers, LOC.

103. https://www.cmohs.org/recipients/francis-w-judge; *OR*, Vol. 31, I, 336, 342; Marvel, *Burnside*, 318–31.

104. Lane, *A Soldier's Diary*, 130; Fish Correspondence, NHHS.

105. Watson, ed., *From Ashby*, 164–68; Mettendorf, *Between Triumph and Disaster*, 74; Albert, ed., *History of the Forty-Fifth*, 97, 109–10; 21st Massachusetts Regimental Correspondence, MSA; Cutcheon, *History*, 92.

106. Paige, *Story*, 97; Committee of the Regiment, *History of the Thirty-Sixth*, 124.

107. Lane, *A Soldier's Diary*, 131–32, 159.

108. *OR*, Vol. 33, 373; Marvel, *Burnside*, 338–42; Morton, *Trusting to Luck*, 476–77.

109. Gould, *The Story*, 147–55; Bosbyshell, *The 48th*, 141–45; Addison Boyce Papers, UM.

110. Eicher and Eicher, *High Commands*, 413, 437; *OR*, Vol. 32, I, 48; Tilton Papers, NHHS.

111. *OR*, Vol. 33, 657, 678; Marvel, *Burnside*, 339–42; Woodbury, *Burnside and the Ninth Corps*, 365–67.

Part Six

1. *OR*, Vol. 33, 1045.

2. John Austin Stevens, Jr., *Report of Committee to Recruit the Ninth Army Corps, February to August, 1864* (New York: John W. Amerman, 1866), 1–14.

3. Jackson, *History of the Sixth*, 205–6, 210.

4. Eicher and Eicher, *High Commands*, 511; this review of Ninth Corps organization is based on *OR*, Vol. 36, I, 113–14.

5. Adjutant General, *Massachusetts Soldiers, Sailors, and Marines in the Civil War*, Vol. IV (Norwood: Norwood Press, 1932), 762; Stephen Minot Weld, *War Diary and Letters of Stephen Minot Weld* (privately printed, Riverside Press, 1912), 259.

6. Warren Wilkinson, *Mother, May You Never See the Sights I Have Seen: The Fifty-Seventh Massachusetts Veteran Volunteers in the Last Year of the Civil War* (New York: Harper and Row, 1990), 1–47.

7. Lydia Minturn Post, ed., *Soldiers' Letters from Camp, Battle-field and Prison* (New York: Bunce and Huntington, 1865), 462.

8. 14th Massachusetts Battery Correspondence, MSA; Adjutant General, *Massachusetts Soldiers*, V, 522–31.

9. Osborne, *The History*, 290–91, 295–301.

10. https://www.findagrave.com/memorial/25126242/charles-cummings; Wipperman, *First*, 235–39; State of Vermont, *Revised Roster of Vermont Volunteers and List of Vermonters Who Served in the Army and Navy of the United States* (Montpelier: Watchman Publishing, 1892), 569.

11. William Elmore Howard letters, VHS, Barre; James Pollard, 1864 diary, VSA.

12. Raymond J. Herek, *These Men Have Seen Hard Service: The First Michigan Sharpshooters in the Civil War* (Detroit: Wayne State University Press, 1998), 1–91.

13. Charles Horace Hodskin, 1864 diary, UM; Boyce Papers, UM; Marvel, *Burnside*, 345–46; Woodbury, *Burnside and the Ninth Corps*, 368–69.

14. https://museum.dmna.ny.gov/unit-history/infantry-2/109th-infantry-regiment; https://www.findagrave.com/memorial/3310/benjamin-franklin-tracy.

15. James M. McPherson, *The Negro's Civil War: How American Negroes Felt and Acted during the War for the Union* (Urbana: University of Illinois Press, 1982), 161–82; William A. Dobak, *Freedom by the Sword: The U.S. Colored Troops, 1862–1867* (Alexandria, VA: St. John's Press, 2016), 1–23; Joseph T. Glatthaar, *Forged in Battle: The Civil War Alliance of Black Soldiers and White Officers* (Baton Rouge: Louisiana State University Press, 1990), 1–10; John J. Hennessy, "I Dread the Spring: The Army of the Potomac Prepares for the Overland Campaign," in *The Wilderness Campaign*, Gary W. Gallagher, ed. (Chapel Hill: University of North Carolina Press, 1997), 77–78.

16. Roy P. Basler, ed., *The Collected Works of Abraham Lincoln*, Vol. VI (New Brunswick, NJ: Rutgers University Press, 1953), 406–10.

17. Towne Papers, NHHS.

18. William A. Gladstone Afro-American Military Collection, LOC.

19. Frank Levstik, "The Civil War Diary of Colonel Albert Rogall," *Polish American Studies*, Spring 1970, Vol. 27, No. 1, 33–36.

20. Correspondence of Alfred F. Dodge, VSA; https://www.findagrave.com/memorial/12419556/albert-francis-dodge.

21. Paul G. Zeller, "'My Soldier Boy Mark': The Civil War Letters of Pvt. Mark B. Slayton," *Vermont History*, Vol. 82, No. 1 (Winter/Spring 2014), 49–50; 58th Massachusetts Death Records, MSA; F. E. C., *History of the 58th Regt. Massachusetts Vols. from the*

15th Day of September, 1863, to the Close of the Rebellion (Washington: Gibson Brothers, 1865), 5; Adjutant General, *Massachusetts Soldiers*, Vol. V, 1.

22. *OR*, Vol. 36, I, 905; Sears, *Lincoln's Lieutenants*, 624; Marvel, *Burnside*, 347; Gordon C. Rhea, *The Battle of the Wilderness, May 5–6, 1864* (Baton Rouge: LSU Press, 1994), 48.

23. Marvel, *Burnside*, 346–49; R. Alfred Allen Diary, Duke.

24. Harlan Closson Diaries, Rauner Library, Dartmouth.

25. Lane, *Story*, 165–66.

26. Larned Papers, LOC; M. G. Bell letter, LVA.

27. *OR*, Vol. 36, II, 363, 371, 380; Rhea, *The Battle*, 184–85; Bruce L. Brager, *Grant's Victory: How Ulysses S. Grant Won the Civil War* (Guilford, CT: Stackpole Books, 2020), 103.

28. Ulysses S. Grant, *Personal Memoirs of U. S. Grant*, Vol. II (New York: Charles L. Webster, 1892), 192–93; *OR*, Vol. 36, I, 906; Lewis Simonds Diary, Dartmouth; 7th Maine Battery Correspondence, MSA.

29. Sauers, ed., *The Civil War Journal*, 198; Rhea, *The Battle*, 326, 337–38; *OR*, Vol. 36, II, 460; Walcott, *History of the Twenty-First*, 315.

30. Hopkins, *The Seventh*, 165–66; Cutcheon, *The Story*, 110; Marvel, *Race*, 204–5; Marvel, *Burnside*, 352–53.

31. Morris Schaff, *The Battle of the Wilderness* (Boston: Houghton Mifflin, 1910), 225–27, 230–33; Rhea, *The Battle*, 330; Sears, *Lincoln's Lieutenants*, 640–41; David M. Jordan, *Winfield Scott Hancock: A Soldier's Life* (Bloomington: Indiana University Press, 1996), 118.

32. Jackson, *History of the Sixth*, 215–16.

33. Bosbyshell, *The 48th*, 148; Bates, *History*, Vol. I, 1066, 1109; *OR*, Vol. 36, I, 131.

34. Committee of the Regiment, *History of the Thirty-Sixth*, 150–51; Robert E. L. Krick, "Like a Duck on a June Bug: James Longstreet's Flank Attack, May 6, 1864," in *The Wilderness Campaign*, Gary W. Gallagher, ed., 237; Byron Cutcheon Autobiography, UM, 248.

35. Clark, ed., *Histories*, I, 721–22; Herek, *These Men*, 118–20.

36. Crater, *History*, 52; *OR*, Vol. 36, I, 132; https://www.findagrave.com/memorial/14230895/william-hill; https://www.findagrave.com/memorial/71727884/mary-hill.

37. Rhea, *The Battle*, 330; *OR*, Vol. 36, I, 906; Scott, ed., *Forgotten*, 512; Byron Cutcheon Autobiography, UM, 250.

38. *OR*, Vol. 36, I, 928; Jackson, *History of the Sixth*, 218–19.

39. *OR*, Vol. 36, I, 321; Regimental Association, *History of the Thirty-Fifth*, 224; Walcott, *History of the Twenty-First*, 314.

40. Eicher and Eicher, *High Commands*, 120; Francis Winthrop Palfrey, *Memoir of William Francis Bartlett* (Boston: Houghton, Osgood and Company, 1879), 1, 98–99.

41. Weld, *War Diary*, 285; Walcott, *History of the Twenty-First*, 315; Rhea, *The Battle*, 340; Z. Boylston Adams, "In the Wilderness," *Civil War Papers Read before the Commandery of the State of Massachusetts, Military Order of the Loyal Legion of the United States*, Vol. II (Boston: F. H. Gilson, 1900), 376.

42. Palfrey, *Memoir*, 99.

43. https://www.findagrave.com/memorial/6285726/joseph-wheeler-gird; *OR*, Vol. 36, I, 13; Fox, *Regimental Losses*, 175; Wilkinson, *Mother*, 78, 87–88, 625.

44. 57th Massachusetts Regimental Correspondence, MSA; Adjutant General, *Massachusetts Soldiers*, IV, 863.

45. John Anderson, *The Fifty-Seventh Regiment of Massachusetts Volunteers in the War of the Rebellion* (Boston: E. B. Stillings, 1896), 65.

46. https://www.findagrave.com/memorial/139715629/charles-edward-griswold; Adams, "In the Wilderness," 378–79; Weld, *War Diary*, 288.

47. Bates, *History*, Vol. III, 562; Walcott, *History of the Twenty-First*, 316; Horace Porter, *Campaigning with Grant* (New York: Century Co., 1906), 60.

48. Krick, "Like a Duck," 240–55; Rhea, *The Battle*, 371–76.

49. *OR*, Vol. 36, II, 444.

50. Rhea, *The Battle*, 380–84; *OR*, Vol. 36, I, 928; Porter, *Campaigning*, 60–61.

51. Lane, *Story*, 168; *OR*, Vol. 36, I, 948, 953, 957.

52. Oates, *The War*, 349–50.

53. William F. Perry, "Reminiscences of the Campaign of 1864 in Virginia," *Southern Historical Society Papers*, Vol. VII, No. 2, 1879, 61.

54. *OR*, Vol. 36, I, 957; Cogswell, *A History*, 341; https://www.findagrave.com/memorial/228707521/moses-n-collins.

55. Cogswell, *A History*, 170–74.

56. Charles Cummings Papers (MS-28), VHS; Steven E. Sodergren, *The Army of the Potomac in the Overland and Petersburg Campaigns: Union Soldiers and Trench Warfare, 1864–1865* (Baton Rouge: LSU Press, 2017), 43.

57. Committee of the Regiment, *History of the Thirty-Sixth*, 152–54; Albert, ed., *History of the Forty-Fifth*, 121.

58. https://www.cmohs.org/recipients/benjamin-f-tracy.

59. *OR*, Vol. 36, I, 953, 957.

60. https://www.findagrave.com/memorial/6554023/frank-graves; *OR*, Vol. 36, I, 948.

61. Cutcheon, *The Story*, 107; *OR*, Vol. 36, I, 132; Crater, *History*, 51.

62. Perry, "Reminiscences," 62.

63. Hopkins, *The Seventh*, 166–67.

64. *OR*, Vol. 36, II, 44–46.

65. Josiah Jones War Memoranda, NHHS; Bosbyshell, *The 48th*, 148; Lane, *Story*, 168; Perry, "Reminiscences," 62.

66. Sauers, ed., *The Civil War Journal*, 199; Stephen F. Brown Papers, VHS.

67. 57th Massachusetts Regimental Correspondence, MSA.

68. Adjutant General, *Massachusetts Soldiers*, V, 48, 85; https://www.findagrave.com/memorial/212614665/swinton-dunlop#.

69. Pollard Diary, VSA; Brager, *Grant's Victory*, 118–20; Jones Memoranda, NHHS; *OR*, Vol. 36, I, 907–8; Parker, *History of the 51st*, 546; Sears, *Lincoln's Lieutenants*, 646–50; Wert, *The Sword*, 343–44; Gordon C. Rhea, *The Battles for Spotsylvania Court House and the Road to Yellow Tavern, May 7–12, 1864* (Baton Rouge: LSU Press, 1997), 13–60; *OR*, Vol. 36, II, 545–46.

70. Lane, *Story*, 168–72.

71. Contemporary and modern sources spell the river either Ni or Ny. Although the later spelling is more phonetic, Ni seems more common in nineteenth-century references to the river.

72. *OR*, Vol. 36, II, 546–48, 550.

73. Rhea, *The Battles*, 103–4; *OR*, Vol. 36, II, 580–81; Ryan T. Quint, "Ambrose Burnside, the Ninth Corps, and the Battle of Spotsylvania Court House," *The Gettysburg College Journal of the Civil War Era*, Vol. 5, 2005, 87–88.

74. Crater, *History*, 54–56; *OR*, Vol. 36, I, 943.

75. *OR*, Vol. 36, I, 968; McKnight, *Blue Bonnets*, 130–34.

76. Eicher and Eicher, *High Commands*, 474.

77. Rhea, *The Battles*, 107–8.

78. Herek, *These Men*, 133–34; *OR*, Vol. 36, I, 941; Scott, ed., *Forgotten*, 520.

79. R. A. Smith, "How General Stevenson Died," *National Tribune*, January 20, 1898, 2; *OR*, Vol. 36, I, 908–9; Eicher and Eicher, *High Commands*, 510–11.

80. Larned Papers, LOC.

81. Rhea, *The Battles*, 212–31; *OR*, Vol. 36, II, 643.

82. Marvel, *Burnside*, 363–64; *OR*, Vol. 36, I, 909.

83. Rhea, *The Battles*, 244–45; Robinson Papers, Dartmouth.

84. J. H. Lane, "Battle of Spotsylvania Court-House," *Southern Historical Society Papers*, Vol. 9, 1881, 146.

85. Henry C. Houston, *The Thirty-Second Maine Regiment* (Portland: Southworth Brothers, 1903), 128; William Kelsey McDaid, *"Four Years of Arduous Service": The History of the Branch-Lane Brigade in the Civil War*, PhD dissertation, Michigan State University, 1987, 269–70.

86. Pollard Diary, VSA.

87. Lord, *History*, 380–81.

88. Houston, *The Thirty-Second*, 131; Clark, ed., *Histories*, Vol. II, 571, 666; Earl J. Hess, *Trench Warfare under Grant and Lee: Field Fortifications in the Overland Campaign* (Chapel Hill: UNC Press, 2007), 69–70.

89. Robinson Papers, Dartmouth.

90. Rhea, *The Battles*, 252–53; Cogswell, *A History*, 364; Canfield, *A History*, 29; Quint, "Ambrose Burnside," 96; Jones Memoranda, NHHS.

91. Committee of the Regiment, *History*, 164–65; Rhea, *The Battles*, 253–54.

92. *OR*, Vol. 36, I, 148–49, 928.

93. Committee of the Regiment, *History*, 167; https://www.findagrave.com/memorial/128012631/amos-buffum.

94. Gavin, ed., *Infantryman*, 135–36; Rhea, *The Battles*, 254–55; Quint, "Ambrose Burnside," 97–98.

95. Rhea, *The Battles*, 323; Herek, *These Men*, 140–41; Sauers, ed., *Civil War Journal*, 202.

96. *OR*, Vol. 36, II, 677–79.

97. *OR*, Vol. 36, I, 944.

98. Scott, ed., *Forgotten*, 521.

99. Furney, ed., *Reminiscences*, 205–7.

100. Parker, *History of the 51st*, 548–49; Crater, *History*, 56.

101. Sauers, ed., *Civil War Journal*, 204, 213; https://www.findagrave.com/memorial/41028912/george-w-bisbing.

102. Lane, "Battle of Spotsylvania Court-House," 149; Clark, ed., *Histories*, Vol. II, 667.

103. Lane, "Battle of Spotsylvania Court-House," 148; *OR*, Vol. 36, I, 939; Rhea, *The Battles*, 297–98.

104. *OR*, Vol. 36, I, 954–55.

105. Quint, "Ambrose Burnside," 98–100; *OR*, Vol. 36, I, 950, 958; John Horn, *The Petersburg Regiment in the Civil War: A History of the 12th Virginia Infantry from John Brown's Hanging to Appomattox* (El Dorado Hills: Savas Beatie, 2019), 248–51; McDaid, *"Four Years,"* 275–78.

106. Weld, *War Diary*, 292; F. E. C., *History*, 7.

107. *OR*, Vol. 36, II, 681.

108. *OR*, Vol. 36, I, 149; Crater, *History*, 57–62; https://www.findagrave.com/memorial/15795469/thomas-gillett.

109. Houston, *The Thirty-Second*, 137; Cogswell, *A History*, 368.

110. 57th Massachusetts Regimental Correspondence, MSA; Wilkinson, *Mother*, 113; https://www.findagrave.com/memorial/175156970/james-maynard-stetson.

111. Marvel, *Burnside*, 365–66; https://www.cmohs.org/recipients/samuel-n-benjamin.

112. McKnight, *Blue Bonnets*, 135; Eicher and Eicher, *High Commands*, 399.

113. *OR*, Vol. 36, I, 149, 910; Larned Papers, LOC; Marvel, *Burnside*, 366–68; Scott, ed., *Forgotten*, 522; Gordon C. Rhea, *To the North Anna River: Grant and Lee, May 13–25* (Baton Rouge: LSU Press, 2000), 65–198, 212–79.

114. *OR*, Vol. 36, I, 951.

115. Houston, *The Thirty-Second*, 171–75; *OR*, Vol. 36, III, 134–35.

116. *OR*, Vol. 36, III, 169–70; Marvel, *Burnside*, 372.

117. *OR*, Vol. 36, I, 985; Hodskin Diary, UM.

118. Regimental Association, *History of the Thirty-Fifth*, 238; Anderson, *The Fifty-Seventh*, 98.

119. Eicher and Eicher, *High Commands*, 190, 342; Marvel, *Burnside*, 369–73.

120. Walcott, *History of the Twenty-First*, 327.

121. Ent, *Pennsylvania Reserves*, 274–75; O. R. Howard Thomson and William H. Rauch, *History of the "Bucktails," Kane Rifle Regiment of the Pennsylvania Reserve Corps (13th Pennsylvania Reserves, 42nd of the Line)* (Philadelphia: Electric Printing Company, 1906), 316; Regimental Association, *History of the Thirty-Fifth*, 238–39.

122. Anderson, *The Fifty-Seventh*, 99–100; *Lt. Col. Charles Lyon Chandler* (Cambridge, MA: 1864), 11–12; Regimental Association, *History of the Thirty-Fifth*, 239; *OR*, Vol. 36, I, 316.

123. Weld, *War Diary*, 296.

124. Adjutant General, *Massachusetts Soldiers*, IV, 817; Anderson, *The Fifty-Seventh*, 101–2; https://www.cmohs.org/recipients/leopold-karpeles.

125. Weld, *War Diary*, 296–97; Anderson, *The Fifty-Seventh*, 100–104; Rhea, *To the North Anna*, 339–41; *Lt. Col. Charles Lyon Chandler*, 13; Wilkinson, *Mother*, 121, 141.

126. *OR*, Vol. 36, I, 161; Peter Cozzens, *This Terrible Sound: The Battle of Chickamauga* (Urbana: University of Illinois Press, 1996), 7–9, 522–26; William F. G. Shanks, *Personal Recollections of Distinguished Generals* (New York: Harper & Brothers, 1866), 266.
127. Rhea, *To the North Anna*, 342.
128. *OR*, Vol. 36, III, 198–99.
129. Rhea, *To the North Anna*, 325–26; Walcott, *History of the Twenty-First*, 327; Hess, *Trench Warfare*, 131–32.
130. *OR*, Vol. 36, I, 932; F. E. C., *History*, 7–8; Paige, *Story*, 117.
131. Jackson, *History of the Sixth*, 268.
132. *OR*, Vol. 36, I, 936–37; Houston, *The Thirty-Second*, 176.
133. Gordon C. Rhea, *Cold Harbor: Grant and Lee, May 26–June 3, 1864* (Baton Rouge: LSU Press, 2002), 27–31; Houston, *The Thirty-Second*, 189; Jackson, *History of the Sixth*, 269.
134. *OR*, Vol. 36, I, 929; Upton Papers, NHHS.
135. Jackson, *History of the Sixth*, 269; *OR*, Vol. 36, I, 929; https://www.findagrave.com/memorial/16135170/henry-h-pearson; Towne Papers, NHHS.
136. Hopkins, *The Seventh*, 179.
137. Weld, *War Diary*, 298.
138. Sauers, ed., *The Civil War Journal*, 209; Regimental Association, *History of the Thirty-Fifth*, 241; Fisher Cleaveland Papers, Duke.
139. *OR*, Vol. 36, I, 932.
140. https://museum.dmna.ny.gov/index.php/?cID=1960.
141. Faron Anderson Papers, UM.
142. William Randall Reminiscences, 1867, UM.
143. Furney, ed., *Reminiscences*, 211; *OR*, Vol. 36, I, 983, 985; Hess, *Trench Warfare*, 139–41.
144. Diary of Eldin J. Hartshorn, 1864, VHS; Marvel, *Burnside*, 374–75; *OR*, Vol. 36, III, 426.
145. Gavin, ed., *Infantryman*, 139; Grant, *Personal Memoirs*, Vol. II, 252–54; Rhea, *Cold Harbor*, 19–64.
146. Walcott, *History of the Twenty-First*, 329; Sauers, ed., *The Civil War Journal*, 209; Scott, ed., *Forgotten*, 526.
147. *OR*, Vol. 36, III, 330–31, 335–36, 346, 360; Jackson, *History of the Sixth*, 273; Herek, *These Men*, 169.
148. Rhea, *Cold Harbor*, 118.
149. *OR*, Vol. 36, I, 913, 955, and III, 376; Weld, *War Diary*, 299.
150. Albert, ed., *History of the 45th*, 131; Bates, *History*, Vol. I, 1096; https://www.findagrave.com/memorial/81833435/thomas-j-davies.
151. *OR*, Vol. 36, III, 404–10; Marvel, *Burnside*, 375.
152. https://www.findagrave.com/memorial/59988806/joseph-a-gilmour; Gould, *The Story*, 187; Bosbyshell, *The 48th*, 152–53; *OR*, Vol. 36, III, 930.
153. Eicher and Eicher, *High Commands*, 364–65; *OR*, Vol. 36, I, 149.
154. https://museum.dmna.ny.gov/index.php/?cID=1867.
155. Rhea, *Cold Harbor*, 231.

156. Robinson Papers, Dartmouth.

157. Regimental Association, *History of the Thirty-Fifth*, 244–45.

158. *OR*, Vol. 36, III, 436–38.

159. Weld, *War Diary*, 300; Rhea, *Cold Harbor*, 256–59.

160. https://museum.dmna.ny.gov/application/files/9715/4834/3944/14thArtCW
_Roster.pdf; https://www.findagrave.com/memorial/28245535/lorenzo-c-newton;
https://www.findagrave.com/memorial/51145405/george-w-vansant.

161. Regimental Association, *History of the Thirty-Fifth*, 245.

162. Scott, ed., *Forgotten*, 526; Clark, ed., *Histories*, I, 727.

163. Randall Reminiscences, UM.

164. *OR*, Vol. 36, I, 952; Sauers, ed., *The Civil War Journal*, 210; Parker, *History of the 51st*, 559.

165. *OR*, Vol. 36, I, 918.

166. Houston, *The Thirty-Second*, 212.

167. Grant, *Personal Memoirs*, Vol. II, 268; Rhea, *Cold Harbor*, 279–80.

168. *OR*, Vol. 36, I, 162; Weld, *War Diary*, 301–2.

169. Gavin, ed., *Infantryman*, 139; Moses and Matthew Whitehill Letters, VHS.

170. Larned Papers, LOC; Albert, ed., *History of the 45th*, 259.

171. Jackson, *History of the Sixth*, 283.

172. Rhea, *Cold Harbor*, 279–81.

173. *OR*, Vol. 36, III, 498–500; Rhea, *Cold Harbor*, 283.

174. Rhea, *Cold Harbor*, 295–97.

175. https://museum.dmna.ny.gov/index.php/?cID=1960.

176. Grant Diaries, UM; *OR*, Vol. 36, I, 971; Cutcheon, *The Story*, 128–29.

177. Walcott, *History of the Twenty-First*, 330–31; Fox, *Regimental Losses*, 165.

178. Gavin, ed., *Infantryman*, 139–49.

179. Marvel, *Burnside*, 377–78.

180. Committee of the Regiment, *History of the Thirty-Sixth*, 191; Bosbyshell, *The 48th*, 153.

181. *OR*, Vol. 36, 914, 930; John A. Sloan, *Reminiscences of the Guilford Grays* (Washington: R. O. Polkinhorn, 1883), 96; Clark, ed., *Histories*, I, 746.

182. Hopkins, *The Seventh*, 184.

183. Committee of the Regiment, *History of the Thirty-Sixth*, 191.

184. Gould, *The Story*, 189.

185. Albert, ed., *History of the 45th*, 133–34; Bates, *History*, Vol. I, 1068; *OR*, Vol. 36, I, 175; Fox, *Regimental Losses*, 265.

186. Clark, ed., *Histories*, III, 76–77; Hopkins, *The Seventh*, 184.

187. *OR*, Vol. 36, I, 952; F. E. C., *History*, 9.

188. Parker, *History of the 51st*, 560–61; Sauers, ed., *The Civil War Journal*, 211.

189. *OR*, Vol. 36, I, 983, 985; 32nd Maine Regimental Correspondence, MSA; https://www.findagrave.com/memorial/121343006/william-r-ham.

190. 58th Massachusetts Regimental Correspondence, MSA.

191. https://www.findagrave.com/memorial/88644496/barnabas-ewer; F. E. C., *History*, 9–10; *OR*, Vol. 36, I, 175.

192. Rhea, *Cold Harbor*, 382; Marvel, *Burnside*, 378.

193. *OR*, Vol. 36, III, 585; Marvel, *Burnside*, 379–81.

194. Lord, *History*, 426; Albert, ed., *History of the 45th*, 259; Crater, ed., *History*, 63.

195. Upton Papers, NHHS.

196. Larned Papers, LOC.

197. Hodskin Diary, UM; Hopkins, *The Seventh*, 187–88.

198. Tilton Papers, NHHS; Towne Papers, NHHS; Ayling, *Revised Register*, 301.

199. *OR*, Vol. 36, III, 598–99; A. Wilson Greene, *A Campaign of Giants: The Battle for Petersburg, Vol. 1, From the Crossing of the James to the Crater* (Chapel Hill: University of North Carolina Press, 2018), 42–45.

200. Eicher and Eicher, *High Commands*, 422.

201. Edwin P. Rutan II, *"If I Have Got to Go and Fight, I Am Willing": A Union Regiment Forged in the Petersburg Campaign* (Park City, UT: RTD Publications, 2015), 43–50.

202. *OR*, Vol. 40, I, 582–83; R. C. Eden, *The Sword and Gun: A History of the 37th Wis. Volunteer Infantry* (Madison: Atwood & Rublee, 1865), 7–12.

203. *OR*, Vol. 36, I, 176; S. W. Pierce, *Battlefield and Camp Fires of the Thirty-Eighth* (Milwaukee: Daily Wisconsin Printing, 1866), 12–18.

204. *OR*, Vol. 36, I, 985.

205. Hopkins, *The Seventh*, 189.

206. Regimental Association, *History of the Thirty-Fifth*, 251.

207. Greene, *A Campaign*, 46, 54–55, 72; Gordon C. Rhea, "Grant's Disengagement from Cold Harbor: June 12–13, 1864," in *Cold Harbor to the Crater: The End of the Overland Campaign*, Gary W. Gallagher and Caroline E. Janney, eds. (Chapel Hill: University of North Carolina Press, 2015), 194–95; *OR*, Vol. 36, I, 915, 931; Hopkins, *The Seventh*, 189; Marvel, *Burnside*, 382–83.

208. *OR*, Vol. 40, I, 544, 581, 583; Tilton Papers, NHHS; Sauers, ed., *The Civil War Journal*, 214; Walcott, *History of the Twenty-First*, 334; Diary of Eldin J. Hartshorn, 1864, VHS; Weld, *War Diary*, 310.

209. *OR*, Vol. 40, I, 522, 593–94, and II, 50, 68–69; Greene, *A Campaign*, 129–30; Albert S. Twitchell, *History of the Seventh Maine Light Battery, Volunteers in the Great Rebellion* (Boston: E. B. Stillings, 1892), 27; Cummings Papers (MS-28), VHS; Hodskin Diary, UM.

210. *OR*, Vol. 40, II, 68–70; Marvel, *Burnside*, 384.

211. Sears, *Lincoln's Lieutenants*, 704–5; Cogswell, *A History*, 376; George W. Ward, *History of the Second Pennsylvania Veteran Heavy Artillery from 1861 to 1866* (Philadelphia: Geo. W. Ward, 1904), 189; Osborne, *The History*, 302; Walcott, *History of the Twenty-First*, 335; Sargent Papers, Dartmouth.

212. *OR*, Vol. 40, II, 88–91; Lawrence A. Kreiser, Jr., *Defeating Lee: A History of the Second Corps, Army of the Potomac* (Bloomington: Indiana University Press, 2011), 193–99.

213. *OR*, Vol. 40, I, 545, 565, and II, 87, 95, 134; Greene, *A Campaign*, 146–50; Jordan, *Winfield*, 147–48.

214. *OR*, Vol. 40, I, 569; Hartshorn Diary, VHS; Sargent Papers, Dartmouth.

215. Houston, *The Thirty-Second*, 273–74; Cogswell, *A History*, 376–77.

216. Orlando Wales Dimick Autobiography, Dartmouth.

217. Houston, *The Thirty-Second*, 278; https://www.findagrave.com/memorial/96712415/reuben-vining; https://www.findagrave.com/memorial/104173003/marcellus-vining; *OR*, Vol. 40, I, 569.

218. Committee of the Regiment, *History of the Thirty-Sixth*, 207–8.

219. https://www.findagrave.com/memorial/149305501/otis-worthington-holmes; Committee of the Regiment, *History of the Thirty-Sixth*, 208.

220. Gould, *The Story*, 197; *OR*, Vol. 40, I, 522.

221. *OR*, Vol. 40, II, 135.

222. See 31st Maine Regimental Correspondence, MSA; Greene, *A Campaign*, 151–52; *OR*, Vol. 40, I, 522.

223. Fox, *Regimental Losses*, 381; Hodskin Diary, UM.

224. Hess, *Trench Warfare*, 3–4; Cullum, *Biographical Register*, Vol. II, 437–38.

225. Greene, *A Campaign*, 157–59; *OR*, Vol 40, I, 577, 588.

226. Eden, *The Sword and Gun*, 20–21; *OR*, Vol 40, I, 577.

227. See 2nd Michigan Regimental Records, https://michiganology.org/civil-war; https://www.findagrave.com/memorial/2597283/sanford-g-rogers; https://www.findagrave.com/memorial/35050742/lyman-heath.

228. *OR*, Vol. 40, I, 571.

229. Cullum, *Biographical Register*, Vol. II, 438; Eden, *The Sword and Gun*, 22; *OR*, Vol. 40, I, 588.

230. Crater, *History*, 65–66.

231. https://museum.dmna.ny.gov/index.php/?cID=2994.

232. https://museum.dmna.ny.gov/application/files/3215/4894/3211/24thCavCW_Roster.pdf; https://www.findagrave.com/memorial/70964137/calvin-p-burch.

233. Greene, *A Campaign*, 163–64; Osborne, *The History*, 302; Walcott, *History of the Twenty-First*, 336.

234. *OR*, Vol. 40, I, 228–29, 532–33.

235. Walcott, *History of the Twenty-First*, 337.

236. Wilkinson, *Mother*, 178–79; https://www.findagrave.com/memorial/22532723/julius-massena-tucker.

237. Herek, *These Men*, 178–87; https://www.findagrave.com/memorial/14764738/levant-c-rhines.

238. Ward, *History*, 190–91.

239. *OR*, Vol. 40, I, 229, 231; https://museum.dmna.ny.gov/application/files/9715/4834/3944/14thArtCW_Roster.pdf.

240. https://www.findagrave.com/memorial/82798691/job-clark-hedges; https://museum.dmna.ny.gov/unit-history/artillery/14th-artillery-regiment-heavy/newspaper-clippings.

241. *OR*, Vol. 40, I, 540; Greene, *A Campaign*, 166–67.

242. Weld, *War Diary*, 312.

243. *OR*, Vol. 40, I, 523, 545, 572–73; Marvel, *Burnside*, 387–89; Sauers, ed., *Civil War Journal*, 218–19; Sears, *Lincoln's Lieutenants*, 707–14; Greene, *A Campaign*, 170–212; Nutting Papers, NHHS.

244. Gary W. Gallagher, "The Two Generals Who Resist Each Other: Perceptions of Grant and Lee in the Summer of 1864," in *Cold Harbor*, Gallagher and Janney, eds., 5; *OR*, Vol. 40, I, 177.

245. *OR*, Vol. 40, I, 177, 228–31.

246. William T. King Letters, VHS; Ward, *History*, 195.

247. Correspondence of Dodge, VSA; *OR*, Vol. 40, I, 231.

248. Jim Corrigan, *The 48th Pennsylvania in the Battle of the Crater: A Regiment of Coal Miners Who Tunneled under the Enemy* (Jefferson, NC: McFarland & Company, 2006), 17–18; Bosbyshell, *The 48th*, 163–66; *OR*, Vol. 40, 523; Marvel, *Burnside*, 390–91; Wert, *The Sword*, 380.

PART SEVEN

1. *OR*, Vol. 40, I, 545.

2. Crater, *History*, 68–69; *OR*, Vol. 40, I, 248, 261; John Cooper Letter, LVA.

3. Walter Pingree Papers, Dartmouth; https://www.findagrave.com/memorial/1154 15100/hiram-k-little; Cogswell, *A History*, 485.

4. Levstik, "The Civil War Diary," 46–47.

5. Jones Memoranda, NHHS; Muchmore Correspondence, NHHS; Henry Muchmore Diary, Dartmouth.

6. Correspondence of Dodge, VSA.

7. Gilbert Family Papers, RIHS; Walcott, *History of the Twenty-First*, 341.

8. Albert, ed., *History of the 45th*, 143–44; Letters of Albert Camp Raymond, VHS; Richard B. Loomis letter, LVA.

9. George B. Codman Papers, Dartmouth; Sargent Papers, Dartmouth; Muchmore Correspondence, NHHS; Letters of Raymond, VHS; Henry Eaton letter, LVA.

10. John Gross Barnard Papers, Duke; Marvel, *Burnside*, 392–94; Henry Pleasants, Jr., *The Tragedy of the Crater* (Boston: Christopher Publishing House, 1938), 55–59.

11. Richard Slotkin, *No Quarter: The Battle of the Crater, 1864* (New York: Random House, 2009), 33–35; Greene, *A Campaign*, 379–80; Eicher and Eicher, *High Commands*, 431; Earl J. Hess, *Into the Crater: The Mine Attack at Petersburg* (Columbia: University of South Carolina Press, 2010), 1, 11–17; Pleasants, Jr., *The Tragedy*, 38; *OR*, Vol. 40, I, 557.

12. *OR*, Vol. 40, I, 556–58; Pleasants, Jr., *The Tragedy*, 41–45; Slotkin, *No Quarter*, 34; Corrigan, *The 48th*, 33.

13. *OR*, Vol. 40, I, 558. July 30, 1864, marked the detonation of the mine and the horrible brawl immediately after. Few battles of the Civil War have received as much detailed treatment as the Crater, especially in recent years. Multiple monographs published in the twenty-first century, or excellent general works, provide extensive tactical depth and nearly minute-by-minute accounts of the dreadful engagement. While *Burnside's Boys* discusses the horrendous fight so costly to Burnside personally and his troops, the extensive amount of readily available modern scholarship is highly recommended for those wishing to delve into the battle in greater detail. The leading secondary sources I used to understand the Crater's construction and the fiendish combat that followed are Greene, *A Campaign*, 373–516; Slotkin, *No Quarter*; Hess, *Into the Crater*;

Corrigan, *The 48th Pennsylvania*; Kevin M. Levin, *Remembering the Battle of the Crater: War as Murder* (Lexington: University Press of Kentucky, 2017), 7–51; Kevin M. Levin, "The Devil Himself Could Not Have Checked Them: Fighting with Black Soldiers at the Crater," in *Cold Harbor*, Gary W. Gallagher and Caroline E. Janney, 264–82.

14. *OR*, Vol. 40, I, 45, 70–71.

15. Marvel, *Burnside*, 392–93; Slotkin, *No Quarter*, 71–72; Morton, *Trusting to Luck*, 526; Corrigan, *The 48th*, 59–60.

16. Hess, *Into the Crater*, 55–56; Morton, *Trusting to Luck*, 512–17; Greene, *A Campaign*, 421–22; Sears, *Lincoln's Lieutenants*, 727–28; White, *American Ulysses*, 376–77.

17. Slotkin, *No Quarter*, 80–83, 325.

18. Pleasants, Jr., *The Tragedy*, 54; Corrigan, *The 48th*, 18; *OR*, Vol. 40, III, 479; Greene, *A Campaign*, 390; Slotkin, *No Quarter*, 182, 184.

19. James Chatham Duane Papers, LVA; Slotkin, *No Quarter*, 207–8; Greene, *A Campaign*, 420.

20. Pleasants, Jr., *The Tragedy*, 70–71.

21. Upton Papers, NHHS.

22. Greene, *A Campaign*, 432–37; *OR*, Vol. 40, I, 139–40.

23. F. W. McMaster, "The Battle of the Crater, July 30, 1864," *Southern Historical Society Papers*, Vol. X, No. 3, 1879, 119–20; Hess, *Into the Crater*, 85; Charles Moulton Letter, NHHS.

24. Weld, *War Diary*, 353.

25. Heisler Papers, LOC.

26. Ward, *History*, 87; Lyman Knapp Papers, VHS.

27. John F. Sale Papers, LVA; *OR*, Vol. 40, I, 604; Furney, ed., *Reminiscences*, 247; Frank Kenfield, "Captured by Rebels: A Vermonter at Petersburg, 1864," *Vermont History*, Autumn 1968, Vol. 36, No. 4, 232.

28. *OR*, Vol. 40, I, 43–44.

29. Slotkin, *No Quarter*, 322; Greene, *A Campaign*, 422–23; Wert, *The Sword*, 383; Sears, *Lincoln's Lieutenants*, 727–28.

30. *OR*, Vol. 40, I, 158, 535; Marvel, *Burnside*, 395–96.

31. *OR*, Vol. 40, I, 541; Hess, *Into the Crater*, 58–60; *OR*, Vol. 40, I, 158–59.

32. Ward, *History*, 196–97; Hess, *Into the Crater*, 88–90; Greene, *A Campaign*, 439–42; Rutan II, *"If I Have Got to Go,"* 94–96.

33. Regimental Association, *History of the Thirty-Fifth*, 269.

34. *OR*, Vol. 40, I, 527; United States Senate, 38th Cong., 2nd Sess., *Report of the Committee on the Conduct of the War on the Attack on Petersburg on the 30th Day of July, 1864* (Washington: GPO, 1865), 105; William H. Powell, "The Tragedy of the Crater," *The Century*, Vol. 34, No. 5, 767.

35. *OR*, Vol. 40, I, 64, 103; U.S. Senate, *Report of the Committee*, 222.

36. Palfrey, *Memoir*, 119.

37. Marvel, *Burnside*, 398–400; Walcott, *History of the Twenty-First*, 346; Anderson, *The Fifty-Seventh*, 175–78.

38. U.S. Senate, *Report of the Committee*, 99.

39. *OR*, Vol. 40, I, 567; Daniel White, "Charging the Crater," *National Tribune*, June 21, 1883, 5; Hess, *Into the Crater*, 92–95; Clark, ed., *Histories*, Vol. II, 299.

40. Allen, *Forty-Six Months*, 286; *OR*, Vol. 40, I, 553–54; Committee of the Regiment, *History of the Thirty-Sixth*, 235.

41. Albert, ed., *History of the 45th*, 153; *OR*, Vol. 40, I, 553; Bates, *History*, Vol. I, 1108; https://www.findagrave.com/memorial/100546198/rees-griffith-richards; https://www.findagrave.com/memorial/63574979/theodore-eyde.

42. Vol. 40, I, 549–50, 564; Allen, *Forty-Six Months*, 287; Hess, *Into the Crater*, 117–20.

43. Scott, ed., *Forgotten Valor*, 554–57.

44. *OR*, Vol. 40, I, 574, 578.

45. Eden, *The Sword and Gun*, 31; *OR*, Vol. 40, I, 247, 584; Pierce, *Battlefield*, 38.

46. *OR*, Vol. 40, I, 586, 591–92; Mettendorf, *Between Triumph and Disaster*, 92–93.

47. *OR*, Vol. 40, I, 247; Crater, *History*, 69.

48. *OR*, Vol. 40, I, 139–40.

49. *OR*, Vol. 40, I, 70–71, 86, 108, 122, 161–62.

50. Marvel, *Burnside*, 401–3; *OR*, Vol. 40, I, 147–48.

51. Greene, *A Campaign*, 444–46; *OR*, Vol. 40, I, 148–49.

52. *OR*, Vol. 40, I, 140–43.

53. Powell, "The Tragedy," 771; Anderson, *The Fifty-Seventh*, 210–11.

54. Ervin T. Case, *The Battle of the Mine* (Providence: Sidney S. Rider, 1879), 28; Andrew A. Humphreys, *The Virginia Campaign of '64 and '65* (New York: Scribner's Sons, 1883), 258.

55. Eicher and Eicher, *High Commands*, 121; Greene, *A Campaign*, 459–60; Free S. Bawley, "The Crater," *National Tribune*, November 6, 1884, 1.

56. F. S. Bowley, *A Boy Lieutenant* (Philadelphia: Henry Altemus Company, 1906), 93–95; J. M. Mickley, *The Forty-Third Regiment United States Colored Troops* (Gettysburg: J. E. Wible, 1866), 74–75; https://www.cmohs.org/recipients/delavan-bates.

57. Henry Seymour Hall, "Personal Experience of a Staff Officer," *A Paper Prepared and Read before the Kansas Commandery of the Military Order of the Loyal Legion of the United States, October 3, 1894*, 18–19.

58. *OR*, Vol. 40, I, 596–97.

59. https://www.findagrave.com/memorial/74998135/christopher-pennell; *OR*, Vol. 40, I, 598.

60. Frank Holsinger, "The Colored Troops at the Mine," *National Tribune*, October 19, 1905; *OR*, Vol. 40, I, 248; Greene, *A Campaign*, 498–505.

61. https://www.findagrave.com/memorial/59062696/cleaveland-john-campbell; Eicher and Eicher, *High Commands*, 160; *OR*, Vol. 40, I, 599.

62. *Memorial of Colonel John A. Bross, Twenty-Ninth U.S. Colored Troops* (Chicago: Tribune Book and Job Office, 1865), 17–20.

63. Greene, *A Campaign*, 461–63; W. A. Day, "Battle of the Crater," *Confederate Veteran*, August 1903, 355.

64. For a monograph about Fort Pillow, see Andrew Ward, *River Run Red: The Fort Pillow Massacre in the American Civil War* (New York: Penguin Group, 2005); Greene, *A Campaign*, 502–5; Levin, *Remembering*, 74–75.

65. Sale Papers, LVA; Slotkin, *No Quarter*, 232–38; Horn, *The Petersburg Regiment*, 289; Ward, *River Run Red*, 71–73; Lord, *History of the Ninth*, 489.

66. Bowley, *A Boy*, 95; Bawley, "The Crater"; William Fielding Baugh Letter, LVA.

67. Robinson Papers, Dartmouth.

68. *OR*, Vol. 40, I, 597; Albert, ed., *History of the 45th*, 260.

69. *OR*, Vol. 40, I, 143–44; Slotkin, *No Quarter*, 207–8.

70. https://www.findagrave.com/memorial/3268445/benjamin-f-trail.

71. Solomon Oakley Papers, NYSL.

72. Levin, *Remembering*, 18–19; *OR*, Vol. 40, I, 599; Glatthaar, *Forged*, 150.

73. https://www.findagrave.com/memorial/20094/decatur-dorsey; https://www.cmohs.org/recipients/decatur-dorsey.

74. https://www.findagrave.com/memorial/7980551/abraham-cohn; https://www.cmohs.org/recipients/abraham-cohn.

75. https://www.findagrave.com/memorial/20631/nathaniel-gwynne.

76. Louis Martin Pension File, NARA; Levin, *Remembering*, 22.

77. *OR*, Vol. 40, I, 177–78; Smith Papers, NYSL.

78. *Recollections*, Dartmouth; Hess, *Into the Crater*, 235.

79. Albert, ed., *History of the 45th*, 261.

80. *OR*, Vol. 40, I, 248; Greene, *A Campaign*, 500–505.

81. *OR*, Vol. 40, I, 246–48; Codman Papers, Dartmouth; Charles Lancaster Letter, LVA; Jackson, *History of the Sixth*, 322.

82. 31st Maine Regimental Correspondence, MSA; *OR*, Vol. 40, I, 249–50; Whitehill Letters, VHS.

83. Walcott, *History of the Twenty-First*, 347–48.

84. https://www.findagrave.com/memorial/24961837/jacob-parker-gould.

85. *OR*, Vol. 40, I, 172–76; Marvel, *Burnside*, 403–4, 408–13.

86. Sears, *Lincoln's Lieutenants*, 731–32; *OR*, Vol. 40, I, 42–43, 531–32; Slotkin, *No Quarter*, 321–24.

87. Eicher and Eicher, *High Commands*, 342.

88. *OR*, Vol. 40, I, 50.

89. *OR*, Vol. 40, I, 45–49, 64–65.

90. *OR*, Vol. 40, I, 76, 78.

91. *OR*, Vol. 40, I, 88–91.

92. The testimonies of Ferrero, Willcox, and Griffin are at *OR*, Vol. 40, I, 92–96, 99–101.

93. *OR*, Vol. 40, I, 108–9.

94. *OR*, Vol. 40, I, 125–29.

95. United States Senate, 38th Cong., 2nd Sess., *Report of the Committee*.

96. Marvel, *Burnside*, 410–14; Eicher and Eicher, *High Commands*, 416.

97. *OR*, Vol. 40, I, 525–26.

98. Jones Memoranda, NHHS.

99. *OR*, Vol. 42, II, 10; George Codman Papers, Dartmouth; Allen, *Forty-Six Months*, 292–93.

100. Parker, *History of the 51st*, 579; Jones Memoranda, NHHS.

101. 7th Maine Battery Correspondence, MSA; Twitchell, *History*, 30.

102. *OR*, Vol. 42, II, 32, 45; Walcott, *History of the Twenty-First*, 350; Adjutant General, *Massachusetts Soldiers*, II, 634; https://www.findagrave.com/memorial/13912177 /richard-baxter-loomis.

103. *OR*, Vol. 42, II, 44, 59; Eicher and Eicher, *High Commands*, 565–66.

104. Correspondence of Dodge, VSA.

105. *OR*, Vol. 42, II, 153–54.

106. Cuffel, *History*, 202.

107. *OR*, Vol. 42, I, 544–45, and II, 251–53; Scott, ed., *Forgotten Valor*, 565–66; Wert, *The Sword*, 387–88.

108. *Battles and Leaders of the Civil War*, Vol. 4 (New York: Century Company, 1888), 568–70; Scott, ed., *Forgotten Valor*, 567–68; *OR*, Vol. 42, I, 595; Ward, *History*, 215.

109. *OR*, Vol. 42, I, 593.

110. Parker, *History of the 51st*, 579–80; Mettendorf, *Between Triumph and Disaster*, 94–95; Bates, *History*, Vol. II, 13, 28.

111. *OR*, Vol. 42, I, 594; Herek, *These Men*, 242.

112. *OR*, Vol. 42, I, 72, 551; Walcott, *History of the Twenty-First*, 350; https://www .findagrave.com/memorial/93310095/william-b-phipps.

113. Osborne, *The History*, 319.

114. Walcott, *History of the Twenty-First*, 352; Regimental Association, *History of the Thirty-Fifth*, 285–86; Dunlap Family Papers, LVA.

115. Horn, *The Petersburg Regiment*, 309–18; *OR*, Vol. 42, I, 127–28, 564.

116. https://www.findagrave.com/memorial/38434577/eli-hunt; Crater, *History*, 70–71.

117. *OR*, Vol. 42, I, 545, 550; Dunlap Family Papers, LVA.

118. Nutting Papers, NHHS.

119. Levstik, "The Civil War Diary," 54–55.

120. Robinson Papers, Dartmouth; Salmon K. Gates Papers, VHS.

121. *OR*, Vol. 42, II, 603–4.

122. Cleaveland Papers, Duke.

123. Howard Aston, *History and Roster of the Fourth and Fifth Independent Battalions and Thirteenth Regiment Ohio Cavalry Volunteers* (Columbus: Fred J. Heer, 1902), 22; Osborne, *The History*, 320.

124. Cummings Papers (MS-28), VHS.

125. *OR*, Vol. 42, II, 1047–48, 1069, 1076, 1119, 1131, 1137.

126. Committee of the Regiment, *History of the Thirty-Sixth*, 258–59; *OR*, Vol. 42, I, 545–46, 565, 581.

127. *OR*, Vol. 42, I, 578–79, 587.

128. Houston, *The Thirty-Second*, 392; Lord, *History of the Ninth*, 524; Clark, ed., *Histories of the Several Regiments*, III, 249.

129. Jackson, *History of the Sixth*, 336–37.

130. *OR*, Vol. 42, I, 581–82; Albert, ed., *History of the 45th*, 164.

131. *OR*, Vol. 42, I, 582, 585.

132. Bosbyshell, *The 48th*, 181–82; Hopkins, *The Seventh*, 216.

133. *OR*, Vol. 42, I, 565–66; Cutcheon, *The Story*, 155–56; Jones Memoranda, NHHS.

134. *OR*, Vol. 42, I, 142; Diary of Lewis Simonds, Dartmouth.

135. Jackson, *History of the Sixth*, 338–39; https://www.findagrave.com/memorial/3492 0771/hiram-drown; Ayling, *Revised Register*, 302.

136. https://www.findagrave.com/memorial/58090482/orange-scott-sampson.

137. F. E. C, *History*, 17; Adjutant General, *Massachusetts Soldiers*, V, 9, 14.

138. Cummings Papers (MSA 829.9), VHS.

139. Jones Memoranda, NHHS; Aston, *History and Roster*, 23; Sears, *Lincoln's Lieutenants*, 742; *OR*, Vol. 42, I, 157–60.

140. *OR*, Vol. 42, I, 580, and III, 1121–22.

141. Sears, *Lincoln's Lieutenants*, 742; Charles Rundlett Letters, LVA; *OR*, Vol. 42, I, 157–60.

142. Codman Papers, Dartmouth; Hartshorn Diary, VHS.

143. Dunlap Family Papers, LVA.

144. Rundlett Letters, LVA; Sargent Papers, Dartmouth.

145. John T. Andrews Letters, LVA.

146. Wert, *The Sword*, 391; Sears, *Lincoln's Lieutenants*, 742–43; Zachery A. Fry, *A Republic in the Ranks: Loyalty and Dissent in the Army of the Potomac* (Chapel Hill: University of North Carolina Press, 2020), 155–83, 210–24; Herek, *These Men*, 268–71; Marvel, *Race*, 322–24; Houston, *The Thirty-Second*, 413; Sauers, ed., *The Civil War Journal*, 236; Jones Memoranda, NHHS; Muchmore Diary, Dartmouth.

147. Albert, ed., *History of the 45th*, 170.

148. *Recollections*, Dartmouth; Regimental Association, *History of the Thirty-Fifth*, 316.

149. *OR*, Vol. 42, I, 39–40, 162.

150. Hopkins, *The Seventh*, 234.

151. Rundlett Letters, LVA.

152. Cogswell, *A History*, 431.

153. Milton A. Embick, ed., *Military History of the Third Division, Ninth Corps, Army of the Potomac* (Harrisburg: C. E. Aughinbaugh, 1913), 1–4.

154. Letters of Charles Read, private collection of John Gardiner, Carroll, NH.

155. Committee of the Regiment, *History of the Thirty-Sixth*, 272–73.

156. Houston, *The Thirty-Second*, 426–31.

157. Andrews Letters, LVA.

158. Jameson Papers, LOC.

159. Post, ed., *Soldiers' Letters*, 462–63.

160. Robinson Papers, Dartmouth.

161. Pendleton Family Papers, RIHS.

162. Andrew Fitch letters, LVA.

163. Committee of the Regiment, *History of the Thirty-Sixth*, 278.

164. Cutcheon, *The Story*, 162; Crater, *History*, 78.

165. Letters of Raymond, VHS; Eden, *The Sword and Gun*, 40–41.

166. Read Letters, Gardiner Collection.

167. Boston Diary, UM; https://www.findagrave.com/memorial/30421394/samuel -waldron; Pride Collection, NHHS; Ayling, *Revised Register*, 326.

168. Sargent Papers, Dartmouth.

169. 31st Maine Regimental Correspondence, MSA.

170. *OR*, Vol. 46, II, 565, 570–71.

171. *OR*, Vol. 46, I, 600, and II, 737; Albert, ed., *History of the 45th*, 174.

172. *OR*, Vol. 46, I, 107; Jay Winik, *April 1865: The Month That Saved America* (New York: Harper Perennial, 2006), 41.

173. Clark, ed., *Histories of the Several Regiments*, I, 329; William H. Hodgkins, *The Battle of Fort Stedman, March 25, 1865* (Boston: privately printed, 1889), 10–11.

174. James A. Walker, "Gordon's Assault on Fort Stedman," *Southern Historical Society Papers*, Vol. XXXI, 1879, 23; Clark, ed., *Histories of the Several Regiments*, I, 329, and III, 424.

175. Eicher and Eicher, *High Commands*, 381.

176. *OR*, Vol. 46, I, 70, 331; Scott, ed., *Forgotten Valor*, 616.

177. *OR*, Vol. 46, I, 337, 341; Hodgkins, *The Battle*, 24–25.

178. Osborne, *The History*, 328; *OR*, Vol. 46, I, 338.

179. W. C. Beck, "Fort Steadman," *National Tribune*, September 24, 1885; Hodgkins, *The Battle*, 25–26; *OR*, Vol. 46, I, 342.

180. *OR*, Vol. 46, I, 336; https://www.findagrave.com/memorial/89615615/joseph-henry-pentecost.

181. *OR*, Vol. 46, I, 340–41.

182. Furney, ed., *Reminiscences*, 263; *OR*, Vol. 46, I, 364.

183. 11th Massachusetts Battery Correspondence, MSA.

184. *OR*, Vol. 46, I 325–30; Herek, *These Men*, 307–8.

185. *OR*, Vol. 46, I, 345; W. C. Beck, "Fort Steadman."

186. Hodgkins, *The Battle*, 30–36; *OR*, Vol. 46, I, 345–46.

187. Walker, "Gordon's Assault," 28; Hodgkins, *The Battle*, 39–43.

188. Clark, ed., *Histories of the Several Regiments*, III, 424; *OR*, Vol. 46, III, 121; Embick, ed., *Military History*, 14–15.

189. Scott, ed., *Forgotten Valor*, 614–15, 619–36; W. C. Beck, "Fort Steadman"; *OR*, Vol. 46, I, 70–71.

190. *OR*, Vol. 46, III, 110.

191. *OR*, Vol. 46, III, 109; Samuel Emerson Diary, Dartmouth.

192. 11th Massachusetts Battery Correspondence, MSA; *OR*, Vol. 46, I, 71; https://www.findagrave.com/memorial/104739725/ephraim-bassett-nye.

193. https://museum.dmna.ny.gov/index.php/?cID=1867.

194. https://www.cmohs.org/recipients/joseph-f-carter.

195. Robinson Papers, Dartmouth.

196. Clark, ed., *Histories of the Several Regiments*, III, 425; Winik, *April 1865*, 99; Grant, *Personal Memoirs*, Vol. II, 616–18; Eden, *The Sword and Gun*, 47.

197. *OR*, Vol. 46, III, 233, 265; Nathaniel Talbot Letters, LVA; Emerson Diary, Dartmouth.

198. Sears, *Lincoln's Lieutenants*, 749–52; *OR*, Vol. 46, I, 62, and III, 274–75.

199. *Recollections*, Dartmouth; *OR*, Vol. 46, I, 1072.

200. Jackson, *History of the Sixth*, 357–58; *OR*, Vol. 46, I, 1054, 1059.

201. Thomas P. Beals, "In a Charge Near Fort Hell, Petersburg, April 2, 1865," *War Papers*, Vol. II (Portland, ME: Lefavor-Tower Company, 1902), 109.

202. *Recollections*, Dartmouth; *OR*, Vol. 46, I, 1059.

203. *OR*, Vol. 46, I, 1042–43.

204. Beals, "In a Charge," 109–10.

205. Bates, *History*, Vol. V, 753; *OR*, Vol. 46, I, 1068.

206. *OR*, Vol. 46, I, 1061–62.

207. Jackson, *History of the Sixth*, 359.

208. Clark, ed., *Histories of the Several Regiments*, III, 16–17.

209. Houston, *The Thirty-Second*, 451; Read Letters, Gardiner Collection.

210. Bosbyshell, *The 48th*, 186.

211. Pierce, *Battlefield*, 116; *OR*, Vol. 46, I, 1068.

212. *OR*, Vol. 46, I, 1017–18, 1062–63.

213. Pierce, *Battlefield*, 123.

214. *OR*, Vol. 46, I, 588–90, 600–1; Fox, *Regimental Losses*, 153; *Biographical Notes on the Life of Cassius Wirt Ellsworth*, VHS; *Recollections*, Dartmouth.

CONCLUSION

1. Embick, ed., *Military History*, 22; Cutcheon, *The Story*, 167.

2. Herek, *These Men*, 322–27; Scott, ed., *Forgotten Valor*, 641–42; Sauers, ed., *The Civil War Journal*, 256–57; *OR*, Vol. 46, I, 1019, 1065.

3. Weld, *War Diary*, 393, 395.

4. Sauers, ed., *The Civil War Journal*, 259; Allen, *Forty-Six Months*, 356.

5. *Recollections*, Dartmouth; William Boston Diary, UM; Osborne, *The History*, 336–37.

6. King letters, VHS.

7. Read Letters, Gardiner Collection.

8. Pendleton Family Papers, RIHS; Albert, ed., *History of the 45th*, 181.

9. Wert, *The Sword*, 411–13; Sears, *Lincoln's Lieutenants*, 757; Herek, *These Men*, 339–40; Rutan II, *"If I Have Got to Go,"* 236–37; Albert, ed., *History of the 45th*, 183; Jackson, *History of the Sixth*, 367–68.

10. 58th Massachusetts Regimental Correspondence, MSA; Fox, *Regimental Losses*, 174–76.

11. Fox, *Regimental Losses*, 190, 265.

12. Eicher and Eicher, *High Commands*, 120; https://www.findagrave.com/memorial/5890597/william-francis-bartlett.

13. Cullen, *Biographical Register*, II, 781–82.

14. Marvel, *Burnside*, 412–25; https://bioguideretro.congress.gov/Home/Member Details?memIndex=B001130.

15. Mannie Dorsey pension file, NARA.

16. Eicher and Eicher, *High Commands*, 233.

17. Eicher and Eicher, *High Commands*, 269.

18. Eicher and Eicher, *High Commands*, 284.

19. https://www.findagrave.com/memorial/25112407/samuel-haynes.

20. http://100thpenn.com/drleasure.htm#:~:text=he%20was%20awarded%20a%20par
tial%20pension--%247.50%20a%20month,Army%20surgeon%20to%20St.%20Paul%20
to%20examine%20Leasure.

21. Charles Edward Potter, ed., *Genealogies of the Potter Families and Their Descendants in America* (Boston: Alfred Mudge and Son, 1888), Part 10, 43; https://www.findagrave
.com/memorial/8045/robert-brown-potter.

22. Marvel, *Race*, 359–65; Robinson Papers, Dartmouth.

23. Cullen, *Biographical Register*, II, 280.

24. Weld, *War Diary*, 404-11; https://www.findagrave.com/memorial/111214867
/stephen-minot-weld.

25. Eicher and Eicher, *High Commands*, 568.

26. Eicher and Eicher, *High Commands*, 570.

BIBLIOGRAPHY

MANUSCRIPTS

Antietam National Battlefield, Sharpsburg, MD
89th New York Regimental File
9th New Hampshire Regimental File
9th New York Regimental File
103rd New York Regimental File

Auburn University Digital Library, Auburn, AL
Jabez Smith Letters

Civil War Collections Online, Bentley Historical Library, University of Michigan, Ann Arbor, MI
Faron Anderson Papers
Belcher Diary, McCreery-Fenton Family Papers
William Boston Diary
Addison Boyce Papers
Claudius Buchanan Grant Papers
Charles Horace Hodskin, 1864 diary
Byron Mac Cutcheon Autobiography
William Randall Reminiscences, 1867
William Herbert Withington Papers

Delaware State Archives, Dover, DE
John V. Harrington Papers
James Harrison Wilson Papers

Library of Congress, Washington, DC
William A. Gladstone Afro-American Military Collection
Henry Heisler Papers
Robert Jameson Papers
Daniel Read Larned Papers

George B. McClellan Papers
Edwin McMasters Stanton Papers

Library of Virginia, Richmond, VA
John T. Andrews Letters
William Fielding Baugh Letter
M. G. Bell Letter
John Cooper Letter
Crofut-Humiston Family Papers
James Chatham Duane Papers
Dunlap Family Papers
Henry Eaton Letter
Andrew Fitch Letters
Charles Lancaster Letter
Richard B. Loomis Letter
Charles Rundlett Letters
John F. Sale Papers
Nathaniel Talbot Letters
George B. Tracy Papers

Maine State Archives, Augusta, ME
7th Maine Battery Correspondence
31st Maine Regimental Correspondence
32nd Maine Regimental Correspondence

Massachusetts State Archives, Boston, MA
8th Massachusetts Battery Correspondence
11th Massachusetts Battery Correspondence
14th Massachusetts Battery Correspondence
58th Massachusetts Death Records
57th Massachusetts Regimental Correspondence
35th Massachusetts Regimental Correspondence
36th Massachusetts Regimental Correspondence
21st Massachusetts Regimental Correspondence

National Archives, Washington, DC
Mannie Dorsey Pension File
Louis Martin Pension File

New Hampshire Historical Society, Concord, NH
John Batchelder Bailey Papers
Brigham Family Papers

George Henry Chandler Papers
Chase Family Papers
Dodge Family Papers
William W. Fish Correspondence
Biography of George W. Gove
Daniel Emerson Hurd, "My Experiences in the Civil War"
Josiah Jones War Memoranda
Charles Moulton Letter
Henry S. Muchmore Correspondence
Theodore Nutting Papers
Charles Paige Collection
Alonzo Pierce Papers
Mike Pride Collection
George H. P. Rowell Papers
Aaron Stevens Papers
Sewell D. Tilton Papers
Hosea Towne Papers
George Upton Papers
John E. Wilcox Diary

New York State Library, Albany, NY
Henry Heffron Papers
Harvey Henderson Diaries
Solomon Oakley Papers
Jerry Smith Letters

Personal Collection of John Gardiner, Carroll, NH
Letters of Charles Read

Rauner Library, Dartmouth College, Hanover, NH
Elmer Bragg Papers
Harlan Closson Diaries
George B. Codman Papers
Orlando Wales Dimick Autobiography
Samuel Emerson Diary
Letter extracts from James W. Lathe
Henry Muchmore Diary
Recollections of Simon Goodell Griffin
Walter Pingree Papers
Oscar Robinson Papers
Ransom F. Sargent Civil War Papers
Lewis Simonds Diary

Rhode Island Historical Society, Providence, RI

John F. Austin Papers
Burnside Letterbooks, Vol. 6
William Stillwell Chace Papers
General Orders No. 6, January 6, 1863, Court Martial of Pvt. Edwin Gallagher
Herreshoff-Lewis Family Papers
Ives-Gammell-Safe Papers,
    Diary of Robert Hale Ives, Jr., Box 5, folder 3
    Memorials to Robert Hale Ives, Jr., Box 5, folder 5
    Robert Hale Ives, Jr. Correspondence, Box 4, folder 12
Gilbert Family Papers
Pendleton Family Papers
Henry Spooner Papers

Rubenstein Library, Duke University, Durham, NC

Alfred Allen Diary
John Gross Barnard Papers
Fisher A. Cleaveland Papers
Thomas Read Rootes Cobb Papers

South Carolina Department of Archives and History, Columbia, SC

Campbell Family Papers

Vermont State Archives, Middlesex, VT

Correspondence of Alfred F. Dodge
James Pollard, 1864 Diary

Vermont Historical Society, Barre, VT

Biographical Notes on the Life of Cassius Wirt Ellsworth
Stephen F. Brown Papers
Charles Cummings Papers (MS-28)
Charles Cummings Papers (MSA 829.9)
Salmon K. Gates Papers
Diary of Eldin J. Hartshorn, 1864
William Elmore Howard Letters
William T. King Letters
Lyman Knapp Papers
Letters of Albert Camp Raymond
Moses and Matthew Whitehill Letters

GOVERNMENT PUBLICATIONS

Adjutant General, *Massachusetts Soldiers, Sailors, and Marines in the Civil War*, 5 Vols. (Norwood: Norwood Press, 1932).

Adjutant General's Office, *Record of Service of Connecticut Men in the Army and Navy of the United States during the War of the Rebellion* (Hartford: Case, Lockwood & Brainard Company, 1889).

Annual Report of the Adjutant General of the State of Maine for the Year Ending 1863 (Augusta: Stevens & Sayward, 1864).

House of Representatives, 37th Congress, 3rd Session, *Report of the Joint Committee on the Conduct of the War*, Part I (Washington: GPO, 1863).

State of Vermont, *Revised Roster of Vermont Volunteers and Lists of Vermonters Who Served in the Army and Navy of the United States* (Montpelier: Watchman Publishing, 1892).

United States Senate, 38th Cong., 2nd Sess., *Report of the Committee on the Conduct of the War on the Attack on Petersburg on the 30th Day of July, 1864* (Washington: GPO, 1865).

U.S. War Department, *The War of the Rebellion: A Compilation of the Official Records of the Union and Confederate Armies*, 128 vols. (Washington: U.S. Gov't Printing Office (1880–1901).

WEBSITES

https://www.ancestry.com
http://bioguide.congress.gov
http://www.cmohs.org
http://dmna.ny.gov/
http://www.findagrave.com
https://48thpennsylvania.blogspot.com
https://historicalpubs.njstatelib.org
https://michiganology.org/civil-war
https://museum.dmna.ny.gov/unit-history/conflict/us-civil-war-1861-1865
https://sites.google.com/site/generalwelsh/lastcampaign
https://southfromthenorthwoods.blogspot.com
https://www.sstephens.org/history

BOOKS, ARTICLES, DISSERTATIONS, AND THESES

Adams, Z. Boylston, "In the Wilderness," *Civil War Papers Read Before the Commandery of the State of Massachusetts, Military Order of the Loyal Legion of the United States*, Vol. II (Boston: F. H. Gilson, 1900).

Albert, Allen D., ed., *History of the Forty-Fifth Regiment Pennsylvania Veteran Volunteer Infantry, 1861–1865* (Williamsport, PA: Grit Publishing Company, 1912).

Alexander, Ted, *The Battle of Antietam: The Bloodiest Day* (Charleston, SC: History Press, 2011).

Allen, George H., *Forty-Six Months with the Fourth R. I. Volunteers in the War of 1861 to 1865* (Providence, RI: J. A. & R. A. Reid, 1887).

Ammen, Daniel, *The Navy in the Civil War, Vol. 2—The Atlantic Coast* (New York: Charles Scribner's Sons, 1883).

Anders, Curt, *Henry Halleck's War: A Fresh Look at Lincoln's Controversial General-in-Chief* (Carmel, IN: Guild Press, 2000).

Anderson, John, *The Fifty-Seventh Regiment of Massachusetts Volunteers in the War of the Rebellion* (Boston: E. B. Stillings, 1896).

Arnold, Jennie Porter, "At Antietam," *National Tribune*, October 18, 1888.

Aston, Howard, *History and Roster of the Fourth and Fifth Independent Battalions and Thirteenth Regiment Ohio Cavalry Volunteers* (Columbus: Fred J. Heer, 1902).

Ayling, Augustus D., *Revised Register of the Soldiers and Sailors of New Hampshire in the War of the Rebellion, 1861–1866* (Concord: Ira C. Evans, 1895).

Banks, John, *Connecticut Yankees at Antietam* (Charleston, SC: History Press, 2013).

Barnard, Sandy, ed., *Campaigning with the Irish Brigade: Pvt. John Ryan, 28th Massachusetts* (Terre Haute, IN: AST Press, Terre, 2001).

Bartlett, John Russell, *Memoirs of the Rhode Island Officers Who Were Engaged in the Service of Their Country during the Great Rebellion of the South* (Providence: Sidney S. Rider & Brother, 1867).

Basler, Roy P., *The Collected Works of Abraham Lincoln*, 8 Vols. (New Brunswick, NJ: Rutgers University Press, 1953).

Bates, Samuel, *History of Pennsylvania Volunteers, 1861–1865*, 5 Vols. (Harrisburg: B. Singerly, 1869).

Bawley, Free S., "The Crater," *National Tribune*, November 6, 1884.

Beals, Thomas P., "In a Charge Near Fort Hell, Petersburg, April 2, 1865," *War Papers*, Vol. II (Portland, ME: Lefavor-Tower Company, 1902).

Beck, W. C., "Fort Steadman," *National Tribune*, September 24, 1885.

Benning, H. L., "Notes by General H. L. Benning on the Battle of Sharpsburg," *Southern Historical Society Papers*, Vol. XVI, 393–95.

Blackburn, George M., ed., *The Diary of Captain Ralph Ely of the Eighth Michigan Infantry* (Mount Pleasant: Central Michigan University Press, 1965).

Blakeslee, B. F., *History of the Sixteenth Connecticut Volunteers* (Hartford: Case, Lockwood & Brainard, 1875).

Bosbyshell, Oliver Christian, *The 48th in the War* (Philadelphia: Avil Printing Company, 1895).

Bowen, James L., *Massachusetts in the War, 1861–1865* (Springfield: Clark W. Bryan, 1889).

Bowley, F. S., *A Boy Lieutenant* (Philadelphia: Henry Altemus Company, 1906).

Brager, Bruce L., *Grant's Victory: How Ulysses S. Grant Won the Civil War* (Guilford, CT: Stackpole Books, 2020).

Brennan, Patrick, *Secessionville: Assault on Charleston* (Campbell, CA: Savas Publishing Company, 1996).

Brinkerhoff, Henry R., *History of the Thirtieth Regiment Ohio Volunteer Infantry* (Columbus: James W. Osgood, 1863).

Burnside, Ambrose E., "The Burnside Expedition," *Personal Narratives of the Events in the War of the Rebellion, Being Papers Read before the Rhode Island Soldiers and Sailors Historical Society,* No. 6, 2nd Series (Providence, RI: N. Bangs Williams & Company, 1882).

Burton, Brian K., *Extraordinary Circumstances: The Seven Days Battles* (Bloomington: Indiana University Press, 2001).

Byron Cutcheon, *The Story of the Twentieth Michigan Infantry* (Lansing: Robert Smith Printing Co., 1904).

Caldwell, James Fitz James, *The History of a Brigade of South Carolinians* (Bedford, MA: Applewood Books, 1866).

Canfield, William A., *A History of Army Experience* (Manchester: C. F. Livingston, 1869).

Case, Ervin T., *The Battle of the Mine* (Providence: Sidney S. Rider, 1879).

Clark, Walter, ed., *Histories of the Several Regiments and Battalions from North Carolina in the Great War, 1861–'65,* 5 Vols. (Goldsboro, NC: Nash Brothers, 1901).

Cogswell, Leander W., *A History of the Eleventh New Hampshire Regiment Volunteer Infantry in the Rebellion War, 1861–1865* (Concord: Republican Press Association, 1891).

Commemorative Biographical Record of Hartford County, Connecticut (Chicago: J. H. Beers & Co., 1901).

Committee of the Regiment, *History of the Thirty-Sixth Regiment Massachusetts Volunteers, 1862–1865* (Boston: Rockwell and Churchill, 1884).

"Commodore," "The Funny Side of Army Life," *National Tribune,* April 25, 1889.

Cooling, Benjamin Franklin, *Counter-Thrust: From the Peninsula to the Antietam* (Lincoln: University of Nebraska Press, 2007).

Cooney, Thomas T., "Sykes' Regulars," *National Tribune,* February 9, 1893.

Corrigan, Jim, *The 48th Pennsylvania in the Battle of the Crater: A Regiment of Coal Miners Who Tunneled under the Enemy* (Jefferson, NC: McFarland & Company, 2006).

Cox, Jacob D., "Forcing Fox's Gap and Turner's Gap," *Battles and Leaders of the Civil War,* Vol. 2 (New York: Century Company, 1884).

Cox, Jacob, "The Battle of Antietam," *Battles and Leaders of the Civil War,* Vol. 2 (New York: Century Company, 1884).

Cox, Jacob Dolson, *Military Reminiscences of the Civil War, Volume I, April 1861–November 1863* (New York: Charles Scribner's Sons, 1900).

Cozzens, Peter, *This Terrible Sound: The Battle of Chickamauga* (Urbana, University of Illinois Press, 1996).

Cozzens, Peter, *General John Pope: A Life for the Nation* (Urbana: University of Illinois Press, 2000).

Crater, Lewis, *History of the Fiftieth Regiment, Penna. Vet. Vols., 1861–1865* (Reading, PA: Coleman Printing House, 1884).

Croffut, W. A., and John M. Morris, *The Military and Civil History of Connecticut during the War of 1861–65* (New York: Ledyard Bill, 1868).

Crummel, A. B., "Reno's Death," *National Tribune,* August 23, 1883.

Cuffel, Charles A., *History of Durell's Battery in the Civil War, Independent Battery D, Pennsylvania Volunteer Artillery* (Philadelphia: Craig, Finely, and Co., 1903).

Cullom, George W., *Biographical Register of the Officers and Graduates of the United States Military Academy at West Point, New York, since Its Establishment in 1802*, 2 Vols. (Boston: Houghton, Mifflin, and Company, 1891).

Cullum, George W., *Biographical Register of the Officers and Graduates of the U.S. Military Academy at West Point, N.Y.*, 2 Vols. (Boston: Houghton, Mifflin and Company, 1891).

Day, W. A., "Battle of the Crater," *Confederate Veteran*, August 1903, 355–56.

Diman, George Waters, *Autobiography and Sketches of My Travels by Sea and Land* (Bristol: Bristol Phoenix, 1896).

Dobak, William A., *Freedom by the Sword: The U.S. Colored Troops, 1862–1867* (Alexandria, VA: St. John's Press, 2016).

Draper, William F., *Recollections of a Varied Career* (Boston: Little, Brown, and Company, 1909).

Early, Jubal Anderson, *Autobiographical Sketch and Narrative of the War between the States* (Philadelphia: J. B. Lippincott, 1912).

Eby, Cecil D., Jr., ed., *A Virginia Yankee in the Civil War: The Diaries of David Hunter Strother* (Chapel Hill: University of North Carolina Press, 1961).

Eden, R. C., *The Sword and Gun: A History of the 37th Wis. Volunteer Infantry* (Madison: Atwood & Rublee, 1865).

Eicher, John H., and David J. Eicher, *Civil War High Commands* (Stanford: Stanford University Press, 2001).

Embick, Milton A., ed., *Military History of the Third Division, Ninth Corps, Army of the Potomac* (Harrisburg: C. E. Aughinbaugh, 1913).

Ent, Uzal W., *The Pennsylvania Reserves in the Civil War* (Jefferson, NC: McFarland and Company, 2014).

F. E. C., *History of the 58th Regt. Massachusetts Vols. From the 15th Day of September, 1863, to the Close of the Rebellion* (Washington: Gibson Brothers, 1865).

Faulkner, Terry, and Charles H. Faulkner, *Rediscovering Fort Sanders: The American Civil War and Its Impact on Knoxville's Cultural Landscape* (Knoxville: University of Tennessee Press, 2020).

Fishel, Edwin, *The Secret War for the Union: The Untold Story of Military Intelligence in the Civil War* (Boston: Houghton Mifflin Company, 1996).

Fisher, Noel C., *War at Every Door: Partisan Politics and Guerrilla Violence in East Tennessee, 1860–1869* (Chapel Hill: University of North Carolina Press, 1997).

Fox, Wells B., *What I Remember of the Great Rebellion* (Lansing, MI: Darius D. Thorp, 1892.

Fox, William F., *Regimental Losses in the American Civil War, 1861–1865* (Albany: Brandow Printing Company, 1889).

Francis Winthrop Palfrey, *Memoir of William Francis Bartlett* (Boston: Houghton, Osgood and Company, 1879).

Fry, Zachery A., *A Republic in the Ranks: Loyalty and Dissent in the Army of the Potomac* (Chapel Hill: University of North Carolina Press, 2020).

Furney, L. A., ed., *Reminiscences of the War of the Rebellion, 1861–1865, By Bvt. Maj. Jacob Roemer* (Flushing, NY: Estate of Jacob Roemer, 1897).

Gallagher, Gary W., "The Two Generals Who Resist Each Other: Perceptions of Grant and Lee in the Summer of 1864," in Gallagher and Janney, eds., *Cold Harbor to the Crater: The End of the Overland Campaign* (Chapel Hill: University of North Carolina Press, 2015), 1–32.

Gavin, William Gilfillan ed., *Infantryman Pettit: The Civil War Letters of Corporal Frederick Pettit* (New York: Avon Books, 1990).

Glatthaar, Joseph T., *Forged in Battle: The Civil War Alliance of Black Soldiers and White Officers* (Baton Rouge: Louisiana State University Press, 1990).

Goodrich, Ira B., "Second Bull Run," *National Tribune*, May 4, 1893.

Gordon C. Rhea, *The Battle of the Wilderness, May 5–6, 1864* (Baton Rouge: Louisiana State University Press, 1994).

Gordon, Lesley J., "All Who Went into That Battle Were Heroes: Remembering the 16th Regiment Connecticut Volunteers at Antietam," in *The Antietam Campaign*, Gary Gallagher, ed. (Kent: Kent State University Press, 1989), 169–91.

Gordon, Lesley J., *A Broken Regiment: The 16th Connecticut's Civil War* (Baton Rouge: Louisiana State University Press, 2014).

Gottfried, Bradley M. *The Maps of Antietam: An Atlas of the Antietam (Sharpsburg) Campaign, Including the Battle of South Mountain, September 2–20, 1862* (New York: Savas Beatie, 2013).

Gottfried, Bradley, *The Maps of Fredericksburg* (El Dorado Hills: Savas Beatie, 2018).

Gould, Joseph, *The Story of the Forty-Eighth* (Slocum Company, 1908).

Grabau, Warren E., *Ninety-Eight Days: A Geographer's View of the Vicksburg Campaign* (Knoxville: University of Tennessee Press, 2000).

Graham, Matthew J., *The Ninth Regiment New York Volunteers (Hawkins Zouaves)* (New York: F. P. Coby, 1900).

Grant, J. W., *The Flying Regiment: Journal of the Campaign of the 12th Regt. Rhode Island Volunteers* (Providence: Sidney S. Rider, 1865).

Grant, Ulysses S., *Personal Memoirs of U. S. Grant*, 2 Vols. (New York: Charles L. Webster, 1892).

Greene, A. Wilson, "Morale, Maneuver, and Mud: The Army of the Potomac, December 16, 1862–January 26, 1863," in Gary W. Gallagher, ed., *The Fredericksburg Campaign: Decision on the Rappahannock*, 171–227.

Greene, A. Wilson, *A Campaign of Giants: The Battle for Petersburg, Vol. 1, From the Crossing of the James to the Crater* (Chapel Hill: University of North Carolina Press, 2018).

Hadley, Amos, *Life of Walter Harriman, With Selections from His Speeches and Writings* (Boston: Houghton, Mifflin and Company, 1888).

Hall, Henry Seymour, "Personal Experience of a Staff Officer," *A Paper Prepared and Read before the Kansas Commandery of the Military Order of the Loyal Legion of the United States, October 3, 1894.*

Harsh, Joseph L., *Taken at the Flood: Robert E. Lee and Confederate Strategy in the Maryland Campaign of 1862* (Kent, OH: Kent State University Press, 1999).

Hartwig, D. Scott, "Who Would Not be a Soldier: The Volunteers of '62 in the Maryland Campaign," in Gary W. Gallagher, ed., *The Antietam Campaign* (Chapel Hill: University of North Carolina Press, 1999), 143–68.

Hartwig, D. Scott, *To Antietam Creek: The Maryland Campaign of September 1862* (Baltimore: Johns Hopkins University Press, 2012).

Haupt, Herman, *Reminiscences of General Herman Haupt* (Milwaukee: Wright & Joys, 1901).

Hays, Gilbert Adams, *Under the Red Patch: Story of the Sixty-Third Regiment Pennsylvania Volunteers, 1861–1864* (Pittsburgh: Regimental Association, 1908).

Hebert, Walter H., *Fighting Joe Hooker* (Lincoln: University of Nebraska Press, 1999).

Hennessy, John J., *Return to Bull Run: The Campaign and Battle of Second Manassas* (New York: Simon & Schuster, 1993).

Hennessy, John J., "I Dread the Spring: The Army of the Potomac Prepares for the Overland Campaign," in Gary W. Gallagher, ed., *The Wilderness Campaign* (Chapel Hill: University of North Carolina Press, 1997), 66–105.

Herberger, Charles F., ed., *A Yankee at Arms: The Diary of Lieutenant Augustus D. Ayling, 29th Massachusetts Volunteers* (Knoxville: University of Tennessee Press, 1999).

Herek, Raymond J., *These Men Have Seen Hard Service: The First Michigan Sharpshooters in the Civil War* (Detroit: Wayne State University Press, 1998).

Hess, Earl J., *Trench Warfare under Grant and Lee: Field Fortifications in the Overland Campaign* (Chapel Hill: UNC Press, 2007).

Hess, Earl J., *Into the Crater: The Mine Attack at Petersburg* (Columbia: University of South Carolina Press, 2010).

Hess, Earl J., *The Knoxville Campaign: Burnside and Longstreet in East Tennessee* (Knoxville: University of Tennessee Press, 2012).

Hodgkins, William H., *The Battle of Fort Stedman, March 25, 1865* (Boston: privately printed, 1889).

Holsinger, Frank, "The Colored Troops at the Mine," *National Tribune,* October 19, 1905.

Hopkins, William P., *The Seventh Regiment Rhode Island Volunteers in the Civil War, 1862–1865* (Providence: Snow & Farmham, 1903).

Hoptak, John David, *The Battle of South Mountain* (Charleston: History Press, 2011).

Horn, John, *The Petersburg Regiment in the Civil War: A History of the 12th Virginia Infantry from John Brown's Hanging to Appomattox* (El Dorado Hills: Savas Beatie, 2019).

Horton, J. H., and Soloman Teverbaugh, *A History of the Eleventh Regiment (Ohio Volunteer Infantry)* (Dayton: W. J. Shuey, 1866).

Houston, Henry C., *The Thirty-Second Maine Regiment* (Portland: Southworth Brothers, 1903).

Huffman, William H., "A Roundhead Who Was with Pope's Army at Chantilly," *National Tribune,* April 13, 1899.

Humphreys, Andrew A., *The Virginia Campaign of '64 and '65* (New York: Scribner's Sons, 1883).

Jackson, Lyman, *History of the Sixth New Hampshire Regiment in the War for the Union* (Concord, NH: Republican Press Association, 1891).

Jermann, Donald R., *Antietam: The Lost Order* (Gretna, LA: Pelican Publishing, 2006).

Johnson, Charles F., *The Long Roll* (East Aurora, NY: Roycrofters, 1911).

Jordan, Brian Matthew, *Unholy Sabbath: The Battle of South Mountain in History and Memory* (New York: Savas Beatie, 2012).

Jordan, David M., *Winfield Scott Hancock: A Soldier's Life* (Bloomington: Indiana University Press, 1996).

Kenfield, Frank, "Captured by Rebels: A Vermonter at Petersburg, 1864," *Vermont History,* Autumn 1968, Vol. 36, No. 4, 230–35.

Kimball, Orville Samuel, *History and Personal Sketches of Company I, 103 N. Y. S. V, 1862–1864* (Elmira: Facts Printing Co., 1900).

Kreiser, Lawrence A., Jr., *Defeating Lee: A History of the Second Corps, Army of the Potomac* (Bloomington: Indiana University Press, 2011).

Krick, Robert E. L., "Like a Duck on a June Bug: James Longstreet's Flank Attack, May 6, 1864," in Gary W. Gallagher, ed., *The Wilderness Campaign*, 236–64.

Lane, David, *A Soldier's Diary: The Story of a Volunteer* (self-published, 1905).

Lane, J. H., "Battle of Spotsylvania Court-House," *Southern Historical Society Papers*, Vol. 9, 1881, 145–54.

Lapham, Oscar, "Recollections of Service in the Twelfth Regiment, R. I. Volunteers," *Personal Narratives of the Events in the War of the Rebellion,* Third Series, No. 11 (Providence: Rhode Island Soldiers and Sailors Historical Society, 1885).

Leasure, Daniel, "Personal Observations and Experiences in the Pope Campaign in Virginia," Military Order of the Loyal Legion of the United States, Minnesota Commandery, *Glimpses of the Nation's Struggle* (St. Paul: St. Paul Book and Stationery Company, 1887).

Levin, Kevin M., "The Devil Himself Could Not Have Checked Them: Fighting with Black Soldiers at the Crater," in Gary W. Gallagher and Caroline E. Janney, eds., *Cold Harbor,* 264–82.

Levin, Kevin M., *Remembering the Battle of the Crater: War as Murder* (Lexington: University Press of Kentucky, 2017).

Levstik, Frank, "The Civil War Diary of Colonel Albert Rogall," *Polish American Studies,* Spring 1970, Vol. 27, No. 1.

Longacre, Edward G., *General John Buford: A Military Biography* (Cambridge: Da Capo Press, 1995).

Longstreet, James, *From Manassas to Appomattox* (New York: Da Capo Press, 1992).

Lord, Edward O., *History of the Ninth Regiment, New Hampshire Volunteers in the War of the Rebellion* (Concord: Republican Press, 1895).

Lt. Col. Charles Lyon Chandler (Cambridge, MA: 1864).

Lusk, William, *War Letters of William Thompson Lusk* (New York: self-published, 1906).

Marvel, William, "The Making of a Myth: Ambrose E. Burnside and the Union High Command at Fredericksburg," in *The Fredericksburg Campaign: Decision on the Rappahannock,* Gary W. Gallagher, ed. (Chapel Hill: University of North Carolina Press, 1995), 1–25.

Marvel, William, *Burnside* (Chapel Hill: University of North Carolina Press, 1991).

Marvel, William, *Lincoln's Darkest Year: The War in 1862* (New York: Houghton Mifflin, 2008).

Marvel, William, *Race of the Soil: The Ninth New Hampshire Regiment in the Civil War* (Wilmington, NC: Broadfoot Publishing Company, 1988).

Marvel, William, *The Great Task Remaining: The Third Year of Lincoln's War* (Boston: Houghton Mifflin Harcourt, 2010).

McClellan, George B., *McClellan's Own Story* (New York: Charles L. Webster, 1887).

McClendon, W. A., *Recollections of War Times* (Montgomery: Paragon Press, 1909).

McConnell, William F., *Remember Reno: A Biography of Major General Jesse Lee Reno* (Shippensburg, PA: White Mane Publishing, 1996).

McDaid, William Kelsey, *"Four Years of Arduous Service": The History of the Branch-Lane Brigade in the Civil War,* PhD dissertation, Michigan State University, 1987.

McKnight, William Mark, *Blue Bonnets O'er the Border: The 79th New York Cameron Highlanders* (Shippensburg, PA: White Mane Books, 1998).

McMaster, F. W., "The Battle of the Crater, July 30, 1864," *Southern Historical Society Papers,* Vol. X, No. 3, 1879, 119–30.

McPherson, James M., *The Negro's Civil War: How American Negroes Felt and Acted during the War for the Union* (Urbana: University of Illinois Press, 1982).

Members of the Regiment, *The Story of the Twenty-First Regiment Connecticut Volunteer Infantry during the Civil War, 1861–1865* (Middletown: Stewart Printing, 1900).

Memorial of Colonel John A. Bross, Twenty-Ninth U.S. Colored Troops (Chicago: Tribune Book and Job Office, 1865).

Mettendorf, Ernest, *Between Triumph and Disaster: The History of the 46th New York Infantry, 1861–1865* (Eden, NY: self-published, 2012).

Mickley, J. M., *The Forty-Third Regiment United States Colored Troops* (Gettysburg: J. E. Wible, 1866).

Mixson, Frank, *Reminiscences of a Private* (Columbia: State Company, 1910).

Morton, Julia Jenkins, *Trusting to Luck: Ambrose E. Burnside and the American Civil War,* PhD dissertation, Kent State University, August 1992.

Motlow, Felix, "Campaigns in Northern Virginia," *Confederate Veteran,* Vol. 2, Sept. 1894, 310.

Napier, J. L., "M'Intosh's Battery at Sharpsburg," *Confederate Veteran,* Vol. 19, Sept. 1911, 429.

Nichols, G. W., *A Soldier's Story of His Regiment* (privately printed, 1898).

Norton, H. R., "The Ninth Corps," *National Tribune,* March 3, 1904.

O'Reilly, Francis Augustin, *The Fredericksburg Campaign: Winter War on the Rappahannock* (Baton Rouge: Louisiana State University Press, 2003).

Oates, William C., *The War between the Union and the Confederacy and Its Lost Opportunities* (New York: Neale Publishing Company, 1905).

Olcott, Charles S., *William McKinley,* Vol. 1 (Boston: Houghton Mifflin, 1916).

Osborne, William H., *The History of the Twenty-Ninth Regiment of Massachusetts Volunteer Infantry in the Late War of the Rebellion* (Boston: Albert J. Wright, 1877).

Paige, Charles C., *Story of the Experiences of Lieut. Charles C. Paige in the Civil War of 1861–5* (Franklin, NH: Journal-Transcript Press, 1906).

Palfrey, Francis Winthrop, *The Antietam and Fredericksburg* (New York: Charles Scribner's Sons, 1912).

Parker, Thomas H., *History of the 51st Regiment of P. V and V. V.* (Philadelphia, PA: King & Baird, 1869).

Patch, Eileen Mae Knapp, ed., *This from George: The Civil War Letters of Sergeant George Magusta Englis* (Binghamton: Broome County Historical Society, 2001).

Patchan, Scott C., *Second Manassas: Longstreet's Attack and the Struggle for Chinn Ridge* (Washington: Potomac Books, 2011).

Paul G. Zeller, "'My Soldier Boy Mark': The Civil War Letters of Pvt. Mark B. Slayton," *Vermont History*, Vol. 82, No. 1 (Winter/Spring 2014), 45–62.

Perry, William F., "Reminiscences of the Campaign of 1864 in Virginia, *Southern Historical Society Papers*, Vol. VII, No. 2, 1879, 49–63.

Phisterer, Frederick, *Statistical Record of the Armies of the United States* (New York: Charles Scribner's Sons, 1883).

Pierce, S. W., *Battlefield and Camp Fires of the Thirty-Eighth* (Milwaukee: Daily Wisconsin Printing, 1866).

Pierro, Joseph, ed., *The Maryland Campaign of September 1862: Ezra A. Carman's Definitive Study of the Union and Confederate Armies at Antietam* (New York: Routledge, 2008).

Pleasants, Jr., Henry, *The Tragedy of the Crater* (Boston: Christopher Publishing House, 1938).

Poore, Ben Perle, *The Life and Public Services of Ambrose E. Burnside, Soldier—Citizen—Statesman* (Providence: J. A. & R. A. Reid, 1882).

Pope, John, "The Second Battle of Bull Run," *Battles and Leaders of the Civil War*, Vol. 2 (New York: Century Company, 1888).

Porter, Horace, *Campaigning with Grant* (New York: Century Co., 1906).

Post, Lydia Minturn, ed., *Soldiers' Letters from Camp, Battle-field and Prison* (New York: Bunce and Huntington, 1865).

Powell, William H., "The Tragedy of the Crater," *The Century*, Vol. 34, No. 5, 774–76.

Pratt, Fletcher, *Civil War in Pictures* (Garden City, NY: Garden City Books, 1955).

Priest, John Michael, *Antietam: The Soldiers' Battle* (New York: Oxford University Press, 1989).

Priest, John Michael, *Captain James Wren's Civil War Diary: From New Bern to Fredericksburg* (New York: Berkley Books, 1990).

Priest, John Michael, *Before Antietam: The Battle for South Mountain* (Shippensburg: White Mane Publishing, 1992).

Priest, John Michael, ed., "Tired Soldiers Don't Go Very Fast," *Civil War Times Illustrated*, Jan./Feb. 1992, Vol. 30, #6.

Public Services of Brvt. Maj. Gen. John F. Hartranft, Union Candidate for Auditor General (Norristown, PA: Wills, Fredell & Jenkins, 1865).

Quint, Ryan T., "Ambrose Burnside, the Ninth Corps, and the Battle of Spotsylvania Court House," *The Gettysburg College Journal of the Civil War Era*, Vol. 5, 2005, 80–107.

Rable, George C., *Fredericksburg! Fredericksburg!* (Chapel Hill: University of North Carolina Press, 2002).

Rafuse, Ethan, *McClellan's War: The Failure of Moderation in the Struggle for the Union* (Bloomington: Indiana University Press, 2005).

Rafuse, Ethan S., "'Poor Burn?': The Antietam Conspiracy That Wasn't," *Civil War History*, Vol. 54, No. 2, June 2008, 146–75.

Reese, Timothy J., *Sealed with Their Lives: Battle of Crampton's Gap* (Baltimore: Butternut and Blue, 1999).

Reese, Timothy J., *High Water Mark: The 1862 Maryland Campaign in Strategic Perspective* (Baltimore: Butternut and Blue, 2004).

Regimental Association, *History of the Thirty-Fifth Regiment Massachusetts Volunteers, 1862–1865* (Boston: Mills, Knight & Co., 1884).

Rhea, Gordon C., "Grant's Disengagement from Cold Harbor: June 12–13, 1864," in *Cold Harbor to the Crater: The End of the Overland Campaign*, Gary W. Gallagher and Caroline E. Janney, eds. (Chapel Hill: University of North Carolina Press, 2015), 176–209.

Rhea, Gordon C., *Cold Harbor: Grant and Lee, May 26–June 3, 1864* (Baton Rouge: Louisiana State University Press, 2002).

Rhea, Gordon C., *The Battle of the Wilderness, May 5–6, 1864* (Baton Rouge: Louisiana State University Press, 1994).

Rhea, Gordon C., *The Battles for Spotsylvania Court House and the Road to Yellow Tavern, May 7–12, 1864* (Baton Rouge: Louisiana State University Press, 1997).

Rhea, Gordon C., *To the North Anna River: Grant and Lee, May 13–25* (Baton Rouge: Louisiana State University Press, 2000).

Richards, J. Stuart, *A History of Company C, 50th Pennsylvania Veteran Volunteer Infantry Regiment: From the Camp, the Battlefield, and the Prison Pen* (Charleston, SC: History Press, 2006).

Robertson, James I., Jr, *Stonewall Jackson: The Man, the Soldier, the Legend* (New York: Macmillan Publishing, 1997).

Robertson, Jr., James I., ed., "A Federal Surgeon at Sharpsburg," *Civil War History*, Vol. 6, No. 2, June 1960, 134–51.

Rutan II, Edwin P., *"If I Have Got to Go and Fight, I am Willing": A Union Regiment Forged in the Petersburg Campaign* (Park City, UT: RTD Publications, 2015).

Sauers, Richard, ed., *The Civil War Journal of Colonel Bolton, 51st Pennsylvania* (Conshohocken, PA: Combined Publishing, 2000).

Schaff, Morris, *The Battle of the Wilderness* (Boston: Houghton Mifflin, 1910).

Schildt, John W., *Roads to Antietam* (Shippensburg, PA: Burd Street Press, 1997).

Schmitt, Martin F., ed., *General George Crook: His Autobiography* (Norman: University of Oklahoma Press, 1946).

Scott, Robert Garth, ed., *Forgotten Valor: The Memoirs, Journals, and Civil War Letters of Orlando B. Willcox* (Kent, OH: Kent State University Press, 1999).

Sears, Stephen W., ed., *The Civil War Papers of George B. McClellan: Selected Correspondence* (Cambridge, MA: Da Capo Press, 1992).

Sears, Stephen W., *George B. McClellan: The Young Napoleon* (Cambridge: Da Capo Press, 1999).

Sears, Stephen W., *Landscape Turned Red: The Battle of Antietam* (Boston: Houghton Mifflin, 1983).

Sears, Stephen W., *Lincoln's Lieutenants: The High Command of the Army of the Potomac* (Boston: Mariner Books, 2017).

Sears, Stephen W., *To the Gates of Richmond: The Peninsula Campaign* (Boston: Houghton Mifflin, 1992).

Shanks, William F. G., *Personal Recollections of Distinguished Generals* (New York: Harper & Brothers, 1866).

Shildt, John W., *The Ninth Corps at Antietam* (Gaithersburg, MD: Olde Soldier Books, 1998).

Simpson, Brooks D., "General McClellan's Bodyguard: The Army of the Potomac after Antietam," *The Antietam Campaign,* Gary W. Gallagher, ed. (Chapel Hill: University of North Carolina Press, 1999), 44–73.

Sloan, John A., *Reminiscences of the Guilford Grays* (Washington: R. O. Polkinhorn, 1883).

Slotkin, Richard, *No Quarter: The Battle of the Crater, 1864* (New York: Random House, 2009).

Slotkin, Richard, *The Long Road to Antietam: How the Civil War Became a Revolution* (New York: Liveright Publishing, 2012).

Smith, R. A., "How General Stevenson Died," *National Tribune,* January 20, 1898.

Smith, Sol. R., "South Mountain, *National Tribune,* January 17, 1895.

Sodergren, Steven E., *The Army of the Potomac in the Overland and Petersburg Campaigns: Union Soldiers and Trench Warfare, 1864–1865* (Baton Rouge: Louisiana State University Press, 2017).

Stevens, Hazard, *The Life of Isaac Ingalls Stevens,* Vol. II (Boston, MA: Houghton, Mifflin and Company, 1900).

Stevens, John Austin, Jr., *Report of Committee to Recruit the Ninth Army Corps, February to August, 1864* (New York: John W. Amerman, 1866).

Stiles, Robert, *Four Years under Marse Robert* (New York: Neale Publishing Company, 1903).

Stine, J. H., *History of the Army of the Potomac* (Washington: Gibson Bros, 1893).

Stone, James Madison, *Personal Recollections of the Civil War* (Boston: self-published, 1918).

Stotelmyer, Steven R., *Too Useful to Sacrifice: Reconsidering George B. McClellan's Generalship in the Maryland Campaign from South Mountain to Antietam* (El Dorado Hills: Savas Beatie, 2019).

Taylor, Paul, *He Hath Loosed the Fateful Lightning: The Battle of Ox Hill (Chantilly), September 1, 1862* (Shippensburg: White Mane Books, 2003).

Thayer, William Roscoe, *The Life and Letters of John Hay,* 2 Vols. (London: Constable & Co., 1915).

Thompson, S. Millett, *History of the Thirteenth Regiment of New Hampshire Volunteer Infantry in the War of the Rebellion, 1861–1865* (Boston: Houghton, Mifflin and Company, 1888).

Thomson, O. R. Howard, and William H. Rauch, *History of the "Bucktails," Kane Rifle Regiment of the Pennsylvania Reserve Corps (13th Pennsylvania Reserves, 42nd of the Line)* (Philadelphia: Electric Printing Company, 1906).

Thorp, Gene M., and Alexander B. Rossino, *The Tale Untwisted: George McClellan and the Discovery of Lee's Lost Orders, September 13, 1862* (El Dorado Hills, CA: Savas Beatie, 2019).

Thorpe, Sheldon B., *The History of the Fifteenth Connecticut Volunteers in the War for the Defense of the Union* (New Haven: Price, Lee & Adkins Co., 1893).

Todd, William, *The Seventy-Ninth Highlanders: New York Volunteers in the War of the Rebellion* (Albany: Brandow, Barton & Co., 1886).

Tucker, Phillip Thomas, *Burnside's Bridge: The Climactic Struggle of the 2nd and 20th Georgia at Antietam Creek* (Mechanicsburg: Stackpole Books, 2000).

Twitchell, Albert S., *History of the Seventh Maine Light Battery, Volunteers in the Great Rebellion* (Boston: E. B. Stillings, 1892).

Walcott, Charles F., *History of the Twenty-First Regiment Massachusetts Volunteers in the War for the Preservation of the Union* (Boston, MA: Houghton, Mifflin and Company, 1882).

Walker, James A., "Gordon's Assault on Fort Stedman," *Southern Historical Society Papers,* Vol. XXXI, 1879, 19–31.

Walton, J. E., "Some Reminiscences of the Battle of Antietam," *National Tribune,* December 31, 1885.

Ward, Andrew, *River Run Red: The Fort Pillow Massacre in the American Civil War* (New York: Penguin Group, 2005).

Ward, George W., *History of the Second Pennsylvania Veteran Heavy Artillery from 1861 to 1866* (Philadelphia: Geo. W. Ward, 1904).

Warner, Ezra J., *Generals in Blue: Lives of the Union Commanders* (Baton Rouge: Louisiana State University Press, 1992).

Watson, Ronald G., ed., *From Ashby to Andersonville: The Civil War Diary and Reminiscences of George A. Hitchcock* (Campbell, CA: Savas Publishing, 1997).

Waugh, John C., *Lincoln and McClellan: The Troubled Partnership between a President and His General* (New York: Palgrave Macmillan, 2010).

Weld, Stephen Minot, *War Diary and Letters of Stephen Minot Weld* (privately printed, Riverside Press, 1912).

Welker, David A., *Tempest at Ox Hill: The Battle of Chantilly* (Cambridge, MA: Da Capo Press, 2002).

Wert, Jeffry D., *The Sword of Lincoln: The Army of the Potomac* (New York: Simon & Schuster, 2005).

West, Robert, "Reno's Death," *National Tribune,* August 9, 1883.

White, Daniel, "Charging the Crater," *National Tribune,* June 21, 1883.

White, Ronald C., *American Ulysses: A Life of Ulysses S. Grant* (New York: Random House, 2016).

Whitney, J. H. E., *The Hawkins Zouaves: Their Battles and Marches* (New York, self-published, 1866).

Wilkinson, Warren, *Mother, May You Never See the Sights I Have Seen: The Fifty-Seventh Massachusetts Veteran Volunteers in the Last Year of the Civil War* (New York: Harper and Row, 1990).

William McKinley: Memorial Address Delivered by John Hay, Secretary of State, in the Hall of the House of Representatives, February 27th, 1902 (Lexington, KY: Transylvania Press, 1902).

Williams, Charles Richard, *The Life of Rutherford Birchard Hayes, Nineteenth President of the United States*, Vol. I (Boston: Houghton Mifflin, 1914).

Williams, Charles Richard, ed., *Diary and Letters of Rutherford Birchard Hayes*, Vol. II, 1861–1865 (New York: Kraus Reprint Co., 1971).

Williams, Horace N., "Rodman's Brigade at Antietam," *National Tribune*, December 9, 1886.

Wilmer, Allison, J. H. Jarrett, and Geo. W. F. Vernon, *History and Roster of Maryland Volunteers, War of 1861–5, Vol. I* (Baltimore: Guggenheimer, Weil, Co., 1898).

Winik, Jay, *April 1865: The Month That Saved America* (New York: Harper Perennial, 2006).

Wipperman, Darin, *First for the Union: Life and Death in a Civil War Army Corps from Antietam to Gettysburg* (Guilford, CT: Stackpole Books, 2020).

Wood, A. H., "How Reno Fell," *National Tribune*, July 26, 1883.

Wood, William N., *Reminiscences of Big I* (Charlottesville: Michie Company, 1909).

Woodbury, Augustus, *Major General Ambrose E. Burnside and the Ninth Corps* (Providence, RI: Sidney S. Rider and Brother, 1867).

Yates, Walter J., ed., *Souvenir of Excursion to Antietam and Dedication of Monuments* (New London: E. E. Darrow, 1894).

Index

Page numbers in *italics* and **bold** refer to photographs and tables, respectively.